If They Hadn't Gone

How World War II Affected Major League Baseball

By Thomas E. Allen

Southwest Missouri State University
901 South National Avenue
Springfield, Missouri 65804

© Copyright 2004 by Southwest Missouri State University

International Standard Book Number: 0-974-8190-2-6

Manufactured in the United States
Printing by A&J Printing, Inc.
Nixa, Missouri

ACKNOWLEDGMENTS

I would like to express my thanks to those who have played a part in the preparation of this book. I particularly want to thank my daughter-in-law, Shelly, for her work in reading the manuscript for form and my son, Michael, for his reading for content. In addition, I would like to thank Jennifer Purvis for her work in combining text with numbers to make the final product. Also, thanks to Dr. John H. Keiser, president; Mr. Greg Burris, vice president for administration and finance; and the publications staff at Southwest Missouri State University for their encouragement and help during the process. Finally, I want to thank Alyssa Medlin for her editing work. Without her help, the end product would not have been as good.

TABLE OF CONTENTS

FOREWORD
by
Jerry Lumpe

U. S. Army, 1953-54; New York Yankees 1956-59; Kansas City Athletics 1959-63; Detroit Tigers 1964-67; 1957-1958 World Series; 1964 All-Star Game

Since the time of the Civil War there has been an interaction between baseball and war. The game of baseball was introduced to a new section of the United States following that war, and baseball players took their turn on the battlefield during the First World War. The major impact of war on baseball occurred during the 1940s when the United States entered World War II after the December 7, 1941, attack on Pearl Harbor.

During all of these wars, baseball careers were interrupted because of the players' service to their country, and the records these players achieved were curtailed because of that service. Since baseball is a game of statistics, as well as a game on the field, people have often wondered what a player would have achieved had he not lost playing time during his military service. This is where *If They Hadn't Gone* comes to the front.

The predictions listed in *If They Hadn't Gone* are sure to invoke a lot of discussion and comment as the reader reviews the estimates of what might have been. The technique used in the book does provide a reasonable estimate for the lost performances. Adjusting for the age of the player while he was in the military should make the predictions of performance closer to what would have happened if the player had carried out his career without interruption.

In addition, the narrative brings together a lot of information about the baseball players' roles in World War II. Presenting it in a biographical format allows readers to easily find the relevant information about the players in whom they are interested. The research from newspapers of the period, personal letters from more than 120 of the players listed, and the use of other published material brings new insight and information to light. *If They Hadn't Gone* is excellent reading for the true baseball fan.

INTRODUCTION

It is a bright autumn day in Boston's Fenway Park in 1961. Ted Williams steps into the batter's box, digs in his back foot, and begins his warm-up ritual, all the while sizing up the pitcher and anticipating the pitch. The pitcher glances at the runner on second and then looks in for the sign. The catcher gives the sign for a fastball low and away. The pitcher stretches, looks at second to check the runner, and then delivers the pitch. The pitch is low enough—just below the belt—but catches the heart of the plate. Williams begins that picture-perfect swing as the pitch heads toward the plate. The bat makes solid contact, and the ball screams toward the right field seats, landing in the tenth row. As fans scramble for the souvenir, the crowd stands as one to salute Williams' 700th career home run.

"But wait a minute," you say, "Ted Williams didn't have 700 home runs in his career."

You are right! But how many home runs would Williams have had if he hadn't missed all or part of five seasons while serving his country, three full seasons while serving in World War II and most of two other seasons while serving in the Korean conflict?

The purpose of this book is to estimate what effect World War II had on the career statistics of Ted Williams and the other major league baseball players who took part in that war.

Between 1942 and 1945, many major league players took part in the war effort. Because of this service, many of these players, like Ted Williams, have career statistics that do not reflect their potential. The numbers are lower than they would have been had they not missed from one to five years in their careers. In many cases, the years they missed would have been some of the most productive years of their careers. As Herbert Hoover said, "Older men declare war. But it is youth that must fight and die. And it is youth who must inherit the tribulation, the sorrow, and the triumphs that are the aftermath of war" (Braun and Getzed, 1996, 165). Baseball, like war, is for young men.

The National Baseball Hall of Fame and Museum, Inc., provided me with a list of baseball people who served in World War II. That list contained 526 names, including umpires, baseball executives, and men who played in the Negro League in addition to players from the major leagues. Unfortunately, the records for the Negro League are limited and are not included in the career statistics at the major league level. The Hall of Fame list was supplemented with players listed in *The Sports Encyclopedia: Baseball* as serving in the war effort. Based on those sources, the number of players with major league experience prior to entering their military service was 472. Information on those 472 players is included in the following chapters.

To a lesser degree, I also looked at the effect that World War I, the Korean conflict, and the war in Vietnam had on the players who took part in those wars. The players who served during those conflicts are listed in the chapter, "Other Wars and Other Players." Fewer players took part in the other wars, and the time they missed was not as long as that missed by the players who served in World War II. For the most part, the players who served in World War I missed the 1918 season. A few were gone for 1917, and/or 1919 or 1920. In addition, the 1918 and the 1919 seasons were cut short for all players.

The Korean War lasted a little longer with players serving in the military from 1951 through 1955. Most players who served missed only one or two years. However, some of the players who served do rank at the top of the list in career statistics. Willie Mays, who is in the Top 10 in many categories, missed almost two years because of his military service. The Vietnam War did not have a large impact on most players. The *Encyclopedia* lists only 17 major league players as serving during 1959 through 1964.

During World War II some of the men listed got to play in the major leagues because of the war. When a regular player was called into military service, another player was called up from the minor leagues to replace him. As time passed, these replacement players were also called into service and others took their place on the major league roster. Some of those only had a short time at the major league level and based on their career statistics, estimates would be impossible. They are listed with their actual numbers; estimates are not included. Also listed are the names of players from the Negro League.

To determine what might have happened for those players who missed time because of service, I sampled the career records of several long time major leaguers (who did not miss years due to war) to determine the relationship of their age to their average seasonal statistics. By using these people, who played in the majors from 17 to 25 years, I was able to establish some benchmarks to estimate the production of a player at different ages. These benchmark numbers were used along with the actual numbers put up by the player in the years just before and just after the years of military service to predict the numbers the player would have had during the years he missed because of that service.

The actual career numbers for each player are included on the first line of statistical information. The estimated figures for the years missed because of the war are on the second line. This is followed by an estimated total for the player's career if he had not served in the war. The change that might have occurred in the top 25 ranking in a number of statistical categories is included in Appendix A.

A number of personal information items are included for each player. The date and place of his birth and death (if applicable) are listed. His weight, height, nicknames and whether he was right or left handed are listed. The teams that he played on are listed. Where there were two teams from the same city the letter "N" is used to identify the National League team and an "A" is used to specify the American League team. The following is a list of symbols used in the statistical section:

For position players:

Age	The age of the player when he served in the military
Yrs	The years the player was in the military
ML	The number of major league seasons played
G	The number of games played
BA	Batting average
SA	Slugging average
AB	The number of at-bats
H	The number of hits
2B	The number of doubles
3B	The number of triples
HR	The number of home runs
HR%	The percent of home runs to times
R	The number of runs scored
RBI	The number of runs batted in
BB	The number of bases on balls received
SO	The number of times struck out
SB	The number of stolen bases

For pitchers:

Age	The age of the pitcher when he served in the military
YRS	The years that the pitcher was in the military
ML	The number of major league seasons played
W	The number of wins
L	The number of losses
Pct	The winning percentage
ERA	The earned run average
G	The number of games pitched
GS	The number of games started
CG	The number of complete games pitched
IP	The number of innings pitched
H	The number of hits allowed
BB	The number of bases on balls given
SO	The number of strikeouts achieved
Sho	The number of shutouts pitched
Sv	The number of saves received

The men listed in this book are part of the generation that was called upon to sacrifice themselves and their careers for the benefit of their country. In many cases that sacrifice was given willingly by men who volunteered to serve in the military. Baseball players, as well as the average American, were among those who volunteered. Mel Ott predicted this would happen when he was named manager of the New York Giants on December 2, 1941. He said, "Young fellows eligible for military service, whether they are clerks or ballplayers, are going to rush to the colors....The first thought by everybody is the defense of our country" (*Sports Illustrated,* July 16, 2001). The freedom that we enjoy today was preserved by the sweat and blood of the men and women who fought in World War II. Baseball players were part of that group. In some cases, they provided support roles for those who fought. However, in many cases the baseball player was also on the front line shooting a gun and getting shot at by the enemy. "It doesn't take a hero to order men into battle. It takes a hero to be one of those men who go into battle," H. Norman Schwarzkopf said (Braun and Getzen 1996, 568). These men were some of the heroes of World War II.

George Washington, as part of his farewell speech, said, "You have in common cause fought and triumphed together. The independence and liberty you possess are the work of joint councils and joint efforts, of common dangers, sufferings and successes" (Braun and Getzen 1996, 26). That is what could be said about the United States of America during the period from 1941 to 1945. The country came together to face the common foe. They faced the danger together; they fought the enemy together; they had the sufferings together; they, in the end, had the successes together. Many individuals paid a very high price for that victory. But together those individuals triumphed and sustained the American way of life.

I have spent the last several years accumulating the data and compiling this book. I hope that you enjoy the information contained on the pages of this book as much as I enjoyed putting it together.

CHAPTER 1

At the 21st Annual Dinner of the New York Chapter Baseball Writers Association of America, a song was sung that shows the affection America had for its fighting men. This song featured baseball players since that was the group doing the singing. The country was at war and those who remained behind supported those who were on foreign soils defending the American way of life, which had been threatened when the Japanese attacked Pearl Harbor. Now we were fighting back. This song shows how one group felt about those players who were taking part in that defense.

BLESS 'EM ALL*

We're warm and well-fed and we're havin' a time,
We've done it all before;
Fun and good spirits are seldom a crime,
You can't ask for anything more;
But now give a thought to the hope of the world:
Kids who in battle may fall;
Lift voices and prayers for stout-hearted players
Who honor our game. Bless 'em all!

CHORUS

Bless 'em all! Bless 'em all!
The players who answered the call;
Start with Mulcahy, the first to go in,
Yell, "Captain Greenberg!" and set up a din,
For we're singin' good luck to 'em all,
And pray they'll be back to play ball—
The Powells and Fellers, the Rowells and Kellers—
Unbutton your lips! Bless 'em all!

Bless 'em all! Bless 'em all!
The humble, the short and the tall,
Arnovich, Mulligan, Pesky and Klein,
Reiser, Krakauskas and young Gantenbein;
Make your pray'rs echo out in the hall,
They'll need 'em with backs to the wall,
For Pytlaks, Sylvestris, the Dusaks, Majeskis,
Let's whoop it aloud! Bless 'em all!

Bless 'em all! Bless 'em all!
Our homage they'll always enthrall—
Dickey, Bonura, Dejan, Posedel,
Gehringer, Lyons, McCoy and Blackwell,
Padgett, Schumacher, Marshall and Mize,
Di Maggios, Campbells and Fryes,
Sib Sisti and Graham, and Crespi and Nahem—
They're bringin' us fame. Bless 'em all!

Bless 'em all! Bless 'em all!
Rizzuto, a hero one Fall,
Beazley and Martin, now John Vander Meer,
Williams, and Wakefield, the kid of the year!
For they're sayin' good-by to us all,
And some of 'em beyond recall;
Just think of the futures, the shell-shock and sutures,
And lost boyhood dreams! Bless 'em all!

Bless 'em all! Bless 'em all!
Let's put our best stuff on the ball;
You had a tough break in losin' Gene Stack—
Our Jackie Singer will never be back;
It's good-by to a few, but not all,
And some days the list will appall,
But don't pull the blunder of stoppin' to wonder,
Keep doin' your best. Bless 'em all!

Bless 'em all! Bless 'em all!
Our boys who are winnin' the brawl;
Face 'em in darkness and ask your Divine:
"Safeguard his future; he's prolongin' mine!"
And then vow not to grumble or squall,
As into warm blankets you crawl;
Just liken your ease to his jungles and fleas, to
The horror he sees! Bless 'em all!

Bless 'em all! Bless 'em all!
Our heroes who used to play ball,
Lyin' in foxholes, in mud and the rain,
Fight for the right to play baseball again;
Oh, you can't let 'em down, not at all,
You'll play out the schedule till Fall—
Status quo ipso facto, a goal to come back to
When victory's won! Bless 'em all!

* Meaning every player, official and executive of Organized
Baseball now serving his country.

THE HOME NEWS PRESS

Originally sung at the 21st Annual Dinner of the New York Chapter,
Baseball Writers Association of America.

Reprint of this song courtesy of the Baseball Hall of Fame Library.

Any war brings about many changes in the countries that fight in it. World War II was no different for the United States. Baseball was among the things changed in America. Baseball had just experienced some of its best years. The Gas House Gang was over. The great Yankee teams were continuing to dominate the American League. Joe DiMaggio, Ted Williams, and Bob Feller had just come on the scene. Feller had set the strikeout record for a game. Williams had batted over .400. DiMaggio had his 56-game hitting streak. Hank Greenberg had come close to Babe Ruth's 60 home runs by hitting 58 in 1938. The Hall of Fame had been dedicated in 1939 in Cooperstown, New York. Baseball was in high gear.

The thought of country was not at the forefront of everyone's mind. The national anthem was not played on a regular basis before all ball games. It was only played on special occasions such as the All-Star Game or the World Series. The country was still not a part of the war that was going on in Europe. It was a long way from our coast and, for the most part, Americans were letting other countries take care of their own problems.

That was not the case for everyone. Many of the nation's leaders were very concerned about what was going on in foreign countries. All-star teams made several exhibition trips to other countries before the United States became involved in World War II. One of those trips was to Japan. Among the players making the trip was a catcher named Moe Berg. In addition to his work playing baseball, Berg also photographed a number of the military locations in Japan. His work, while several years before the start of the war, was helpful to the United States.

The war also affected the families of the United States. When it started, most families consisted of a husband working and a wife and children staying at home. When it was over, because of the need for women to work the plants, women had moved from the homeplace to the workplace. This changed the structure of the family in the United States forever. Many women were no longer content to be homemakers after they had tasted the freedom that comes from money of their own generated by a job.

Also, the outlook of those soldiers who had seen foreign places for the first time was changed. They were no longer content to "stay down on the farm." This was a rebirth of the World War I song, "How You Gonna Keep 'em Down on the Farm After They've Seen Paris." America had just come out of the Great Depression; travel, which had been reduced, was open again.

The method of travel had also changed. No longer would trains and automobiles on bad roads be the preferred way of travel. Roads were improved and airplanes provided a quick and safe way to get to a destination. Airplanes made the transition from propeller to jet. A new age of travel was born. The world became smaller and other cultures had a greater influence on the American people. This greater influence was also enhanced by better communications.

War, many times, provides improvements in products and new technology. The atomic bomb closed World War II. It also opened the Nuclear Age. Other improvements also came as the result of the country working on new ways to win the war. In all, the war caused change to the American family and the way it lived.

THE WHITE HOUSE
WASHINGTON

January 15, 1942.

My dear Judge:-

Thank you for yours of January fourteenth. As
you will, of course, realize the final decision about the
baseball season must rest with you and the Baseball Club
owners -- so what I am going to say is solely a personal
and not an official point of view.

I honestly feel that it would be best for the
country to keep baseball going. There will be fewer people
unemployed and everybody will work longer hours and harder
than ever before.

And that means that they ought to have a
chance for recreation and for taking their minds off
their work even more than before.

Baseball provides a recreation which does
not last over two hours or two hours and a half, and
which can be got for very little cost. And, incidentally,
I hope that night games can be extended because it gives
an opportunity to the day shift to see a game occasionally.

As to the players themselves, I know you agree
with me that individual players who are of active military
or naval age should go, without question, into the services.
Even if the actual quality of the teams is lowered by the
greater use of older players, this will not dampen the
popularity of the sport. Of course, if any individual
has some particular aptitude in a trade or profession,
he ought to serve the Government. That, however, is a
matter which I know you can handle with complete justice.

Here is another way of looking at it -- if
300 teams use 5,000 or 6,000 players, these players are
a definite recreational asset to at least 20,000,000
of their fellow citizens -- and that in my judgment is
thoroughly worthwhile.

With every best wish,

Very sincerely yours,

Franklin D Roosevelt

Hon. Kenesaw M. Landis,
333 North Michigan Avenue,
Chicago,
Illinois.

Reprint of this letter courtesy of the Baseball Hall of Fame Library.

Baseball continued while the war went on. During World War I, General Enoch Crowder, the provost marshall of the armed forces, issued a statement that required men either to fight or work in an essential, war-related job. Baseball was not considered essential at that time. Because of this order, the 1918 baseball season closed on September 1. Baseball was concerned how it would be treated when World War II started. *The Sporting News*, baseball's best-known paper, ran articles and front page layouts to show how baseball was supporting the war effort and how important it was to continue playing the game. The answer came in President Franklin Roosevelt's "Green Light" letter, seen on the previous page.

The letter, addressed to Commissioner Kenesaw Landis, stated that baseball was good for the morale of the people, and it gave the citizens an activity to be involved with other than the war. Commissioner Landis was given credit for getting this concession. However, Washington Senators' owner Clark Griffith's friendship with President Roosevelt was probably the driving force behind the decision. Whatever the reason, baseball would continue to be played as the country fought the war.

At that time there were sixteen teams and each team had twenty-five players. This made a total of 400 players on major league rosters at any one time. Almost 500 players with major league experience fought in the war. In other words, major league baseball contributed $1 \frac{1}{4}$ times the number of players on the total rosters. Also, some players couldn't serve. They had physical problems that made them unfit for service or their family responsibilities were such that they couldn't go to war.

During this period, baseball became a game played by older men, very young men, and men who couldn't pass the military's physical examination. As the war went on, from 1942 to 1945, the pool of "regular" major league players went down. More and more the job of playing major league baseball was done by those who would have been passed over in an earlier time.

This, however, did not cause the intensity of the pennant races or the World Series to lessen. In 1942 most of the teams were not feeling the effect of the military involvement. The Cardinals and the Dodgers battled the whole season before the Cardinals pulled away at the end. The 1942 St. Louis Cardinal team is considered to be one of the best teams of all time. They went on to defeat the Yankees in five games in the World Series.

From 1943 to 1945 the teams that won were the ones less affected by the military call-up. The Cardinals were able to keep Stan Musial for 1943 and 1944, and they continued to win. The Yankees won again in 1943 but fell back in 1944 as almost all of their regulars were activated.

This gave the St. Louis Browns a chance to win their only pennant. In 1945 the Detroit Tigers were led by Hal Newhouser and bolstered by the return of Hank Greenberg. The Chicago Cubs also took advantage of the player shortage to win the National League flag. The St. Louis Browns were hurt in their quest for a second flag by the use of Pete Gray, the outfielder with just one arm. Many feel that the Browns played Gray in an attempt to draw fans rather than to win games.

Another effect on major league baseball during this time was the restriction on travel. This led to changes in spring training and to the way series were set up during the season. All

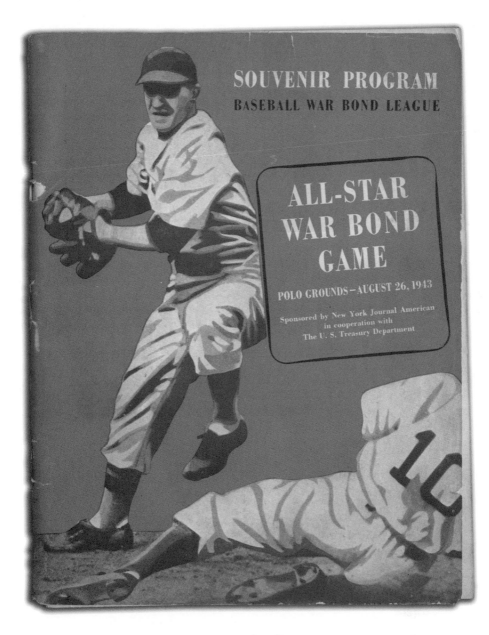

Front cover of the game program from August 26, 1943.

Reprint courtesy of author's private collection.

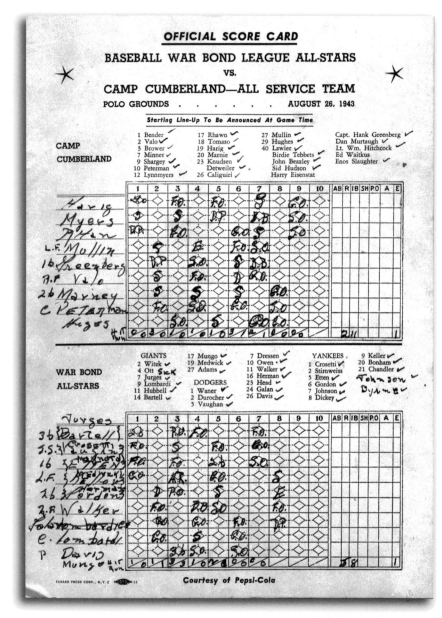

This used scorecard lists the roster of all the players who were on both teams.

Reprint courtesy of author's private collection.

were designed to reduce the amount of travel done by the teams. For spring training, the teams were restricted to sites north of the Mason-Dixon line and east of the Mississippi River. The exception was made for the teams from St. Louis. However, the Cardinals trained just east of the river at Cairo, Illinois, and the St. Louis Browns trained just west of the river at Cape Girardeau, Missouri. The rest of the teams chose sites close to their home base. Pictures in *The Sporting News* during this period show teams warming up in the snow and standing around fires. But baseball went on.

The war-related reduction in travel that affected all Americans had an effect on a planned move in baseball. The St. Louis Browns were in the process of getting approval to transfer their franchise to Los Angeles when the Japanese attacked Pearl Harbor. To avoid increased travel, baseball's expansion to the west coast was put on hold until 1958. By that time the Browns had moved to Baltimore.

Major league baseball also contributed to the war effort in a number of different ways. Wrigley Field in Chicago was known for many years as the only major league baseball park that didn't have lights. However, many don't know that in 1942 Philip K. Wrigley had announced that he was installing lighting in Wrigley Field. When the war started, instead of installing the lights, he gave the electrical equipment to be used in the war effort. Wrigley Field remained dark for another fifty years.

There were other activities in which baseball helped the war effort. Some of the Boston Red Sox players took part in coast watches. Some of the Brooklyn Dodgers visited plants to encourage workers to invest in war bonds. In New York, Dodger, Giant, and Yankee players were "auctioned" off to different companies. After the initial "price," the companies also bought additional war bonds based on the players' performances. Over $7 million of war bonds were sold using this technique. Other major leaguers became members of all-star teams that visited military bases to entertain the troops. These players were in addition to those players in the military who played for the entertainment of troops. Others put teams together to play games to raise money for Army/Navy relief and for war bonds.

Many of these games were against military all-star teams made up of major league players who were already in the military. Some of the games raised large amounts of money to help the war effort. The game that generated the most money in this series of "war bond games," was played in The Polo Grounds in New York on August 26, 1943. This game featured the "War Bond All-Stars" (made up of Yankee, Giant, and Dodger players) against the team from Camp Cumberland. The War Bond All-Stars featured Mel Ott, Carl Hubbell, and Dick Bartell of the Giants; Leo Durocher, Mickey Owen, and Billy Herman of the Dodgers; and Joe Gordon, Bill Dickey, Charley Keller, and Spud Chandler of the Yankees. Additional players from each of the teams played as well. The Camp Cumberland team featured major leaguers who had already been taken into the service. They included Hank Greenberg, Enos Slaughter, Elmer Valo, Birdie Tebbets, and Johnny Beazley. A number of other major leaguers were also on the roster. In addition to playing the game, a number of other activities took place in the Polo Grounds that day. The program for the day stated that seven of the twelve living Hall of Fame members would be at the game dressed "in the uniforms they wore when they flamed the big league greatness" (All-Star War Bond Game program). Also appearing that day were a number of show business personalities. They included Don Ameche, Milton Berle, Irving Berlin, Jimmy Cagney, Bennie Goodman and his Orchestra, Fred Waring and his Glee Club, Ethel Merman, and several others. The event's master of ceremonies was New York's mayor, James J. Walker.

They raised $816 million that day through the sale of advertising in the sixty-eight page program and through seat purchases. The attitude of the people who committed $816 million for war bond purchases and of the players and performers who took part in the activities is summed up in a statement made by Branch Rickey, Dodger president. He said, "The Dodgers are 'All Out' to aid the war effort and our entire organization—players, officials and employees—have pledged their full cooperation to the cause of Victory" (All-Star War Bond Game program).

Some of the major league players suffered more than just the loss of time. Ted Williams lost almost five years because of his time in the Marines. His three years in World War II were spent in training and giving training. However, during the Korean conflict he was assigned to combat duty as a pilot and almost lost his life. On a combat mission his plane was hit and he was forced into a crash landing. Luckily he was not injured. During his time in Korea, Williams served as a wingman for future astronaut and U.S. Senator John Glenn when they were flying with the 311 Marine fighter squadron near Pohang Dong Ni, Korea, in February 1953.

Not all were that lucky. Cecil Travis was one of the best infielders in the American League prior to being called into the Army. During the 1941 season, when Ted Williams batted .406, Travis was second in the batting race. He batted higher than Joe DiMaggio despite DiMaggio's fifty-six game batting streak. His career average, after eight full seasons, was .327 at the time he entered the service. His success was based partly on his speed and agility. During his military service, he was involved in the Battle of the Bulge, where his feet were frozen. When he returned to the Washington Senators, he had lost some of his speed and agility. His batting average went down, and he was out of baseball at age thirty-four, only two years after returning from the Army. After the war he batted only .241. He had a potential Hall of Fame career before the war. After the war, he not only didn't have a Hall of Fame career, he couldn't even continue to play at the major league level.

There are many other stories of suffering that took place as men, including baseball players, fought for their country. Phil Marchildon was a Canadian citizen and a pitcher for the Philadelphia Athletics. He joined the Canadian Air Force and turned down a job to be a physical fitness trainer so he could fight. On August 16, 1944, he was one of seven crew members on a Halifax bomber making a bombing run over Northern Europe. His plane was shot down over Kiel Bay, one of the inlets off the coast of Denmark. Denmark was controlled by the Germans. He parachuted into the water and spent four hours there before he was picked up by a fisherman. Marchildon and one other crew member survived the crash. He was turned over to the Germans and spent nine months in a prisoner of war camp in Poland before the British liberated the camp in May 1945. He lost thirty to forty pounds and suffered a bad case of nerves. Although he returned to pitch in the major leagues, he was never the same after his service.

While it is true that a number of major league baseball players did not take part in combat, a number of them did fight. Even the ones who entertained were exposed to some risk. They

ORIGINAL w/ Ted Spencer TW 5/3/95

NATIONAL LEAGUE SERVICE BUREAU
30 ROCKEFELLER PLAZA
NEW YORK 20, N. Y.

The National League is interested, for purposes of publicity and historical record, to have in its Service Bureau files, the war record of its baseball players who served with the Armed Forces during World War II. So that your part in this war may be available to the league, would you kindly fill out the following questionnaire and return same to this office.

Ford Frick

Name WARREN E SPAHN Club BOSTON BRAVES

Date of Entry Into Service NOVEMBER 10-42 Branch of Service C.E.

What outfits (corps, divisions, fleet, etc) served in 14TH ARM'D DIV
276TH COMBAT ENGR BN, 1257 C ENGR BN 1265 C ENGR BN 34RD REGS by general sv.

Length of overseas service, dates AUG-44 TO MAY 46. Where? ENGLAND
FRANCE BELGIUM + GERMANY

Campaigns BATTLE OF BULGE - RHINE CROSSING-CENTRAL GERMANY

Decorations, battle stars, campaign ribbons, etc,,,
AMER. THEATER - EUROPEAN THEATER - 3 BATTLE STARS PURPLE HEART

Promotions in rank WAS DISCHARGED 1st LT BATTLEFELD Com.

Wounds or injuries sustained
SHRAPNEL WOUND LEFT FOOT

Where were you V-E Day? GIESSEN GERMANY V-J Day KASSEL GERMANY

Please give any other interesting details of your time in service. (Use back of page if necessary.

Signature Warren E Spahn

Reprint of this form courtesy of the Baseball Hall of Fame Library.

9

were stationed in war zones and flew to places where the enemy was still present. However, the group that did actual fighting was exposed to the most extreme dangers. A number of those did suffer injuries and did take part in significant battles. Warren Spahn, in response to an inquiry from Ford Frick, National League president, filled out a questionnaire about his service. It shows that Spahn took part in the Battle of the Bulge as well as the Rhine Crossing. It also indicates that Spahn was wounded during his service. He was promoted with a battlefield commission to end his service as a 1st Lieutenant. A copy of his form, from the Warren Spahn file in the Baseball Hall of Fame, is shown.

Minor league players also suffered. As a group, they were exposed to more danger than major league players because they were not as well known. Several good prospects suffered injuries that kept them from having a major league career. One of those prospects was Bert Shepard. He had been with Bisbee in the Arizona-Texas League in 1941 before entering the Army Air Corps on May 26, 1942. He became a fighter pilot. On May 21, 1944, on his thirty-fourth mission with the 55th Fighter group, he was shot down. He was flying a P-38 Lightning. While he was strafing a truck convoy north of Berlin, he was brought down by anti-aircraft fire. He was injured in the crash and the injuries necessitated the amputation of his right leg between the ankle and the knee. A fellow prisoner made an artificial leg for him from supplies provided by the British Red Cross. In February 1945, he was released from the prison camp and returned home. Even though he had suffered this injury, he was determined to resume his baseball career. After additional recovery in Walter Reed Army Hospital, Shepard was allowed to work out with the Washington Senators. Other baseball owners, along with the Senators, knew the positive public relations that could be had by letting Shepard take part in baseball activities. His chance for a major league career was over as a player so the Senators signed him as a player/coach. While mostly a batting practice pitcher, Shepard did get to pitch in some exhibition games. He pitched in two games against military teams and in one game against the Dodgers. He did get to pitch in one official game during the year. On August 4, 1945, manager Ossie Bluege brought Shepard into a game where the Senators were well behind. His one game was successful. He pitched five and one-third innings, allowing only three hits and one run. Because of the injury he suffered in the war, his major league career consisted of that one game. Rather than being resentful or angry about what could have been, he had a good disposition and was grateful for the chance he had with the Senators.

Billy Southworth, Jr., was the first baseball player to enlist. He joined the Army Air Corps in December 1940. He had reached the Triple-A level in the minor leagues before he enlisted. He became a bomber pilot and had twenty-five bombing runs over Europe without being hit. He had christened his B-17 "The Winning Run," and he always wore the St. Louis Cardinal baseball cap his father, the Cardinal manager, had sent to him. He rose to the rank of major and earned the Distinguished Flying Cross and Air Medal. However, his luck ran out February 15, 1945, as he tried to make an emergency landing at New York's LaGuardia Field. He overshot the runway and went into Flushing Bay. Southworth's body was not found until six months later when it washed up on a beach in the Bronx—another career taken away by the war.

Lou Brissie was another who suffered very severe wounds in the fighting in Italy. However, after twenty-three operations and the use of a steel brace and shin guard on his left leg when pitching, Brissie was able to overcome and have two years with the Philadelphia Athletics. His wounds were caused by shell fragments, and it was reported that "both feet were broken, his left ankle was smashed, his left leg was broken between the knee and ankle, and both hands and shoulders were wounded" (Mead 1985, 200). Brissie's story was told in the movie "The Comeback" starring Chuck Connors.

There are many other examples of men who were thought to be major league prospects whose careers ended because of injuries suffered during the war. Johnny Beazley had just helped the Cardinals win the pennant and beat the Yankees in the 1942 World Series. Johnny Grodzicki was the number one prospect in the Cardinal organization before the war. He was with a paratrooper unit engaged in some of the last battles with the Germans when he was wounded in his right thigh only five days before VE day. When he came back, he couldn't control his leg well enough to field his position or to throw the ball in an effective manner.

The minor leagues suffered during this time. Many of the minor leagues were forced to close down because of the lack of players and other wartime restrictions. In 1941, there were forty-one minor leagues with 292 teams. The total ballplayers in the minor league system would have totaled close to 6,000 team members. By the 1943 season, the number of minor leagues had been reduced to ten with only sixty-six teams. This reduced the number of players from approximately 6,000 to less than 1,500. The lack of players was so severe that the St. Louis Cardinals advertised for players in *The Sporting News*. The number of leagues and players stayed about the same during the next two years. Four teams were added to the ten leagues in 1944, and two additional leagues with a total of sixteen teams resumed action in 1945. For the most part, minor league baseball was taken away from the people during the course of the war.

To make up for some of loss of baseball, the All-American Girls Professional Baseball League was formed. It was financed by Philip K. Wrigley, president of the Chicago Cubs, and its Board of Trustees, including Branch Rickey, general manager of the Brooklyn Dodgers. The teams were located in the general Chicago area, and the rules evolved over time. Play started in 1943 using a 12" ball and pitching underhand. The ball was reduced in size as the years progressed until, by its last season in 1954, the ball measured 9". The method of pitching also changed. After four seasons of pitching underhand, players pitched sidearm for two seasons before overhand pitching was allowed in 1948. The distance from the pitching rubber to home plate also was increased as the pitching methods changed. Starting at 40', the distance was increased to 60' by the last season. According to *The Baseball Encyclopedia*, the league drew more than one million fans for the ten teams in the league in 1948 (Bucek 1996, 3007).

The style of play used when the league was formed caused the baseball record magazine, *Major League Baseball*, to call the league the All-American Girls Softball League (Salsinger, Heilmann, and Black 1945, 129). The teams played between eighty and one hundred and twenty games per season during the time the league existed. The magazine started reporting the statistics of the league in their 1945 edition. The coverage continued in 1946. In that year the record book featured a picture of Harold Newhouser, player of the year in major league baseball in 1945, on the cover and a picture on Connie Wisniewski, player of the year in the All-American Girls Baseball League in 1945, on the back cover.

Wrigley sold the league after the 1944 season. At that time it was apparent that major league baseball was going to be allowed to continue to play. It was after Wrigley sold the league that it reached its greatest popularity. The war had caused a vacuum to be created with the removal of many of the professional baseball players, and Wrigley stepped up and filled that vacuum. The league continued after the close of the war and folded only after management problems when the central control of the league ceased. The league's last season was 1954.

The war caused many baseball careers to be interrupted. Even with this interruption in their careers and the dangers they faced when they were put in harm's way, most baseball players realized the need of their country. They knew that the country was in trouble and needed its citizens to step up and support the war effort. Their feelings are represented by what they said. Enos Slaughter lost three prime years of his career. He said, "I was glad to serve my country. I am proud to [have] come back and have some great years in baseball" (Slaughter letter 1997).

Bob Feller missed almost four years in his career. He was also the support of his family because of his dad's illness. He could have sat out the war on his farm in Iowa, but he didn't. He said, "We were outraged about Pearl Harbor and what Hitler was doing in Europe. We didn't just fight to protect ourselves. We wanted to take those guys on and beat the living hell out of them, and I wanted to be a part of that" (Feller and Gilbert 1990, 116). Feller's actions bore out his words. After enlisting he could have been part of a recreation program somewhere and not have been in active combat. However, after training, he requested and got assigned to a battleship and saw a good deal of combat.

Hank Greenberg was one of the early draftees when the draft was reinstated. He was drafted in 1941. After serving his year, Greenberg was discharged from the Army on December 5, 1941, at age thirty. When Pearl Harbor was bombed by the Japanese two days later, Greenberg reenlisted. He would not have had to at that time because of his age. However, he said, "We are in trouble and there is only one thing for me to do—return to the service" (Mead 1985, 32). He went on to add "...This doubtless means I am finished with baseball, and it would be silly for me to say I do not leave it without a pang. But all of us are confronted with a terrible task—the defense of our country and the fight for our lives" (Mead 1985, 32). Here was a man who only a few years earlier had come the closest to breaking Babe Ruth's sixty home run record and, when faced with a decision that meant choosing between himself and his country, he chose his country. He was able to return after the war for a few years, but he missed over four years in service to his country.

Many others had the same attitude as these three players. Many had names that are not household words. Sometimes that lack of identity was caused by their service to their country. William R. (Billy) Johnson had his career interrupted with the Yankees. Despite that he said, "My feeling is there is no service as wonderful as serving one's country" (Johnson letter 1998). Hank Sauer wrote, "Yes, [I] missed three years, but so did a lot of players. But it was for our country" (Sauer letter 1998). Tommy Byrne said, "[I] have always enjoyed and [am] proud to have served my country during World War II" (Byrne letter 1997). Albert Milnar, who pitched for the Indians, Browns, and A's, wrote, "I am not sorry I served my country. I am proud of it" (Milnar letter 1997). He wrote this even though he lost two years of his career after he was called into the military at age thirty-one. These are but examples of the attitude that was shown by most baseball players, yes, by most Americans.

Damon Phillips, who played for the Cincinnati Reds in 1942 and the Boston Braves in 1944 and 1946, may have summed it up the best. He wrote in a letter, "Two years away from baseball may or may not have had a bearing on my career. But it really doesn't matter. Thousands died in that war and thousands of others sustained injuries that would affect their lives for as long as they would live. I did not. For that I am grateful—I wish no one had" (Phillips letter 1998).

The question is always raised, "Who suffered the most because of their military service?" Many say that Ted Williams, Hank Greenberg, and Bob Feller are the ones. They missed the most time and had the best career marks during the time they actually played. Bob Savage, who pitched for the A's and the Browns, agrees with that statement even though his career was hurt because of wounds he suffered during his service. He downplayed his own losses when he said, "I do not believe the wounds caused me any problems as far as baseball was concerned, other than lost time. Friends like Ted Williams were the ones more affected by the war, because they were the ones that were going to set records" (Savage letter 1997). That's one theory.

However, what about the player who had just started his career and was not established? Joe DiMaggio, Ted Williams, Bob Feller, and Stan Musial had their old jobs back when they returned because of who they were and the records they had achieved before they entered the service. On the other hand, a player who was just getting started when he entered the service returned after three years with rust on his skills. Somewhat older than the other players, he was out of luck. In spite of the G.I. Bill, major league baseball found a way around the requirement to reemploy former players. Because of their handling of these cases, several of the "journeyman" players missed out on a baseball pension, some by only a few days of service.

So the question remains, "Who paid the most: the name players who lost a chance for a record or a journeyman player who lost his chance to ever have a meaningful major league career?" Both paid a very severe price. However, for the most part they paid that price willingly and with pride. They knew there was a need and moved to fill the country's requirements.

The country was fighting for its survival. Japan had tried to cripple the United States with its sneak attack on Pearl Harbor. What it really did was awake a sleeping giant. It brought the country together with a common purpose—to preserve the American way and to defeat the evil Germans and Japanese. Baseball players took their role in that effort as seriously as did all other Americans. Because of that united effort by all Americans, the United States was successful.

CHAPTER 2

The players listed in this chapter are those position players who had careers that lasted at least eleven years at the major league level. Also, these players had experience in the major leagues before their service in the military. The exceptions to this rule were those who were included on the list of players obtained from the Hall of Fame. Those players were included even though they did not reach the majors until after the war. Because of the length of their careers, many of these players will be known to baseball fans. In addition, the totals they achieved when playing place some of them among the all-time career leaders in different statistical categories.

ADAMS, ROBERT H. (BOBBY)   BR TR 5' 10" 160 lbs.
Born December 14, 1921, Tuolumne, Ca. — Died February 13, 1997, Gig Harbor, Wa.
Played for Cincinnati (1946-55), Chicago (A) (1955), Baltimore (1956), and Chicago (N) (1957-59)

Bobby Adams did not reach the majors until after the war. He was identified as an infield prospect when the players for Cincinnati were listed. His 1942 season was in Syracuse before going into the Army Air Force for three years. He was stationed at Santa Rosa, California, for a while in late 1942 and early 1943. He arrived back from the Pacific on November 2, 1945, aboard the transport *Cecil* and landed at Los Angeles. After his time in the Army, he joined the Cincinnati Reds for the 1946 season. He had an extended career as a infielder, playing both second base and third base. He played in over one hundred games per season for six consecutive years (1949-1954). His best years were 1952 and 1953 when he was the full-time third baseman for the Reds. Because his career did not begin until after the war, no additions to his career totals were necessary.

AGE	YRS	ML	G	BA	SA	AB	H	2B	3B	HR	HR%	R	RBI	BB	SO	SB
21-23	43-45	14	1281	0.269	0.368	4019	1082	188	49	37	0.9	591	303	414	447	67
(NO PRIOR		0	0	0	0	0	0	0	0	0	0	0	0	0	0	0
MAJOR EXP)		14	1281	0.269	0.368	4019	1082	188	49	37	0.9	591	303	414	447	67

APPLING, LUCIUS B. (LUKE)   BR TR 5' 10" 183 lbs.
Born April 2, 1907, High Point, N.C. — Died January 3, 1991, Cummings, Ga.
Played for Chicago (A) (1930-43, 1945-50)

Luke Appling, a Hall of Fame shortstop, played for the White Sox for fourteen years before going into the Army. He was one of the best hitting shortstops of all time. He led the league in hitting on two different occasions (1936 and 1943). His .388 average in 1936 is the highest average ever achieved by a shortstop. He was not known as a good fielder when he arrived in the majors. However, under the tutoring of Jimmy Dykes, Appling became a good shortstop. He was known for always having some kind of ailment. Because of this, his nickname became "Old Aches & Pains." Because of his reputation, it is ironic that Appling got assigned to Lawson General Hospital, Atlanta, Georgia, to spend most of his 21 months in the service. He said when he was inducted on November 27, 1943, "ducking bullets can't be much worse than ducking some of those bad hops in the infield" (Goldstein 1980, 236). Instead of bullets, Appling got assigned to be the manager/shortstop on the quartermaster post team at Camp Lee, Virginia, after he completed his basic training at Fort Sheridan, Illinois. Appling's wife had an optimistic outlook when he left for the Army. She said, "The war will soon be over because outside of baseball, Luke never held a job for over two weeks" (Gilbert 1992, 107).

Appling was thirty-six years old when he entered military service. He served for almost two years before being discharged on August 30, 1945, in Georgia. While in many cases a baseball player of that age is well past his prime, Appling led the American League in batting in 1943, the year he was inducted. In addition, he hit over .300 for the four years after he was released from the Army. It would then be easy to project that he would have been able to maintain the .300 average if he had not served his country. Appling was also noted for his ability to foul off the pitches he did not like until something was thrown that he could hit. Once he was credited with fouling off seventeen straight pitches before hitting a triple. He was so good at this that Bob Feller admitted in his book, *Now Pitching Bob Feller* (1990, 96) that he walked Appling on purpose when he was in the process of pitching his no-hitter on opening day 1940. It was in the ninth with two out; Appling, with a count of two and two, fouled off four or five pitches. Feller decided that he would not try to get the third strike and walked Appling to get to the next hitter.

Since he maintained a .300 batting average for an additional two years (minus eighteen games), it is also reasonable to assume that he would have been able to reach the three-thousand-hit level. He also would have been close to the record number of games for a shortstop in a career. The record is held by Luis Aparicio with 2,581 games. Appling retired with 2,218 games at shortstop. With an additional two seasons he would be very close to that record. In addition, Appling is second to Ernie Banks in the number of games played without a post-season appearance (Banks 2,528 and Appling 2,422). Appling's career covered twenty years, and he was elected to the Hall of Fame in 1964.

AGE	YRS	ML	G	BA	SA	AB	H	2B	3B	HR	HR%	R	RBI	BB	SO	SB
37-38	44-45	20	2422	0.31	0.398	8857	2749	440	102	45	0.5	1319	1116	1302	528	179
(2 YRS MINUS		1	275	0.303	0.372	1043	316	50	5	4	0.4	129	104	143	56	26
18 GAMES)		21	2697	0.31	0.396	9900	3065	490	107	49	0.5	1448	1220	1445	584	205

BARTELL, RICHARD W. (DICK)   BR TR 5'9" 160 lbs.
Born November 22, 1907, Chicago, Il. — Died August 4, 1995, Alameda, Ca.
Played for Pittsburgh (1927-30), Philadelphia (N) (1931-34), New York (N) (1935-38, 1941-43, 1946), Chicago (N) (1939), and Detroit (1940-41)

Dick Bartell earned the nickname "Rowdy Richard." His aggressive style of play earned him both respect and contempt. He was known as a fierce competitor who sometimes wore out his welcome after a while because of his attitude. He played for six teams over the course of his eighteen-year major league career. Considered a good shortstop, he played in the first All-Star game in 1933. He also had the ability to "spark" a team. After he was traded to the New York Giants, they won the pennant during his second and third years with the team. Bartell was considered to be a very important part of these teams. The Detroit Tigers also won the pennant the year that Bartell was traded to them.

On April 17, 1944, following the 1943 season, he was inducted into the Navy at Camp Farragut, Idaho. He was thirty-six years old and his career was winding down. He did get to play baseball for the Bainbridge, Maryland, Naval Training Station team in 1944 and at Treasure Island, California, in 1945. When he was discharged on October 5, 1945, he was almost thirty-eight years of age, and younger players were taking over. Bartell appeared in only five games following his return from the Navy. Even though Bartell was known for aggressive behavior, Bill Rigney sees him in a different light. Rigney remembers Bartell taking him aside and working with him when he was a rookie in 1946. This even though they knew that only one of them would make the team. Rigney made the Giants team, and Bartell became a coach. Rigney said, "I never forgot his generosity" (Peary 1994, 5).

AGE	YRS	ML	G	BA	SA	AB	H	2B	3B	HR	HR%	R	RBI	BB	SO	SB
36-37	44-45	18	2016	0.284	0.391	7629	2165	442	71	79	1	1130	710	748	627	109
		2	159	0.272	0.366	554	151	24	2	8	1.4	77	47	77	49	8
		20	2175	0.283	0.39	8183	2316	466	73	87	1.1	1207	757	825	676	117

BERARDINO, JOHN (JOHNNY)   BR TR 5' 11" 175 lbs.

Born May 1, 1917, Los Angeles, Ca. — Died May 19, 1996, Los Angeles, Ca.
Played for St. Louis (A) (1939–42, 1946–47, 1951), Cleveland (1948–50, 1952), and Pittsburgh (1950, 1952)

Although he played baseball for eleven years, Johnny Berardino is probably best known for playing Dr. Steve Hardy on the soap opera *General Hospital*. He also played in the movie *North by Northwest* starring Cary Grant. He is one of two former major leaguers to be included in the Hollywood Walk of Fame. (Chuck Conners is the other.) He played most of his playing career for the St. Louis Browns. He was the regular second baseman for the Browns for three years before he entered the service and for a year after he was discharged. He was known as a one-man infield because of his ability to play all infield positions.

Times were tough, playing for the Browns. It was tough losing all the time. The Browns had a habit of trading away or selling their best players to pay operating expenses. Because of this, the teams was never very successful (except for 1944). The pay was low, so Berardino had to draw his unemployment of $15.00 per week during the off-season, as well as do some acting to make ends meet. Bill Veeck, always known for his publicity stunts, once had Berardino's face insured for $1,000,000 against line drives and other mayhem.

Berardino applied for admission to the Army Air Force at Los Angeles, January 14, 1942, and was sent to Higley Field, Chandler, Arizona, for flight training. He received a medical discharge from the Air Force in mid-June 1942. He then enlisted in the Navy on September 28, 1942, and served there until he was discharged on October 26, 1945. He was a physical instructor stationed in the States for most of the war and he was listed as the manager of the baseball team at the Naval Air Station at Terminal Island, California. Later (June 1945) he was listed as a recent arrival at Pearl Harbor, where he played some baseball. A back injury suffered while stationed at Pearl Harbor required a good deal of therapy and caused problems during the rest of his playing career. He only had one season as a regular after the war despite being only twenty-nine years of age.

AGE	YRS	ML	G	BA	SA	AB	H	2B	3B	HR	HR%	R	RBI	BB	SO	SB
25-28	42-45	11	912	0.249	0.355	3028	755	167	23	36	1.2	334	387	284	268	27
(4 YRS MINUS		3	475	0.263	0.38	1806	475	106	14	26	1.4	207	252	147	155	14
29 GAMES)		14	1387	0.254	0.365	4834	1230	273	37	62	1.3	541	639	431	423	41

BERRA, LAWRENCE P. (YOGI)   BL TR 5'7" 185 lbs.
Born May 12, 1925, St. Louis, Mo.
Played for New York (A) (1946–63) and New York (N) (1965)

If you are talking to any person who knows anything about baseball, all you have to do is mention "Yogi" and he or she knows immediately who you are talking about. More has been said about Yogi and his comments than almost anyone else. Yogi was listed by the Hall of Fame as a major league veteran of World War II. His major league career didn't start until 1946, so his career statistics have not been adjusted. He enlisted in the Navy in 1944 and was discharged in 1946. He was in the third wave to hit Omaha Beach on "D" day when the Allies started their operation to reclaim Europe from Germany by landing on the coast of France. In addition to being involved in the Normandy invasion, he also fought in southern France. He suffered a hand wound and was returned to the States for hospitalization early in 1945.

I cannot say enough about this Hall of Fame catcher. It wasn't always easy for Yogi. He first tried out for the St. Louis Cardinals but rejected a $250 bonus offer (they offered Joe Garagiola $500). When he started playing for the Yankees, he was not accepted. They said he "didn't look like a Yankee" (Ward and Burns 1994, 311). Larry MacPhail said, "He looked like the bottom man on an unemployed acrobatic team" (Okrent and Wulf 1989, 207). He was not considered to be a good catcher when he arrived in New York, so the Yankees brought back Bill Dickey to work with Yogi to improve his catching skills. It worked because he later became known as a good catcher and handler of pitchers. He was best known, however, for his hitting skills. A notorious "bad ball" hitter, he made a career of getting the big hit in pressure games. He holds or has held most of the career records for batting in the World Series. He hit the first pinch-hit homer in the World Series on October 2, 1947. This three-time American League MVP (1951, 1954, and 1955) and Hall of Fame catcher (elected in 1972) held the record for most home runs by a catcher (306) until it was broken by Carlton Fisk.

For all his World Series records and all his hitting and fielding records, Yogi is perhaps most famous for the things he said or is given credit for saying. "It ain't over 'til it's over;" "baseball is ninety percent mental. The other half is physical;" "you can observe a lot by watching;" "it's deja vu all over again" are but a few of the remarks that Yogi is given credit for saying. However, Gene Woodling, one of Yogi's teammates, said, "For the public, Yogi built an image of being a dumb, funny guy. He did make those absurd nonsensical statements he was famous for—I'd say, 'Yogi, what are you talking about?'—but he was a serious player. He wasn't dumb.

He didn't read comics. Bobby Brown came up with that; he said he was reading medical books, and Yogi was over there reading comic books. Yogi got good mileage out of the publicity" (Peary 1994, 107-108).

AGE	YRS	ML	G	BA	SA	AB	H	2B	3B	HR	HR%	R	RBI	BB	SO	SB
19-20	44-45	19	2120	0.285	0.482	7555	2150	321	49	358	4.7	1175	1430	704	415	30
(NO PRIOR	0	0	0	0	0	0	0	0	0	0	0	0	0	0	0	0
MAJOR EXP)	19	2120	0.285	0.482	7555	2150	321	49	358	4.7	1175	1430	704	415	30

BLOODWORTH, JAMES H. (JIMMY)   BR TR 5' 11   180 lbs.

Born July 26, 1917, Tallahassee, Fl. — Died August 17, 2002, Apalachicola, Fl.
Played for Washington (1937, 1939-41), Detroit (1942-43, 1946), Pittsburgh (1947),
Cincinnati (1949-50), and Philadelphia (N) (1950-51)

Jimmy Bloodworth was considered to be a journeyman second baseman. He is described as being an "adequate second baseman over eleven ML seasons but a subpar hitter"(Shatzkin 1990, 84). He was Bob Feller's 348th strikeout victim in 1946. He missed all of the 1944 and 1945 seasons and most of the 1946 season in the military. He entered the Army in November 1943 and was discharged in May 1946. He only got to play about 30 games while in the service even though he was stationed at Fort Leonard Wood, Missouri, for most of his time. He said, "I just went in and did what I was told and hoped and prayed that the war ended as soon as it could" (Van Blair 1994, 15). He was a weapons and demolitions instructor at Fort Leonard Wood, Missouri, for most of the war. He also said, "I never look back and wonder or use my Army years as an excuse. However, '44 and '45 were the middle years of my baseball career and should have been the best, but who knows?" He continued, "When I joined the Tigers, May 1946, I was not in baseball condition. I played very little baseball during the two and a half years in service. I played in the greatest era of baseball that anybody could have played and enjoyed every minute of it, and I have no regrets" (Bloodworth letter 1997). Bloodworth was the regular second baseman for the Senators and Tigers for the three years before going into the service. He was never able to regain that regular status after he returned.

AGE	YRS	ML	G	BA	SA	AB	H	2B	3B	HR	HR%	R	RBI	BB	SO	SB
26-28	44-46	11	1002	0.248	0.358	3519	874	160	20	62	1.8	347	453	200	407	19
(3 YRS MINUS	2	290	0.249	0.361	1082	269	53	3	21	1.9	102	126	68	121	3
76 GAMES)	13	1292	0.248	0.359	4601	1143	213	23	83	1.8	449	579	268	528	22

CAMILLI, ADOLF L. (DOLF)   BL TL 5' 10"   185 lbs.

Born April 23, 1907, San Francisco, Ca. — Died October 21, 1997, San Mateo, Ca.
Played for Chicago (N) (1933-34), Philadelphia (N) (1934-37), Brooklyn (1938-43), and
Boston (A) (1945)

Dolf Camilli's career was almost over before spending any time in the military. *The Sports Encyclopedia, Baseball 1999* lists him on the Dodgers' military roster for 1944. Early he was considered to be safe from the draft because of a large family. This slick-fielding first baseman was a regular from 1934 to 1943, first for the Phillies and then for the Dodgers. He is considered to be one of the best fielding first basemen of all time. He was also a good hitter both for average and power. While he only had two seasons over .300, he regularly batted around .285. For eight straight years (1935 to 1942) he hit more than 20 home runs. Named the National League's MVP in 1941, he led the league in home runs and RBIs as the Dodgers won the pennant. As a former boxer, not many challenged his authority and he is credited as a quiet leader in the clubhouse. He was considered to be the first piece of the puzzle Larry MacPhail used to start rebuilding the Dodgers in 1938. They traded Eddie Morgan and $45,000 to the Phillies to get his contract. Once he became a Dodger, he was a Dodger through and through. Dodgers hated the Giants with a passion. In 1943, the Dodgers traded him to the Giants. He retired rather than play for the Giants. He managed and played in Oakland of the Pacific Coast League rather than playing for the Giants. He made his last appearance in 1945 for the Boston Red Sox.

AGE	YRS	ML	G	BA	SA	AB	H	2B	3B	HR	HR%	R	RBI	BB	SO	SB
37-38	44-45	12	1490	0.277	0.492	5353	1482	261	86	239	4.5	936	950	947	961	60
(2YRS MINUS		1	127	0.26	0.407	508	132	25	10	10	2	88	67	95	58	2
63 GAMES)		13	1617	0.275	0.484	5861	1614	286	96	249	4.2	1024	1017	1042	1019	62

CAMPBELL, BRUCE D.   BL TR 6' 1" 185 lbs.

Born October 20, 1909, Chicago, Il. — Died June 17, 1995, Fort Myers Beach, Fl.
Played for Chicago (A) (1930-32), St. Louis (A) (1932-34), Cleveland (1935-39), Detroit (1940-41) and Washington (1941-42)

The war ended Bruce Campbell's career. He was 33 years old when he joined the Army Air Force in November 1942 at the urging of Birdie Tebbetts. He was a physical instructor at Waco, Texas, where Tebbetts was the manager of the baseball team. Later he was transferred to a base at Liberal, Kansas. He rose to the rank of sergeant during his tenure in the Air Force. After serving three years, he was 36 years old when he was released in October 1945. He went to spring training in 1946 but was released by the Senators after 35 days. He was paid off with 15 days salary per the GI bill for players who were released. He went to veterans' organizations to get help in getting one year's salary ($9,000). Buffalo signed him but then released him after the story broke about his dispute with Washington. Ultimately, he signed with Minneapolis, and Clark Griffith made up the difference between his actual salary and $9,000. This member of the 1933 American League All-Star team once had a 27-game hitting streak (1938) and a six-for-six performance (July 2, 1936). After recovering from spinal meningitis in 1935 to play again, he was given the most courageous athlete award by Philadelphia sports writers.

AGE	YRS	ML	G	BA	SA	AB	H	2B	3B	HR	HR%	R	RBI	BB	SO	SB
32-35	42-45	13	1360	0.29	0.455	4762	1382	295	87	106	2.2	759	766	548	584	53
(4 YRS MINUS		3	326	0.28	0.446	1197	336	66	18	32	2.7	223	191	161	140	15
122 GAMES)		16	1686	0.288	0.454	5959	1718	361	105	138	2.3	82	957	709	724	68

CHAPMAN, SAMUEL B. (SAM)   BR TR 6' 0"   180 lbs.
Born April 11, 1916, Tiburon, Ca.
Played for Philadelphia (A) (1938–41, 1945–51) and Cleveland (1951)

Sam Chapman volunteered for the Navy in November 1941. He was accepted as an athletic instructor and rose to the rank of chief petty officer while serving at Norfolk. Giving up his rank, he tried for a commission in Naval Aviation and won his wings at Corpus Christi, Texas. He was commissioned an ensign on February 26, 1943. His rank was lieutenant (j.g.) when he was an executive officer for one of the Navy's composite air squadrons at Arlington, Washington. Because of his training, it was assumed that he would soon be in the Pacific aboard an aircraft carrier seeing combat against the Japanese. However, he indicated that he did not see any combat but did play for the baseball team at Norfolk (Chapman letter., 1997). He was discharged on September 22, 1945.

Chapman was at the height of his career when he volunteered for the Navy. He had just finished the 1941 season during which he batted .322, hit 25 home runs, drove in 106 runs, and received MVP votes. Known for his defense, he was a regular center fielder for four years before the war and for an additional five years after he returned. Eddie Joost said, "He [Sam Chapman] was one of the best center fielders in the American League including Joe DiMaggio. Not many people gave him the credit he deserved" (Peary 1994, 40). The four years he lost would have been the heart of his career.

AGE	YRS	ML	G	BA	SA	AB	H	2B	3B	HR	HR%	R	RBI	BB	SO	SB
26-29	42-45	11	1368	0.266	0.438	4988	1329	210	52	180	3.6	754	773	562	682	40
(4 YRS MINUS		3	550	0.277	0.463	2047	568	89	25	80	3.9	335	335	246	287	23
9 GAMES)		14	1918	0.27	0.445	7035	1897	299	77	260	3.7	1089	1108	808	969	63

COOPER, WILLIAM W. (WALKER)   BR TR 6' 3"   210 lbs.
Born January 8, 1915, Atherton, Mo. — Died April 11, 1991, Scottsdale, Az.
Played for St. Louis (N) (1940–45, 1956–57), New York (N) (1946–49), Cincinnati (1949–50), Boston (N) (1950–52), Milwaukee (N) (1953), Pittsburgh (1954), and Chicago (N) (1954–55)

Walker Cooper had a physical problem that caused him to be classified as "available for limited service" and gave him a 4-F status for much of the war. In 1945, the director of War Mobilization and Reconstruction led a campaign to get all the athletes classified 4-F reclassified and into the war effort. They adopted a policy that said "if you were an athlete, you were automatically qualified for military service" (Mead 1985, 222). However, Congress put pressure on the War Department to rescind this campaign. The War Department gave in to Congress but not until after Cooper had been drafted. He entered the Navy on May 2, 1945, and was discharged on April 4, 1946. He was inducted at Jefferson Barracks, Missouri, and shipped to Great Lakes, where he spent most of his Navy time. He also played on the Great Lakes baseball team during that time. He was transferred to the Lambert Naval Air Station, Missouri, after the baseball season was over at Great Lakes.

Cooper was known as one of the most intelligent and capable catchers to play the game. He was named to every All-Star team from 1942 to 1950. (The All-Star game was canceled in 1945.) He finished second in MVP voting in 1943. He, along with his brother Mort, were mainstays on the Cardinal teams of 1942, 1943, and 1944 when they won three pennants and two World Series.

There were also stories of incidents where he was known for his fighting, drinking, and intimidating players. Enos Slaughter tells the story that Cooper would spit tobacco juice across batters' shoes when they came to bat and say, "Well, what are you going to do about it?" (Peary 1994, 161).

His best hitting year came in 1947 while with the Giants. During that year, he batted .305, hit 35 home runs, and had 122 RBIs. The Giants thought enough of Cooper and his skills that they paid $175,000 for his contract on January 5, 1946, while he was still in the service. This was the largest cash transaction to purchase a player up to that time.

AGE	YRS	ML	G	BA	SA	AB	H	2B	3B	HR	HR%	R	RBI	BB	SO	SB
30	45	18	1473	0.285	0.464	4702	1341	240	40	173	3.7	573	812	309	357	18
(1 YR MINUS		0	115	0.305	0.495	410	125	22	4	16	3.9	54	80	20	23	2
4 GAMES)		18	1588	0.287	0.466	5112	1466	262	44	189	3.7	627	892	329	380	20

COX, WILLIAM R. (BILLY)   BR TR 5' 10"   150 lbs
Born August 29, 1919, Newport, Pa. — Died March 30, 1978, Harrisburg, Pa.
Played for Pittsburgh (1941, 1946-47), Brooklyn (1948-1954), and Baltimore (1955)

Billy Cox was a very good third baseman. It was said of him, "No better defense third baseman ever lived" (Ritter and Honig 1984, 243). It seems most players agree with that statement. Stan Musial called him one of the finest fielding third basemen he had ever seen (Broeg 1964, 126). Bob Kuzava agreed. "Like I said, I saw a lot of great fielders: Kell, Nettles, Brooks Robinson and both Boyer brothers were great fielders too. But at third base Billy Cox was the premier third baseman" (Van Blair 1994, 99). Cox was a shortstop when he came to the Pirates in 1941. He continued to play shortstop until he was traded to the Dodgers.

After getting in ten games at the end of the season with the Pirates, Cox entered the Army on February 9, 1942. He spent some time at New Cumberland Gap. He helped an engineer baseball team win the "championship of Sicily." This was baseball played in the war zone. He was discharged on July 29, 1945, suffering from malaria. He looked very weak and frail. It took some time to recover from this illness and the emotional effects of the war. After the war he had two seasons as the Pirates shortstop before he was traded to the Dodgers along with Preacher Roe, in 1948. It was one of the worst trades ever made by the Pirates. In Brooklyn, he was transferred to third where he anchored the Dodger infield for seven years.

AGE	YRS	ML	G	BA	SA	AB	H	2B	3B	HR	HR%	R	RBI	BB	SO	SB
22-25	42-45	11	1058	0.262	0.38	3712	974	174	32	66	1.8	470	351	298	218	42
		4	410	0.271	0.405	1485	403	73	19	29	2	195	143	102	64	18
		15	1468	0.265	0.387	5197	1377	247	51	95	1.8	665	494	400	282	60

DESAUTELS, EUGENE A. (GENE)   BR TR 5' 11"   170 lbs.

Born June 13, 1907, Worcester, Ma. — Died November 5, 1994, Flint, Mi.

Played for Detroit (1930–33), Boston (A) (1937–40), Cleveland (1941–43, 1945), and Philadelphia (A) (1946)

Gene Desautels' career lasted for thirteen years. However, he was only considered a regular for four of those years. He was a back-up catcher for the Tigers for four years, back to the minors for three years, a regular with the Red Sox for four years, traded to the Indians to again be a reserve for three years, and in the service for two years before closing out his career with the A's in 1946. He was 36 years old when he went into the Marines on February 29, 1944. He rose to the rank of T/sergeant while stationed at Parris Island, South Carolina. He coached the basketball team and managed and played for the baseball team there. He was discharged on July 29, 1945 at age 38. His baseball career lasted only one more year after serving in the Marines.

AGE	YRS	ML	G	BA	SA	AB	H	2B	3B	HR	HR%	R	RBI	BB	SO	SB
37-38	44-45	13	712	0.233	0.285	2012	469	73	11	3	0.1	211	186	233	168	12
(2 YRS MINUS		1	95	0.228	0.281	285	65	10	1	1	0.4	29	28	40	21	1
10 GAMES)		14	807	0.232	0.284	2297	534	83	12	4	0.2	240	214	273	189	13

DICKEY, WILLIAM M. (BILL)   BL TR 6' 1"   185 lbs.

Born June 6, 1907, Bastrop, La. — Died November 12, 1993, Little Rock, Ar.

Played for New York (A) (1928–43, 1946)

This Hall of Fame catcher was selected to the American League All-Star team eleven times out of twelve chances, despite the fact that the All-Star games did not start until he had been in the league for five years. He was selected as a reserve for the first game in 1933 but didn't get to play when Rick Ferrell started and caught the whole game. For his skill, Dickey had the respect of both Yankee and opposing pitchers. Spud Chandler, Yankee pitcher, said, "He was a great guy to work with. He was real patient with a young pitcher; he'd always encourage you, and he seemed to know what to call for" (Honig 1975, 232). An opposing pitcher said, "With Dickey catching, I would have won five more games a year" (Hirshberg 1970, 124). Bob Feller agreed, "I'd have to rate Bill Dickey of the Yankees in the 1930s and '40s as the best I ever saw. He was as good as anyone behind the plate, and better with the bat" (Feller and Gilbert 1990, 65).

Dickey was the leading catcher of the late 1930s and early 1940s. He was the connecting force on the Yankees between Ruth and Gehrig and DiMaggio as a player, and during the Mantle period as a coach. Known as a good handler of pitchers, he was the regular catcher for eight of the Yankee pennants. He was also durable. He caught more than 100 games for thirteen seasons, a record that stood until Johnny Bench tied it in 1980. However, defense was not the only thing that Dickey could do. He was a lifetime .300 hitter with power. He batted .362 in 1936 to set a record for catchers in the American League that still stands. Dan Daniel, *New York World-Telegram* sportswriter, wrote in 1939, "You have to watch this man, day in and day out, to appreciate him to the full. You have to see the Yankees when he is not in the line-up to know how much he means to them…before you are able to realize how completely he dominates his field" (Dickson 1991, 102).

Dickey was drafted March 15, 1944, shortly before his thirty-seventh birthday, even though he suffered from a bad sinus condition. He was commissioned a lieutenant in the Navy after training at Great Lakes. He also graduated from the Naval Training School at Fort Schuyler, New York. He spent most of his two years in the Navy playing exhibition games in the South Pacific. He played for the Navy in the Pacific "World Series" in late 1944. He managed a team of the Navy's biggest stars which played exhibition games on a tour of Pacific fighting areas. He was discharged in January 1946.

At 39 years old during the 1946 season, he could no longer be more than a part-time player and pinch hitter. He became a playing manager during 1946 when Joe McCarthy was fired, but he resigned as manager at the close of the season and didn't manage in the major leagues again. He also retired as a player at the close of the 1946 season. Later he came back to coach on the Yankee team and help Yogi Berra develop his defensive skills. Dickey is rated as one of the top ten catchers of all time.

AGE	YRS	ML	G	BA	SA	AB	H	2B	3B	HR	HR%	R	RBI	BB	SO	SB
37-38	44-45	17	1789	0.313	0.486	6300	1969	343	72	202	3.2	930	1209	678	289	36
		2	147	0.31	0.415	429	133	26	2	5	1.2	45	53	57	23	3
		19	1936	0.312	0.481	6729	2102	369	74	207	3.1	975	1262	735	312	39

DIMAGGIO, DOMINIC P. (DOM)   BR TR 5'9"   168 lbs.
Born February 12, 1917, San Francisco, Ca.
Played for Boston (A) (1940–42, 1946–53)

How Dom DiMaggio got into service is an example of how Americans felt about their country at this time. He was known during his baseball career as "The Little Professor" in part because of his glasses. He was one of the first position players to wear glasses. Because of his poor eyesight, Army doctors rejected him. Rather than say, "I've done my duty," and go on playing baseball, he went to the Navy and asked to be reexamined. "There was no rejoicing if you were declared 4-F. Every man in his twenties or thirties wanted to do his part in helping America prepare for whatever dangers we would face…" (Gilbert 1992, 22). DiMaggio served as a volunteer aircraft spotter while he was still playing during 1942. Upon reexamination, the Navy accepted him. He was called in November after the 1942 season and served for three years.

DiMaggio completed his boot camp at Treasure Island, California. He had the rank of coxswain there and was later transferred to Norfolk to receive training for chief petty officer. While in Norfolk he played on the baseball team. He went back to California and then to the Pacific. He played for the Navy in the Pacific "World Series" in late 1944. Also, in late 1944 and early 1945, he was in Australia managing and playing on a Navy team. Later it was reported that he was stationed on a tiny island in a hangar on the western coast of Luzon. While there he helped convert part of the island into a well-equipped recreation center. In a letter he said he spent time in the Pacific Theater, didn't see any action, and lost some sight in his right eye because of an infection (DiMaggio letter, 1997).

He was almost twenty-six when he went into the Navy and almost twenty-nine when he came out January 13, 1946, the prime years of a baseball player's career. He knew what he was giving up. He said upon returning from service, "We had added pressure on us because we knew that those war years were lost forever...The limited number of years available to us had been reduced to an even lower number...We knew that what was going to be a short career anyhow was going to be even shorter now" (Gilbert 1992, 264-265).

Despite losing these valuable years, Dom DiMaggio was recognized as a very good baseball player by his peers. Mace Brown said, "The two best center fielders I saw in my career were the Cardinals' Terry Moore and the Red Sox's Dom DiMaggio. They were something" (Van Blair 1994, 27-29). Buddy Lewis said, "Dom DiMaggio was a fantastic fielder" (Van Blair 1994, 108).

In 1948 he set an American League record for making 503 outfield putouts. However, he was always in the shadow of his brother Joe. Because of this, he never got the kind of recognition that he deserved. He was also a good hitter but did not have the power of Joe. He played on some very good Red Sox teams, but they were not quite as good as the Yankee teams where Joe played. Dom had a 34-game hitting streak in 1949 and a 27-game streak in 1951 but again not quite as good as brother Joe. Dom led the league in stolen bases in 1950 with 15. This is the lowest number ever to lead the league.

This seven-time all-star should be considered as one of the better players in baseball. His lifetime .298 batting average and his average of 105 runs scored per season for his ten full years show that he was a great lead-off man, a brilliant fielder with a good arm, and a good hitter.

AGE	YRS	ML	G	BA	SA	AB	H	2B	3B	HR	HR%	R	RBI	BB	SO	SB
26-28	43-45	11	1399	0.298	0.419	5640	1680	308	57	87	1.5	1046	618	750	571	100
		3	418	0.292	0.419	1660	484	95	18	27	1.6	298	192	221	167	33
		14	1817	0.296	0.419	7300	2164	403	75	114	1.6	1344	810	971	738	133

DIMAGGIO, JOSEPH P. (JOE)   BR TR 6' 2"   193 lbs.
Born November 25, 1914, San Francisco, Ca. — Died March 8, 1999, Hollywood, Fl.
Played for New York (A) (1936-42, 1946-51)

When you start reading about Joe DiMaggio's career, you are overwhelmed by the comments made about him. His teammates said very positive things. Billy Johnson said, "Our star, of course, was Joe DiMaggio. He was a quiet player, but he was a leader who did whatever it took to win. He didn't play for himself, but for the team" (Peary 1994, 50). Gene Woodling said, "I expected him to be great, but still his talent surprised me" (Peary 1994, 50). Spud Chandler put it this way. "For all-around ability and everyday play, DiMaggio was the greatest player I ever saw" (Honig 1975, 228). Vic Raschi added, "He was the greatest all-around ballplayer I ever saw" (Honig 1976, 177). Non-Yankee baseball players also were impressed by DiMaggio. Bob Feller said, "DiMaggio was the greatest all-around player" (Feller and Gilbert 1990, 91). Ted Williams said "He is the greatest ballplayer I've ever seen" (Johnson and Stout 1991, 51). Stan Musial gave similar comments.

DiMaggio's career started in San Francisco in 1932. After a year in the Pacific Coast league, many major league teams were looking at him; however, a knee injury suffered in 1934 turned off all but the Yankees, who bought him from the Seals for $25,000. After an additional year in the minors, he joined the Yankees in 1936.

Starting with his rookie year, he put up great numbers for the seven years he played before going into military service. However, the 1942 season was not as good as the previous six. He volunteered to go into the Army Air Force on February 17, 1943, after a period of deferment for which he was criticized. In a column on January 31, 1942, in the *New York Times*, M. M. Caretti wrote, "Men have been drafted into the Army who never have earned more than a small salary in civilian life, who had no sideline returns to fall back on, and who had wives and children to support. On the other hand, especially in baseball, there are quite a few, too many, high-salaried players, some of them with businesses on the side, who have been exempted from the service. A case in point is Joe DiMaggio of the Yankees. Why he ever was exempted from service is beyond comprehension" (Mead 1985, 96). DiMaggio enlisted at the reception center at Monterey, California. By August 1943, he was stationed at the Santa Ana Army Air Field in California and had risen to the rank of corporal. While there he played for the baseball team. By mid-1944 he was transferred to Honolulu as a member of the Seventh Army Air Force with the rank of staff sergeant.

He spent the summer of 1944 playing for the Seventh Air Force team. In a Honolulu hospital for treatment of a stomach disorder, DiMaggio learned he had an ulcer. By October he was back on the mainland "for medical observation and treatment at Hamilton Field, California hospital. Nature of illness not revealed. But earlier reports stated he was under treatment for a stomach ailment" (*The Sporting News*, From the Service Front 10-26-1944, page 11). DiMaggio was transferred to San Francisco, then to Atlantic City, New Jersey, and then to St. Petersburg, Florida. In each case he was being treated for stomach ulcers. He was discharged on September 14, 1945. All during his hitch in the Air Force he was given special treatment. He was not put in harm's way but rather used for morale purposes for the other troops, playing baseball and giving demonstrations wherever he was stationed. He had not played ball in over a year, so he opted not to report to the Yankees when he was discharged. He waited until spring 1946 before reporting. He said, "I said to myself that when I come back to baseball it would only be after long preparation" (Turner 1996, 29).

Joe was always concerned that the fans thought of him in the best light. He was asked, in the spring of 1945, if he would rejoin the Yankees immediately if he was released from the Army because of the ulcer. He replied, "You say the fans would not hoot a man with a medical discharge. Well, I would not take the chance" (Goldstein 1980, 199). Joe was never quite the same player after the war as he was before. Nineteen forty-eight was the only great season he had following the war. By the end of 1951 he called it a career. "I no longer have it. You start chasing a ball and your brain immediately commands your body to 'run forward! Bend! Scoop up the ball! Peg it to the infield!' Then your body says, 'Who, me?'" (Ward and Burns 1994, 324). "The Yankee Clipper" (for grace and class) and "Joltin' Joe" (for power and batting) describe his career which consisted of ten pennants in thirteen years, nine world championships, two batting crowns, two home run titles, two RBI championships, three MVPs (although Ted Williams probably should have won two of the three years if he could have gotten along with the media), and the 56-game hitting streak. When baseball fans mention "the streak," most are referring to Joe's 56-game streak. His only weakness was physical. He was prone to injuries and was slow to recover. He missed an average of twenty games per year over his thirteen-year career. He had a great career that could have been even better had it not been for the three years spent serving his country.

AGE	YRS	ML	G	BA	SA	AB	H	2B	3B	HR	HR%	R	RBI	BB	SO	SB
28-30	43-45	13	1736	0.325	0.579	6821	2214	389	131	361	5.3	1390	1537	790	369	30
		3	436	0.33	0.583	1697	560	95	32	90	5.3	325	380	215	83	9
		16	2172	0.326	0.58	8518	2774	484	163	451	5.3	1715	1917	1005	452	39

DOERR, ROBERT F. (BOBBY)   BR TR 5' 11"   175 lbs.
Born April 7, 1918, Los Angeles, Ca.
Played for Boston (A) (1937-44, 1946-51)

Eddie Collins, Boston Red Sox scout, made a very successful trip to San Diego in 1936. He signed both Ted Williams and Bobby Doerr. They would be the backbone of the Red Sox for about fifteen years. Sometimes Doerr was overlooked because of Williams' great hitting; however, Doerr was a nine-time All-Star in his own right. He was called "The Silent Captain" by Ted Williams (MacLean 1990, 84). Ted also considered Doerr to be one of his few close friends. "I liked every one of my teammates, but I just didn't socialize with them. The only one I was real close to then and for a long time was Bobby Doerr. Bobby liked the same things I did" (Williams and Underwood 1988, 77). While he is known for his hitting, Doerr was also a very good second baseman. He led or tied the American League in fielding at second six times. He led in double plays five times. In 1948, he handled a string of 414 chances without an error. (He also had 349 chances in a row without an error in 1943.) In his book, *Ranking Baseball's Elite*, A.W. Laird rated Doerr as the seventh best second baseman of all time, including ranking first in home runs per season and career fielding range.

After being rejected and classified 4-F, Doerr was later reclassified 1-A and then drafted on September 19, 1944. He was inducted at Fort Lewis, Washington, and was leading the American League in hitting when he was taken. He was transferred to Camp Roberts, California, for basic training and then stayed there for the duration of his service. The Red Sox were in the thick of the pennant race with the Browns, Yankees, and Tigers when Doerr, along with two other Red Sox players, was drafted. With Doerr and the others gone, the Red Sox soon fell back. Doerr missed a little over one year of playing because of his service before being discharged in December 1945. He rejoined the Red Sox in 1946 to help lead them to the pennant that year. He was elected to the Hall of Fame in 1986. Tommy Henrich of the Yankees said, "Bobby Doerr is one of the few who played the game hard and retired with no enemies" (Dickson 1991, 179).

AGE	YRS	ML	G	BA	SA	AB	H	2B	3B	HR	HR%	R	RBI	BB	SO	SB
26-27	44-45	14	1865	0.288	0.461	7093	2042	381	89	223	3.1	1094	1247	809	608	54
(2 YRS MINUS		1	179	0.279	0.443	688	192	37	8	20	2.9	97	116	76	68	6
125 GAMES)		15	2044	0.287	0.459	7781	2234	418	97	243	3.1	1191	1363	885	676	60

EDWARDS, HENRY A. (HANK)   BL TL 6' 0"   190 lbs.
Born January 29, 1919, Elmwood Place, Oh. — Died June 22, 1988, Santa Ana, Ca.
Played for Cleveland (1941-43, 1946-49), Chicago (N) (1949-50), Brooklyn (1951), Cincinnati
(1951-52), Chicago (A) (1952), and St. Louis (A) (1953)

Hank Edwards played eleven seasons in the majors but only played in 100 games in two of
those seasons. He suffered a number of injuries which cut down his playing time early in
his career and ended his status as a regular later in that career. In 1943 he suffered a broken
collarbone in a collision with another player and was out for three weeks. In 1947, he was
injured in training camp and didn't play until June 9. In 1948, he suffered the injury that
ended his days as a regular. On August 1, he dislocated his shoulder making a leaping catch
and was out for the rest of the season. However, at the time he was drafted he was the
Indians' regular center fielder. So the years he missed in the Army could have been some of
his most productive. He batted .301 and led the American League in triples (16) in 1946.
He entered the Army in October 1943 and was released in March 1946, missing the 1944
and 1945 seasons. It was reported that he was stationed somewhere in the Pacific and later
reported that he was playing for the 13th Replacement Depot team at Schofield Barricks in
Hawaii. Edwards (like many other players) did defense work during the off-season. Edwards
worked at Republic Steel.

AGE	YRS	ML	G	BA	SA	AB	H	2B	3B	HR	HR%	R	RBI	BB	SO	SB
24-26	43-45	11	735	0.28	0.44	2191	613	116	41	51	2.3	285	276	208	264	9
(3 YRS MINUS		2	256	0.284	0.484	980	278	50	22	34	3.5	136	141	81	120	2
92 GAMES)		13	991	0.281	0.453	3171	891	166	63	85	2.7	421	417	289	384	11

EVANS, ALFRED H. (AL)   BR TR 5' 11"   190 lbs.
Born September 28, 1916, Kenly, N.C. — Died April 6, 1979, Wilson, N.C.
Played for Washington (1939-42, 1944-50) and Boston (A) (1951)

Al Evans was a journeyman catcher for his entire twelve-year career. Only one year did he play
at least 100 games. He was considered to be a good defensive catcher but not a good hitter.
His best year hitting was 1949 when he played 109 games. That year he hit .271, batted in 42
runs, and led American League catchers in fielding percentage. He was originally classified 1A
but appealed it because he was married and supported an invalid father. The deferment was
granted. Later he enlisted in the Navy on November 11, 1942, and was stationed for a while at
Norfolk Naval Air Station. He was discharged in May 1944 and rejoined the Senators on June 1,
1944. He was the Senators' starting catcher on opening day 1946, when baseball returned to
normal. President Truman threw out the first ball that day and baseball was back.

AGE	YRS	ML	G	BA	SA	AB	H	2B	3B	HR	HR%	R	RBI	BB	SO	SB
26-27	43-44	12	704	0.25	0.326	2053	514	70	23	13	0.6	188	211	243	206	13
(2 YRS MINUS		1	114	0.267	0.35	363	97	14	5	2	0.6	32	42	43	32	4
14 GAMES)		13	818	0.253	0.329	2416	611	84	28	15	0.6	220	253	286	238	17

EVERS, WALTER A. (HOOT)   BR TR 6' 2"   180 lbs.
Born February 8, 1921, St. Louis, Mo. — Died January 25, 1991, Houston, Tx.
Played for Detroit (1941, 1946-52, 1954), Boston (A) (1952-54), New York (N) (1954),
Baltimore (1955, 1956), and Cleveland (1955-56)

Hoot Evers was considered one of the top prospects in the Tiger organization when he
was drafted after the 1942 season. He had a good year in the Texas League in 1942 and was
expected to be with the Tigers in 1943. This outstanding prospect never achieved the kind
of stardom that was anticipated. Part of the reason was the three years he spent in the Army.
When he returned, Evers was hampered in 1946 when he suffered a broken ankle. This caused
him to miss almost half the season after being the starting center fielder. However, he did
have four good years for the Tigers (1947–1950). During that time he was part of a very good
outfield. Vic Wertz and Johnny Groth made up the other two players. In 1950 they all batted
over .300 with Evers leading the way with a .323 average. He spent most of his military career
(early 1944 until late 1945) at Waco, Texas, Army Air Force Base. He achieved the rank of
sergeant, and he was able to play both baseball and basketball.

His career was shortened by both the military and injuries. He didn't get his first major league
hit until he was twenty-five years old. After having his finest year in 1950, he slumped badly
in 1951 and suffered a hand injury in 1952 that hurt his batting grip. He never recovered
his batting swing. In 1952, he became part of one of the largest trades of regulars. The Tigers
sent him along with Dizzy Trout, Johnny Lipon, and George Kell to the Red Sox for Johnny
Pesky, Walt Dropo, Fred Hatfield, Don Lenhardt, and Bill Wight. He did make two All-Star game
appearances, hitting a home run in 1948.

AGE	YRS	ML	G	BA	SA	AB	H	2B	3B	HR	HR%	R	RBI	BB	SO	SB
22-24	43-45	12	1142	0.278	0.426	3801	1055	187	41	98	2.6	556	565	415	420	45
		3	202	0.285	0.454	694	198	37	10	20	2.9	104	107	68	54	9
		15	1344	0.279	0.43	4495	1253	224	51	118	2.6	660	672	483	474	54

FLETCHER, ELBURT P. (ELBIE)   BL TL 6' 0"   180 lbs.
Born March 18, 1916, Milton, Ma. — Died March 9, 1994, Milton, Ma.
Played for Boston (N) (1934-35, 1937-39, 1949) and Pittsburgh (1939-43, 1946-47)

Elbie Fletcher may be the only player to get to the majors by winning a newspaper contest.
Living in the Boston area, he was aware of a contest put on by a Boston newspaper. The
paper wanted people to write in and recommend a high school player who might have the
ability to become a major league player. He got all of his relatives to write and recommend
him for the tryout. He won the prize which was a trip to spring training with the Braves. That
experience gave him the chance he needed. In 1934, he signed with the Braves and spent the
first part of his career with them. By 1937 he was the regular first baseman for the Braves. He
was considered to be a line-drive-hitting, good-fielding first baseman. He never hit with great
power, but he was good at getting walks. He led the National League in walks in 1940 and
1941. He also led the league in on-base percentage three straight years, 1940, 1941, and 1942.
Elbie entered the Navy in December 1943 and served until December 1945.

After basic training, he was assigned to the physical instructor school at Bainbridge, Maryland, Naval Training Station. While at Bainbridge, he continued to play baseball. He was their leading hitter during the 1944 season. He stayed there from early 1944 until the service "super" teams were broken up when he was transferred to the Pacific. Starting in Hawaii, he played for a Navy team that toured the South Pacific playing exhibitions for soldiers in the war zone. These islands included Saipan, Guam, and others. When the tour was over, he was assigned to an island called Pelelise in the Western Caroline Islands. There he organized activities for the soldiers. Following his release in December 1945, he returned to the Pirates in 1946 as their regular first baseman. However, with the acquisition of Hank Greenberg in 1947, Fletcher became a back-up. After being out of the majors in 1948, he finished his career in 1949 where he started, with the Boston Braves.

AGE	YRS	ML	G	BA	SA	AB	H	2B	3B	HR	HR%	R	RBI	BB	SO	SB
28-29	44-45	12	1415	0.271	0.39	4879	1323	228	58	79	1.6	723	616	851	495	32
		2	299	0.278	0.395	1051	293	50	15	14	1.3	172	134	214	100	5
		14	1714	0.273	0.391	5930	1616	278	73	93	1.6	895	750	1065	595	37

FREY, LINUS R. (LONNY)   BB TR 5' 10"   160 lbs.
Born August 23, 1910, St. Louis, Mo.
Played for Brooklyn (1933–36), Chicago (N) (1937, 1947), Cincinnati (1938–43, 1946), New York (A) (1947–48), and New York (N) (1948)

Lonnie Frey was thirty-three years old and had three sons when he was drafted into the Army on December 11, 1943. By that time he had been a regular middle infielder for nine of the ten full seasons he had spent in the majors. The exception was 1937 in Chicago when he was back-up for Billy Herman at second base and Bill Jurges as shortstop. He started as a shortstop in Brooklyn and was converted to a second baseman in Cincinnati. His best success came as a member of the pennant-winning teams in Cincinnati in 1939 and 1940. Only a career .269 hitter, he batted .290 in 1939 with eleven homers as the Reds won the pennant. The next year he led the National League with twenty-two stolen bases. He was considered to be a fine defensive second baseman. He was the first to use a glove with a solid piece of leather between the thumb and the index finger. Discussing the Cincinnati Reds' improvement, which led to the pennant in 1939 and 1940, Harry Craft said, "Lonny Frey came over from the Cubs in nineteen thirty-eight; he was a fine second baseman" (Van Blair 1994, 32).

Frey led the league in fielding percentage twice and in double plays twice. He played in three all-star games and in three World Series. The Reds considered him a major loss when he was drafted. Taking his basic training at Fort Riley, Kansas, and staying there, he didn't see any combat and didn't suffer any injuries from the war. However, when he was released on November 14, 1945, he was thirty-five years old. In 1946, he lost his starting job to a twenty-four year old and was sold or traded three times before he retired in 1948. Having to compete against younger players after spending two years in the Army brought his career to an end. The same thing happened to many of the players who were slightly older when they served their country.

AGE	YRS	ML	G	BA	SA	AB	H	2B	3B	HR	HR%	R	RBI	BB	SO	SB
33-34	44-45	14	1535	0.269	0.374	5517	1482	263	69	61	1.1	848	549	752	525	105
		2	271	0.259	0.343	993	257	41	11	7	0.7	134	83	149	81	18
		16	1806	0.267	0.37	6510	1739	304	80	68	1	982	632	901	606	123

GEHRINGER, CHARLES L. (CHARLIE)   BL TR 5' 11" 180 lbs.
Born May 11, 1903, Fowlerville, Mi. — Died January 21, 1993, Bloomfield Hills, Mi.
Played for Detroit (1924–42)

Charlie Gehringer was called "The Mechanical Man." Teammate Doc Cramer said, "You wind him up on Opening Day and forget him" (Shatzkin 1990, 383). Manager Mickey Cochrane put it this way, "Charlie says 'hello' on Opening Day, 'goodbye' on closing day, and in between hits .350" (Shatzkin 1990, 383). He earned his title by doing everything well on a consistent basis, year in and year out. From his second full year (1927) until his next to last full year (1940), he batted over .300 every year except for 1932 when he hit .298. He scored more than 100 runs in all but two of those fourteen years. Seven times he drove in more than 100 runs. In 1937 he won the American League batting title by hitting .371. He also won the MVP award that year. The list could go on and on. Gehringer was part of a very special hitting infield. The infield of the 1934 Tigers drove in 462 runs for the year. They had Hank Greenberg at first (139 RBIs), Gehringer at second (127 RBIs), Bill Rozell at short (100 RBI's), and Marv Owen at third (96 RBIs). The 462 RBIs in 1934 set a record for production by an infield. They followed that up by driving in 420 runs in 1935.

Gehringer was also a great second baseman. He had the ability to make plays in the field look easy. He seemed to be where the ball was hit and to know what the batter would be able to do with the pitch the pitcher was about to throw. Some downplayed his ability because he made it look so easy. But he covered a lot of ground and got to balls others would have only watched go by to the outfield. Once he got there, he had sure hands and a good arm to complete the play. He led the league in fielding percentage nine times, in assists seven times, and in putouts three times. From the late '20s until the late '30s "The Mechanical Man" was one of, if not *the* best, second baseman in the major leagues.

World War II ended Gehringer's career. He was thirty-nine when he enlisted in the Army Air Force in November 1942. He realized that his career was probably over. "I hardly expect to play again. But I'd like to come back as a coach or a manager" (*The Sporting News*, Lieut. Gehringer after 17 seasons, 1-7-43 page 2). He was given a commission as a lieutenant in the Navy and he completed his naval indoctrination at preflight school in Chapel Hill, North Carolina. Early in 1943 he was transferred to St. Mary's preflight school in California. He was in charge of baseball at St. Mary's. He also played on the team and was on the service all-star team in California. In the spring of 1945, he was transferred to a naval air station at Jacksonville, Florida. When he arrived, the commander told him of the wonderful plans he had to have a baseball team at the base.

Gehringer, being 41 years old and tired of playing, told the commander that he would be happy to manage the team, but he didn't want to play. However, the commander had different plans. He said, "If you don't play, I'll send you so far they won't know where to find you" (Goldstein 1980, 229). He played. Later, when Ted Williams was transferred to the same base, he told Gehringer that he just wanted to concentrate on his flying. Gehringer told him that he would play. Williams said no. However, after a discussion with the commander, Williams played. Gehringer said, "Those commanding officers took the whole baseball thing pretty seriously" (Honig 1975, 57). Rear Admiral Ralph E. Davidson commended Gehringer for being a good officer. He was promoted to lieutenant commander in the fall of 1945 while stationed at Jacksonville. He was released from service November 5, 1945, after serving in the Navy for thirty-four months.

He chose not to try to rejoin the Tigers in 1946, retiring with a lifetime batting average of .320 and a total of 2,839 hits. He later said he regretted not getting 3,000 hits. If he had the three years he had spent in the service added to his totals, he would have had more than the 3,000 hits that he wanted. Gehringer played in three World Series and batted .321 in twenty World Series games. He also hit .500 in six All-Star games. He was called quiet, deadly, and efficient. His manager, Mickey Cochrane, put it this way, "He was a hard loser, the hardest loser I think I ever saw…Always hustling, always battling" (Ward and Burns 1994, 209). Dick Bartell commented, "…as far as I'm concerned, the best of all second basemen—ever" (Van Blair 1994, 8).

AGE	YRS	ML	G	BA	SA	AB	H	2B	3B	HR	HR%	R	RBI	BB	SO	SB
39-42	42-45	19	2323	0.32	0.48	8860	2839	574	146	184	2.1	1774	1427	1185	372	182
(4 YRS MINUS		3	362	0.283	0.396	1400	396	77	14	18	1.3	219	201	178	50	13
45 GAMES)		22	2685	0.315	0.469	10260	3235	651	160	202	2	1993	1628	1363	422	195

GORDON, JOSEPH L. (JOE)   BR TR 5' 10"   180 lbs.
Born February 18, 1915, Los Angeles, Ca. — Died April 14, 1978, Sacramento, Ca.
Played for New York (A) (1938-43, 1946) and Cleveland (1947-50)

This All-Star second baseman replaced Tony Lazzeri in the Yankee infield in 1938. He remained with the Yankees until 1946. When people talk about the great Yankee teams of the late '30s and early '40s, Gordon is always included. In 1947 he was traded to Cleveland and helped the Indians win the pennant and World Series in 1948. Overall, he played in six World Series, winning five. He was considered to be one of the better fielding second basemen of his time. Some say he could make plays other second basemen could only dream about. While he was noted for his fielding, he was also a good hitter with power. He holds the American League record for career home runs by a second baseman (246) and for a season (32). Gordon was selected for the All-Star game for nine consecutive years, every year of his career except the first and the last year. He was also named MVP for the American League in 1942. (He had a good year, but Ted Williams should have been named.)

Gordon was drafted on May 8, 1944, after controversy concerning a hunting trip he took in the fall of 1943. Someone took a picture of him holding the ducks he had killed. The picture led to someone writing the War Department to say he should be shooting Germans instead of ducks. He was drafted into the Army Air Corps the following spring. He reported to the Army in San Francisco and was transferred to the Army Transport Command Replacement Center at Camp Luna near Las Vegas. Later he was transferred to Camp Hamilton, California, and then to Honolulu. He was able to play baseball on a regular basis at each of his stops. While in Hawaii, he played for the Seventh Army Air Force team and took part in the "Pacific World Series" between the Army and the Navy in the fall of 1944. After the stint in Hawaii, he was transferred back to Camp Hamilton near San Francisco where he managed the baseball team. In the summer of 1945, he returned to Hawaii where he was selected to be on an all-star team that would tour the South Pacific. He was part of the first group to play in such places as Saipan, Guam, Tinian, and Iwo Jima. He was discharged from the Army on November 14, 1945.

Gordon had a bad year in 1946. It may have been the time away from the majors, or it may have been the spike-wound injury to his hand which caused him to miss the start of the season. He returned to the lineup faster than anticipated, but this early return might have hurt him in the long run. He began to have leg problems and was never able to play at his normal level that season. After that season, the Yankees traded him to the Indians for Allie Reynolds. Working with Lou Boudreau, he solidified the middle of the infield. Together they helped bring the Indians a world championship in 1948. Bob Feller said, "Joe was one of our most valuable players in 1948 with a .280 average, 32 home runs, and 124 runs batted in" (Feller and Gilbert 1990, 148).

AGE	YRS	ML	G	BA	SA	AB	H	2B	3B	HR	HR%	R	RBI	BB	SO	SB
29-30	44-45	11	1566	0.268	0.466	5707	1530	264	52	253	4.4	914	975	759	702	89
		2	305	0.279	0.472	1115	311	55	11	44	3.9	182	176	155	149	17
		13	1871	0.27	0.466	6822	1841	319	63	297	4.4	1096	1151	914	851	106

GORDON, SIDNEY (SID)   BR TR 5' 10"   185 lbs.
Born August 13, 1917, Brooklyn, N.Y. — Died June 17, 1975, New York, N.Y.
Played for New York (N) (1941-43, 1946-49, 1955), Boston (N) (1950-52), Milwaukee (N) (1953), and Pittsburgh (1954-55)

Sid Gordon had been a regular for the Giants for one year when he entered the Coast Guard in October 1943. He first was sent to the Coast Guard station at Manhattan Beach, New York. Later he was transferred to the station at Curtis Bay, Maryland, where he spent most of his time in the service and where he continued to play ball. In the fall of 1945 he did spend time in the South Pacific. He was discharged on January 12, 1946.

Gordon was not known as a power hitter when he first arrived in the majors. However, later in his career he became a person who would hit with power. He was on the Giants team that set the (then) major league record by hitting 221 home runs in 1947. He also hit three grand slams in 1948 for the Giants and in 1950 for the Braves. He was involved in a major trade between the Giants and the Braves that changed the complexion of both clubs. Gordon, Buddy Kerr, Willard Marshall, and Sam Webb were traded to the Braves for Eddie Stanky and Alvin Dark. Gordon had some good years for the Braves; however, his best year was probably 1948 when he hit 30 home runs, drove in 107 runs, and batted .299. He was selected for the All-Star game that year as a reserve but didn't get to play. Selected again in 1949, he got into the game and had a double and a walk in three plate appearances.

AGE	YRS	ML	G	BA	SA	AB	H	2B	3B	HR	HR%	R	RBI	BB	SO	SB
26-27	44-45	13	1475	0.283	0.466	4992	1415	220	43	202	4	735	805	731	356	19
		2	264	0.272	0.397	907	247	29	15	18	2	114	110	102	53	3
		15	1739	0.282	0.456	5899	1662	249	58	220	3.7	849	915	833	409	22

A baseball player has a limited number of years to play the game. A career usually starts slowly and develops to a peak and then declines in the later years. "This was so with Billy Herman, Terry Moore, and Hank Greenberg, stars whose great days were now behind them, lost to the war, not through injury but simply through the passage of time" (Turner 1996, 83). Hank Greenberg gave a great deal of his prime years to his country. He gave those years willingly because he saw the need for his service.

AGE	YRS	ML	G	BA	SA	AB	H	2B	3B	HR	HR%	R	RBI	BB	SO	SB
30-34	41-45	13	1394	0.313	0.605	5193	1628	379	71	331	6.4	1051	1276	852	844	58
(5 YRS MINUS		3	626	0.311	0.652	2313	719	150	29	194	8.4	521	592	428	381	26
19 & 78 GAMES)		16	2020	0.313	0.62	7506	2347	529	100	525	7	1572	1868	1280	1225	84

HAMNER, GRANVILLE W. (GRANNY)   BR TR 5' 10"   163 lbs.
Born April 26, 1927, Richmond, Va. — Died September 12, 1993, Philadelphia, Pa.
Played for Philadelphia (N) (1944-59), Cleveland (1959), and Kansas City (1962)

Granny Hamner was one of the kids who got to play because of the war. He was different because he was good enough to play after he came back from the war as well. He signed with the Phillies in 1944 at age 17 along with his brother Wesley. However, his brother did not play again after the war. Granny played twenty-one games in 1944 and fourteen games in 1945 before he went into the military late in 1945. He spent some time at Fort Meade where he was able to play on their baseball team. He spent most of 1946 in the service. He got to play in only two games for the Phillies in 1946. After spending 1947 in the minors, he was able to establish himself as a regular in 1948, first at second base and then as the regular shortstop in 1949. It was there that he would find his spot. He was a member of the 1950 Philadelphia Phillies "Whiz Kids" that won the National League pennant, the first for Phillies the since 1915. Even though the Yankees swept them in four games and the Phillies batted only .203 as a team, Hamner batted .429. His teammate, catcher Andy Seminick, said, "When he played short, he was the best at that time at making a relay throw to third or home. He had such a good arm" (Peary 1994, 68). Teammate Del Ennis added, "He was a take-charge guy" (Peary 1994, 122). This three-time All-Star spent most of his seventeen-year career with the Phillies before retiring in 1962.

AGE	YRS	ML	G	BA	SA	AB	H	2B	3B	HR	HR%	R	RBI	BB	SO	SB
18	45	17	1531	0.262	0.383	5839	1529	272	62	104	1.8	711	708	351	432	35
(1 YR MINUS		0	44	0.208	0.3	120	25	4	2	1	0.8	10	8	4	3	1
2 GAMES)		17	1575	0.261	0.381	5959	1554	276	64	105	1.8	721	716	355	435	36

HEGAN, JAMES E. (JIM)   BR TR 6' 2"   195 lbs.
Born August 3, 1920, Lynn, Ma. — Died June 17, 1984, Swampscott, Ma.
Played for Cleveland (1941-42, 1946-57), Detroit (1958), Philadelphia (N) (1958-59), San Francisco (1959), and Chicago (N) (1960)

Jim Hegan was a great defensive catcher. You have to be a great defensive catcher to play in the majors for seventeen years and have a career batting average of .228, especially when twelve of those seventeen years you are the regular catcher for the Indians. He is widely acclaimed as the finest defensive catcher of his generation. Some say he is the best defensive catcher in the American League in the post-World War II period. The Indians' pitching staff of his era included Bob Feller, Bob Lemon, Early Wynn, Mike Garcia, Gene Bearden, and Herb Score. With this staff, he holds the record handling eighteen twenty-game winners in his career (Lemon 7, Wynn 4, Feller 3, Garcia 2, Bearden 1, and Score 1). He also caught three no-hitters, which ties him for the most by any catcher.

His teammates, as well as his opponents, recognized his great defensive skills. Johnny Berardino said, "Our catcher was Jim Hegan, who was the best. He called a great game and was the best defensive receiver in baseball. He had soft hands, which he needed for Feller and Lemon" (Peary 1994, 74–75). Bob Feller added, "Jim Hegan became the best catcher I ever had. He didn't hit as well as some others, but nobody was his equal as a catcher, especially with his arm" (Feller and Gilbert 1990, 65). Ted Williams said, "Jim Hegan of Cleveland was the real stylish catcher. He wasn't the hitter Berra was, but for handling a pitcher nobody could beat Jim Hegan" (Williams and Underwood 1988, 237). Bill Dickey, the Hall of Fame catcher, said, "When you can catch like Hegan, you don't have to hit" (Shatzkin 1990, 458).

This five-time All-Star was a durable catcher. He caught 152 games in 1949 and 1629 for his career. He was twenty-two years old when he enlisted in the Coast Guard on December 7, 1942. At that time he was called "a promising prospect" and was listed among the "losses to war" by the Indians. He was a specialist first class. He was discharged on December 11, 1945, after spending three years in the military. He was able to have a good career after returning from service. However, he did give up three of his prime years as a baseball player.

AGE	YRS	ML	G	BA	SA	AB	H	2B	3B	HR	HR%	R	RBI	BB	SO	SB
22-24	43-45	17	1666	0.228	0.344	4772	1087	187	46	92	1.9	550	525	456	742	15
		3	270	0.242	0.347	803	194	32	10	11	1.4	85	82	73	123	7
		20	1936	0.23	0.345	5575	1281	219	56	103	1.8	635	607	529	865	22

HEMSLEY, RALSTON B. (ROLLIE)   BR TR 5' 10"   170 lbs.
Born June 24, 1907, Syracuse, Oh. — Died July 31, 1972, Washington, D.C.
Played for Pittsburgh (1928-31), Chicago (N) (1931-32), Cincinnati (1933, 1942), St. Louis (A) (1933-37), Cleveland (1938-41), New York (A) (1942-44), and Philadelphia (N) (1946-47)

Rollie Hemsley had the nickname of "Rollickin' Rollie" which he earned early in his career. He had a real problem with alcohol. He drank himself off four teams before he was able to overcome his problem while with the Indians. At that time, he went on the wagon, joined Alcoholics Anonymous, and didn't drink again. However, the stories about him when he was drinking are legendary. Some of the incidents led to him being traded to another team. For instance, the Pirates traded him to the Cubs in 1931 after an incident with water-filled bags being thrown around a hotel room. The Cubs traded him to the Reds in 1933. They kept him for only forty-nine games before passing him on to the Browns. All this time he served in the role as back-up catcher. Finally in 1934, with the Browns, he was able to get a starting role.

Hemsley had several incidents while with the Browns but Rogers Hornsby, the manager, liked how he worked behind the plate. The final incident occurred when Hemsley rented a car

He missed over three full seasons. With those seasons his home run total should have been over 250 and his RBI total in excess of twelve hundred. Henrich did not have a good year in 1946. He called it a "lousy season." While 1946 was a "lousy season," 1948 was a career year. He hit twenty-five homers, drove in 100 runs, and batted .308. This five-time All-Star played on eight pennant winners. Henrich was involved in one of the best-known baseball bloopers. He was at bat when catcher Mickey Owen missed the third strike in the 1941 World Series. He reached first base on the passed ball and later scored as the Yankees got three more hits, won the game, and the next day the World Series.

AGE	YRS	ML	G	BA	SA	AB	H	2B	3B	HR	HR%	R	RBI	BB	SO	SB
29-32	42-45	11	1284	0.282	0.491	4603	1297	269	73	183	4	901	795	712	383	37
(4 YRS	MINUS	3	455	0.285	0.525	1758	501	126	31	78	4.4	368	299	257	157	9
127 GAMES)		14	1739	0.283	0.501	6361	1798	395	104	261	4.1	1269	1094	969	540	46

HERMAN, WILLIAM J. B. (BILLY)   BR TR 5' 11" 180 lbs.
Born July 9, 1909, New Albany, In. — Died September 5, 1992, West Palm Beach, Fl.
Played for Chicago (N) (1931–41), Brooklyn (1941–43, 1946), Boston (N) (1946), and Pittsburgh (1947)

Billy Herman was a ten-time All-Star who helped his teams to four pennants. They were the Cubs in 1932, 1935, and 1938 and the Dodgers in 1941. Herman was called the spark plug of those teams and his addition to the Dodgers in 1941 is thought to have put them over the top in their quest for a National League flag. He was considered to be the best National League second basemen of the 1930s and early '40s. He was good on defense, including turning the double play. He led the league in putouts at second base seven times, which tied a National League record. Kirby Higbe said, "Herman stood out at second base over any other second baseman I ever saw" (Shatzkin 1990, 465). In addition to his fielding, he also was a very good hitter. He had a career batting average of .304, batting over .300 eight times and scoring over 100 runs five times. He may have been the best hit-and-run man of all time. Because of his ability to hit behind the runner, Brooklyn manager Leo Durocher said, "Herman was...universally accepted as the classic number-two hitter...an absolute master at hitting behind the runner" (Shatzkin 1990, 466). He was also known for changing his batting stances. He might change even during the game. Casey Stengel said, "He's an unusual hitter. Sometimes he stands straight up, and sometimes his head is so close to the plate he looks like John the Baptist" (Okrent and Wulf 1989, 148). He had a reputation for being a great competitor and for being one of the most intelligent players of his day. Gene Woodling added, "Billy Herman had better baseball sense than any guy I've ever been around" (Mead 1985, 192).

Before he went into military service, Herman devoted time to help raise money for war bonds. He would go to employers to try to get employees to put part of their salaries into war bonds. Herman entered the Navy in March 1944 and was assigned to Great Lakes Naval Training Station for basic training. He had a leg injury that kept him out of some games that summer.

In the winter of 1944–45, he was transferred to Hawaii. He played for a Naval team that toured the South Pacific playing exhibitions in the war zone. Upon returning to Honolulu he played, managed, and did some umpiring for the 14th Naval District. He played and managed the AIEA

Barracks team. He was named to the 14th Naval District all-star team after being named MVP of that league. Herman was discharged in December 1945.

He didn't have much left when he came back. He was slower around second, and his reaction time was slower as well. Herman knew this. He said he was "fifteen pounds late and thirty-eight years old" (Turner 1996, 159). Actually, he was only thirty-six.

Durocher decided that he was no longer an everyday player. Herman could still hit, but he could no longer make the plays at second. He was tried at third and first. Branch Rickey thought that a $20,000 salary was too much for a utility player and traded him to the Braves for Stew Hofferth. Herman showed the player he was by his reaction to news of the trade. He was notified by the Dodgers at 2:00 in the morning, gathered his things, got a train from Brooklyn to Boston, and played that afternoon, but the war had taken its toll. Herman was traded to the Pirates after the 1946 season. He only played in fifteen games during the 1947 season before he retired. The war had shortened another Hall of Fame player's career.

AGE	YRS	ML	G	BA	SA	AB	H	2B	3B	HR	HR%	R	RBI	BB	SO	SB
34-35	44-45	15	1922	0.304	0.407	7707	2345	486	82	47	0.6	1163	839	737	428	67
		2	272	0.305	0.41	1084	331	71	9	8	0.7	170	122	115	51	8
		17	2194	0.304	0.408	8791	2676	557	91	55	0.6	1333	961	852	479	75

HIGGINS, MICHAEL F. (PINKY)   BR TR 6' 1"   185 lbs.

Born May 27, 1909, Red Oak, Tx. — Died March 21, 1969, Dallas, Tx.
Played for Philadelphia (A) (1930, 1933–36), Boston (A) (1937–38, 1946), and Detroit (1939–44, 1946)

Three-time All-Star Pinky Higgins started his professional baseball career with the Philadelphia Athletics in 1930, after signing out of the University of Texas, the same year the Athletics played the Cardinals in the World Series. He finished his career after the Red Sox played the Cardinals in the World Series in 1946. While he didn't get to play in the 1930 World Series, he did play in 1946. In addition, he helped the Tigers to the 1940 pennant and hit .375 against the Reds in the World Series. That average led the Tigers in hitting for the series and it included a two-run homer in game three that helped the Tigers gain a win. He had a total of six RBIs to tie for the team lead. During thirteen of the fourteen years he played in the majors, he was the regular third baseman, First with the Athletics, then the Red Sox, the Tigers, and back with the Red Sox. A career .292 hitter, he batted over .300 four times and drove in over 100 runs in both 1937 and 1938. One of his major personal achievements came in 1938. On June 21, 1938, he went eight for eight in a double header. The last hit that day, along with the four he had gotten in the previous game, gave him the major league record for consecutive hits. (It would later be tied by Walt Dropo.) He had gone twelve for twelve. When you add in two walks, he reached base on fourteen consecutive times at bat.

Higgins missed a chance to play in another World Series by missing the 1945 season as the Tigers won the pennant. He was drafted into the Navy on March 24, 1945. He took his pre-induction physical in Dallas, Texas. He was then shipped to Great Lakes Naval Training Station for basic training. After he had completed his boot training, several rumors claimed he would year was 1954 when he hit forty-two home runs, drove in 130 runs, and batted .304. He drove in over 100 runs for seven straight seasons and had twenty or more home runs for eleven straight seasons. Hodges is always listed as one of the stars of the Dodger teams that dominated the National League from 1949 to 1956.

He also made history as a manager. Hodges took over as manager of Mets in 1968. This was a team that had averaged 53 wins in its first six years and had finished last every year except one. In two years, the Mets were the darlings of baseball as they won the National League pennant and beat the Orioles in the World Series. Because of their success under Hodges, the Mets retired his number.

AGE	YRS	ML	G	BA	SA	AB	H	2B	3B	HR	HR%	R	RBI	BB	SO	SB
20-21	44-45	18	2071	0.273	0.487	7030	1921	295	48	370	5.3	1105	1274	943	1137	63
		2	30	0.2	0.313	80	16	4	1	1	1.3	10	8	15	20	1
		20	2101	0.272	0.485	7110	1937	299	49	371	5.2	1115	1282	958	1157	64

KELLER, CHARLES E. (CHARLIE)   BL TR 5' 10" 185 lbs.
Born September 12, 1916, Middletown, Md. — Died May 23, 1990, Frederick, Md.
Played for New York (A) (1939-43, 1945-49, 1952) and Detroit (1950-51)

Charlie Keller was part of the famous Yankee outfield of the early '40s that also included Joe DiMaggio and Tommy Henrich. In 1941 each of the three hit more than thirty home runs, led by Keller's thirty-three. From 1940 to 1943 he averaged twenty-eight home runs, 102 RBIs, 102 runs, and 107 walks per season. After Keller was promoted to the Yankees in 1939, they won the pennant four of the next five years along with three world championships. On occasion he was called a "hairy-armed, beetle-browed slugger" because of his black, bushy eyebrows and his muscular body. These features earned him the nickname King Kong, which he did not appreciate.

Keller joined the Merchant Marines on January 20, 1944. He was commissioned an ensign and reported to St. Petersburg, Florida. In the spring he was transferred to Sheepshead Bay, New York, for further training. When asked what effect the war would have on his career, Keller said, "It's hard to tell, but a lot of the fellows are playing some sort of regular schedules with their branch of the service." He added, "I will complete my training at Sheepshead Bay here as a purser-pharmacist's mate in a few weeks. Then I'll go to sea aboard a merchant vessel. I haven't touched a bat or ball" (Kaam 1944, 13). When Keller was interviewed by *The Sporting News* he had not been able to play any baseball since the 1943 World Series.

By September 1944, he had completed his training and had shipped out on a merchant ship. The first trips he made were in the North Atlantic, where they encountered rough seas. Later he also had service in the Pacific, visiting Guam. When he returned to New York on the ship *Santa Cecila*, which was carrying troops returning from the European theater, he had been at sea for over one year going back and forth to Europe and the Marianas. He was released from service on August 17, 1945.

Keller was able to rejoin the Yankees for the last forty-four games of the 1945 season. He had a good record for those games, batting .301, hitting ten home runs, and batting in twenty-six runs in only 163 at-bats. Keller had a good year in 1946 even though his batting average was below normal. He said, "I had a good half year, but then I ran out of gas. I still had my sea legs" (Gilbert 1992, 265). As it turned out, 1946 was the only full season he would have after the war. In 1947 he suffered a back injury (a ruptured disk) and in 1948 a broken hand. These injuries caused him a lot of pain. Unable to play full time, he spent the next five years as a part-time outfielder and pinch hitter. This five-time All-Star is always listed as one of the Yankee stars of the 1939 to 1946 period.

AGE	YRS	ML	G	BA	SA	AB	H	2B	3B	HR	HR%	R	RBI	BB	SO	SB
27-28	44-45	13	1170	0.286	0.518	3790	1085	166	72	189	5	725	760	784	499	45
(2 YRS MINUS		1	247	0.282	0.53	888	250	39	16	50	5.6	175	175	187	122	14
44 GAMES)		14	1417	0.285	0.52	4678	1335	205	88	239	5.1	900	935	971	621	59

KELTNER, KENNETH F. (KEN)   BR TR 6' 0"   190 lbs.
Born October 31, 1916, Milwaukee, Wi. — Died December 12, 1991, New Berlin, Wi.
Played for Cleveland (1937–44, 1946–49) and Boston (A) (1950)

When you mention Ken Keltner, most baseball buffs want to talk about the two great plays he made on July 17, 1941, to help end Joe DiMaggio's fifty-six game hitting streak. They were sensational plays made before 67,468 fans in Cleveland. In the first inning he dove for the ball to his right, backhanded it, and got up and threw DiMaggio out. DiMaggio said of that play, "That play Ken made on me in the first inning, when he went behind third for a backhand stop of that hard smash, was a beautiful piece of work" (Feller and Gilbert 1990, 109). The third time DiMaggio came to bat, Keltner duplicated the play he had made in the first inning, diving to his right, getting up, and throwing DiMaggio out at first. These plays were typical of the kind of defense Keltner could play. He was considered one of the best fielding third basemen of the 1940s. He led the American League in assists, double plays, and fielding several times. This seven-time All-Star is considered to be Cleveland's all-time best third baseman. He was also a good clutch hitter. His best year was 1948 as the Indians won the American League pennant and the World Series. In that year he batted .297, hit thirty-one home runs, and drove in 119 runs.

Keltner spent one year in the Navy. He entered the Navy on March 20, 1945 and was discharged in March 1946. He reported for duty in Milwaukee and was transferred to Great Lakes Naval Training Station for basic training. While he was stationed there, he played on the Great Lakes team. By summer he had completed his training and was sent to Shoemaker Field, California. During the rest of the summer he played for the Fleet City, California, Bluejackets and for the Alameda, California, Naval Air Station. Following his release, he rejoined the Indians in time for the 1946 season. He had an off year in 1946, batting only .241 with forty-five RBIs. Following his career year in 1948, he had another off year in 1949 and was out of baseball after the 1950 season. For eleven years he was the regular third baseman for the Indians. During that time he helped anchor the infield with great defensive play. Bob Feller said, "He was an outstanding third baseman. He was a devoted team player" (Feller and Gilbert 1990, 67).

AGE	YRS	ML	G	BA	SA	AB	H	2B	3B	HR	HR%	R	RBI	BB	SO	SB
28	45	13	1526	0.276	0.441	5683	1570	308	69	163	2.9	737	852	514	480	39
		1	136	0.29	0.458	507	147	29	7	14	2.8	74	77	55	48	5
		14	1662	0.277	0.442	6190	1717	337	76	177	2.9	811	929	569	528	44

plant were deferred. Laabs qualified. Browns general manager Bill DeWitt got Laabs a job in a St. Louis defense plant. Laabs said, "Bill got me a job in his father-in-law's plant in St. Louis. They made pipes—ten, twelve, fourteen inches in diameter. Our job was to inspect them. I found out later that these pipes were sent down to Tennessee for the atom bomb project. I got to St. Louis about the first of June" (Mead 1985, 148).

With the job in Detroit, Laabs could only play on weekends. After moving to the St. Louis job, he could also play in night games during the week. Finally, around the first of August, he quit his job and began playing full-time. He had an off season during 1944 because he was playing out of shape. He had missed spring training and his only time to practice, because of his job, was when he was playing in the game.

While his overall numbers were not great, he did have a number of key hits that helped the Browns win their only pennant. He hit two home runs (a two-run and a three-run) to help the Browns beat the Yankees on the last day of the season to clinch the pennant. No longer working in the war plant, Laabs was drafted in 1945 and spent most of that season in the service. In 1946, at age thirty-four, he returned to the Browns to play part-time. After a trade to the A's in 1947, his career was over.

AGE	YRS	ML	G	BA	SA	AB	H	2B	3B	HR	HR%	R	RBI	BB	SO	SB
32-33	44-45	11	950	0.262	0.452	3102	813	151	44	117	3.8	467	509	389	595	32
(2 YRS MINUS		0	86	0.26	0.425	308	80	15	3	10	3.2	49	49	42	56	3
66 & 35 GAMES)		11	1036	0.262	0.45	3410	893	166	47	127	3.7	516	558	431	651	35

LEMON, ROBERT G. (BOB)   BL TR 6' 0"   180 lbs.
Born September 22, 1920, San Bernardino, Ca. — Died January 11, 2000, Long Beach, Ca.
Played for Cleveland (1941–42, 1946–58)

Yes, Bob Lemon, the Hall of Fame pitcher, is listed among the position players. Prior to his going into the service in 1943, he was a third baseman for the Indians. He was considered a promising youngster before going into service. He had two trials with the Indians but failed to make the grade because of poor hitting. Stan Musial, who saw him play in the service, said, "He could hit righthanders fairly well, but he couldn't hit the lefthander" (Boerg 1964, 277). Lemon enlisted in the Navy in late 1942. He spent some time at the San Diego Naval Training Center in 1944 where he was able to play on their team.

By early 1945 he had been transferred to Hawaii. He did play baseball while stationed there. He took part in the Navy "Little World Series" in Hawaii in October 1945. He played on the AIEA barracks team and was named to the 14th Naval District All-Star Team. As far as his baseball career was concerned, going into service was the best thing that happened to Bob Lemon. Bill Dickey saw him pitch in Hawaii and told Lou Boudreau, Indians manager, that he should let Lemon pitch on a permanent basis. He got that chance when he returned to the Indians in 1946. Boudreau used him as a relief pitcher that year.

Lemon was wild but showed promise. In 1947 he was converted to a starter, and as they say, the rest is history. When the Indians won the pennant in 1948, Lemon was one of the main pitchers. Starting in 1948, Lemon won twenty or more games per season during seven of the next nine years. The people who played against and with Bob Lemon were the ones who admired him the most. Les Moss, catcher for the Browns, said, "Bob Lemon was the toughest right-hander in the league and had been since after the war" (Peary 1994, 270). Eddie Joost, A's shortstop, added, "Bob Lemon was the most intimidating pitcher I faced" (Peary 1994, 271). Ted Williams also said that Lemon was one of the five toughest pitcher he faced. Williams was noted for taking a pitch. One day he hit a homer off Lemon on the first pitch. When asked why he was swinging instead of taking, he said, "There is one guy I don't want to get ahead of me" (Williams and Underwood 1988, 145). On a staff that featured Feller, Wynn, Garcia, Bearden, and Score, Lemon was one of the most underrated pitchers of the decade.

In 1952 Garcia, Lemon, and Wynn finished one, two, three in earned run average and in innings pitched in the American League. Lemon had one other problem when he was playing third base. His throws sank. What is a problem for a third baseman is a gift for a pitcher. Lemon's sinker was very hard to hit. Also, a poor-hitting third baseman can be a good-hitting pitcher. He ended up with thirty-seven career home runs, one behind Wes Ferrell. Most players' numbers were hurt by their time in service. However, Lemon's time in service gave him a chance to show what he could do as a pitcher. With that chance he became a member of the Hall of Fame.

AGE	YRS	ML	G	BA	SA	AB	H	2B	3B	HR	HR%	R	RBI	BB	SO	SB
22-24	43-45	15	615	0.232	0.386	1183	274	54	9	37	3.1	148	147	93	241	2
		3	130	0.237	0.412	257	61	12	3	9	3.5	33	32	17	38	0
		18	745	0.233	0.391	1440	335	66	12	46	3.2	181	179	110	279	2

LEWIS, JOHN K. (BUDDY)

BL TR 6' 1"   175 lbs.

Born August 10, 1916, Gastonia, N.C.
Played for Washington (1935-41, 1945-47, 1949)

Buddy Lewis was the regular third baseman for the Senators in 1936 at age nineteen. Starting with that year until he enlisted in the Army on November 18, 1941, he batted between .291 and .319 each year. For six years he was a model of consistency. He was not a home run hitter but hit lots of doubles and triples. Tommy Henrich was impressed with Lewis. He said, "I'll tell you another great man with that bat—Buddy Lewis of the old Washington Senators. Talk about bat control, he was an artist. I used to drool watching Buddy Lewis handle a ball bat. He could hit a pitch just about anywhere he wanted" (Honig 1976, 41). He scored over one hundred runs four times in that six-year period.

Lewis had an interest in flying before the war. He had taken an airplane ride while at spring training one year and was hooked. Clark Griffith, Senators' owner, gave specific instructions that he was not to fly. Lewis liked it so well he took flying lessons under the assumed name of John Kelley. By the time he entered the service, he was an accomplished pilot. This training would serve him well. He was inducted at Fort Bragg, North Carolina, in November 1941. This was before Pearl Harbor. He then moved to Fort Knox, Kentucky, for basic training where he was in an Armored Force Replacement Training Center and there he made corporal. The day he was to ship out to North Africa he got orders to report to Texas for flight training. In January 1942 he took and passed the test necessary to be transferred to the Air Corps. By the fall of 1942 he had reported to Lubbock Field to complete advanced twin-engine bomber training. By March 1943 he been transferred to Fort Benning, Georgia, with the air transport service and had risen to the rank of lieutenant.

While he was stationed at Fort Benning, he flew a group of VIPs to Washington, D.C. During his stay there, he went out to the ball park to visit his former teammates. The Senators were playing a double-header, and Lewis had to leave before the games were over. He promised that he would buzz the field as he left Washington. In the fourth inning of the second game, an airplane came in low over the center field wall and headed straight for the home plate area. George Case told it this way, "I'm in the on-deck circle in the second game, ready to hit, and here comes this DC-3 straight out of center field, breaking all air regulations. The fans didn't know who it was, but we did. He cut the field in half, almost hit the flagpole. He wiggled his wings, and I threw my bat in the air. That was the most thrilling thing that ever happened to me. He told me later he got reprimanded for it" (Goldstein 1980, 249). When asked how low he was, Lewis answered, "I could almost read the letters on their uniforms." There were strict flying restrictions around Washington at that time and pilots were to follow them to the letter. Lewis said, "We had to stick to corridors. Well, I didn't do that. I didn't stick to the minimum altitude either" (Gilbert 1992, 56).

Lewis's military service took him to the China-Burma-India theater. To get there he had to fly his C-47 (the military name for a DC-3) from West Palm Beach, Florida, to Puerto Rico, then to South America, then to Ascension Island, then to Africa, then across the Red Sea, then over the Indian Ocean, and finally to Karachi. This flight in the C-47, with its top speed of 150 mph, took two weeks. While serving in the China-Burma-India theater, Lewis flew many missions over "The Hump," the name flyers gave to the Himalayan Mountains. The mountain barrier is located between India and China. It was the world's most dreaded and dangerous strip of airway. With treacherous cross-currents above and jagged peaks below, a mistake by a pilot or a mishap with a plane opened the door to eternity. One account put the number of Lewis's missions at 213 and another at over 500. Either way Lewis was exposed to dangers of war. He received the Distinguished Flying Cross for his work with Wingate's Raiders. They made a sneak landing 200 miles behind Japanese lines in Burma. This was one of the most important aerial operations up to that time.

Lewis flew a C-47 transport fully loaded pulling two gliders over the treacherous, enemy-occupied territory without a fighter escort. Sometimes, he flew these missions as often as three times a day. This went on for six straight days. The citation on the Distinguished Flying Cross read, "For extraordinary achievement in aerial flight during which exposure to enemy fire was probable and expected, flying transport aircraft carrying a normal load. In addition to towing two heavily-loaded gliders, he took off at night for a point 200 miles beyond the enemy positions in Burma, . . . Due to the proximity of the enemy and the necessity of surprise, the entire flight was made without radio aid, requiring the highest degree of piloting skill to avoid mid-air crashes either with aircraft in the towing unit or near-by units on the same mission" (*The Sporting News,* "Flying Cross Awarded Buddy Lewis for Feats" June 22, 1944, page 12). By this time he had been promoted to the rank of captain. By the time he was ready to return home, he had also won the air medal with oak leaf cluster and distinguished unit citation badge in addition to the Distinguished Flying Cross.

By June 1945 he had been transferred back to the States and was stationed at Stout Field, Indianapolis, Indiana. While stationed there he got his first real chance to play baseball since he went overseas. He was discharged on July 23, 1945, and rejoined the Senators as soon as he could. He was able to get into sixty-nine games in 1945 and batted .333 in 258 at-bats. "The good pitchers were not in baseball, and with the good pitchers gone my timing came rapidly." He added, "I was four years older but still right in my prime, and I had no difficulty hitting" (Mead 1985, 227). However, Buddy Lewis's career was short-lived after returning from war. He had a good year in 1946 and an off year in 1947. He missed all of 1948 with an injury, couldn't regain his form in 1949 while playing only part-time, and retired at age 32. Rick Van Blair, author of *Dugout to Foxhole*, commented, "The war didn't just cut his baseball career short—it really ended it" (Van Blair 1994, 112). Even with those comments, Lewis said, "The Air Corps was probably more glamorous in World War II than baseball, and flying to me was the most wonderful thing in the world. Oh, my God almighty, I just wouldn't take anything for my years of flying. You could say my record in baseball might have been better otherwise. But fate injected me into this thing, and I liked it" (Mead 1985, 98).

He could have done like many major leagues baseball players: stay at some camp and play baseball for the camp team. Lewis chose to fly. He wanted to make a difference in the war effort. In doing so, he put his life on the line by flying over some of the most dangerous areas in the world. Floyd (Bucky) Walters, former sports writer in San Francisco, said, "I'd say Lewis is the major leaguer who has had the most hazardous mission to date" (*The Sporting News*, "C-B-I Editor Catches Up on Sports" August 3, 1944, page 13). Lewis was another of baseball's war heros.

AGE	YRS	ML	G	BA	SA	AB	H	2B	3B	HR	HR%	R	RBI	BB	SO	SB
25-28	42-45	11	1349	0.297	0.42	5261	1563	249	93	71	1.3	830	607	573	303	83
(4 YRS MINUS		3	518	0.303	0.441	2029	614	104	43	30	1.5	325	218	250	104	39
69 GAMES)		14	1867	0.299	0.426	7290	2177	353	136	101	1.4	1155	825	823	407	122

LINDELL, JOHN H. (JOHNNY)   BR TR 6' 4"   217 lbs.
Born August 30, 1916, Greeley, Co. — Died August 27, 1985, Newport Beach, Ca.
Played for New York (A) (1941–50), St. Louis (N) (1950), Pittsburgh (1953), and Philadelphia (N) (1953–54)

Johnny Lindell had always been a pitcher in the minors. When he was promoted to the Yankees in 1941 it was as a pitcher. In 1942 he continued to make the club in that role. However, he did not have a good fast ball and had to rely on a knuckleball and a curve ball. These were not good enough. He did show promise as a hitter. In 1943 the Yankees switched him to the outfield. This, in part, was the result of the shortage of players caused by their induction into the armed forces. Lindell made the most of this opportunity, and in 1944, he had his best year. He hit eighteen home runs, drove in 103 runs, and batted .300. He tied for the league in triples in both 1943, with twelve, and 1944, with sixteen.

While he was listed as one who had been accepted for service as early as April 1944, he was not drafted until June 8, 1945. Early in 1945 he toured with a group playing ball in the Pacific including the Philippians. He took his examination in Camden, New Jersey, on April 17 but was inducted in New York. He spent the summer of 1945 at Camp Lee where he played on the camp baseball team. He was discharged on March 22, 1946. He only missed part of one year. Although he didn't serve long in military service, he did work off-season 1943-44 at the Western Pipe and Steel shipyard in Wilmington, California.

With the return of DiMaggio, Henrich, and Keller in 1946, Lindell was forced into a reserve role. He got more playing time in 1947 and 1948 when Charlie Keller was injured. However, the balance of his career was spent as a reserve. He started as a pitcher, made it to the majors, was converted to an outfielder, played ten years, was demoted to the minors, became a pitcher again, and returned to the majors one more time. His return in 1953 as a pitcher with the Pirates and later that year with the Phillies was short lived, and he retired in 1954.

AGE	YRS	ML	G	BA	SA	AB	H	2B	3B	HR	HR%	R	RBI	BB	SO	SB
28	45	12	854	0.273	0.429	2795	762	124	48	72	2.6	401	404	289	366	17
(1 YR MINUS		0	84	0.268	0.46	302	81	14	7	10	3.3	37	45	23	47	1
41 GAMES)		12	938	0.272	0.431	3097	843	138	55	82	2.6	438	449	312	413	18

LITWHILER, DANIEL W. (DANNY)   BR TR 5' 10"   198 lbs.
Born August 31, 1916, Ringtown, Pa.

Played for Philadelphia (N) (1940-43), St. Louis (N) (1943-44, 1946), Boston (N) (1946-48), and Cincinnati (1948-51)

Danny Litwhiler was one of the 4-F athletes who were drafted under a Selective Service rule that said if you were good enough to play ball you were good enough to serve in the military. James E. Byrnes, director of War Mobilization and Reconstruction, ordered the re-examination of all professional athletics. Litwhiler was 4-F because of his badly damaged knee. He had two operations to remove cartilage in 1939. Litwhiler said, "I had had six physicals and they rejected me every time because I had no cartilage in my left knee. In fact, I had tried to enlist because of the harassment we had, not so much from the fans, but writers would kind of take off in general about ballplayers not going. I felt I might as well try to get in. I had tried to enlist in the Navy and they rejected me." He added, "It was in January when I was called and the doctor had had me I guess five or six times in a row, and he said 'not you again?'" (Goldstein 1980, 206). The doctor rejected him again, but as he was leaving a captain stopped him and said that he was in anyway and had been accepted for "limited service."

He entered the Army on March 20, 1945, and was accepted for active duty on April 19, 1945, at Jefferson Barracks, Missouri. By May 1945, he had been transferred to Fort Lewis, Washington, where he spent the balance of his military service. While there he was the Director of Recreation and Entertainment for Basic Training. Also, he was able to play for the fort's baseball team. They had some additional major leaguers on the team and were the 9th Service Command champions. In addition, he coached the basketball team to the championship of the same area. In a letter Litwhiler indicated he was proud that the basketball team had beaten the "Globe Trotters."

He was discharged on April 24, 1946. Before he was drafted Litwhiler had contributed to the morale of the soldiers. In the winter of 1943-44 he went, along with a group of players, to the Aleutian Islands to entertain troops.

Litwhiler's career began in 1940 with the Phillies, and by 1941, he was a regular outfielder. He had one major problem. He led outfielders in the National League with fifteen errors, most coming on ground balls. The next spring the manager made him take infield practice every day to improve his ability to handle ground balls. The practice worked. In 1942, he became the first major league regular to play a whole season without an error. He had 308 putouts and nine assists in 151 games without an error. Although he had helped the Cardinals to the pennant in 1944 before he was drafted, including hitting a homer to help win game five of the World Series, Litwhiler was traded to the Braves after playing in only six games in 1946. He spent the balance of his career as a platoon player for the Braves and the Reds.

AGE	YRS	ML	G	BA	SA	AB	H	2B	3B	HR	HR%	R	RBI	BB	SO	SB
28-29	45-46	11	1057	0.281	0.438	3494	982	162	32	107	3.1	428	451	299	377	11
(2 YRS MINUS		1	137	0.297	0.471	488	145	22	6	17	3.5	71	60	52	62	2
85 GAMES)		12	1194	0.283	0.442	3982	1127	184	38	124	3.1	499	511	351	439	13

LOCKMAN, CARROLL W. (WHITEY)   BL TR 6' 1"   175 lbs.

Born July 25, 1926, Lowell, N.C.
Played for New York (N) (1945, 1947-56, 1957), St. Louis (N) (1956), San Francisco (1958), Baltimore (1959), and Cincinnati (1959-60)

Whitey Lockman got to play in one of the most famous games of all time on October 3, 1951, the day Bobby Thomson hit his shot "heard around the world." Many people remember that. However, most people don't know that it was Whitey Lockman's double that knocked Don Newcombe off the pitcher's mound and led to Ralph Branca being in the game to pitch to Thomson. Lockman drove in one run with his hit and sent another to third, setting the stage for the homer.

Lockman was eighteen when was he promoted to the Giants on July 5, 1945. He started his career by hitting a home run in his first at bat. He played in thirty-two games that year before he was drafted into the Army on August 10. He was inducted at Newark, New Jersey.

By late August the Army had transferred him to Washington Military Camp to serve as an athletic instructor. He also spent some time at Fort Dix, New Jersey. He remained in the Army for the balance of 1945 and all of 1946. He was discharged in time to go to the Giants' spring training camp in 1947. His luck was bad as he broke his leg in an exhibition game and didn't play with the Giants until September. He only appeared in two games in 1947. Throughout his career Lockman was known as a good .280 hitter with some home run power. In an effort to get the Giants going in 1951, Leo Durocher moved Lockman from outfield to first base during that year. Over his career he played almost the same number of games at first (771) as he did in the outfield (752). He was a very hard man to double up. During his playing years, Lockman grounded into a double play only once in every 87.4 at-bats, putting him among the leaders of all time. Lockman was always known as a consistent contributor.

AGE	YRS	ML	G	BA	SA	AB	H	2B	3B	HR	HR%	R	RBI	BB	SO	SB
18-19	45-46	15	1666	0.279	0.391	5940	1658	222	49	114	1.9	836	563	552	383	43
(2 YRS MINUS	1		80	0.292	0.415	212	62	12	1	4	1.9	22	25	21	16	1
32 GAMES)		16	1746	0.28	0.391	6152	1720	234	50	118	1.9	858	588	573	399	44

LOWREY, HARRY L. (PEANUTS)   BR TR 5'8"   170 lbs.

Born August 27, 1918, Culver City, Ca. — Died July 2, 1986, Inglewood, Ca.
Played for Chicago (N) (1942-43, 1945-49), Cincinnati (1949-50), St. Louis (N) (1950-54), and Philadelphia (N) (1955)

Harry (Peanuts) Lowrey had a shorter stay than most in the military. He was drafted in February 1944 and discharged in October 1944. He spent some time with the 5th Ferrying Group in California and later at Fort Custer, Michigan. He was able to play baseball for both of the groups.

Lowrey was known as "Peanuts" his whole career. There are two stories on how he got his nickname. The first is that a relative (some say grandfather and some say uncle) took a look at him when he was born and said, "He's no bigger than a peanut." The other story is that when he was working as a child actor, actress Thelma Todd promised him peanuts if he would behave. (Incidentally he did do some additional acting later in his life. He had a speaking part in the movie, "The Winning Team" in which Ronald Reagan starred as Grover Cleveland Alexander.)

Lowrey was a regular player for the Cubs and Reds in the late '40s. However, he also made his mark as a pinch hitter later in his career. He led the league in pinch hits in 1952 and 1953. In 1953 he set a record when he got twenty-two pinch hits. (The record has since been broken.) During that year he got seven straight pinch hits, also a record at the time. Stan Musial said, "He could hit, not for power, but always close to .300, because he knew how to hit the ball and punch it around" (Broeg 1964, 279). Lowrey was a consistent player who had a good career.

AGE	YRS	ML	G	BA	SA	AB	H	2B	3B	HR	HR%	R	RBI	BB	SO	SB
25	44	13	1401	0.273	0.362	4317	1177	186	45	37	0.9	564	479	403	226	48
		1	139	0.276	0.377	514	142	24	8	4	0.8	69	69	46	24	11
		14	1540	0.273	0.364	4831	1319	210	53	41	0.8	633	548	449	250	59

MAJESKI, HENRY (HANK)   BR TR 5'9"   174 lbs.

Born December 13, 1916, Staten Island, N.Y. — Died August 9, 1991, Staten Island, N.Y.
Played for Boston (N) (1939-41), New York (A) (1946), Philadelphia (A) (1946-49, 1951-52), Chicago (A) (1950-51), Cleveland (1952-55), and Baltimore (1955)

Hank Majeski won the batting championship in the International League in 1942. In 1943 he was expected to take over third base for the Yankees, replacing Red Rolfe who had retired. But the war changed that. Instead of playing for the Yankees, he was a member of the United States Coast Guard. He had trials before, playing a full season with the Braves in 1939 and partial years in 1940 and 1941. This would have been his chance to play for the world champions. The war took that chance and also three years out of his career.

He entered the Coast Guard on January 27, 1943. He was stationed at the U. S. Coast Guard Academy in New London, Connecticut, in late 1943. By the spring of 1945 he was located at Curtis Bay Station. He was able to play for the base team at that location. In the fall of 1945, he was shipped to the South Pacific. He was discharged on November 27, 1945.

The chance to play for the Yankees ended quickly. After only eight games the Yankees sold him to the A's. Starting in 1947 and continuing through 1951, he was considered one of the leading third basemen in the American League. Majeski was known for fielding. Eddie Joost, Majeski's teammate with the A's, said, "Majeski was a great third baseman, as good as I ever saw defensively. He set a major league record for fielding percentage that year [1947]" (Peary 1994, 41). While known for his fielding, Majeski also had some good years with the bat. In 1948 he batted .310 with twelve homers and 120 runs driven in. He once had six doubles in a doubleheader on August 27, 1948. If he had stayed with the Yankees, he might have played in many World Series. Because of the teams he played on, Majeski got to play in only one World Series. In 1954 he played for the Cleveland Indians, mostly as a pinch hitter. He hit a three-run homer for the Indians in a losing cause.

AGE	YRS	ML	G	BA	SA	AB	H	2B	3B	HR	HR%	R	RBI	BB	SO	SB
26-28	43-45	13	1069	0.279	0.398	3421	956	181	27	57	1.7	404	501	299	260	10
		3	275	0.29	0.411	898	260	50	7	15	1.7	114	138	83	70	4
		16	1344	0.282	0.401	4319	1216	231	34	72	1.7	518	639	382	330	14

MARSHALL, WILLARD W. BL TR 6' 1" 205 lbs.
Born February 8, 1921, Richmond, Va. — Died November 5, 2000, Norwood, N.J.
Played for New York (N) (1942, 1946-49), Boston (N) (1950-52), Cincinnati (1952-53), and Chicago (A) (1954-55)

Willard Marshall was called "a slow footed, sure handed outfielder with one of the most powerful throwing arms" (Shatzkin 1990, 673). He was an unheralded rookie when he arrived at Giants' spring training in 1942. He had a good spring, made the team, and was the regular left fielder that season. It was anticipated that he would be drafted in early October 1942, so he enlisted in the Marines on September 19 to report on September 29.

By June 1943, he had been promoted to the rank of corporal and assigned to the Quartermaster's Division, Washington, D.C. The December 2, 1943, issue of *The Sporting News* listed his address as U.S. Marine Corps, 403 - 50th. Avenue, Capital Heights, Md. He was transferred to the Pacific by the summer of 1945. He had been promoted to the rank of sergeant and was playing on the base baseball team. He played on the FMF team in the 14th Naval District League in Hawaii. According to Marshall, he did not see combat while he was in the Marines (Marshell letter, 1998). He was not discharged until April 2, 1946.

Marshall was able to make the transition back to baseball without a drop in his statistics. He had his career year in 1947 when the Giants set the team record for the most home runs in a season with 221. (The record has since been broken.) Marshall was second on the team with thirty-six home runs, including three home runs on July 18, 1947. He never had more than seventeen in any other season. In addition to the team record, Johnny Mize, Marshall, and Walker Cooper set the record for the most homers by three teammates (since broken). Marshall was part of the major trade the Giants made on December 14, 1949, as they tried to remake the nature of the team. The Giants had been a home-run hitting, slow-running team. Leo Durocher wanted speed and defense. The Giants traded Marshall, Sid Gordon, Buddy Kerr, and Sam Webb to the Braves for Eddie Stanky and Alvin Dark. It worked for the Giants as they won the pennant in 1951 and 1954.

AGE	YRS	ML	G	BA	SA	AB	H	2B	3B	HR	HR%	R	RBI	BB	SO	SB
22-24	43-45	11	1246	0.274	0.423	4233	1160	163	39	130	3.1	583	604	458	219	14
		3	358	0.278	0.443	1254	349	49	17	41	3.3	176	178	114	47	4
		14	1604	0.275	0.428	5487	1509	212	56	171	3.1	759	782	572	266	18

MCCARTHY, JOHN J. (JOHNNY)   BL TL 6' 1"   185 lbs.
Born January 7, 1910, Chicago, Il. — Died September 13, 1973, Mundelein, Il.
Played for Brooklyn (1934–35), New York (N) (1936–41, 1948), and Boston (N) (1943, 1946)

Johnny McCarthy got more than seventy-five percent of his career at-bats and career hits during three seasons, even though he played in eleven seasons. After trials with Brooklyn, he was touted as the replacement for Bill Terry with the Giants when the 1937 season got under way. In fact he was the regular first baseman for the Giants during the 1937 and 1938 seasons. In 1939 he lost out when the Giants acquired Zeke Bonura. He spent three more seasons with the Giants but played very little. After being out of the majors in 1942, he got another chance as the military took away players for the war effort. In 1943 he became the first baseman for the Braves. He played in seventy-eight games and batted .304. He got in that one year before he too was inducted.

He entered the Navy on January 24, 1944, and was assigned to the Great Lakes base. During 1944 he was listed as a member of the Great Lakes' baseball team. Early in 1945, McCarthy was listed as a new arrival in Hawaii. When his wife had a daughter that spring, he was still with the Navy in the Southwest Pacific. He was discharged from the Navy in December 1945.

His playing days were almost over. While his status as a regular was limited, he did make a mark as a pinch hitter. He led the National League in pinch hit at-bats and in pinch hits in both 1940 and 1948.

AGE	YRS	ML	G	BA	SA	AB	H	2B	3B	HR	HR%	R	RBI	BB	SO	SB
33-35	43-45	11	542	0.277	0.392	1557	432	72	16	25	1.6	182	209	90	114	7
(3 YRS MINUS		2	86	0.279	0.402	122	34	7	1	2	1.6	13	20	6	9	0
78 GAMES)		13	628	0.278	0.393	1679	466	79	17	27	1.6	195	229	96	123	7

MCCOSKY, WILLIAM B. (BARNEY)   BL TR 6' 1"   184 lbs.
Born April 11, 1917, Coal Run, Pa. — Died September 6, 1996, Venice, Fl.
Played for Detroit (1939–42, 1946), Philadelphia (A) (1946–48, 1950–51), Cincinnati (1951), and Cleveland (1951–53)

Barney McCosky was a big hit in Detroit starting at the time he made the team. First, the fans liked him, and second, he could hit the ball. While he never hit for power—he hit only twenty-four home runs lifetime—he did hit for average. He had speed and made an excellent lead-off man. He had fourteen triples his rookie year and led the league in triples his second year with nineteen. He batted .340 in 1940 to help the Tigers win the pennant.

Barney entered the Navy on December 11, 1942. He was sent to Wooster, Ohio, in April 1943 to start pilot training. "I enlisted, wanted to be a pilot. I went somewhere in Ohio to pre-flight school and, hell, I was 25 at the time, and when I got in that school there were kids 19 and 20, just out of college. I couldn't keep up with those guys. I said, 'What the hell am I doing here?' So I called Great Lakes; Mickey Cochrane was a commander there; I said, 'Mickey get me out of this end of it. Get me over there, I'll be a sailor'" (Mead 1985, 194). He was transferred to Great Lakes in about a week. While he was there, he got to play for the Great Lakes team. They had a very good team with a number of major leaguers.

Early in 1944 McCosky was transferred to Bainbridge, Maryland, for more intense training. There he went through Gene Tunney's physical fitness program. Following Bainbridge, he was sent to Treasure Island just outside San Francisco. Under orders from Admiral Nimitz to, "get those ballplayers out here" (Mead 1985, 195). McCosky and others finally left for Hawaii on board the USS *Birmingham*. The good players were not all put on one team. They were spread among several teams with the balance of the players from the minors or amateurs. McCosky managed the AIEA barracks team. His daily duties in addition to playing ball were giving exercises, setting up basketball tournaments, umpiring games, and being an instructor. His rank was chief specialist in recreation.

Stationed in Hawaii, McCosky got to take part in the Army/Navy World Series in the fall of 1944. As the war in the Pacific pushed closer to Japan and more islands were captured, the Navy sent teams from Hawaii to the Pacific islands to play exhibition games to entertain the troops. They went on a six-week tour of these islands, including Tinian, Saipan, and Guam. The fields were makeshift flat spaces cleared off by bulldozers. Many times long hits went into the ocean. The islands were secure, but there were still Japanese soldiers who had not given up. They liked baseball. When the game was going on, they would find a high place to watch. After the tour was over, the different players were split up to go to different islands. McCosky was sent to Saipan to run the recreation program. He was discharged on October 14, 1945.

McCosky did have some trouble picking up where he left off. His game had been based on speed. The spring he came back he was plagued by leg and ankle problems. By the middle of May 1946, the Tigers had some additional problems. They had a shortage of infielders and a surplus of outfielders. McCosky was hitting .198. A trade was made: Barney McCosky, outfielder, to the A's for George Kell, infielder. McCosky turned his year around with the A's. He batted .354 the rest of season to give him an overall average of .318. He also had good years in 1947 and 1948, batting .328 and .326, respectively. However, he lost all of 1949 to a back injury and never regained form despite playing four more years.

AGE	YRS	ML	G	BA	SA	AB	H	2B	3B	HR	HR%	R	RBI	BB	SO	SB
26-28	43-45	11	1170	0.312	0.414	4172	1301	214	71	24	0.6	664	397	497	261	58
		3	406	0.321	0.421	1571	505	78	27	8	0.5	247	152	190	92	18
		14	1576	0.314	0.416	5743	1806	292	98	32	0.6	911	549	687	353	76

MCCULLOUGH, CLYDE E.   BR TR 5' 11"   180 lbs.
Born March 4, 1917, Nashville, Tn. — Died September 18, 1982, San Francisco, Ca.
Played for Chicago (N) (1940-43, 1946-48, 1953-56) and Pittsburgh (1949-52)

Clyde McCullough was a journeyman catcher for fifteen years in the major leagues. He appeared in one hundred games in only three seasons. He was platooned much of his career because of weak hitting; however, he was a good defensive catcher with a strong arm. It is reported that he was the last catcher to play without a chest protector. He was not a good home run hitter with only fifty-two in his career. However, on July 26, 1942, he hit three home runs in a row. Those three, along with his two others, made his total five for the year.

McCullough entered the Navy on December 31, 1943. He was stationed at Great Lakes during 1944. While there he played on their baseball team. Early in 1945 he was transferred to Norfolk Naval Training Station. He spent 1945 playing on that baseball team. He was discharged from the Navy on September 26, 1945.

Although he did not arrive back in Chicago in time for the regular season, he did get back in time for the World Series. He was called on to pinch-hit in the series. By doing that, he became the only man to play in a World Series without making a regular season appearance.

AGE	YRS	ML	G	BA	SA	AB	H	2B	3B	HR	HR%	R	RBI	BB	SO	SB
27-28	44-45	15	1098	0.252	0.358	3121	785	121	28	52	1.7	308	339	265	398	27
		2	190	0.251	0.349	578	145	23	5	8	1.4	58	59	47	77	7
		17	1288	0.251	0.357	3699	930	144	33	60	1.6	366	398	312	475	34

MIKSIS, EDWARD T. (EDDIE)   BR TR 6' 0"   185 lbs.
Born September 11, 1926, Burlington, N.J.
Played for Brooklyn (1944, 1946-51), Chicago (N) (1951-56), St. Louis (N) (1957), Baltimore (1957-58), and Cincinnati (1958)

Miksis was just out of high school and seventeen years old when he made his first appearance with the Dodgers. The year was 1944 and he was one of several teenagers to play during that time. The player shortage was being felt. Many older players and many younger players were filling out the rosters. He only got to play the balance of 1944 before he entered military service.

He entered the Navy and by December was stationed at Bainbridge, Maryland. He had the rank of apprentice seaman. He was still at Bainbridge in September 1945. He got to play some ball while he was stationed there. Miksis also missed most of the 1946 season. He returned to the Dodgers in time to get into twenty-three games that year.

Miksis was a good utility man who struggled with the bat. He did get a chance to play more when he was traded to the Cubs in 1951. Frank Baumholtz said, "He was a nice guy and played a good second base when he got the chance" (Peary 1994, 144). He never got very many chances because of his weak hitting, even though he was able to play for fourteen years. However, he did get to take part in one very exciting game. It was the fourth game of the 1947 World Series. Bill Bevens was pitching a no-hitter. It was the bottom of the ninth. After an out,

Furillo walked. After another out, Gionfriddo, who was running for Furillo, stole second. Reiser batted for Casey and was intentionally walked. Miksis ran for him. Lavagetto batted for Stanky and hit a double off the right field wall. Gionfriddo scored, and Miksis scored the winning run as the Dodgers came from behind and beat the Yankees three to two on only one hit.

AGE	YRS	ML	G	BA	SA	AB	H	2B	3B	HR	HR%	R	RBI	BB	SO	SB
18-19	45-46	14	1042	0.236	0.322	3053	722	95	17	44	1.4	383	228	215	313	52
(2 YRS MINUS		1	52	0.229	0.3	140	32	5	1	1	0.7	14	6	4	7	3
23 GAMES)		15	1094	0.236	0.321	3193	754	100	18	45	1.4	397	234	219	320	55

MIZE, JOHN R. (JOHNNY)   BL TR 6' 2"   215 lbs.
Born January 7, 1913, Demorest, Ga. — Died June 2, 1993, Demorest, Ga.
Played for St. Louis (N) (1936–41), New York (N) (1942, 1946–49), and New York (A) (1949–53)

This Hall of Famer had two careers, one as a power-hitting first baseman for the Cardinals and the Giants and another as a pinch-hitter for the Yankees. Both of the careers were successful. When Mize joined the Cardinals in 1936, he beat longtime favorite Ripper Collins for the first base job. He remained a fixture there until he was traded by the Cardinals to the Giants in 1942. The Cardinals of that era had a history of trading off good veterans, whose salaries were going up, for cash and young prospects. Mize fell into that category in 1942. He had led the league in home runs in 1939 and 1940. Also in 1939 and 1940, he missed the triple crown by one category each year. In 1939 he won the batting and home run titles and finished third in the RBI race.

In 1940 he won the home run and RBI titles and finished fifth in batting. In 1938 he led the league in triples by hitting sixteen. During that year he had no stolen bases. In 1939 he hit fourteen triples and again did not have any stolen bases. These two years rank as the most and second most triples hit in a year where the batter did not have any stolen bases. He had batted over .300 every year since he had come into the league. He had driven in over 100 runs every year except his first. So instead of paying the increased salary, the Cardinals traded him to the Giants. He continued his success with the Giants. First, in the one year before going into service, he led the league in RBIs. After the war he led the league twice in home runs and once in RBIs. In addition to hitting over .300 for the first nine years of his career, he also had power, power without a wild swing. Stan Musial said, "Johnny Mize had a classic swing. It was smooth, seemed almost effortless, yet Big John had a good follow-through and was one of the best home-run hitters baseball has known" (Broeg 1964, 251). He went on to say, "John Mize had the best eye of any hitter I've seen in the National League" (Broeg 1964, 282).

This compact swing and keen eye gave him a statistic unheard of in today's home run hitters. In 1947 he hit fifty-one home runs for the Giants. During that year he struck out only forty-two times. He followed that up by hitting forty home runs and striking out only thirty-seven times in 1948. For two years, while hitting ninety-one home runs, he was able to hit more home runs than the number of times he struck out. He is the only major leaguer to hit fifty home runs and strike out fewer than fifty times. Mize's nickname was "The Big Cat." Bill Rigney says it wasn't because he was a great fielder around first base. He said, "…he couldn't move at all around first base" (Peary 1994, 27). He was recognized as an adequate fielder with limited range. He said about himself, "I can get to any ball hit within a foot of me in either direction" (Blake 1994, 62). Mize was called "The Big Cat" because of his graceful batting style, not for his quickness. When Stan Musial introduced Mize at his Hall of Fame induction he said, "Did you ever see a pitcher knock him down at the plate? Remember how he reacted when brushed back? He'd just lean back on his left foot, bend his body back and let the pitch go by. Then he'd lean back into the batter's box and resume his stance, as graceful as a big cat" (Shatzkin 1990, 750).

Mize had been classified 3-A when the Cardinals traded him to the Giants in December 1941. He played for the Giants in 1942 and entered the Navy on March 24, 1943. He started his military service at Great Lakes, spending the spring and summer there getting his basic training. While he was stationed at Great Lakes, he did play for the base team in 1943. By fall of 1943, he was transferred to Bainbridge, Maryland, to receive further training in the physical instructors' school. When this training was completed, he was transferred to the Pacific. By May 1944 he was stationed at Kaneohe Naval Air Base in Honolulu. Mize played for a Navy team while stationed in Honolulu. He also took part in the Army/Navy World Series in the fall of 1944. The Navy team beat the Army team in five games. Mize was part of the Navy teams that toured the Pacific war zone playing exhibitions for the fighting troops. He ended up in the Marianas. It was from this location that he departed as he came back to the States to be discharged. He was among the group on board *The General Weigel* that docked in San Francisco on September 24, 1945. He reached the rank of specialist first class before he was discharged on October 9, 1945.

There was concern that Mize, at age thirty-three, would not be able to play at the same level he had before he went into service. His speed was not as good, based on the number of triples hit, but his power was still there. He played only 101 games in 1946, but it was because of a broken arm and not because of war injuries. He hit .337 in 1946. His second career came after the Giants sold him to the Yankees in 1949. He had spent the first ten years being a starting first baseman. Now he would become a part-time player and pinch hitter. He was just as successful in the second role as he had been in the first. He played five years for the Yankees. In each of those five years, the Yankees won the pennant and the World Series.

Mize was a big part of those victories. In the 1952 World Series, he batted .400 with three home runs and was voted the most valuable player for the series. He led the league in pinch hits for the last three years of his career. Mize gave his philosophy on hitting, "The pitcher has to throw the ball in the strike zone sooner or later and the rules allow the batter to hit only one fair ball each time he bats, so why not hit the pitch you want to hit and not the one he wants you to hit" (Dickson 1991, 295).

AGE	YRS	ML	G	BA	SA	AB	H	2B	3B	HR	HR%	R	RBI	BB	SO	SB
30-32	43-45	15	1884	0.312	0.562	6443	2011	367	83	359	5.6	1118	1337	856	524	28
		3	415	0.309	0.576	1558	482	83	18	99	6.4	296	340	221	119	12
		18	2299	0.312	0.565	8001	2493	450	101	458	5.7	1414	1677	1077	643	40

MOORE, TERRY B.   BR TR 5' 11"   195 lbs.

Born May 27, 1912, Vernon, Al. — Died March 29, 1995, Collinsville, Il.

Played for St. Louis (N) (1935-42, 1946-48)

In his book, *Dugout to Foxhole*, Rick Van Blair starts the chapter on Terry Moore as follows, "In the history of baseball there have been many great center fielders, including such greats stars as Tris Speaker, Joe and Dom DiMaggio, Max Carey, Willie Mays, Mickey Mantle, Duke Snider, Cool Papa Bell, Harry Craft and Curt Flood. One name, however, stands at the top of the list, and he just might have been the greatest ever to play the position. His name is Terry Moore" (Van Blair 1994, 138). That is indeed high praise for any player. While some would disagree, many of those who played in the Terry Moore era would agree with Van Blair's statement. Max Lanier said, "He was the greatest center fielder I ever played with, and I played with Willie Mays when I was on the Giants" (Van Blair 1994, 210). Jimmy Bloodworth, Mace Brown, Harry Danning, and Harry Gumbert made similar statements about Terry Moore's ability to play center field. He was a good team player and was one of the reasons the Cardinals had such a good team in 1942. Harry Walker said, "Terry Moore was our captain and the glue that held that 1942 team together" (Van Blair 1994, 206)

Moore entered the Army on May 31, 1943. He did not play any baseball in 1943 because he served in civilian government physical training instruction in Panama before entering the Army. After he completed his basic training, he was stationed in the Canal Zone as part of the Army Air Force. He served his entire time in that location. From that base, they patrolled into the Southwest Pacific. During that time, he went on several flying missions where he witnessed the sinking of several Japanese ships. He manned a machine gun on some of these sorties. He was assigned to the Sixth Air Force and rose to the rank of sergeant. There was also time to play on the base baseball team during his stay in the Canal Zone.

Moore was discharged on January 12, 1946. "I was gone for all of forty-three, forty-four, and forty-five. It did hurt to be away from baseball, but there was a war on so what are you going to do? That't the way it was." He went on to say, "I wasn't the same player after I came back from the service. Those years I lost in the service should have been my best years…when I went into the service during the war, I was in the prime of my baseball career. But when I came back after the war, I was an old man trying to keep up with the younger players" (Van Blair 1994, 141-142).

Stan Musial said, "It was apparent early that a few of the Cardinals' brightest stars never would be the same. Terry Moore was having trouble with his legs in center field" (Broeg 1964, 86). Now he would be required to go all out for fly balls that he could have caught with ease before. He was thirty-four when he returned to the Cardinals in 1946. Leg injuries limited his playing time that year. After a good year in 1947 and a bad one in 1948 Moore retired. He was a five-time All-Star when he went into service. He was an "old man" trying to keep up when he returned. The war took a lot from Terry Moore.

AGE	YRS	ML	G	BA	SA	AB	H	2B	3B	HR	HR%	R	RBI	BB	SO	SB
31-33	43-45	11	1298	0.28	0.399	4700	1318	263	28	80	1.7	719	513	406	368	82
		3	375	0.28	0.391	1367	383	77	7	20	1.5	220	144	127	100	24
		14	1673	0.28	0.399	6067	1701	340	35	100	1.6	939	657	533	468	106

MUELLER, RAY C.   BR TR 5' 9"   175 lbs.

Born March 8, 1912, Pittsburg, Ks. — Died June 29, 1994, Dauphin County, Pa.
Played for Boston (N) (1935–38, 1951), Pittsburgh (1939–40, 1950), Cincinnati (1943-44, 1946–49), and New York (N) (1949–50)

Ray Mueller got to play because of the war. He had been a back-up catcher for the Braves and the Pirates from 1935 till 1939, never playing in more than eighty-six games in any one year. In 1940 he was sent down to the minors and stayed there until the player shortage became severe. He was able to return to the majors in 1943. At age thirty-one the Reds called him up to replace Ray Lamanno who had entered the military. Mueller made the most of his chance. He caught 140 games and batted .260 in 1943 and batted .286 and caught all 155 games in 1944, making the All-Star team. In all, counting the sixteen games he caught when he returned from the service, he caught 233 games in a row.

He had been classified 4-F during the early part of the war because he had a stomach ulcer. However, when the war department reexamined athletes, he was drafted. He entered the Army on February 8, 1945, at New Cumberland, Pennsylvania. He was sent to Fort Lewis, Washington, for training. While there he was able to play on their baseball team. By August 1945, he had been transferred to Moore General Hospital, North Carolina. He was also able to play some baseball there. He had the rank of private when he was discharged on November 16, 1945.

He was the regular catcher for the Reds in the 1946 season. Following that year he reverted to a back-up status for the remainder of his career. His last season in the majors was 1951.

AGE	YRS	ML	G	BA	SA	AB	H	2B	3B	HR	HR%	R	RBI	BB	SO	SB
33	45	14	982	0.252	0.368	2911	733	123	23	56	1.9	281	373	250	322	14
		1	76	0.247	0.361	227	56	10	2	4	1.8	23	27	22	24	1
		15	1058	0.251	0.367	3138	789	133	25	60	1.9	304	400	272	346	15

MUSIAL, STANLEY F. (STAN)   BL TL 6' 0"   175 lbs.

Born November 21, 1920, Donora, Pa.
Played for St. Louis (N) (1941–44, 1946–63)

Say "Stan the Man" and any Brooklyn Dodger fan knows who you mean. They named him. Over his career Musial had some of his best moments against the Dodgers, especially in Brooklyn. It may have been the atmosphere. It may have been that the Cardinals and the Dodgers were usually fighting for the pennant. Whatever the reason, Musial killed the Dodgers over the years. This twenty-four time All-Star also had good success against everybody else. His career was filled with great moments. That great career was almost over before it started. Musial was signed by the Cardinals as a pitcher. Because he was hitting so well when he was pitching, he also played outfield on days when he wasn't pitching. In late August 1940, the event happened that changed his career. While playing outfield, he dived for a line drive and hurt his shoulder. The pitching career was over. Musial became a full-time outfielder.

Over the course of his career, he led the National League in forty-six major offensive categories. That includes seven batting titles, most hits six times, leading in doubles eight times, in triples five times, runs scored five times, RBIs twice, and slugging percentage six times. He got within one home run of tying for that title in 1948. Also in 1948, he hit thirty-nine home runs and struck out thirty-four times. He averaged striking out only thirty-one times per year for his whole career. In addition, he was voted the most valuable player three times. He holds the distinction of hitting the most home runs in a career without ever winning a home run title.

Many of the players who played at that time consider Musial to be one of the best players of all time. Warren Spahn said, "He was the toughest hitter for me to get out" (Reichler 1981, 10). Preacher Roe put it this way, "I throw him four wide ones and then I try to pick him off first base" (Shatzkin 1990, 778). The comments go on and on. Dick Groat said, "When I first come up in 1952 Stan Musial could fly. At that time, he went to first base in a class with Mantle, before Mickey hurt his knee. He was that quick" (Peary 1994, 180). Joe Garagiola put it this way, "He could hit .300 with a fountain pen" (Liebman 1994, 81). Noted author Bill James summarized how many view Musial when he compared Musial with Ted Williams. "I think he [Ted Williams] was the second-greatest left-fielder who ever lived. That's not criticism. But if I had to choose between the two of them, I'd take Musial in left field, Musial on the base paths, Musial in the clubhouse, and Williams only with the wood in his hand. And Stan Musial could hit a little too" (Lahsche 1994, 3).

Musial missed only 1945 because of the war. He did, however, work to help the war effort before he went into the Navy. In the off-season in 1943 he worked for the American Steel & Wire Co. in Donora, Pennsylvania. He also went on a goodwill trip to the Aleutian Islands, along with some other players, to visit the troops stationed there. He also was scheduled to make a trip to the Pacific in September of 1943; however, the trip was canceled by the War Department.

While Musial was not drafted until 1945, there was never a hint that he sought or received special treatment. Musial was ordered by the draft board to report for a physical. He was first scheduled to take it in Pennsylvania, but he got it transferred to Jefferson Barracks just outside St. Louis. On May 16, 1944, he passed the physical and was told he had been accepted for the Navy. Although he expected to be called up within a few weeks, the call didn't come until January 1945. On January 22, 1945, he entered the Navy and was assigned to Bainbridge, Maryland, for basic training. While at Bainbridge, Musial was able to play in a few games. Two things happened that would affect his baseball career. First, he played first base for the first time. He was not good at first but developed with experience. He would play over 1,000 games at first base before his career was over. Second, the sailors liked to see home runs. Musial adjusted his stance slightly to give him more power. Prior to entering the Navy, he had never hit more than thirteen home runs in any season. The changed stroke would help him hit 475 home runs over his career, including setting a record by hitting five home runs in a double-header on May 2, 1954.

He completed his basic training in April 1945 and was shipped out. He reported to Shoemaker, California, Naval Base to be assigned to duty overseas. His assignment took him to Honolulu. There he was assigned to a ship repair unit in the 14th Naval District. His job was to run a liberty launch transporting men and officers from the dock out to the ships needing repair and back. He did this in the morning and played ball in the afternoons. He was named to the 14th Naval District's all-star team while playing for the ship repair unit team. Musial was still stationed in Hawaii when VJ day occurred.

Later his father became ill and was not expected to live. His mother applied and got an emergency leave for him. His father survived, but Musial was not sent back overseas. When his leave was up, he was transferred to a ship repair unit in the Philadelphia Navy Yard. While his title was a ship repairman, he had never worked as one. After he was assigned to help take apart a destroyer, he requested and got his assignment changed. He was discharged on March 1, 1946, at Bainbridge, where he started. Transportation was not good during those times. After getting a train to Philadelphia, he could not get to Pittsburgh. He and a friend had to hitchhike. They were picked up by two members of the Pennsylvania legislature. When they found out who the sailors were, they delivered them right to the front door. He only missed one year, but it cost him a chance at 2,000 runs and RBIs as well as 3,800 hits.

Musial picked up right where he left off in 1946. He led the Cardinals to the National League pennant and a World Series victory. The Cardinals played in the World Series the first four years of Musial's career. However, they would not play in another World Series during the remaining seventeen years of his career. To try to list his accomplishments would take a whole book by itself. As important as Musial the player was, more important was Musial the man. Hershell Freeman said, "Stan Musial, with all his notoriety and accomplishments, was one of the friendliest, everyday common people you'd ever want to be around" (Peary 1994, 366). His attitude about himself and about the game would be an example to the modern day player.

After he had a sub-par year in 1959, he told the Cardinals to cut his salary the maximum amount permitted by baseball rules. The cut was from $100,000 to $80,000. Musial was the first National League player to make $100,000. His salary was good for the times. However, it was reported that when he signed his 1961 contract for $75,000 that he now had career earnings of $1,128,177. This was for a nineteen-year career at the time. Musial's career lasted to age forty-three. While these later years added to his career numbers, they also hurt his lifetime batting average. His career average at the end of the 1958 season was .340. By the time he retired in 1963 that lifetime number had dropped to .331. At age 41 he became the oldest player to hit three home runs in a game. He followed that up with one the first time at bat the next day to hit four in a row. In fact, he leads the league in most home runs hit by a grandfather. He hit nineteen home runs in 1962 and twelve more in 1963.

He is the only player to be ranked in the top twenty for a career in singles, doubles, triples, and home runs. His best year was 1948 when he led the league in every offensive category except for home runs. He missed the home run title by one round tripper. During that season he tied a Ty Cobb record by getting five hits in a game on four occasions. When Musial appeared in the All-Star game in Washington in 1962, President John F. Kennedy said to him, "A couple of years ago they told me I was too young to be president and you were too old to be playing baseball. But we fooled them" (Dickson 1991, 220). Kennedy was forty-five when he made the remark and Musial was three years younger. When Musial hurt his shoulder in 1940 diving for a fly ball in the outfield, no one could have predicted that the injury would produce one of baseball's best hitters. A sore-armed pitcher does not have much of a future. But one that can hit like Stan the Man could hit will go far.

AGE	YRS	ML	G	BA	SA	AB	H	2B	3B	HR	HR%	R	RBI	BB	SO	SB
24	45	22	3026	0.331	0.559	10972	3630	725	177	475	4.3	1949	1951	1599	696	78
		1	153	0.357	0.569	603	215	50	18	14	2.3	115	93	78	26	8
		23	3179	0.332	0.56	11575	3845	775	195	489	4.2	2064	2044	1677	722	86

NORTHEY, RONALD J. (RON)   BL TR 5' 10"   195 lbs.

Born April 26, 1920, Mahanoy City, Pa. — Died April 16, 1971, Pittsburgh, Pa.
Played for Philadelphia (N) (1942-44, 1946-47, 1957), St. Louis (N) (1947-49),
Cincinnati (1950), Chicago (N) (1950, 1952), and Chicago (A) (1955-57)

Ron Northey was the first baseball player taken as a result of the war department's campaign against professional athletes. Their position was if they are fit enough to play sports, they are fit enough to serve in the military. He had been turned down and classified 4-F on two previous occasions for three reasons. He had a punctured eardrum, a heart condition, and high blood pressure. Two weeks after his second physical he was ordered to take another at Valley Forge Army Hospital near Philadelphia. He again was stamped unfit for service. Without notice, his 4-F was changed and he was ordered to report for induction into the Army. Northey then tried to join the Navy but was turned down because he couldn't pass the physical. So, on January 29, 1945, he was inducted into the Army at New Cumberland, Pennsylvania, Army Reception Center. Northey said, "It was not my fault that I was not in the Army long ago and now that I'm here I want to do my part, the same as any other American, to get this war over in a hurry" (*The Sporting News,* "In The Service–Northey a Rookie Again," 02-08-45, page 12).

After taking his recruit training at New Cumberland, Pennsylania, Northey was transferred to Fort Lewis, Washington. He spent the spring there and by summer had moved on to Moore General Hospital, Asheville, North Carolina. What did he do to help the war effort? He became a valuable member of each of the baseball teams at each of the bases where he was stationed. Northey was discharged on November 4, 1945.

Northey was known as slow-moving outfielder. However, he was gifted with an exceptional arm. He got his start in the majors at the beginning of the war and became a regular during the war. However, after 1946, his playing time started slipping, and after spending 1951 on the disabled list, he was back in the minors. After four years in the minors, he returned to the majors as a pinch hitter and played for two additional years. One unique thing about Ron Northey is that he was traded for Harry Walker twice. In 1947 the Phillies traded him to the Cardinals for Walker, and after the 1949 season, the Cardinals traded him to the Reds, again for Harry Walker.

AGE	YRS	ML	G	BA	SA	AB	H	2B	3B	HR	HR%	R	RBI	BB	SO	SB
25	45	12	1084	0.276	0.45	3172	874	172	28	108	3.4	385	513	361	297	7
		1	129	0.277	0.453	433	120	23	4	15	3.5	55	66	46	42	1
		13	1213	0.276	0.45	3605	994	195	32	123	3.4	440	579	407	339	8

OWEN, ARNOLD M. (MICKEY)   BR TR 5' 10" 190 lbs.
Born April 4, 1916, Nixa, Mo.
Played for St. Louis (N) (1937–40), Brooklyn (1941–45), Chicago (N) (1949–51), and
Boston (A) (1954)

Mickey Owen is known for two events in his baseball career. These two things overshadow
the fact that he was a good defensive catcher for a number of years. After splitting the catching
duties for the Cardinals in 1937, Owen became their regular catcher the next three years. When
the Dodgers bought him after the 1940 season, he was considered to be one of the pieces
needed to put the Dodgers over the top. It was a success. The Dodgers won the pennant in
1941, and Owen played a major role in the pennant chase. The winning of the pennant led to
the World Series and this led to one of the events for which Owen is remembered.

It was the ninth inning of game four. The Dodgers had a four to three lead in a game that
would have tied the series. There were two out and three balls and two strikes on Yankee
batter Tommy Henrich. Hugh Casey was the pitcher and was in his fifth inning of relief work.
Casey threw a breaking pitch that Henrich swung at and missed. However, Owen also missed
catching the pitch, and it went all the way to the back stop. Henrich was able to get to first
before Owen could retrieve the ball. The Yankees went on to score four runs before the
Dodgers could get the third out. The Dodgers didn't score in the bottom of the ninth, lost the
game, and lost the next day and the World Series. When Mickey Owen is pictured, it is as he
turns to run back to the screen to get the ball. Tommy Henrich said of the pitch, "...it was the
best curve ball Hugh Casey ever threw. Casey didn't have a good curve, but this ball exploded."
He continued, "...it started out belt-high. It looked like a fast ball. Then when it broke, it broke
so sharply that it was out of the strike zone" (Honig 1976, 34). Some have said over years
that it was spitter. Pee Wee Reese called it, "a little wet slider" (Shatzkin 1990, 835). Fellow
catcher Harry Danning said, "Mickey Owen was a great receiver. That passed ball...could have
happened to anybody" (Van Blair 1994, 47). Tommy Henrich also added, "People should stop
treating Mickey Owen as if he had misplayed it. He didn't" (Blake 1994, 97).

A few players were not so kind to Owen. Teammate Billy Herman said, "I think Owen might
have 'nonchalanted' the ball, putting his glove out for it instead of shifting his whole body
to make the catch" (Honig 1975, 152). Owen himself indicates that, "Sure it was my fault.
The ball was a low curve that broke down. It hit the edge of my glove and glanced off, but
I should have had him out anyway" (Hanks, et al. 1989, 280). It doesn't make any difference
what exactly happened. Mickey Owen will always wear the goat horns for the 1941 World
Series. What people forget is that he set a National League record that year by handling 476
consecutive chances without an error and that he had a fielding percentage of .995, making
only three errors all year.

Owen had been classified 2-C by the military. However, he enlisted in the Navy at the start of
the 1945 season. He had been called for a pre-induction physical at Brookline, Missouri, in the
summer of 1944 and was accepted for service after examination at New York on September
1, 1944. He started the 1945 season with the Dodgers but entered the Navy after twenty-four
games. He started his training at the Naval Training Center at Sampson, New York, on June 4,
1945. He spent the summer of 1945 at Sampson and was able to play on the base baseball

team. He was released from the Navy in early 1946. This time leads to the second event that dominates Mickey Owen's career.

In 1946, Jorge Pasquel, a Mexican millionaire, tried to get several major leaguers to join his Mexican League. Mickey Owen was one who was contacted, and he signed with that league. The baseball commissioner, Happy Chandler, banished for life any player who was not back with his team for spring training. Owen had gone down to Mexico and played in several games. Some of the conditions and other things were not as they had been presented to him. He tried to return to the Dodgers. He was ahead of the deadline given by the commissioner, but Branch Rickey, Dodger general manager, would not take him back. Owen was forced to return to Mexico where he played and managed for four years.

One of the players who had jumped to Mexico sued baseball for the banishment. In 1949 the players who had gone to Mexico were reinstated. However, Owen's best years were behind him. He had been a starting catcher for pennant contenders for the first eight years of his career. After a year in the Navy and four years in Mexico, he was a backup catcher for second-division teams. He had a good career, but these two events overshadow the other events of his career.

AGE	YRS	ML	G	BA	SA	AB	H	2B	3B	HR	HR%	R	RBI	BB	SO	SB
29	45	13	1209	0.255	0.322	3649	929	163	21	14	0.4	338	378	326	181	36
(1 YR MINUS		0	100	0.25	0.293	324	81	7	2	1	0.3	35	35	25	14	5
24 GAMES)		13	1309	0.254	0.32	3973	1010	170	23	15	0.4	373	413	351	195	41

PHILLEY, DAVID E. (DAVE)   BB TR 6' 0"   188 lbs.
Born May 16, 1920, Paris, Tx.
Played for Chicago (A) (1941, 1946-51, 1956-57), Philadelphia (A) (1951-53), Cleveland (1954-55), Baltimore (1955-56, 1960-61), Detroit (1957), Philadelphia (N) (1958-60), San Francisco (1960), and Boston (A) (1962)

Dave Philley had a ten-year career as a regular outfielder and another six-year career as a part-time player and pinch hitter. At first he was considered an outfielder with excellent speed and a good arm. He was a team player. Bob Feller said, "… Philley was able and willing to do that little extra something that separate life's winners from the also-rans" (Feller and Gilbert 1990, 194). His attitude about how you should play the game was noticed by his teammates. Gus Zernial said, "He was a hard-nosed all-around player, a switch-hitting outfielder with some power and good speed" (Peary 1994, 133). Ed Bouchee added, "He thought there was only one way to play—as hard as you can from the get go, and I believed him" (Peary 1994, 396).

In his second career, he became a very good pinch hitter. For his career he batted .299 (93 of 311) as a pinch hitter. However, during the last six years he played in the majors, he hit .324. This includes his last year, at age forty-one, when he hit only .143. During those last six years, he led the league in pinch hits for two years, and in 1958, he ended the season by getting eight pinch hits in a row. He opened the 1959 season by getting another to set the major league record of nine pinch hits in a row. In 1961 he set a major league record (still an American League record) by getting twenty-four pinch hits for the Orioles.

Philley had gotten into seven games in 1941 with the White Sox. He was sent back to St. Paul in the American Association in 1942 before he entered military service during that season. By 1944 he was stationed at Camp Pickett, Virginia, where he was able to play some baseball. Later, in 1945, he was transferred to Camp Lee. He stayed there during the summer of 1945. Upon getting out of service, he spent most of the 1946 season with Milwaukee in the American Association before making it back to the White Sox late in 1946.

AGE	YRS	ML	G	BA	SA	AB	H	2B	3B	HR	HR%	R	RBI	BB	SO	SB
23-25	43-45	18	1904	0.27	0.377	6296	1700	276	72	84	1.3	789	729	596	551	102
(3 YRS-EST		2	50	0.272	0.344	125	34	5	2	0	0	12	10	8	9	5
1 YR-MINORS)		20	1954	0.27	0.376	6421	1734	281	74	84	1.3	801	739	604	560	107

PRIDDY, GERALD E. (GERRY)   BR TR 5' 11" 180 lbs.

Born November 9, 1919, Los Angeles, Ca. — Died March 3, 1980, North Hollywood, Ca.
Played for New York (A) (1941–42), Washington (1943, 1946-47), St. Louis (A) (1948-49), and Detroit (1950–53)

Gerry Priddy had two outstanding years at Kansas City in 1939 and 1940. The Yankees then brought him up to backup Joe Gordon at second and the rest of the infield. He served in that role for 1941 and 1942. He then was traded to Washington in January 1943. Two reasons are usually given for the trade. Some say he was traded because he had no children and he was probably going to be drafted early. Others say he was traded because he criticized Yankee manager Joe McCarthy for not playing him. Priddy was known for being an outspoken player who had a reputation for being a clubhouse lawyer. He did get in one full year with Washington before he was drafted into the Army Air Corps in December 1943. He was assigned to McClellan Field, California, with the sixth ferrying group.

By summer 1944, he had been transferred to the 7th Air Force in Honolulu, where he was able to play on their baseball team. He played with Joe DiMaggio and the other "ground-based" airmen of the 7th Air Force. His stay in Hawaii was short since his asthma forced a transfer back to the mainland. In September 1944, he was assigned to Fairfield-Suisun Air Base near San Francisco. He had reached the rank of sergeant. Priddy also spent some time in an Army-Navy hospital in Hot Springs, Arkansas, suffering from arthritis. This was in early 1945. He had one more assignment in California before being released in January 1946.

His best years were to come after the war. The two best batting years came in 1948 with the Browns when he batted .296 and in 1950 with the Tigers when he scored 104 runs and drove in 75. Priddy was a good fielder and double-play man. In 1950 he set the American League record by taking part in 150 double plays. Along with Johnny Lipon, he set the record for the most double plays by a double-play combination. Together they took part in 276 double plays in 1950.

AGE	YRS	ML	G	BA	SA	AB	H	2B	3B	HR	HR%	R	RBI	BB	SO	SB
24-25	44-45	11	1296	0.265	0.373	4720	1252	232	46	61	1.3	612	541	624	639	44
		2	292	0.26	0.363	1068	278	56	12	10	0.9	130	124	136	149	13
		13	1588	0.264	0.371	5788	1530	288	58	71	1.2	742	665	760	788	57

PYTLAK, FRANK A. (FRANKIE)   BR TR 5' 7"   160 lbs.

Born July 30, 1908, Buffalo, N.Y. — Died May 8, 1977, Buffalo, N.Y.
Played for Cleveland (1932–40) and Boston (A) (1941, 1945–46)

He was a back-up catcher for most of his twelve-year career. He had a small build for a
catcher and injuries did not allow him to complete very many full seasons. He was a good
hitter but usually split the catching time with others. He was catching with the Indians when
Bob Feller made his appearance with the Tribe. On October 2, 1938, Bob Feller struck out
eighteen Tigers. Frankie Pytlak caught that game for the Indians. Bob Feller said of Pytlak's
performance, "Another who deserved much was my catcher, Frankie Pytlak. Behind every
good pitching performance is a good catching performance. A no-hitter or a game with a lot
of strikeouts means the catcher did an excellent job of knowing what pitch to call for in a
given situation and of setting up each hitter with a successful sequence of different pitches.
That's what Frankie did. So I bought him a new suit" (Feller and Gilbert 1990, 84).

He is also known for catching a ball dropped from the 52th floor of the Terminal Tower
Building in Cleveland. He said, "It stung more than Bob Feller's fastball" (Cataneo 1991, 205).
Pytlak enlisted in the Navy on April 17, 1942. He spent 1942 at the Great Lakes Naval Base and
had the rank of Yeoman 3rd class. While there he was listed as a member of the 1942 Great
Lakes baseball team. On July 7, 1942, he took part in an all-star game that pitted the service all-
stars against the American League All-Stars. The game raised $193,000 for war relief.

In 1943 he was transferred from Great Lakes to Buffalo for gunnery duty. He was discharged
on September 1, 1945, in time to rejoin the Red Sox for a couple of weeks. At age thirty-seven,
he could no longer compete with the younger players. He only played four games in 1946
before his major league career was over. He was never a great player, but the years in the
service ended his chance to extend his playing days.

AGE	YRS	ML	G	BA	SA	AB	H	2B	3B	HR	HR%	R	RBI	BB	SO	SB
33-36	42-45	12	795	0.282	0.363	2399	677	100	36	7	0.3	316	272	247	97	56
(4 YRS MINUS		3	275	0.283	0.359	835	236	35	10	3	0.4	113	97	93	31	15
9 GAMES)		15	1070	0.282	0.362	3234	913	135	46	10	0.3	429	369	340	128	71

REESE, HAROLD H. (PEE WEE)   BR TR 5' 10"   160 lbs.

Born July 23, 1918, Louisville, Ky. — Died August 14, 1999, Louisville, Ky.
Played for Brooklyn (1940–42, 1946–58)

Pee Wee Reese was a fixture in the Brooklyn Dodger infield from 1940 to 1957. He got the
nickname "Pee Wee" not because he was small but rather because he was the City of Louisville
marble champion when he was twelve years old. (Pee wee is a type of marble.) He originally
belonged to the Red Sox. The Dodgers purchased him from the Red Sox's Louisville farm team
to replace the aging Leo Durocher. He fulfilled the expectations that they had when he was
acquired. He was considered the glue that held it all together, the unofficial captain of the
team even before he was selected officially to fill the role in 1950. He helped the Dodgers to
the pennant in 1941 in his second year.

He entered the Navy on January 30, 1943. He had originally been classified 3-A because of family obligations but by April 1942 was reclassified to 1-A. Before he entered the Navy, he had been employed in a defense plant since the close of the 1942 season. Reese, an apprentice seaman, was assigned to Norfolk Naval Base for training for the ranking of chief petty officer in early 1943. While there he played for the Norfolk Naval Air Station team during the 1943 season but was unable to beat out Phil Rizzuto for shortstop. He had achieved the rank of chief petty officer when he was transferred. He went to San Francisco for assignment and then on to Hawaii.

He spent the summer of 1944 playing ball for the Aila Hospital team to entertain the regular troops in Honolulu. He also took part in the Army/Navy World Series in September 1944. In the spring of 1945, following the "World Series," the Navy team toured some of the islands that had recently been won from the Japanese. These islands included Tinian, Saipan, Guam, and others, which were still considered part of the war zone. His rank was changed to chief specialist when he helped coach the Third Marine Division all-star team.

When VJ day happened on August 14, 1945, Reese was still in the Pacific. He was discharged on November 11, 1945. He picked up his career where he left off. In the next eleven years, he would help the Dodgers to six pennants and one World Series victory. He was considered to be a very good shortstop by his peers. Spider Jorgenson said, "I thought he was the best shortstop in the league. He had a very strong and accurate arm and knew exactly where to play hitters" (Peary 1994, 24). Bill Rigney added, "Of the other shortstops in the league, I thought Reese was the best" (Peary 1994, 29). Stan Musial also thought highly of Reese. When Musial picked his National League All-Star team, he said, "I had the most indecision at shortstop, where I finally chose Pee Wee Reese over Marty Marion and Ernie Banks" (Broeg 1964, 292).

As good as Reese was as a shortstop and player, he may have made his best contribution to baseball and the Dodgers by the way he treated Jackie Robinson. Reese was a skeptic at first, but when it counted the most, he openly supported Robinson. One incident happened on the field early in the season. Reese went over to Robinson and put his arm around him, showing to the world that Robinson was a teammate and he would support him. At Reese's death, Mrs. Robinson indicated that was one of the most important happenings in the first year of Jackie Robinson's career. This was a very strong gesture from a Southerner. Reese was a true leader. When some of his teammates were signing a petition asking to be traded rather than play with a black man, Reese said, "If he can take my job, he's entitled to it" (Ward and Burns 1994, 290).

This ten-time All-Star played in all of the Yankee-Brooklyn Dodger World Series. After losing to the Yankees five times, he was part of the team that won the World Series in 1955. Finally the Dodgers didn't have to wait till next year. "If I had my career to play over, one thing I'd do differently is swing more. Those 1,200 walks I got, nobody remembers them" (Nemec and Palmer 1993, 173). Reese made the move with the Dodgers from Brooklyn to California in 1958. That was his last year as active player. He was inducted into the Hall of Fame on August 12, 1984, a fitting end to a good career.

AGE	YRS	ML	G	BA	SA	AB	H	2B	3B	HR	HR%	R	RBI	BB	SO	SB
24-26	43-45	16	2166	0.269	0.377	8058	2170	330	80	126	1.6	1338	885	1210	890	232
		3	452	0.267	0.372	1680	448	73	16	24	1.4	276	190	268	181	47
		19	2618	0.269	0.376	9738	2618	403	96	150	1.5	1614	1075	1478	1071	279

RIZZUTO, PHILIP F. (PHIL)   BR TR 5'6"   150 lbs.
Born September 25, 1917, New York, N.Y.
Played for New York (A) (1941-42, 1946-56)

When Phil Rizzuto attended a Dodger tryout camp in 1935 at age seventeen, Casey Stengel said, "Kid, you're too small. You ought to go out and shine shoes" (Dickson 1991, 420). Another version went this way, "You're too small. You'll get hurt…Go on, get outa here. Go get a shoebox" (Solomon 1997, 359). Whichever is the correct quotation, Phil Rizzuto proved Casey Stengel wrong. Rizzuto went on to provide the Yankees with solid shortstop play for many years. This put-down may have been one of the reasons that Rizzuto was not happy when Stengel was named as Yankee manager in 1949. By that time, however, Rizzuto had established himself as the regular shortstop. He continued to play that position for Stengel as the Yankees won the pennant and World Series for the first four years of Stengel's reign.

Rizzuto took over as Yankee shortstop from Frankie Crosetti in 1941 after two successful years with the Kansas City Blues. He got in two years with the Yankees before going into the military. In both of those years the Yankees went to the World Series, beating the Dodgers in 1941 and losing to the Cardinals in 1942.

Rizzuto entered the Navy on October 10, 1942. (He had been classified 3-A because he was the main support of his parents, kid brother, and himself.) He was sent to Norfolk Naval Training Station for training. While he was stationed there he played on the baseball team. There was a lot of discussion over the years about who was the better shortstop, Rizzuto or Reese. At least at one time Rizzuto won out. While at Norfolk, both Reese and Rizzuto competed for the shortstop position. Rizzuto won out and Reese was transferred to another unit. Rizzuto played for the Norfolk team during the 1943 season. Many baseball players used their celebrity status to help with the war effort. Rizzuto was no different. While a seaman at Norfolk, he presented the bat he used to hit a home run in the 1942 World Series to the Norfolk Lions Club to help in a war bond drive. He also took part in a game to help the war bond effort. Admission to the game was to buy a war bond. There were songs by Bing Crosby and speeches by Babe Ruth and others urging people to buy bonds. Rizzuto said, "I always thought the first World Series I played in was the most thrilling event I would ever take part in or see, but the show in Washington outdid that" (Mead 1985, 4).

By April 1944, he had been transferred to Shoemaker Naval Receiving Barracks in California. He also played on their team for awhile. He then was sent to Australia in the summer of 1944. He had the responsibility of organizing recreational activities for wounded sailors at a fleet hospital at Brisbane, Australia. Rizzuto said, "You'd be surprised how much sports can do to help men who have just returned from battle" (Romeo 1944, 11). While in Australia, he continued to play baseball for one of the Navy teams. When the officers set up the Army/Navy World Series in September 1944 in Hawaii, Rizzuto was flown from Australia to play for the Navy team. After it was over he was returned to Australia. He had twelve hits in the eleven games.

By 1945 he had been transferred to the Philippines to organize a recreation program for that area. He was running three leagues for forty teams and also playing for a Navy team. While in the South Pacific, Rizzuto picked up a bad case of malaria. He was discharged on October 28, 1945.

During his career he was known as a good shortstop. He led the league three times in double plays and total chances. Teammate Bob Kuzava said, "Phil Rizzuto was a great fielder. He had a weak arm, but he knew the speed of all the hitters" (Van Blair 1994, 95). He compensated for the weak arm with a quick release on his throws.

He was also known for being a great bunter. Stan Musial said, "Phil was…the best right-handed bunter I ever saw" (Broeg 1964, 286). He led the league in sacrifice bunts for four straight years. His nickname "Scooter" came from the bunting. He would drop a bunt and scoot to first base. His career year was 1950 as far as batting was concerned. He hit .324 (one of his two years over .300), had two hundred hits, and scored 125 runs. He was passed over many times by the selection committee for the Hall of Fame. Rizzuto said, "I'll take any way to get into the Hall of Fame. If they want a batboy, I'll go as a batboy" (Solomon 1997, 997). Finally a sympathetic veterans committee selected him in 1994.

AGE	YRS	ML	G	BA	SA	AB	H	2B	3B	HR	HR%	R	RBI	BB	SO	SB
25-27	43-45	13	1661	0.273	0.355	5816	1588	239	62	38	0.7	877	562	651	397	149
		3	419	0.275	0.358	1583	436	61	18	11	0.7	225	163	147	102	43
		16	2080	0.274	0.356	7399	2024	300	80	49	0.7	1102	725	798	499	192

ROBINSON, WILLIAM E. (EDDIE)   BL TR 6' 2"   210 lbs.
Born December 15, 1920, Paris, Tx.
Played for Cleveland (1942, 1946-48, 1957), Washington (1949-50), Chicago (A) (1950-52), Philadelphia (A) (1953), New York (A) (1954-56), Kansas City (1956), Detroit (1957), and Baltimore (1957)

Eddie Robinson got into only eight games with the Indians in 1942 before he began his military service. He volunteered to go into the Navy in October after the 1942 season. He was called a "promising prospect" at the time he entered the Navy. He was assigned to Norfolk Naval Training Station for basic training and spent most of the next two years at that location. He played for the Station team for both the 1943 and 1944 seasons. Robinson suffered a leg injury while he was stationed at Norfolk. An operation there failed to fix the leg. When he was transferred to Hawaii in February 1945, he still had to wear a brace on the leg. He had another operation in Hawaii, and his career was considered to be in doubt.

By May 1945 he was sent back to the States and was a patient in a Baltimore hospital. He later was transferred to Bethesda Naval Hospital to complete the recovery from the surgery done at Pearl Harbor. Still on the Indians' defense list in December 1945, he was released in time for the 1946 season. Eddie Robinson had a good career. However, he was always getting traded to someone else. In 1948 he was the regular first baseman for the pennant-winning Indians and batted .300 in the World Series. To reward him, the Indians traded him to the Senators on December 14, 1948. So it was, he was usually being traded for another good player as teams tried to fill their needs. The trades came quickly after that: to the White Sox on May 30, 1950; the Athletics on January 27, 1953; the Yankees on December 16, 1953; the Kansas City A's on June 15, 1956; the Tigers on December 3, 1956; the Indians on May 20, 1957; and the Orioles on June 29, 1957. By the time he was done, he had played for every American League team except the Red Sox.

It's not that he was a bad player; it was that someone else always wanted him. He hit more than twenty home runs for five straight seasons and drove in more than one hundred runs for three seasons. During his prime years (1949-1952), his batting average ranged from .282 to .295. During that time he was traded twice. Eddie Robinson had a solid career at first base for a number of teams.

AGE	YRS	ML	G	BA	SA	AB	H	2B	3B	HR	HR%	R	RBI	BB	SO	SB
22-24	43-45	13	1315	0.268	0.44	4282	1146	172	24	172	4	546	723	521	359	10
		3	196	0.256	0.421	672	172	23	5	26	3.9	88	111	54	51	2
		16	1511	0.266	0.437	4954	1318	195	29	198	4	634	834	575	410	12

ROSAR, WARREN V. (BUDDY)   BR TR 5' 9"   190 lbs.

Born July 3, 1914, Buffalo, N.Y. — Died March 13, 1994, Rochester, N.Y.
Played for New York (A) (1939-42), Cleveland (1943-44), Philadelphia (A) (1945-49), and Boston (A) (1950-51)

Buddy Rosar was a backup catcher for Bill Dickey with the Yankees for four years before being traded to the Indians. With the Indians and later with the A's, he was able to earn the starting position. With the chance to play more, he got more recognition and played in the All-Star game for three straight years (1946-1948).

Rosar was always known as an outstanding defensive catcher. In 1946 he set a fielding record for catchers. He had a fielding percentage of 1.000. He was the first catcher to go through a season without an error. He was able to extend the errorless streak to 147 games in 1947 before making another error. (The record has since been broken by Yogi Berra with 148 games.) He led the American League in assists three years, fielding average two years, and double plays one year.

Rosar was classified 2-B for the draft. He did not serve in the military. He is included because he did miss part of both 1944 and 1945 working in defense plants. He worked in the Whitehead Aircraft plant in Cleveland and caught part-time. He also worked in a war plant in Buffalo. In addition he played in a game to help raise money for relief. The game on July 7, 1942, was the American League All-Stars vs. the service all-stars. The game raised $193,000 for war relief. He did not face some of the things others faced, but his career was affected by the war.

AGE	YRS	ML	G	BA	SA	AB	H	2B	3B	HR	HR%	R	RBI	BB	SO	SB
29	44	13	988	0.261	0.334	3198	836	147	15	18	0.6	335	367	316	161	17
(1 YR MINUS		0	9	0.257	0.286	35	9	1	0	0	0	3	3	4	2	0
99 GAMES)		13	997	0.261	0.333	3233	845	148	15	18	0.6	338	370	320	163	17

RYAN, CORNELIUS J. (CONNIE)   BR TR 5' 11"   175 lbs.

Born February 27, 1920, New Orleans, La. — Died January 3, 1996, Metairie, La.
Played for New York (N) (1942), Boston (N) (1943-44, 1946-50), Cincinnati (1950-51, 1954), Philadelphia (N) (1952-53), and Chicago (A) (1953)

Connie Ryan was a journeyman infielder who was able to maintain a regular status for a number of different teams despite a lifetime batting average of .248. He was able to do this because of his fielding. Also, he was considered a very good team player. Ryan played in the 1944 All-Star game. His hitting achievements came in 1953 while playing for the Phillies. On April 16, 1953, he went six for six, and on April 26, 1953, he got five straight hits. Both of these games were against the Pirates.

Ryan entered the Navy on July 25, 1944. He was assigned to the Sampson New York Naval Training Center. He spent the rest of the summer there and was able to play on the base team. On September 1, 1944, he got orders to go overseas. This led to his transfer to the Pacific, arriving in Hawaii in late January or early February. He played on a Navy team that toured the South Pacific war zone playing exhibitions for the other service men. For part of 1945 he was stationed in Guam. Ryan was discharged on January 18, 1946.

He returned to the Braves for the 1946 season. He played for five different teams during his career including playing for the Reds on two different occasions.

AGE	YRS	ML	G	BA	SA	AB	H	2B	3B	HR	HR%	R	RBI	BB	SO	SB
24-25	44-45	12	1184	0.248	0.357	3982	988	181	42	56	1.4	535	381	518	514	69
(2 YRS MINUS		1	195	0.254	0.354	670	170	39	8	4	0.6	74	75	81	79	8
88 GAMES)		13	1379	0.25	0.356	4652	1158	220	50	60	1.3	609	456	599	593	77

SAUER, HENRY J. (HANK)   BR TR 6' 3"   198 lbs.
Born March 17, 1917, Pittsburgh, Pa. — Died August 24, 2001, Burlingame, Ca.
Played for Cincinnati (1941–42, 1945, 1948–49), Chicago (N) (1949–55), St. Louis (N) (1956), New York (N) (1957), and San Francisco (1958–59)

Hank Sauer was not able to attain regular status until he was thirty-one years old. He had trials in 1941 and 1942 before the war and in 1945 after serving in the military. But it took a fifty-home run, 141-RBI, .336-batting average year at Syracuse in 1947 before he got a real chance.

Sauer was drafted by the Coast Guard after the 1943 season in late October. He was stationed at the Coast Guard in Manhattan Beach, New York. By early 1944 he was transferred to Coast Guard station at Curtis Bay, Maryland, where there he was able to play on the station baseball team. He spent the balance of 1944 and most of 1945 at that location. However, Sauer indicated in a letter that he did see some combat in the Pacific but didn't suffer any injuries. He also said, "Yes, [I] missed three years, but so did a lot of players. But, it was for our country" (Sauer letter 1998).

When he was released in September 1945, he returned to the Reds and played the balance of the 1945 season with them. After spending two years with the Syracuse, New York, team in the International League, he finally got his regular job in the majors in 1948. He had been in line for the first base job in 1947 until he hurt his knee. After getting to play on a regular basis, he made his mark on the league. He hit thirty or more home runs for six of the next seven seasons. He was slowed in 1953 by a broken finger.

His home run ratio of 16.65 puts him in the top twenty of home run sluggers. Sauer's best year was 1952. He led the league in home runs and in RBIs and was named most valuable player, one of the few players to win that honor while playing for a second-division team. He was a slow-footed outfielder but he had a strong arm. He tied for the league lead in assists in 1949. He made the All-Star team two times. After hitting a home run in the 1952 game, Sauer said, "It was a tremendous thrill. I felt as if I were flying on air as I circled the bases" (Smith 1993, 155). He did lead the National League in strikeouts in 1948; however, he was the last person to lead the league while striking out fewer than 90 times. After two tough years in 1955 and 1956, Sauer won the comeback player of the year in 1957 while playing for the Giants. He hit twenty-six home runs and drove in seventy-six runs while playing in 127 games.

AGE	YRS	ML	G	BA	SA	AB	H	2B	3B	HR	HR%	R	RBI	BB	SO	SB
27-28	44-45	15	1399	0.266	0.496	4796	1278	200	19	288	6	709	876	561	714	11
(2 YRS MINUS		1	38	0.297	0.428	145	43	1	0	6	4.1	22	25	8	20	3
31 GAMES)		16	1437	0.267	0.494	4941	1321	201	19	294	6	731	901	569	734	14

SISTI, SEBASTIAN D. (SIBBY) BR TR 5' 11" 175 lbs.
Born July 26, 1920, Buffalo, N.Y.
Played for Boston (N) (1939-42, 1946-52) and Milwaukee (N) (1953-54)

Sibby Sisti was a regular on the Braves infield before he went into the Coast Guard. When he came back, he was never able to nail down a regular position. He stayed with the Braves for his entire career. From 1946 until he retired in 1954, he served as a utility infielder. In fact, Sisti did not make the 1946 team and spent all but one game in the minors. He had a good year there and was able to return to the Braves for the 1947 season. During his career, he played two games at first, 359 games at second, 290 games at third, 179 games at shortstop, and 74 games in the outfield.

He enlisted in the Coast Guard on December 11, 1942. He was released in Seattle in October 1945. Sisti indicated in a letter that he did not see active combat nor did he suffer any injuries. He did say, "[I] spent 3 years in service and I was one of thousands who had a career interrupted by being in service" (Sisti letter 1997). From being a starting infielder to the minors, the war did have an effect on Sibby Sisti.

After their baseball careers are over, baseball players try many different occupations to finish their productive work years. The same was true for Sisti. After retiring in 1954 he tried his hand at acting. He got a small part in the movie *The Natural*. He played the part of the opposing manager.

AGE	YRS	ML	G	BA	SA	AB	H	2B	3B	HR	HR%	R	RBI	BB	SO	SB
22-24	43-45	13	1016	0.244	0.324	2999	732	121	19	27	0.9	401	260	283	440	30
		3	266	0.246	0.323	891	219	34	7	7	0.9	124	75	85	123	9
		16	1282	0.244	0.324	3890	951	155	26	34	0.9	525	335	368	563	39

SLAUGHTER, ENOS B. BL TR 5' 9" 180 lbs.
Born April 27, 1916, Roxboro, N.C. — Died August 12, 2002, Durham, N.C.
Played for St. Louis (N) (1938-42, 1946-53), New York (A) (1954-55, 1956-59), Kansas City (1955-56), and Milwaukee (N) (1959)

When people mention Enos Slaughter, they always want to talk about the 1946 World Series and Slaughter's "mad dash for home." Although this play typifies the way he played, Slaughter's career was a lot more than that one moment in a World Series game. This hustling attitude started back in the minors. During one game when he didn't run off the field after an inning, Manager Eddie Dyer said to him, "Are you tired, kid? If so, I'll get some help for you" (Coleman 1998, 73). After that he always hustled at whatever he did. Stan Musial said, "Enos had to be the greatest hustler of all time. He was a great competitor and all-around player…" (Broeg 1964, 288–289).

Slaughter always hustled. It didn't matter where the game was played. It could be for the Cardinals, or it could be for an Army team in the South Pacific. Pinky May said, "To show you how much Enos Slaughter hustled, one time playing in the Mariana Islands during the war, Enos hit a pop-up and when it was caught he was rounding second base. That's how Enos Slaughter hustled" (Van Blair 1994, 134). Slaughter talked about how he played in the service. "We had some real battles. Major league quality? Ok, heck, yes. I slid and played just as hard over there as I played here. Everybody played to win" (Mead 1985, 199).

This ten-time All-Star joined the Cardinals in 1938. He helped lead the Cardinals to the 1942 pennant and to the World Series win over the Yankees. Slaughter said, "That '42 Cardinal team was the best team I ever played on, better than all the Yankee teams and anything else" (Mead 1985, 46). He was an established star at that time. When the World Series in 1942 was over, Slaughter enlisted in the Army Air Corps. He was interviewed for Armed Forces Radio after the fourth game of that series. He said, "Hi fellows, we played a great game today and we won again. And we are going to finish this thing tomorrow. Then I'm going to report for duty in the Army Air Corps and join you" (Mead 1985, 48)

Slaughter was twenty-six, in the prime of his career, when he entered the Air Corps. He would be almost thirty before he would get to play again. He enlisted in the Army Air Corps on August 27, 1942, but wasn't called to active duty until January 23, 1943. The delay let him complete the 1942 season and take part in the World Series. He was sent to San Antonio for training. Slaughter wanted to be a pilot when he entered the service. However, they found out that he was color blind, which prevented him from becoming a pilot. The Army wanted him to be a bombardier, but he said if he couldn't be the one flying the plane, he would just as soon not fly. So he became a physical education instructor. On afternoons and weekends he played baseball against other base teams.

When he completed his training his commanding officers didn't want him shipped out because he was a valuable member of their baseball team. So he remained in San Antonio for some time. He spent 1943 and 1944 stationed in San Antonio as a physical training instructor. A series of games played in Hawaii changed all that. The Army and Navy played a "Pacific World Series" in Honolulu, and the Navy won rather easily. This did not set too well with the Army brass. Larry MacPhail was given the task of assembling a team of Army personnel that could compete with the Navy. Slaughter said, "In seven days' time [after Army was defeated] I had my orders, and I was at a base in Utah. There were forty-eight of us." He went on, "We stayed there and got shots, and they were supposed to fly us to Honolulu. Instead they took the football players and flew them over there and we went by boat. When we got there, it was too late; all the Navy was gone and the Marines were gone" (Mead 1985, 197).

Slaughter was a sergeant when he was sent to Kerns, Utah, then on to Seattle before going to Hawaii. His transfer to Utah was effective by March 1945, and he was on to Hawaii by May 1945. He played at Hickam Field, Hawaii, for a while. The players were told that if they would volunteer to play exhibition games on some of the islands, they would get to go home sooner. They were sent by ship and landed on Saipan on July 4, 1945. The games they played followed closely behind the advance of the front lines. Slaughter played for the B-29s of the 58th Bomb Wing on Tinian. He said, "See, the Japanese really like baseball. On Saipan, there were plenty of 'em back in those holes and caves. They'd sneak around and watch the ball game" (Mead 1985, 199). He played on Iwo Jima, Saipan, Tinian, and Guam. In several cases, the ball fields had to be built before a game could be played. The players would work with the SeaBees to help design and build the diamonds. It was from the airstrip on Tinian that the B-29 took off to drop the atomic bomb on Japan.

After the war was over, the players were gathered on Guam and shipped home. After surviving a typhoon on the way, the ship with Slaughter and the others arrived in Los Angeles on November 2, 1945. He was discharged on January 23, 1946. Slaughter said in a letter, "I ask no favors. Did whatever I was asked to do. Missed three of my prime years. I was glad to serve my country. I am proud to come back and have some great years in baseball" (Slaughter letter 1997).

Indeed he did have some of his best years after the war. In 1946, at age thirty and after three years away from professional baseball, he had his best year as the Cardinals won the pennant and defeated the Red Sox in the World Series. Slaughter played a major role in the Cardinals' World Series win in addition to the "mad dash." In total he scored five runs and had eight hits while batting .320. There are many versions of what happened on October 15, 1946. Some say Johnny Pesky was at fault. Some say other Red Sox players should have let Pesky know that Slaughter was running for home. The key thing, whatever the other reasons, is that Slaughter scored the winning run because he, like always, was hustling. He was giving everything he had for the benefit of the team. Because of that, he scored and the Cardinals won the World Series.

Slaughter continued with the Cardinals until just before the start of the 1954 season. He had just been told by the new owner, August Busch, "Enos, you're a credit to the game and you'll always be with us" (Honig 1976, 167). Shortly after that statement, the Cardinals traded Slaughter to the Yankees for Bill Virdon and two others. He was called into the general manager's office and told he been traded to the Yankees. "Well, it floored me. It cut my heart out. I cried. I cried like a baby. I couldn't help it. I'd been a Cardinal since 1935, and I don't think anybody who's ever worn a Cardinal uniform was ever more loyal to it than I was or put out as hard as I did or gave so much" (Honig 1976, 168). Slaughter continued, "I never felt as bad when my father died as I did when I was released by the Cardinals" (Dickson 1991, 397). Slaughter was always a Cardinal regardless of the team on which he was playing.

After the trade he had to make the transition from a regular, everyday player to a spot player and pinch hitter. He competed in that role just as he had done as a regular, with all he had. In fact, he led the American League in pinch hits in 1955. By going to the Yankees, he was able to take part in three more World Series. In the 1956 World Series, at age forty, Slaughter batted .350 as the regular left fielder, including hitting a three-run home run in game three to help the Yankees win 5-3. His nickname was "Country" because he was from rural North Carolina, but his real nickname should have been "hustle" because that's how he played the game.

AGE	YRS	ML	G	BA	SA	AB	H	2B	3B	HR	HR%	R	RBI	BB	SO	SB
27-29	43-45	19	2380	0.3	0.453	7946	2383	413	148	169	2.1	1247	1304	1019	538	71
		3	427	0.305	0.476	1636	500	83	36	41	2.5	279	277	200	95	19
		22	2807	0.301	0.458	9582	2883	496	184	210	2.2	1526	1581	1219	633	90

SNIDER, EDWIN D. (DUKE)   BL TR 6' 0"   198 lbs.

Born September 19, 1926, Los Angeles, Ca.

Played for Brooklyn (1947-57), Los Angeles (1958-62), New York (N) (1963), and San Francisco (1964)

Duke Snider did not play any major league games until 1947; however, he was listed by the Hall of Fame as a major league player who took part in World War II. He was signed by Branch Rickey at age seventeen and kept in training camp with the Dodgers. At the end of training camp, he was sent to the minors in the spring of 1944. After spending 1944 in the Piedmont League, Snider was drafted by the Navy and spent all of 1945 and part of 1946 in service. He spent some time in Honolulu during this time.

After being released in 1946, he spent the balance of the season in the Texas League. After a trial in 1947 and in 1948, he took over the center field job in 1949. That would be the start of a long run in that position. He would spend the next nine years as one of the best players in the game. He was part of the Dodger teams that dominated the '50s. The Dodgers won five pennants during the nine years Snider played for them in Brooklyn. He is in the top ten of six offensive categories in World Series' play. He hit forty or more home runs for five straight seasons (1953 to 1957), drove in ninety or more runs for nine straight seasons (1949 to 1957), and led the league in runs scored three consecutive years.

During the time Snider played in Brooklyn, he, Mickey Mantle, and Willie Mays were often compared. Who was the better center fielder? The fans of each team thought their player was the best. Ben Wade, Dodger pitcher of the time, said, "The biggest arguments were about center field. Duke Snider wasn't as good a fielder as Mickey Mantle or Willie Mays, but he was a good fielder. He wasn't as exciting as the other two and didn't get the same publicity, but his average, homers, and RBIs during the fifties matched them. He was a great hitter, especially in Ebbets Field" (Peary 1994, 185).

Snider's best all-around season was in 1954 when he hit .341 with forty homers and 130 RBIs. His game was hurt when the Dodgers moved to Los Angeles. They played their games in The Coliseum, a football field that had been converted to baseball. The right field fence was too far for anybody to reach. Snider's home run total fell from forty (the last year in Brooklyn) to fifteen. His effectiveness was hurt, and he went from a regular to a part-time player. His career four hundred home runs would have been a lot higher had the Dodgers remained in Brooklyn. Snider commented about the move, "We wept; Brooklyn was a lovely place to hit. If you got a ball in the air, you had a chance to get it out. When they tore down Ebbetts Field, they tore down a little piece of me" (Dickson 1991, 404). This Hall of Famer, selected in 1980, was an eight-time All-Star selection. The Dodgers retired his number four.

AGE	YRS	ML	G	BA	SA	AB	H	2B	3B	HR	HR%	R	RBI	BB	SO	SB
18-19	45-46	18	2143	0.295	0.54	7161	2116	358	85	407	5.7	1259	1333	971	1237	99
(NO PR MAJOR		0	0	0	0	0	0	0	0	0	0	0	0	0	0	0
LEAGUE EXP)		18	2143	0.295	0.54	7161	2116	358	85	407	5.7	1259	1333	971	1237	99

SUDER, PETER (PETE)   BR TR 6' 0"   175 lbs.
Born April 16, 1916, Aliquippa, Pa.
Played for Philadelphia (A) (1941–43, 1946–54) and Kansas City (1955)

Pete Suder was a fancy-fielding, versatile infielder who played his whole career for the A's. He showed his versatility in his first three years. His rookie year he played third base, his second year he played shortstop, and his third year he moved to second base where he would spend most of his career. Suder led the league in fielding average at second base for two years. He was the last of the good infielders for the A's to go into service. He was drafted on March 30, 1944. He was sent to the New Cumberland, Pennsylvania, Army Reception Center where he was a member of Company C. He was discharged on January 5, 1946, in time for spring training. Suder was a very good second baseman. Nellie Fox, twelve-time All-Star, was unable to displace him as the regular second baseman for the A's, and Fox was traded to the White Sox.

In 1947, along with Eddie Joost and Farris Fain, Suder set a team record for double plays with 217. Joe DeMaestri, shortstop for the A's in 1953, said, "My second-base partner was Pete Suder, who was as good a fielder as there was in those days." He added, "He was always in the right spot. [And]…made everything look so easy" (Peary 1994, 228). His best year with the bat was 1953. He batted .286 that year with his lifetime average only .249. Suder moved with the A's from Philadelphia to Kansas City in 1955. After one year in Kansas City, he retired.

AGE	YRS	ML	G	BA	SA	AB	H	2B	3B	HR	HR%	R	RBI	BB	SO	SB
28-29	44-45	13	1421	0.249	0.337	5085	1268	210	44	49	1	469	541	288	456	19
		2	266	0.249	0.33	967	241	41	8	7	0.7	80	103	46	80	3
		15	1687	0.249	0.336	6052	1509	251	52	56	0.9	549	644	334	536	22

SULLIVAN, WILLIAM J., JR. (BILLY)   BL TR 6' 0"   170 lbs.
Born October 23, 1910, Chicago, Il. — Died January 4, 1994, Sarasota, Fl.
Played for Chicago (A) (1931–33), Cincinnati (1935), Cleveland (1936–37), St. Louis (A) (1938–39), Detroit (1940–41), Brooklyn (1942), and Pittsburgh (1947)

Billy Sullivan was the son of a White Sox catcher of the early 1900s. He was signed out of Notre Dame and began his career in 1931. He continued with his education, missing part of the 1932 and 1933 seasons to go to school. While his father was a catcher, Billy Jr. started out as an infielder and didn't switch to catching until he was traded to the Indians in 1936. He was a good hitter, with a lifetime batting average of .289, but he did not have many years where he was the regular in his position. He never caught more than ninety-nine games in any one year. He was a catcher in Cleveland when Bob Feller arrived in the majors in 1936. It is ironic that he got the only hit against Bob Feller in a game on April 20, 1938. It was a drag bunt that he beat out for a single. He got the most playing time after he was traded to the Browns for Rollie Hemsley in 1938. He shared the catching duties with Birdie Tebbetts in 1940 after he was traded to the Tigers. He got to play in the World Series for the Tigers that year.

After a trade to the Dodgers in 1942, he was listed on their voluntarily retired list in 1943, probably working in the war industry. He spent 1944 through 1946 in the military while listed on the Pirates reserved list. He played in only thirty-eight games in 1947 after he returned from the military. Sullivan was a good contact hitter while he was playing. He only struck out 119 times in 2,840 at-bats. He was also considered to be a good pinch hitter.

AGE	YRS	ML	G	BA	SA	AB	H	2B	3B	HR	HR%	R	RBI	BB	SO	SB
33-35	44-46	12	962	0.289	0.395	2840	820	152	32	29	1	347	388	240	119	30
		3	121	0.265	0.342	234	62	8	2	2	0.9	18	33	27	14	3
		15	1083	0.287	0.391	3074	882	160	34	31	1	365	421	267	133	33

TEBBETTS, GEORGE R. (BIRDIE)   BR TR 5' 11"   170 lbs.

Born November 10, 1912, Burlington. Vt. — Died March 24, 1999, Manatee, Fl.
Played for Detroit (1936–42, 1946–47), Boston (A) (1947–50), and Cleveland (1951–52)

George (Birdie) Tebbetts had been with the Detroit Tigers since 1936 when he enlisted in the Army Air Force in late 1942. During that time, he had played in a World Series (1940) and had been considered the "regular" catcher for the Tigers for four years. He received his nickname from his classmates at Providence College because he had a high-pitched voice and he liked to talk a lot.

Tebbetts enlisted in the Army Air Corps on August 21, 1942. He went to officers candidate school after basic training and graduated a 2nd lieutenant on March 3, 1943, in Miami. He was then assigned to the Army Air Base at Waco, Texas. By November 1943, he had been promoted to 1st lieutenant. He was a physical instructor while stationed there and was given the assignment of organizing an athletic program that included a baseball team. Using his connections as a former major leaguer, Tebbetts urged a number of major and minor leaguers to join the Air Corps. He worked on getting them assigned to Waco to be part of the team he played on and managed. He had been slated for overseas duty until he broke his toe playing ball during the summer of 1944.

By February 1945, he had been promoted to captain and was still stationed at Waco. When the Navy beat the Army in the Pacific World Series, the Army brass were unhappy. Tebbetts was one of the players who were assembled by the Army to go to Hawaii to make a better showing. However, the group arrived too late because the other groups had been reassigned. While in Honolulu, he was stationed at Hickam Field. He managed and played for a team there and was selected to the Army Air Force all-star team. Later in 1945 he visited Tinian with a squad of major leaguers. While in the Marianas he managed the 58th Wing Team of the 20th Air Force. He stayed in the South Pacific until the end of the war. He arrived back in the United States in Los Angeles aboard the transport ship *Cecil* on November 2, 1945. He was discharged in March 1946. He was thirty-three when he was discharged. He played with the Tigers, Red Sox, and Indians for seven more years. Some of his best years came with the Red

Sox between 1947 and 1950. Although he was a four-time All-Star, he was, for the most part, a platoon catcher for much of his career. However, he did catch 1,108 games total.

Tebbetts made the following statement about his career and about the Hall of Fame. He said, "The Hall of Fame, let them have it. Let them put all the great players in it. But I'd like to put a wing on it for fellows like Phil Rizzuto and myself—not that I'm putting myself in a class with Rizzuto. I'm speaking of a type now. Fellows like Rizzuto and Billy Martin" (Dickson 1991, 435). Tebbetts was talking about the steady team players who did not put up the great individual numbers. At the time Tebbetts said this in August of 1950, Rizzuto was still playing and not in the Hall of Fame. However, Tebbetts has never been able to achieve that status.

AGE	YRS	ML	G	BA	SA	AB	H	2B	3B	HR	HR%	R	RBI	BB	SO	SB
30-32	43-45	14	1162	0.27	0.358	3705	1000	169	22	38	1	357	469	389	261	29
		3	323	0.272	0.352	1058	288	51	6	7	0.7	98	126	113	74	8
		17	1485	0.27	0.357	4763	1288	220	28	45	0.9	455	595	502	335	37

TRAVIS, CECIL H.

BL TR 6' 1"   185 lbs.

Born August 8, 1913, Riverdale, Ga.
Played for Washington (1933–41, 1945–47)

There may not be anyone whose career was more affected by World War II than Cecil Travis. This All-Star shortstop for the Washington Senators was never the same after he came back from the war. He was just coming off his best year, 1941, when he was drafted into the Army. He had finished second in the batting race to Ted Williams' .406 by batting .359. Travis' average that year was higher than Joe DiMaggio's even with his fifty-six game hitting streak. He had more hits that year than either Williams or DiMaggio. He also scored 106 runs and drove in 101 runs that year. His career batting average at the end of the 1941 season was .327. By the time he was drafted, he had completed eight seasons as a regular, batting over .300 in seven of those seasons. He was only twenty-eight years old.

His Georgia draft board announced in April 1941 that he would be drafted, but he received a deferment until after the 1941 season. The deferment may have been because of Clark Griffith's friendship with an Army general. (Griffith owned the Senators.) Travis was drafted on January 7, 1942, one month after the Japanese bombed Pearl Harbor. He reported to Fort McPherson, Georgia, for his physical and was then transferred to Camp Wheeler, Georgia. He was a member of Company A, 15th Training Battalion. While he was stationed at Camp Wheeler, he was able to play some baseball for the base team. He was promoted to corporal and then to sergeant and remained at Camp Wheeler for 1942 and 1943. In the spring of 1944, he was transferred to Camp McCoy, Wisconsin. He was able to play on the 76th Combat Infantry team during that summer.

In the fall of 1944, he was sent to Europe along with his 76th Infantry Division. Travis served in Scotland, England, France, Belgium, and Germany during his stay in Europe. He suffered his career-ending injury in Belgium. Adolf Hitler ordered thirty-eight German divisions to attack the Allies along a fifty-mile front in the Ardennes Forest in Belgium. The attack was launched on December 16, 1944, but it took the Allies until December 27 to halt the German offensive.

Washington teams. He was a good hitter, a good first baseman, and just as nice a person as there was in baseball" (Peary 1994, 310).

He had played three full seasons when he entered the Navy on October 16, 1943. At first he was at the training station at Sampson, New York. By the summer of 1944, he had been transferred to Norfolk and spent the summer playing ball for the Norfolk Naval Air Station team. Herman Franks was the manager of the Norfolk team that summer. Following the 1944 season, the Navy transferred several players to Hawaii. They were shipped out of San Francisco for the trip to Honolulu. Vernon became seasick almost as soon as the voyage started. He remained that way for the entire eleven-day trip. One day there was a submarine scare. Vernon said, "That was around the fifth day of the trip and I'll tell you, by that time, I was so sick I was almost hoping that baby would come around and sink us" (Honig 1976, 116). Because he was too sick to shave and too sick to eat, when he got to Hawaii he had a sunken face and a beard. They started calling him "Abe" because of his looks.

He was in Honolulu for five months before he, along with others, was sent to the islands in the South Pacific to play exhibition games for the fighting soldiers. After the tour, instead of going back to Honolulu, the group was split up and sent to different islands. Vernon was sent to Ulithi and ended up on an atoll about a mile long by a quarter mile wide. He was kept there for ten months. He helped organize a softball league there. Major leaguers Larry Doby and Billy Goodman were in that league. Vernon stayed there until he was sent home to be discharged. He was discharged on December 22, 1945.

Vernon came out of the service to have his best year. In 1946 at age twenty-eight, he led the American League in hitting with a .353 average. He also led the league in hitting in 1953 with a .337 average. During that time he was President Dwight D. Eisenhower's favorite player. President Eisenhower came to the park and personally presented the Silver Bat to Vernon for winning the batting championship. By winning the batting title that year, Vernon kept Al Rosen from winning the triple crown, beating Rosen by .0005 in the batting race. Satchel Paige said, "I've faced the best in the world just about, but I never could get Mickey out" (Nemec et al. 1992, 238).

This seven-time All-Star's career extended into four decades (1939–1960). During his career, he set an American League record for most games played at first base (2,237), most assists (1,444), most putouts (19,754), and total chances accepted (21,198). Vernon was the best player on several Washington teams. Because those teams weren't very good, he ranks third in the number of games played without a post-season appearance.

AGE	YRS	ML	G	BA	SA	AB	H	2B	3B	HR	HR%	R	RBI	BB	SO	SB
26-27	44-45	20	2409	0.286	0.428	8731	2495	490	120	172	2	1196	1311	934	869	137
		2	295	0.283	0.406	1150	325	66	17	14	1.2	160	156	100	106	33
		22	2704	0.285	0.426	9881	2820	556	137	186	1.8	1356	1467	1034	975	170

WAGNER, HAROLD E. (HAL)   BL TR 6' 0" 165 lbs.
Born July 2, 1915, East Riverton, N.J. — Died August 4, 1979, Riverside, N.J.
Played for Philadelphia (A) (1937–44), Boston (A) (1944, 1946–47), Detroit (1947–48), and
Philadelphia (N) (1948–49)

Hal Wagner was a backup catcher who received additional playing time because of the war.
He had been up and down with the A's starting in 1937; however, he never caught more
than forty-two games in any season until 1942 when major league players started going into
service. He was the A's regular catcher for 1942 and 1943. For a time during that period, he
worked in a factory and played only on weekends when the A's were in town or were within
traveling distance of Philadelphia.

He was the Red Sox regular catcher in 1944 until he was drafted on August 28, 1944, during
his best year. He was batting .330, and his call into the military, along with Tex Hughson and
Bobby Doerr, finished the Red Sox pennant hopes in 1944. Wagner had been accepted for
active duty at Camden, New Jersey, on May 5 but was not summoned to active duty until
August 28. He was sent to Camp Devens, Massachusetts when he entered the Army. In the
spring of 1945 he was stationed at Camp Blanding, Florida. He was discharged on October 4,
1945. Wagner did return to the Red Sox for their 1946 pennant drive, catching 116 games that
year and playing in the All-Star game. His career ended quickly after that, and by 1949, he had
played his last game.

AGE	YRS	ML	G	BA	SA	AB	H	2B	3B	HR	HR%	R	RBI	BB	SO	SB
28-29	44-45	12	672	0.248	0.334	1849	458	90	12	15	0.8	179	228	253	152	10
(2 YRS MINUS		1	141	0.243	0.328	400	97	20	1	4	1	37	49	55	33	2
71 GAMES)		13	813	0.247	0.333	2249	555	110	13	19	0.8	216	277	308	185	12

WAITKUS, EDWARD S. (EDDIE)   BL TL 6' 0" 170 lbs.
Born September 4, 1919, Cambridge, Ma. — Died September 15, 1972, Jamaica Plain, Ma.
Played for Chicago (N) (1941, 1946–48), Philadelphia (N) (1949–53, 1955), and Baltimore
(1954–55)

Eddie Waitkus was one of the "Whiz Kids" who won the National League pennant for the
Philadelphia Phillies in 1950. He made it to the majors with the Cubs in 1941 for a short
stay and then had a good year in the Pacific Coast League in 1942. He joined the Army in
January 1943. He was a member of 554th Engineers Amphibious Command at Fort Devens,
Massachusetts. Waitkus was promoted to corporal and put in charge of a machine gun crew
at Fort Devens. By December 1943, he had been transferred to Camp Gordon Johnston in
Florida, where he suffered a broken arm. He stayed in Florida until early 1944. During 1944 he
was shipped to the Pacific, where he was involved in combat. He was in the first wave of an
American attack on a Japanese-held island in the Pacific. He said, "The strategy employed in
landing the amphibious forces was just like stealing home in a ball game" (*The Sporting News*,
"In the Service—Landing Like Stealing Home" November 25, 1944, page 11).

While in the Pacific, he was able to play some ball. He played for the 544th regiment in Rizal
Stadium in Manila while he was in the service. He was discharged from the Army on January

17, 1946. When he returned, he took over as the regular first baseman for the Chicago Cubs. He held that position until he was traded to the Phillies in time for the 1949 season. On June 23, 1946, while with the Cubs, he and Marv Richert became the first major leaguers to hit back-to-back inside-the-park home runs.

Waitkus' closest brush with death came after he returned from fighting in the Army. The Phillies were on a road trip to Chicago on June 14, 1949. Waitkus came back to his room and received a message that someone wanted to see him in another room. The message was that his father was sick, and this person had information for him. He went up to the room. Robin Roberts, his teammate, related that Waitkus said it happened this way, "He knocked and the girl said, 'come in.' When he walked in there was nobody in the room. He looked around, and all of a sudden the girl jumped out of a closet with a rifle and shot him. Just like that. She just missed his heart" (Honig 1976, 236). He was in critical condition for some time. He had to have four operations to correct the problems associated with the shooting. The girl admitted to the shooting. She had a crush on him and said, "As time went on I just became nuttier and nuttier about the guy, and I knew I would never get to know him in a normal way…and if I can't have him, nobody else can. And I then decided I would kill him" (Peary 1990, 188).

He missed the rest of 1949, but he did come back for the 1950 season. He had a good year in 1950 and was voted the comeback player of the year. He had three games that year when he got five hits, and, at one point he had eight hits in a row. His play helped the Phillies to their first pennant since 1915. Waitkus, who played in the All-Star game in 1948, was a line-drive hitter as well as a top defensive first baseman.

AGE	YRS	ML	G	BA	SA	AB	H	2B	3B	HR	HR%	R	RBI	BB	SO	SB
23-25	43-45	11	1140	0.285	0.374	4254	1214	215	44	24	0.6	528	373	372	204	28
		3	335	0.3	0.402	1288	386	72	18	8	0.6	168	119	101	45	9
		14	1475	0.289	0.38	5542	1600	287	62	32	0.6	696	492	473	249	37

WALKER, HARRY W.   BL TR 6' 2" 175 lbs.
Born October 22, 1916, Pascagoula, Mi. — Died August 8, 1999, Pascagoula, Mi.
Played for St. Louis (N) (1940-43, 1946-47, 1950-51, 1955), Philadelphia (N) (1947-48), Chicago (N) (1949), and Cincinnati (1949)

Harry (The Hat) Walker came from a baseball family. His father, Ewart Walker, was a pitcher for the Senators in the 1910s, his uncle, Ernie Walker, played for the Browns in the 1910s, and his brother, Dixie Walker, played for several teams during the 1930s and 1940s. Harry and Dixie were the first brothers to win a batting title. Harry won his in 1946. He got his nickname because of his habit of tugging at his hat while he was batting. He would wear out several caps over the course of the year. He signed for a bonus of $2500 in 1939. He said, "I felt like one of those instant millionaires" (Liebman 1994, 136). Times have changed since 1939.

Walker played in the 1943 World Series for the Cardinals and then was drafted and entered the Army on November 3, 1943. He remembered it this way, "The next morning after the Series, Al Brazle and I were inducted in the Army at Jefferson Barracks" (Goldstein 1980, 228). They thought they were headed to Memphis, but the commander at Fort Riley, Kansas, was trying to build a ball team. He had pull at Jefferson Barracks, so they were sent to Fort Riley. He had basic training there in the mechanized calvary. The plan of the commander for Walker to play ball didn't work because he came down with spinal meningitis and almost died. After he recovered, he was able to play some baseball while stationed there. He, along with several of the other major leaguers, was transferred to Camp Shelby, Mississippi, during the fall of 1944. There he joined the Sixty-Fifth Division of General Patton's Third Army. This group of players stayed together for much of their military service. "I was in a recon [reconnaissance] outfit. You look at a western movie and see the scouts going forward. That's pretty much what we were doing, except on a mechanized basis. You'd try to find roadblocks or bridges blown up and report back so you wouldn't have your infantry or artillery pieces bottled up where the enemy's artillery or planes could get to them. You'd try to keep out in front, from five to ten miles and one time we got seventy miles back of the enemy lines" (Goldstein 1980, 252).

This out-front position led to Walker meeting the Germans in a shooting situation. "One night about 11 o'clock we were trying to get to a bridge going out of Germany into Austria. It was on a river not too far from Passeau. We didn't have but thirty men. We were just about a half-mile from the bridge when we had to stop. It was sleeting and raining, and we ran into three guys, guards that were patrolling the thing. At first they thought we were Germans because we were so far ahead of the lines." Walker continued. "I tried to get them to surrender. Well, one guy pulled his gun up in my face. I had a .45 revolver that I'd bought in the States. That little thing saved my life. The guy that pulled the gun, I shot him in the chest and then I shot the others. Killed the first two and wounded the third guy. It was so damned quick, it was almost like a machine gun went off. It was just one of those deals that you didn't want to happen, but your reaction was to live and that's about it" (Goldstein 1980, 252).

This was not the only incident where Walker faced death. Once, he was in a jeep with two machine guns mounted on it. They were trying to hold a bridge. The Germans advanced toward their position. Walker remembered, "…here they come, and I'm trying to stop them and they wouldn't stop. So that's when I had to start shooting, and I just cut through the whole mess and they were scattered everywhere, firing back and forth at you, and you're just out there on point like a sitting duck" (Turner 1996, 8). He was wounded twice, neither time seriously. He was hit in the hand and in the rump. He was awarded the Bronze Star as well as the Purple Heart for his bravery in action. "I wouldn't ever want to go through it again, but I certainly feel good that I got to be in this thing, to see what it was all about. It makes you appreciate what you've got here so much more. We've got faults, we bitch and complain, but I think our country is greatest in the world" (Goldstein 1980, 253).

After the combat in 1945, General Reinhart, commanding officer (C.O.), wanted a team to play and to help entertain the other troops. The general wanted Walker to help. Walker said he would rather go home. "He said to me, 'Walker, I didn't ask you if you wanted to do it. I said I wanted you to do it. I have about fifteen thousand GI's here, and I've got to entertain them, or they're going to give me a fit… so I want you to get those teams together and play two or three times a week'" (Turner 1996, 8). They found equipment, built fields, and started playing. They played on converted soccer fields, etc. Once they built a diamond and played at Nuremberg Stadium. There was a runway behind the outfield fence, and the infield was made from finely crushed brick that came from the shell-damaged buildings.

Walker's sixty-fifth division team played in the Third Army championship but lost. He was picked up to play for the winners, the 71st division. The championship was played in Nuremberg Stadium with sixty thousand GIs watching. Walker's 71st division team lost to a team from Reims, France. Walker was added to that team to play the Mediterranean theater champions in Italy. The team from Reims' won the championship playing on a soccer field near the Leaning Tower of Piza. After being discharged in January, Walker struggled during the 1946 season. He batted only .237. However, he did have a very good World Series as the Cardinals won the pennant and the Series. He was the player who hit the ball when Slaughter made his mad dash for home. Walker again struggled at the start of the 1947 season. He was traded to the Phillies on May 3, 1947. At the time he was traded, he was batting .200. The trade woke him up, and he batted .371 the rest of the way for a season batting average of .363. This was good enough to win the National League batting crown that year.

He is the only player to win a batting crown while being traded during the season. Stan Musial commented, "Harry was a good all-around player with speed and an arm" (Broeg 1964, 297). Walker served his country, faced the enemy, and felt good about what he had done. He believed in what he was fighting for. His comment says it best, "We've got faults…but I think our country is the greatest in the world" (Goldstein 1980, 253).

AGE	YRS	ML	G	BA	SA	AB	H	2B	3B	HR	HR%	R	RBI	BB	SO	SB
27-28	44-45	11	807	0.296	0.383	2651	786	126	37	10	0.4	385	214	245	175	42
		2	237	0.306	0.406	807	247	42	15	3	0.4	124	69	72	53	16
		13	1044	0.299	0.389	3458	1033	168	52	13	0.4	509	283	317	228	58

WANER, LLOYD J.

BL TR 5'9"   150 lbs.

Born March 16, 1906, Harrah, Ok. — Died July 22, 1982, Oklahoma City, Ok.
Played for Pittsburgh (1927–41, 1944–45), Boston (N) (1941), Cincinnati (1941), Philadelphia (N) (1942), and Brooklyn (1944)

Lloyd Waner's career was almost over by the time World War II was a problem. He started with the Pirates in 1927. What a start it was. In his rookie year he set a major league record for rookies with 223 hits, including 198 singles. He batted .355, the second highest rookie average since 1900, and he led the league in runs scored with 133. Lloyd and his brother, Paul, had the best combined year that a pair of brothers ever achieved. They combined for 460 hits and a .367 average, scored 247 runs, and drove in 158 runs. Together they led the Pirates to the pennant in 1927. The Yankees swept the Pirates in the World Series that year, but Lloyd batted .400 and Paul .333. They had a higher batting average than Babe Ruth and Lou Gehrig. With Paul, they were the best brother hitting combination of all-time. They combined for a lifetime batting average of .325. Lloyd continued his excellent hitting into the 1930 season. He lost over half of the 1930 season with appendicitis. He was never the same hitter after the illness. His batting average for 1927 through 1930 was .349, but it was .303 for the rest of his career. His strikeout record was the second best all-time in the major leagues. For his career, he only fanned once in every 44.9 at-bats. In 1941 he went seventy-seven straight games without striking out, a National League record.

In 1943 Waner had been traded to the Dodgers. However, he didn't report to them. It was either take a war-related job or be drafted. He said, "They told me, the draft board, that I'd have to work in a government defense business, I couldn't play baseball. Here in Oklahoma City they had Douglas aircraft. I started with Douglas and worked there, I guess, about six months or more then I transferred to Will Rogers Army Air Base" (Goldstein 1980, 176). Waner worked as a fireman there. "I had quite some experiences there; I got a medal here someplace for bravery. We put out a bomber that crashed. He'd come in about a mile short of the field. It was on instruments on a bad night. He shouldn't have been flying. He hit a ditch, just kind of nosed into it. There were three of them in it, they jumped out and ran. When we got down there, the thing had started on fire. They had flares in there and it started throwing those out everyplace. We had quite a job; we were there from three o'clock in the morning till nine o'clock, putting the thing out. A couple of the boys got burned a little, but we saved part of the plane" (Goldstein 1980, 176).

In 1944 the draft board was no longer interested in Waner at age thirty-eight, so he played for the Dodgers and Pirates. World War II did not have a great impact on Lloyd Waner's career because it was almost over when the war started. He didn't enter the military, but he did serve his country through helping the war effort here in the States.

AGE	YRS	ML	G	BA	SA	AB	H	2B	3B	HR	HR%	R	RBI	BB	SO	SB
37	43	18	1992	0.316	0.394	7772	2459	281	118	28	0.4	1201	598	420	173	67
		1	61	0.271	0.306	144	39	3	1	0	0	18	6	8	3	1
		19	2053	0.316	0.392	7916	2498	284	119	28	0.4	1219	604	428	176	68

WANER, PAUL G.   BL TL 5'8" 153 lbs.
Born April 16, 1903, Harrah, Ok. — Died August 29, 1965, Sarasota, Fl.
Played for Pittsburgh (1926-1940), Brooklyn (1941, 1943-44), Boston (N) (1941-42), and New York (A) (1944-45)

The only record found that Paul Waner had military service was in the book *The Sports Encyclopedia: Baseball 1999*. There on page 225, listed with the 1945 Yankees, Paul Waner has the (MS) listed by his name. He is included here because of that reference. He, like his brother Lloyd, was able to play longer because of the war. Paul had the nickname "Big Poison." It was given by a Brooklyn fan, who was saying, with a Brooklyn accent, big person. The nickname stuck. Lloyd had the nickname "Little Poison" because he was the younger brother. Paul Waner was a very good hitter. His career average, for twenty years, was .333. This was down from .342, which represents his years before the wind-down years. Dick Bartell said, "There's no doubt in my mind that Paul was the greatest hitter I ever saw" (Van Blair 1994, 5). With Lloyd, they were the best brother combo ever. They collected 5,611 hits in their careers, which is 1,000 more than the five Delahanty brothers and 500 more than the three DiMaggio brothers. In addition to being a great hitter with three batting titles, Waner was also a major league drinker. Jack Kavanagh wrote that Waner was, "Always a threat to break up a ball game but never a party" (Shatzkin 1990, 1141). There are many stories about his drinking and his ability to play the next day. Buddy Hassett roomed with Waner for a while and had this to say, "…he could also sober himself up in a hurry. He would do back flips. He had remarkable agility, like an acrobat. Fifteen or twenty minutes of back flips and he was cold sober, ready to go out to the ball park and get his three hits" (Honig 1976, 60).

One year he decided to go on the wagon. His batting average suffered, staying around .250. After a while the manager took him to the nearest bar and bought him a drink. He went back to his old ways and his batting average returned to the plus .300 level.

Some players have a favorite bat that they have to use. He believed it was the person not the bat that got the hit. In one game to prove his point he had his teammates grab a different bat for him each time. He went four for five that day. He was also a good hitting teacher. Tommy Holmes, who played with Waner in 1942, credits him with giving Holmes the right approach to hitting. Holmes said, "I would not have been as successful as I was if it had not been for Paul Waner. He made me a smarter hitter" (Goldstein 1980, 174). In 1944 he was playing for the Yankees. Some fan shouted to Waner and asked, "Hey Paul, how come you're in the outfield for the Yankees? Waner answered, 'Because Joe DiMaggio's in the Army'" (Ritter 1985, 332).

The Yankees released him in 1945, and it was reported that he was working for a burial vault business in Pittsburgh. Waner played in four of the first five All-Star games. He was MVP of the National League in 1927 when the Pirates won the pennant. Burleigh Grimes said, "I saw a lot of good hitters but I never saw a better one than Paul Waner. I may have got Waner out but I never fooled him" (Dickson 1991, 170). Stan Musial added, "This old favorite of mine was one of the greatest hitters ever. Pound for pound, he perhaps was the greatest" (Broeg 1964, 291). While he may not have served in military, he did take part in bond drives, both in visiting businesses while in Brooklyn and in playing in All-Star games to raise money for the war effort.

AGE	YRS	ML	G	BA	SA	AB	H	2B	3B	HR	HR%	R	RBI	BB	SO	SB
42	45	20	2549	0.333	0.473	9459	3152	603	190	112	1.2	1626	1309	1091	376	104
(1 YR MINUS		0	87	0.299	0.38	184	55	10	1	1	0.5	23	22	32	9	1
1 GAME)		20	2636	0.333	0.471	9643	3207	613	191	113	1.2	1649	1331	1123	385	105

WEST, SAMUEL F. (SAMMY)   BL TL 5' 11" 165 lbs.
Born October 5, 1904, Longview, Tx. — Died November 23, 1985, Lubbock, Tx.
Played for Washington (1927-32, 1938-41), St. Louis (A) (1933-38), and Chicago (A) (1942)

Sammy West didn't have to go into the military. He was thirty-eight years old when he enlisted in the Army Air Force in December 1942. He did so because he wanted to help his country win the war. His baseball career was almost over. By 1942 he had gone from a regular center fielder to a back-up player and pinch hitter. At that time he had been in the majors for sixteen years, all in the American League. He was an outstanding defensive outfielder. Hall of Famer Tris Speaker taught West how to play center field his rookie year, 1927. West was a very good pupil. He set an American League record for fielding percentage for outfielders of .996 (since broken) in 1928. In addition to being a good outfielder, West was also a good hitter. His lifetime batting average only dipped under .300 during his last year. He ended at .299.

His best year was 1931 when he batted .333 for the Senators. In 1933 he had a streak of eight consecutive hits. He played in the first two All-Star games. When he enlisted he was sent to

Lubbock, Texas. There he was in the Army Flying School. He said, "[this is] one team I'm really trying to make" (*The Sporting News*, "In the Service–Sam West" December 17, 1942, page 8). West spent almost his entire career in the military at Lubbock. He didn't fly, but he did stay there as a physical instructor and coach of one of the teams at the airfield. He rose to the rank of staff sergeant during his time in the military. He was transferred to Fort Bliss, Texas, to await his discharge. He was discharged on June 26, 1945, at age forty. His career had been winding down in 1942 when he enlisted. Now, after three years in the service, his career in the majors was over.

AGE	YRS	ML	G	BA	SA	AB	H	2B	3B	HR	HR%	R	RBI	BB	SO	SB
38-40	43-45	16	1753	0.299	0.425	6148	1838	347	101	75	1.2	934	838	696	540	53
		3	99	0.247	0.307	215	53	8	1	1	0.5	18	37	44	25	2
		19	1852	0.297	0.421	6363	1891	355	102	76	1.2	952	875	740	565	55

WILLIAMS, THEODORE S. (TED)   BL TR 6' 3"   205 lbs.

Born August 30, 1918, San Diego, Ca. — Died July 5, 2002, Crystal River, Fl.
Played for Boston (A) (1939-42, 1946-60)

When Ted Williams arrived on the major league baseball scene in 1939 he had one goal. He said, "All I want out of life is that when I walk down the street folks will say, 'There goes the greatest hitter who ever lived'" (Nemec et al. 1992, 325). At the end of his career many said exactly that. However, that career was not without its ups and downs. The ups and downs did not come because Ted could not hit; they came because of the attitude and personality of this great hitter. He was called, at one time or another, controversial, patriotic, competitive, caustic, a perfectionist, self-confident to the point of cockiness, and several other adjectives.

All of these comments, at times, were true. None of them, however, took away from his ability to hit the baseball. He started out with a bang in his rookie year by hitting .327 and setting a rookie record, while leading the league, for the most runs driven in with 145. Babe Ruth called him the unofficial rookie of the year in 1939. His numbers continued to get better. In 1941, at age 23, and in his third major league season, Williams batted .406 for the season. By doing this he became the only man to bat over .400 since 1930. During that year, Joe DiMaggio got more publicity because of his 56-game hitting streak. However, for the year, Williams out hit DiMaggio by 49 points, out homered him by seven, and was within five RBIs of him. Even during the time when DiMaggio was in his streak, Williams out hit The Yankee Clipper. During the streak, DiMaggio batted .408 and Williams batted .412. Nineteen forty-one was the first of four times Williams would be robbed of the MVP award by a Yankee player (1942, 1947, and 1957 were the other years). He also won the All-Star game for the American League that year by hitting a three-run home run with two out in the bottom of the ninth to win the game by a score seven to five. He followed up 1941 by winning the triple crown in 1942, a year filled with controversy. The United States was in World War II. Many players had already been drafted or had volunteered for military service. Williams had been classified 3-A because of his support of his mother. His mother was a Salvation Army worker, divorced, and unable to support herself. However, early in 1942, the draft board reclassified him to 1-A. Williams consulted an advisor who appealed the classification to the Appeals Board which turned it down. The advisor then took the appeal to General Hershey of the Presidential Board, and the classification was returned to 3-A. This change in deferment incensed the Boston press who did not like Williams.

Harold Kaese's writings give an example of the comments. He wrote, "A youth, healthy and highly paid, is transferred from 3-A to 1-A by his local draft board. He is on the verge of being inducted into the Army, like thousands of other young men, like poor young men and rich young men, like Hank Greenberg, like [Senators shortstop] Cecil Travis, like Hugh Mulcahy. The case goes to Washington. There is a delay. Those with sensitive ears hear strings being pulled. An ominous silence envelops the youth. There is suspicion. There is contempt. There is hatred" (Gilbert 1997, 39).

The Boston press was so suspicious that they hired a detective to see if Williams did actually support his mother. Williams faced detractors when he reported to spring training in 1942. He did make a statement as training started. "Anyone who knows the facts in my case will not condemn me. This is the toughest decision I've ever had to make. I realize I'm going to take a great deal of abuse from the crowds this year. I don't know why I should" (Goldstein 1980, 24). He also stated that, "I am going to play ball this season. My conscience is clear. I have as much right to be exempted as anyone else. I have my mother to support. Before my status was changed to 1-A, I made commitments which I must go through with. I can do so by playing ball this year. When the season is over, I'll get into the Navy as fast as I can" (Mead 1985, 49). Williams carried out his promise. In fact, he volunteered for service in the Navy in the spring of 1942. During 1942 he took math and science classes at Boston's Mechanics Art High School in the Navy's V-5 preflight training program, and he was allowed to play out the season before going on active duty.

In 1942 Williams had another great season. He won the triple crown that year but was robbed in the MVP voting for the second time. This time he lost out to Joe Gordon, even though he batted 34 points higher, hit double the number of home runs (36 to 18), and drove in thirty-four more runs. He was called up November 15, 1942. He was sent to Amherst College with Johnny Sain, Buddy Gremp, Joe Coleman, and Johnny Pesky for preliminary ground school. By May 1943, he had completed the work at Amherst and was transferred to Chapel Hill, North Carolina, for preflight training. This was completed in September 1943, and then he moved on to Bunker Hill Naval Air Station at Kohomo, Indiana, for basic flight training. These training sessions were not without their near misses.

At Amherst he almost hit a power line, and at Kohomo, he tried to take off with flaps set wrong and the propeller at the wrong pitch. He would have crashed if the instructor had not taken over the controls. He was at Bunker Hill three months so he could accumulate one hundred hours of flying time. In December 1943, he had completed the first three phases of his training and was transferred to Pensacola Naval Air Station for advanced training. Williams won his wings at Pensacola in May 1944. He was commissioned a second lieutenant at that time. He became an instructor at Bronson Field, Pensacola. During this time, he was able to play some baseball in addition to his flying duties.

In June 1945, he was sent to Jacksonville, Florida, for a ten-week advanced training, and then he was scheduled to go to the Pacific. Although Williams just wanted to concentrate on flying, his commanding officer ordered him to play some baseball.

He requested that he be assigned to fly fighter planes. He was ordered to report to San Francisco, on September 2, 1945, to join a fighter group flying to Manila. When the Japanese surrendered, Williams was in San Francisco waiting for a ship to go to the Pacific. In spite of the surrender, he was still sent to Hawaii, where he was able to play some ball. He played for the 14th Naval District team and took part in the Navy all-star game in October 1945. In December 1945, with the rank of lieutenant (j.g.), he was transferred back to the States to Camp Miramar, California. Finally, he was released from active duty on January 12, 1946. He had joined the Navy in 1942 and when given the choice, chose the Marines as the branch he would serve. This choice would later come back to haunt him. Talking about returning to baseball in 1946 as well as after service in Korea, Williams said, "Both times I came back real strong. It didn't make that much difference to me, but I could see that there were some who were completely different players. The years of being away took something from them" (Gilbert 1992, 263).

He also talked about his attitude after returning home. He said, "As far as desire was concerned, I had the same desire as before. I appreciated life a little more, but I was at the age (twenty-seven) when three or four years out of the game didn't have the same effect on me as on some of the others. I always had the same desire. I wanted to be first. I didn't want anybody to beat me" (Gilbert 1992, 263). That statement sums up Ted Williams. He had a great desire to be the best baseball hitter that was currently playing or had ever played. Because of this, he was driven to be the best that he could be, and he would not let anything get in the way of being the best hitter of all time. Williams downplayed his role in the war. He added, "The three years that I lost—hell, there were nine billion guys who contributed a lot more than I did" (Gilbert 1992, 267).

In 1946, he picked up right where he had left off by batting .342 and leading the Red Sox to their only pennant during Williams' career. For his effort that year, he did win his first MVP award. His career continued at a very high level. He won his second triple crown in 1947. Also in 1947, he was robbed for the third time of the MVP award. He lost out to Joe DiMaggio, even though he out hit DiMaggio by twenty-eight points, hit twelve more home runs, and drove in seventeen more runs. In 1949 he won his second MVP and missed another triple crown by only .00012 in the batting race. He lost one-half of the 1950 season when he broke his elbow in the All-Star game after running into the wall while trying to catch a ball.

In 1952 the second phase of Williams' military career would start. He had chosen the Marines when he entered World War II. He had remained in the reserves during the intervening years. When the Korean War was underway, the United States needed pilots. Johnny Sain, who had started out with Williams at the beginning of World War II, commented, "During the war, Ted Williams and I received our commissions in the naval aviator program in Chapel Hill, North Carolina, qualifying us for active duty. At that time we were given a choice of going into the Navy or the Marines, which was run by the Navy Department. They had us move to one line or the other. That's when I chose the Navy and Ted chose the Marines. After World War II was over, the Navy had so many reserve pilots I was able to get completely out of the reserves. But Ted had to go to Korea in 1952" (Peary 1994, 201).

The Red Sox had a day for Ted Williams on April 30, 1952, and Williams reported for service on May 1. He didn't have a good feeling about what was going to happen to him. He commented, "I expect to be killed" (Cataneo 1991, 282). First, there was an eight-week refresher course

WOODLING, EUGENE R. (GENE)   BL TR 5'9" 195 lbs.
Born August 16, 1922, Akron, Oh. — Died June 2, 2001, Barberton, Oh.
Played for Cleveland (1943, 1946, 1955-57), Pittsburgh (1947), New York (A) (1949-54),
Baltimore (1955, 1958-60), Washington (1961-62), and New York (N) (1962)

Gene Woodling found success with the Yankees after trials with both the Indians and the
Pirates. He had a very good year in the Pacific Coast League in 1948, leading the league in
hitting with a .385 batting average. After that season, he was purchased by the Yankees for the
1949 season. His timing was good because the Yankees went on to win the pennant and the
World Series for the next five years. Woodling was an important part of those teams.

One thing that Woodling did not like about those teams is that Casey Stengel platooned him
along with Hank Bauer. He did a lot of complaining about his playing time. Woodling had been
signed by the Indians when he was seventeen years old. When he made the Indians team late
in 1943, at age twenty-one, he was considered to be a very good prospect. He had led three
different leagues in hitting in the four years he had been playing. However, his career had to
be put on hold when he was drafted into the Navy after the close of the 1943 season.

Woodling was sent to Great Lakes Naval Training Center for basic training. "I was drafted
into the Navy in the fall of '43 and sent to Great Lakes. I was just going through regular basic
training, and word had gotten out that I was a professional ballplayer. So they called me over
to mainside" (Mead 1985, 192). He was asked if he would like to stay at Great Lakes for a year
and play ball. Woodling responded, "Well, would I like to! Yeah! I like to jump through the
ceiling. And that was not realizing the type of ball club we were going to have" (Mead 1985,
192). He added, "I actually gained a lot that one year by playing with those guys in 1944"
(Sargent 2000, 70). Woodling was a young player getting to play with some of the best veteran
players of the day. He said, "Billy Herman had better baseball sense than any guy I've ever been
around. My Lord, I learned a lot. It helped my career" (Mead 1985, 192). Woodling batted .342
for his year at Great Lakes. Late in 1944, he was sent to Hawaii. While he was there, he played
in the Navy/Army "Pacific World Series" that took place in September 1944. By early 1945, he
was transferred to the Western Pacific islands, with other ballplayers, to play exhibitions for
the other troops. He played on half a dozen different islands, ending up on Saipan where he
did see some combat. He was released by the Navy in January 1946.

Woodling was a good defensive outfielder. He led the league in fielding for two consecutive
years. Casey Stengel considered Woodling "the best defensive left fielder he managed in New
York" (Shatzkin 1990, 1197). He was also a good clutch hitter. Nicknamed in New York "Old
Faithful," he was considered to be a tough out. Ted Williams once signed a picture for him
with the inscription, "The toughest guy to get out in the American League in the years I played
against him" (Peary 1994, 171).

On November 18, 1954, he was part of one of the biggest trades of all time. He was traded
to Baltimore along with eight or nine other players for seven or eight in return. He stayed in
Baltimore for only a part of 1955 before he was sent to Cleveland. He had his best batting
average in Cleveland in 1957 (.321) before being sent back to Baltimore in 1958. Woodling

said, "I consider 1959 my best year in baseball. My stats were slightly higher with the Indians in 1957...but I got more key hits and won more ball games. I even made the All-Star team" (Peary 1994, 445). Woodling ended his career back in New York playing for Casey Stengel. However, this time it was playing for the Mets, and there wasn't a World Series ring at the end of the season.

AGE	YRS	ML	G	BA	SA	AB	H	2B	3B	HR	HR%	R	RBI	BB	SO	SB
20-22	43-45	17	1796	0.284	0.431	5587	1585	257	63	147	2.6	830	830	921	477	29
(3 YRS MINUS		2	83	0.217	0.288	212	46	3	6	0	0	15	19	23	18	1
8 GAMES)		19	1879	0.281	0.426	5799	1631	260	69	147	2.5	845	849	944	495	30

WYROSTEK, JOHN B. (JOHNNY)   BL TR 6' 2" 180 lbs.

Born July 12, 1919, Fairmont City, Il. — Died December 12, 1986, St. Louis, Mo.

Played for Pittsburgh (1942–43), Philadelphia (N) (1946–47, 1952–54), and Cincinnati (1948–52)

Johnny Wyrostek was a two-time All-Star who was signed out of high school by the St. Louis Cardinals in 1937. However, he made the major leagues with the Pirates in 1942. He had brief trials in '42 and '43. In 1944, the Cardinals again had his contract, and he was playing in the American Association where he led the league in hitting.

On July 29, 1944, the Cardinals announced that they had purchased his contract. He didn't get to play for the Cardinals because he was inducted into the Army on August 7, 1944. He spent some time in Germany during his service. In the fall of 1945 he played for the 3rd Army's 71st division team while in Germany. He also helped with a baseball school for German youths while stationed there. He was discharged in January 1946.

When he returned, the Cardinals were loaded with talent, and he was sold to the Phillies. In 1946, with the Phillies, he had his first chance to obtain regular status. In 1948, he was traded to the Reds. It was with the Reds that he had his best batting years, batting .311 in 1951 and hitting seventeen homers in 1948. Wyrostek was never an outstanding hitter; however, Ewell Blackwell said, "He was a good left-handed hitter" (Peary 1994, 70).

AGE	YRS	ML	G	BA	SA	AB	H	2B	3B	HR	HR%	R	RBI	BB	SO	SB
24-25	44-45	11	1221	0.271	0.383	4240	1149	209	45	58	1.4	525	481	482	437	33
		2	98	0.265	0.392	339	90	17	4	6	1.8	46	37	39	35	4
		13	1319	0.271	0.383	4579	1239	226	49	64	1.4	571	518	521	472	37

YOST, EDWARD F. (EDDIE)   BR TR 5' 10" 170 lbs.

Born October 13, 1926, Brooklyn, N.Y.

Played for Washington (1944, 1946–58), Detroit (1959–60), and Los Angeles (A) (1961–62)

Eddie Yost was one of the teenagers who got to play major league baseball because of the war. He was noticed while playing for the Bushwicks semi-pro team in Brooklyn. He had a tryout in Boston but did not like the way it went, so he signed with the Senators for a $500 bonus. He was seventeen years old when he played in August 1944. In his first game, he made a good stop at third and got a single off Eddie Lopat.

The Senators were hopeful that he would be able to play for them in 1945. But on January 23, 1945, Yost wrote the Senators owner the following letter, "I just wanted to write you a few lines to let you know that I am leaving for the armed forces on the 26th of this month. I didn't expect to leave quite so soon but, just as you said, they seem to be taking practically every available man. Before closing I want to thank you for the fine opportunity you gave me in the baseball world. Please give my regards to Joe Cambrie, who has been so swell to me. I hope that I can fulfill that contract before long. Best wishes" (Gilbert 1992, 140).

He was eighteen years old when he entered the Navy. In a letter, Yost gave this account of his service time, "[I] was in the Navy from January 1945 to July 1946 (1½ years). Stationed in Sampson N.Y. Training Center where I was a physical instructor in Unit G for the boots. Played on the baseball team there with some other major leaguers for the entertainment of the new recruits. Mickey Owen, Jim Konstanty, George Fallon and a few others were on that team. I feel very fortunate to have been part of the athletic department at Sampson" (Yost letter 1998).

He rejoined the Senators when he was released by the Navy in 1946. In 1947 he became the regular third baseman for the Senators and remained there for twelve years. Yost was a good fielding third baseman, leading the league in fielding two years, in putouts eight years, in assists two years, and in double plays two years. He holds the career record for the most games at third (2,008), most putouts at third (2,356), and assists at third (3,659). He played in 838 straight games from 1949 to 1955.

His best batting year was 1950 when he hit .295. Fielding or hitting for average were not why Eddie Yost was considered a successful player. His nickname, "The Walking Man," tells it all. His ability to draw the base on balls was one of the best, if not the best, in baseball. From 1946 till 1960 Ted Williams, Mickey Mantle, or Eddie Yost led the American League in walks every year. Williams led six years, Yost led six years, and Mantle led three years. The difference between these players is that Williams had a career batting average of .344 with 521 home runs, Mantle batted .298 with 536 home runs, and Yost batted .254 with 139 career home runs. Williams and Mantle got some of their walks because of their skill in looking at pitches and some of them because the pitcher was afraid to throw them a good pitch. Yost, however, had to earn each one of his because his batting skills were not on the same level as the other two players.

He is the only player with more than 1,500 walks and less than 2,000 hits (1,614 walks and 1,863 hits). He is also the only player with more than 1,500 walks and less than 200 home runs (1,614 walks and 139 home runs). One year, 1956, he had more walks than hits (151 walks and 119 hits). That year he batted only .231. For his career he ranks 9th in walks. Yost was one of the few who was signed to fill in during the war who came back after the war to have a good baseball career.

AGE	YRS	ML	G	BA	SA	AB	H	2B	3B	HR	HR%	R	RBI	BB	SO	SB
18-19	45-46	18	2109	0.254	0.371	7346	1863	337	56	139	1.9	1215	683	1614	920	72
(2 YRS MINUS		1	110	0.224	0.307	326	73	12	3	3	0.9	41	23	38	19	1
8 GAMES)		19	2219	0.252	0.369	7672	1936	349	59	142	1.9	1256	706	1652	939	73

The pitchers who pitched for at least eleven years in the majors are featured in this chapter. Most of the names listed are ones that any baseball fan will remember. Most are the pitchers who led their teams during the time they played the game. Many pitched in World Series games or threw no-hitters. They are the pitchers that batters talk about. Batters like to brag about the time they got a hit off the best pitchers. The pitchers who played for this length of time are usually those pitchers. Some of these players pitched for service teams while others got very little opportunity to keep the rust off their skills while they spent their time in the military. When you look at career statistics, some of these pitchers are the ones who are at the top of the list in a number of different categories. The loss of one to four years cost them dearly when they are compared to those who didn't spend time serving their country.

APPLETON, PETER W. (PETE)   BR TR 5' 11" 180 lbs.
Born May 20, 1904, Terrytown, Co. — Died January 18, 1974, Trenton, N.J.
Played for Cincinnati (1927–28), Cleveland (1930–32), Boston (A) (1932), New York (A) (1933), Washington (1936–39, 1945), Chicago (A) (1940–42), and St. Louis (A) (1942, 1945)

Pete Appleton made his debut with the Cincinnati Reds on September 14, 1927, after spending less than two years in the minors. He had graduated from the University of Michigan and had chosen a baseball career over a musical future as an accomplished pianist and band leader. However, his career in the majors was up and down for several years. He spent part or all of 1927, 1928, 1929, 1932, 1933, 1934, and 1935 in the minors before sticking in the majors in 1936. His best year in the majors was 1936 when he won fourteen games for the Washington Senators. He was used in relief for most of his career but was used as a spot starter for the Senators for the three years between 1936 and 1938. His career was winding down when he was commissioned in the Navy in December 1942. He had been released by the White Sox on July 5, 1942, and signed by the St. Louis Browns on July 10, 1942. He spent his time in the Navy as a member of the Browns.

When Appleton entered the Navy, he reported to Chapel Hill, North Carolina. He had the rank of lieutenant (j.g.). In late 1943, he went to Quonset Point, Rhode Island, to work in the USNR Welfare Department. He continued to be stationed at the Quonset Naval Air Station during 1944. He was released during the 1945 season and returned to the Browns in time to pitch in two games for them before being sent back to the Washington Senators where he pitched six games. Appleton was forty-one years old when he was released in 1945. He was listed on the Senators active roster in December 1945 but did not make the team for the 1946 season. The last season that he played for a major league team was 1945.

AGE	YRS	ML	W	L	PCT	ERA	G	GS	CG	IP	H	BB	SO	SHO	SV
39-41	43-45	14	57	66	0.463	4.3	341	71	34	1141	1187	486	420	6	26
(3 YRS MINUS		2	6	5	0.545	4.9	50	0	0	93	89	41	34	0	7
8 GAMES)		16	63	71	0.47	4.35	391	71	34	1234	1276	527	454	6	33

BENTON, JOHN A. (AL)   BR TR 6' 4" 215 lbs.
Born March 18, 1911, Noble, Ok. — Died April 14, 1968, Lynwood, Ca.
Played for Philadelphia (A) (1934–35), Detroit (1938–42, 1945–48), Cleveland (1949–50), and
Boston (A) (1952)

Al Benton made it to the majors with the Philadelphia Athletics in April 1934. He had a good
rookie year, winning seven and losing nine for a team that finished fifth. He was the fifth
starter and also pitched in relief. He struggled the following year and was sent back to the
minors and did not return to the majors until 1938 with the Detroit Tigers. Benton both
started and relieved during his career. Some years he did both jobs and other years only one.
In 1940, when the Tigers won the pennant, Benton was their relief pitcher, but he didn't
pitch in the World Series. He did not start any games during that year and led the American
League in saves and relief losses. By 1942, he had been converted back to a starter. That year
he started thirty of the thirty-five games in which he appeared. His best year was 1941 when
he won fifteen games while losing six. In that year, he started fourteen games and relieved in
twenty-four.

Benton enlisted in the Navy on November 30, 1942. He was sent to the Naval Air Technical
Training Center in Norman, Oklahoma. He was an athletic specialist and spent his entire
time in the Navy at that location. While stationed in Oklahoma, Benton was able to play some
baseball. In November 1944, he received a medical discharge from the Navy. He was able to
rejoin the Tigers for the 1945 season. He had spent two years in the Navy without suffering
any injuries. However, on May 24, 1945, he was hit by a line drive and suffered a broken right
ankle. He was out of action until July 1. Even with the time off for the injury, Benton started
twenty-seven games for the Tigers as they won the pennant. He pitched in three games in
relief, without a decision, in the 1945 World Series.

In 1946, Benton reverted back to the dual role of starter and reliever and then to reliever.
Released by the Tigers in December 1948, Benton signed with Sacramento before returning
to the majors with the Indians. He spent 1951 in the minors before returning to the Red
Sox in 1952 at age forty-one. His career covered nineteen years (1934 to 1952). He holds the
distinction of giving up home runs to both Babe Ruth (1934) and Mickey Mantle (1952). He
was picked to two All-Star games, pitching five innings in the 1942 game and receiving the save.

AGE	YRS	ML	W	L	PCT	ERA	G	GS	CG	IP	H	BB	SO	SHO	SV
32-33	43-44	14	98	88	0.527	3.66	455	167	58	1689	1672	733	697	10	66
		2	23	17	0.575	2.89	66	45	17	358	323	135	155	4	6
		16	121	105	0.535	3.53	521	212	75	2047	1995	868	852	14	72

BRIDGES, THOMAS J.D. (TOMMY)   BR TR 5' 10" 155 lbs.
Born December 28, 1906, Gordonsville, Tn. — Died April 19, 1968, Nashville, Tn.
Played for Detroit (1930–43, 1945–46)

Tommy Bridges reached the majors after less than two years in the minors. He made his debut
on August 13, 1930, with the Detroit Tigers and stayed with them for the next seventeen years
less the time he spent in the service. After a few years developing, Bridges became one of the

best pitchers in the American League during 1934, 1935, and 1936. During those three years, he won sixty-six games, and the Tigers won the pennant in two of those years. Bridges played in four World Series for the Tigers. In addition to 1934 and 1935, he also pitched in the 1940 and 1945 Series, winning four games and losing one. He was known for having a great curve ball. Charlie Gehringer said, "We had Tommy Bridges on our staff, too. One of the finest curve ball pitchers I ever saw" (Honig 1975, 47). Bridges continued to be part of the Tigers' rotation until he entered the service at age thirty-six.

During his career, he led the American League in games started twice (1934 and 1936), strikeouts twice (1935 and 1936), wins once (1936), and shutouts in 1932. He was inducted into the Army on November 20, 1943, one month shy of his thirty-seventh birthday. He reported to Fort Sheridan, Illinois. He was transferred to Camp Crowder, Missouri, to take a basic course as a member of the Central Signal Corps Replacement Training Center. Bridges was able to play some baseball while stationed at Camp Crowder. He also served as manager of the base team during the time he spent there in 1945. He remained at Camp Crowder through the middle of 1945 when he was transferred to Washington, D.C. He went in as a private and rose to the rank of sergeant.

Bridges was stationed at Fort Meade, Maryland, when he was discharged on August 26, 1945. He was asked in an interview for *The Sporting News* about the ability of former players to return to the game after being away for a while. He said, "Big time athletes have a chance to come back after the war—with a big 'if.' The younger ones can make the grade again, no matter what sport and some of the older ones may get in a season or two if not retained in the service too long. The top flight performer never loses the 'feel' of his game; it is age that keeps gaining on him, not competition. All the angles of performing the easy way, a thorough knowledge of the game, and knowing the tricks of the trade add up to the all-important quality called experience. This asset alone has kept many an athlete in the game when many, ignorant of sports, wonder why he wasn't finished long ago. You can't buy experience and it often outweighs mere youth" (*The Sporting News*, "From the Service Front—Ex-Stars' Future Depends on Pop Time, Says Bridges" 12-7-1944, page 15). Bridges returned to the Tigers' lineup on September 3, 1945, in time to pitch in four games at the end of the 1945 season as the Tigers won the pennant. He also got into one game in the 1945 World Series. However, the age that he spoke about in his *Sporting News* interview caught up with him. He was thirty-eight when he was discharged and thirty-nine when the 1946 season began. The man who had been in the Tigers' regular starting rotation for thirteen years when he was inducted now could no longer compete with the younger players at the major-league level.

After he left the majors, he pitched in the Pacific Coast League for three more years (1947–1949). He won 33 and lost 27 for the Portland team during that time. Regarding his career, Bridges said, "The past is nice. I enjoyed my playing days and the memories are priceless. But you must live in the present" (Dickson 1991, 60).

AGE	YRS	ML	W	L	PCT	ERA	G	GS	CG	IP	H	BB	SO	SHO	SV
37-38	44-45	16	194	138	0.584	3.57	424	362	207	2826	2675	1192	1674	33	10
(2 YRS MINUS		1	21	18	0.538	3	51	47	22	355	311	140	222	4	0
4 GAMES)		17	215	156	0.568	3.51	475	409	229	3181	2986	1332	1896	37	10

By November 1944, Chandler had been assigned to the headquarters detachment of Moore General Hospital at Asheville, North Carolina. He did rehabilitation work with wounded veterans at the hospital. Chandler did get his wish to play some Army baseball. He pitched for the hospital team during the summer of 1945. He was released from the Army on September 14, 1945, at Fort Bragg, North Carolina. He was thirty-eight when he rejoined the Yankees at the close of the 1945 season and pitched in four games. Chandler was right when he told the interviewer that he had two more seasons left. He returned strong in 1946. He began the season by throwing two shutouts. He won twenty again with an ERA of 2.10. He suffered arm problems, as he had off and on during his career, during the 1947 season. This limited him to seventeen games during the season. However, he pitched well when he did pitch. He won his second earned run average title during his last season at age forty. The Yankees released him the next spring on April 12, 1948.

Chandler was known as a competitor. Tommy Henrich said, "He was a bulldog. He would never give a batter a good ball to hit, never give in to him" (Turner 1996, 102). When he retired he had the highest winning percentage of any pitcher with 100 or more victories. His percentage was .717.

AGE	YRS	ML	W	L	PCT	ERA	G	GS	CG	IP	H	BB	SO	SHO	SV
36-37	44-45	11	109	43	0.717	2.84	211	184	109	1485	1327	463	614	26	6
(2 YRS MINUS		0	30	11	0.732	2.15	52	51	17	420	337	130	207	8	1
1 & 4 GAMES)		11	139	54	0.72	2.69	263	235	126	1905	1664	593	821	34	7

DICKSON, MURRY M.

BR TR 5' 10" 157 lbs.

Born August 21, 1916, Tracy, Mo. — Died September 21, 1989, Kansas City, Ks.
Played for St. Louis (N) (1939-40, 1942-43, 1946-48, 1956-57), Pittsburgh (1949-53), Philadelphia (N) (1954-56), Kansas City (1958, 1959), and New York (A) (1958)

Murry Dickson started his professional career in 1937 and reached the major leagues for one game with the Cardinals in 1939. He returned to the Cardinals to pitch in one game in 1940. He arrived in the majors to stay in 1942. He pitched mostly in relief in 1942 and 1943 as the Cardinals won the pennant both years. He entered the Army on September 7, 1943, during the last weeks of the season. He was assigned to Fort Riley, Kansas. When the World Series started, Dickson was given a special ruling and a ten-day pass to be able to pitch in the fall classic. He appeared in game five, getting the final two outs in the ninth inning. He became the only active soldier to pitch in a World Series game.

Dickson stayed at Fort Riley into the summer of 1944. He was able to pitch for the base team during that summer. He was assigned to Fort George G. Meade, Maryland, during July 1944. Dickson was later transferred to the European Theater. He served as a jeep driver and forward observer during that time. At one point during combat, he dove into a fox hole only to have General George S. Patton jump in on top of him. The General later offered to let Dickson be his jeep driver. Dickson declined, telling his commanding officer that, "Patton is nuts. He doesn't think anyone can kill him." Dickson was involved in the Battle of the Bulge while fighting in Europe. He rose to the rank of sergeant during his time in the service.

Following the surrender of Germany, a number of baseball teams were formed. Dickson pitched for the 35th Infantry Division team in a game in Germany in July 1945. He returned to New York on September 10, 1945, on board the *Queen Mary* along with 14,000 other soldiers. He was discharged by the Army on November 5, 1945.

Dickson rejoined the Cardinals for the 1946 season. At that point in his career, he began starting more games as well as relieving. He was always a workhorse of a pitcher. Starting in 1946 he pitched in at least forty games per season for nine straight years. Starting in 1947 he pitched at least 200 innings for ten straight years. The Cardinals won the pennant in 1946, and Dickson had the best winning percentage in the National League. He also started two games in the 1946 series. He lost game three and was ahead in game seven when he was relieved. The score was tied and Brecheen got the win. Dickson was sold to the Pirates on January 29, 1949, for $125,000. Stan Musial speculated that the cash raised by the sale helped finance the purchase of the Cardinals by Fred Saigh. Saigh denied the claim.

Dickson continued to pitch well. However, the Pirates of the 1950s were a very bad team. In 1951 he won twenty games for a team that finished seventh and only won a total of sixty-four games. In 1952 he won fourteen games while the team finished with a record of 42-112. This was the worst record in Pirate history. Because of the poor teams, Dickson led the league in losses for the three straight years (1952-54). He also led the league three times in runs allowed and home runs given up. He was considered to have a "rubber arm," and he liked to pitch a lot. He also was known for the variety of his pitches. He threw a fast ball, slider, curve, sinker, knuckleball, and a change-up. He also threw these pitches from different positions; straight overhand, 3/4 overhand, sidearm, and slightly submarine. Dickson pitched until age forty-three.

He moved to a lot of different teams during his last years. However, even though he pitched for a long time after serving in World War II, he still lost his prime years during the war. He was twenty-seven when entered the Army and was twenty-nine when he rejoined the Cardinals.

AGE	YRS	ML	W	L	PCT	ERA	G	GS	CG	IP	H	BB	SO	SHO	SV
27-28	44-45	18	172	181	0.487	3.66	625	338	149	3052	3024	1058	1281	27	23
		2	21	14	0.6	3.11	81	29	15	327	288	127	152	3	3
		20	193	195	0.497	3.61	706	367	164	3379	3312	1185	1433	30	26

DOBSON, JOSEPH G. (JOE)   BR TR 6' 2"   197 lbs.
Born January 20, 1917, Durant, Ok. — Died June 23, 1994, Jacksonville, Fl
Played for Cleveland (1939–40), Boston (A) (1941–43, 1946–50, 1954), and Chicago (A) (1951–53)

Joe Dobson overcame a childhood accident to play baseball. When he was nine years old he lost the thumb and forefinger of his left hand while playing with a dynamite cap. After playing two years in the minors, he joined the Cleveland Indians for the 1939 season. He served primarily as a relief pitcher for the Indians during 1939 and 1940. Traded to the Red Sox on December 12, 1940, he was converted to a starter and served in that capacity for the balance of his career. He was part of the Red Sox regular rotation for eight years.

Feller was well known enough that his enlistment made the newspapers in Cleveland, New York, and other cities. *The New York Times* announced that "Feller is signed by the Naval Reserve" (*New York Times,* 12-11-1941, 40) and *The Cleveland Plain Dealer* ran a cartoon of Feller alongside Uncle Sam with the caption, "Now Pitching for Uncle Sam" (*Cleveland Plain Dealer*, 12-21-1941, 23). Feller had talked to Gene Tunney about his fitness program in the Navy. He called Tunney to tell him he wanted to enlist. Tunney came to Chicago to swear-in Feller. He was assigned to Norfolk Naval Training Station to do his basic training. He said he would "throw a few strikes for Uncle Sam" (Goldstein 1980, 18). He also began to work with the physical fitness program. He had the rank of chief boatswain mate. His day was full of exercises, drilling, and study.

During the spring of 1942, while at Norfolk, he began pitching for the base team and won nineteen games that year. He pitched in many exhibition games to raise money for war bonds and Navy relief. Those games included a game against the Cleveland Indians where 62,094 fans came to watch him pitch. Again Feller could have taken the easy and safe way but he didn't. After six months as a part of Tunney's fitness program, Feller asked to be transferred. Feller said, "I wanted to do something besides standing around handing out balls and bats or making ball fields out of coral reefs" (Mead 1985, 192).

In May 1942, Feller was transferred to Newport, Rhode Island, to attend gunnery school. However, Mickey Cochrane, who headed the sports program at Great Lakes; Gene Tunney; and Captain Harry McClure, commander of the Norfolk Naval Operating Base, got into an argument about who would have Bob Feller on his base. In the end Captain McClure won and Feller was transferred back to Norfolk to complete his gunnery training. Feller graduated from gunnery school with honors in the fall of 1942 and was assigned to the USS Alabama. It had been commissioned in August 1942, and Feller joined the crew the next month. He was the chief of a 40 mm, anti-aircraft gun crew that consisted of twenty-four men.

The Alabama joined the fleet in early 1943 and spent the spring and summer protecting the shipping lanes of the Allies in the North Atlantic. The ship was reassigned to the Pacific in late summer 1943. After going through the Panama Canal, they joined the action against the Japanese. They remained around the Fiji Islands until the Navy had assembled enough men and material to start a successful assault on the enemy. The Alabama did shore bombardments and anti-aircraft protection for about twenty carriers. They took part in the invasions of The Gilbert Islands, Kwajalein Atoll, The Marshalls, Saipan, The Marianas, New Guinea, Tarawa, Guam, The Philippines, and Iwo Jima. The ship was awarded eight battle stars for helping in these invasions.

These were difficult times. Feller said the worst time was in a hurricane in late 1943. The wind lasted for several days and ranged from 180 to 210 miles per hour. A number of ships sank and hundreds of men were lost during the storm. Between battles Feller worked hard to keep himself in shape. He ran around the deck; he worked out with a heavy bag in the boiler room; he played catch with anybody who could catch him (he put a few fellow sailors out of commission with his fast ball); he did push-ups and chin-ups; he skipped rope. Feller had always believed in a regimented physical fitness program, and he did his best to continue to be physically fit during his time in the Navy.

During the two years in combat, the USS Alabama traveled about 175,000 miles, crossing the Arctic Circle six times and the Equator twenty-four times. Feller returned to the States and landed at Bremerton, Washington, on January 14, 1945. When he returned, "Ralph Cannon wrote in *Esquire Magazine*, 'Feller probably has seen more combat in this war than any other top-ranking American sports celebrity'" (Feller and Gilbert 1990, 120). He was assigned to the Naval base at Great Lakes. That spring he assumed the position that Mickey Cochrane had occupied. Feller managed and pitched for the Great Lakes baseball team. They had a good team in 1945 and played and beat some major league teams including the Chicago Cubs. This time with the Great Lakes team would help Feller as he returned to the major leagues. He had been at sea for about two years and now was given the opportunity to tune his pitching skills in actual games.

The war was winding down, and Feller had spent his time in combat. Still the Navy would not release him. The admiral in charge of Great Lakes tried to stall his release. Feller made a telephone call to the Secretary of the Navy. The next morning the admiral got a radiogram with the following instructions, "Release Feller and nineteen others tomorrow" (Mead 1985, 225). The other nineteen were not baseball players but just sailors who had enough points to be released. He got his release papers at the Navy Pier (where he started), got in a plane, and flew to Cleveland. He was released from active duty on August 22, 1945. Instead of taking the balance of the season off, Feller rejoined the Indians. He had concerns for his future while serving. He reported, "I'd say to myself, 'when is this thing ever gonna be over?' 'Will I ever play ball again?'" (*The Philadelphia Inquirer.* 1976. "War Ball: Read Hardship Draft". August 8). These normal concerns for someone in the time of war were now over.

Feller returned to the Cleveland Indians, and on August 24, 1945, he was the starting pitcher against the Detroit Tigers and Hal Newhouser. Many baseball experts wondered how the war would affect Feller and the other major leaguers who served. The answer for Feller came soon; he struck out the first batter that he faced. The 46,477 fans at Municipal Stadium went wild. He pitched a four-hitter, struck out twelve, and won the game 4–2 against Newhouser and the Tigers. The headline in the Cleveland paper the next morning said, "This is What We've Been Waiting For" (Mead 1985, 226). Bob Feller had returned. He started nine games during the balance of the 1945 season. He won five, lost three, and pitched seven complete games. He also had one shutout while striking out fifty-nine batters in seventy-two innings. He was back at full strength during the 1946 season. It was in 1946 that Feller struck out 348 batters.

He continued to be effective for several more years, but his strikeout totals dropped out dramatically after the 1946 season. Even though he led the American League for two more years, he would never strike out two hundred batters in any season after 1946. After struggling for a few years, Feller came back with one of his best seasons in 1951. The blazing fast ball was gone, but he adjusted and won twenty-two games while losing only eight. He continued with the Indians until the 1956 season. He retired after that season. He never played in the minors, and he only played for one major league team, the Cleveland Indians.

Bob Feller was a special pitcher. Many of the best hitters ever to play the game list Feller as one of the best pitchers they ever faced, batters like Stan Musial and Ted Williams. Umpire Bill Klem said Bob Feller was "faster than Walter Johnson" (Hirshberg 1970, 155). Bill Klem should have known because he worked behind the plate for both pitchers. In addition, to get some feel for the ability of Bob Feller, you only need to look at the number of times he led the American League in different categories. He led the league in wins six times (three years before and three years after Navy service), in winning percentage once (after military service), earned run average once (before service), games pitched three times (two years before and one after), games started five times (two years before and three after), complete games pitched three times (two before and one after), innings pitched five times (three years before and two after), hits allowed three times (once before and twice after), bases on balls four times (three years before and one after), strikeouts seven times (four years before and three after), and shutouts four times (two years before and two after). Feller's service in the Navy came at the time when he was at his best. He won 24, 27, and 25 games respectively the three years before going into the Navy, and he won 26 and 20 respectively in the two years following his release.

Even with his service having a major affect on his career, Feller has always spoken of his duty and his commitment to that duty. "There are many things more important than baseball these days. First we'll have to win the war to keep baseball" (*The New York Times.* 12-11-1941 page 40). He had told his mother before Pearl Harbor, "When it's time for me to do the job I'm ready to do the job. When they want me I'll go" (Mead, 1985, 32). He commented on the war's affect on his pitching totals and said, "I might have had a shot at some others [records] but for the war and the three-year 'vacation' in the Navy. But you can't saw dust" (Dickson 1991, 132). He continued, "I thought what I did was right. I may have lost a chance to break a helluva lot of records, because it cost me a few years, but it was worth it" (*The Philadelphia Inquirer*, 1976. "War Ball: Real Hardship Draft". August 8).

His attitude still remains today. In a letter to Americans in support of donations to a World War II memorial, Feller responded to a question if he regretted his time spent in service to his country. "Well, my friend, I don't regret it at all" (Feller letter, 1997). Bob Feller's enlistment on the day following the attack on Pearl Harbor was a great morale boost for many young men who would serve. Some seemed to think if a national hero, a sports figure, can give up his career to serve his country, then I can. At that point, the country needed all the heroes it could find, and Bob Feller was one of those heroes.

AGE	YRS	ML	W	L	PCT	ERA	G	GS	CG	IP	H	BB	SO	SHO	SV
23-26	42-45	18	266	162	0.621	3.25	570	484	279	3827	3271	1764	2581	46	21
(4 YRS MINUS		3	92	44	0.676	2.69	164	144	104	1232	960	552	990	22	11
9 GAMES)		21	358	206	0.635	0.311	734	628	383	5059	4231	2316	3571	68	32

FRENCH, LAWRENCE H. (LARRY)   BR TL 6' 1"   195 lbs.
Born November 1, 1907, Visalia, Ca. — Died February 9, 1987, San Diego, Ca.
Played for Pittsburgh (1929-34), Chicago (N) (1935-41), and Brooklyn (1941-42)

Larry French began his major league career with the Pirates in 1929 after three years in the minors where he lost more games than he won. Starting in that rookie year of 1929 and continuing for the next fourteen years, until he went into the Navy, French pitched in at least thirty or more games per year. In fact, in nine of those fourteen years he pitched in at least forty games. He pitched in more games than any other pitcher during the 1930s and was second in innings pitched during the same time. He was used both as a starter and a reliever during the time. However, the majority of his games were in the starting role. For six years in a row, he started at least thirty games per year (1930–35). His record with the Pirates was about a .500 winning percentage. When he was traded to the Cubs before the 1935 season, his record improved. His seventeen wins in 1935 helped the Cubs to the pennant that year.

He suffered an injured thumb and the worst season of his career in 1941. It was the first time since his rookie year that he did not win at least ten games. His record that year was five wins and fourteen losses. He was waived to the Dodgers on August 20, 1941. He followed his worst year with his best year. In 1942, his last season in baseball, he won fifteen games while only losing four. With that record he won the National League percentage title with .789 while having an earned run average of 1.83.

During his career, French had a unique statistic: more than twenty percent of his wins were shutouts. He pitched forty shutouts in his 197 wins. At age thirty-five, with 197 wins in his baseball career, French enlisted in the Navy on January 8, 1943. He was a member of the Brooklyn Dodgers when he enlisted. He was assigned to the Brooklyn Naval Yards after his enlistment. He was able to receive a commission as a lieutenant (j.g.) when he entered the Navy. Because of the location of his assignment, French requested permission to pitch for the Dodgers during his off-duty hours. He wanted to win 200 games in his career. He was close, and because he was thirty-five years old he didn't think he would be able to return to the major leagues after the war. He was turned down in his request.

He remained in Brooklyn during the summer of 1943 and was transferred to an undisclosed location that fall. The undisclosed location led him to England as part of an amphibious unit. He reported in the April 13, 1944, issue of *The Sporting News* that "our season will open over here in the not too far distant future. This will be for a bit higher stakes than I have ever played for. However, we have a winner and when it is over, I am still of a mind to return and win the games necessary to make me a 200-game winner" (*The Sporting News*. "In The Service–Overseas Play Developing Prospects, Says French." 4-13-44, page 14). French did take part in the invasion of France. He landed on the beach two days after D-Day and came under heavy fighting. He was cited for meritorious service during the invasion.

During the late summer of 1944, he returned to the States and was dispatched to California. He was going from the beaches of Normandy to the Pacific Theater. After spending about six months training in San Diego, he was assigned to a battleship in the Pacific as a supply officer. His naval duty for World War II ended on November 11, 1945, when he was released from the Navy in Los Angeles, but he remained in the reserves after the war. He had risen to the rank of lieutenant commander. He was thirty-eight years old when he was released and he was unable to rejoin the Dodgers.

During the Korean War he was recalled to active duty. He made the Navy his second career, retiring in 1969 with the rank of captain. French's baseball career ended because of the war and his military career started because of the same war. He is known for being the pitcher who won the most career games (197) without winning twenty games in any one season. He won eighteen three times.

AGE	YRS	ML	W	L	PCT	ERA	G	GS	CG	IP	H	BB	SO	SHO	SV
35-37	43-45	14	197	171	0.535	3.44	570	384	199	3152	3375	819	1187	40	17
		3	30	27	0.526	3.17	105	50	21	453	456	125	195	7	0
		17	227	198	0.534	3.41	675	434	220	3605	3831	944	1382	47	17

GALEHOUSE, DENNIS W. (DENNY)   BR TR 6' 1" 195 lbs

Born December 7, 1911, Marshallville, Oh. — Died October 12, 1998, Doylestown, Oh.
Played for Cleveland (1934–38), Boston (A) (1939–40, 1947–49), and St. Louis (A) (1941–44, 1946–47)

Denny Galehouse made his debut with the Cleveland Indians on April 30, 1934, and pitched in the majors for fifteen seasons. After a trial in 1934 and 1935, Galehouse stuck with the Indians. He always was a workhorse during his career. Starting in 1936, he averaged pitching in over thirty games per year during the next twelve years. Used as a starter and reliever, he struggled to win games. During those same twelve years, Galehouse won ten or more games only three times, with twelve wins being his highest total. He was not drafted when the war started because he was twenty-six years old and had pre-Pearl Harbor children.

In 1944 he went to work in the Goodyear Aircraft Plant in Akron, Ohio. His job was working with the Selective Service to determine whose job was necessary and, therefore, would get a deferment. During that time the baseball commissioner gave permission to those working in plants to play baseball on the weekends. Galehouse, then a member of the St. Louis Browns, took advantage of the ruling. He would take the evening train from Akron to wherever the Browns were playing that weekend. He would pitch the first game of the Sunday doubleheader, get back on the train, and return to Akron ready for work on Monday morning. He pitched reasonably well; however, victories were hard to get.

As the summer wore on, Galehouse's lack of conditioning became more of a problem. He was only able to play some catch at noon other than being in a game. As the baseball season progressed two things happened. The Browns were playing well and contending for the pennant, and Galehouse was getting further behind because he was out of shape. He went to his draft board and asked when he might be drafted if he quit the defense plant job. With the information that he probably would not be drafted till after the season, Galehouse quit his job and joined the Browns full time to help them in their push for the pennant.

The Browns did win the pennant and Galehouse started two of the World Series games. He pitched in game one, winning 2-1 on a seven-hit complete game. He also started game five, losing a complete-game outing by the score of 2-0. He was drafted after the 1944 season and entered the Navy on April 26, 1945. He was thirty-two years old when he entered the Navy. He was inducted in Cleveland and assigned to the Great Lakes Naval Training Center. He spent his entire time in service at that location.

During the summer of 1945, while he was stationed at Great Lakes, he pitched for the Training Center team, winning seven and losing four. He was released on October 19, 1945. He had his best year in 1947 after he had been sold to the Boston Red Sox on June 20, 1947. For the balance of the season, he won eleven games while losing seven, giving him twelve wins for the year. St. Louis Browns manager, Luke Sewell played a hunch and made Galehouse the starting pitcher in game one of the 1944 World Series and was successful. Boston Red Sox manager Joe McCarthy played the same hunch by making Galehouse the surprise starter in 1948 in the Red Sox playoff game with the Indians. However, this time he was the loser as the Indians won the pennant. The playoff game would be his last major league decision. He closed his career the following year without a decision.

AGE	YRS	ML	W	L	PCT	ERA	G	GS	CG	IP	H	BB	SO	SHO	SV
32-33	44-45	15	109	118	0.48	3.98	375	258	106	2003	2148	735	851	17	13
(2 YRS MINUS		1	12	15	0.444	3.47	37	33	18	235	236	83	84	3	1
24 GAMES)		16	121	133	0.476	3.93	412	291	124	2238	2384	818	935	20	14

GOMEZ, VERNON L. (LEFTY)   BL TL 6' 2" 173 lbs.
Born November 26, 1908, Rodeo, Ca. — Died February 17, 1989, Greenbrae, Ca.
Played for New York (A) (1930–42) and Washington (1943)

Vernon "Lefty" Gomez was one of baseball's colorful characters. His actions also earned him the nicknames of "Goofy," "The Gay Castillon," and "El Gomez." All of the names give an indication of Gomez's attitude about life and dealing with people. He was a comedian off the mound but when he was on the mound it was a different story. For an eleven-year period (1931 to 1941), except 1940 when he had a sore arm, Gomez was one of the mainstays of the New York Yankee pitching staff. He was named to the American League All-Star team for seven straight years (1933 to 1939), including starting the first All-Star game in 1933. He pitched three innings that day. He also set the All-Star game record for the longest pitching stint. He pitched six innings in the 1935 game. He won twenty games four times during this stretch, leading the league in wins twice. He also led the league in percentage twice, complete games once, shutouts three times, and strikeouts three times. The Yankees won five pennants while Gomez was pitching for them.

While his regular season record was good, his World Series record was even better. He made seven World Series starts, winning six and losing none. He pitched four complete games and had an earned run average of 2.86. In 1934, he won the triple crown of pitching, leading the league in wins (26), strikeouts (158), and earned run average (2.33). When arm trouble took away his fast ball, he became a finesse pitcher. He said, "I'm throwing as hard as I ever did, the ball's just not getting there as fast" (Shatzkin 1990, 397). He was always known for his quotes. When asked why he was successful, he replied, "Clean living and a fast outfield" (Ritter and Honig 1984, 159). Gomez teamed with Red Ruffing to lead the Yankees for twelve years. Their record from 1930 to 1942 is the best righty/lefty record for a team in baseball history. They won 408 games for the Yankees during that stretch. Bob Feller said, "Red Ruffing and Lefty Gomez were two of the best pitchers in baseball" (Feller and Gilbert 1990, 53).

Gomez was sold by the Yankees to the Boston Braves on January 25, 1943. However, he was released by the Braves on May 19, 1943, without playing in a game in the National League. The Washington Senators signed him on May 24, 1943, and he pitched in one game for them as he closed out his major league career. Gomez did not enter the military during the war. However, during the 1943 season he did work in a defense plant producing war materials. He

MASTERSON, WALTER E. (WALT)   BR TR 6' 2" 189 lbs.
Born June 22, 1920, Philadelphia, Pa.
Played for Washington (1939–42, 1945–49, 1952–53), Boston (A) (1949-52), and Detroit (1956)

Walt Masterson made his major league debut after only playing in two minor league games in which he pitched a total of seven and two-thirds innings. He made his first appearance with the Senators on May 8, 1939, when he was eighteen years old. He struggled in the years before he went into military service because of his youth and playing for a team that spent most of the time in the second division. His best pre-war year was 1942. While only winning five games that year, four of his victories were shutouts. He had an earned run average that year of 3.34 in 142 $^2/_3$ innings. Masterson volunteered for the Navy on September 15, 1942. He took his early training at Norfolk Naval Training Station in late 1942 and the first part of 1943.

While stationed at Norfolk, he was able to play some baseball. He took part in a war bonds game in 1943 against his old team, the Senators. He was transferred to the Pacific by the fall of 1943. Masterson served at sea on board a submarine. He saw action at Midway and Guam during his service. Following this service he was sent back to Hawaii and spent the summer of 1944 stationed in Honolulu. In Hawaii, Masterson was able to play some baseball. He pitched for the 14th Naval District team and also pitched for the Navy in the Army/Navy World Series in Honolulu in October 1944. By the summer of 1945 he had been transferred back to the States and was stationed at New London, Connecticut, where he played for the sub base team. He received his discharge on September 11, 1945. He pitched in four games in 1945 after he returned from the Navy. On September 13, 1945, only two days after his release, he outpitched Bob Feller for a victory.

Masterson wrote in a letter that he did not receive any injuries or wounds. However, his wounds were not ones which showed up physically. The effect of war took its toll on his nerves for over a year. Masterson said, "It was not a happy time coming out of the service, which I guess it should have been. I didn't have a happy time in the service. It messes up your head. When you get to the position where you don't care whether you live or die, you're kind of strange to be around." He also added, "I wasn't the only one" (Gilbert 1992, 262). This was shown by an incident that happened in spring training of 1946. The Senators were playing an exhibition game in Cuba. The evening cannon was shot from the battlement on Morro Castle. Masterson described what happened. "There was a mad scramble for cover among the players who'd been in service" (Turner 1996, 24). Sometimes the psychological adjustment can be more difficult than a physical problem.

After a shaky year in 1946, Masterson recovered to have one of his best years in 1947. He won twelve and lost sixteen with an earned run average of 3.13 in 253 innings for a team that finished seventh. Masterson pitched in the 1947 All-Star game and started the 1948 All-Star game. Masterson closed his major league career by pitching relief in thirty games for the Detroit Tigers after a two-year absence from the big leagues. He later served as the Senators' pitching coach.

AGE	YRS	ML	W	L	PCT	ERA	G	GS	CG	IP	H	BB	SO	SHO	SV
23-25	43-45	14	78	100	0.438	4.15	399	184	70	1650	1613	886	815	15	20
(3 YRS MINUS		2	15	19	0.441	4.3	81	30	11	317	300	193	180	3	6
4 GAMES)		16	93	119	0.439	4.17	480	214	81	1967	1913	1079	995	18	26

MCLISH, CALVIN C.J.C.T. (CAL)   BB TR 6' 0" 179 lbs.

Born December 1, 1925, Anadarko, Ok.

Played for Brooklyn (1944, 1946), Pittsburgh (1947–48), Chicago (N) (1949, 1951), Cleveland (1956–59), Cincinnati (1960), Chicago (A) (1961), and Philadelphia (N) (1962–64)

Calvin Coolidge Julius Caesar Tuskahoma McLish gave a reason for his long name. He said, "There were eight kids in my family, and I was the only one my father was permitted to name, so I guess he figured he'd make up for the situation" (Shatzkin 1990, 719). McLish starred for the American Legion team in Oklahoma City and was signed by the Dodgers. They took him straight to the major league team because of the player shortage in 1944. He was eighteen years old when he made his debut on May 13, 1944. He spent the 1944 season with the Dodgers, winning three games and losing ten until he was called for active duty by the Navy on August 29, 1944. He spent twenty-three months overseas in the European theater before he returned home.

While stationed in Austria during the summer of 1945, McLish pitched on the 3rd Division baseball team. He was not discharged until late in the 1946 season. He returned in time to pitch one-third of an inning in one game during the 1946 season. Following the 1946 season, McLish was traded to the Pirates. This would start a series of moves that would let him play for seven different teams during his fifteen-year career. Starting with 1947, he spent eight of the next nine years trying to return to the majors on a regular basis. Only in 1951 did he spend the entire season with a major league team. The wait was worth it. After two years in the bullpen (1956 and 1957), McLish moved to the starting rotation for the Cleveland Indians. He had his two best years in 1958 and 1959. In 1958 he won sixteen games and lost eight, and in 1959 he won nineteen and lost eight.

In 1959 he was named to the American League All-Star team and pitched the last two innings as the American League won the game. He also finished second in the Cy Young Award voting in 1959. McLish had two bad years after he was traded to the Reds in 1960 and the White Sox in 1961. He rebounded with two good years with the Phillies in 1962 and 1963 before he closed out his career by pitching in two games in 1964. Following his active career, McLish coached and scouted for major league teams until 1981.

AGE	YRS	ML	W	L	PCT	ERA	G	GS	CG	IP	H	BB	SO	SHO	SV
19-20	45-46	15	92	92	0.5	4.01	352	209	57	1609	1684	552	713	5	6
		2	6	8	0.429	5.04	30	15	4	121	125	36	58	0	0
		17	98	100	0.495	4.08	382	224	61	1730	1809	588	771	5	6

MURPHY, JOHN J. (JOHNNY)   BR TR 6' 2" 190 lbs.

Born July 14, 1908, New York, N.Y. — Died January 14, 1970, New York, N.Y.

Played for New York (A) (1932, 1934–43, 1946), and Boston (A) (1947)

Johnny Murphy was one of the first relief specialists in the major leagues. After a brief trial with the Yankees in 1932, he joined the New York team to stay in time for the 1934 season. During his first year, he was used both as a starter and a reliever. During that season he started twenty games and relieved in twenty games. The following season he was used mostly in relief and that's where he stayed. He would only start another twenty games during the balance of his thirteen-year career. Murphy was a successful reliever. He played an important part in the Yankee success of the 1930s and early 1940s. In the ten full seasons he played before World War II, Murphy led the American League in relief wins six times and in saves four times. He held the lifetime record for saves (107) and relief wins (73) until baseball changed the way the game is played in the 1960s.

He also had success in postseason play. The Yankees appeared in the World Series six times during this period, and Murphy recorded two wins and four saves during those series. In 1936 he pitched the final two and two-thirds innings of the sixth and final game as the Yankees won the game thirteen to five. He had come in with the tying runs on base and one out. He retired the side without the Giants scoring a run. On November 1, 1943, following the 1943 season, Murphy went to work in a war-related job. In April 1944, Murphy announced that he would stay on the job and voluntarily retired from baseball to work at his war-related job. He remained on the job at the atomic bomb plant in Oak Ridge, Tennessee, for the 1944 and 1945 seasons. He was supervisor of the service department for the Carbide and Carob Chemicals Corp. He might have pitched on a part-time basis but Yankee president Ed Barrow nixed the idea. He said, "A man is either a major league player, or a war worker or bricklayer. I think that using part-timers would demean big league ball. It would give us a semi-pro tone. The New York club wants none of it in any circumstances" (Mead 1985, 119). So Murphy stayed on the war-plant job and did not pitch for the Yankees during this time.

Murphy returned to the Yankees in time for the 1946 season. He was thirty-six years old, but he pitched reasonably well during that season. The Yankees released him in the spring of 1947, and he signed with the Red Sox where he closed out his playing career in 1947. Murphy was one of the leaders in getting the Major League Players Association started in 1946. He also worked on getting a pension plan set up for the players. He was able to get both television and radio money added to the pension plan. Following his retirement from playing, Murphy directed the Boston Red Sox farm system for fifteen years. He transferred to the New York Mets in 1961. He became vice president in 1964 and general manager in 1967. He was responsible for getting Gil Hodges to New York as manager and also for putting together the main parts of the "Miracle Mets" of 1969. He didn't get to taste the success for long as he died of a heart attack in 1970. Murphy didn't serve in the military, but the time he lost in service to his country cost him as much as if he had been in the service.

AGE	YRS	ML	W	L	PCT	ERA	G	GS	CG	IP	H	BB	SO	SHO	SV
35-36	44-45	13	93	53	0.637	3.5	415	40	17	1045	985	444	378	0	107
		2	16	7	0.695	3	65	0	0	113	96	50	42	0	14
		15	109	60	0.645	3.45	480	40	17	1158	1081	494	420	0	121

OSTERMUELLER, FREDERICK R. (FRITZ)   BL TL 5' 11' 175 lbs.
Born September 15, 1907, Quincy, Il. — Died December 17, 1957, Quincy, Il.
Played for Boston (A) (1934–40), St. Louis (A) (1941–43), Brooklyn (1943–44), and Pittsburgh (1944–48)

Fritz Ostermueller started in the St. Louis Cardinal organization but made it to the majors with the Boston Red Sox in 1934 after three good years in the minors. Early in his career he was one of the pitchers who both started and relieved. During his seven years with the Red Sox, he started 127 games and relieved in 92. Then after three years in the bullpen with the Browns and Dodgers, he became a starting pitcher for the Pirates during his last five years. For his career he started 247 games and relieved in 143.

Ostermueller's win/loss record was marginal during his entire career. He struggled in winning during the early years. His best record during those years was thirteen wins and five losses in 1938. It would be one of the two years in which he would show a winning record during his first seven years. Ostermueller had been classified 4-F because of arthritis. His case was reviewed and referred to Washington. After review he was declared fit for the draft and called for induction at Quincy, Illinois, on May 5, 1945. He was inducted into the Army at Fort Sheridan, Illinois, on May 10, 1945. His military service didn't last very long, however. He was discharged on July 20, 1945.

He rejoined the Pirates and returned to the lineup on August 5, 1945. He had been gone from the Pirates about three months. Ostermueller had better success with the Pirates. In 1944 he won thirteen and lost eight with an earned run average of 2.81. In 1946 he won thirteen and lost ten with an earned run average of 2.84. These were the only two years during his career that he had an earned run average under 3.00. While with the Pirates, Ostermueller coined the phrase about Ralph Kiner, "Home run hitters drive Cadillacs and single hitters drive Fords" (Okrent 1989, 198). Ostermueller closed his major league playing career following the 1948 season.

AGE	YRS	ML	W	L	PCT	ERA	G	GS	CG	IP	H	BB	SO	SHO	SV
37	45	15	114	115	0.498	3.99	390	247	113	2067	2170	835	774	11	15
(1 YR MINUS		0	7	5	0.583	3.7	16	14	10	126	133	30	44	1	0
14 GAMES)		15	121	120	0.502	3.97	406	261	123	2193	2303	865	818	12	15

POLLET, HOWARD J. (HOWIE)   BL TL 6' 1"   175 lbs.
Born June 26, 1921, New Orleans, La. — Died August 8, 1974, Houston, Tx.
Played for St. Louis (N) (1941-43, 1946-51), Pittsburgh (1951-53, 1956), Chicago (N) (1953-55), and Chicago (A) (1956)

Howie Pollet had a record of twenty wins and three losses with an earned run average of 1.16 when the Cardinals called him up to St. Louis on August 20, 1941. With St. Louis he continued the success he had enjoyed in Houston of the Texas League. He won five games and lost two with the Cardinals and had an earned run average of 1.93. After dividing his time between the starting rotation and the bullpen in 1942, Pollet became one of the regular starters in 1943. He won eight games and lost four in 1943 before being called into service. He pitched twelve complete games and five shutouts in his fourteen starts that season. His earned run average was 1.75, good enough to lead the National League even though he missed the last half of the season. He pitched three straight shutouts and had a streak of twenty-eight straight scoreless innings as he entered the service.

Pollet was inducted into the Army Air Force on July 15, 1943. He took his basic training at Miami Beach, Florida. During the winter of 1943-44 he was stationed at Santa Ana Air Field.

He was in pilot training; however, this did not work out and Pollet was sent to the San Antonio Air Cadet Center in Texas. During the summer and fall of 1944, he pitched for the base team. Also on that team was his Cardinal teammate Enos Slaughter. Pollet was one of the Army players who was transferred to Kearns, Utah, and then on to Hawaii to play the Navy in early 1945. The transfer was made after the Navy team had beaten the Army team during a Pacific World Series in October 1944. A rematch did not take place because the Navy team had been disbursed before the new Army team arrived in Hawaii.

Pollet was stationed at Hickam Field when he arrived in Hawaii, and he was able to pitch for them during that time. The Army, as well as the Navy, had baseball teams touring the South Pacific islands to entertain the regular troops. Pollet was assigned to one of those teams. He was attached to the 58th Bomb Wing 20th Air Force during this time.

On July 4, 1945, he boarded the ship PA-101 to make the tour of the islands. They played on Saipan in the Marianas Islands and in Tinian and then assembled at Guam to board a ship for the trip home. Pollet's time in the South Pacific islands lasted about four months. He boarded the transport ship *Cecil* for the trip back to the States that should have taken eleven days. They ran into the tail of a typhoon on the way home and experienced very rough seas, and the trip took nineteen days. For three of those days, Pollet and the other passengers were locked below deck because of the violent pitching of the ship. He arrived in Los Angeles on November 2, 1945. Upon arriving back in the States, he was stationed at Fort Sam Houston, Texas, until his release. Pollet was discharged on November 11, 1945.

He returned to the Cardinals for the 1946 season. It would be the best season of his career. Pollet won twenty-one games to lead the National League and had an earned run average of 2.10 which would also lead the league. The Cardinals won the pennant that year, and Pollet started the first game of the Series. He pitched all ten innings and lost the game in the tenth. He also started game five. However, he suffered arm pain and had to leave the game in the first inning. The pain that he had required surgery, and he did not regain his form again until 1949. In that year he also won twenty games as the Cardinals came in second to the Dodgers. He led the league in shutouts in 1949 with five. His effectiveness suffered after 1949. This led to his movement to other teams as he closed out his career in 1956.

During his prime, Pollet was considered to be one of the best pitchers in the National League. Stan Musial said, "This was an artist, a class pitcher, a stylist with pitching rhythm and a student of the game. Howard knew how to pitch young" (Broeg 1964, 285). Jackie Robinson added, "He was the toughest pitcher for me last season [1949]. It was because of the change of pace. He throws the fastball and the slow ball with the same motion. It's deadly" (Eisenbath 1999, 261). Howard Pollet, at age twenty-two, was just hitting his stride when he was called into service. He missed two and one-half years because of that service. His service cost him a good deal in his baseball career.

AGE	YRS	ML	W	L	PCT	ERA	G	GS	CG	IP	H	BB	SO	SHO	SV
22-24	43-45	14	131	116	0.53	3.51	403	277	116	2107	2096	745	934	25	20
(3 YRS MINUS		2	39	24	0.619	3.44	98	68	32	526	567	192	215	4	4
16 GAMES)		16	170	140	0.548	3.5	501	345	148	2633	2663	937	1149	29	24

RAFFENSBERGER, KENNETH D. (KEN)   BR TL 6' 2" 185 lbs.
Born August 8, 1917, York, Pa. — Died November 10, 2002, York, Pa.
Played for St. Louis (N) (1939), Chicago (N)(1940–41), Philadelphia (N) (1943–47), and
Cincinnati (1947–54)

Ken Raffensberger joined the Cardinals for one game in 1939 after spending the season at
Rochester in the International League. That winter he was traded to the Chicago Cubs. After
spending the entire 1940 season with the major league team, he spent most of the next three
seasons in the minors. In 1944, he emerged as the last-place Phillies' number one pitcher.
He represented them in the All-Star game and pitched two innings of one-hit ball and was
credited with the win as the National League got one of its rare early wins in the All-Star
game. He also led the National League in losses that year with twenty. It was one of the two
years he led the league in losses. The other was 1951 with seventeen. Raffensberger started
the 1945 season with the Phillies. Two weeks into the season, he was drafted into the Navy. It
was on May 7, 1945, that he entered the service at Philadelphia, Pennsylvania. He was sent to
Bainbridge Naval Training Station where he stayed for his entire time in the Navy.

While stationed at Bainbridge, Raffensberger pitched for the base team. He said in a letter
that he won twenty games and lost four during the summer of 1945. Members of that team
included Dick Sisler, Stan Spence, Thurman Tucker, Stan West, Bill Conroy, Bennie Culp, Earl
Naylor, and others according to Raffensberger (Raffensberger letter, 1997). His stay in the Navy
did not last long. He was discharged on October 18, 1945. He spent a total of five months and
twelve days in service. This period of time did cause him to miss most of the 1945 season.
He rejoined the Phillies for the 1946 season. He was then traded to the Cincinnati Reds
during the middle of the 1947 season. It would be with the Reds that Raffensberger would
have his best success. He became the workhorse of the Reds staff. In 1949 he won eighteen
games while losing seventeen for the seventh-place Reds. In 1952 he won seventeen and
lost thirteen with an earned run average of 2.81 as the Reds finished sixth. His performance
declined the next year at age thirty-five, and he closed out his playing career the following
year.

Raffensberger struggled to win games for most of his career because he played with second-
division teams. He suffered a number of one-run losses. Commenting on his twenty losses
in 1944, he said, "I remember I lost a lot of one-run games that year, including one in sixteen
innings against the Cardinals. I pitched the full sixteen innings" (Gilbert 1992, 130). He had ten
1-0 losses in his career to rank him among the leaders in that category. Known for his control,
he walked only 449 batters in 2,151 innings to rank him among the best control pitchers of
all time. His pitching style and delivery gave some batters fits. Stan Musial said, "Actually, the
toughest pitchers for me were Ken Raffensberger..." (Broeg 1964, 264).

AGE	YRS	ML	W	L	PCT	ERA	G	GS	CG	IP	H	BB	SO	SHO	SV
27	45	15	119	154	0.436	3.6	396	282	133	2152	2257	449	806	31	16
(1 YR MINUS		0	10	14	0.417	3.35	33	23	15	203	202	28	98	2	3
5 GAMES)		15	129	168	0.427	3.58	429	305	148	2355	2459	477	904	33	19

ROWE, LYNWOOD T. (SCHOOLBOY)   BR TR 6' 4" 210 lbs.

Born January 11, 1910, Waco, Tx. — Died January 8, 1961, El Dorado, Ar.
Played for Detroit (1933–42), Brooklyn (1942), and Philadelphia (N) (1943, 1946–49)

Schoolboy Rowe got his nickname when he pitched in an adult league in El Dorado, Arkansas, at age fourteen. He signed with the Tigers at age twenty-two, and after one season in the minors, he joined the major league team. He won nineteen games at Beaumont in the Texas League. Rowe was one of the main reasons the Tigers won the pennant in 1934. He won twenty-four games that season, including sixteen in a row, and one more in the World Series. He continued his success over the next two seasons. However, in 1937 he suffered an injury to his pitching arm that caused him to miss most of that season as well as 1938. Rowe was sent down to minors in 1938 to strengthen the arm, so he spent most of the season back at Beaumont. The rehab was successful, and in 1939 he returned to the Tigers. It was then he started the first of his three comebacks. This comeback was successful. In 1940 Rowe led the American League in winning percentage. He won sixteen games while only losing three, a winning percentage of .842. But only two years later he would be sold and back in the minors, again with arm trouble. Then on March 24, 1943, Rowe was sold to the Philadelphia Phillies, and he started the second of his comebacks. In 1943 he was the Phillies' leading pitcher, winning fourteen games for a second-division team. In addition, his earned run average was under 3.00 for the first time in his career.

His time with the Phillies was interrupted by his call to war. Rowe was inducted into the Navy on February 18, 1944. He took his basic training at the Great Lakes Naval Training Center. During the summer of 1944 he pitched for the Great Lakes team. That team won forty-eight games and lost only two during that summer. Their opponents included twelve major league teams. Rowe won six of those games and lost one. Admiral Nimitz had challenged the Army to play some baseball games in Hawaii. The problem was that the Army had several good players, and the Navy didn't have a good team. Rowe, who was at Great Lakes, was transferred to Shoemaker Base in California and then on to Hawaii to represent the Navy. Nimitz also transferred a number of other major leaguers from the mainland to Honolulu as well as others from around the South Pacific. These players were stationed with the 14th Naval District. The movement was successful and the Navy beat the Army team in the Pacific World Series eight games to two in October 1944.

During the spring of 1945, Rowe was hospitalized in the Naval Hospital in Pearl Harbor for treatment of arthritis. There was a good deal of concern whether he would ever pitch again. However, later that summer, Rowe managed and played for a team called the Sub Base Dolphins. He led them to the championship and was named to the 14th Naval District All-Star team. He played in the all-star game and in the Little World Series in the fall of 1945. Rowe was discharged on November 24, 1945. He had the rank of coxswain when he left the Navy.

He was able to rejoin the Phillies for the 1946 season and start his third comeback. He was thirty-six years old when the season started. He returned to the majors with a good season. He didn't pitch in as many games as before but was very successful in the games he did pitch.

He won eleven and lost four with an earned run average of 2.12, the best in his career. Rowe had two more productive years before closing out his major league career in 1949. He pitched three more years in the minors before ending his professional playing career.

Rowe was always considered a very good hitter. During his career he hit eighteen home runs and was used as a pinch hitter on 101 occasions. Three times he batted over .300. In each of those years he had over 100 at-bats during the season. His best hitting year was 1943. During that year the Phillies used him as a pinch hitter forty-nine times. He got fifteen hits for a .306 batting average. Both the forty-nine at-bats and the fifteen hits led the National League that year. He became the first pitcher to hit grand-slam home runs in both leagues. He hit one for the Tigers on July 22, 1939, and then one for the Phillies on May 2, 1943. Rowe had a good career, but he could have had better. His career was interrupted three times. The first two times by a sore arm and the last time by his service to his country. Before he hurt his arm the first time he was one of the best pitchers in baseball. Charlie Gehringer said, "We had a fine pitcher with us in Detroit in those days, Schoolboy Rowe. In fact, when he first came up, he was a great pitcher" (Honig 1975, 47).

AGE	YRS	ML	W	L	PCT	ERA	G	GS	CG	IP	H	BB	SO	SHO	SV
34-35	44-45	15	158	101	0.61	3.87	382	278	137	2219	2330	558	913	23	12
		2	26	14	0.65	3.13	50	46	23	354	359	63	118	4	1
		17	184	115	0.615	3.77	432	324	160	2573	2689	621	1031	27	13

RUFFING, CHARLES H. (RED)   BR TR 6' 1"   205 lbs.
Born May 3, 1904. Granville, Il. — Died February 17, 1986, Mayfield Heights, Oh.
Played for Boston (A) (1924–30), New York (A) (1930–42, 1945–46), and Chicago (A) (1947)

Never has the change from one team to another had a more dramatic affect on a player's record than it did when Red Ruffing moved from the Red Sox to the Yankees. Red Ruffing got a trial with the Red Sox in 1924 after one year (1923) in the minors. After spending most of 1924 in the minors, he joined the Red Sox to stay in 1925. That tenure with the Red Sox is the first part of Ruffing's career. He was with the Red Sox for five full seasons before being traded to the Yankees on May 6, 1930. The record he accumulated for his stay in Boston was thirty-nine wins and ninety-six losses. This gave him a winning percentage of .289 in the 189 games he pitched. He also gave up 575 earned runs in the 1,122 ²/₃ innings or an earned run average of 4.61. During that time he led the American League twice in losses. He lost twenty-five games in 1928 and twenty-two in 1929. The trade to the Yankees was just what he needed for his career. The change he experienced was sudden and dramatic. He went from a winning percentage of .290 in his last year with the Red Sox to .750 in his first year with the Yankees. With the Yankees for almost fifteen full seasons, Ruffing won 231 and lost 124 for a winning percentage of .651. In addition, his earned run average dropped by more than a run a game. It went from 4.61 with the Red Sox to 3.47 for his career with the Yankees. He won at least twenty games four consecutive years between 1936 and 1939. He also led the American League in strikeouts in 1932.

Ruffing helped the Yankee teams of the late '30s and early '40s win seven American League pennants. He was able to get ten World Series starts during this period, pitching seven complete games. His record for those ten games was seven wins and two losses. He ranks high among World Series participants. He rates second in wins, third in innings pitched, and fourth in starts, complete games, and strikeouts. Ruffing was thirty-eight years old in December 1942. He had just pitched two games in the 1942 World Series, earning the Yankees only win as the St. Louis Cardinals won the series 4 to 1.

In addition, he had a wife, children, and a mother-in-law to support. He also had a foot that was missing four toes as the result of a mining accident. He had left school and gone to work in the mines at age fifteen to help the family. All this and Ruffing still got his draft notice. Most thought he would not pass the physical examination. He was living in Long Beach, California, at the time and went to Los Angeles for induction. He talked to a worker at the induction center and was told that he would not be taken. He was examined by the regular doctors and was given a 4-F status. However, he still had to be examined by one Army doctor. Ruffing reported what this doctor wrote, "He put on his report that what I could do on the outside I could on the inside. He would have drafted any ballplayer. So that's how I got in" (Mead 1985, 93). Ruffing entered the Army Air Force on December 29, 1942. He was classified 1-B, certified for non-combat duty, and sent to Camp MacArthur.

After basic training he was assigned to the Air Transport Command, Ferrying Division, Long Beach, California. He arrived there in January 1943. Ruffing stayed at Long Beach until the summer of 1944. He pitched for the Sixth Ferrying Command during that time. He spent his days as a physical instructor at the base. In the fall of 1943, he pitched the Long Beach team to the Southern California service championship. In the summer of 1944, Ruffing got orders to go to Hawaii. He didn't want to go and worked an agreement to give Hawaii a try, and he could return to his original assignment if he chose to do so. Ruffing commented on the trip. "I had to fly to San Francisco first to catch a plane. I got there in the evening" (Mead 1985, 197). The personnel at San Francisco thought he would be there for a week; however, the next morning he got orders to head on to Honolulu. They wanted him in Hawaii right away; a general was bumped off the plane so Ruffing could make the trip. He arrived in time to play in the Army/Navy World Series in October 1944. He played for the 7th Army Air Force team while stationed in Honolulu. He suffered a twisted knee in September which curtailed his playing. Following the "World Series," Ruffing exercised his option to return to his former assignment. He returned to Long Beach and the Sixth Ferrying Group.

In the spring of 1945, because he was over forty years old, it was assumed that he would soon be discharged under the "over 40 ruling." He continued to believe that he should be released from the service. However, the Army was making other plans. Ruffing said, "I was 41 years old, and they were letting men out. But they were going to send me over to Italy, across the ocean, entertaining the troops. So I decided to contact my congressman, Jerry Voorhis. I told him I'd like to have an interview with the Secretary of War" (Mead 1985, 224). Ruffing got his interview, and he told the secretary of his age, his dependents, and his responsibilities. He was sent to Camp Lee, Virginia, in May 1945 to prepare to make the trip to Italy. The next morning after he arrived at Camp Lee, he was to report to be shipped out. That morning the captain called Ruffing aside and told him there had been a mixup and he was to report to New York to get his papers. Ruffing said, "We go to New York. The moment we hit the door, some Colonel in the back room says, 'Sergeant Ruffing, come back here!' I says, 'Yes Sir.' He says, 'We can't send you over to Italy.' I says, 'That's what I hear.' He says, 'Your orders don't call for it'" (Mead 1985, 225). Ruffing was discharged at Fort Dix, New Jersey, on June 5, 1945. He had the rank of sergeant when he was discharged. He was twenty-five pounds overweight, forty-one years old, and had spent two and one-half years away from the major leagues. He returned to the Yankee lineup on July 16, 1945, just over a month after he had been released. He had eleven starts during the balance of the 1945 season. He won seven, lost three, and pitched eight complete games.

Ruffing was off to a great start in 1946 when he broke his ankle and missed the rest of the season. He had won five games and lost one with an earned run average of 1.77. He was released by the Yankees in September 1946 and signed with the White Sox in December. Nineteen forty-seven would be Ruffing's last year. His pitching suffered during the year. However, the White Sox picked him up to pinch-hit as well as pitch. This season, as well as his career, ended when he suffered a knee injury. The White Sox had acquired Ruffing for his bat as well as his arm. He was a very good hitting pitcher throughout his career. During his career he batted over .300 eight times with a career average of .269. He hit thirty-six home runs. This ranks him third all-time for home runs by a pitcher behind Wes Ferrell and Bob Lemon. He is also third in career hits by a pitcher with 521, after Cy Young and Walter Johnson. He had the second best season batting average for a pitcher in 1930 when he batted .364 (Walter Johnson batted .433 in 1925). He ranks first in career RBIs for a pitcher with 273. As a pinch hitter, Ruffing had fifty-eight hits in 228 at-bats. The fifty-eight hits rank him second in pinch hits by a pitcher. Even though Ruffing was a good hitter, he was a better pitcher. Teaming up with Lefty Gomez, the two became one of the best righty/lefty duos in baseball history. They won 408 games for the Yankees between 1930 and 1942. Bill Dickey said, "If I were asked to choose the best pitcher I ever caught, I would have to say Ruffing" (Nemec and Palmer 1993, 157).

AGE	YRS	ML	W	L	PCT	ERA	G	GS	CG	IP	H	BB	SO	SHO	SV
39-40	43-44	22	273	225	0.548	3.8	624	536	335	4344	4294	1541	1987	48	16
		2	20	11	0.645	3.48	35	35	20	269	254	77	97	4	0
		24	293	236	0.554	3.78	659	571	355	4613	4548	1618	2084	52	16

SAIN, JOHN F. (JOHNNY)   BR TR 6' 2"   185 lbs.
Born September 25, 1917, Havana, Ar.
Played for Boston (N) (1942, 1946–51), New York (A) (1951–55), and Kansas City (1955)

Johnny Sain was half of the duo that was immortalized by the saying, "Spahn and Sain and pray for rain" as the Boston Braves won the National League pennant in 1948. Sain had joined the Braves in time for the 1942 season after spending six seasons in the minors. He was used as a reliever during that season and was called the Braves' top reliever when he left to go into service. He joined the Navy when he received his draft notice. He went into Naval Aviation on August 21, 1942, but didn't have to report to aviation cadet training until November 15. This allowed him to finish the 1942 baseball season. He started his training along with several other major league players. They included Ted Williams, Johnny Pesky, Buddy Gremp, and Joe Coleman. They started their preliminary ground school at Amherst College.

During this time his training kept him occupied fifteen hours a day. In May 1943, he completed his preliminary training and was transferred to Chapel Hill, North Carolina, to start his preflight instruction. During his stay at Chapel Hill, Sain was able to pitch some baseball. In July 1943, a team made up of servicemen played a Red Cross benefit game against a team made up of Indian and Yankee players, and Sain pitched for the Chapel Hill team. Sain, along with Ted Williams, received his commission at Chapel Hill. Sain said, "At that time we were given a choice of going into the Navy or the Marines, which was run by the Navy." He continued, "That's when I chose the Navy and Ted chose the Marines. After World War II was over, the Navy had so many reserve pilots I was able to get completely out of the reserves. But Ted had to go to Korea in 1952" (Peary 1994, 202). After three months at Chapel Hill he completed Sain indoctrination training. He graduated from Corpus Christi Naval Air Training as an ensign in August 1944. He later taught flying at Corpus Christi. Ted Williams said, "He (Sain) was a damned good airplane pilot and did a tremendous job." He continued, "We went to flight training together in Springfield [Massachusetts] during the war. Johnny became a flight instructor. He is a well thought of guy" (*Sports Collector Digest*, July 17, 1992).

Sain was able to play for the base team while he was stationed at Corpus Christi, Texas. He was ready to be shipped out when the war ended. He had stayed at Corpus Christi for over a year when he was discharged on November 25, 1945. He did not suffer any injuries during his time in service. He said that the time spent in service actually made him a better pitcher. He said, "I think learning to fly an airplane helped me as much as anything. I was twenty-five years old. Learning to fly helped me to concentrate and restimulated my ability to learn" (Gilbert 1992, 262). When he rejoined the Braves in 1946 his entire baseball career consisted of one season in which he had started a total of three games. His performance during the next three seasons did not give any indication of the lack of experience. In 1946 he became one of the Braves regulars in the starting rotation. During those three years he won 20, 21 and 24 games, respectively.

The latter came in 1948 as the Braves won the pennant. One of his most famous games took place during the 1948 World Series. He outdueled Bob Feller one to nothing with the Braves' only run coming on a bad call on Feller's pickoff play at second. He was a workhorse during that time. He pitched seventy-four complete games out of 118 starts in those three years. In 1949 Sain suffered some arm problems. The pain he had when pitching affected his ability. His record dropped to ten wins and seventeen losses. The pain didn't go away, so Sain changed his delivery for the 1950 season, and he returned to the twenty-win category. The pain returned in 1951. Sain was ineffective as a starter for the Braves, so they traded him to the Yankees for Lou Burdette. Sain told a doctor friend about his shoulder problems. The doctor took x-rays and discovered a fibrous tissue had formed in the muscle. The doctor treated it with radiation, and in three weeks the pain was gone. Sain then became an effective member of the Yankee teams that would win pennants in three straight years.

His role changed from dominant starter to spot starter and set-up man to closer. He led the American League in saves during the 1954 season with twenty-two. Sain closed out his playing career with the Kansas City Athletics in 1955. Following his playing career, he developed another career as a pitching coach. He coached several teams and was noted for his innovative training ideas. Jim Bouton called him, "the greatest pitching coach who ever lived" (Shatzkin 1990, 956). He became known for developing twenty-game winners. During his coaching career with four different teams, he had pitchers who won twenty or more games sixteen times. Sain was able to transfer his success as a player to the players he coached.

AGE	YRS	ML	W	L	PCT	ERA	G	GS	CG	IP	H	BB	SO	SHO	SV
25-27	43-45	11	139	116	0.545	3.49	412	245	140	2126	2145	619	910	16	51
		3	45	33	0.577	3.21	115	72	46	628	569	229	329	6	9
		14	184	149	0.553	3.43	527	317	186	2754	2714	848	1239	22	60

SCHEIB, CARL A.   BR TR 6' 1"   192 lbs.
Born January 1, 1927, Gratz, Pa.
Played for Philadelphia (A) (1943–45, 1947–54) and St. Louis (N) (1954)

Carl Scheib was the youngest player to ever appear in an American League game. He was signed by the Athletics right out of high school and taken to the major league team without appearing in a minor league game. He was sixteen years eight months and five days old when he made his major league debut on September 6, 1943. He pitched two-thirds of an inning that day and took the loss as the Yankees beat the Athletics. He was a hard thrower, and the A's needed bodies as the war had taken many of their regular players. Scheib appeared in six games during the balance of the 1943 season. He continued with the major league team during 1944. As a seventeen year old, he was underage and not eligible for the draft. When he became eighteen on January 1, 1945, he became eligible, and early in the 1945 season Scheib was drafted into the Army Infantry. He was inducted on May 12, 1945, at the New Cumberland Training Center. He did get to play some baseball for the Indiantown Gap team during July 1945. After taking his training, he was in the process of being sent to European Theater for combat duty. Scheib said, "in the middle of the ocean the war was over and we changed our destination to Germany. We were the first occupational troops to land directly in Germany. So I saw no action" (Scheib letter 1998). His tour of duty lasted for the rest of 1945 and 1946.

He was discharged from the Army in time to return to the Athletics for the 1947 season. He was still only twenty years old when he rejoined the A's. He matured in 1948 and had his best major league season. He won fourteen games and lost eight with an earned run average of 3.94. That season gave him his most wins, best winning percentage, and lowest ERA of his career. He struggled with his pitching during the 1950 and 1951 seasons. During those two years, he won only four games and lost twenty-two. His earned run average during those two years was 5.64. He recovered in 1952 to have his second-best year. He won eleven and lost seven during that season. Despite his pitching record of 1–12, Seheib received a raise after the 1951 season because of his good hitting. That year he batted .396 with a slugging percentage of .623. He was used as a pinch hitter throughout his career.

In 1948, he made sixteen pinch hitting appearances and fourteen in 1952. Playing for the A's teams in that era was not a good experience. Scheib would have liked to have moved on to another team. He said, "I really would have liked to have been traded by my team, and I would have liked to have played the outfield" (Kaufman and Kaufman 1995, 144). He got his wish to be traded in 1954. However, it was after he had suffered a sore arm in 1953 which led to the end of his career. He played only in three games for the Cardinals after he was traded. He was twenty-seven years old when he called it quits as a major league pitcher. Scheib was one of the "kids" that was taken to major leagues to meet the player shortage during World War II. He might have had a chance if he had been given the opportunity to develop in the minors before being thrown into baseball at the major league level. He didn't have that chance, and he struggled through his eleven-year career.

AGE	YRS	ML	W	L	PCT	ERA	G	GS	CG	IP	H	BB	SO	SHO	SV
18-19	45-46	11	45	65	0.409	4.88	267	107	47	1072	1130	493	290	6	17
(2 YRS MINUS		1	3	6	0.333	4.1	20	8	3	65	72	28	20	0	0
4 GAMES)		12	48	71	0.403	4.84	287	115	50	1137	1202	521	310	6	17

SCHMITZ, JOHN A. (JOHNNY)   BR TL 6'0" 170 lbs.
Born November 27, 1920, Wausau, Wi.
Played for Chicago (N) (1941-42, 1946-51), Brooklyn (1951-52), New York (A) (1952, 1953), Cincinnati (1952), Washington (1953-55), Boston (N) (1956), and Baltimore (1956)

Johnny Schmitz joined the Chicago Cubs on September 6, 1941, after spending most of the 1941 season with Milwaukee in the American Association. He spent a total of four years in the minors before joining the Cubs. Schmitz stayed with the major league club in 1942 until he was drafted into the Navy on August 2, 1942. He spent 1943 at Great Lakes where he was able to play for the base team during the summer. He was assigned to the South Pacific during 1944 but did not see any combat. His rank was specialist second class in athletics.

Schmitz indicated in a letter that he did not suffer any injuries during his time in the Navy (Schmitz letter, 1997). He was discharged on January 7, 1946. He returned to the Cubs in time for the 1946 season. At age twenty-five, he became one of the regulars in the starting rotation for the Cubs for the next five years. Schmitz led the National League in strikeouts during the 1946 season with 135. His winning percentage was not good because he pitched for Chicago Cubs teams that were not strong. However, his earned run average for 1946 and 1948 was under 2.65, and he won eighteen games in 1948. During his time with the Cubs, he was known as a "Dodger Killer." Between 1941 and 1950 he had almost twenty percent of the Cubs' victories against the Dodgers. That may be why the Dodgers traded for him in 1951. He also gave the Cardinals trouble during his career.

On the final day of the 1946 season, the Cubs went to St. Louis to play the Cardinals. Schmitz was in the hospital because of an infection in his right foot. He had contracted the infection months earlier while he was stationed in the South Pacific during the war. It had been dormant, but at this time it became a boil between this fourth and fifth toes of his right foot. The Cubs manager, Charlie Grimm, called the hospital and asked him to pitch the final game. Schmitz said, "They had to cut out part of my shoe so that the foot could kind of spread. The foot had been bandaged. In the sixth, I got a hit and drove in a run and when I hit second base that infection broke wide open. I felt a little funny in the seventh, and I told 'em to get somebody warmed up, but I finished the game" (Turner 1996, 213). He won the game, and because of the Cubs' win, the Cardinals and the Dodgers finished the 1946 season in a tie.

Starting with the trade to the Dodgers, Schmitz became part of a number of multiple-player deals during the balance of his career. The trade to the Dodgers involved eight players. The following year, after being sold to the Yankees, he was part of a deal that totaled five players. In 1953 he was sold back to the Yankees and then released to the Washington Senators. He had one of his better years with the Senators during the 1954 season. Again, a major deal involving nine players sent Schmitz to the Red Sox on November 8, 1955. The stay didn't last long as he was sold to the Baltimore Orioles on May 14, 1956. He closed his major league career at the end of the 1956 season. Schmitz's best and most productive years came from 1946 to 1950 with the Chicago Cubs following his return from the Navy.

AGE	YRS	ML	W	L	PCT	ERA	G	GS	CG	IP	H	BB	SO	SHO	SV
22-24	43-45	13	93	114	0.449	3.55	366	235	86	1813	1766	757	746	17	19
		3	22	27	0.449	3.09	80	54	20	404	356	171	220	4	6
		16	115	141	0.449	3.47	446	289	106	2217	2122	928	966	21	25

SCHUMACHER, HAROLD H. (HAL)   BR TR 6'0" 190 lbs.
Born November 23, 1910, Hinckley, N.Y. — Died April 21, 1993, Cooperstown, N.Y.
Played for New York (N) (1931–42, 1946)

Hal Schumacher made it to the majors after only five weeks in the minors. He had signed with Giants out of St. Lawrence University and was sent to Bridgeport in the Eastern League. Five weeks later he made his debut with the Giants on April 15, 1931. He would spend his entire career, which lasted thirteen seasons, with the Giants. In 1933, after spending one year as a spot starter and reliever, Schumacher became part of the regular Giant rotation. Dick Bartell said, "Hal Schumacher was a real workhorse for us on the mound. He was a winner that threw an overhand curve that broke straight down and his sinker gave us infielders plenty of business" (Van Blair 1994, 9). He teamed with Carl Hubbell to help the Giants win the National League pennant in 1933, 1936, and 1937. The Giants were World Champions in 1933 with Schumacher winning one game. Between 1931 and 1942, Hubbell and Schumacher were one of the most effective righty/lefty pitching duos in major league baseball history. Together they won 358 games in this period. Harry Danning, Giants' catcher, said, "Hal Schumacher had a great fastball and was a low-ball pitcher. He also had a good fast curveball; his used to break a foot" (Van Blair 1994, 43). In addition to his pitching, Schumacher was also a good hitter. He hit fifteen home runs during his playing career.

Schumacher suffered a shoulder injury that caused him problems during his career. He had an operation on his shoulder in 1938 to help with the problem. With the arm problems came a loss of some of the speed on his fastball. He adjusted and developed a palm ball. He was not as effective after the injury, but he became a steady and dependable pitcher. After winning nineteen, twenty-three, and nineteen games in his first three years as a starter, Schumacher won eleven, twelve, or thirteen games in each of the next seven years, the years up to the time he entered military service. He applied for a commission in the Navy after the end of the 1942 season. He received it and enlisted in the Naval Reserves in December 1942 as a lieutenant. He reported for duty on January 7, 1943. He was sent to Chapel Hill, North Carolina, for Naval indoctrination at the preflight school. When it was completed he was transferred from there to the Naval Training School near Memphis, Tennessee, in February 1943. He then was sent that fall to Lambert Field, Missouri. Schumacher's sea duty was aboard an aircraft carrier. He was the athletic and physical conditioning officer. He spent 1945 in this duty. He returned to the States in the late summer of 1945. He was expecting to be discharged at Newport News, Virginia; however, the discharge did not come until November 8, 1945.

He returned to the Giants for the 1946 season. His age (35) and his three years away from major league baseball had taken its toll. In 1946, Schumacher's role was that of a spot starter and reliever. He won four and lost four games that year. He closed his playing career with the 1946 season. After retirement he helped found the Adirondack Bat Company. He remained with the company until 1967.

AGE	YRS	ML	W	L	PCT	ERA	G	GS	CG	IP	H	BB	SO	SHO	SV
32-34	43-45	13	158	120	0.568	3.36	391	329	138	2481	2424	902	906	29	7
		3	32	30	0.516	3.67	88	75	28	557	544	238	205	5	2
		16	190	150	0.559	3.42	479	404	166	3038	2968	1140	1111	34	9

SHOUN, CLYDE M.   BL TL 6' 1"   188 lbs.

Born March 20, 1912, Mountain City, Tn. — Died March 20, 1968, Mountain Home, Tn. Played for Chicago (N) (1935-37), St. Louis (N) (1938-42), Cincinnati (1942-44, 1946-47), Boston (N) (1947-49), and Chicago (A) (1949)

Clyde Shoun got a five-game trial with the Cubs in his first year of professional baseball in 1935. He spent most of that season at Birmingham in the Southern League. He got another four-game trial in 1936 and made the major league team to stay in 1937. He was used primarily in relief that season, as he would be throughout his career. On April 16, 1938, he became part of the headline deal that sent Dizzy Dean from the Cardinals to the Cubs. He led the National League in saves in 1939 with nine for the Cardinals. He also led the National League in games pitched in both 1939 and 1940.

During 1940 he also became a spot starter. He won thirteen games and pitched in 197 innings in 1940. After being sold to the Reds during the 1942 season, Shoun had two of his best years in 1943 and 1944. In 1943 he pitched in relief. He won a total of fourteen games (thirteen wins in relief) and lost five. The thirteen wins in relief constituted the second highest number of wins at that time (currently it ranks 16th). In 1944 he became a starter as well as a reliever. He won thirteen games that season and pitched in 202 innings. As a starter on May 15, 1944, Shoun pitched a no-hitter. He missed a perfect game when he walked the opposing pitcher, Jim Tobin, in the third inning. He had been accepted by the Navy on March 22, 1944, at Fort Oglethorpe, Georgia. However, he wasn't called to active duty until January 1945. He was stationed at Great Lakes for his basic training. It was thought that he would be able to play baseball, but his stay was not long at Great Lakes.

In April 1945, he was transferred from Great Lakes to another base. The assignments led him to the South Pacific. Bob Feller, who was the manager of the Great Lakes team, commented why his stay did not last long at Great Lakes. Feller said, "We had Clyde Shoun, too. He was a little bit of a screwball. He gave me some lip, and I threw him off the ball club. I sent him out to OGU (outgoing unit) and they sent him to the South Pacific. No bullshit, either; tomorrow, pack your sea bag. Zoom!" (Mead 1985, 194). He was stationed in Hawaii in October 1945 and took part in the Navy's Little World Series at that time. Shoun was discharged in January 1946. He rejoined the Reds in time for the 1946 season. The return proved to be a rough time. Shoun had only one win and six losses with no saves during the 1946 season. After being sold to the Braves in June 1947, he had two good years as a middle reliever. He closed his career the following season after being sold to the Chicago White Sox.

AGE	YRS	ML	W	L	PCT	ERA	G	GS	CG	IP	H	BB	SO	SHO	SV
33	45	14	73	59	0.553	3.91	454	85	34	1287	1325	404	483	3	29
		1	8	6	0.571	3.67	36	8	4	129	125	35	41	0	3
		15	81	65	0.555	3.89	490	93	38	1416	1450	439	524	3	32

SPAHN, WARREN E.   BL TL 6' 0" 172 lbs.
Born April 23, 1921, Buffalo, N.Y. — Died November 24, 2003, Broken Arrow, OK.
Played for Boston (N) (1942, 1946–52), Milwaukee (N) (1953–64), New York (N) (1965), and San Francisco (1965)

Warren Spahn was one of the best left-handed pitchers of all time. His career was interrupted early by his service in World War II. He signed with the Boston Braves in 1940 at age nineteen and was sent to Bradford in the Pony League. He spent the following season at Evansville, Indiana, in the III League. On April 19, 1942, he made his major league debut. He only lasted four games before he was sent down to Hartford in the Eastern League. He was successful at both Evansville and Hartford. At Evansville he led the league in wins, and at both places, his earned run average was under 2.00. That four-game experience would be his only major league time before he joined the Army. He was inducted on October 10, 1942. He spent some of his early time in the Army at Camp Chaffee. However, it was not long before he was sent to the European Theater. He was a member of the 14th Armored Division, 276th Engineer Combat Battalion, 1257c Engineer Battalion. He went overseas in August 1944 and stayed there until May 1946.

Spahn's movement in Europe in late 1944 put him in Belgium. He was there on December 16, 1944, when the Germans started their counteroffensive against the Allied troops. He had the rank of staff sergeant at that time. The Germans tried to impersonate American troops. Spahn said, "The Germans had our equipment, our uniforms, even our dog tags." He also said there was one thing they lacked: a knowledge of baseball. He went on to say, "Our password used to be something like, 'who's the second baseman for the Bums?' They wouldn't know who the 'Bums' were. I used to pity any guy in our outfit who wasn't a baseball fan because he would be in deep trouble" (Gilbert 1992, 157). The Allies rebuffed the Germans by the first of January 1945 and were again moving toward Germany. Again Spahn was in the forefront of the action. He saw action in the Battle of Ardennas, the Rhine crossing, and the battle for Central Germany.

On March 7, he was with the advance troop that arrived at the Remagan Bridge on the Rhine River before the Germans could blow it up. Because they were able to take the bridge, the

Allies were able to make a beachhead on the east side of the Rhine. This helped shorten the war in Europe by several months. Spahn received a battlefield commission because of his bravery and leadership during this period. He continued to be stationed at the Remagan Bridge for several days. On March 17, 1945, he and a squad of troops were preparing to go on guard duty on the bridge. His duty was to start at 4:00. At 3:59 he stopped to talk to a fellow officer before taking up his position. While they talked, the bridge collapsed. The strain of the traffic of equipment and men traveling over it for ten days was too much. Spahn said, "The rivets just popped out of that bridge. They sounded like machine gun fire." He continued, "I felt like a pretty lucky guy and I guess that luck followed me through my baseball career" (Gilbert 1997, 171). If Spahn had been any earlier in arriving at the bridge, he could have been a casualty. He did suffer a shrapnel wound during the fighting. He received the Purple Heart because of his wound, and he also received the Bronze Star for bravery.

After the German surrender, Spahn spent several more months in Germany with the Army of Occupation. He replaced a fellow officer who had been killed. After the surrender he was also able to pitch for a team at Heidelberg, Germany. In four games he struck out seventy-three batters, not too much of a test for someone of Spahn's ability. Spahn was not discharged until June 2, 1946. He missed spring training and the first part of the 1946 season. He did join the Braves when he was released. He made the most of the opportunity by winning eight games that year with an earned run average of 2.94 in the partial season.

Spahn was twenty-five years old when he was released from the Army and when he won his first major league game. In 1947 he became part of the Braves regular rotation. This was a position he would retain until 1964. He won twenty-one games in 1947. This would start a string of years in which he would win at least twenty games in thirteen of the next seventeen seasons. His success was outstanding. He led the National League in wins in eight seasons, in winning percentage once, in earned run average three times, in starts twice, in complete games nine times (his percentage of complete games is second only to Bob Feller during his era), in innings pitched four times, in bases on balls once, in strikeouts in four seasons, and in shutouts four times. His total wins (363) places him fifth all-time; he ranks eighth in innings pitched and sixth in shutouts, respectively. The 363 wins is the most in baseball history by a left-hander. He holds the record for the most wins by a thirty-eight-year-old pitcher (21), a thirty-nine-year-old pitcher (21), a forty-year-old pitcher (21), a forty-one-year-old pitcher (18), and a forty-two-year-old pitcher (23).

In 1963, at age forty-two, Spahn won twenty-three games and lost seven. He had an earned run average of 2.60 that year. He started thirty-three games and pitched twenty-two complete games. Spahn and Lou Burdette are the best righty/lefty combination in baseball history. Between 1951 and 1963 the duo won 443 games and lost 278 for the Braves. Other baseball players recognized Spahn's ability. Dick Groat said, "Warren Spahn was the greatest pitcher of my era..." (Peary 1994, 564). Stan Musial added, "The best pitchers were Bob Feller and Warren Spahn" (Broeg 1964, 264). Musial went on to say, "He was one of the great athletes as well as the best National League pitcher of my era" (Broeg 1964, 289). After an off season for the Braves in 1964, Spahn was sold to the New York Mets. Spahn rejoined Casey Stengel who had been his manager in Boston in 1942. Spahn said, "I played for Casey Stengel before and after he was a genius" (Hanks et al. 1989, 304). Yogi Berra, who also joined the Mets to catch Spahn, said, "I don't know if we're the oldest battery, but we're certainly the ugliest" (Dickson 1991, 42). Spahn closed his major league career with the San Francisco Giants in 1965 after being released by the Mets and signed by the Giants. He was forty-four years old in his last major league season. He was very successful during his career. Discussing his philosophy of pitching, he said, "Hitting is timing. Pitching is upsetting timing" (Dickson 1991, 404). Based on his record, it is apparent that this simple outlook was correct. He won 363 games, the most ever by a left-hander.

Many have asked him if would have won 400 games had he not served in World War II. The probable answer is yes. However, Spahn said, "People say that my absence from the big leagues may have cost me a chance to win 400 games. But I don't know about that. I matured a lot in three years, and I think I was better equipped to handle major league hitters at 25 than I was at 22. Also, I pitched until I was 44. Maybe I wouldn't have been able to do that otherwise" (Pietrusza 2000, 1062).

AGE	YRS	ML	W	L	PCT	ERA	G	GS	CG	IP	H	BB	SO	SHO	SV
22-25	43-46	21	363	245	0.597	3.09	750	665	382	5244	4830	1434	2583	63	29
(4 YRS MINUS		3	56	36	0.609	3.01	115	106	64	836	761	244	372	16	3
24 GAMES)		24	419	281	0.599	3.08	865	771	446	6080	5591	1678	2955	79	32

TRUCKS, VIRGIL O.   BR TR 5' 11"   198 lbs.
Born April 26, 1917, Birmingham, Al.
Played for Detroit (1941–43, 1945-52, 1956), St Louis (A) (1953), Chicago (A) (1953–55), Kansas City (1957–58), and New York (A) (1958)

Virgil Trucks started his professional career with a bang. The Tigers signed him in 1938 as a nineteen year old, and he was assigned to Andalusia in the Alabama-Florida league. During the 1938 season, Trucks pitched in 273 innings and won twenty-five games. He also had an earned run average of 1.25 that season. His two biggest feats were pitching two no-hitters and striking out 418 batters. He averaged more than one-and-a-half strikeouts per inning, a major achievement in anybody's league. He would go on to pitch two additional no-hitters during his four-year minor league career. He joined the Tigers at the end of the 1941 season and pitched in one game without a decision. The following season he became part of the Tigers' regular rotation. His first two seasons (1942 and 1943) before his service in World War II were successful. He won fourteen and sixteen games and had an earned run average of 2.74 and 2.84, respectively.

He enlisted in the Navy in February 1944. Trucks had heard of the baseball program that was being run at Great Lakes by Mickey Cochrane. He contacted Cochrane about joining his team. Cochrane gave Trucks the directions on what to do to make this happen. Trucks got his papers transferred from Birmingham, Alabama, to Chicago. He went to Chicago, and two days later, he got the notice he was to report to the Great Lakes Naval Training Station. He took his boot training there and stayed during the summer of 1944 to pitch for the base team. The team won forty-eight games and lost two. Trucks won ten and lost none that summer. In the fall of 1944, Trucks was home in Birmingham on leave. He got an order canceling his leave and ordering him to report back to Great Lakes. He then flew out of Chicago the next day, destination Hawaii. He, along with two other ballplayers, flew "high priority" during the trip. They bumped other military personnel, including officers, to make the trip as quickly as possible. The reason? Admiral Nimitz had been enduring the Army beating the Navy in baseball for some time, and he wanted a team in Hawaii that could win a challenge series. Bill Dickey was given the task of rounding up the best baseball players in the Navy and getting them to Hawaii. They were brought from the States, Australia, and other places. They were assigned to the 14th Naval District. When the players were in place, Nimitz challenged the Army to the Army/Navy Pacific World Series. There were 18,000 fans in the stands for the first game. Trucks pitched and won that game, and the Navy beat the Army eight games to two.

The series took place in October 1944. After the series was completed, the Navy, in early 1945, divided the players into two teams and sent them out to entertain the troops on the islands of the South Pacific. Some of the islands were so small that an airplane could not land. On those islands, they would land on an island nearby and use a landing craft for the final part of the journey. They went to Kwajalein, Eniwetok, Peleliu, Tinian, Saipan, Roi-Namur, Ulithi, and Guam. Trucks was left on Guam, along with Johnny Vander Meer and Del Ennis, after the teams were broken up. The rest of the players were disbursed among other Pacific Islands. While he was in the Marianas, he was attached to the Fleet Recreation Center and was in charge of four softball fields. Trucks commented about playing before the troops. He said, "The soldiers loved it" (*Sarasota Herald-Tribune*. 1997. "Baseball Had to Wait for Pitcher". December 8). They had other duties in addition to baseball. Trucks remembers standing guard at night on a Pacific Island when the remaining Japanese soldiers, who had not given up, would slip down from the hills and steal food and clothing from the American bases. Trucks had problems with his knee while stationed on Guam. He said, "I had a bad knee for a long time and the problem recurred on Guam. The war was about over and I wanted to get out, so I turned in to sick bay in Guam and stayed there about three weeks, a month, and they decided to send me back to Hawaii. I stayed there a few weeks and they shipped me back to San Francisco and then to the Norman Naval Station" (Goldstein 1980, 260). Trucks thought his discharge would come through as early as July 1945; however, the paperwork was delayed until the end of September. He was discharged on September 27, 1945.

There was not a baseball team at Norman. He had found someone to play catch with and did a lot of running during this time. As soon as he was released, he boarded a train to St. Louis and was immediately started by the Tigers against the Browns. Trucks pitched five innings during the game. The Tigers won as they were on their way to winning the American League pennant, but Trucks did not get the victory. Trucks did get two starts in the 1945 World Series. He started game two and won the game four to one. It was the only time a starting pitcher has won a World Series game without winning a game during the regular season. Trucks had continued success with the Tigers except in 1950 and 1952. In 1950 he was limited to pitching in seven games because of a sore arm.

After a comeback in 1951, Trucks suffered in 1952 by pitching for the last-place Tigers. The year was a paradox. Trucks won five games while losing nineteen. However, during that year, he pitched two no-hitters. This would bring his career total to six. The two no-hitters in 1952 were both 1–0 games, the first on May 15th against the Senators and the second on August 25 against the Yankees. In 1953 Trucks was traded to the St. Louis Browns and then on to the Chicago White Sox. With the White Sox, Trucks would regain his pitching success. He enjoyed three good years as a starter with the White Sox. After several more moves, he closed out his major league career with the Yankees in 1958. In an interview with the *Sarasota Herald-Tribune* in the December 8, 1997, edition, Trucks said, "I had just finished a minor league season and heard on the radio that Pearl Harbor was attacked. I didn't know what the outcome was going to be, but I thought then that it ended my career and a lot of other ballplayers...." He continued, "I don't regret the two years I spent in the service—even though from a baseball standpoint it cost me two prime years. If Americans didn't serve, it might have cost us a lot more. I was just happy to get back. I am very proud that I was able to serve my country. I think if you ask every ballplayer that was in the war they would say the same thing" (*Sarasota Herald-Tribune*. 1997. "Baseball Had to Wait for Pitcher". December 8).

AGE	YRS	ML	W	L	PCT	ERA	G	GS	CG	IP	H	BB	SO	SHO	SV
25-26	44-45	17	177	135	0.567	3.39	517	328	124	2682	2416	1088	1534	35	30
(2 YRS MINUS		1	27	20	0.574	3.33	64	49	21	390	357	138	236	5	2
1 GAME)		18	204	155	0.568	3.38	581	377	145	3072	2773	1226	1770	40	32

VANDER MEER, JOHN S. (JOHNNY)   BB TL 6' 1" 190 lbs.
Born November 2, 1914, Prospect Park, N.J. — Died October 6, 1997, Tampa, Fla.
Played for Cincinnati (1937–1943, 1946–1949), Chicago (N) (1950), and Cleveland (1951)

You mention the name Johnny Vander Meer and most baseball fans can tell you that this is the man who threw back-to-back no-hitters. Vander Meer had originally signed with the Brooklyn Dodgers. They sent him to Dayton in the Mid-Atlantic League for his first season in 1933. It wasn't until three years later at Durham in the Piedmont League that he really excelled. *The Sporting News* named him the minor league player of the year in 1936, and the Cincinnati Reds paid $10,000 to the Dodgers for his contract. He made his major league debut in April 1937 but only stayed with the Reds for part of the year before being sent out to Syracuse. In 1938 he established himself as part of the Reds' regular starting rotation. It was in 1938 that he threw his consecutive no-hitters. On June 11, 1938, he beat the Braves by the score of three to nothing. Four days later he beat the Dodgers six to nothing. In the following start he threw three innings of hitless ball. In total, he went twenty-one and one-third consecutive innings without allowing a hit. The game on June 15, 1938, in Brooklyn had another distinction. It was the first night game ever played in New York City.

The next two years were difficult for Vander Meer. As he was pitching in Pittsburgh on a rainy day, his feet slipped and he heard something pop in his shoulder. He had torn the muscles underneath his shoulder. He struggled for the balance of 1939 and was finally sent down to Indianapolis in the American Association in 1940 to try to work out his problems. He was at Indianapolis from June 28 to August 29. He returned to the Reds in time to help with their pennant drive. He won three games in 1940. His recovery was complete, and he returned to the regular rotation in 1941.

During the next three years (1941–1943), Vander Meer led the National League in strikeouts each year. His win/loss record was not great, but he had a good earned run average each year. Vander Meer had been 4-F for a while but was reexamined on November 23, 1943. He was approved for service and was inducted into the Navy on January 27, 1944, at Newark, New Jersey, and reported for duty on March 3, 1944. He had worked as in investigator for Curtiss-Wright Aeronautical Corp. in Clifton, New Jersey, from the close of the season until he was drafted. He was sent to Sampson, New York, Naval Training Station for basic training. He remained at Sampson until that fall.

During the summer of 1944 he pitched for the base baseball team. The team was strong enough to beat the Red Sox and Indians during that summer. He got his orders to go overseas on September 1, 1944. He was sent along several other major league players to Hawaii. He would spend a total of about five months in Hawaii. The Navy was getting together a team to challenge the Army. The Army/Navy Pacific World Series took place in October 1944. Vander Meer pitched the second game of the series for the Navy and won the game. The Navy took the series eight games to two. Following that series, in January 1945, the Navy team was broken up into two teams of fourteen players and sent out to the islands of the South Pacific to entertain the troops. They would play baseball games for the regular soldiers. During those times, they played on Kwajalein, Eniwetok, Peleliu, Tinian, Saipan, Roi-Namur, Ulithi, and Guam. After the tour of the islands was complete, Vander Meer ended up stationed on Guam. He spent most of the rest of 1945 in the South Pacific. In October 1945, he was still in Guam. He was sent back to the States and was discharged from the Navy on December 20, 1945. He returned to the Reds for the 1946 season. He commented on returning to major league baseball. He said, "Nineteen forty-six was the hardest year for most of the guys from the physical end of it. We had to play another year just to get back into shape. We had to build up our stamina again. It was the same thing with our coordination" (Gilbert 1992, 266).

Johnny Vander Meer was not the same pitcher after the war that he had been before the war. The three years before the war, he led the National League in strikeouts. The three years after the war, he struck out over one hundred batters only one time. The three years before the war, his earned run average had averaged 2.71. The three years after, it averaged 3.66. Things were not the same. He was sold to the Chicago Cubs in 1950 after a poor season with the Reds in 1949. He then closed out his career with the Indians in 1951 by pitching in one game. Vander Meer was a good pitcher before the war. Stan Musial said, "One of the toughest I ever hit against. An extremely hard thrower and wild" (Broeg 1964, 290). He will always be known as the pitcher who pitched two consecutive no-hitters. He is the only pitcher in major league baseball history to perform that feat.

AGE	YRS	ML	W	L	PCT	ERA	G	GS	CG	IP	H	BB	SO	SHO	SV
29-30	44-45	13	119	121	0.496	3.44	346	285	131	2105	1799	1132	1294	30	2
		2	26	27	0.491	3.22	64	62	31	462	389	214	267	8	0
		15	145	148	0.495	3.4	410	347	162	2567	2188	1346	1561	38	2

WARNEKE, LONNIE (LON)   BR TR 6' 2"   185 lbs.
Born March 28, 1909, Mt. Ida, Ar. — Died June 23, 1976, Hot Springs, Ar.
Played for Chicago (N) (1930–36, 1942–43, 1945) and St. Louis (N) (1937–42)

Lon Warneke had experience with two major league organizations, the St. Louis Cardinals and the Chicago Cubs. He was originally signed by the Cardinals in 1928 after he had made the trip from Mt. Ida, Arkansas, to Houston, Texas, to take part in a Cardinal tryout camp. He was assigned to Laurel, Mississippi, in the Cotton States League. He was not successful that year and left the Cardinals organization. The following season he played for Alexandra, also in the Cotton States League, and was successful. Following that season he was sold to the Chicago Cubs for $100. He pitched in one game for the Cubs at the start of the 1930 season and was then sent down to Reading in the International League. He rejoined the Cubs to stay in 1931. After a year in the bullpen, Warneke joined the regular starting rotation. He would retain that position until he was traded to the Cardinals in time for the 1937 season. In 1932, he led the National League in wins with twenty-two, winning percentage with .786, earned run average with 2.37, and shutouts with four.

His first full year as a starter would be his best. He helped the Cubs win the pennant that year. In 1933, he pitched four innings in the first All-Star game. He allowed one run in a losing cause. The Cubs won the pennant again in 1935, and Warneke was a pitching leader. In the World Series that year, he started two games and relieved in one. He won both of his starts and had an earned run average of 0.54 in sixteen innings. On October 8, 1936, he was traded to the St. Louis Cardinals. For the next five years, he was in the Cardinals' regular starting rotation. His best year with the Redbirds was 1941 when he won seventeen games and pitched a no-hitter on August 30, 1941.

The Cardinals sold him back to the Cubs on July 8, 1942, in order to reduce their payroll and to make room for younger players. Warneke was making $15,000 a year and was the highest paid player on the Cardinal roster. After finishing strong with the Cubs in 1942, Warneke struggled in 1943 and was used as a spot starter and reliever. After having his preinduction physical on March 23, he entered the Army in April 1944 at age thirty-five. His release date from the Army is unclear. By the spring of 1945, he was in charge of the Naval Ordinance Plant team at Camden, Arkansas. On June 5, 1945, he applied for reinstatement into major league baseball. He was listed on the voluntary retired list as a civilian employee at an Army camp. He was reinstated and made his first start for the Cubs on July 18, 1945. He pitched in nine games that summer but did not appear in the 1945 World Series.

He retired from playing baseball following the 1945 season. With the help of P.K. Wrigley, Cubs owner, Warneke changed his career. He became an umpire. Wrigley helped get him a job in the Pacific Coast League in 1946. He remained there until he was promoted to the National League for the 1949 season. He umpired in the National League for seven seasons (1949–1955). He was one of the umpires in the 1952 All-Star game and in the 1954 World Series. This feat makes him the only man to have played and umpired in both the World Series and the All-Star game. Warneke was a good pitcher for several years but not as good an umpire. Stan Musial said, "The old Arkansas Hummingbird was a real fine pitcher with good control and a dry sense of humor. As an umpire, Lon seemed indecisive" (Broeg 1964, 291).

AGE	YRS	ML	W	L	PCT	ERA	G	GS	CG	IP	H	BB	SO	SHO	SV
35	44	15	193	121	0.615	3.18	445	343	192	2783	2726	739	1140	31	13
		1	5	5	0.5	3.18	20	10	4	85	80	15	25	0	0
		16	198	126	0.611	3.18	465	353	196	2868	2806	754	1165	31	13

WHITE, HAROLD G. (HAL)   BL TR 5' 10"   165 lbs.
Born March 18, 1919, Utica, N.Y. — Died April 21, 2001, Venice, Fl.
Played for Detroit (1941-43, 1946-52), St. Louis (A) (1953), and St. Louis (N) (1953-54)

Hal White was promoted to the Detroit Tigers for the start of the 1941 season after winning sixteen and losing four at Buffalo in the International League. He got into only four games that year and spent the balance of the season in Buffalo. He became one of the Tigers' starters in 1942. He had a great start to his career as a starter that year. White said, "I pitched back to back shutouts in April, my first major league starts as a pitcher. In my first start in 1942 I shut out the St. Louis Browns 4-0. In my second major league start I shut out the Chicago White Sox 9-0" (White letter 1998). It would be difficult to do better at the beginning of a career. His record for his rookie year was twelve wins and twelve losses with an earned run average of 2.91. He slumped to a record of seven wins and twelve losses, and his earned run average went up almost a half a run per game. Following the 1943 season, White was drafted into military service. He said, "I was drafted into the U.S. Navy on December 23, 1943. Had to report to the Sampson Naval Base in Geneva, N.Y." (White letter 1998). He remained at Sampson during the summer of 1944 and pitched for the Sampson, New York, Naval Training Center team.

On September 1, 1944, he got his orders to go overseas. He was part of the players who were sent to Hawaii in the fall of 1944 to play the Army in the Army/Navy Pacific World Series. In early 1945, after completion of the "World Series," White was one of the twenty-eight players the Navy shipped to the smaller islands of the South Pacific to play baseball to entertain the troops. They played on Kwajalein, Eniwetok, Peleliu, Tinian, Saipan, Guam, Roi-Namur, and Ulithi. The mission was to last for six weeks, but after it was completed, the teams were broken up and the players shipped to different islands to run recreation programs. In some cases there was no field and they had to use a bulldozer to clear and level a playing field. White said, "When I arrived at Guam on November of 1944 the island was secured but there were still a few Japanese soldiers hiding in the hills but were later captured or turned themselves in" (White letter 1998).

While he was in the war zone, White did not see any combat. He was discharged in January 1946. He rejoined the Tigers in time for the 1946 season. However, his role had changed. Before the war he was a starting pitcher. After the war he spent the balance of his career in the bullpen. He struggled following the war and spent most of the 1949 season back in the minors. He closed his career with the St. Louis Browns and the St. Louis Cardinals in 1953 and 1954 without much success. The war changed his opportunity. He said, "I won nineteen games in my first two years. I think I missed the prime time being in the service but I'm proud to have served" (White letter 1998).

AGE	YRS	ML	W	L	PCT	ERA	G	GS	CG	IP	H	BB	SO	SHO	SV
25-26	44-45	12	46	54	0.46	3.78	336	67	23	920	875	450	349	7	25
		2	12	15	0.444	3.34	56	28	10	253	244	108	98	3	3
		14	58	69	0.457	3.69	392	95	33	1173	1119	558	447	10	28

WILHELM, JAMES H. (HOYT)   BR TR 6' 0"   190 lbs.
Born July 26, 1923, Huntersville, N.C. — Died August 24, 2002, Sarasota, Fl.

Played for New York (N) (1952–56), St. Louis (N) (1957), Cleveland (1957–58), Baltimore (1958–62), Chicago (A) (1963–68), California (1969), Atlanta (1969–70, 1971), Chicago (N) (1970), and Los Angeles (1971–72)

Hoyt Wilhelm's major league career did not begin until 1951, so his career numbers have not been adjusted for the time he spent in the military. He is included because his name was included on a list provided by the Baseball Hall of Fame as a major leaguer who served in World War II. Wilhelm signed a professional baseball contract out of high school and was assigned to Mooresville, North Carolina, in the North Carolina State League for the 1942 season. He was drafted into the Army following the 1942 season and spent the next three years in the military. He was an infantryman in the European Theater with the rank of staff sergeant.

During the winter of 1944–45, he was stationed in Belgium. He was part of the American Army that was attacked by the Germans as they made their push during the Battle of the Bulge. Wilhelm was wounded during the battle and received the Purple Heart. The wound left him with a permanently crooked neck. He was discharged by the Army in time to return to the Mooresville team for the 1946 season.

Wilhelm was successful when he returned from the service. He won over twenty games the first two years back. With that success he was drafted by the New York Giants in 1948. He moved up in the organization of the New York Giants and continued to pitch well. He was a starting pitcher during this time. However, it took him six full years in the minors before he was promoted because Leo Durocher didn't like knuckleball pitchers. Wilhelm had developed the knuckleball while he was in high school. He said, "I learned the knuckler myself. Fooled around with it in high school. I used to read about Freddie Fitzsimmons and Dutch Leonard, but nobody showed me anything. I developed it myself" (Pietrusza 2000, 1225).

Wilhelm was finally promoted to the Giants for the 1952 season at age twenty-eight. Leo Durocher converted him from a starting pitcher to a reliever. He had a very successful rookie year. He led the National League in winning percentage, earned run average, games pitched, and relief wins. However, he did not win the rookie of the year as the Giants did not win the pennant. Also in his rookie year, he hit a home run in his first major league at-bat. He would play for twenty more years and never hit another home ru Wilhelm was a very bad batter. His career batting average was .088, the lowest of any player in the Hall of Fame. After having another very good year in 1954 and helping the Giants to the World Championship, Wilhelm's career slipped. He was not as effective the next two years and was traded to the Cardinals in February, 1957. After part of 1957 in St. Louis and parts of 1957-1958 in Cleveland, he was released to the Baltimore Orioles on waivers on August 23, 1958.

The sale to Baltimore would add another chapter to Wilhelm's career. Paul Richards, Baltimore's manager, needed starting pitching. He converted Wilhelm to a starting pitcher. In 1959 he started twenty-seven of the thirty-two games in which he pitched. He had a good year. He won fifteen games and led the American League in earned run average. Wilhelm is one of the few pitchers to lead both leagues in earned run average. He also pitched a no-hit game against the Yankees during that season. He continued spot starting in 1960, and by 1961 he was back in the bullpen full time. During the three years (1958-1960), Wilhelm started forty-eight of the fifty-two games he would start during his career.

Wilhelm was very durable. He pitched in forty-six to seventy-three games per season from 1961 to 1970. He was forty-seven years old during the 1970 season. The knuckleball was easy on the arm, so he could continue to pitch after most other players of his age were long gone. He caused lots of batters problems during his career. Ted Williams is quoted as saying, "Wilhelm had a sure-strike knuckler, then a real good knuckler, then with two strikes, a real bastard of a knuckler, dancing in your face. The closest thing to an unhittable ball I ever saw" (Williams 1988, 200). Billy Goodman added, "But if I had to pick myself one guy that I wouldn't want to hit against when he was right, it would be Hoyt Wilhelm" (Honig 1976, 226).

Wilhelm is considered to be one of the best relief pitchers of all time. When he retired at age forty-nine, he held the record for the most games pitched and most relief wins and was the first pitcher to reach 200 saves. However, during the twenty-one years of his career, he never did lead the league in saves in any one season. Also during the course of his twenty-one year career, he was given his unconditional release on nine different occasions. Quite a record for someone elected to the Hall of Fame. Another record that Wilhelm holds is being the last World War II veteran to be playing in the major leagues. His career came to an end in 1972.

AGE	YRS	ML	W	L	PCT	ERA	G	GS	CG	IP	H	BB	SO	SHO	SV
19-21	43-45	21	143	122	0.54	2.52	1070	52	20	2254	1757	778	1610	5	227
		0	0	0	0	0	0	0	0	0	0	0	0	0	0
		21	143	122	0.54	2.52	1070	52	20	2254	1757	778	1610	5	227

WYNN, EARLY

BB TR 6' 0" 190 lbs.

Born January 6, 1920, Hartford, Al. — Died April 4, 1999, Venice, Fl.
Played for Washington (1939-44, 1946-48), Cleveland (1949-57, 1963), and Chicago (A) (1958-62)

Early Wynn signed a professional baseball contract with the Washington Senators at age sixteen. He started playing at Sanford in the Florida State League in 1937 and spent another two years in the minors before getting a trial with the Senators at the end of the 1939 season. He made his debut on September 13, 1939, and pitched in three games that year. Then he pitched another two years on the farm before getting a second chance in 1941. He pitched in five games in 1941. In 1942 Wynn became part of the regular starting rotation and kept that position until he entered the military in late 1944. After a good year in 1943 (he won 18 games), Wynn struggled during the 1944 season before he left for the Army.

In 1944 he won eight games and lost seventeen as the Senators finished last. He entered the Army on August 21, 1944, at the Armored Replacement Training Center at Fort Knox, Kentucky. By the fall of 1945 Wynn had been transferred to the Pacific. He was stationed in the Philippines. While stationed there, he played on a baseball team managed by Kirby Higbe. Wynn played shortstop as well as pitcher. They played an exhibition game in Rizal Stadium in Manila. It had a hole in the outfield fence where an American tank had come through to get at a Japanese machine gun position which had been located in the dugout. While they were in

Manila, "Manager Higbe requisitioned the living quarters designated for the umpires, and from there he and Senators' pitcher Early Wynn sold Filipinos beer Higbe got from the Seabees" (Turner 1996, 115).

Wynn was not discharged until July 5, 1946. He rejoined the Senators in the middle of the 1946 season, winning eight games while losing five. He continued to be part of the Senators' starting rotation. The year 1948 was a disastrous season for Wynn. He won only eight games and lost nineteen with an earned run average of 5.82. Then, on December 14, 1948, Wynn got his biggest break. He was traded to the Cleveland Indians. He had struggled pitching for the Senators, who were usually in the second division. His record up to this time was seventy-two wins and eighty-seven losses. After he arrived at Cleveland, he worked with Indians pitching coach, Mel Harder, who taught Wynn a number of things about pitching. Up to this time, Wynn had been strictly a fastball pitcher. Harder showed Wynn how to throw a curve, a knuckleball, a slider, and a change-up. He went from winning forty percent of his games to winning over sixty percent. He became part of the Indians' pitching staff that had the best four-man rotation of the era, featuring Wynn, Bob Feller, Bob Lemon, and Mike Garcia. Wynn was part of the 1954 Indians that won 111 games and finished eight games ahead of the Yankees. He continued to be a dominant force for the Indians until 1956.

In 1957, Wynn had an off year and, at age thirty-seven, was traded to the Chicago White Sox on December 4, 1957. He rebounded in 1959 to help lead the White Sox to their first pennant in forty years. He won twenty-two games for the Sox that year. He remained with the White Sox until November 20, 1962. He closed out that season with 299 wins, one short of the coveted 300. The Indians signed him in June 1963 to give him a chance to get the 300th win, and he got his one additional win on July 13, 1963. He ended his playing career that year with the 300 wins at age forty-three after twenty-three years in the majors.

During his career, he led the American League in wins twice, losses once, earned run average once (although in 1954 the Indian pitchers Garcia, Lemon and Wynn ranked 1-2-3 in the League), innings pitched three times, and strikeouts twice. Wynn was known as a tough competitor. His reputation was he would knock down his own mother if she crowded the plate. Mickey Mantle said that Early Wynn was "so mean he'd knock you down in the dugout" (Pietrusza 2000, 1260). Vic Power said, "Wynn was the toughest pitcher for me. He was too smart. He'd find a batter's weakness" (Peary 1994, 262). Wynn's attitude was the batter was the enemy. He said, "A pitcher had to look at the hitter as his mortal enemy. A pitcher will never be a big winner until he hates batters" (Dickson 1991, 482). This competitive attitude was also shown when someone asked him about retiring when he was still pitching in his forties. He said, "Somebody will have to come out and take the uniform off me, and the guy who comes after it better bring help" (Nemec and Palmer 1993, 257).

AGE	YRS	ML	W	L	PCT	ERA	G	GS	CG	IP	H	BB	SO	SHO	SV
24-26	44-46	23	300	244	0.551	3.54	691	612	290	4564	4291	1775	2334	49	15
(3 YRS MINUS		1	29	21	0.58	3.63	50	47	16	379	396	146	119	4	0
33 & 17 GAMES)		24	329	265	0.554	3.55	741	659	306	4943	4687	1921	2453	53	

CHAPTER 4

This chapter consists of position players who played at the major league level at least six years but less than eleven years. Also, these players had at least some of their major league experience prior to being called into military service. Some of these players were wartime replacements who got the chance to play at the major league level because of the war. However, some of these players, who had promising careers before going into the military, were never able to regain the same level of skills that they had prior to being inducted. The time away from professional baseball and/or an injury caused them to not be able to compete at the same level after they returned.

ARNOVICH, MORRIS (MORRIE)   BR TR 5' 10"   168 lbs.
Born November 16, 1910, Superior, Wi. — Died July 20, 1959, Superior, Wi.
Played for Philadelphia (N) (1936–40), Cincinnati (1940), and New York (N) (1941, 1946)

Morrie Arnovich's career was winding down before he entered the Army. However, the war did put the finishing touches on it. He was thirty-one when he entered the service. He had been a regular for the Phillies from 1937 to 1939 but had lost his regular status when traded to the Reds in 1940. He volunteered for service in 1941 but was not taken because of bad teeth. He was accused of seeking a deferment for himself, but he produced documents showing the reason he was deferred as well as removing his false teeth to prove the point. However, in February 1942, he was reexamined and passed the physical. He was inducted into the Army on March 5, 1942, at Fort Sheridan, Illinois. After completing basic training he was transferred to Fort Lewis, Washington where he managed the baseball team for two years (1942 and 1943). Arnovich's only major injury suffered during his military service was a severe laceration on his arm after he slipped in the shower, which caused no permanent damage. By 1944, he was in New Guinea where he served as an Army postal clerk. He spent over a year in New Guinea and was then transferred to Manila in the Philippines where he was able to play some baseball. Arnovich played for the Fifth Replacement Depot team and was still playing for them as late as November 1945. Arnovich was released in time to play in 1946. However, he got into only one game before being released by the Giants. This stocky, line-drive hitter was done at age thirty-six.

AGE	YRS	ML	G	BA	SA	AB	H	2B	3B	HR	HR%	R	RBI	BB	SO	SB
31-34	42-45	7	590	0.287	0.383	2013	577	104	12	22	1.1	234	261	185	139	17
		4	344	0.261	0.33	1034	270	37	11	4	0.4	102	102	93	72	6
		11	934	0.278	0.365	3047	847	141	23	26	0.9	336	363	278	211	23

BAKER, WILLIAM P. (BILL)   BR TR 6' 0"   200 lbs.
Born February 22, 1911, Paw Creek, N.C.
Played for Cincinnati (1940–41), Pittsburgh (1941–43, 1946), and St. Louis (N) (1948–49)

Bill Baker was always a backup catcher. The most at-bats he got in any one season was one hundred seventy-two in 1943. The seven seasons that he played netted him a total of one hundred forty-five hits in 588 career at-bats. He hit only two career home runs. However, on July 30, 1943, he did hit a grand-slam homer. He was drafted into the Navy in March 1944. In early summer of 1944 he was listed on the Iowa Seahawks club roster, and later that same year, he was listed as a member of the Great Lakes team. Baker was discharged in December 1945 and rejoined the Pirates in time for the 1946 season.

AGE	YRS	ML	G	BA	SA	AB	H	2B	3B	HR	HR%	R	RBI	BB	SO	SB
33-34	44-45	7	263	0.247	0.316	588	145	25	5	2	0.3	45	68	68	30	6
		2	80	0.247	0.32	178	44	8	1	1	0.6	14	20	22	8	2
		9	343	0.247	0.317	766	189	33	6	3	0.4	59	88	90	38	8

BONURA, HENRY J. (ZEKE)   BR TR 6' 0" 210 lbs.
Born September 20, 1908, New Orleans, La. — Died March 9, 1987, New Orleans, La.
Played for Chicago (A) (1934–37), Washington (1938, 1940), New York (N) (1939), and Chicago (N) (1940)

Zeke's career was short but legendary. His nickname was "banana nose" for obvious reasons and the White Sox fans loved him. In his rookie year in 1934, Bonura hit twenty-seven home runs and drove in one hundred and ten runs. He was a regular during his entire seven-year career. He achieved a career batting average of .307 even though he was very slow. In fact, in his best year, 1937, he batted .345. Zeke did have some liabilities. He was not a good fielder even though he did lead the American League in fielding percentage three times. He did not have much mobility and didn't get too many grounders. Manager Jimmy Dykes told him, "You can't miss what you can't get" (Karst and Jones 1973, 86). In addition to his liability as a fielder and runner, Bonura was not a quick thinker. Dykes called him "my pet ox" (Okrent and Wulf 1989, 149).

When Zeke was traded from the White Sox to the Senators, the White Sox didn't bother to change their signs. Again Dykes said, "Why should we? He couldn't remember them when he was with us" (Okrent and Wulf, 1989, 149). He did remember the signs one time. The Senators (his new team) were playing the White Sox (his old team) and Bonura made it to third base as a runner. He saw Dykes swing his scorecard—the White Sox steal sign—and he took off for home and was safe. When asked why he tried to steal home, Bonura said, "I saw Dykes give the sign to steal, and I forgot I wasn't on his team anymore" (Okrent and Wulf 1989, 149).

He was one of the first baseball players to be drafted. Early in 1941 he entered the Army and spent that year in the service. He spent his training time at Camp Livingston, Louisiana. He was released late in 1941 because of his age. He was thirty-two years old when he entered the service and was released because of the new twenty-nine-year-old requirement. This was a pre-Pearl Harbor ruling that allowed men over the age of twenty-nine to be released from military service. It looked like Bonura would be able to make it back to the majors. Joe McCarthy, Yankee manager, contacted him at the winter meetings about signing with the Yankees to play first base in 1942. McCarthy was talking to him about playing when the radio broadcast the news that Japan had bombed Pearl Harbor. On January 19, 1942, Bonura was asked to again report for duty. He was back in the service, and his major league baseball career was over. Zeke realized that because of his age, coming back would be difficult. He said, "If I miss another season, I'll probably be through with baseball for all time, because it's not so easy to get back in the swing of this sport after a lengthy absence. But I guess Uncle Sam needs me more than baseball" (*The Sporting News*, "From the Army Front" 1-8-1942, page 8). When he reported for Army duty at Camp Shelby, Mississippi, he added, "It will be bullets for the Japanese instead of big league baseball for me" (*The Sporting News*, "From the Army Front" 1-15-1942, page 8).

While at Camp Shelby, Bonura changed his role in the war. The GIs needed a place to play, so he and some other GIs made a ball diamond. His work as a promotor and as someone who got things done was noted. So after spending some time as a rifle instructor there and some time in special training at Camp Butner, North Carolina, he was transferred to North Africa early in 1943. He was put in charge of organizing recreation for the battle weary troops. Under Major General Arthur A. Wilson, Bonura constructed twenty baseball diamonds using salvaged materials and volunteer labor. By the summer of 1943, he had ten leagues in place with eighty teams taking part. He also had other events.

On one New Years' Day he put on a show that included camel and donkey races, paratroopers, cowboys roping Arabian horses, and a football game. Because of his efforts he was given the Legion of Merit medal. General Eisenhower personally pinned the medal on Bonura. Eisenhower said, "He made a substantial contribution to the morale and efficiency of troops in the field" (Goldstein 1980, 248). The inscription on the medal said in part, "By his resourcefulness, enthusiasm and leadership he was able to overcome..." (Rumill 1946, 256). This recognition presents a paradox when you compare it to the reputation Bonura had as a player. As a player he was considered to be a slow thinker and as a soldier he was considered a resourceful leader. He had risen to the rank of master sergeant while stationed in North Africa. Late in 1944 he spent some time in Marseilles, France, where he again organized activities for the entertainment of the troops. By September 1945, he was stationed in Switzerland. Bonura was finally released on October 7, 1945, after spending almost five years in the Army. He was thirty-two when he was drafted, and he was thirty-eight when released. His major league career was over. He only got to play for seven seasons. But as a batter he made the most of his time. For his seven years, he averaged seventeen home runs, one hundred RBIs, and batted .307.

AGE	YRS	ML	G	BA	SA	AB	H	2B	3B	HR	HR%	R	RBI	BB	SO	SB
32-36	41-45	7	917	0.307	0.487	3582	1099	232	29	119	3.3	600	703	404	180	19
		5	630	0.304	0.474	2419	736	155	17	74	3.1	359	455	236	115	13
		12	1547	0.306	0.482	6001	1835	387	46	193	3.2	959	1158	640	295	32

BRAGAN, ROBERT R. (BOBBY)   BR TR 5' 10" 175 lbs.
Born October 30, 1917, Birmingham, Al.
Played for Philadelphia (N) (1940-42) and Brooklyn (1943-44, 1947-48)

Bobby Bragan did not have a long career as a player. However, he also had a number of other roles in professional baseball. He also was a coach, manager, scout, executive, and president of a minor league. He started out with the Phillies as a shortstop and later switched to catcher. The Dodgers picked him up as a wartime replacement. He wasn't drafted until after the season was over in 1944.

Bragan entered the Army on April 15, 1945. He reported to Fort McClellan, Alabama, for induction. Later that year he helped put on a baseball school at Camp Wheeler for kids. Bragan was commissioned a second lieutenant at Fort Benning, Georgia. He was in the infantry, but he never left the States during his tour of duty. He was discharged in February 1947. Bragan had three brothers who also served. One spent three years in the Air Force in England, one went to Paris in General Patton's 3rd Army infantry and another made five voyages across the Atlantic with armed guard duty. All four came out of the service without injury. Bragan was only able to get into thirty-four games in two seasons after the war. Not getting out until 1947 left him way behind the others who had returned from service the previous year.

AGE	YRS	ML	G	BA	SA	AB	H	2B	3B	HR	HR%	R	RBI	BB	SO	SB
27-28	45-46	7	597	0.24	0.309	1900	456	62	12	15	0.8	136	172	110	117	12
		2	128	0.261	0.325	348	91	11	4	1	0.3	31	29	23	22	2
		9	725	0.243	0.311	2248	547	73	16	16	0.7	167	201	133	139	14

BROWN, JAMES R. (JIMMY)   BB TR 5' 8" 165 lbs.
Born April 25, 1910, Jamesville, N.C. — Died December 29, 1977, Bath, N.C.
Played for St. Louis (N) (1937–43) and Pittsburgh (1946)

Jimmy Brown was a utility infielder who got his at-bats whether he was playing second, short, or third. Between 1937 and 1942 he was a regular in the line-up stationed at one of the infield positions. Stan Musial said, "Jimmy was another great competitor and wonderful team man, a three-position infielder who could get on base as a lead off man" (Broeg 1964, 268). His best year was 1942 when he batted .306 and played in the All-Star game. In 1943, at age thirty-three, he had lost his starting job before he was drafted.

He entered the Army on July 13, 1943. After basic training, he was assigned to Fourth Ferrying Group in Memphis. By January 1944, he had been promoted to sergeant. He continued to be assigned to that group and played baseball for their team. He was named manager of that team early in 1945. Also, during this same time he suffered a hand infection which kept him from playing for a period of time. While being treated for the infection, he was confined to the Army Air Force hospital at Maxwell Field, Alabama. When he was discharged on October 28, 1945, he had risen to the rank of staff sergeant.

The Cardinals had too many players when they started returning home after the war. So the Cardinals sold Brown to the Pirates for $30,000. However, at age thirty-five, he had lost his edge. The years in service had taken something away from him. He lasted through the 1946 season, which would be his last in the majors.

AGE	YRS	ML	G	BA	SA	AB	H	2B	3B	HR	HR%	R	RBI	BB	SO	SB
34-35	44-45	8	890	0.279	0.352	3512	980	146	42	9	0.3	465	319	231	110	39
		2	172	0.243	0.295	638	155	25	4	0	0	69	61	51	11	5
		10	1062	0.273	0.343	4150	1135	171	46	9	0.2	534	380	282	121	44

BROWN, THOMAS M. (TOMMY)   BR TR 6' 1" 170 lbs.

Born December 6, 1927, Brooklyn, N.Y.

Played for Brooklyn (1944-45, 1947-51), Philadelphia (N) (1951-52), and Chicago (N) (1952-53)

Tommy Brown was one of the "kids" signed by the Dodgers as they tried to fill out their rosters during the war. They also were trying to sign the good young prospects for the future. He was signed at age sixteen. He had been working on docks since age twelve, playing ball against older boys since age fourteen, so he had a chance to develop. In 1943 the Dodgers set up a try-out camp and about 2000 boys came. They played for several days, and every day some were sent home. Finally, in early December 1943, Brown signed a Dodger contract. He started the year in the minors but was called up during the year. So on August 3, 1944, at age sixteen, he started a doubleheader against the Cubs. He was the youngest player to see regular action. For the most part he was overmatched with major league pitching. However, he also became the youngest player to ever hit a home run. The following year on August 20, 1945, he hit a homer off Preacher Roe. He was 17 years, 8 months, and 14 days old when he hit the first home run. His early nickname was "Buckshot" because of his throwing problems. Brown was drafted into the Army in March 1946 and was discharged in April 1947. His baseball career never developed. It lasted nine years but only consisted of 1,280 at-bats. The greatest amount of playing time came after the Dodgers traded him to the Phillies and then the Cubs in 1951 and 1952.

AGE	YRS	ML	G	BA	SA	AB	H	2B	3B	HR	HR%	R	RBI	BB	SO	SB
18-19	46-47	9	494	0.241	0.355	1280	309	39	7	31	2.4	151	159	85	142	7
(2 YRS MINUS		1	84	0.232	0.307	254	59	6	2	3	1.2	28	30	13	23	2
15 GAMES)		10	578	0.24	0.347	1534	368	45	9	34	2.2	179	189	98	165	9

CAMPBELL, PAUL M.   BL TL 5' 10" 185 lbs.

Born September 1, 1917, Paw Creek, N.C.

Played for Boston (A) (1941-42, 1946) and Detroit (1948-50)

Paul Campbell was a very good fielding first baseman who got a brief trial with the Red Sox prior to entering the military. He had a good record in the minors but was never able to make the successful jump to the majors. Prior to being drafted he had been working in a defense plant, married, classified 2-A, and did not expect the draft call. After being inducted in February 1943, he was stationed at Camp Croft, South Carolina. He later was transferred to Morris Field, North Carolina, and then to the Jacksonville, Florida, Army Air Base. By August 1943, he was stationed somewhere in England with the Army Air Force doing clerical and athletic work. Campbell had been promoted to the rank of corporal. He was still in England in 1945. He had risen to the rank of sergeant and was able to play baseball for an Army team in London. He was still listed on the Red Sox defense list in December 1945 and was able to return to baseball for the 1946 season. His best year was 1949 with the Tigers when he got into eighty-seven games and had 255 at-bats.

AGE	YRS	ML	G	BA	SA	AB	H	2B	3B	HR	HR%	R	RBI	BB	SO	SB
25-27	43-45	6	204	0.255	0.358	380	97	17	5	4	1.1	61	41	28	54	4
		3	112	0.27	0.395	215	58	10	4	3	1.4	37	25	15	28	3
		9	316	0.261	0.371	595	155	27	9	7	1.2	98	66	43	82	7

CAREY, THOMAS F.A. (TOM)   BR TR 5'8"   170 lbs.
Born October 11, 1906, Hoboken, N.J. — Died February 21, 1970, Rochester, N.Y.
Played for St. Louis (A) (1935-37) and Boston (A) (1939-42, 1946)

Tom Carey was a regular infielder for the Browns in 1936 and 1937. After he was traded
to the Red Sox in time for the 1939 season, his role became limited. He never played more
than fifty-four games in any one season for the Red Sox. He was inducted into the Navy on
February 23, 1943. On September 1, 1944, he was ordered overseas to the Pacific. While in
Hawaii, he was able to play baseball. He was named to the 14th Naval District second team all-
stars in 1945. Carey was discharged on October 10, 1945. He returned to the Red Sox in 1946
but played in only three games. He then became a Red Sox coach.

AGE	YRS	ML	G	BA	SA	AB	H	2B	3B	HR	HR%	R	RBI	BB	SO	SB
34-36	43-45	8	465	0.275	0.348	1520	418	79	13	2	0.1	169	169	66	75	3
		3	25	0.2	0.2	30	6	0	0	0	0	5	5	2	2	0
		11	490	0.274	0.345	1550	424	79	13	2	0.1	174	174	68	77	3

CONROY, WILLIAM G. (BILL)   BR TR 6'0"   185 lbs.
Born February 26, 1915, Bloomington, Il. — Died November 13, 1997, Bloomington, Il.
Played for Philadelphia (A) (1935-37) and Boston (A) (1942-44)

Bill Conroy had brief trials with the A's in 1935, 1936, and 1937 before he was even able
to achieve part-time status with the Red Sox in 1942. During that year he caught in eighty-
three games. His hitting was always a problem. His lifetime batting average was only .199.
He entered the Navy in February 1945. He had been classified 2-B but was accepted for
active service after examination at Boston on October 5, 1944. He spent the summer of 1945
stationed at Bainbridge playing for their baseball team. He was still listed on the Red Sox
defense list in December 1945. Conroy was never able to return to the majors following the
time he spent in the Navy.

AGE	YRS	ML	G	BA	SA	AB	H	2B	3B	HR	HR%	R	RBI	BB	SO	SB
30	45	6	169	0.199	0.274	452	90	13	3	5	1.1	45	33	77	85	3
		1	29	0.205	0.269	78	16	2	0	1	1.3	8	6	15	14	1
		7	198	0.2	0.274	530	106	15	3	6	1.1	53	39	92	99	4

DALLESSANDRO, NICHOLAS D. (DOM)   BL TL 5'6"   168 lbs.
Born October 3, 1913, Reading, Pa. — Died April 29, 1988, Indianapolis, In.
Played for Boston (A) (1937) and Chicago (N) (1940-44, 1946-47)

Dom Dallessandro started his baseball career as part of the Boston Red Sox. He was traded to
the San Diego team of the Pacific Coast League in the deal that brought Ted Williams to the
Red Sox. San Diego got Dallessandro, Al Niemiec, Bunny Griffith, Spencer Harris, and $25,000.
The Red Sox got Ted Williams. After two years in San Diego, Dallessandro returned to the
majors with the Chicago Cubs, where he stayed for the rest of his career. His nickname was
"Dim Dom." This was short for "Diminutive Dominick," which was a reference to his height of
5'6". Dom had his best year in 1944.

He was classified 1-A until he had his physical at Reading, Pennsylvania, in early 1944. After that he was changed to 4-F. He retained that classification until 1945 when the government started their crackdown of people classified 4-F. As a result, Dom was reexamined and changed back to 1-A. He was inducted into the Army on March 8, 1945, at Philadelphia. He was stationed at Fort Lewis, Washington, for most of 1945. He was able to play some baseball while stationed at Fort Lewis. Dom was discharged on April 2, 1946, in time to rejoin the Cubs for the 1946 season. Because he was in the Army during the 1945 season, he missed the only Cubs pennant during his career. He played part-time during 1946 and 1947 before leaving the majors for good.

AGE	YRS	ML	G	BA	SA	AB	H	2B	3B	HR	HR%	R	RBI	BB	SO	SB
31	45	8	746	0.267	0.381	1945	520	110	23	22	1.1	242	303	310	150	16
		1	95	0.268	0.374	246	66	14	3	2	0.8	32	36	42	17	2
		9	841	0.267	0.381	2191	586	124	26	24	1.1	274	339	352	167	18

DANNING, HARRY

BR TR 6' 1" 190 lbs.

Born September 6, 1911, Los Angeles, Ca.
Played for New York (N) (1933–42)

Harry Danning was an All-Star catcher for four years. He spent the first part of his career as back-up for Gus Mancuso and then took over in 1937 as the regular catcher for the next six years until he went into the Army. Danning became a catcher because he wanted to play and nobody wanted to catch. He became good at catching. Terry Moore picked Danning as one of the best catchers he saw during his career. His manager, Bill Terry, said this, "Harry, you make everything look easy" (Van Blair 1994, 46). Danning's nickname was "Harry the Horse" because of his durability. He caught a lot of games during this time, including playing through injuries. His batting average suffered because he was willing to play when he was hurt.

Danning was drafted into the Army Air Force on April 6, 1943, at Los Angeles. He said, "I'm through with baseball. From now on I'm going to be in there pitching instead of catching" (*Herald Tribune*, 4-7-1943). He was assigned to the Sixth Ferrying Group at McClennan Field in Long Beach, California. In December 1943, he was promoted to the rank of sergeant. He was able to play on the baseball team at the base and in 1944 was the manager of the base team. In spring of 1945 Danning found himself in the base hospital because of injuries to his knees. The Army doctors recommended a medical discharge, but the War Department wanted additional treatment. He indicated in a letter that he didn't suffer any wounds, but he had arthritis in both knees when he went into service and that they got worse. He was ultimately given a medical discharge. He was told that he should not try to play baseball again. Danning said, "Bearing in mind that in 1946 they didn't know a lot about knee operations, I was told when leaving the service that if I played again and slid that there was a good chance that my leg would lock up and [I] would spend the rest of my life with a stiff leg. The diagnosis was concurred by my personal orthopedic doctor. In a way you can say that the service hastened my departure from baseball" (Danning letter 1997). Harry Danning took the advice of his doctors and quit baseball. Because he didn't play after the war, he didn't qualify for the baseball pension plan.

AGE	YRS	ML	G	BA	SA	AB	H	2B	3B	HR	HR%	R	RBI	BB	SO	SB
31-33	43-45	10	890	0.285	0.415	2971	847	162	26	57	1.9	363	397	187	216	13
		3	283	0.285	0.405	951	271	52	7	16	1.7	122	123	64	65	4
		13	1173	0.285	0.412	3922	1118	214	33	73	1.9	485	520	251	281	17

DICKEY, GEORGE W.   BB TR 6' 2"   180 lbs.
Born July 10, 1915, Kensett, Ar. — Died June 16, 1976, DeWitt, Ar.
Played for Boston (A) (1935-36) and Chicago (A) (1941-42, 1946-47)

George Dickey might be best known as Bill Dickey's little brother. He spent his entire major league career as a back-up catcher for the Red Sox and the White Sox. He played the most games in any one season during his last year in 1947 when he caught 83 games. On October 12, 1942, after the 1942 season, Dickey enlisted in the Navy. He did his training at Great Lakes Naval Training Station and became an instructor in the anti-aircraft school there. He played on their team while stationed at Great Lakes. In March 1944, he was transferred to Bainbridge for more intensive training. After it was completed, he was sent to Pearl Harbor to assist with physical conditioning. He did play on a Navy team while stationed in Honolulu during the summer of 1944. In 1945, as the United States took control of the islands of the Pacific, Dickey was one of the professional ball players who toured the islands playing to entertain the other troops. He was discharged on October 13, 1945. He did play two more years, after being discharged, before leaving major league baseball.

AGE	YRS	ML	G	BA	SA	AB	H	2B	3B	HR	HR%	R	RBI	BB	SO	SB
26-29	42-45	6	226	0.204	0.253	494	101	12	0	4	0.8	36	54	63	62	4
(4 YRS MINUS		3	152	0.212	0.262	344	73	8	0	3	0.9	29	36	51	45	4
59 GAMES)		9	378	0.208	0.257	838	174	20	0	7	0.8	65	90	114	107	8

DUSAK, ERVIN F. (ERV)   BR TR 6' 2"   185 lbs.
Born July 29, 1920, Chicago, Il. — Died November 6, 1994, Glendale Heights, Il.
Played for St. Louis (N) (1941-42, 1946-51) and Pittsburgh (1951-52)

Dusak had a brief trial with the Cardinals before he entered the Army. He tried to enlist in the Navy in December 1942 but was rejected for a minor physical problem. He wanted to serve his country, so he said he would undergo a minor operation and try to enlist again. He did make it into the Army early in 1943. He was stationed at Fort Sheridan. By the fall of 1944 he had been promoted to the rank of staff sergeant and was playing on an Army team that was barnstorming through the Southwest Pacific bases. During 1945, he was stationed in the Philippines where he was able to play for the 8th Army Base Force team. By October 1945, he was scheduled to board a transport ship from Yokohama to be home between November and December. He was still listed on the Cardinals' defense list as of December 6, 1945. He left the service in time to rejoin the Cardinals for the 1946 season.

Starting in 1946, Dusak received more playing time. For the next three years he would be the number four outfielder with the Cardinals. Dusak's nickname became "Four-Sack Dusak" after he hit a home run in 1946 to beat the Dodgers and put the Cardinals in first place. He was a strong-armed outfielder who had trouble with the curve ball. Stan Musial said, "Inability to hit the curve ball cost Dusak a great career and the Cardinals a fine center fielder. He had everything but..." (Broeg 1964, 270). Because of his strong arm, he tried to make a comeback as a pitcher. After one year of reasonable success in the minors as a pitcher, he had a brief trial in the majors but without success.

AGE	YRS	ML	G	BA	SA	AB	H	2B	3B	HR	HR%	R	RBI	BB	SO	SB
22-24	43-45	9	413	0.243	0.355	1035	251	32	6	24	2.3	168	106	142	188	12
		3	252	0.244	0.356	706	172	21	5	16	2.3	118	69	101	119	8
		12	665	0.243	0.355	1741	423	53	11	40	2.3	286	175	243	307	20

EARLY, JACOB W. (JAKE)   BL TR 5' 11" 168 lbs.
Born May 19, 1915, King's Mountain, N.C. — Died May 31, 1985, Melbourne, Fl.
Played for Washington (1939–43, 1946, 1948–49) and St. Louis (A) (1947)

After alternating with Rick Ferrell in the beginning of his career, Early became the regular Senators' catcher when Ferrell was traded to the Browns. He was known as a colorful player. He would sing, do play-by-play, and talk to the batter while catching, all to distract the hitter. During the time he was the regular Senators' catcher (1941–1943), they had four knuckleball pitchers. Early did a good job of catching the elusive butterfly pitch. Early was named to and caught the entire 1943 All-Star game. He entered the Army in March 1944. He went from Fort Bragg, North Carolina, to Camp Butner, North Carolina, in spring 1944. He was able to play on the 78th Infantry team at Camp Pickett, Virginia, while stationed there in June 1944. He did do some fighting with the 87th division in Europe. He was discharged on December 19, 1945. He was able to return to the Senators for the 1946 season. His career lasted through the 1949 season, but he spent the last years as a back-up catcher for the Senators and Browns.

AGE	YRS	ML	G	BA	SA	AB	H	2B	3B	HR	HR%	R	RBI	BB	SO	SB
29-30	44-45	9	747	0.241	0.35	2208	532	98	23	32	1.4	216	264	280	259	7
		2	199	0.242	0.358	660	160	31	6	11	1.7	61	89	68	72	2
		11	946	0.241	0.351	2868	692	129	29	43	1.5	277	353	348	331	9

FRANKS, HERMAN L.   BL TR 5' 10" 187 lbs.
Born January 4, 1914, Price, Ut.
Played for St. Louis (N) (1939), Brooklyn (1940–41), Philadelphia (A) (1947–48), and New York (N) (1949)

Herman Franks was a weak-hitting back-up catcher during his career. He never played in more than sixty-five games in any one season. He achieved greater baseball success as a manager. He managed for seven years, leading the Giants to four consecutive second-place finishes. Franks was a member of the 1941 Dodger team that won the pennant. He entered the Navy on May 16, 1942, in Buffalo, New York, as an ensign. He was assigned to Annapolis as a P.E. instructor. Franks was in the "Tom Hamilton" program. In January 1943, he was transferred to Ellyson Field, Pensacola, Florida. He was ordered overseas in late 1944 which sent him to the Pacific. He rose to the rank of lieutenant. Franks was able to play some baseball while stationed in Hawaii during 1945. In October 1945, he played in the Navy "Little World Series." He was released from the Navy in time for the 1946 season. However, he spent that season in Montreal of the International League. He made it back to the majors briefly in 1947 and in 1948 with the A's. After playing one game with the Giants in 1949 he became a coach.

AGE	YRS	ML	G	BA	SA	AB	H	2B	3B	HR	HR%	R	RBI	BB	SO	SB
28-31	42-45	6	190	0.199	0.275	403	80	18	2	3	0.7	35	43	57	37	2
		4	139	0.203	0.275	295	60	13	1	2	0.7	27	31	47	27	2
		10	329	0.201	0.275	698	140	31	3	5	0.7	62	74	104	64	4

GILBERT, CHARLES M. (CHARLIE) BL TL 5' 9" 165 lbs.
Born July 8, 1919, New Orleans, La. — Died August 13, 1983, New Orleans, La.
Played for Brooklyn (1940), Chicago (N) (1941-43, 1946), and Philadelphia (N) (1946-47)

Charlie Gilbert was a weak-hitting, fast outfielder. His best year was the first one after he returned from service, playing in 103 games and batting .234. He took his preinduction physical on March 24, 1944, and was added to the national defense list that spring. In July 1944, he was in San Diego at the Naval Training Center. By October 1944, he had been transferred to Bainbridge, Maryland, for physical training instructor school. In January 1945, he finished the school and was sent to Naval Air Technical Training Center at Millington Station near Memphis, Tennessee. Spring 1945 found him on his way to Hawaii. He was able to play baseball while he was stationed in Hawaii. He played in the Navy "Little World Series" in the fall of 1945. Gilbert was named to the 14th Naval District all-star team, finishing third in the most valuable player voting. He did this while playing for the sub base team. Gilbert rose to the rank of lieutenant commander while serving in the Navy. He was still listed on the Cubs defense list in December 1945, but he returned in time for the 1946 season.

AGE	YRS	ML	G	BA	SA	AB	H	2B	3B	HR	HR%	R	RBI	BB	SO	SB
24-25	44-45	6	364	0.229	0.299	852	195	27	9	5	0.6	109	55	86	82	7
		2	135	0.244	0.329	328	80	12	5	2	0.6	45	23	29	23	3
		8	499	0.233	0.307	1180	275	39	14	7	0.6	154	78	115	105	10

GRACE, JOSEPH L. (JOE) BL TR 6' 1" 180 lbs.
Born January 5, 1914, Gorham, Il. — Died September 18, 1969, Murphysboro, Il.
Played for St. Louis (A) (1938-41, 1946) and Washington (1946-47)

Joe Grace was just starting to build a career when he entered the Navy in 1942. He had served as the fourth outfielder for the Browns for three years with 1941 being his best year. The left-handed line-drive hitter got into 115 games and batted .309. Grace entered the Navy on January 10, 1942, about a month after Pearl Harbor. He was stationed at Great Lakes during 1942 and 1943. He played on the baseball team there during that time. Early in 1944 he was transferred from Great Lakes to Bainbridge, Maryland, for more intensive training. When this training was completed, he was scheduled to be transferred to Pearl Harbor to assist in physical conditioning. He made it to Hawaii by July 1944. He was slowed during this time because of a broken wrist.

Grace played baseball for the Navy while stationed in Hawaii. He was a member of the Navy team that beat the Army team in the "Pacific World Series" during September 1944. In fact, Grace hit a grand-slam homer to beat Army in game two. Following the "Pacific World Series," the Navy team was broken up, and groups toured the islands that had been captured from the Japanese. These islands included Johnston Island, Kwajalein, Peleliu, Tinian, Saipan, Guam, Roi-Namur, and Ulithi. This tour started in the spring of 1945. Grace was discharged from the Navy on October 16, 1945. He returned to the Browns for the 1946 season but was traded to the Senators during the season. Between the two teams Grace played in more games in 1946 than any other season. However, he lasted only one more year, with 1947 being his last year in the majors.

AGE	YRS	ML	G	BA	SA	AB	H	2B	3B	HR	HR%	R	RBI	BB	SO	SB
28-31	42-45	6	484	0.283	0.393	1561	442	76	18	20	1.3	225	172	179	135	9
		4	398	0.278	0.39	1307	363	64	16	17	1.3	183	146	158	108	6
		10	882	0.281	0.392	2868	805	140	34	37	1.3	408	318	337	243	15

HAAS, BERTHOLD J. (BERT)   BR TR 5' 11" 178 lbs.
Born February 8, 1914, Naperville, Il. — Died June 23, 1999, Tampa, Fl.
Played for Brooklyn (1937-38), Cincinnati (1942-43, 1946-47), Philadelphia (N) (1948-49),
New York (N) (1949), and Chicago (A) (1951)

Bert Haas made it to the majors as a regular in 1942 with the Reds. He was a utility player who played third base, first base, and outfield, serving as a regular at each of the positions at one time or another. His career started in Brooklyn where in his first year he pinch-hit four games in a row. He got a single and three doubles in those four appearances. Haas entered the Army on September 18, 1943. By June 1944 he was serving in Italy. He saw action at several points in the European Theater during the time he spent in the Army. He was discharged in December 1945. He rejoined the Reds for the 1946 season. He had good years in both '46 and '47. He was named to and played in the 1947 All-Star game. He suffered a concussion in 1948 and saw limited playing time the rest of his career. He was traded to the Giants in 1949 and saw very limited action with the White Sox in 1951.

AGE	YRS	ML	G	BA	SA	AB	H	2B	3B	HR	HR%	R	RBI	BB	SO	SB
30-31	44-45	9	723	0.264	0.355	2440	644	93	32	22	0.9	263	263	204	188	51
		2	265	0.262	0.354	967	253	39	13	8	0.8	106	107	86	74	21
		11	988	0.263	0.355	3407	897	132	45	30	0.9	369	370	290	262	72

HASSETT, JOHN A. (BUDDY)   BL TL 5' 11" 180 lbs.
Born September 5, 1911, New York, N.Y. — Died August 23, 1997, Westwood, N.J.
Played for Brooklyn (1936-38), Boston (N) (1939-41), and New York (A) (1942)

Buddy Hassett signed with the Yankees but could not make the majors with them because of Lou Gehrig. Given a chance after a trade to Brooklyn, he was able to produce on the major league level. After the war started taking a toll on the available players, the Yankees traded one of their top prospects to reacquire Hassett. He was the regular first baseman for the Yankees during the 1942 season. He batted .333 in the '42 World Series. He got to play in only three of the games because he suffered a broken finger while attempting to bunt. Hassett enlisted in the Navy in December 1942. He spent 1943 at the Navy preflight school in Chapel Hill, North Carolina. While stationed in North Carolina he was able to play some baseball.

By the spring of 1944 he had achieved the rank of lieutenant and was appointed as recreation officer on an aircraft carrier nearing completion at Newport, Rhode Island. He continued in the role of recreation and physical conditioning during 1945. His ship was in the first carrier raids on Tokyo. His ship also gave air support for the Iwo Jima and Okinawa campaigns. Hassett was discharged on November 16, 1945. He had seen thirty-seven months of service as a line officer. In spite of being only thirty-four old when released and having a lifetime batting average of .292, Hassett did not play in the majors after his release from the Navy.

AGE	YRS	ML	G	BA	SA	AB	H	2B	3B	HR	HR%	R	RBI	BB	SO	SB
31-33	43-45	7	929	0.292	0.362	3517	1026	130	40	12	0.3	469	343	209	116	53
		3	422	0.292	0.357	1608	469	60	15	5	0.3	226	151	103	50	24
		10	1351	0.292	0.36	5125	1495	190	55	17	0.3	695	494	312	166	77

HERMANSKI, EUGENE V. (GENE)   BL TR 5' 11" 185 lbs.
Born May 11, 1920, Pittsfield, Ma.
Played for Brooklyn (1943, 1946-51), Chicago (N) (1951-53), and Pittsburgh (1953)

Gene Hermanski had two hitches in the military. He served in the Coast Guard in 1942 and again in 1944-1945. The first time was before he had reached the major league level and the second was after a brief trial with the Dodgers in 1943. He was able to play a lot of baseball during his time in the Coast Guard. He played almost every day during the summer. He was able to stay in the New York area by signing up for one training course after another. In January 1945, he was stationed at Floyd Bennett, New York, Air Station Coast Guard. During the summer he played for the Coast Guard, the Navy, and a good semi-pro team in the area. With all the playing time he got while in the service, he came out of the military a better player than when he entered. He was still listed on the Dodgers' defense list in December 1945 and was able to join the Dodgers in time for spring training in 1946. He also was in great physical shape when spring training started in 1946. His best year was 1948 when he batted .290 with fifteen home runs. Three of the home runs came in one game on August 5. He was always a good hitter, but his problems in the field kept him from being a regular for most of his career.

AGE	YRS	ML	G	BA	SA	AB	H	2B	3B	HR	HR%	R	RBI	BB	SO	SB
23-25	43-45	9	739	0.272	0.404	1960	533	85	18	46	2.3	276	259	289	212	43
(3 YRS MINUS		2	161	0.256	0.368	359	92	11	4	7	1.9	57	59	56	24	8
18 GAMES)		11	900	0.27	0.398	2319	625	96	22	53	2.3	333	318	345	236	51

HITCHCOCK, WILLIAM C. (BILLY)   BR TR 6' 1" 185 lbs.
Born July 31, 1916, Inverness, Al.
Played for Detroit (1942, 1946, 1953), Washington (1946), St. Louis (A) (1947), Boston (A) (1948-49), and Philadelphia (A) (1950-52)

Billy Hitchcock was the regular shortstop for the Tigers in his rookie year in 1942, the year before he entered the Army. He had received a commission as a 2nd lieutenant while in college at Auburn. He entered the Army on August 13, 1942. The commission he received was in field artillery but after he entered the military he was transferred to the Air Force. One of his first duties was to be in charge of physical training at Boca Raton, Florida. In December 1943, he was transferred to Greenville, South Carolina, to assist the special services officer. Early in 1945 he was stationed at Alameda, California, Air Station. Hitchcock was one of forty-eight Army personnel sent to Utah to work out, get shots, and then be transferred to Hawaii to play the Navy baseball team who had just beaten the Army team in the "Pacific World Series." They were sent to Hawaii by ship instead of plane, and the Navy team had left by the time they got there.

During the spring and summer of 1945, Hitchcock was stationed in Hawaii and was able to play some baseball. He was stationed at Hickem Field. He was selected to the Army all-star team that summer. He achieved the rank of captain and was put in charge of the Army Air Force Sports Program in Hawaii. That fall the teams were sent to the Pacific islands to play. In a letter, Hitchcock said, "We had an Air Force team (42 players mostly major leaguers) that played in Honolulu. In July 1945 we were ordered to the Mariannas and played exhibition games at Tinian, Saipan, Iwo Jima, and Guam for the entertainment of the service personnel in these areas. But losing four years in pro ball certainly affected my career as well as many other players" (Hitchcock letter 1997). He was awarded the Bronze Star for his service in the Pacific. Hitchcock was discharged on February 19, 1946. His career lasted until 1953. However, for most of that time he served the role of a utility infielder. Only in 1950 and 1952 with the A's did he play more than one hundred games for a team in a season.

AGE	YRS	ML	G	BA	SA	AB	H	2B	3B	HR	HR%	R	RBI	BB	SO	SB
26-28	43-45	9	703	0.243	0.299	2249	547	67	22	5	0.2	231	257	264	230	15
		3	261	0.214	0.263	852	182	24	6	2	0.2	79	82	74	89	8
		12	964	0.235	0.289	3101	729	91	28	7	0.2	310	339	338	319	23

HODGIN, ELMER R. (RALPH)   BL TR 5' 10" 167 lbs.
Born February 10, 1916, Greensboro, N.C.
Played for Boston (N) (1939) and Chicago (A) (1943-44, 1946-48)

Ralph Hodgin was drafted out of the Pacific Coast League by the Chicago White Sox as a wartime replacement. He had a good record in the minors as a hitter. He played in over one hundred games in both of his first two years (1943 and 1944) before being drafted. He batted .314 in his rookie year, one of the few to bat over .300 in their rookie year and never bat .300 again. Hodgin entered the Army in February 1945. He was almost twenty-nine years old when he started his service. He had been classified 4-F but was accepted after re-examination. He was accepted at Guilford, North Carolina. He was discharged in December 1945. His service was shorter than most. He said, "Military service interrupted my career at its pinnacle and I was never able to return at that level after discharge" (Hodgin letter 1997). His career was further damaged in April 1947 when Hal Newhouser hit Hodgin in the head. He never was the same aggressive batter after the beaning. His last season in the majors was 1948.

AGE	YRS	ML	G	BA	SA	AB	H	2B	3B	HR	HR%	R	RBI	BB	SO	SB
29	45	6	530	0.285	0.367	1689	481	79	24	4	0.2	198	188	97	63	7
		1	102	0.295	0.38	329	97	15	5	1	0.3	42	38	20	13	2
		7	632	0.286	0.369	2018	578	94	29	5	0.2	240	226	117	76	9

JOHNSON, WILLIAM R. (BILLY)   BR TR 5' 10" 180 lbs.
Born August 30, 1918, Montclair, N.J.
Played for New York (A) (1943, 1946-51) and St. Louis (N) (1951-53)

Billy Johnson was called up to the Yankees in 1943 to fill in for Red Rolfe who had retired. He had a good minor league career before 1943 and was ready for the major leagues. He proved that he was ready by coming back after the war and contributing to the Yankee pennant winners. He played every game in 1943, batted .280, drove in 94 runs, and helped the Yankees to a World Series win that year. Johnson was classified 1-A early in 1944, and it was anticipated that he would be drafted. He joined the Merchant Marines while he was waiting for his call. He entered that service on March 1, 1944. While in the Merchant Marines, he was stationed at New London, Connecticut, where he was able to play some baseball. Johnson was then inducted into the Army on September 1, 1944. He took his boot training at Camp Blanding, Florida, and served in the European theater with an armored division as a member of a mortar crew. He saw combat with the 87th division while stationed in Germany. He served in Europe for about one year.

In August 1945, Johnson returned home for a furlough and then was transferred to Fort Benning, Georgia. That fall he did get to play for the Fort Benning baseball team. He didn't receive his discharge until May 1946, which put him behind for the 1946 season. He said, "When I came back, it took a month or two to get adjusted and get back into form. I batted .260 in less than 300 at-bats" (Peary 1994, 50). Johnson recovered the next season. Two of his best years were 1947 and 1948. In 1947 he again helped the Yankees to a world title. With the arrival of Casey Stengel, Johnson was platooned at third with Bobby Brown and never had another season at the same level. He was traded to the Cardinals in 1951 and retired with arm problems in 1953. Johnson was another one whose career was hurt because of the war. However, his attitude about his service was remarkable. He said in a letter, "My feeling is there is no service as wonderful as serving one's country. The military service came during the prime years of my baseball career. After serving two-and-a-half years in the Army I never fully regained my playing potential. Those are just the breaks of life. We cannot live our lives thinking what might have been. It was my privilege to serve my country and I enjoyed the rest of the time spent in baseball after I returned home. I suffered an injury to my throwing arm and had to retire from baseball at age 33" (Johnson letter 1998).

AGE	YRS	ML	G	BA	SA	AB	H	2B	3B	HR	HR%	R	RBI	BB	SO	SB
25-27	44-46	9	964	0.271	0.391	3253	882	141	33	61	1.9	419	487	347	290	13
(3 YRS MINUS		2	310	0.285	0.405	1100	313	42	12	22	2	132	197	108	68	3
85 GAMES)		11	1274	0.275	0.394	4353	1195	183	45	83	1.9	551	684	455	358	16

JUDNICH, WALTER F. (WALT)   BL TL 6' 1" 205 lbs.
Born January 24, 1917, San Francisco, Ca. — Died July 12, 1971, Glendale, Ca.
Played for St. Louis (A) (1940-42, 1946-47), Cleveland (1948), and Pittsburgh (1949)

Walt Judnich was an outfielder with a lot of potential when he was in the Yankee farm system. Unfortunately for him, the Yankees had an outfield full of good outfielders. He wasn't able to reach the majors until he was traded to the St. Louis Browns. A good outfielder with a strong arm, he led the American League in fielding three out of the four years he was eligible. For the three years before he entered military service, he averaged eighteen home runs and batted .299. Judnich entered the Army Air Force on March 3, 1943. He was stationed at McClellan Air Field, Sacramento, California. He stayed there for about a year, serving with the Sixth Ferrying Group. He achieved the marksman rating with a rifle while at that base. He did play baseball while stationed there. Judnich was transferred to Hawaii in the spring of 1944 and spent the summer as a member of the 7th Air Force team in Honolulu.

In September 1944 Judnich was a member of the Army team that played Navy in the "Pacific World Series." He played with a group at Hickem Field. He continued in Hawaii into 1945, playing for the Bellow Flyers, taking part in a baseball school for kids, and being named to the Army Air Force all-star team. There was a group of professional players that the Army sent on a tour of the newly captured islands in the Pacific. Judnich was among that group. He played for the 313th flyers in the Marianas, including Saipan, Guam, and Tinian. He arrived back in Los Angeles in November 1945 aboard the transport ship *Cecil*. He was discharged from the Air Force on November 30, 1945. He had two more years as a regular before he was traded to the Indians in 1948. He did get to take part in the 1948 World Series for the Indians even though he played on a part-time basis, but he was never able to hit at the same level after the war. His batting average had been .299 for the three years before he entered the service, and it was .259 for four years after service.

AGE	YRS	ML	G	BA	SA	AB	H	2B	3B	HR	HR%	R	RBI	BB	SO	SB
26-28	43-45	7	790	0.281	0.452	2786	782	150	29	90	3.2	424	420	385	298	20
		3	421	0.284	0.463	1520	431	82	16	53	3.5	230	234	197	164	11
		10	1211	0.282	0.456	4306	1213	232	45	143	3.3	654	654	582	462	31

KAMPOURIS, ALEXIS W. (ALEX)   BR TR 5' 8" 155 lbs.

Born November 13, 1912, Sacramento, Ca. — Died May 29, 1993, Sacramento, Ca.
Played for Cincinnati (1934–38), New York (N) (1938–39), Brooklyn (1941–43), and Washington (1943)

Alex Kampouris was a light-hitting second baseman during the late '30s. He had been relegated to part-time status before the start of World War II. While he only hit forty-five home runs in his career, he did hit three in one game on May 9, 1937. He had eight RBIs that day. His best batting average as a regular was .249. He entered the Army Air Force in 1944 and was stationed at Buckley Field, Colorado. That summer he was transferred to Stockton Field, California, where he stayed and played ball for the rest of 1944 and into 1945. In the fall of 1945 he played for an Army Air Force team in Canada. Kampouris was still listed on the Senators defense list on December 6, 1945. He was not able to resume his baseball career at the major league level after the war.

AGE	YRS	ML	G	BA	SA	AB	H	2B	3B	HR	HR%	R	RBI	BB	SO	SB
31-32	44-45	9	708	0.243	0.367	2182	531	94	20	45	2.1	272	284	244	360	22
		2	70	0.238	0.372	231	55	13	3	4	1.7	33	29	44	42	3
		11	778	0.243	0.367	2413	586	107	23	49	2	305	313	288	402	25

KINER, RALPH M.   BR TR 6' 2"   195 lbs.

Born October 27, 1922, Santa Rita, N.M.
Played for Pittsburgh (1946–53), Chicago (N) (1953–54), and Cleveland (1955)

Ralph Kiner did not play in the majors before entering the Navy in 1943. However, he had been called up from Albany in March 1943 before he enlisted as a Navy cadet, although he did not get into a game with the Pirates and spent the time before he went into active duty at Toronto in the International League. He entered the Navy on June 6, 1943, to begin his Naval Cadet training. He did his preflight school training at St. Mary's in California. While in the Navy, he did see some combat as a Navy flyer in the South Pacific. Kiner was discharged on December 9, 1945. He said, "I had the opportunity to stay in the reserve program, along with most of the guys I flew with, but I wanted no part of it." He added, "The war had been so catastrophic that all of us who went through it, either overseas or on the home front, were greatly affected by it" (Peary 1994, 3).

Kiner knew that there would be lots of competition for the 400 major league jobs, and unlike some, he hadn't gotten to play in more than a few games during the two-and-a-half years he had spent in the Navy. In addition to the players who had played during the war, young players were trying for their chance at the "bigs" as well as the returning war veterans. He said, "I was discharged in December 1945. As soon as I got home I began working out. I worked out every day for two months before spring training started, so when I joined the ball club in San Bernardino I was in great shape. I was ready" (Honig 1976, 107). He was ready. He had a great spring training and was kept with the Pirates even though he had been scheduled to go to the minors. The Pirates made a good decision to keep him. He became the first National League rookie to lead the league in home runs. He hit twenty-three, starting a streak that would last for seven years. Kiner led or tied for the lead in home runs for the first seven years of his career, also a major league record. Stan Musial said, "For a number of years, Kiner was the most consistent home-run hitter in the National League" (Broeg 1964, 275). He was the best slugger in the National League in the late '40s and early '50s. At the close of his career, Kiner had the second highest home run percentage of alltime (Babe Ruth was number one). He was traded to the Cubs in 1953, and his streak as home run leader came to an end. A bad back shortened his career. He retired at age thirty-two. In a letter Kiner said, "Other than the two-and-a-half years I spent in the service, [time I lost] to pro ball, I don't believe there were too many adverse effects [on my career]" (Kiner letter, 1997).

AGE	YRS	ML	G	BA	SA	AB	H	2B	3B	HR	HR%	R	RBI	BB	SO	SB
20-22	43-45	10	1472	0.279	0.548	5205	1451	216	39	369	7.1	971	1015	1011	749	22
(3 YRS-EST 2		2	216	0.276	0.523	789	218	33	9	48	6.1	140	145	107	83	3
YRS MAJORS)		12	1688	0.278	0.545	5994	1669	249	48	417	7	1111	1160	1118	832	25

LAVAGETTO, HARRY A. (COOKIE)   BR TR 6' 0"   170 lbs.

Born December 1, 1912, Oakland, Ca. — Died August 10, 1990, Orinda, Ca.
Played for Pittsburgh (1934–36) and Brooklyn (1937–41, 1946–47)

The event that made Cookie Lavagetto famous came in the World Series of the last year that he played major league baseball. It happened in game four of the 1947 World Series when

Lavagetto's Dodgers played the Yankees. Yankees' starter Bill Bevens had taken a no-hitter into the ninth. He had a one-to-nothing lead. After two outs and two walks, Lavagetto came up to pinch-hit for Eddie Stanky. Lavagetto then doubled off the right field wall, two runs scored, and the Dodgers had the victory. This was the only hit Bevens gave up that day. That hit would be the last hit that Lavagetto ever got wearing a major league uniform. While he did pinch-hit in the next three games, he was unsuccessful each time. He closed his career with the hit that made him famous.

Cookie got his nickname from the man who gave him his first chance in baseball, Cookie DeVincenzi of the Oakland Oaks. He had come up with the Pirates in 1934 but did not become a regular until he was traded to the Dodgers in 1937. Over the next five years he would be a regular infielder for the Dodgers. That run was stopped when he entered the Navy on January 31, 1942. He was an All-Star four of those five years. He waived his 2-A deferment and enlisted in the Navy. He wanted to show his loyalty to America because of his Italian background.

By 1943 he had graduated from the Naval Aviation Physical Education School at Bainbridge, Maryland, and had been transferred to Livermore, California, as an instructor. In December 1944 he reached the rank of Specialist First Class and was sent to Alameda, California, Naval Air Field. He spent the spring at Alameda, playing and managing the baseball team. That summer he was slated for overseas duty and shipped out of San Francisco to the Pacific. While in Hawaii he was able to continue to play baseball. He was named to the 14th Naval District all-star team while playing for the Ship Repair Unit team. Lavagetto was discharged on October 8, 1945. He returned to the Dodgers in 1946 and played in 1947 as well. However, in both years he was a reserve, and he had only gotten eighteen hits in 1947 before the one in the World Series.

AGE	YRS	ML	G	BA	SA	AB	H	2B	3B	HR	HR%	R	RBI	BB	SO	SB
29-32	42-45	10	1043	0.269	0.377	3509	945	183	37	40	1.1	487	486	485	244	63
		4	448	0.275	0.381	1516	417	79	14	18	1.2	223	208	226	101	33
		14	1491	0.271	0.378	5025	1362	262	51	58	1.2	710	694	711	345	96

LIPON, JOHN J. (JOHNNY)   BR TR 6'0" 175 lbs.
Born November 10, 1922, Martins Ferry, Oh. — Died August 17, 1998, Houston, Tx.
Played for Detroit (1942, 1946, 1948–52), Boston (A) (1952–53), St. Louis (A) (1953), and Cincinnati (1954)

Johnny Lipon played in thirty-four games with the Tigers at the end of the 1942 season before he entered military service. He was sworn in on December 11, 1942, as an apprentice seaman at the Great Lakes base. In March 1944, he set the best accuracy mark with a .50 caliber machine gun at Jacksonville Naval Air Station. Later that year he was stationed in California, played baseball, and was named to an all-star team in the Army-Navy league. In the spring of 1945, he was flying casualties from the Okinawa area. He was picked from Navy Aviation Rescue Squad for duty at Manila late in 1945. He would not be available to the Tigers for a while. He was still listed on the Tigers' defense list on December 6, 1945, and he rejoined the Tigers in 1946 but played in only fourteen games. After a year in the minors in 1947, Lipon returned to the Tigers in 1948 as their regular shortstop for four years. While he wasn't a great shortstop, he did team with Gerry Priddy to form a very good double play combination. In 1950 they combined for 276 double plays, the second highest number ever. Lipon became a respected minor league manager following his playing days. He was voted manager of the year on two different occasions. He had one shot at major league managing but was not successful.

AGE	YRS	ML	G	BA	SA	AB	H	2B	3B	HR	HR%	R	RBI	BB	SO	SB
20-22	43-45	9	758	0.259	0.324	2661	690	95	24	10	0.4	351	266	347	152	28
		3	72	0.208	0.221	226	47	3	0	0	0	14	15	18	15	2
		12	830	0.255	0.316	2887	737	98	24	10	0.3	365	281	365	167	30

LIVINGSTON, THOMPSON O. (MICKEY)   BR TR 6' 1" 185 lbs.

Born November 15, 1914, Newberry, S.C. — Died April 3, 1983, Newberry, S.C.
Played for Washington (1938), Philadelphia (N) (1941-43), Chicago (N) (1943, 1945-47), New York (N) (1947-49), Boston (N) (1949), and Brooklyn (1951)

Mickey Livingston was a backup catcher for most of his career. His only year to play at least 100 games came in 1943 when he split time between the Phillies and the Cubs. He entered the Army in March 1944, and his time in the Army went from Fort Bragg, North Carolina, to Camp Butner, North Carolina, to Camp Pickett, Virginia, to Camp Atterbury, Indiana. These transfers occurred during a short time, ending at Camp Atterbury in the summer of 1944. While there he was first gunner in a machine gun outfit and won expert rating with the machine gun and rifle. He was able to play for the 106th Infantry team while stationed at Camp Atterbury.

Livingston was discharged in November 1944 because of a medical problem. In 1939, while playing in the minors, Livingston ran into a concrete dugout trying to catch a pop foul. He received a concussion because of the accident. It was discovered that when he wore a metal helmet for a period of time, he got headaches and became dizzy. The problem was not noticed during basic training because they did not wear metal helmets during that time, but when it came time to get ready to go to Europe, they wore helmets and the problem surfaced. After examination by Army doctors, Livingston was given an honorable discharge. He returned to baseball in time for the 1945 season. He was a part-time catcher for the Cubs that year as they made their drive for the pennant. He had a very good World Series in a losing cause against the Tigers. He batted .364 and had four RBIs. He continued his back-up role for several more seasons, retiring in 1951.

AGE	YRS	ML	G	BA	SA	AB	H	2B	3B	HR	HR%	R	RBI	BB	SO	SB
29	44	10	561	0.238	0.326	1490	354	56	9	19	1.3	128	153	144	141	7
		1	88	0.238	0.32	244	58	9	1	3	1.2	21	23	23	22	1
		11	649	0.238	0.325	1734	412	65	10	22	1.3	149	176	167	163	8

LODIGIANI, DARIO A.   BR TR 5' 8" 150 lbs.

Born July 16, 1916, San Francisco, Ca.
Played for Philadelphia (A) (1938-40) and Chicago (A) (1941-42, 1946)

Dario Lodigiani grew up in San Francisco playing baseball with the DiMaggio brothers. He was considered to have a regular position for three of five years before he went into service.

However, only one year in his career did he play at least one hundred games. He enlisted in the Army Air Force on March 3, 1943, and went to McClellan Field in Sacramento, California. He stayed there for 1943 and part of 1944. He achieved the sharpshooter rating with a rifle there and was assigned to the Sixth Ferrying Group at that location. By June 1944 Lodigiani had been transferred to Hawaii, stationed at Hickem Field. He was able to play baseball while stationed there. He was a member of the 7th Air Force team in Honolulu, and was also a member of the Army team that played Navy in the "Pacific World Series" in September 1944. He was named to the Honolulu league all-star team while stationed in Hawaii.

The summer of 1945 saw Lodigiani shipped out, along with other ballplayers, to the Pacific Islands to play for the other troops. He said, "We were the first ones out there to play ball there" (Van Blair 1994, 114). In a letter, Lodigiani said, "While in the States and assigned to a special service outfit, we played a lot of games to entertain the troops. While stationed at Hickem Field in Hawaii, we played a lot of ball for the troops." He continued, "Down under in the South Pacific, we were assigned to a B29 outfit that had a great many bombing runs over Japanese Islands and Japan itself. Our base on Saipan and Tinian was a long way from the targets and we didn't see any of the actual bombings. Our jobs were servicing the planes that did the bombings." He went on to say, "While on Tinian, we saw the Enola Gay take off that dropped the first atomic bomb on Japan. There were many major league players in the South Pacific and nearing the end of the war, we played a number of games against the Navy" (Lodigiani letter 1998). He arrived in Los Angeles on November 2 on board the transport *Cecil* and was discharged on November 16, 1945, with the rank of sergeant. Lodigiani returned to the White Sox in time for the 1946 season. Forty-four games into the season, he was hit on the elbow and broke a big piece of bone. He was sent home to heal. However, in 1947 he still could not throw very well, so he was given his release. Lodigiani is still employed by the White Sox as a scout on the West Coast.

AGE	YRS	ML	G	BA	SA	AB	H	2B	3B	HR	HR%	R	RBI	BB	SO	SB
27-29	43-45	6	405	0.26	0.358	1364	355	71	7	16	1.2	142	156	141	86	12
		3	190	0.251	0.329	645	162	34	2	4	0.6	60	68	65	43	7
		9	595	0.257	0.348	2009	517	105	9	20	1	202	224	206	129	19

LUCADELLO, JOHN (JOHNNY)   BB TR 5' 11" 160 lbs.
Born February 22, 1919, Thurber, Tx. — Died October 30, 2001, San Antonio, Tx.
Played for St. Louis (A) (1938–41, 1946) and New York (A) (1947)

The year 1941 was Johnny Lucadello's first chance to play on a regular basis in the major leagues. He served the role of a utility infielder and pinch hitter before that time. That was the only year that he played in over one hundred games in one season in his career. No one will know if he could have had a good career because he enlisted in the Navy on March 25, 1942. He joined in Chicago and was assigned to the Great Lakes base. He took part in a game that matched service all-stars against American League All-Stars. This took place in the summer of 1942 and raised money for war relief. Lucadello stayed at Great Lakes until the spring of 1944 when he was transferred to Bainbridge, Maryland. There he received more intensive training before shipping out of San Francisco on the way to Pearl Harbor to assist with physical conditioning. He had been able to play baseball at Great Lakes, and he was also able to play in Honolulu. While in Hawaii, Lucadello was a member of the Navy team that defeated the Army in the "Pacific World Series" in September 1944. After five months in Honolulu, he, along with several others, was sent to the Pacific Islands to entertain the troops in those areas. The islands included Guam, Saipan, and Tinian. He was discharged on October 16, 1945. In 1946, he served as a backup in the infield and as a pinch hitter. His major league career ended the next season at age twenty-eight.

AGE	YRS	ML	G	BA	SA	AB	H	2B	3B	HR	HR%	R	RBI	BB	SO	SB
23-26	42-45	6	239	0.264	0.359	686	181	36	7	5	0.7	95	60	93	56	6
		4	388	0.267	0.353	1122	300	58	10	6	0.5	158	92	168	86	10
		10	627	0.266	0.355	1808	481	94	17	11	0.6	253	152	261	142	16

LUPIEN, ULYSSES J. (TONY)   BL TL 5' 10"   185 lbs.
Born April 23, 1917, Chelmsford, Ma.
Played for Boston (A) (1940, 1942-43), Philadelphia (N) (1944-45), and Chicago (A) (1948)

Tony Lupien replaced Jimmie Foxx as first baseman for the Boston Red Sox in 1942. He was with the Red Sox again in 1943 and was waived to the Phillies for the 1944 season. He had been classified 2-B with the Red Sox before being waived. Lupien entered the Navy on March 5, 1945. He was stationed at Sampson, New York, during that spring, and was able to play baseball for the Sampson team. He played his last game for them on May 31, 1945, and left Sampson to enter the V-12 Naval course at Colgate University. As the war ended, he was released from the Navy in time to play fifteen games for the Phillies at the close of the 1945 season. He batted .315 during that stretch.

The problem developed the following spring. The Phillies had traded for Frank McCormick and Lupien didn't fit into their plans. They put Lupien on waivers, and when no major league team claimed him, they traded him to Hollywood in the Pacific Coast League. Lupien protested. The basis of his protest was a provision of the G.I. Bill which stated that an employer had to reemploy his former workers who had been in service if they were still qualified for their former position. Baseball had set up their own version of this reemployment provision. They said they would give a player thirty days of spring training or fifteen days of regular season to prove his ability. After that they had three choices. They could keep the player; they could send him to the minors if he cleared waivers; or they could give him his outright release. If they kept the player, he got his previous pay or higher; if sent to the minors, he got one year at his old salary; and if released, he got fifteen days' pay.

Lupien had gotten to play fifteen games at the end of the 1945 season, so the Phillies said they had met the requirements of the reemployment law as far as baseball was concerned. Lupien disagreed. This Harvard graduate did not accept what he considered to be a violation of his rights. With no players' association, he protested to "Happy" Chandler, baseball's commissioner. When he did not get action, he filed a complaint with the U.S. Attorney's office in Philadelphia. His contention was that the general reemployment provision of the G.I. Bill should apply to baseball as well as other professions. His lawyer was concerned that baseball would drag the matter out for a long time. When the Hollywood team offered him the same salary as he had before the war with Phillies, he gave up and reported there. He said, "I had kids and no money. So I dropped the case and went out there" (Mead 1985, 240). Lupien would make it back to the majors for one more year. After two years at Hollywood, he was the regular first baseman for the White Sox in 1948. Following his active career, he managed in the minors, coached at Dartmouth, and wrote a book called *The Imperfect Diamond*, a book on baseball's reserve clause.

AGE	YRS	ML	G	BA	SA	AB	H	2B	3B	HR	HR%	R	RBI	BB	SO	SB
28	45	6	614	0.268	0.355	2358	632	92	30	18	0.8	285	230	241	111	57
(1 YR MINUS		0	130	0.267	0.367	502	134	22	8	4	0.8	69	53	47	24	13
15 GAMES)		6	744	0.268	0.357	2860	766	114	38	22	0.8	354	283	288	135	70

MACK, RAYMOND J. (RAY)   BR TR 6' 0"   200 lbs.
Born August 31, 1916, Cleveland, Oh. — Died May 7, 1969, Bucyrus, Oh.
Played for Cleveland (1938–44, 1946), New York (A) (1947), and Chicago (N) (1947)

Ray Mack was a good fielding second baseman for the Indians for the four years before the war. He was able to field the ball to get the final out in two of Bob Feller's no-hitters. On April 16, 1940, he went to his left after a sharp grounder. He was able to knock it down and throw out Taft Wright of the White Sox on a great play. On April 30, 1946, he fielded a high hopper hit by Charley Keller of the Yankees and threw to first for the final out. He was selected to and played in the 1940 All-Star game. He and Lou Boudreau formed a good double play combination. They combined for 245 double plays in 1943. Mack's playing time was curtailed in 1944 as he worked in a defense plant. He was a plant layout engineer for the Thompson Aircraft Product Company. Mack asked to play as much baseball as possible in 1944, as long as he did not let the job at the defense plant suffer. His draft board and baseball's Commissioner Kenesaw Mountain Landis agreed. His baseball playing probably did suffer because of his part-time status, however.

The draft board changed his classification from 2-B to 2-A and then to 1-A-L, meaning he would be inducted for limited service. He entered the Army on April 17, 1945. He was inducted in Cleveland and sent to Camp Atterbury, where he was able to play some baseball. After boot camp, he was sent to Fort Leonard Wood, Missouri, as an engineer trainee in Company D, 28th Engineer Trainee Battalion. He was also able to play baseball at Fort Leonard Wood. He spent the summer there and was discharged on November 15, 1945. He returned to the Indians in 1946 but was never able to regain his position as the regular second baseman. After the Indians traded for Joe Gordon in 1947, Mack was sent to the Yankees in a trade that brought Gene Bearden to the Indians. After playing only one game with the Yankees, Mack finished his career that year with the Cubs.

AGE	YRS	ML	G	BA	SA	AB	H	2B	3B	HR	HR%	R	RBI	BB	SO	SB
28	45	9	791	0.232	0.329	2708	629	113	24	34	1.3	273	278	261	365	35
		1	80	0.222	0.319	270	60	13	2	3	1.1	26	28	26	37	4
		10	871	0.231	0.328	2978	689	126	26	37	1.2	299	306	287	402	39

MACON, MAX C.   BL TL 6' 3"   175 lbs.
Born October 14, 1915, Pensacola, Fl. — Died August 5, 1989, Jupiter, Fl.
Played for St. Louis (N) (1938), Brooklyn (1940, 1942–43), and Boston (N) (1944, 1947)

Max Macon came to the Cardinals in 1938 as a pitcher. His best year was 1943 with the
Dodgers when he won seven games and lost five with an earned run average of 3.37. Although
he wasn't an outstanding pitcher, Macon was always a decent hitter, being used several times
as a pinch hitter. In 1942 he had a streak of five consecutive pinch hits. So when the shortage
of players was becoming acute in 1944, he switched to play first base and outfield. Playing in
106 games, he batted .273 and drove in thirty-six runs. He had been classified 2-B, but he was
accepted for active service by the Navy at Boston on July 27, 1944. He was allowed to finish
the year with Boston before becoming active. Starting at Fort McClelland, Alabama, he was
transferred to Fort Meade, Maryland, in April 1945. Macon was injured in a dynamite explosion
and was hospitalized for twenty-nine days because of his injuries. He also spent some time in
the summer of 1945 playing baseball for the team at Bainbridge, Maryland. His tour of duty
extended through 1946. He returned for the 1947 season, and the one game he pitched for
the Braves was the last game of his major league career.

AGE	YRS	ML	G	BA	SA	AB	H	2B	3B	HR	HR%	R	RBI	BB	SO	SB
29-30	45-46	6	226	0.265	0.333	502	133	17	4	3	0.6	54	46	16	32	9
		2	83	0.276	0.335	185	51	6	1	1	0.5	21	17	7	12	5
		8	309	0.268	0.333	687	184	23	5	4	0.6	75	63	23	44	14

MARTIN, STUART M. (STU)   BL TR 6' 0"   155 lbs.
Born November 17, 1913, Rich Square, N.C. — Died January 11, 1997, Serevn, N.C.
Played for St. Louis (N) (1936–40), Pittsburgh (1941–42), and Chicago (N) (1943)

Stu Martin was brought up from the minor leagues by the Cardinals in 1936 to relieve Frankie
Frisch at second base. He served in that role well and was selected to the All-Star team in 1936
as a reserve, although he did not play. Martin secured a starting role in 1938 and held that role
until he was sold to the Pirates in 1941. He was a good fielder, leading the National League
in fielding for the 1939 season. Martin lost part of the season in 1942 when he served in the
merchant marines. He closed out his major league career in 1943 with the Chicago Cubs.

AGE	YRS	ML	G	BA	SA	AB	H	2B	3B	HR	HR%	R	RBI	BB	SO	SB
28	42	8	722	0.268	0.361	2237	599	112	24	16	0.7	322	183	190	185	36
(1 YR MINUS		0	42	0.225	0.317	120	27	4	2	1	0.8	16	12	8	10	1
42 GAMES)		8	764	0.266	0.359	2357	626	116	26	17	0.7	338	195	198	195	37

MAUCH, GENE W.   BR TR 5' 10"   165 lbs.
Born November 18, 1925, Salina, Ks.
Played for Brooklyn (1944, 1948), Pittsburgh (1947), Chicago (N) (1948–49), Boston (N)
(1950–51), St. Louis (N) (1952), and Boston (A) (1956–57)

Gene Mauch was signed by the Dodgers out of a Fremont, California, high school in 1944 at
age 18. He was part of the host of youngsters that Branch Rickey signed as he tried to stock

the warriddled rosters. But Rickey was also looking toward the future of baseball after the war. Some did make it big from that group, but Mauch did not. Mauch was given a shot at the shortstop job in 1944 but was sent down after only five games. After the 1944 season, Mauch enlisted in the Army Air Corps with the intent of being a pilot. However, the cadet program was discontinued before he could complete the training, so he became a physical fitness instructor. He did not see any combat during the time he spent in the Army Air Corps. He said about his career and his military service, "The only thing I lost was time" (Mauch letter 1998). He was released in time for the 1946 season, which he spent at St. Paul in the American Association. Traded to the Pirates in 1947, he began a career that ended in 1957 in which he served as a backup infielder for a number of major league teams.

Mauch was more noted as a manager, a position he held for twenty-five years. This ties him for fourth in the most years managed by any person. However, he did not win a pennant in any of those years. He came close in 1964, 1982, and 1986, but his teams were not able to close the victory. He said, "The worst thing is the day you realize you want to win more than the players do" (Dickson 1991, 277).

AGE	YRS	ML	G	BA	SA	AB	H	2B	3B	HR	HR%	R	RBI	BB	SO	SB
18-19	44-45	9	304	0.239	0.312	737	176	25	7	5	0.7	93	62	104	82	6
(2 YRS MINUS		1	29	0.232	0.286	56	13	1	1	0	0	5	3	4	2	0
5 GAMES)		10	333	0.238	0.31	793	189	26	8	5	0.6	98	65	108	84	6

MCCORMICK, MYRON W. (MIKE)   BR TR 6'0" 195 lbs.

Born May 6, 1917, Angel's Camp, Ca. — Died April 14, 1976, Ventura, Ca.
Played for Cincinnati (1940–43, 1946), Boston (N) (1946–48), Brooklyn (1949), New York (N) (1950), Chicago (A) (1950), and Washington (1951)

Mike McCormick helped the Reds win the pennant in his rookie year in 1940. He had a good World Series, batting .310 and setting a World Series record, making twenty-four putouts in the outfield as the Reds beat the Tigers. He lost much of the 1942 season with a broken leg, and he entered the Army in May 1943. McCormick spent most of 1943 and the early part of 1944 at McClellan Field, California, where he was part of the Sixth Ferrying Group. He earned a sharpshooter award while stationed at McClellan.

The summer of 1944 found McCormick stationed in Hawaii at Hickem Field. He had risen to the rank of corporal and was playing on the 7th Air Force team in Honolulu. He was named to the all-star team and played for the Army in the "Pacific World Series" against the Navy. In June 1945 he was managing the "Wheeler Wingmen" team in Hawaii. Again in 1945 he was selected to the all-star team. When the Army sent the ballplayers out to the islands to play exhibitions for the troops, McCormick was in the first group that was sent. In the summer of 1945, he went to the Marianas, playing for the 73rd Wing Team from the 20th Air Force in such places as Saipan, Guam, and Tinian. McCormick was discharged in October 1945.

After twenty-three games with the Reds in 1946, McCormick was traded to the Braves. He was an important part of the Braves as they made their pennant drive in 1948. Traded to the

Dodgers in 1949, he also took part in their pennant drive as a reserve. His career ended with the Senators in 1951, one of his better hitting years in several seasons.

AGE	YRS	ML	G	BA	SA	AB	H	2B	3B	HR	HR%	R	RBI	BB	SO	SB
26-28	43-45	10	748	0.275	0.361	2325	640	100	29	14	0.6	302	215	188	174	16
(3 YRS MINUS		2	271	0.287	0.376	878	252	41	11	5	0.6	119	84	62	67	3
4 GAMES)		12	1019	0.278	0.365	3203	892	141	40	19	0.6	421	299	250	241	19

MEYER, LAMBERT D. (DUTCH)   BR TR 5' 10"   185 lbs.

Born October 6, 1915, Waco, Tx. — Died January 19, 2003, Ft. Worth, Tx.
Played for Chicago (N) (1937), Detroit (1940–42), and Cleveland (1945–46)

Dutch Meyer had a few trials with the Tigers before he entered the Army Air Corps on November 1, 1942. He spent part of his Air Force service at Fort Worth, Texas. In August 1944 he was stationed at Waco, Texas, and was playing for the base team. He was discharged on April 15, 1945. On April 29, 1945, the Tigers traded him to the Indians. Meyer got to play on a regular basis for the 1945 season as a replacement for Ray Mack, who was in the military. He had a good year, batting .292. The All-Star game was canceled that year because of the war. However, Meyer was considered to be one of the two best second basemen in the American League in 1945. The following year, his final major league season, Meyer served as a backup at second.

AGE	YRS	ML	G	BA	SA	AB	H	2B	3B	HR	HR%	R	RBI	BB	SO	SB
27-28	43-44	6	286	0.264	0.367	994	262	49	12	10	1	113	93	82	75	5
		2	105	0.272	0.383	371	101	19	5	4	1.1	46	36	34	29	3
		8	391	0.266	0.371	1365	363	68	17	14	1	159	129	116	104	8

MILLS, COLONEL B. (BUSTER)   BR TR 5' 11"   195 lbs.

Born September 16, 1908, Ranger, Tx. — Died December 1, 1991, Arlington, Tx.
Played for St. Louis (N) (1934), Brooklyn (1935), Boston (A) (1937), St. Louis (A) (1938), New York (A) (1940), and Cleveland (1942, 1946)

Buster Mills must have had an interesting time in the Army with a first name of Colonel. Soldiers wouldn't have known what to call him. He was an officer, receiving a commission in April 1942 as a 2nd lieutenant. Mills didn't achieve regular status in the majors until 1937 with the Red Sox. That status lasted for only one more year, 1938, with the Browns. He was used as a leadoff man because of his speed. The rest of his career he served the role of reserve. He was sent back to the minors in 1941 only to be called back to the majors with the Indians in 1942 as the player shortage began to take effect.

Mills entered the Army Air Force after the 1942 season and was sent to the base at Waco, Texas, where he served as a physical instructor. While he was stationed at Waco, he was able to play baseball. He was stationed there for almost two years, and he helped make the Waco team famous, being voted the outstanding player in a tournament in 1944. In the summer of 1944, he was transferred to Aloe Army Air Field, Victoria, Texas, as assistant physical training officer. After the Navy beat the Army in the "Pacific World Series" in September 1944, the Army assembled a group of men in Utah to train, go to Hawaii, and take on the Navy. However, when they got there in the summer of 1945, the Navy team was already gone from the island. When arriving in Hawaii, he was assigned to Bellows Field, about twenty miles outside Honolulu. He was the base athletic officer in charge of the baseball team. By mid-summer, the ball players were transferred out to the South Pacific to entertain the troops who had captured the islands from the Japanese.

Mills managed the 73rd Wing Bomber, 20th Air Force team in the Marianas. They were headquartered in Saipan but also played games on Guam, Tinian, and Iwo Jima. He was on Tinian when the bomber "Enola Gay" took off for her run on Japan. He arrived back in Los Angeles on November 2, 1945, from the Pacific aboard the transport ship *Cecil* with the rank of 1st lieutenant. Mills was still on the Indians' defense list on December 6, 1945, but he did return for the 1946 season. At age thirty-eight, he played in only nine games before becoming a coach for the Indians.

AGE	YRS	ML	G	BA	SA	AB	H	2B	3B	HR	HR%	R	RBI	BB	SO	SB
34-35	43-45	7	415	0.287	0.39	1379	396	62	19	14	1	200	163	131	137	24
		3	190	0.285	0.382	625	178	28	6	7	1.1	91	75	65	54	8
		10	605	0.286	0.388	2004	574	90	25	21	1	291	238	196	191	32

MULLIN, PATRICK J. (PAT)

BL TR 6' 2" 190 lbs.

Born November 1, 1917, Trotter, Pa. — Died August 14, 1999, Brownsville, Pa.
Played for Detroit (1940–41, 1946–53)

Pat Mullin batted .345 in his rookie year with the Tigers in 1941 as a part-time player. He then enlisted in the Army on March 13, 1942, at Pittsburgh. He was stationed at New Cumberland, Pennsylvania, Reception Center, awaiting assignment. That summer he played with the service all-stars against the American League All-Stars to raise money for war relief. By October 1942 he had been promoted to corporal and by December to sergeant. He remained at the New Cumberland Reception Center in the records and assignment section. By March 1944, he was transferred to Camp Siebert, Alabama, as a physical training instructor. While stationed there he was able to play on the camp baseball team, and he received a commission. Mullin said, "I attended officer training—Medical Administrate Corp—and was discharged a first lieutenant from Washington & Lee University in Lexington, Virginia, [as an] instructor in sports and games with or without equipment. If you didn't have a ball you used a taped-up sock. I also gave calisthenics to the troops. I spent four years in the service, didn't go overseas" (Mullin letter 1998). He also indicated he trained at Great Lakes Naval Base and played on the all-service team that was managed by Mickey Cochrane.

Mullin was discharged on April 2, 1946. He returned to the Tigers for the 1946 season, but he looked rusty and, with some shoulder problems, remained in a slump for most of the year. His best year was 1948 when he got to play in the All-Star game. He batted .288 that year with twenty-three home runs and eighty RBIs.

AGE	YRS	ML	G	BA	SA	AB	H	2B	3B	HR	HR%	R	RBI	BB	SO	SB
24-27	42-45	10	864	0.271	0.453	2493	676	106	43	87	3.5	381	385	330	312	20
		4	381	0.284	0.493	1137	323	53	26	44	3.9	184	189	141	121	12
		14	1245	0.275	0.465	3630	999	159	69	131	3.6	565	574	471	433	32

a stroke, he'd go right down, and he flew an airplane like he had stone arms." He added, "They finally got Pesky out of there. In an airplane he was a menace to himself and everybody else, but he was certainly officer material so they moved him into O.C.S. [Officer Candidate School] and he actually got his rank before I did" (Williams and Underwood 1988, 101).

After Bainbridge, Pesky was sent to Atlanta Naval Training Station for gunnery training in March 1944. He was eligible for a commission when the training was completed. He served as manager of the base baseball team while stationed in Atlanta. Pesky graduated from the Assistant Operations Officers' School on June 13, 1944, and was commissioned an ensign. He continued to be stationed in Atlanta at Gordon Field. Pesky stayed there until March 1945 when he was detached from Atlanta and assigned to Welfare and Recreation in the South Pacific. He was attached to the 14th Naval District in Hawaii. When stationed in Honolulu, he was able to play some baseball. He played in the Navy all-star game and "Pacific World Series" in the fall of 1945. He also was voted runner-up in the MVP voting in the 14th Naval District League. He was discharged from the Navy in December 1945 with the rank of lieutenant (j.g.). Pesky picked up his career right where he left off. He again led the American League in hits in 1946 and 1947, getting over 200 hits each year. He set a major league record by starting his career with three consecutive years of over 200 hits. He helped the Red Sox to the pennant in 1946.

An event happened during that World Series that will continue to haunt Pesky forever. In game seven of the 1946 World Series, the score was tied 3 to 3. With two outs, Enos Slaughter, Cardinal outfielder, ran with the pitch. Harry Walker hit the ball into center field. The center fielder retrieved the ball and threw it to the relay man, Pesky. Slaughter didn't stop at third and headed for home plate. When Pesky saw Slaughter running, he threw home but too late. The Cardinals won the World Series. Pesky has been accused of hesitating before throwing, thereby allowing the run to score and becoming the scapegoat because he didn't react quickly enough. Most of the players who were playing that day say it was not Pesky's fault. Harry Walker said, "Johnny Pesky did not hold the ball that long. He just turned, looked, then threw. There really wasn't any play at the plate anyway" (Cataneo 1991, 244). Terry Moore added, "They didn't let Pesky know that Slaughter was going home" (Van Blair 1994, 143). Boo Ferris said, "Yes, it wasn't Pesky's fault. Bobby Doerr and Pinky Higgins at third were yelling at Pesky to throw home, but John couldn't hear because thirty-five thousand Cardinal fans were yelling" (Van Blair 1994, 57). Enos Slaughter added, "You know, they've made Pesky the goat...Well, I don't go along with that. Anytime an infielder has to go out to take a relay his back is to the plate and it's up to his teammates to let him know where the runner is" (Honig 1976, 166). Ted Williams said, "...you can't blame Pesky" (Williams and Underwood 1988, 117).

Pesky also talked about the incident, saying, "I didn't hesitate...but I'll never convince the baseball world of that" (Blake 1994, 113). He added, "...as far as the forty-six World Series goes, I've learned to live with it. I never dreamed the way the ball was hit, that Slaughter would try to score. But he did" (Van Blair 1994, 163). Johnny Pesky had a good career, but he never lived down the "hesitation" from the '46 World Series. He switched to third base after Vern Stephens joined the Red Sox in 1948 and was never quite as productive as the first three years. He concluded his career in 1954 with a .307 lifetime batting average.

AGE	YRS	ML	G	BA	SA	AB	H	2B	3B	HR	HR%	R	RBI	BB	SO	SB
23-25	43-45	10	1270	0.307	0.386	4745	1455	226	50	17	0.4	867	404	663	218	53
		3	448	0.316	0.397	1829	578	91	20	6	0.3	337	161	227	83	26
		13	1718	0.309	0.389	6574	2033	317	70	23	0.3	1204	565	890	301	79

PETERS, RUSSELL D. (RUSTY)   BR TR 5' 11"   170 lbs.

Born December 14, 1914, Roanoke, Va. — Died February 21, 2003, Harrisonburg, Va.

Played for Philadelphia (A) (1936–38), Cleveland (1940–44, 1946), and St. Louis (A) (1947)

Rusty Peters was a middle infielder who was a good fielder but struggled with the bat. His best year was 1937. He was with the A's, and he batted .260 in one hundred sixteen games. The only other two years he played at least seventy-five games were the war years when he was a replacement for those already in service. In six of the other seven years, he played less than forty games in any one year. He was called for a preinduction physical on June 5, 1944, by the Roanoke, Virginia, draft board. He requested a transfer to Cleveland where he was playing. He was drafted in April 1945. In June 1945 he was at Fort Knox, Kentucky, taking tank training. After that he was sent to Germany as part of the army of occupation in November 1945. He was sent home the middle of August 1946.

Peters said, "At Ft. Knox, I lost most of the little finger on my throwing hand, which caused shoulder problems the rest of my career. I was refused any compensation by the Army." He added, "I think Bill Veeck was the best thing that ever happened to baseball. He gave me the only decent contract I ever received in my years of playing, which was 17 years total" (Peters letter 1997). Peters was discharged on September 8, 1946. He played a little for the Indians that year and closed his career with the Browns the following year.

AGE	YRS	ML	G	BA	SA	AB	H	2B	3B	HR	HR%	R	RBI	BB	SO	SB
30-31	45-46	10	471	0.236	0.326	1222	289	53	16	8	0.7	123	117	98	199	9
2 YRS MINUS		1	88	0.235	0.335	230	54	11	3	2	0.8	26	21	21	36	2
9 GAMES)		11	559	0.236	0.327	1452	343	64	19	10	0.7	149	138	119	235	11

RADCLIFF, RAYMOND A. (RIP)   BL TL 5' 10"   170 lbs.

Born January 19, 1906, Kiowa, Ok. — Died May 23, 1962, Enid, Ok.

Played for Chicago (A) (1934–39), St. Louis (A) (1940–41), and Detroit (1941–43)

Rip Radcliff didn't reach the majors until age twenty-eight and did not achieve regular status until the following year when he was twenty-nine years old. This outfielder did well when he got the chance. In 1936, his second full year, he batted .335 and played in the All-Star game. He made a game-saving catch in that game for the American League. The year 1940 was also very good for Radcliff. He led the league with 200 hits and batted .342. He continued his full-time status through the 1941 season. Starting in 1942, he lost his regular status with the Tigers. He was, however, a good pinch hitter during the last two years of his career. Radcliff entered the Navy on April 26, 1944. He was thirty-eight years old when he was drafted. He reported to San Diego, California.

By February 1945, Radcliff was stationed at the Norman, Oklahoma, Naval Air Station where he played some baseball. Later that spring he was shipped out of Norman. In December 1945, Radcliff was discharged from the Navy as a specialist (a) 2-C. He was almost forty years old when he was released, and was not able to continue his major league baseball career. It ended with a career batting average of .311 while playing in 1,081 games.

AGE	YRS	ML	G	BA	SA	AB	H	2B	3B	HR	HR%	R	RBI	BB	SO	SB
38-40	44-46	10	1081	0.311	0.417	4074	1267	205	50	42	1	598	532	310	141	40
		3	161	0.256	0.301	316	81	11	0	1	0.3	20	37	27	11	1
		13	1242	0.307	0.408	4390	1348	216	50	43	1	618	569	337	152	41

REISER, HAROLD P. (PETE)   BL TR 5'11" 185 lbs.

Born March 17, 1919, St. Louis, Mo. — Died October 25, 1981, Palm Springs, Ca.
Played for Brooklyn (1940-42, 1946-48), Boston (N) (1949-50), Pittsburgh (1951), and Cleveland (1952)

If there ever was a career made up of "what if's" it was Pete Reiser's. After being freed from the Cardinal farm system by Commissioner Kenesaw Mountain Landis, Pete made his way to the majors with the Dodgers in 1940. His first full year was 1941, and in that year he led the league in batting (.343), runs (117), doubles (39), triples (17), and slugging average (.558). Reiser was the youngest National League player to win the batting title. He was twenty-two years, six months, and eight days old when he won the title. He continued his exceptional hitting into the 1942 season. Then came the problems with injuries. On July 2, 1942, he ran into the wall in St. Louis trying to catch a flyball off the bat of Enos Slaughter. When the accident happened he was batting .383 and leading the league. The injury was severe—a skull fracture—and it had lingering effects. His batting suffered as he tried to make a comeback, falling from the .383 at the time of the accident to .310 for the entire year.

During 1942 his military classification changed from 3-A (because of family obligations) to 1-A, back to 3-A, and back to 1-A. At the close of the 1942 season, Reiser decided to enlist in the Navy. After taking his physical, he was turned down by the Navy because of the injuries he had suffered playing baseball. They told him no induction center would take him. However, the Army called. After the Army physical, he was told to sit with the rejects. A captain found out that this Harold Reiser was actually Pete Reiser the ballplayer. He asked Reiser what he would do if he was rejected. Reiser recounts what happened. "Play ball, I said. He turned around, 'Sergeant,' he said, 'fingerprint this guy and induct him.'" Reiser added, "I'm in" (Honig 1975, 308).

Reiser entered the Army on January 13, 1943. He was sworn in as a private at Jefferson Barracks, Missouri and was assigned to the Calvary Replacement Training Center at Fort Riley, Kansas. Two days after arriving at Fort Riley, in January, they were required to go on a fifty-mile forced march. Reiser took pneumonia and woke up in the hospital. The Army doctor who was treating him examined his chart and told him that he would be out of the Army in two weeks. The doctor had seen the account of all the injuries that Reiser had suffered. After waiting a while, Reiser checked on why nothing had happened about his release. The colonel, a sports fan, asked what he would do if released. Again Reiser answered that he would play for the Dodgers. The colonel wanted a good baseball team at Fort Riley and tore up the release papers. He wanted Reiser to play for the post team. The colonel gave Reiser no duties. All he had to do was play baseball. He had a pass to go anywhere between six a.m.

and six p.m. ("Just be back for the game.") He stayed at Fort Riley for about two years. He had incessant headaches and dizziness, and his condition kept him from being certified for combat duty, but he was kept at Fort Riley because the colonel wanted a good baseball team.

Late in 1944, Reiser was transferred to Camp Livingston, Louisiana. He again played baseball on the post team during his stay there. With the rank of sergeant, he made his last appearance with the team in June 1945 before leaving on an Army Special Service assignment. In July he reported to Camp Lee, Virginia, for advanced training. While playing baseball at Camp Lee, Reiser fell into a ditch chasing a fly ball and reinjured his shoulder, which had been hurt while he was playing in the majors. Reiser was scheduled to be shipped to Europe, but before he left he was given another physical. This time the person who reviewed the file wanted to know how he, with all his problems, was still in the Army. This colonel signed his medical discharge papers, and Reiser was out of the Army within twenty-four hours. He was discharged on November 30, 1945.

Reiser rejoined the Dodgers in time for the 1946 season. However, his shoulder was not up to par when he reported, and he separated the shoulder again during spring training. In addition, he suffered a broken ankle during the season. His worst accident came in 1947. Again he ran into a wall. This time it was in Brooklyn. He suffered a skull fracture, dislocated both shoulders, and was administered the last rites in the clubhouse. The injury happened on June 4, 1947, and he remained hospitalized until June 14. This event ended Reiser's career as a productive player. He never played in more than eighty-four games or batted more than .271 the rest of his career. In all, he was carried off the field eleven times because of injuries, and nine of those times he didn't wake up until he was off the field, either in the clubhouse or the hospital. Pete Reiser's career was the career that wasn't because of all the injuries he suffered. Kirby Higbe said, "That Reiser was a ballplayer to remember, too. If he hadn't had those injuries, he might have been one of the greatest that ever lived. He had speed, power, could field, throw, and he hit it inside, too" (Honig 1976, 95). Tommy Holmes added, "But talk about great ballplayers, what about Pete Reiser? There wasn't a thing he couldn't do on that ball field" (Honig 1976, 209). Stan Musial said about Reiser, "He could have been great if he hadn't crashed into the wall in St. Louis in 1942 and hurt his head and shoulders in other reckless collisions with the concrete. Until then, he could hit, run, field, and throw with any—or all—of them" (Broeg 1964, 286). Leo Durocher, who managed for many years, said, "He was the best I ever had, with the possible exception of Mays. At that he was even faster than Willie" (Dickson 1991, 120). The career that might have been. What if?

AGE	YRS	ML	G	BA	SA	AB	H	2B	3B	HR	HR%	R	RBI	BB	SO	SB
24-26	43-45	10	861	0.295	0.45	2662	786	155	41	58	2.2	473	368	343	369	87
		3	371	0.312	0.474	1370	428	87	22	30	2.2	262	194	163	161	54
		13	1232	0.301	0.458	4032	1214	242	63	88	2.2	735	562	506	530	141

RICKERT, MARVIN A. (MARV)   BL TR 6' 2" 195 lbs.
Born January 8, 1921, Longbranch, Wa. — Died June 3, 1978, Oakville, Wa.
Played for Chicago (N) (1942, 1946–47), Cincinnati (1948), Boston (N) (1948–49), Pittsburgh (1950), and Chicago (A) (1950)

Marv Rickert got into eight games in 1942 with the Cubs after spending most of the year at Tulsa in the Texas League. After the close of the season, on September 28, 1942, Rickert joined the Coast Guard. He was stationed out of Seattle after completing his training in December 1942, and he stayed on the West Coast in 1943 after being transferred to Tacoma, Washington. By June 1944, he was again stationed in Seattle. He was able to play on the Coast Guard Repair Yard team while stationed there. He spent part of the time in the Coast Guard hauling ammunition to the Aleutians. He was discharged on November 9, 1945, after serving in the Pacific.

Rickert had a good spring in 1946. He made the Cubs roster and had his best year in the majors. He took part in a first on June 23, 1946. He, along with Eddie Waitkus, hit back-to-back inside-the-park home runs. This was a major league first. He slumped badly in 1947 and found himself back in the minors in 1948. When the Braves outfielder Jeff Heath broke his ankle late in the 1948 season as the Braves were driving for the pennant, they picked Rickert up from the minors to fill the gap. He only played three games for the Braves during the season, but he played in five of the World Series games and even hit a home run in game four. He had another good year as a part-time player in 1949 before ending his career in 1950.

AGE	YRS	ML	G	BA	SA	AB	H	2B	3B	HR	HR%	R	RBI	BB	SO	SB
22-24	43-45	6	402	0.247	0.352	1149	284	45	9	19	1.7	139	145	88	161	4
		3	180	0.25	0.363	531	133	21	6	9	1.7	65	67	34	54	2
		9	582	0.248	0.355	1680	417	66	15	28	1.7	204	212	122	215	6

RIGGS, LEWIS S. (LEW)   BL TR 6' 0"   175 lbs.
Born April 22, 1910, Mebane, N.C. — Died August 12, 1975, Durham, N.C.
Played for St. Louis (N) (1934), Cincinnati (1935–40), and Brooklyn (1941–42, 1946)

Lew Riggs was the regular third baseman for the Reds for four years after he was purchased from the Cardinals in 1935. He made the All-Star team in 1936. However, when the Reds traded for Billy Werber in 1939, Riggs lost his job. The rest of his career he spent as a defensive specialist and pinch hitter. He was a good glove man but had trouble with the bat as a regular. He had been traded to the Dodgers when he enlisted in the Army Air Force. Riggs entered the service on October 26, 1942. He said, "With a war on, it seems as though I ought to be in there tossing something besides baseballs" (*The Sporting News*, "In The Service," 11-12-1942, page 9). He started his military career at Fort Jackson and then on to Fort Myers, Florida. He had orderly room duty there but applied for an airplane mechanics assignment. June 1944 found him at Buckingham Field. While stationed there he was able to play baseball. After the Navy beat Army in the "Pacific World Series," Riggs was one of the players who gathered in Utah to train and to go to Hawaii to challenge Navy. They arrived in Hawaii in early 1945, but the Navy team had already left. Riggs was stationed at Wheeler Field in Honolulu. He played on the Wheeler Wingman team and was selected to the Army Air Force all-star team. After a few months in Hawaii, the players were sent out to the Pacific Islands to entertain the troops. He went to the Marianas, playing and managing the 313th Flyers team during the summer of 1945. He played on Guam, Iwo Jima, Saipan, and Tinian during this time. Riggs was released by the military in November 1945. He returned to the Dodgers for the 1946 season but appeared in only one game that year, his last year in the majors.

AGE	YRS	ML	G	BA	SA	AB	H	2B	3B	HR	HR%	R	RBI	BB	SO	SB
33-35	43-45	10	760	0.262	0.375	2477	650	110	43	28	1.1	298	271	181	140	22
		3	158	0.282	0.416	365	103	20	4	7	1.9	45	51	27	22	2
		13	918	0.265	0.381	2842	753	130	47	35	1.2	343	322	208	162	24

ROBERTSON, SHERRARD A. (SHERRY)   BL TR 6' 0" 180 lbs.
Born January 1, 1919, Montreal, Quebec, Canada — Died October 23, 1970, Houghton, S.D.
Played for Washington (1940-1941, 1943, 1946-52) and Philadelphia (A) (1952)

Sherry Robertson was Senators' owner Clark Griffith's adopted son. It was the Senators
who brought him up to the majors even though his minor league record was not good. The
fans never let him forget that he was the owner's son. After he was killed in an automobile
accident while hunting in South Dakota, his obituary still mentioned this relationship. It said,
"He probably was the most booed player in the Senators history, starting in 1940" (Gilbert
1992, 93). He went into the Navy following the 1943 season. He completed his basic training
at Sampson Naval Training Station, Seneca Lake, New York, in December 1943. The summer
of 1944 found him stationed at Bainbridge, Maryland, where he was able to play baseball.
On September 1, 1944, he received orders to go to the Pacific. Robertson left Bainbridge in
October 1944 and arrived in Hawaii during the winter of 1944-45. He played in the Navy
"Pacific World Series" in October 1945 and was named to the 14th Naval District second team
all-stars. Robertson had some of his best success as a ballplayer against the major league talent
that was assembled in Hawaii. While still listed on the Senators' defense list of December
6, 1945, he was able to return to them in time for the 1946 season. He was to play seven
more seasons in the majors, but he played in only one hundred games in one season, 1949.
Robertson had a ten-year major league career, but the entire time was spent in a reserve role.

AGE	YRS	ML	G	BA	SA	AB	H	2B	3B	HR	HR%	R	RBI	BB	SO	SB
25-26	44-45	10	597	0.23	0.342	1507	346	55	18	26	1.7	200	151	202	238	32
		2	119	0.218	0.32	325	71	10	4	5	1.5	41	28	42	60	5
		12	716	0.228	0.338	1832	417	65	22	31	1.7	241	179	244	298	37

ROBINSON, AARON A.   BL TR 6' 2" 205 lbs.
Born June 23, 1915, Lancaster, S.C. — Died March 9, 1966, Lancaster, S.C.
Played for New York (A) (1943, 1945-47), Chicago (A) (1948), Detroit (1949-51), and Boston
(A) (1951)

Aaron Robinson got into one game in 1943 with the Yankees before he entered the Coast
Guard on June 19, 1943. He served with the Coast Guard until he was discharged on July 6,
1945. After leaving service in 1945, he played in fifty games with the Yankees. He took over
as the regular catcher in 1946. He had his best year in 1946, hitting sixteen home runs and
batting .297. However, the next year (1947) he lost his starting job to Yogi Berra even though
he was named to the All-Star team that year. He figured in two key trades. The Yankees traded
him to the White Sox for Eddie Lopat in 1948, and the White Sox traded him to the Tigers
for Billy Pierce the following year. Both Lopat and Pierce would go on to have good careers

with their new teams. After serving as the Tigers' regular catcher in 1949 and 1950, Robinson closed his major league career the following season.

AGE	YRS	ML	G	BA	SA	AB	H	2B	3B	HR	HR%	R	RBI	BB	SO	SB
28-30	43-45	8	610	0.26	0.412	1839	478	74	11	61	3.3	208	272	337	194	0
(3 YRS MINUS		1	129	0.275	0.425	433	119	14	3	15	3.5	30	42	41	25	0
1 & 50 GAMES)		9	739	0.263	0.414	2272	597	88	14	76	3.3	238	314	378	219	0

ROJEK, STANLEY A. (STAN)   BR TR 5' 10" 170 lbs.
Born April 21, 1919, North Tonawanda, N.Y. — Died July 9, 1997, North Tonawanda, N.Y. Played for Brooklyn (1942, 1946–47), Pittsburgh (1948–51), St. Louis (N) (1951), and St. Louis (A) (1952)

Stan Rojek enlisted in the Army Air Corps as a ground mechanic on February 6, 1942. He was sworn in as an Air Cadet during the summer but was allowed to continue to play baseball until he was called to active duty after the end of the 1942 season. Rojek got into one game with the Dodgers in 1942 as a pinch runner. In January 1943 he was a student at the San Antonio Aviation Cadet School. In the spring of 1943 he was attached to the 58th Training Group, Keesler Field, Mississippi. Rojek was one of the players the Army assembled in Utah for training to be sent to Hawaii after the Navy had beaten the Army in the "Pacific World Series." When they arrived in Hawaii, the Navy team was gone and they did not play again. He was selected to the Army Air Force all-star team in Hawaii. After a period of time in Hawaii he was transferred to the South Pacific. He spent the rest of the summer and fall of 1945 playing baseball on islands captured from the Japanese. He played for the 73rd Wing Bombers of the 20th Air Force in Saipan. He also played in Guam, Iwo Jima, and Tinian.

He arrived back in Los Angeles on November 2, 1945, aboard the transport ship *Cecil.* He had achieved the rank of sergeant. He had ribbons and two battle stars for forty-three months of service. After arriving in the States he was stationed at Fort Dix. He had gotten to play in more than two hundred games and had led the Pacific all-stars in batting. He was still on the Dodgers' defense list on December 6, 1945, and he was able to rejoin the Dodgers for the 1946 season. What Rojek wanted was Pee Wee Reese's job. What he got was two years of sitting on the bench playing second, short, or third as needed. Following the 1947 season, he was traded to the Pirates. This gave him his first chance to play on an everyday basis. He responded with his best year in 1948. He batted .290 and led National League shortstops in assists. The following year he slumped with the bat and the year after that was back to the role of a reserve. His major league career closed out in 1952.

AGE	YRS	ML	G	BA	SA	AB	H	2B	3B	HR	HR%	R	RBI	BB	SO	SB
24-26	43-45	8	522	0.266	0.326	1764	470	67	13	4	0.2	225	122	152	100	32
		3	116	0.267	0.314	191	51	3	3	0	0	27	14	17	6	3
		11	638	0.266	0.325	1955	521	70	16	4	0.2	252	136	169	106	35

ROSS, CHESTER J. (CHET)   BR TR 6' 1" 195 lbs.
Born April 1, 1917, Buffalo, N.Y. — Died February 21, 1989, Buffalo, N.Y.
Played for Boston (N) (1939–44)

Chet Ross's career started out well. In his rookie year in 1940, he hit seventeen home runs, had eighty-nine RBIs, and batted .281. The two negative things were he led the National League in strikeouts with one hundred twenty-seven and outfielders with fourteen errors. On March 8, 1941, he severely pulled the lateral ligament in his left ankle, and on July 18 that same year, he fractured a fibula and suffered a recurrence of the ankle injury. As a result, he played in only twenty-nine games that year and batted .120. Although a fine outfielder, he could never regain the hitting level he achieved during his rookie year. After playing a backup role in 1943 and 1944 for the Braves, he took and passed his preinduction physical at Boston on July 27, 1944. He had been classified as 2-B in the spring of 1944 but by summer he was accepted by the Navy. He spent the summer of 1945 playing for Sampson, New York, Naval Training team. He was still listed on the Braves' defense list on December 6, 1945. He did not play any games in the majors after his release.

AGE	YRS	ML	G	BA	SA	AB	H	2B	3B	HR	HR%	R	RBI	BB	SO	SB
28	45	6	413	0.241	0.392	1309	316	53	21	34	2.6	156	170	124	281	6
		1	75	0.214	0.355	220	47	9	2	6	2.7	22	26	18	42	1
		7	488	0.237	0.387	1529	363	62	23	40	2.6	178	196	142	323	7

ROWELL, CARVEL W. (BAMA)   BL TR 5' 11" 185 lbs.
Born January 13, 1916, Citronelle, Al. — Died August 16, 1993, Citronelle, Al.
Played for Boston (N) (1939–41, 1946–47) and Philadelphia (N) (1948)

Bama Rowell (he was from Alabama) batted .305 during his rookie season (1940) as the second baseman for the Braves. His batting slumped in 1941 when he hit .267. In addition his errors increased from thirty to forty. The forty errors in 1941 led National League second basemen. He was inducted into the Army following the 1941 season. He entered the Army on December 4, 1941, three days before Pearl Harbor. At first he was assigned to Company C, 1st Chemical Warfare Service Training Battalion. By April 1942 he was the athletic director at the Replacement Center at Edgewood Arsenal, Maryland. In January 1943 he was at Camp Sibert, Alabama. At Camp Sibert, he achieved the rank of sergeant. April 1944 found him attached to Billings Hospital in Indianapolis. That summer he was transferred to Camp McCoy where he played baseball for the 76th Infantry Combat Team. By January 1945 he was sent to Europe. He played second base on the baseball team, and handled athletic equipment, movies, radio programs, daily news bulletins, and other morale builders. He was in Germany at the end of his service overseas before being discharged in October 1945. He returned to the Braves for the 1946 season, but he had lost his second base job. He played outfield for the Braves in 1946 and 1947 before he closed out his major league career with the Phillies in 1948.

AGE	YRS	ML	G	BA	SA	AB	H	2B	3B	HR	HR%	R	RBI	BB	SO	SB
26-29	42-45	6	574	0.275	0.382	1901	523	95	26	19	1	200	217	113	105	37
		4	430	0.285	0.4	1451	414	75	23	16	1.1	164	173	92	82	41
		10	1004	0.28	0.391	3352	937	170	49	35	1	364	390	205	187	78

SCHEFFING, ROBERT B. (BOB)   BR TR 6' 2"   180 lbs.

Born August 11, 1913, Overland, Mo. — Died October 26, 1985, Phoenix, Az.

Played for Chicago (N) (1941–42, 1946–50), Cincinnati (1950–51), and St. Louis (N) (1951)

Bob Scheffing spent two years with the Cubs as a backup catcher before going into the Navy. He entered the Navy in October 1942, reporting to Lambert Field in St. Louis when he was inducted. He stayed at Lambert Field for almost all of 1943. In December 1943 he was transferred from Lambert Field to Bainbridge, Maryland, to the Navy Physical Instructor School. He was able to play some baseball while stationed at Lambert Field. His stay at Bainbridge lasted for all of 1944 and into 1945. He continued to be able to play baseball during 1944. On April 13, 1945, he passed through the processing mill at Bainbridge. The procedure got personnel ready for transfer to another post.

Scheffing went to San Francisco where he boarded a ship headed for Hawaii. There were about ten other players in the group who traveled with Scheffing. He arrived in Honolulu in the late spring or summer of 1945. He played in the Navy "Pacific World Series" in Hawaii during the fall of 1945 before being discharged in November 1945. He returned to the Cubs in 1946 in the same backup role as when he left for the Navy. However, in 1947 and 1948 he took over as the regular catcher for the Cubs. He had his best year batting in 1948 when he hit .300. An illness limited playing time in 1949, and he never was able to reassume the role of a regular catcher.

AGE	YRS	ML	G	BA	SA	AB	H	2B	3B	HR	HR%	R	RBI	BB	SO	SB
29-31	43-45	8	517	0.263	0.36	1357	357	53	9	20	1.5	105	187	103	127	6
		3	207	0.269	0.368	546	147	21	3	9	1.6	45	74	45	49	3
		11	724	0.265	0.362	1903	504	74	12	29	1.5	150	261	148	176	9

SELKIRK, GEORGE A.   BL TR 6' 1"   182 lbs.

Born January 4, 1908, Huntsville, Ontario, Canada — Died January 19, 1987, Ft. Lauderdale, Fl.

Played for New York (A) (1934–42)

George Selkirk took over an outfield position with the Yankees in 1935 and helped them to win pennants in six of the following eight years. He replaced Babe Ruth in right field when he broke into the regular lineup after spending eight years in the minors. He earned the nickname "Twinkletoes" in the minors because of the way he ran on the balls of his feet. His two best years were 1936 and 1939 when he made the All-Star team both years. In 1936, he was part of the Yankee team that had a record five players who drove in over one hundred runs. In 1939, he again drove in over one hundred runs.

Selkirk's career was winding down when he enlisted. He was classified 3-A and was not in danger of being drafted. In spite of that, close to age thirty-five, he enlisted in the Navy on November 24, 1942. He spent the early days at the Newport, Rhode Island, Naval Station as a boatswain. He still had the same address at the end of 1943. He rose to the rank of ensign and assisted the training of Naval recruits in shooting. Selkirk was still listed on the Yankees' defense list on December 6, 1945. After he got out of the Navy, he was not able to continue his major league career. He would have been thirty-eight years old if he had been able to play in the 1946 season.

AGE	YRS	ML	G	BA	SA	AB	H	2B	3B	HR	HR%	R	RBI	BB	SO	SB
35-37	43-45	9	846	0.29	0.483	2790	810	131	41	108	3.9	503	576	486	319	49
		3	100	0.211	0.312	218	46	7	0	5	2.3	41	32	40	34	1
		12	946	0.285	0.47	3008	856	138	41	113	3.8	544	608	526	353	50

SILVESTRI, KENNETH J. (KEN)   BB TR 6'1"   200 lbs.

Born May 3, 1916, Chicago, Il. — Died March 31, 1992, Tallahassee, Fl.
Played for Chicago (A) (1939-40), New York (A) (1941, 1946-47), and Philadelphia (N) (1949-51)

The most at-bats that Ken Silvestri ever got in any one season was his rookie year of 1939 when he batted seventy-five times. He served in the third-string catcher role for a career that lasted eight years. During those eight years, he batted only 201 times with forty-four hits. He was one of the early players to enter the service. He entered the Army in December 1941. In January 1942, he reported to Fort Custer. In September 1943, he received the marksman rating with a rifle at McClellan Field, Alabama. During the fall of 1944 Silvestri played on an Army barnstorming team that toured the Southwest Pacific playing baseball for the troops stationed on those bases. He had the rank of staff sergeant. During the summer of 1945 he played for and managed the 8th Army team stationed in the Philippines. He played in an all-star game in the Marianas on August 26, 1945. He reached the rank of first sergeant before he was shipped home. He was scheduled to board a transport for home from Yokohama in November 1945. Silvestri was discharged on November 17, 1945. He returned to the Yankees in 1946 in the same role he had when he entered the Army four years before, a third-string catcher.

AGE	YRS	ML	G	BA	SA	AB	H	2B	3B	HR	HR%	R	RBI	BB	SO	SB
26-29	42-45	8	102	0.217	0.355	203	44	11	1	5	2.5	26	25	31	41	0
		4	57	0.224	0.362	116	26	7	0	3	2.6	16	15	19	24	0
		12	159	0.219	0.357	319	70	18	1	8	2.5	42	40	50	65	0

SPENCE, STANLEY O. (STAN)   BL TL 5'10"   180 lbs.

Born March 20, 1915, South Portsmouth, Ky. — Died January 9, 1983, Kinston, N.C.
Played for Boston (A) (1940-41, 1948-49), Washington (1942-44, 1946-47), and St. Louis (A) (1949)

Stan Spence got his chance to play as a regular in 1942 when some of the players were called into the military. He made the most of his chance. He batted .323 and led the league in triples with fifteen in 1942 and made the All-Star team. He had another very good year in 1944, driving in 100 runs and batting .316, also playing in the 1944 All-Star game. Spence had been classified 4-F during the early part of the war. However, when the Defense Department made the ruling that if someone was healthy enough to play baseball he was good enough to go in to the Army, Spence was drafted. The government later rescinded this rule, but Spence had already been inducted. He entered the Navy on March 28, 1945, at Bainbridge Naval

Training Station. He spent the summer of 1945 playing for the base team. He was discharged on November 8, 1945.

Spence returned to the Senators for the 1946 season and was able to do well against the other returning players. He was always known as a very good outfielder with good range and a fine throwing arm. His hitting remained strong as well. In 1946, he batted .292 and hit fifty doubles. He played in the All-Star game in both 1946 and 1947, hitting a single to bring home the winning run in the 1947 game. Bob Feller said, "Guys like…Stan Spence gave me more trouble than most of the long-ball hitters" (Feller and Gilbert 1990, 91). However, after the 1947 season, his hitting trailed off, and he closed his major league career in 1949.

AGE	YRS	ML	G	BA	SA	AB	H	2B	3B	HR	HR%	R	RBI	BB	SO	SB
30	45	9	1112	0.282	0.437	3871	1090	196	60	95	2.5	541	575	520	248	21
		1	150	0.296	0.452	575	170	31	10	13	2.3	79	85	72	31	4
		10	1262	0.283	0.439	4446	1260	227	70	108	2.4	620	660	592	279	25

STEWART, EDWARD P. (BUD)   BL TR 5'11" 160 lbs.
Born June 15, 1916, Sacramento, Ca. — Died June 21, 2000, Palo Alto, Ca.
Played for Pittsburgh (1941–42), New York (A) (1948), Washington (1948–50), and Chicago (A) (1951–54)

Bud Stewart made the Pirates team in 1941 as a reserve outfielder and pinch hitter. He continued in that role during 1942 even though his hitting fell off sharply. He led the National League in pinch hits in 1941 with ten. He was on the Pirates' voluntary retired list in 1943, probably working in some war-related endeavor. He spent 1944 in the Army after being drafted, but he got out in time to play sixty-three games in the 1945 season. However, the games were played with Hollywood in the Pacific Coast League. He remained in the minors for two more years before being called up by the Yankees and traded to the Senators in 1948. The time he spent in the majors as a regular came during the three years he spent with the Senators. Stewart was used a pinch hitter throughout his career. In fact, 202 (or 10%) of his 2,041 career at-bats came as a pinch hitter.

AGE	YRS	ML	G	BA	SA	AB	H	2B	3B	HR	HR%	R	RBI	BB	SO	SB
27-29	43-45	9	773	0.268	0.393	2041	547	96	32	32	1.6	288	260	252	157	29
2 YRS (1945		2	171	0.272	0.346	367	100	17	5	0		58	35	42	38	8
IN MINORS)		11	944	0.269	0.386	2408	647	113	37	32	1.3	346	295	294	195	37

STRINGER, LOUIS B. (LOU)   BR TR 5'11" 173 lbs.
Born May 13, 1917, Grand Rapids, Mi.
Played for Chicago (N) (1941–42, 1946) and Boston (A) (1948–50)

Lou Stringer was bought by the Cubs to replace Billy Herman. He filled that role in 1941 and 1942. He led the National League second basemen in assists in 1941 and led them in errors in 1942. However, his hitting was never very strong. He enlisted in the Army Air Force on October 29, 1942. He was a private at Williams Field, Chandler, Arizona. While stationed in Arizona, he attended mechanics school and graduated in January 1943. Stringer continued to be stationed there throughout the summer. He was able to play some baseball and played in a benefit game on August 21, 1943. In the fall of 1945, he played an exhibition game in California before being discharged on December 11, 1945. He rejoined the Cubs in time for the 1946 season. His hitting continued to be weak, and he lost his starting job at second. After spending the 1947 and 1948 seasons in the minors, Stringer was called up by the Red Sox when Bobby Doerr was injured in 1948 and stayed with them in a backup role for two more seasons.

AGE	YRS	ML	G	BA	SA	AB	H	2B	3B	HR	HR%	R	RBI	BB	SO	SB
26-28	43-45	6	409	0.242	0.348	1196	290	49	10	19	1.6	148	122	121	192	7
		3	228	0.251	0.365	680	171	30	7	11	1.6	90	73	73	111	6
		9	637	0.246	0.354	1876	461	79	17	30	1.6	238	195	194	303	13

STURGEON, ROBERT H. (BOBBY)   BR TR 6' 0"   175 lbs.
Born August 6, 1919, Clinton, In.
Played for Chicago (N) (1940-42, 1946-47), and Boston (N) (1948)

Bobby Sturgeon became the Cubs regular shortstop in his rookie year of 1941. The 1942 season would not be so good. Sturgeon said in a letter, "Unfortunately, I was spiked [cut by the cleats or spikes on baseball shoes] the third day of the season in '42 and used only sparingly the rest of the year." He enlisted in the Navy in December 1942. In March 1944 he was stationed at Roosevelt Base in California before being transferred to Camp Elliott in the 11th Naval District in Oregon in March 1945. He was able to play baseball while stationed at Camp Elliott. He was discharged in December 1945. He rejoined the Cubs for the 1946 season, his best batting year. He hit .296 in one hundred games as a utility infielder. His playing time and his batting average decreased in 1947, and he was traded to the Braves in 1948 where he backed up Eddie Stanky at second in the Braves' pennant year. When Sturgeon discussed the impact of his service on his career, he said, "It has never been a bone of contention with me" (Sturgeon letter 1997). His comments were intended to show that he placed service to country above his own personal goals for his baseball career. Because he played before his enlistment and after for at least five years, he was eligible for a baseball pension. "Some players were unfortunate in not playing major league ball prior to their enlistment," he said (Sturgeon letter 1997).

AGE	YRS	ML	G	BA	SA	AB	H	2B	3B	HR	HR%	R	RBI	BB	SO	SB
23-25	43-45	6	420	0.257	0.318	1220	313	48	12	1	0.1	106	80	34	79	7
		3	284	0.26	0.322	841	219	33	8	1	0.1	71	56	23	55	5
		9	704	0.258	0.32	2061	532	81	20	2	0.1	177	136	57	134	12

SULLIVAN, JOHN PAUL   BR TR 5' 10"   170 lbs.
Born November 2, 1920, Chicago, Il.
Played for Washington (1942-44, 1947-48) and St. Louis (A) (1949)

John Sullivan was a wartime replacement who held down the shortstop position for the Washington Senators for three years. His hitting was suspect with his best average as a regular at .251 in 1944. He also had some trouble in the field as he led the American League shortstops in errors in both 1943 and 1944. Despite being classified 4-F earlier that year and having two children, he was drafted on March 27, 1945. He was inducted at Fort Sheridan, Illinois, and he served in the Special Services unit in Japan. He arrived in Japan after the bomb in 1945. While stationed there he played and managed a service team in Osaka. He was discharged on October 24, 1946, and returned to the Senators in time for the 1947 season. He was a year behind all the other returning servicemen and was not able to regain his starting job at shortstop. He served the balance of his career with the Senators and Browns as a utility infielder.

AGE	YRS	ML	G	BA	SA	AB	H	2B	3B	HR	HR%	R	RBI	BB	SO	SB
24-25	45-46	6	605	0.23	0.27	1833	422	52	9	1	0.1	203	162	216	206	18
		2	225	0.245	0.296	706	173	23	5	1	0.1	84	68	74	58	8
		8	830	0.234	0.277	2539	595	75	14	2	0.1	287	230	290	264	26

TABOR, JAMES R. (JIM)   BR TR 6' 2" 175 lbs.
Born November 5, 1916, New Hope, Al. — Died August 22, 1953, Sacramento, Ca.
Played for Boston (A) (1938–44) and Philadelphia (N) (1946–47)

Jim Tabor was the regular Red Sox third baseman from his first full season in 1939 until he was taken into service after the 1944 season. He had a good rookie year but was overshadowed by another Red Sox rookie, Ted Williams. Tabor drove in 95 runs that year and followed it up in 1941 by driving in 101 runs. He had one of his best days that rookie year. On July 4, 1939, in a doubleheader, he hit four home runs and drove in eleven runs. He had three homers with nine RBIs in the first game. While he led the American League in assists in 1939 and putouts in 1942, he also led third basemen in errors for five consecutive years, 1939 to 1943. His nickname was "rawhide," which fit his personality and style. Ted Williams said, "Tabor was from Alabama, a strong-built guy, about six feet two, with a trim waist." He continued, "A sort of tough, rough-hewn guy" (Williams and Underwood 1988, 130).

Tabor enter the Army on October 23, 1944. He was accepted for active service after examination at Boston in the summer even though he had been classified 2-B in the spring. He spent some time during his service at Camp Croft, South Carolina. He was discharged on December 14, 1945. He returned to baseball in time for the 1946 season. However, the Red Sox sold him to the Phillies in January 1946, so he missed the chance to play for the pennant winner. He was the regular third baseman for the Phillies in 1946 and closed his major league career in 1947.

AGE	YRS	ML	G	BA	SA	AB	H	2B	3B	HR	HR%	R	RBI	BB	SO	SB
30-31	44-45	9	1005	0.27	0.418	3788	1021	191	29	104	2.7	473	598	286	377	69
(2 YRS MINUS		1	150	0.257	0.377	567	146	23	3	13	2.3	64	80	44	58	6
116 GAMES)		10	1155	0.268	0.412	4355	1167	214	32	117	2.7	537	678	330	435	75

TUCKER, THURMAN L.   BL TR 5' 10" 165 lbs.
Born September 26, 1917, Gordon, Tx. — Died May 7, 1993, Oklahoma City, Ok.
Played for Chicago (A) (1942–44, 1946–47) and Cleveland (1948–51)

Thurman Tucker was one of the American League's fastest runners. After struggling with the bat in his rookie year (1943), he started strong in 1944. He was hitting almost .400 for the first part of the year and was named to the All-Star team that year as the leadoff hitter. However, after the All-Star game he went into a deep slump, so bad he was benched for a while. After the great start he finished the year hitting .287—not a bad year but a big comedown from the start. His nickname became "Joe E." because of the resemblance to comedian Joe E. Brown. Tucker entered the Navy on November 18, 1944. He took his basic training at the Naval Training Center, San Diego, California. During the spring of 1945, he was able to play baseball for the base team.

By May 1945 he was transferred to Bainbridge, Maryland. His stay there extended through the summer. He was able to play ball at Bainbridge as well. He was discharged on November 26, 1945. Jimmy Dykes had said he thought Tucker would be able to return to baseball. He did. In 1946 he batted .288 and returned to his position in the White Sox outfield. The following year his batting average slumped and so did his playing time. He was traded to the Indians in January 1948. With the Indians he got to play in the 1948 World Series. He was a good center fielder. Bob Feller said, "Thurman…was one of the league's better center fielders" (Feller and Gilbert 1990, 154). He led the American League in putouts in 1943 and fielding percentage in 1944.

AGE	YRS	ML	G	BA	SA	AB	H	2B	3B	HR	HR%	R	RBI	BB	SO	SB
27	45	9	701	0.255	0.325	2231	570	79	24	9	0.4	325	179	291	237	77
		1	118	0.264	0.338	417	110	15	5	2	0.5	58	35	57	46	15
		10	819	0.257	0.327	2648	680	94	29	11	0.4	383	214	348	283	92

VAN ROBAYS, MAURICE R.   BR TR 6'0"   190 lbs.
Born November 15, 1914, Detroit, Mi. — Died March 1, 1965, Detroit, Mi.
Played for Pittsburgh (1939–43, 1946)

Maurice Van Robays had a very good rookie year with the Pirates. He had eleven home runs, 116 RBIs, and batted .273. These would be the best numbers that he would post during his career. He batted higher the following year but the production numbers were less. His playing time went down as his batting average fell to .232 in 1942. He spent part of the 1943 season back in the minors before he entered the Army on September 18, 1943. March 1944 found him at Camp Crowder, Missouri. In December 1944 he was stationed at Camp Chaffee, Arkansas, where he managed the baseball team during the summer. Other duties, he indicated, included considerable cooking in the mess hall. During this time he expected and received orders for overseas duty. He was in France with an armored infantry battalion in April 1945. That fall he got to play with the 71st Division team in Germany. He also helped with a baseball school for German youths while stationed in Germany. He was discharged on April 6, 1946, causing him to get a late start for the 1946 season. He played in fifty-nine games that year but only batted .212. It was the last year of his major league career.

AGE	YRS	ML	G	BA	SA	AB	H	2B	3B	HR	HR%	R	RBI	BB	SO	SB
29-30	44-45	6	529	0.267	0.38	1844	493	94	27	20	1.1	232	303	139	155	2
		2	128	0.259	0.385	382	99	22	10	2	0.5	46	47	29	34	0
		8	657	0.266	0.381	2226	592	116	37	22	1	278	350	168	189	2

VOLLMER, CLYDE F.   BR TR 6' 1" 185 lbs.

Born September 24, 1921, Cincinnati, Oh.

Played for Cincinnati (1942, 1946-48), Washington (1948-50, 1953-54), and Boston (A) (1950-53)

Clyde Vollmer got into twelve games with the Reds in 1942 before he entered the military. He did, however, make some impression during those twelve games. On the first pitch that was thrown to him in the majors, he hit a home run and became one of the few to ever hit a home run that soon. He was listed on the Reds' military list in December 1942. He was still on that list on December 6, 1945. He spent some time in Iran while in the military. He returned to baseball in time for the 1946 season. However, he did spend that year in the minors. He was not able to establish himself as a regular until the 1949 season with the Senators. His best home run year came in 1951 when he hit twenty-two homers. Al Kozar said, "He was an outfielder with pretty good power. He hit homers in every ballpark in 1949 and 1950" (Peary 1994, 130). On July 26, 1951, he hit three home runs in one game.

AGE	YRS	ML	G	BA	SA	AB	H	2B	3B	HR	HR%	R	RBI	BB	SO	SB
21-23	43-45	10	685	0.251	0.402	2021	508	77	10	69	3.4	283	339	243	330	7
		3	80	0.194	0.274	175	34	8	0	2	1.1	17	14	9	21	1
		13	765	0.247	0.392	2196	542	85	10	71	3.2	300	353	252	351	8

WAKEFIELD, RICHARD C. (DICK)   BL TR 6' 4" 210 lbs.

Born May 6, 1921, Chicago, Il. — Died August 26, 1985, Redford, Mi.

Played for Detroit (1941, 1943-44, 1946-49), New York (A) (1950), and New York (N) (1952)

Dick Wakefield signed with the Tigers for the largest bonus ever paid at that time. The amount they paid was $52,000 for an unproven player from the University of Michigan. After about a year and a half in the minors, Wakefield made a big splash with the Tigers in 1943. That year, even though it was against war replacements, was a very good year. He led the American League in hits, doubles, and at-bats. He batted .316, second only to Luke Appling and made the All-Star team. After the season was over, Wakefield entered the Naval Aviation Cadet program in October 1943. He did this even though his father was dead and he supported his mother and two younger brothers. However, he had been denied an appeal of his 1-A status in the draft. In the spring of 1944, he began a three-month program in physical, military, and academic training at the Navy Preflight School at Iowa City, Iowa. He was working for his Navy wings. In July 1944 he completed the preflight program. However, the Navy decided that it did not need as many pilots as it had training, so the ones who didn't finish in the top half of the class were not allowed to continue in the program. Wakefield had a good passing grade but was not in the top half of his class, so on July 7, 1944, he was discharged from the Navy. He was required to register for the draft again.

While he was waiting for what was going to happen next, he rejoined the Tigers. His rookie year had been good, but his second season was even better. Rejoining the Tigers on July 13 and playing until the end of the season, Wakefield batted .355, hit twelve home runs, and fifteen doubles in seventy-eight games. He passed the draft physical in Chicago in September 1944 and was inducted back into the Navy on November 30, 1944, at Great Lakes.

He completed his boot training at Great Lakes in January 1945. Wakefield tried to get back into flight school. He spent a month at Iowa City, where he had been discharged, trying to qualify. He was unsuccessful and returned to Great Lakes. In April 1945, he was transferred to Bainbridge, Maryland, for training in the physical instructors' program. He was able to play baseball while stationed at Bainbridge. He had the rank of seaman 2nd class in June 1945. A foot injury slowed his progress while at Bainbridge. He graduated in June 1945 from the physical instructors' school and was transferred to Shoemaker Field in California, awaiting overseas duty. In July 1945, he was transferred from Shoemaker Field to Hawaii. That fall he was able to play in the Navy "Pacific World Series" in Hawaii.

He was discharged from the Navy for the second time in January 1946 and came back to the Tigers in time for the season. He suffered some setbacks in that season. He had problems with blisters on his hands in spring training and also missed part of the season with a broken arm. Whether it was the difference in the talent level of the other players, the layoff, the physical problems, or his attitude, Wakefield was not the same player that he had been before he went into service. Some thought that baseball had always come so easy to him that he developed an attitude where he did not play with the intensity needed to be a star. The balance of his career was filled with disappointments. His career had started out so well but his best year after coming back from the military he hit only .283. Not bad, but not what was expected from someone who showed so much talent in the beginning. His career was characterized by a by author Burt Solomon who said, "he was a player of enormous—but mostly unfulfilled—talent" (Solomon 1997, 890). He lived up to what was expected for only one-and-a-half seasons.

AGE	YRS	ML	G	BA	SA	AB	H	2B	3B	HR	HR%	R	RBI	BB	SO	SB
23-24	44-45	9	638	0.293	0.447	2132	625	102	29	56	2.6	334	315	360	269	10
2 YRS MINUS		1	188	0.294	0.422	695	204	32	9	13	1.9	107	94	100	79	4
78 GAMES)		10	826	0.293	0.441	2827	829	134	38	69	2.4	441	409	460	348	14

WARREN, BENNIE L.　　　　　　　　　　　　　　　BR TR 6' 1"　184 lbs.

Born March 2, 1912, Elk City, Ok. — Died May 11, 1994, Oklahoma City, Ok.

Played for Philadelphia (N) (1939–42) and New York (N) (1946–47)

Bennie Warren was the regular catcher for the Phillies for three years before he entered the Navy. He enjoyed this status even though he had a career batting average of .224 when he entered the service. He led the National League in assists, double plays, and errors as a catcher in 1941. He was sold to the Cubs on November 17, 1942, and spent his military career as a member of the Cubs even though he would never play for the Cubs. He entered the Navy in January 1943. He was stationed at Norman, Oklahoma, in April 1943 and stayed there during the rest of 1943, 1944, and into 1945. *The Sporting News* reported in its April 12, 1945, edition that he was being transferred from Norman, however, his destination was not given. He was discharged from the Navy on October 19, 1945. Instead of joining the Cubs, he was sold to the Giants on April 11, 1946. For 1946 and 1947, his last two seasons, he was the third-string catcher behind Walker Cooper and Ernie Lombardi.

AGE	YRS	ML	G	BA	SA	AB	H	2B	3B	HR	HR%	R	RBI	BB	SO	SB
31-33	43-45	6	377	0.219	0.36	989	217	26	7	33	3.3	97	104	129	177	1
		3	200	0.22	0.343	527	116	14	3	15	2.8	55	53	74	89	1
		9	577	0.22	0.354	1516	333	40	10	48	3.2	152	157	203	266	2

infielder. He was inducted into the Army on December 7, 1941, at Fort Bragg. He had been sold to the Pirates before his induction and was listed on the Pirates' defense list. He was stationed at Daniel Field, Georgia, in November 1943 and at Lincoln, Nebraska, in June 1944. He was listed as a combination trainer and equipment manager for the 2nd Air Force football team in November 1944. He had the rank of staff sergeant. He was transferred to Colorado Springs, Colorado, in January 1945 and was able to play on the 2nd Air Force team that spring. He was released in time to join the Pirates for the 1946 season, his last in the majors. He played in only fifty-five games that year.

AGE	YRS	ML	G	BA	SA	AB	H	2B	3B	HR	HR%	R	RBI	BB	SO	SB
32-35	42-45	9	924	0.266	0.331	3316	883	100	31	17	0.5	415	245	150	138	51
		4	440	0.266	0.33	1584	422	49	12	9	0.6	208	117	78	59	21
		13	1364	0.266	0.33	4900	1305	149	43	26	0.5	623	362	228	197	72

WITEK, NICHOLAS J. (MICKEY)   BR TR 5' 10" 170 lbs.
Born December 19, 1915, Luzerne, Pa. — Died September 24, 1990, Kingston, Pa.
Played for New York (N) (1940-43, 1946-47) and New York (A) (1949)

Mickey Witek filled in for Billy Jurges who was beaned in 1940. Even though he batted .362 in twenty-three games in 1941, he was sent back to the minors when injuries to the other players were not a problem. He returned to the Giants as the regular second baseman in 1942 when Burgess Whitehead entered the Navy. He performed well during that season and in 1943. In 1942 he led National League second basemen in assists and fielding percentage, and in 1943 he led the league in games played, putouts, and assists while batting .314. He took part in an all-star game that raised $800,000,000 for war bonds on August 27, 1943. He entered the Coast Guard in November 1943 and was stationed at Manhattan Beach, New York. In 1944 he was transferred to the Curtis Bay, Maryland, Coast Guard Station. He stayed there until the fall of 1945 when he was sent to the South Pacific. He was able to play baseball while stationed at Curtis Bay. He was released from the Coast Guard in January 1946 and returned to the Giants. He suffered with arm problems in both 1946 and 1947 and did not regain his status as a regular after the war.

AGE	YRS	ML	G	BA	SA	AB	H	2B	3B	HR	HR%	R	RBI	BB	SO	SB
28-29	44-45	7	580	0.277	0.347	2147	595	65	9	22	1	239	196	148	84	7
		3	192	0.29	0.362	715	207	22	3	8	1.1	88	67	56	30	3
		10	772	0.28	0.35	2862	802	87	12	30	1	327	263	204	114	10

WRIGHT, TAFT S. (TAFFY)   BL TR 5' 10" 180 lbs.
Born August 10, 1911, Tabor City, N.C. — Died October 22, 1981, Orlando, Fl.
Played for Washington (1938-39), Chicago (A) (1940-42, 1946-48), and Philadelphia (A) (1949)

Taffy Wright was a good hitter. He had a lifetime batting average of .328 when he entered the Army. He led the American League in pinch hits during his rookie year with the Senators in 1938 while batting .350 in one hundred games. After being traded to the White Sox in December 1939, he continued his good hitting with his new team. He was considered to be the best hitter on the White Sox team when he entered the Army. In fact he set an American

League record on May 20, 1941, by driving in a run in thirteen consecutive games. Wright had been classified 3-A because of his dependent mother, but his status was changed, and he was ordered to report for a physical in July 1942.

He passed his physical and entered the Army on September 4, 1942, at Fort Bragg, North Carolina. He made corporal and was in Miami taking a course to prepare for assignment as a physical instructor in July 1943. He was assigned to Greensboro, South Carolina, after completing the course, and he achieved the rank of sergeant by November 1944. He was concerned about servicemen after the war and what their status would be with major league clubs. The White Sox assured him that he would receive at least one year of pay at the major league level after the war. Wright was one of the players the Army assembled in Utah after they lost to Navy in the "Pacific World Series." He, along with the others, was transferred to Hawaii in the spring of 1945.

The Navy team was gone so the Army team didn't get to confront them. He was stationed at Wheeler Field in Honolulu and played baseball for the Wheeler Wingmen team while stationed there. Wright was selected to the all-star team that summer. After about three months in Hawaii, the players, including Wright, were sent out to the South Pacific islands to play baseball and entertain the troops. During that time he played on Guam, Saipan, Tinian, and other islands in the Marianas. He played for the 73rd Wing Bombers of the 20th Air Force in the Marianas and was named to the all-star team. Wright had returned to the States and was stationed at Fort Bragg when he was discharged in November 1945.

He returned to the White Sox for the 1946 season, but he had lost some of the skills he had before entering the service. His lowest batting average before the war was .309. After coming back he had only one year when he batted over .300. He was thirty-one years old when he went in. At thirty-four, it wasn't the same. He had three years as a regular after service but the production wasn't the same. He closed his career in 1949 with the A's.

AGE	YRS	ML	G	BA	SA	AB	H	2B	3B	HR	HR%	R	RBI	BB	SO	SB
31-33	43-45	9	1029	0.311	0.423	3583	1115	175	55	38	1.1	465	553	347	155	32
		3	363	0.312	0.415	1274	397	62	17	12	0.9	174	190	133	52	11

YOUNG, NORMAN R. (BABE)   BL TL 6' 2"   185 lbs.

Born July 1, 1915, Astoria, N.Y. — Died December 25, 1983, Everett, Ma.
Played for New York (N) (1936, 1939–42, 1946–47), Cincinnati (1947–48), and St. Louis (N) (1948)

Babe Young was the regular first baseman for the Giants in 1940 and 1941 but lost that status in 1942 when the Giants traded for Johnny Mize. He hit twenty-five home runs in 1941 and had driven in over one hundred runs in both seasons. In 1942 he played outfield, backed up Mize at first, and pinch-hit. He had been classified 3-A because of dependency requirements. Early in 1942 he was reclassified to 1-A. He appealed the change but was rejected. He then was subject to immediate call-up. He was not called during the summer of 1942 and joined the Coast Guard on October 11, 1942. He was commissioned a lieutenant. In November 1944, he was on convoy duty between Cuba and European ports. By May 1945 he had risen to the rank of lieutenant (j.g.). He was discharged in October 1945. He rejoined the Giants in 1946 and returned to the same duty he had in 1942, backup at first and in the outfield and pinch hitting. He was traded to the Reds during 1947 and to the Cardinals during 1948. In each of these locations, he hit reasonably well but could not achieve regular status. He was invited to the Yankees spring training camp in 1949 but hurt his leg and retired from baseball.

AGE	YRS	ML	G	BA	SA	AB	H	2B	3B	HR	HR%	R	RBI	BB	SO	SB
28-30	43-45	8	728	0.273	0.436	2403	656	121	17	79	3.3	320	415	274	161	9
		3	305	0.284	0.458	1012	287	51	7	37	3.7	146	176	131	70	5
		11	1033	0.276	0.442	3415	943	172	24	116	3.4	466	591	405	231	14

ZARILLA, ALLEN L. (AL)   BL TR 5' 11" 180 lbs.
Born May 1, 1919, Los Angeles, Ca. — Died August 28, 1996, Honolulu, Hi.
Played for St. Louis (A) (1943–44, 1946–49, 1952), Boston (A) (1949–50, 1952–53), and Chicago (A) (1951–52)

Al Zarilla was a wartime replacement who had a good career after the war. Zarilla's name came up for induction in 1943. Because he had two small children, his California draft board gave him a week to find a war job or be drafted. He found the job. He got his draft notice in April 1944, and he requested that it be transferred to Jefferson Barracks, Missouri. This later turned out to be a good move. He was summoned for his preinduction physical on May 9, 1944, and was accepted on May 11. He was batting well and the St. Louis Browns were in the battle for the pennant. Brown's owner Bill DeWitt talked to an officer at Jefferson Barracks, which is just outside St. Louis. He said, "Here's our right fielder. Is there any way I can bring this guy down and get him inducted and then get him a leave until after the baseball season is over?" (Mead 1985, 165).

They let him continue to play baseball for the Browns that summer, including the World Series. Zarilla was the batting star in game three of the '44 Series, scoring and driving in a run as the Browns won 6–2. He was finally inducted on November 8, 1944, and sent to Fort Warren, Wyoming. He stayed in Wyoming and was discharged on October 1, 1945, at the Fort Francis Warren Separation Center, Cheyenne, Wyoming.

He rejoined the Browns for the 1946 season. After two years of struggling with the bat, Zarilla had one of his best years in 1948. He batted .329 with thirty-nine doubles and twelve homers. He was named to the All-Star team in 1948. After being traded to the Red Sox in 1949, Zarilla had another very good year in 1950. He batted .325 and helped the Red Sox to a second-place -finish that year. His batting skills diminished following the 1950 season. After moving from the Red Sox to the White Sox and back to the Browns and the Red Sox, Zarilla retired in 1953.

AGE	YRS	ML	G	BA	SA	AB	H	2B	3B	HR	HR%	R	RBI	BB	SO	SB
26	45	10	1120	0.276	0.405	3535	975	186	43	61	1.7	507	456	415	382	33
		1	113	0.279	0.398	359	100	18	5	5	1.4	45	43	32	37	4
		11	1233	0.276	0.404	3894	1075	204	48	66	1.7	552	499	447	419	37

1942 SERVICE ALL-STARS *in Service Uniforms*

ALL-STARS IN SERVICE UNIFORM

Front row, left to right – Vincent Smith, Norfolk Training Station; Don Padgett, Great Lakes Training Station; Ernest Andres, Great Lakes; Herman Fishman, Great Lakes; Fred Schaffer, Great Lakes; Frank Pytlak, Great Lakes; Russell Meers, Great Lakes; Johnny Lucadello, Great Lakes.

Center row – Don Dunker, Great Lakes; O.V. Mulkey, Great Lakes; Fred Hutchinson, Norfolk Training Station; Sam Chapman, Naval Aviation Station, Washington, D.C.; Bob Feller, Norfolk; George Earnshaw, Naval Aviation Station, Jacksonville, Fla.; Manager Mickey Cochrane, Great Lakes; Hank Gowdy, (coach), Reds; Joe Grace, Great Lakes; Cecil Travis, Camp Wheeler, Ga.; Mickey Harris, Canal Zone; John Rigney, Great Lakes.

Back Row – Ken Silvestri, Fort Custer, Mich.; Pat Mullin, 1301 Service Unit, New Cumberland, Pa.; Johnny Sturm, Jefferson Barracks, Mo.; Sam Harshany, Great Lakes; Chester Hajduk, Great Lakes; Bob Peterson, Great Lakes; John Groszicki, Fort Knox, Ky.; Mush Esler, Great Lakes; Benny McCoy, Great Lakes; Emmett Mueller, Jefferson Barracks; Morris Arnovich, Port Lewis, Wash.

The location of the troops was not an issue. The game was played wherever they were stationed. Here a game is located in London.

The condition of the field didn't matter as long as you had a bat and ball. Here an old peice of cloth serves as home plate and none of the players were using a glove.

The game begins as fellow soldiers watch the action.

The South Pacific jungles also provided a place to "get up" a game. In the warmer climate, the game could go on year-round.

Sergeant Joe DiMaggio, Vice Admiral Robert L. Ghormley USN, Chief Specialist Harold "Pee Wee" Reese and Brigadier General William J. Flood USA. Here the "brass" receive an autograph from the "enlisted men."

Luke Appling models his new uniform. The baseball uniform has been put away for now.

Captain Hank Greenberg, shown here in his Army uniform, spent more time in service than almost all major league players.

Yankee Stadium was also located at Camp Marshall, Lyautey, Africa, in addition
to New York City.

"Out at the Plate." Baseball games provided enjoyment for the troops
regardless of the men who were playing the game.

He returned to the Indians in 1944 in time to pitch in thirteen games. Although Bagby's time in the military was short, he was never the same after he returned. He lasted three more years in the majors; however, he never won more than eight games in any season during this time.

AGE	YRS	ML	W	L	PCT	ERA	G	GS	CG	IP	H	BB	SO	SHO	SV
27	44	10	97	96	0.503	3.96	303	198	84	1666	1815	608	431	13	9
(1 YR MINUS		0	9	4	0.692	3.92	23	18	9	146	144	34	38	1	1
13 GAMES)		10	106	100	0.515	3.95	326	216	93	1812	1959	642	469	14	10

BARNEY, REX E.   BR TR 6' 3"   185 lbs.
Born December 19, 1924, Omaha, Ne. — Died August 12, 1997, Baltimore, Md.
Played for Brooklyn (1943, 1946–50)

Rex Barney was one of the fastest pitchers to ever pitch in the major leagues. The hitters who played against him thought so, as well as one of the other very fast pitchers. Stan Musial said, "He was one of the fastest pitchers I ever saw and had great physical make-up" (Broeg 1964, 266). Ralph Kiner added, "I think Rex Barney threw harder than any pitcher is baseball. He really brought that ball up there in a hurry, at over 100 mph" (Peary 1994, 89). Johnny Mize commented, "He [Bob Feller] was fast all right, but probably not as fast as Rex Barney" (Honig 1975, 104). Bob Feller agreed, "Fastest pitcher I ever saw?…Rex Barney. Barney could throw as hard as anybody, but he couldn't get the ball near the plate. Anyway, speed alone isn't enough" (Honig 1975, 280). Barney was signed out of high school in 1943 at age eighteen. After eleven games at Durham, North Carolina, in the Piedmont League and four games at Montreal in the International League, he was promoted to the Dodgers because of the personnel shortage. He made his first appearance on August 18, 1943, and pitched in nine games, eight of which were starts, during the balance of the 1943 season. He went two and two during that time.

Barney was then drafted into the Army before the start of the 1944 season. He was stationed at Fort Riley, Kansas, and was able to play some baseball during the summer of 1944. He was there with a group of major leaguers led by Harry Walker. At Fort Riley, Barney and the team won the national amateur tournament in Wichita, Kansas. After winning, Barney, along with at least five other major leaguers, was transferred to Camp Shelby, Mississippi, and then overseas. They went overseas together and landed at Le Havre, France. They were with the 65th Calvary Reconnaissance Group and went about 500 miles into France and Germany where they saw combat. They arrived in Europe in early 1945. Following V-E Day, Barney was able to play some baseball on the 65th Infantry Division team in Austria that summer. He was still listed on the Dodgers' defense list in December 1945. He returned to the Dodgers for the 1946 season.

When he returned, he was still only twenty-one years old and as wild as a March hare. He continued to struggle with control in 1946 and 1947. He seemed to mature in 1948 as he won fifteen games while losing thirteen. He also pitched a no-hitter on September 9 that year against the Giants. It would be the only year in his career that he would strike out more hitters than he walked.

The wildness got worse, and at age twenty-five, in 1950, his major league career ended. His speed and his wildness are remembered in Durham, where, in 1943, he threw a pitch that the catcher missed. It crashed through the screen and hit one of the baseball writers in the face, blackening his eyes as he sat in the press box. Barney said, "In *USA Today* I was voted one of the 21 all-time hardest throwers. But I would trade it all to have had great control. The thing I'll think about all my life—the frustrating thing—is what that lack of control cost me. Bull on that throwing hard" (Nemec and Palmer 1993, 186).

AGE	YRS	ML	W	L	PCT	ERA	G	GS	CG	IP	H	BB	SO	SHO	SV
19-20	44-45	6	35	31	0.53	4.34	155	81	20	598	474	410	336	6	1
		2	4	5	0.444	5	30	17	3	110	89	80	68	0	0
		8	39	36	0.52	4.45	185	98	23	708	563	490	404	6	1

BAUERS, RUSSELL L. (RUSS)   BL TR 6' 3" 195 lbs.
Born May 10, 1914, Townsend, Wi. — Died January 21, 1995, Hines, Il.
Played for Pittsburgh (1936–41), Chicago (N) (1946), and St. Louis (A) (1950)

Russ Bauers started his pitching career on a high note. He led Pittsburgh starting pitchers in winning percentage and earned run average during his rookie year in 1937. He followed that year with another solid year, again winning thirteen games. In 1939 he developed a sore arm and never approached those numbers again. He continued with the Pirates during the next three years. He was used mostly in relief and as a spot starter. His last season with the Pirates before World War II was 1941. After spending two years in the minors, he entered the military following the 1943 season. He was listed on the Pirates' defense list in November 1943. He was known to be in England at the time of the invasion. He was also listed in July 1943 as "doing rehab" in England. Following V-E Day, Bauers was on the OISE Headquarters Command team in Rheims, France. He was still listed on the Pirates' defense list in December 1945. Bauers returned to major league baseball in 1946, this time as a member of the Chicago Cubs. He played 1946 in Chicago and then reappeared with the St. Louis Browns for one game in 1950. Bauers spent two years in the military. However, his career was cut short by arm problems rather than his service to his country.

AGE	YRS	ML	W	L	PCT	ERA	G	GS	CG	IP	H	BB	SO	SHO	SV
30-31	44-45	8	31	30	0.508	3.53	129	71	27	599	562	271	300	5	6
		2	4	6	0.4	4.75	26	8	2	82	86	43	33	0	0
		10	35	36	0.493	3.75	155	79	29	681	648	314	333	5	6

BEAZLEY, JOHN A. (JOHNNY)   BR TR 6' 1" 190 lbs.
Born May 25, 1918, Nashville, Tn. — Died April 21, 1990, Nashville, Tn.
Played for St. Louis (N) (1941–42, 1946) and Boston (N) (1947–49)

Johnny Beazley had a rookie season most baseball players could only dream about. After winning his only start with a complete game when he was brought up in September 1941, Beazley carried that winning attitude into his first full year. In 1942 he won twenty-one games, had an earned run average of 2.13, and had a winning percentage of .778. He ranked second in the National League in all three of these categories in 1942. He topped off his rookie year by beating the Yankees twice in the World Series in games two and five. The latter was against Red Ruffing and clinched the championship for the Cardinals. He was voted to the all-rookie team by *The Sporting News* and named rookie of the year by the Chicago baseball writers. In the fall of 1942 Beazley turned down a state job in Tennessee to apply for a place in the

Navy's physical fitness program, but his Navy application was turned down. He then enlisted in the Army and was sworn into the Army Air Force as a mechanic at Nashville, Tennessee, on November 3, 1942. In two months he was promoted to corporal and transferred to Miami, Florida, to begin officer training. He graduated from officer candidate school on March 3, 1943, and was given the rank of 2nd lieutenant. By March 1944 he had been transferred to the Fourth Ferrying Group at Memphis, Tennessee, as the athletic officer. He was the physical fitness director for this group. He spent part of the summer of 1944 receiving training in the Army's specialized program at Virginia Military Institute before being sent back to Memphis and the 4th Ferrying Group.

The Army Chief of Staff did a survey and discovered that 280 former professional baseball players were still located on domestic bases. He ordered them to be dispersed. Beazley was sent first to Fairfield-Suisun Air Base near San Francisco and then on to Hawaii. He arrived in Hawaii in September 1944. He was stationed for a while at Hickam Field in Hawaii. Later he was sent along with others on a tour of the South Pacific islands. These were islands that had just been captured from the Japanese, and the ballplayers entertained the regular troops by playing exhibition games. They played at Saipan, Guam, Tinian, and other islands. The team Beazley was on included Joe DiMaggio, Joe Gordon, and Red Ruffing, all Yankees who Beazley had helped defeat just two years earlier. He was promoted to captain on April 27, 1945. He returned to the States in the fall of 1945 after a ten-month tour of duty in the South Pacific as a Physical Education and Training officer. He reported to Hamilton Field, California, on January 8, 1946. He was discharged on March 17, 1946. Beazley was able to play baseball while he was in the Army. This opportunity led to the end of his professional career.

He played in an All-Star game in New York in April 1944 to raise money for war bonds. The game raised $816 million. He played for the Army Transport Command while stationed near San Francisco. He played for the Berry Field Flyers in the summer of 1944. He played on an Army team at Hickam Field in Hawaii. He pitched for the Army in the Army/Navy World Series in October 1944 in Honolulu. After the tour of the islands, he came back to Hawaii and pitched for the Air Transport Command Base team and in the postseason series in the fall of 1945. However, his professional career really ended at a base in Texas when the Cardinals came through to play an exhibition game. The commanding officer of the base wanted Beazley to pitch against his old teammates. Beazley told the commander that he was not ready to try to pitch against major league competition, but the officer then ordered Beazley to pitch. After giving up several hits, he tried to reach back and put something extra on a pitch. The result was a lingering pain in his pitching shoulder.

In 1946, when he was discharged, the Cardinals were counting on him to return to his old form, but he never was able to regain his pitching skill. Joe Garagiola said, "He'd had that good overhand curve ball, but now it was a shame to watch him try to pitch. You could catch him with a Kleenex" (Turner 1996, 119). Stan Musial called him, "the most promising pitcher of the era" (Broeg 1964, 86). Musial added, "If he hadn't hurt his arm, he would have had many, many big years" (Broeg 1964, 266). In one season, plus one game, before the war Beazley won twenty-two games and lost six. After the war he won nine games and lost six in four seasons. He had an earned run average of 2.09 before the war and an ERA of 4.39 after the war. Beazley didn't get shot in the war but his service in the war ended his ability to be an effective major league pitcher. He retired by age thirty.

AGE	YRS	ML	W	L	PCT	ERA	G	GS	CG	IP	H	BB	SO	SHO	SV
25-27	43-45	6	31	12	0.721	3.01	76	46	21	374	349	157	147	3	3
		3	42	17	0.712	3	93	62	27	477	435	192	191	5	5
		9	73	29	0.716	3.01	169	108	48	851	784	349	338	8	8

BEGGS, JOSEPH S. (JOE)   BR TR 6' 1" 182 lbs.
Born November 4, 1910, Rankin, Pa. — Died July 19, 1983, Indianapolis, In.
Played for New York (A) (1938), Cincinnati (1940-44, 1946-47), and New York (N) (1947-48)

Joe Beggs had a trial with the Yankees in 1938 after a good year at Newark. He didn't stick and after another year at Newark was traded to the Reds on January 4, 1940. His National-League leading twelve relief wins and seven saves helped the Reds to the World Championship in 1940. Harry Craft said, "In 1940, Joe Beggs was our ace in the bullpen. In '40 he won twelve and saved seven and was a wonderful mop-up man" (Van Blair 1994, 32). He continued as the Reds relief man until the time he entered the military. He played in one game in 1944 (a winning complete-game start) before he entered the Navy with a commission as a 2nd lieutenant (j.g.) on April 26, 1944. He was thirty-three years old when he was called. Beggs graduated from the Fort Schuyler Naval Training School on June 23, 1944, after attending an indoctrination class.

During the summer of 1944, he was stationed at Camp Shelton where he pitched for the Armed Guard School team. December 1944 found him waiting to be shipped out with a gun crew while he was stationed at Brooklyn Armed Guard Center. He returned to Camp Shelton in the fall of 1945 and managed the Armed Guard School team. He was released from the Navy in February 1946. Beggs rejoined the Reds for the 1946 season. This time, however, he served the 1946 season as a starter. He started twenty-two games and pitched 190 innings. At age thirty-five, he was the leading starter for a Reds team that finished sixth. He won twelve games and had an ERA of 2.32. He returned to the bullpen in 1947 and closed his career by pitching in one game in 1948 for the Giants.

AGE	YRS	ML	W	L	PCT	ERA	G	GS	CG	IP	H	BB	SO	SHO	SV
33-34	44-45	9	48	35	0.578	2.96	238	41	23	694	687	189	178	4	29
(2 YRS MINUS		1	14	10	0.583	2.75	71	10	6	202	186	59	53	1	10
1 GAME)		10	62	45	0.579	2.9	309	51	29	896	873	248	231	5	39

BLACKWELL, EWELL   BR TR 6' 6" 195 lbs.
Born October 23, 1922, Fresno, Ca. — Died, October 29, 1996, Hendersonville, N.C.
Played for Cincinnati (1942, 1946-52), New York (A) (1952-53), and Kansas City (1955)

Ewell Blackwell signed with the Reds in December 1941 because they agreed to take him to spring training in 1942. He had played at Laverne College. He stayed with the Reds that spring long enough to get into two games before they sent him down to Syracuse in the International League. After the 1942 season, Blackwell tried to enlist in the Navy, but

President Roosevelt canceled all enlistments and Blackwell ended up in the infantry. He entered the Army on December 17, 1942.

Originally he was stationed in California and then transferred to Howze, Texas, to take his basic training. Hank Gowdy, who had been a Cincinnati coach, got Blackwell transferred to Fort Benning, Georgia. He was there from late 1943 until early 1945 when he was sent to Europe. While stationed at Fort Benning, Blackwell played a lot of baseball. He pitched for the Parachute School team and later for the Third Student Training Regiment Rifles, both at Fort Benning. He was part of General Patton's Third Army when he went to Europe. With that Army he saw action in France, Germany, and Austria. He was with the Third Army in Austria when they met the Russians as the two Allied armies came together. Following V-E Day on May 8, 1945, Blackwell got to play baseball in Europe during the balance of the summer of 1945. He pitched the 71st Division to the Third Army championship. However, they did lose the European Championship, which was played at Nuremberg, Germany. He also helped run a baseball school for German youths during this time.

Blackwell was discharged from the Army on March 19, 1946. He said, "I was in the Army three years, three months and three days" (Peary 1994, 4). He got to the Reds' spring training site the day the team broke camp and started north. He stayed in Florida to work out with the minor league teams to get ready for the season. Blackwell said, "I knew I was going to make the team because I had gotten stronger and improved in the Army, pitching 6 no-hitters" (Peary 1994, 4). In Blackwell's case the time spent in the Army did improve his game. He had gotten stronger and the experience of pitching against some good competition had matured him as a pitcher. He had been nineteen when he pitched for the Reds in 1942 and now he was twenty-three and had a good deal more experience. He made the Reds in 1946, winning nine while losing thirteen. However, his earned run average was only 2.45, and he led the National League in shutouts with six. The year 1946 was a good start; however, 1947 was Blackwell's year.

In 1947 he led the National League with twenty-two wins, twenty-three complete games, and 193 strikeouts. In addition his earned run average was only 2.47. He also had a streak of sixteen consecutive wins during 1947. On June 18, 1947, he pitched a no-hitter against the Braves. He followed this up by taking a no-hitter into the ninth on June 22. Eddie Stanky broke it up with a one out dribbler up the middle. With his sidearm delivery, he became the most feared pitcher in baseball. "The Whip," as he was called, gave the impression to right-handed batters that the ball was coming right down the third base line. For his entire career, hitters only batted .235 against his pitches.

Johnny Sain said, "I figured that Ewell Blackwell and I were considered the best pitchers in the league at this time. Blackwell was more of a superstar because he was a power pitcher" (Peary 1994, 18). The hitters felt the same way. Ralph Kiner commented, "Ewell Blackwell was a scary pitcher because he was mean and would throw at you anytime" (Peary 1994, 35). Combine that attitude with an exploding sidearm fastball and it's easy to see why Blackwell was so effective during 1947. In the spring of 1948 in an exhibition game in Columbia, South Carolina, Blackwell pitched for the Reds. It was a cold and windy day and after the game his shoulder was hurting. The team couldn't figure out why, so he continued to try to pitch. He would never be quite the same pitcher again. In addition, Blackwell also had kidney problems in 1949, which hurt his performance. The shoulder continued to be a problem but he won seventeen games in 1950 and sixteen games in 1951. He continued to be a feared pitcher all during his career. Stan Musial said, "Blackie was one of the fastest and greatest pitchers I've seen." Musial added, "Ill health hurt Blackwell more than opposing hitters did" (Broeg 1964, 81-82).

AGE	YRS	ML	W	L	PCT	ERA	G	GS	CG	IP	H	BB	SO	SHO	SV
20-22	43-45	10	82	78	0.513	3.3	236	169	69	1321	1150	562	839	16	11
		3	21	21	0.5	3	67	51	25	359	309	170	237	8	4
		13	103	99	0.51	3.25	303	220	94	1680	1459	732	1076	24	15

BRAZLE, ALPHA E. (AL)   BL TL 6' 2"   185 lbs.
Born October 19, 1913, Loyal, Ok. — Died October 24, 1973, Grand Junction, Co.
Played for St. Louis (N) (1943, 1946-54)

Al Brazle joined the Cardinals in July 1943 after having a good year at Sacramento in the Pacific Coast League. His eleven-win and eight-loss season at Sacramento was only the second winning season he had in eight minor league seasons. He was twenty-nine years old when he made the majors. Brazle made the most of his chance in the majors. During the balance of the 1943 season, he won eight games and lost only two with a 1.53 earned run average. He was used both as a starter and relief pitcher as the Cardinals took the second of their three consecutive pennants.

He was inducted into the Army at Jefferson Barracks, St. Louis, Missouri, the day following the end of the 1943 World Series. He was sent to Fort Riley, Kansas, to take his basic training, and he was able to play baseball for the Fort's all-star team during the summer of 1944. He was transferred to Camp Shelby, Mississippi. There he joined the 65th Division and became a member of the 65th Cavalry Reconnaissance Troop. Included in the troop were a number of former major league players. They were at Camp Shelby together and they stayed together as they were sent to Europe in early 1945 and into battle. As a reconnaissance troop they were out in front of the other troops, many times operating behind enemy lines. Included in the group were Harry Walker, George Archie, Kenny Heintzelmann, Rex Barney, and George Scharein.

They landed at Le Havre, France, and moved across France and Germany as the Allied moved toward Berlin. They saw battle action while they were there. Stan Musial said, "Al Brazle captured a division that was surrendering" (Turner 1996, XIII). After the fighting ended in Europe, Brazle was able to play some baseball. During the summer of 1945 he played for the 65th Infantry Division Team in Austria. At age thirty-two, Brazle was discharged on April 24, 1946, in time to join the Cardinals for the 1946 season.

He returned to his role as both a spot starter and reliever. He won between ten and fourteen games in each of the next five years. Then at age thirty-seven he switched to the bullpen almost full time. He was successful in that role. In 1952 he led the National League in saves with sixteen to go along with eight relief wins. He also led the league in saves in 1953 with eighteen. Brazle was not much of a hitter, with a career batting average of .177. However, on

September 12, 1951, he got the only hit off Warren Spahn as Spahn tried for a no-hitter. He closed out his career in 1954 at age forty.

AGE	YRS	ML	W	L	PCT	ERA	G	GS	CG	IP	H	BB	SO	SHO	SV
30-31	44-45	10	97	64	0.602	3.31	441	117	47	1377	1387	492	554	9	60
		2	22	14	0.611	3.15	81	36	14	308	316	100	120	3	2
		12	119	78	0.604	3.25	522	153	61	1685	1703	592	674	12	62

BROWN, MACE S.

BR TR 6' 1" 190 lbs.

Born May 21, 1909, North English, Ia. — Died March 24, 2002, Greensboro, N.C.
Played for Pittsburgh (1935–41), Brooklyn (1941), and Boston (A) (1942–43, 1946)

Mace Brown was one of the first pitchers to start his major league career as a relief pitcher. Over his career he would only start fifty-seven of the 387 appearances he had on the mound. He was successful at his trade. During the course of his career he led his league in relief wins three times and in saves two times. In 1938 he led the Pirates in wins, all in relief. Sometimes one event becomes a player's legacy. Brown had such an event. In 1938 he had a great year, 15 wins and an appearance in the All-Star game, yet in that year Brown had his infamous moment. On September 28, 1938, in the bottom of the ninth with darkness falling, Mace Brown pitched to Gabby Hartnett. This was the time when Hartnett hit the home run that came to be called the "Homer in the Gloamin" and the Cubs won the pennant. Brown was sold to the Dodgers in 1941 and on to the Red Sox in 1942. He was in a Red Sox uniform when he entered the Navy.

Brown was commissioned a lieutenant (j.g.) in the Navy Reserves on March 13, 1944. During the summer of 1944 he was stationed at Camp Shelton and was able to pitch for the Armed Guard School team. During late 1944 or early 1945 Brown was sent to Hawaii. During the spring, the Navy divided the players who were stationed in Hawaii into two teams and sent them out to the islands that had just been captured from the Japanese. The players were to play exhibition games for the regular troops. Brown was the captain of one of those teams. The players included a number of former major league players, including Mickey Vernon, Johnny Mize, Pee Wee Reese, as well as many others. They played in Kwajalein, Eniwetok, Peleliu, Tinian, Saipan, Guam, Roi-Namur, and Ulithi.

The team played before 15,000 troops the night before the troops left for the invasion of Okinawa. Brown said, "I was in Hawaii for three months and then went to other Pacific islands, ending up in Guam." He added, "I saw many a B-29 take off. Some didn't make it." He was released from the Navy on January 6, 1946. Brown said, "I was overweight and hadn't played for quite a long time" (Van Blair 1994, 25). He went to spring training early to try to get into shape, but he pulled a ligament in his elbow during the training and his arm hurt the whole year. His record in 1946 for the pennant-winning Red Sox was not bad, however. He won three and lost one with an earned run average of 2.05. He only appeared in eighteen games and pitched only twenty-six innings. At age thirty-seven his career was over. He accepted a job as a Red Sox scout in 1947 and retired from his playing career.

AGE	YRS	ML	W	L	PCT	ERA	G	GS	CG	IP	H	BB	SO	SHO	SV
35-36	44-45	10	76	57	0.571	3.47	387	57	18	1075	1125	388	435	3	48
		2	12	8	0.6	2.83	70	0	0	158	150	68	66	0	10
		12	88	65	0.583	3.35	457	57	18	1233	1275	456	501	3	58

CANDINI, MARIO C. (MILO)   BR TR 6' 0" 187 lbs.

Born August 3, 1917, Manteca, Ca. — Died March 17, 1998, Manteca, Ca.

Played for Washington (1943-44, 1946-49) and Philadelphia (N) (1950-51)

Milo Candini won seven games without a loss at the start of his major league career. This was a good start for a pitcher the Yankees thought had a sore arm and was a throw-in included in the trade of Jerry Priddy for Bill Zuber on January 29, 1943. He finished 1943 with a record of eleven wins and seven losses and an earned run average of 2.49. The next year was not as good. His record slipped to six wins and seven losses and went from a starter to pitching mostly out of the bullpen. He entered the Army in March 6, 1945, after spending the winter working in a war plant in Stockton, California. He was stationed at Camp Beale awaiting assignment. That assignment took him to Korea, where he was able to play on a baseball team. After the war, because of his play in Korea, he was asked to play for an Army team in Tokyo. He played with that team about three months during late 1945. They also played in Manila in the Philippines. Candini was very successful pitching for these teams.

He was released from the Army in February 1946. He returned to the Senators in 1946 and played for them and the Phillies for six more years. After his return, he was used strictly in relief. His record for the two seasons before the war was seventeen wins and fourteen losses. His record after the war in six seasons was nine wins and seven losses, never winning more than three games in any one year.

AGE	YRS	ML	W	L	PCT	ERA	G	GS	CG	IP	H	BB	SO	SHO	SV
27	45	8	26	21	0.553	3.92	174	37	13	538	530	250	183	5	8
		1	5	4	0.556	3.8	28	10	3	94	92	43	32	1	1
		9	31	25	0.554	3.91	202	47	16	632	622	293	215	6	9

CASEY, HUGH T.   BR TR 6' 1' 207 lbs.

Born October 14, 1913, Atlanta, Ga. — Died July 3, 1951, Atlanta, Ga.

Played for Chicago (N) (1935), Brooklyn (1939-42, 1946-48), Pittsburgh (1949), and New York (A) (1949)

Hugh Casey started out as a spot starter and reliever. As his career progressed, he moved more and more toward the bullpen. He only started fifty-six of his 343 appearances on the mound. He was successful with that move. He led the National League in relief win three times and in saves twice. For his career, he had a winning percentage of .641 with seventy-five wins and forty-two losses. He holds the record for the highest winning percentage among relief pitchers. His mark was .709. However, his most famous moment came in a loss.

In the 1941 World Series, his pitch struck out Tommy Henrich, but Mickey Owen couldn't handle the pitch; Henrich reached first base on the passed ball, and the Yankees won game four. Casey got the first two out in that ninth inning but, after the passed ball, he gave up a single, a double, a walk, a double, and another walk before he got the final out. Instead of tying the World Series at two games each, the Dodgers were done three games to one and the Yankees went on to close out the World Series with a win in game five.

The Sporting News reported that Casey would either enter the Army or the Coast Guard (November 19, 1942, page 9). However, on January 29, 1943, he enlisted in the Navy as an apprentice seaman at Atlanta. He took his boot training at Norfolk Naval Air Station in 1943 and took a course to be a physical instructor. In the spring of 1944 he was transferred from Norfolk to Hawaii, where he was able to play baseball during the summer. He made an all-star team and also pitched for the Navy team in the Army/Navy World Series in October 1944. His rank was chief specialist when he was pitching for a Navy team in the Pacific during the summer of 1945. He stayed in Hawaii into the fall and pitched for the AIEA Hospital team in the 14th Naval District League, making the all-star team. He also played in the Navy Little World Series in Hawaii in October 1945. He was discharged by the Navy on December 12, 1945.

He returned to the Dodgers in 1946 and pitched very well. He led the league in relief wins that season and his ERA was 1.99. He also had a good season as the Dodgers won the pennant in 1947. He led the league in relief wins and saves in 1947. The 1941 World Series did not go well for Casey. However, the 1947 World Series was one in which he performed very well. In 1947 he picked up two of the Dodgers' wins and had an earned run average of 0.87. He only allowed five hits and one run in ten and a third innings of work. His career lasted until 1949 as he closed it out with the Yankees. Allegedly despondent over the breakup of his marriage, Casey committed suicide on July 3, 1951, at age thirty-seven.

AGE	YRS	ML	W	L	PCT	ERA	G	GS	CG	IP	H	BB	SO	SHO	SV
29-31	43-45	9	75	42	0.641	3.45	343	56	24	940	935	321	349	3	55
		3	28	12	0.7	2.25	140	3	0	290	280	116	130	0	36
		12	103	54	0.662	3.1	483	59	24	1230	1215	437	479	3	91

COLEMAN, JOSEPH P. (JOE)   BR TR 6' 2"   200 lbs.

Born July 30, 1922, Medford, Ma. — Died April 9, 1997, Fort Myers, Fl.

Played for Philadelphia (A) (1942, 1946–51, 1953), Baltimore (1954–55), and Detroit (1955)

Joe Coleman joined the Philadelphia A's on September 19, 1942. He got in one game that fall, pitching six innings of relief, allowing two earned runs, and taking the loss. He had joined the A's after two years in the minors. Both years were in the lower classification leagues. He had been 18-9 at Wilmington of the Inter-State League before being called up to the A's. In November 1942 Coleman was called into the Navy. He joined Ted Williams, Johnny Pesky, Buddy Gremp, and Johnny Sain at Amherst College to do their preliminary ground school training for Naval Aviation. After completing their training, they were transferred to Chapel Hill, North Carolina, for preflight work in the spring of 1943. In the late summer of 1943, Coleman completed his preflight work and was sent on for primary flight training.

He remained in the Navy until late in 1945. He was listed on the A's active roster in December 1945. He spent most of the 1946 season at Toronto of the International League. He rejoined the A's in time to pitch in four games during that season. He made the majors in 1947 and had three good years pitching for a very bad Philadelphia A's team. He pitched three innings in the 1948 All-Star game. After three very bad years with the A's and one year back in the minors, Coleman had one good year for the Baltimore Orioles before he closed his career in 1955. His son, Joseph H. Coleman, pitched in the majors from 1965 to 1979.

AGE	YRS	ML	W	L	PCT	ERA	G	GS	CG	IP	H	BB	SO	SHO	SV
20-22	43-45	10	52	76	0.406	4.38	223	140	60	1134	1172	566	444	11	6
		3	12	21	0.363	4.38	58	40	19	279	285	134	111	4	1
		13	64	97	0.398	4.38	281	180	79	1413	1457	700	555	15	7

DEAN, ALFRED L. (CHUBBY)   BL TL 5' 11"   181 lbs.
Born August 24, 1916, Mt. Airy, N.C. — Died December 21, 1970, Riverside, Ca.
Played for Philadelphia (A) (1936-41) and Cleveland (1941-43)

When Chubby Dean signed with the Philadelphia A's off the Duke University campus, he
was a first baseman. He went straight to the majors from college. During 1936 he appeared
in 111 games, seventy-seven games at first and thirty-four pinch hitting appearances. The
following year, he played first in seventy-eight games, pinch-hit in 23 games, and pitched in
two. He had batted .287 in 1936 and .262 in 1937. Even after he was converted to a pitcher,
Dean continued to pinch-hit on a regular basis. During his career he made 191 pinch hitting
appearances and got forty-nine pinch hits. His overall career batting average was a respectable
.274 in 1,047 at-bats. Starting with the 1938 season, Dean was used almost completely as a
pitcher, first in relief and then as a spot starter also. His best year as a pitcher was 1942 when
he won eight and lost eleven for the Cleveland Indians.

He went into the Army in November 1943. He went to Fort Jackson, South Carolina, for
processing and by April 1944 was stationed at Daniel Field Fliers, Georgia. In the spring of
1945 he was sent to Hawaii. He was able to play some baseball while in Hawaii. He played
for the Bellows Flyers in Honolulu and then was sent to the islands of the South Pacific
during the summer of 1945. Dean was part of the major leaguers that played exhibition
games on the various islands. He played on Iwo Jima, Saipan, Guam, and Tinian. While
stationed at Tinian he pitched for the 58th Wing of the 20th Air Force. He arrived back in
Los Angeles on November 2, 1945, aboard the transport ship *Cecil*. He was still listed on the
Indians' defense list in December 1945. He was released by the Indians in 1946. Dean sued
the Indians under the GI bill. He wanted $4450 of a $7000 contract that he said was due
him. He also complained that, by being released when he was, he missed getting a pension
by one day of service. Dean was not able to return to the majors following his release from
the Army.

AGE	YRS	ML	W	L	PCT	ERA	G	GS	CG	IP	H	BB	SO	SHO	SV
26-28	43-45	7	30	46	0.395	5.08	162	68	23	686	781	323	195	1	9
(3 YRS MINUS		2	12	27	0.308	5.08	66	47	17	385	454	154	91	0	1
17 GAMES)		9	42	73	0.365	5.08	228	115	40	1071	1235	477	286	1	10

EARLY, THOMAS F.A. (TOM)   BR TR 6' 0"   180 lbs.
Born February 19, 1917, Roxbury, Ma. — Died April 5, 1988, Nantucket, Ma.
Played for Boston (N) (1938–42, 1945)

Tom Early made the Braves' roster for the full year in 1941. He had three years (1938, 1939,
and 1940) in which he spent time with both the Braves and in the minors. He was a spot
starter and reliever during the 1941 and 1942 seasons. He won six games in both of those

years while losing eight and eleven. He entered the Navy on November 7, 1942, and took his training at Norfolk Naval Training Station. He pitched for the station during the summer of 1943. Early was transferred to the South Pacific by the summer of 1944. He managed a baseball team while stationed in the Pacific. That fall he was moved and was stationed in Australia. While playing first base in the service, he tore ligaments so badly that his arm could not be repaired. He received a medical discharge in December 1944. He rejoined the Braves in 1945 and pitched in eleven games but could not continue because of his injuries.

AGE	YRS	ML	W	L	PCT	ERA	G	GS	CG	IP	H	BB	SO	SHO	SV
26-27	43-44	6	18	24	0.429	3.78	91	37	15	360	349	143	104	2	5
		2	10	15	0.4	4	55	27	10	240	240	90	65	1	3
		8	28	39	0.418	3.85	146	64	25	600	589	233	169	3	8

EISENSTAT, HARRY
BL TL 5' 11' 185 lbs.

Born October 10, 1915, Brooklyn, N.Y. — Died March 21, 2003, Beachwood, Oh.
Played for Brooklyn (1935-37), Detroit (1938-39), and Cleveland (1939-42)

Harry Eisenstat had trials with the Dodgers in 1935, 1936, and 1937 before sticking with the Detroit Tigers in 1938. He both started and relieved during the 1938 and 1939 seasons. After he was traded to Cleveland during the 1939 season, he was used almost exclusively as a relief pitcher. He was not used a lot even as a relief pitcher after 1939 even though he remained with the major league club. One of his better efforts came on the last game of the 1938 season. He pitched against Bob Feller as Hank Greenberg was trying to hit home run 59 and 60. Feller struck out eighteen Detroit batters that day. Greenberg didn't hit any home runs, but Harry Eisenstat won the game four to one on a four-hitter.

Eisenstat worked in a defense plant during the winter of 1942-43. He continued to work in the defense plant until he was drafted by the Air Force in June 1943. By December 1943, he was stationed at Mitchell Field, Long Island, and had been promoted to private 1st class. In January 1944 he was transferred to Miami, Florida, where he attended classes in officers' training school. He was later sent to the South Pacific where he did see combat. He was still on the Indians' defense list in December 1945.

Following his release from the Air Force, Eisenstat chose to return to his defense plant job rather than rejoin the Indians. He said, "It seemed more important to help this country than to play baseball." He continued, "Thompson Products in Detroit was manufacturing airplane parts—a defense plant setup—and it seemed to be the right thing to do" (Blake 1994, 78). He later became a vice-president for Curtis Industries in Cleveland. Eisenstat's baseball career was not spectacular but his service to country was an example for all. He did not play major league baseball after he left for the service in 1942.

AGE	YRS	ML	W	L	PCT	ERA	G	GS	CG	IP	H	BB	SO	SHO	SV
28-30	43-45	8	25	27	0.481	3.84	165	33	11	479	550	114	157	1	14
		3	4	6	0.4	3.3	77	4	0	153	179	34	57	0	8
		11	29	33	0.468	3.8	242	37	11	632	729	148	214	1	22

EMBREE, CHARLES W. (RED)   BR TR 6' 0" 165 lbs.
Born August 30, 1917, El Monte, Ca. — Died September 24, 1996, Eugene, Or.
Played for Cleveland (1941-42, 1944-47), New York (A) (1948), and St. Louis (A) (1949)

Red Embree made the Cleveland Indians team in 1942 after pitching one game at the close of
the 1941 season. He came to the Indians with a good reputation in the minors. He was listed
among the "minor aces among new faces in major leagues" and called the "Feller of small
leagues" (*The Sporting News*, "Minor Aces Among New Faces in Major Races" 2-5-42, page 1). He
pitched mostly in relief. In 1943, with the war going on, Embree elected to stay and work on his
farm. This was a time when farm products were needed by the country. In 1944 he returned to
play baseball and spent most of the 1944 season at Baltimore in the International League.

In the spring of 1944 he was rejected by the California draft board after a physical examination.
He continued to be listed as 4-F. In May 1945, Embree was summoned to take another physical.
This time his papers were sent from California to Cleveland, where he took the physical. He was
accepted for military service on May 15, 1945. He was inducted into the Army on June 11, 1945,
in Glendora, California. He remained in the Army until January 18, 1946.

Embree rejoined the Indians in 1946 and became part of their starting rotation. He pitched
200 innings in 1946, winning eight while losing twelve. He continued to be an Indian starter
the following season before going to the Yankees in 1948 and the Browns in 1949. He closed
his career following the 1949 season.

AGE	YRS	ML	W	L	PCT	ERA	G	GS	CG	IP	H	BB	SO	SHO	SV
27-28	45-46	8	31	48	0.392	3.72	141	90	29	707	653	330	286	1	1
(2 YRS MINUS		0	6	6	0.5	2.5	20	18	8	130	104	56	56	0	0
8 & 28 GAMES)		8	37	54	0.407	3.6	161	108	37	837	757	386	342	1	1

FERRICK, THOMAS J. (TOM)   BR TR 6' 2" 220 lbs.
Born January 6, 1915, New York, N.Y. — Died October 15, 1996, Lima, Pa.
Played for Philadelphia (A) (1941), Cleveland (1942, 1946), St. Louis (A) (1946, 1949-50),
Washington (1947-48, 1951-52), and New York (A) (1950-51)

Tom Ferrick was a starting pitcher the two years he played in the minors. However, when he
arrived at the major league level he was converted into a relief pitcher. During his career he
started only seven of the 323 pitching appearances he had in the major leagues. While his
overall win/loss record was even (40 wins and 40 losses), Ferrick was considered to be a good
relief pitcher. He spent two seasons in the majors before he entered the Navy.

He enlisted in the Navy on December 25, 1942. His original rank was a shipfitter 3rd class. He
was stationed at the Great Lakes Naval Base during the summer of 1943. He was able to pitch
for the Great Lakes team during the time he was stationed at that location. His rank changed
to 3rd class petty officer.

In the fall of 1943 he was transferred to the Naval Training Center at Bainbridge, Maryland, for further training. He finished that training in January 1944 and was sent to Hawaii. The trip to Hawaii included a stop in San Francisco. There, Ferrick, along with a number of other major league players, went by ship to Honolulu. Mickey Vernon became very seasick during the trip. In Hawaii, Ferrick helped with physical conditioning as well as playing baseball. During the summer of 1944 he pitched for the Kanchoe Naval Base team. He played for Navy in the Pacific "World Series" against Army in October 1944. Following that series against the Army, the Navy sent the players, including Ferrick, out to the islands in the Pacific that had just been captured from the Japanese. They played on Johnston Island, Kwajalein, Eniwetok, Peleliu, Tinian, Saipan, Guam, Roi-Namur, and Ulithi. He played for the Fifth Fleet team. Ferrick was discharged in January 1946.

He rejoined the Indians when he returned. However, he didn't stay long and began a career in which he would play for six teams in seven years. Twice he led the American League in relief losses (1941 and 1947). Both years, however, were with teams that lost a lot more games than they won. His best year was 1950 when he was traded to the Yankees during the year and played an important part in their pennant drive. He had nine relief wins (led the league) as well as eleven saves during that year. Nineteen fifty-two was his final year in the major leagues.

AGE	YRS	ML	W	L	PCT	ERA	G	GS	CG	IP	H	BB	SO	SHO	SV
28-30	43-45	9	40	40	0.5	3.47	323	7	4	674	654	227	245	1	56
		3	16	15	0.516	3.34	125	3	1	267	252	90	99	0	20
		12	56	55	0.505	3.43	448	10	5	941	906	317	344	1	76

FLEMING, LESLIE F. (BILL)   BR TR 6' 0" 190 lbs.
Born July 31, 1913, Rowland, Ca.
Played for Boston (A) (1940-41) and Chicago (N) (1942-44, 1946)

Bill Fleming had a good year at Hollywood in the Pacific Coast League in 1940 before being called up the Red Sox in August. He was listed as one of "minor aces among new faces in major leagues" in *The Sporting News* in February 1942. However, success did not come at the major league level. He divided his time between the majors and minors in 1940, 1941, and 1943. Only with the Cubs in 1942 and 1944 did he spend the entire year with the major league club. The year 1944 was his best as he won nine games and lost ten as a spot starter and reliever. He was drafted into the Army in January 1945 and, after a short time at Camp Beale, California, awaiting assignment for training, he spent his entire time at Fort Lewis, Washington. He was able to pitch for the post team during 1945. There were a number of major league players there and the team didn't lose a game for three years. They won seventy-two games.

He was a member of the First Platoon, Company A, First Battalion Basic Training Section. His platoon got top honors on their training test. Lieutenant Henry Rosensweig said, "In addition to being fine ball players, they are excellent soldiers. Their attitude fills our men with a spirit of pride in their platoon that will be hard to beat" (*The Sporting News*, "From Service Front— Players in Star Platoon" 3-15-45, page 16). Fleming was discharged in December 1945. He was concerned that, at least for the early part of the season, he and the other players would not be ready for the 1946 season because they hadn't had enough good competition during the time in the Army. He added, "You never had to bear down and go all out as you do in the majors" (Turner 1996, 20). Fleming's record for 1946 proved him correct. He pitched in fourteen games that season. He won no games and lost one with an ERA of 6.14. The best moment of his career was a game in 1944 against the Boston Braves when he pitched a one-hitter with the only hit being a little blooper by Tommy Holmes. Fleming won the game 1–0 when Andy Pafko hit a home run in the bottom of the ninth.

AGE	YRS	ML	W	L	PCT	ERA	G	GS	CG	IP	H	BB	SO	SHO	SV
31	45	6	16	21	0.432	3.79	123	40	14	442	442	193	167	3	3
		1	5	8	0.385	3.94	28	10	4	110	110	48	42	1	0
		7	21	29	0.42	3.82	151	50	18	552	552	241	209	4	3

FOWLER, RICHARD J. (DICK)   BR TR 6' 4" 215 lbs.
Born March 30, 1921, Toronto, Ont., Canada — Died May 22, 1972, Oneonta, N.Y.
Played for Philadelphia (A) (1941-42, 1945-52)

Dick Fowler spent his entire career with the Philadelphia Athletics. He joined the team in September 1941 after spending most of the year with Toronto of the International League. The following season he became one of the A's regular pitchers. During 1942 he was used as a spot starter and reliever. Being from Canada, Fowler joined the Canadian Army in January 1943. He served almost three years in the service. He was discharged on August 15, 1945. He rejoined the A's for the close of the 1945 baseball season. He pitched in seven games in 1945, getting three starts. Fowler had some success that fall even though he had been away from baseball for three years. On September 9, 1945, he started a game against the St. Louis Browns and pitched a no-hitter. He won the game by the score of 1–0, walking four batters. This was only a few days after he had been released from the Army. Fowler continued to be one of the mainstays of the A's staff. The team was bad during those years so fifteen games was the most wins he had in a season. He did that twice (1948 and 1949). A severe bursitis condition bothered him during his career. It limited him to eleven games and only sixty-six innings in 1950. This condition forced a premature exit from the A's after the 1952 season.

AGE	YRS	ML	W	L	PCT	ERA	G	GS	CG	IP	H	BB	SO	SHO	SV
22-24	43-45	10	66	79	0.455	4.11	221	170	75	1303	1367	578	382	11	4
(3 YRS MINUS		2	33	32	0.508	3.71	88	75	37	557	567	220	156	5	2
7 GAMES)		12	99	111	0.471	3.93	309	245	112	1860	1934	798	538	16	6

GORSICA, JOHN H.P. (JOHNNY)   BR TR 6' 2" 180 lbs.
Born March 29, 1915, Bayonne, N.J. — Died December 16, 1998, Charlottesville, Va.
Played for Detroit (1940-44, 1946-47)

Johnny Gorsica started out as a first baseman and was converted to a pitcher in his second year of professional baseball. He was able to make the major leagues with the Tigers after only two years of being a pitcher. During his first two years with the Tigers he both started games as well as relieved. During the 1940 World Series, his rookie year, he pitched in two games in relief. The Tigers lost both of the games but Gorsica pitched eleven and one-third innings, giving up only six hits and one earned run. After two years in the bullpen, he returned to spot starting during the 1944 season as the talent pool went down.

He entered the Navy on March 29, 1945, at Huntington, West Virginia. He was sent to the Great Lakes Naval Training Station for his basic training. It was rumored that he would be shipped out to the Pacific, but he remained at Great Lakes during the summer of 1945. While stationed there he pitched for their baseball team, winning five games and losing none. Gorsica was discharged on March 18, 1946. He was slow in returning to form. During 1946 he pitched in fourteen games without a decision. He closed his major league career the following year. Although Gorsica was both a starter and reliever during his career, his record was much better as a reliever. He won fourteen and lost eight while pitching in relief. As a starter, he won seventeen, but he lost thirty-one.

AGE	YRS	ML	W	L	PCT	ERA	G	GS	CG	IP	H	BB	SO	SHO	SV
30-31	45-46	7	31	39	0.443	4.18	204	64	22	724	778	247	272	4	17
(2 YRS MINUS		1	10	12	0.455	4.08	46	17	7	201	209	62	70	1	1
14 GAMES)		8	41	51	0.446	4.15	250	81	29	925	987	309	342	5	18

GRISSOM, LEE T.   BB TL 6' 3"   200 lbs.
Born October 23, 1907, Sherman, Tx. — Died October 4, 1998, Corning, Ca.
Played for Cincinnati (1934–39), New York (A) (1940), Brooklyn (1940–41), and Philadelphia (N) (1941)

Lee Grissom made the Reds in 1937 after trials in 1934, 1935, and 1936. He made a good contribution to the 1937 Reds, starting thirty games and pitching in relief in another twenty. He won twelve and lost seventeen while leading the National League with five shutouts. He was expected to pick up where he left off in 1938. However, after pitching in fourteen games, he tried to steal a base and broke his ankle. He was out for the rest of the season. He returned in 1939 and helped the Reds win the pennant that year. The following two years were not as successful. As a result, he was traded or sold four times, including one time to a minor league team.

He enlisted in the Army on June 30, 1942. Earlier his classification had been changed from 3-A to 1-A and he was expecting an early call. In May 1943, he was stationed with an infantry outfit in Nashville, Tennessee. Later that fall, his address was HDQ Second Army, Memphis, Tennessee. He continued to be stationed in Tennessee. In the spring of 1944 he was at Camp Tyson, Tennessee, in the military police (MP). During 1944 he went to Keesler Field, Biloxi, Mississippi, and then on to Lincoln Field, Nebraska. January 1945 found him at Grand Island, Nebraska.

During the summer of 1945 he was able to pitch for the 2nd Air Force Falcons in Colorado Springs, Colorado. He was an MP attached to the headquarters at that location. Grissom was discharged on October 10, 1945. He was thirty-four years old when he enlisted in the Army. He was almost thirty-eight years old when he was released. Grissom was not able to play at the major league level following his discharge.

AGE	YRS	ML	W	L	PCT	ERA	G	GS	CG	IP	H	BB	SO	SHO	SV
34-37	42-45	8	29	48	0.377	3.89	162	95	23	702	668	305	379	6	7
		4	15	25	0.375	3.89	90	52	10	400	374	175	199	1	1
		12	44	73	0.376	3.89	252	147	33	1102	1042	480	578	7	8

GUMPERT, RANDALL P. (RANDY)   BR TR 6' 3"   185 lbs.

Born January 23, 1918, Monocacy, Pa.

Played for Philadelphia (A) (1936–38), New York (A) (1946–48), Chicago (A) (1948–51), Boston (A) (1952), and Washington (1952)

Randy Gumpert was signed by the Philadelphia A's right out of high school as an eighteen year old. He joined the A's for the 1936 season and pitched in twenty-two games, all but three in relief. He spent parts of 1937 and 1938 with the A's and in the minors. He went to the minors full-time and did not return to the major leagues until after he returned from his time in the service. He spent four years in the minors before he was drafted after the 1942 season.

Gumpert was accepted for induction March 5, 1943. He applied and got accepted into the Coast Guard. He did his training in the spring of 1943 at the Coast Guard Station at Manhattan Beach, New York. He spent the balance of 1943 and most of 1944 at Manhatten Beach before he was transferred to the Coast Guard Station at New London, Connecticut. He was at New London from August 1944 until the summer of 1945. Gumpert said, "I was lucky as I could keep my hand in baseball, pitching for the base team, and on Sundays, for the Connecticut Telephone Co., which was in a semi-pro league in the New London area" (Gumpert letter 1997).

He was discharged in November 1945 after thirty-two months. Gumpert had become the property of the Yankee minor league system before he was drafted. When he returned to baseball it was with the Yankees. He had his best year in 1946 with the Yankees. He was used as a spot starter and reliever. He won eleven games and lost three with an earned run average of 2.31 that year. He pitched in the most innings of his career in 1949 with the White Sox. That year he threw 234 innings while winning thirteen games and losing sixteen. During his time with White Sox, he had at least one distinction. On May 1, 1951, he gave up the first home run that Mickey Mantle had during his career.

AGE	YRS	ML	W	L	PCT	ERA	G	GS	CG	IP	H	BB	SO	SHO	SV
25-27	43-45	10	51	59	0.464	4.17	261	113	47	1053	1099	346	352	6	7
		3	18	10	0.643	3.98	90	32	14	340	340	100	125	1	1
		13	69	69	0.5	4.12	351	145	61	1393	1439	446	477	7	8

HALLETT, JACK P.   BR TR 6' 4"   215 lbs.

Born November 13, 1914, Toledo, Oh. — Died June 11, 1982, Toledo, Oh.

Played for Chicago (A) (1940–41), Pittsburgh (1942–43, 1946), and New York (N) (1948)

Jack Hallett spent six seasons in the minors before making his debut on September 13, 1940. After spending the 1941 season with the White Sox, he was traded to the Philadelphia A's on December 9, 1941, only two days after Pearl Harbor. He then was released by the A's and spent most of 1942 in the minors before joining the Pirates. He started the 1943 season with the Pirates before being drafted into the Navy on June 24, 1943. He started out at Great Lakes where he pitched for the base team over the summer before going to an East Coast base for further training in the fall of 1943. After completing that extended training, he was sent to Pearl Harbor in early 1944. In Hawaii he assisted with physical conditioning. During

League in appearances (53), saves (15), and relief losses (9). He also led the league in relief losses in 1951.

AGE	YRS	ML	W	L	PCT	ERA	G	GS	CG	IP	H	BB	SO	SHO	SV
25-28	42-45	9	59	71	0.454	4.18	271	109	42	1050	1097	455	534	2	21
		4	42	44	0.488	3.65	120	92	43	707	727	295	379	2	0
		13	101	115	0.468	3.97	391	201	85	1757	1824	750	913	4	21

HUGHSON, CECIL C. (TEX)   BR TR 6' 3" 198 lbs.
Born February 9, 1916, Buda, Tx. — Died August 6, 1993, Austin, Tx.
Played for Boston (A) (1941–44, 1946–49)

Tex Hughson split his playing time between Boston and Louisville of the American Association in 1941. The following year he became a part of the Red Sox's regular rotation and one of the best pitchers in the American League. In 1942, his first full year in the majors, he led the league in wins (22), innings pitched (281), strikeouts (113), and complete games (22). Hughson's won/loss record went down in 1943 as the Red Sox fell from second place to seventh place, but his overall pitching performance continued to be good. His earned run average was almost the same; strikeouts were one more but his win/loss record fell to twelve wins and fifteen losses. The Red Sox were in the middle of the pennant drive in 1944 when Hughson, Bobby Doerr, and Hal Wagner were drafted in late August and early September. That ended the Red Sox pennant hopes that year. Hughson's record was eighteen wins and five losses with an earned run average of 2.26 when he was drafted on August 24, 1944.

Before he was drafted Hughson had been a part of the war effort. He served as an aircraft spotter in Boston, atop Carey Hill, while he was still with the Red Sox. He also pitched in an all-star game in Cleveland in July 1942. The game pitted American League All-Stars against a military all-star team and raised $193,000 for benefit of war relief. Hughson said, "I don't recall anyone being unhappy. I know definitely that I wasn't. I was very happy and considered myself fortunate to be on the ball club, and I thought this was a very minor sacrifice as far as myself personally was concerned. I thought it was the least thing we could do" (Goldstein 1980, 68).

Hughson was late going into the service because he had children before Pearl Harbor, he was over twenty-five years old, and he had a high draft number. He was first called to duty by the Navy and it was later changed to the Army. He took his basic training in his home state of Texas. He did pitch a little that fall after being inducted. After basic training at Sheppard Field in Wichita Falls, Texas, he went to an Army Air Force navigation school at San Antonio, Texas. In March 1945, he was transferred to Kearns Field in Salt Lake City. The Army gathered together a group of several former major league players in Salt Lake City to be sent to Hawaii to play the Navy. This was after the Navy had beaten the Army team in the Army/Navy World Series in Honolulu in October 1944. Hughson relates what happened. "The baseball players spent several weeks at least in Salt Lake City and went through basic training all over again and then went to Seattle and then by Liberty Ship to the Hawaiian Islands" (Goldstein 1980, 242). Because of the delays, the Navy team was gone before the Army got their players to the islands. The Army's chance to get even was gone. Hughson added, "The other ballplayers over there who'd waited on us wanted to know where we'd been. It was an Army screw-up on the orders" (Goldstein 1980, 242). Since the Navy was gone, the Army divided the major league players into three teams. Some went to Hickam Field, some to Camp Wheeler, and some to a fighter base about twenty miles outside Honolulu. Hughson was assigned to that base and pitched for the Bellows Flyers while stationed in Hawaii.

He spent late spring and early summer of 1945 in Hawaii. In mid-summer, after six weeks in Hawaii, the groups were shipped out to the Marianas Islands which had just been captured from the Japanese. Hughson was stationed in Saipan but played in Tinian, Guam, Iwo Jima, and the other islands. Hughson's team was in Tinian on August 6, 1945, to play a game. That was the day the B-29 bomber nicknamed "Enola Gay" took off Tinian to drop the first atomic bomb on Hiroshima, Japan. Hughson said, "There was a lot of scuttlebutt that something big was going to happen. But you know how rumors can get around in the Army. We had no inkling of the magnitude of what it was, of course. We weren't too far from where they took off with the atomic bomb" (Goldstein 1980, 243).

He pitched for the 73rd Wing Bombers, 20th Air Force while stationed in Saipan. He played in an all-star game on August 26, 1945, in the Marianas. Hughson continued to play baseball in the Marianas into October 1945. He returned to the States, arriving in Los Angeles aboard the transport ship *Cecil*, on November 2, 1945. He was discharged on January 12, 1946.

Hughson picked up where he left off in his baseball career. In 1946 he helped to Red Sox to the American League pennant, winning twenty games with an earned run average of 2.75. In 1947 he suffered a finger injury and in 1948 came down with a sore arm. The sore arm limited him to nineteen innings pitched in 1948, all in relief. He attempted a comeback in 1949 but had limited success. He closed his major league career in 1949.

AGE	YRS	ML	W	L	PCT	ERA	G	GS	CG	IP	H	BB	SO	SHO	SV
28-29	44-45	8	96	54	0.64	2.94	225	156	99	1376	1270	372	693	19	17
(2 YRS MINUS		1	21	13	0.618	2.71	44	38	24	317	289	84	162	5	3
28 GAMES)		9	117	67	0.636	2.9	269	194	123	1693	1559	456	855	24	20

HUTCHINSON, FREDERICK C. (FRED)   BL TR 6' 2" 190 lbs.
Born August 12, 1919, Seattle, Wa. — Died November 12, 1964, Bradenton, Fl.
Played for Detroit (1939–41, 1946-53)

Fred Hutchinson's father wanted a $5,000 bonus from the Tigers before he would let him sign. The Tigers refused so Hutchinson signed with Seattle in the Pacific Coast League. Hutchinson won twenty-five games during the 1938 season, and the Tigers paid the Seattle team $50,000 and four players to get him in the Tiger organization. He spent the next three years, 1939 to 1941, dividing his time between the Tigers and their top minor league teams. His record during that time was only six wins and thirteen losses. During 1941 he made only two appearances with the Tigers, both as a pinch hitter. He spent the year at Buffalo in the International League where he was named the most valuable player.

Hutchinson enlisted in the Navy on October 30, 1941. He was assigned to the Norfolk Naval Training Station. During the summer of 1942 he pitched for the base team. He, along with Bob Feller, led that team to a record of ninety-two wins and eight losses during 1942. Hutchinson's record was twenty-three wins and one loss. He continued to be stationed at Norfolk during 1943. That season the team had seventy-five wins and twenty-five losses. Hutchinson was one of the pitchers for the military in an all-star game against the American League in July 1942 in Cleveland. The proceeds of the games were used for war relief. During his time at Norfolk, he rose to the rank of chief petty officer and was drillmaster on the rifle range.

During 1944 he was transferred to Pasco, Washington, Naval Station with the rank of chief specialist. In early 1945 he was awarded a Navy medal for expert pistol shooting at Farragut, Idaho, Naval Training Station. In March 1945 he was transferred from the security department at Farragut, Idaho, to overseas duty. He arrived in Hawaii during the summer of 1945. While stationed there he pitched for the AIEA Barracks team in the 14th Naval District League. He also pitched in the Navy's Little World Series during October 1945. He was named to the 14th Naval District Team that year. Hutchinson was discharged from the Navy on October 18, 1945. He rejoined the Tigers for the 1946 season. The opportunity that he had to play baseball during his time in the military had developed him as a pitcher.

He was twenty-two years old when he went into the Navy, and he was twenty-six years old as he rejoined the Tigers. He assumed a role in the regular Tiger rotation and maintained that position for six years starting in 1946. He won eighty-seven games during that six-year period. Hutchinson was an intense person. He didn't like or accept losing. Yogi Berra said, "When we followed Detroit into a city, we could always tell how Hutch fared. If we got stools in the dressing room, we knew he had won. If we got kindling, we knew he had lost" (Dickson 1991, 45). In 1952, with the Tigers in last place, Hutchinson was named manager of the Tigers. He continued to be an active pitcher during 1952 and 1953. He was the last pitcher to serve as a playing manager.

His playing career was winding down when he was named as manager on July 5, 1952. He played only sparingly during the last two years. Hutchinson was a good hitter. He had a lifetime batting average of .263 with four home runs. He was used ninety-one times as a pinch hitter during his career. After his playing career ended, he continued to manage.

His best year as a manager was 1961 when he led the Cincinnati Reds to the National League pennant. Hutchinson was diagnosed with cancer during the winter of 1963. He continued to manage the Reds during the 1964 season, resigning on October 19, 1964. The Reds finished the 1964 season in second place, one game behind the St. Louis Cardinals. He died from the disease on November 12, 1964.

AGE	YRS	ML	W	L	PCT	ERA	G	GS	CG	IP	H	BB	SO	SHO	SV
22-25	42-45	10	95	71	0.572	3.73	242	169	81	1464	1487	388	591	13	7
		4	50	39	0.562	3.73	120	100	60	800	765	230	400	8	5
		14	145	110	0.569	3.73	362	269	141	2264	2252	618	991	21	12

JOHNSON, EARL D. BL TL 6'3" 190 lbs.
Born April 2, 1919, Redmond, Wa. – Died, December 3, 1994, Seattle, Wa.
Played for Boston (A) (1940-41, 1946-50) and Detroit (1951)

Earl Johnson was one of baseball's heroes of World War II. He made it to the major leagues after spending less than one season in the low minors. He joined the Red Sox on July 20, 1940, after starting that season at Rocky Mount of the Piedmont League. He continued with the Red Sox during the 1941 season. In both seasons he had the role of starter and reliever. He enlisted in the Army on January 5, 1942, less than a month after Pearl Harbor. When he was inducted, he was assigned to Camp Roberts, California. He was a member of Company A, 87th Infantry Training Battalion, Platoon 3. He went overseas as a rifle platoon sergeant with Company B of the 120th Infantry, assigned to the 30th Division. Johnson took part in a number of the battles in Europe: the Vire and Taute Canal Crossings, Bradley's St. Lo Breakthrough following the Normandy invasion, the stand against the German counterattack at Mortain, the pursuit of the Nazis through France and Belgium, and finally, the defense of Malmedy against Von Rudstedt's winter offensive.

During his service he was awarded the Silver Star and the Bronze Star with a cluster for heroism. He also received a battlefield commission to second lieutenant. The citation for his Bronze Star read "On September 30, 1944, in Germany, during heavy concentration of hostile fire, a friendly truck was struck by an enemy shell and had to be abandoned. The fact that the vehicle contained vital radio equipment made it imperative that it be recovered before falling into enemy hands. Sergt. Earl Johnson and several other members of his unit were assigned to this hazardous mission. They courageously braved a severe hostile fire and were completely successful in dragging the vehicle over an area in plain view of the enemy" (*The Sporting News*, "In The Service—Red Sox Southpaw—Cited for Bravery" 3-15-45, page 13). Johnson commented on the event in a letter to Eddie Collins, general manager of the Red Sox. "I have been in combat for six months. It sure has been a long road. It really has been tough. It seems like I have been fighting for years. I sure will be glad when it is over. I received a Bronze Star medal a couple of weeks ago. There was a jeep that was knocked out in front of our lines and only about 200 yards from the pill boxes of the Siegeried Line, and a couple of others and I went out and towed it in. The reason for [me] getting it was that it had valuable equipment" (The Sporting News, "In The Service—Red Sox Southpaw—Cited for Bravery" 3-15-45, page 13). He won the Silver Star and a promotion to first lieutenant during the Battle of the Bulge, again being cited for bravery under fire.

In another letter Johnson commented on the difficulty in getting sleep and the problems of having any food other than K rations. While many of the major league players spent their military time playing baseball to entertain the troops, Johnson was a real soldier, an infantryman who knew the horrors of war and the hardship of battle. He spent his time in the Army winning the war and doing it with bravery and honor for the defense of his country. He was discharged on November 27, 1945.

Johnson rejoined the Red Sox for the 1946 season. Pitching mostly in relief, he won five games and lost four as the Red Sox won the pennant. He picked up the win in the opening game of the 1946 World Series, pitching three and one-third innings in relief, allowing only one hit.

Johnson's best season was 1947. He won twelve games and lost eleven while pitching both in relief and as a starter. Converting to a relief pitcher in 1948, he led the American League in relief wins with nine. After spending part of the 1950 season back in the minors, Johnson signed with the Tigers for the 1951 season after the Red Sox released him in October 1950. He only pitched in six games with the Tigers in 1951 before closing out his major league career.

AGE	YRS	ML	W	L	PCT	ERA	G	GS	CG	IP	H	BB	SO	SHO	SV
23-26	42-45	8	40	32	0.556	4.3	179	50	14	546	556	272	250	4	17
		4	30	21	0.588	4	115	30	11	380	371	186	177	3	13
		12	70	53	0.569	4.18	294	80	25	926	927	458	427	7	30

KLINGER, ROBERT H. (BOB)   BR TR 6' 0" 180 lbs.
Born June 4, 1908, Allenton, Mo. — Died August 19, 1977, Villa Ridge, Mo.
Played for Pittsburgh (1938–43) and Boston (A) (1946–47)

Bob Klinger spent nine years in the minors before he joined the Pirates when he was almost thirty years old. He joined the Pirates starting rotation in 1938 and won twelve games while losing only five. His earned run average that year was a good 2.99. In 1939 he was the Pirates' leading winner with fourteen wins even though he led the National League with seventeen losses. Starting with the 1940 season, he pitched both in relief and as a starter. He also had a good year in 1943, winning eleven while losing eight.

He entered the Navy on April 9, 1944. He reported for duty at Jefferson Barracks in St. Louis and then took his basic training at Camp Farragut, Idaho. When he completed his basic training, he was transferred to the Great Lakes Naval Base. He was able to pitch for Great Lakes during the summer of 1944. He won nine games and lost zero while pitching for Great Lakes. In February 1945, Klinger was a new arrival in Hawaii. After a short time in there, he was sent out to the islands of the South Pacific to play baseball to entertain the troops. That is where he spent his time during the summer of 1945. He played on Kwajalein, Eniwetok, Peleliu, Tinian, Saipan, Guam, Roi-Namur, and Ulithi. He was discharged on December 11, 1945.

Klinger was almost thirty-six years old at the start of the 1946 season. After spring training, the Pirates released him on May 9, 1946. This would turn out to be a break for him because on May 10, 1946, he was signed by the Boston Red Sox. During the 1946 season, the Pirates finished seventh and the Red Sox won the pennant. Klinger played a major role for the Red Sox that season. He pitched out of the bullpen, getting three relief wins and leading the American League with nine saves. His only appearance in the 1946 World Series was in game seven. Klinger came in to pitch for the Red Sox after George Metkovich hit a double batting for pitcher Joe Dobson as the Red Sox scored two runs in the top half of the eighth inning to tie up the game. Enos Slaughter opened the Cardinals' half of the eighth with a single against Klinger, and after two outs, Harry Walker singled. This was the single that gave Slaughter the chance to score all the way from first base and give the Cardinals the World Series victory. Klinger took the hard luck loss. He closed his major league career with the 1947 season.

AGE	YRS	ML	W	L	PCT	ERA	G	GS	CG	IP	H	BB	SO	SHO	SV
36-37	44-45	8	66	61	0.52	3.68	265	130	48	1090	1153	358	357	7	23
		2	12	11	0.522	3.05	63	22	10	224	214	76	76	2	8
		10	78	72	0.52	3.57	328	152	58	1314	1367	434	433	9	31

KRAKAUSKAS, JOSEPH V.L. (JOE)   BL TL 6' 1"   203 lbs.
Born March 28, 1915, Montreal, Quebec, Canada — Died July 8, 1960, Hamilton, Ont., Canada
Played for Washington (1937–40) and Cleveland (1941–42, 1946)

Joe Krakauskas joined the Washington Senators on September 9, 1937, and pitched in five games that fall. He started four and had a record of 4-1 during that year. His most active year was 1939 when he won eleven and lost seventeen. He pitched in 217 innings during 1939. After the 1940 season when he won only one game while losing six, he was traded to the Cleveland Indians for Ben Chapman. Following his trade, Krakauskas couldn't make the Indians club on a regular basis. He spent part of both the 1941 and 1942 seasons in the minors. In 1941 he was at Syracuse and in 1942 at Baltimore. Following the 1942 season he joined the Air Force. Since Krakauskas was a Canadian he joined the Royal Canadian Air Force. He was listed as a radio mechanic located in Britain during the summer of 1943. He was discharged by the Royal Canadian Air Force in December of 1945. He rejoined the Indians for the 1946 season. He appeared in twenty-nine games that year with five starts. He won only two games and lost five during 1946, his last major league season.

AGE	YRS	ML	W	L	PCT	ERA	G	GS	CG	IP	H	BB	SO	SHO	SV
28-30	43-45	7	26	36	0.419	4.53	149	63	22	584	605	355	347	1	4
		3	5	10	0.333	4.8	70	15	3	140	150	81	70	0	2
		10	31	46	0.403	4.58	219	78	25	724	755	436	417	1	6

KRIST, HOWARD W. (HOWIE)   BL TR 6' 1"   175 lbs.
Born February 28, 1916, West Henrietta, N.Y. — Died April 23, 1989, Buffalo, N.Y.
Played for St. Louis (N) (1937–38, 1941–43, 1946)

Howie Krist had trials with Cardinals in both 1937 and 1938, but he could not make the team until after he had a great season at Houston in the Texas League in 1940. He won twenty-two and lost nine for the 1940 Houston team. Krist's role with the Cardinals was as a reliever and spot starter. He was very effective in the three years before the war. During those years, he won thirty-four games and lost eight. In 1941, he won ten games without losing a single game. This set the National League record for the most wins in a season without a loss and currently is the third longest win total without a loss in major league history. He led the National League in relief wins in 1942 with eight. In 1943, when pitching was thinned out by men going into service, Krist stepped in as a starter. During 1943 he pitched three shutouts while winning eleven games.

He entered the Army in April 1944. He was stationed at Camp Craft in July 1944. He was transferred to Europe during the last half of 1944. He received a combat infantry medal for courage in late 1944. While serving in France in 1944 Krist badly injured his leg while carrying ammunition. Earlier he had injured his neck while diving head first into a foxhole and had received a Purple Heart. The leg injury put him in an Army hospital for almost a year. He was placed on "limited service" duty following his injury. Krist was discharged on January 23, 1946. In addition to his war injuries, Krist also suffered additional injuries when he was involved in an automobile accident near his home in upstate New York.

He reported for spring training with the Cardinals in 1946, but he could not overcome the problems he had experienced during the war and later. He was unable to regain the skill he had when he left for the Army in 1944. He pitched in fifteen games in 1946, without winning any games. His earned run average was 6.75. He won thirty-seven games and only lost nine during the time before he went into service. After he returned, he won no games and lost two. The injury he suffered during his time in the service put an end to his baseball career.

AGE	YRS	ML	W	L	PCT	ERA	G	GS	CG	IP	H	BB	SO	SHO	SV
28-30	44-46	6	37	11	0.771	3.32	128	37	15	444	408	158	150	3	6
(3 YRS MINUS		2	35	10	0.777	3.15	100	30	13	396	351	140	140	2	6
15 GAMES)		8	72	21	0.774	3.24	228	67	28	840	759	298	290	5	12

KUSH, EMIL B.   BR TR 5' 11" 185 lbs.
Born November 4, 1916, Chicago, Il. — Died November 26, 1969, River Grove, Il.
Played for Chicago (N) (1941-42, 1946-49)

Emil Kush had brief trials with the Cubs in 1941 and 1942 before he entered the military. He pitched in a total of three games during the two years. He joined the Navy on October 1, 1942, after spending most of the 1942 season with the Milwaukee team of the American Association. He spent 1943 and 1944 stationed at Lambert Field, St. Louis, Missouri, where he was able to play baseball for the Lambert Field team. He was transferred to Norfolk Naval Training Station during 1945. He also was able to play for the Norfolk team. Kush was discharged on February 8, 1946. He rejoined the Cubs for the 1946 season and spent his career as a relief pitcher. He started only eight of the 150 games in which he made an appearance. He had a natural sidearm sinker and enjoyed success out of the bullpen during the 1946 and 1947 seasons. An arm injury and resulting surgery cut short his career. He closed his career following the 1949 season.

AGE	YRS	ML	W	L	PCT	ERA	G	GS	CG	IP	H	BB	SO	SHO	SV
26-28	43-45	6	21	12	0.636	3.48	150	8	2	346	324	158	150	1	12
		3	13	6	0.692	3.37	89	4	1	197	180	93	89	0	8
		9	34	18	0.654	3.44	239	12	3	543	504	251	239	1	20

MARCHILDON, PHILIP J. (PHIL)   BR TR 5' 10" 170 lbs.
Born October 25, 1913, Penetanguishene, Ontario, Canada — Died January 10, 1997, Toronto, Ontario, Canada
Played for Philadelphia (A) (1940-42, 1945-49) and Boston (A) (1950)

Phil Marchildon was from a remote mining town in northern Ontario and began his professional baseball career with the Toronto team in the International League. At the close of his second year in baseball, he was promoted to the Philadelphia Athletics. He made his debut on September 22, 1940. He became a regular in the A's rotation starting with the 1941 season. He pitched well for the last place A's. He won twenty-seven and lost twenty-nine during 1941 and 1942.

Marchildon enlisted in the Royal Canadian Air Force in November 1942. He wanted to be a pilot. When the Canadian government offered to let him be a fitness instructor because he was a professional athlete, he refused. He insisted that he wanted to serve on active duty. He didn't make it as a pilot, but he was an air crewman. He served as a tail gunner on a Halifax bomber. He had been in combat service for some time, flying twenty-six missions out of England. It was the night of August 16, 1944, and his bomber was flying a mission to lay mines over Kiel Bay off the coast of Nazi-controlled Denmark. During the mission the plane was shot down and Marchildon had to bail out over the water. His plane was flying at eighteen thousand feet and it was at night. After landing in the water he swam for four hours before a Danish fisherman picked him up. After being rescued from the water, he then was turned over to the Germans. The Germans placed him in a prisoner of war camp in Poland. Only the navigator and Marchildon survived the crash. The rest of the crew, five men, died.

Marchildon spent nine months as a prisoner of war. During that time he survived on three slices of black bread and some watery soup a day. He lost about forty pounds. When the Russians got close to the camp where he was held, the Germans marched him and his fellow prisoners to another camp. When the British got close to that camp, they were marched to another. One of the camps where he was kept was Stalag III. Some of the camps housed large numbers of prisoners. One of the camps that he spent time housed as many as 16,000 prisoners. Marchildon saw his comrades shot down for trivial offenses while in the camps. The British liberated the camp where he was housed on May 2, 1945.

When he was released, he was evacuated to an English hospital because of the mental anguish he had suffered and because he was very malnourished. After he had been released for a while, he said, "I don't feel strong. I get weak much quicker than I ever did" (*The Sporting News*, "Looping The Loops" 8-2-45, page 2). He went on, "Baseball is tough on the nerves of a pitcher. But the strain is only for a few moments. Gosh, over there I was under a strain five and six hours at a time, peering into the darkness, looking for fighters, facing flak and we were playing for keeps. I got rigid and this, of course, took a lot out of me. I hope I can get it back" (*The Sporting News*, "Looping The Loops" 8-2-45, page 2). He was discharged on July 27, 1945.

After Marchildon had been released from the Air Force in July 1945, he had returned to Canada to try to recuperate. However, the A's were doing badly and not drawing many fans to their games. Connie Mack wanted to do something to draw a crowd. He invited Marchildon to come to Philadelphia and take part in a "Phil Marchildon Night." When A's coach, Al Simmons, took a look at Marchildon, he pleaded with Mack not to ask him to pitch in a game. He was still feeling the effects of being a prisoner and was in terrible shape. However, the game was played. The A's had a crowd of about 35,000 fans. Connie Mack had his big gate, and he paid Marchildon with a $1000 dollar war bond (which cost $750). One of the downsides to the game was that Marchildon tore a groin muscle. This injury continued to bother him into spring training of 1946. He returned to the A's full-time during the 1946 season and continued to be part of the A's regular rotation for three more years. He developed a sore arm in 1949 that brought his career to an end. He pitched in only seven games in 1949 and one game in 1950.

The experience of being a prisoner of war left him with a bad case of nerves. He didn't sleep well nor did he eat well. The problem of his nerves continued after he returned to baseball. Teammate Eddie Joost said, "We called him 'Fidgety Phil.' He could never sit still or stop moving his hands" (Peary 1994, 72). George Kell commented that Marchildon was a different person than he had been before the war. "He could still pitch, but he had a funny look in his eyes that hinted his thoughts were about the war and not baseball" (Peary 1994, 72). Sometimes he would fool around the mound and with the resin bag for some time. Joost added, "You'd know something was wrong. And sure enough the next pitch was in the dirt or up in the screen—one day in Detroit he threw one up in the stands." Joost went on, "Every once in a while he'd start to shake and not be able to concentrate. We'd walk to the mound, but we couldn't settle him down" (Peary 1994, 72).

Marchildon commented on his return to baseball following his war experience. "I'd kind of drift away from concentration. I'd think about how lucky I was to get out of it all." He kept thinking of the five crew members who died. He didn't know until after the war the other members of the bombers crew had perished. He went on, "I was more fidgety than before. I was always pretty serious, but I guess I was more so now. 'War nerves,' people were calling this, and of course, many others, both in and out of the game, had the condition" (Turner 1996, 24).

It is easy to see why he would have felt the effects of the war. Seeing fellow prisoners shot, having to endure the hardships of prison, using the concentration needed to fly combat missions, all would have caused the nerves to be tested. Marchildon served his country in combat when he could have stayed out of the line of fire. He paid the price with his health.

AGE	YRS	ML	W	L	PCT	ERA	G	GS	CG	IP	H	BB	SO	SHO	SV
29-31	43-45	9	68	75	0.476	3.93	185	162	82	1214	1084	684	481	6	2
(3 YRS MINUS		2	44	40	0.524	3.6	101	90	52	713	621	385	305	4	2
3 GAMES)		11	112	115	0.493	3.81	286	252	134	1927	1705	1069	786	10	4

MELON, REUBEN F. (RUBE)   BR TR 6' 5" 205 lbs.
Born February 27, 1917, Cramerton, N.C. — Died September 11, 1971, Greer, S.C.
Played for Philadelphia (N) (1941-42) and Brooklyn (1943-44, 1946-47)

Rube Melon was signed by the Cardinal organization and then drafted by the Phillies in October 1940. After a year in the bullpen he became a regular starter for the Phillies in 1942, winning nine and losing twenty. He led the National League in walks during the 1942 season. On December 12, 1942, he was traded to the Brooklyn Dodgers and became a wartime replacement. He both started and relieved during the 1943 and 1944 seasons. He was classified for the draft as 3-A during this time. However, he was drafted by the Army in January 1945. He took his training at Camp McClellan, Georgia, during the early part of 1945. Being 6' 5" he was a standout basketball player on the camp team while he was stationed in Georgia. He was discharged on May 22, 1946, and rejoined the Dodgers.

Melon had his best year in 1946. During the time he was with the Dodgers, he won six games and lost three. His earned run average was 1.99. He started twelve games and relieved in another twelve. When his ERA ballooned to 12.80 in 1947 and the Dodgers developed some new pitchers, Melon's activity was cut to four games. He closed his major league career with the 1947 season.

AGE	YRS	ML	W	L	PCT	ERA	G	GS	CG	IP	H	BB	SO	SHO	SV
28-29	45-46	6	30	50	0.375	3.62	162	87	25	704	620	395	363	6	5
(2 YRS MINUS		1	9	18	0.333	3.62	43	28	7	206	208	123	110	1	0
24 GAMES)		7	39	68	0.364	3.62	205	115	32	910	828	518	473	7	5

MILNAR, ALBERT J. (AL)   BL TL 6' 2"   195 lbs.
Born December 26, 1913, Cleveland, Oh.
Played for Cleveland (1936, 1938–43), St. Louis (A) (1943, 1946), and Philadelphia (N) (1946)

Al Milnar joined the Indians to stay in 1938 after a brief trial in 1936. After a year in the bullpen (1938), he joined the starting rotation in 1939. He was one of the Indians' regular starters for three years. His best year was 1940 when he won eighteen games while losing ten. He also led the league in shutouts that year with four. During the 1941 season, he had the distinction of giving up the last hit Joe DiMaggio got during his fifty-six game hitting streak. Milnar said, "Ken Keltner [Indians' third baseman] didn't get any great stops for me" (Blake 1994, 97).

Milnar had some control problems during his career. His strikeout-to-walk ratio of .71 was bad. During his career he walked 495 batters while striking out 350 in 996 innings. His pitching success decreased as his control problems got worse. In 1942, he was reduced to a spot starter and reliever and in 1943 was sold to the St. Louis Browns. Milnar was drafted by the Army on March 30, 1944. He had been working as a guard in the Thompson Aircraft Product Company during the off-season. He reported for duty at Fort Benjamin, Indiana. He was transferred during that summer to Fort McClellan, Alabama, for training in intelligence work.

By June 1945 he had been sent to the Philippines. He went overseas with an Army engineering outfit and then transferred into athletic work. While stationed in Leyte, Philippines, he developed two baseball leagues, one with fourteen teams and another with ten teams. Milnar was discharged in January 1946. Milnar said in a letter that he didn't see any combat or suffer any injuries while in service. He also said, "I am not sorry I served my country. I am proud of it. It may have hurt or shortened my career because I was called at the age of 31 years old. Losing two years at that age is harmful" (Milnar letter 1997). Milnar rejoined the Browns for the 1946 season. However, he only pitched in four games for them before being sent to the Phillies. He pitched one game for the Phillies before ending his major league career.

AGE	YRS	ML	W	L	PCT	ERA	G	GS	CG	IP	H	BB	SO	SHO	SV
30-31	44-45	8	57	58	0.496	4.22	188	127	49	996	1043	495	350	10	7
		2	8	12	0.4	4.22	47	27	9	210	220	129	54	1	0
		10	65	70	0.481	4.22	235	154	58	1206	1263	624	404	11	7

MOORE, LLOYD A. (WHITEY)   BR TR 6' 1"   195 lbs.
Born June 10, 1912, Tuscarawas, Oh. — Died December 10, 1987, Uhrichsville, Oh.
Played for Cincinnati (1936–42) and St. Louis (N) (1942)

Whitey Moore was the number three starter for the pennant-winning Cincinnati Reds in 1939. He had trials in 1936 and 1937 before sticking in the majors in 1938. He continued to be in the starting rotation in 1940 as the Reds won another pennant and, this time, the World Series. After the 1940 season, Moore spent his time in the bullpen. His won-loss record out of the bullpen was better than when he started. He won ten while losing three in relief and won twenty and lost twenty-six when he started the game.

Moore was sent to the Cardinals during the 1942 season. He entered the Army after the 1942 season and remained there through the 1945 season. In February 1945 it was reported that he was in an Army hospital near London with an infected foot that resulted from an injury he received during training in England. Moore was not able to return to baseball at the major league level after his release from the Army.

AGE	YRS	ML	W	L	PCT	ERA	G	GS	CG	IP	H	BB	SO	SHO	SV
31-33	43-45	7	30	29	0.508	3.75	133	60	18	513	450	292	228	4	4
		3	6	6	0.5	4.2	50	6	1	110	110	92	28	0	0
		10	36	35	0.507	3.83	183	66	19	623	560	384	256	4	4

MULCAHY, HUGH N.   BR TR 6' 2" 190 lbs.
Born September 9, 1913, Brighton, Ma. — Died October 19, 2001, Aliquippa, Pa.
Played for Philadelphia (N) (1935-40, 1945-46) and Pittsburgh (1947)

Hugh Mulcahy was the first major league player to be drafted. Being the first one to go fits right in with his whole career. He toiled for the Phillies as one of their regular starters for four years at a time when the team finished next to last, last, last, and last in the National League. He was a durable pitcher who was good enough to pitch every fourth day for a very bad team. The sportswriters gave him the nickname "Losing Pitcher" because of the number of times the letters L.P. appeared after his name in the box score.

During the four years as a regular starter, Mulcahy led the league in a number of categories. Most, however, were not of a positive nature. He led the league one time in appearances (1937), hits allowed (1940), sacrifice hits allowed (1939), bases on balls (1937), wild pitches (1939), relief losses (1937), and balks (1940). He led the league twice in earned runs allowed (1938 and 1939), hit batsmen (1937 and 1939), and losses (1938 and 1940). He led the league three times in runs allowed (1938, 1939, and 1940). A pitcher has to be the best that a bad team has to offer to get the chance to pitch enough to have records like Mulcahy. The Phillies had a history of money problems during this time. They would sell off their best players to raise money to keep the team operating.

During the winter of 1940-41 Mulcahy was the best player the Phillies had to offer. Most thought that he would be sold to a contender who needed pitching. He said, "I was the next fellow to be sold. I knew the Dodgers were after me, and Cincinnati and the Cubs were trying to get me. Any move would have been a move upstairs; you'd have a better chance" (Mead 1985, 28). Keeping with his "Losing Pitcher" image, he was drafted into the Army and the Phillies sold their next best player.

Kirby Higbe went to the Dodgers for $100,000 and Mulcahy went to the Army. Higbe helped the Dodgers to a pennant in 1941 when he won twenty-two games. Mulcahy was drafted into the Army on March 8, 1941. This was nine months before Pearl Harbor. He was a member of the 101st Artillery at Camp Edwards on Cape Cod, Massachusetts. He drove a truck, learned the machine gun, and managed the baseball team while stationed at Camp Edwards. When he was drafted it was for a year. He anticipated that he would be available for spring training in 1942. He said, "It might be a little tougher and might take a little longer for me to get into shape when I report for spring training next season, but I don't think this year of Army life will hamper my pitching any" (Gilbert 1992, 12). It didn't work out that way.

When the Japanese attacked Pearl Harbor, the United States was at war. He also commented when he was drafted that, "I am 100 percent in favor of military training and will do my best" (Mead 1985, 27). Mulcahy had been released from the Army only days before the attack. He then was recalled immediately and was stationed at Fort Devens, Massachusetts. He did not try to get out of his service to his country. He said, "I should say not; I'm in to stay until it's over. I never applied for my discharge and I never intend to" (*The Sporting News*, "From Army Front" 2-5-42, page 7).

He had the rank of sixth class specialist and drove a quartermaster truck while stationed at Providence, Rhode Island, during early 1942. He was promoted to corporal in June 1942 and was given a chance for a commission by attending Army Air Force Officers Candidate School in Miami Beach, Florida. He reported on June 25, 1942. Mulcahy's attitude was good about his service to his country. "My losing streak is over for the duration. I lost a lot of close ones with the Phils, but my luck is due to change. I am on a winning team now" (*The Sporting News*, "In The Service—Hugh and Hank Teammates" 7-9-42, page 6).

During the next two years, Mulcahy served at several bases as athletic or recreation officer. In October 1942, he was at Fort DuPont, Delaware; in February 1943, he was at Fort Jackson, South Carolina; in July 1943, at Camp Gordon, Georgia; and in November 1943, in Memphis, Tennessee, with the Second Army Headquarters of the Transport Command. He was able to pitch some baseball while stationed in Memphis. He had the rank of sergeant. He stayed at Memphis during the summer of 1944 and rose to the rank of staff sergeant.

In late summer or early fall of 1944, Mulcahy was sent to the Pacific. He managed and played for a barnstorming team that toured the Southwest Pacific bases. His rank was master sergeant. By February 1945 he was stationed in the Philippines with the Eighth Army. He was to organize a serviceman's sports program in Manila. His efforts were successful. He was the manager and pitched for the 8th Army base team. He continued to be stationed in the Philippines until he was ready to be released. He was discharged at Fort Devens, Massachusetts, on August 5, 1945. He started in Massachusetts and ended up in Massachusetts. In between he just about circled the globe. In addition to his stateside service, he also served in New Guinea, Leyte, Luzon, and the Philippines.

He rejoined the Phillies on August 26, 1945. He pitched in five games during the remainder of the 1945 season. The players looked up to Mulcahy because of his service. Bobby Bragan, one of Mulcahy's teammates said, "Hugh Mulcahy was a hero in the minds of all ballplayers at that time" (*Boston Globe*, April 27, 1978). Mulcahy suffered from weight loss when he returned from the Army. He had contracted dysentery while stationed in the Philippines, and it continued to affect him. He stayed with the Phillies during the 1946 season. However, he was never able to regain his pitching skills. The Phillies released him after the 1946 season, and he signed with the Pirates. After pitching only two games for the Pirates in 1947, they also released him. He then spent five more years pitching in the minors before he closed his professional career in 1951.

Mulcahy suffered through playing for a very bad Philadelphia Phillies team. Pinky May said, "Hugh Mulcahy was a fine gentleman. He lost a lot because we never got him enough runs" (Van Blair 1994, 133). Mulcahy had a good attitude toward his professional baseball career. He said, adapting Shakespeare, "Tis better to have pitched and lost, than never to have pitched at all" (Blake 1994, 68).

AGE	YRS	ML	W	L	PCT	ERA	G	GS	CG	IP	H	BB	SO	SHO	SV
27-31	41-45	9	45	89	0.336	4.49	220	145	63	1161	1271	487	314	5	9
(5 YRS MINUS		4	40	75	0.348	4.49	176	127	59	989	1079	401	285	5	8
5 GAMES)		13	85	164	0.341	4.49	396	272	122	2150	2350	888	599	10	17

MUNGER, GEORGE D.   BR TR 6' 2"   210 lbs.
Born October 4, 1918, Houston, Tx. — Died July 23, 1996, Houston, Tx.
Played for St. Louis (N) (1943–44, 1946–52) and Pittsburgh (1952, 1956)

George Munger joined the Cardinals in the spring of 1943 after six years in the minors. He was a wartime replacement who succeeded both during the wartime and after he returned from service. He was a spot starter and reliever during 1943. In 1944 he had a very good record of eleven wins and only three losses with an earned run average of 1.34. He was selected to play in the 1944 All-Star game. However, the morning of the game Munger was inducted into the Army. That night, instead of pitching in the All-Star game, he pitched for a team from Jefferson Barracks as they beat a team from Lambert Field, two to one.

The date he was inducted was July 11, 1944. Munger had been classified 2-B in April 1944 but was summoned for a preinduction physical at Mobile, Alabama, on May 4. He requested a change of location to St. Louis and was accepted for active duty for the Army at Jefferson Barracks on May 23. He took his basic training at Camp Roberts, California, before taking training in machine guns and mortars. He served as a squad leader in basic training. Munger went to officer candidate school at Fort Benning, Georgia. He was commissioned a second lieutenant on April 14, 1945. He remained at Fort Benning after graduation to serve as an officer at the camp prison. He also attended infantry school at Fort Benning. While stationed at Fort Benning during the summer of 1945, he was able to pitch for the 3rd Student Training Regiment Rifles team. In September 1945, he also played on the base team at Ellington Field, Houston, Texas, while on leave from Fort Benning. Munger was transferred to Germany in late 1945 or early 1946. The Cardinals had hoped he would be released for the start of the 1946 season, but he remained in Germany. While stationed in Germany, he did not do much pitching. He returned home on a troop ship and because of his lack of activity in Germany, Munger had gained some weight and his arm was out of shape. He wasn't discharged until August 27, 1946. He rejoined the Cardinals for the balance of the 1946 season.

Eddie Dyer, the manager, brought him along slowly to try to get him into shape to help the team at the end of the year. When the Cardinals won the National League pennant, Munger did get into postseason play that year. He started game four of the World Series and beat the Red Sox, allowing one run while pitching a complete game. Munger had his best year in 1947. He won sixteen games while losing five. He had another good year in 1949, winning fifteen and losing eight. Arm trouble limited his career after 1949. He was traded to the Pirates during the 1952 season. After five games with the Pirates, they sent him to Hollywood in the Pacific Coast League. He stayed at Hollywood until 1955. In 1955, he won twenty-three games with an earned run average of 1.85. This season earned Munger another chance in the majors. He pitched for the Pirates during the 1956 season as a spot starter and reliever, winning three and losing four. Munger's final season in the majors was 1956.

AGE	YRS	ML	W	L	PCT	ERA	G	GS	CG	IP	H	BB	SO	SHO	SV
25-27	44-46	10	77	56	0.579	3.83	273	161	54	1229	1243	500	564	13	12
(3 YRS MINUS		1	25	10	0.714	3.83	72	40	18	317	319	118	168	6	5
21 & 10 GAMES)		11	102	66	0.607	3.83	345	201	72	1546	1562	618	732	19	17

PEARSON, ISSAC O. (IKE)   BR TR 6' 1"   180 lbs.
Born March 1, 1917, Grenada, Mi. — Died March 17, 1985, Sarasota, Fl.
Played for Philadelphia (N) (1939–42, 1946) and Chicago (A) (1948)

Ike Pearson is another pitcher who suffered through playing for the Philadelphia Phillies during the late 1930s and early 1940s. During the four years he played for the Phillies prior to World War II, the team finished last every year. Pearson was signed out of the University of Mississippi and joined the Phillies on June 6, 1939. He pitched both as a starter and as a reliever. Winning was very hard when playing for the Phillies during those days. Pearson has the lowest winning percentage of any major league pitcher who has at least fifty decisions. For his career, he won thirteen games while losing fifty. That is a winning percentage of .206. He had more success in relief than he did as a starter. In 1941, he won four and lost four with an earned run average of 2.07 as a relief pitcher in thirty-six appearances. In 1941 he started ten games. He lost all ten of the starts. His lack of success as a starter raised his total earned run average for the entire forty-six games he pitched that year to 3.57.

Pearson enlisted in the Marines on September 22, 1942. He commented, "I want to be on a first-place team" (Kaufman and Kaufman 1995, 95). He took his basic training at Paris Island. He was discharged from the Marines in February 1946. He rejoined the Phillies that year but only pitched in five games. After being out of the majors in 1947, he joined the White Sox for the 1948 season. He won two and lost three for the Sox in twenty-three appearances. During his career, Pearson started fifty-four games and relieved in 110. In his fifty-four starts, he had a record of seven wins and forty losses. In relief he won six, lost ten, and had eight saves. He finished seventy-five of the 110 games in which he pitched relief.

AGE	YRS	ML	W	L	PCT	ERA	G	GS	CG	IP	H	BB	SO	SHO	SV
26-28	43-45	6	13	50	0.206	4.83	164	54	10	559	611	268	149	2	8
		3	8	25	0.242	4.67	97	27	6	319	340	157	88	1	5
		9	21	75	0.235	4.77	261	81	16	878	951	425	237	3	13

PETERSON, KENT F.   BR TL 5' 10" 170 lbs.
Born December 21, 1925, Goshen, Ut. — Died April 27, 1995, Highland, Ut.
Played for Cincinnati (1944, 1947-51) and Philadelphia (N) (1952-53)

Kent Peterson was signed by the Reds out of high school and sent straight to the majors. He
made his debut on July 15, 1944, as an eighteen year old. He pitched in one game, retiring the
three men he faced. He was called into active service by the Salt Lake City draft board during
August 1944. He went into the Navy and spent part of 1945 stationed in the Philippines. While
there he played for the Fifth Replacement Depot team. He was still on the Reds' defense list
in December 1945 and continued to serve his country during the 1946 season. He rejoined
the Reds for the 1947 season. He pitched as a starter and reliever in 1947 and 1948 before
going full time to the bullpen. Wins were hard to come by for Peterson. His combined record
for 1947 and 1948 was eight wins and twenty-eight losses. After 1949 his pitching time was
limited for the Reds and later the Phillies. He closed his major league career by pitching in
fifteen games for the Phillies in 1953. During his career, Peterson won thirteen games and lost
thirty-eight. He was nine and twenty-eight as a starter with forty-three starts.

AGE	YRS	ML	W	L	PCT	ERA	G	GS	CG	IP	H	BB	SO	SHO	SV
19-20	45-46	8	13	38	0.255	4.95	147	43	7	420	434	215	208	1	5
		2	2	6	0.25	6.22	24	6	1	59	61	27	32	0	0
		10	15	44	0.254	5.11	171	49	8	479	495	242	240	1	5

QUEEN, MELVIN J. (MEL)   BR TR 6' 0" 204 lbs.
Born March 4, 1918, Maxwell, Pa. — Died April 4, 1982, Fort Smith, Ar.
Played for New York (A) (1942, 1944, 1946-47) and Pittsburgh (1947-48, 1950-52)

Mel Queen was a wartime replacement for the Yankees. After a trial in April 1942, he rejoined
the Yankees during the 1944 season after spending part of the year at Newark. His only
winning season in the majors was 1944, going six and three as the Yankees came in third
behind the Browns and the Tigers. He entered the Army in February 1945. He served until
June 13, 1946, and rejoined the Yankees in time to pitch in fourteen games that year. He was
sold to Pittsburgh on July 11, 1947, and spent the balance of 1947 and 1948 with the Pirates.
After winning twenty-two games for the Indianapolis team in the American Association in
1949, Queen rejoined the Pirates in 1950. He was a starter and reliever during the next two
years. He pitched the most innings of his career in 1951. That year he won seven and lost nine
while striking out 123 batters in 168 innings. He closed his major league career by pitching
in two games in 1952. Melvin J. Queen is the father of Melvin D. Queen who played for the
Reds and Angels during the 1960s and 1970s.

AGE	YRS	ML	W	L	PCT	ERA	G	GS	CG	IP	H	BB	SO	SHO	SV
27-28	45-46	8	27	40	0.403	5.09	146	77	15	557	567	329	328	3	1
(2 YRS MINUS		1	8	9	0.47	5.09	29	16	3	131	120	75	72	1	0
14 GAMES)		9	35	49	0.417	5.09	175	93	18	688	687	404	400	4	1

RIGNEY, JOHN D. (JOHNNY)

BR TR 6' 2"   190 lbs.

Born October 28, 1914, Oak Park, Il. — Died October 21, 1984, Lombard, Il.
Played for Chicago (A) (1937-42, 1946-47)

Johnny Rigney joined the White Sox in the spring of 1937 and, after spending two years mostly in the bullpen, joined the regular starting rotation in the 1939 season. He would be the number one pitcher for Chicago over the next three-plus years until he entered the Navy. When Comiskey Park was opened in 1939, Rigney pitched the first game. He averaged starting more than thirty games a year for the three-year period 1939–41. Rigney enlisted in the Navy on May 8, 1942, shortly after Pearl Harbor. He had been summoned by the Army in 1941, during the early draft, but was rejected because of a punctured eardrum. He was classified as 4-F for a while but then returned to 1-A, available for service. He started his training at Great Lakes Naval Training Station. On July 7, 1942, while stationed there, he pitched for the military all-stars against the American League All-Stars to raise money for war bonds and war relief. The game raised $193,000. He had the rank of coxswain in charge of athletic equipment.

In early 1943 he spent some time at St. Mary's California Pre-Flight School. He returned to Great Lakes for a while and left again in September 1943. He was able to play baseball while stationed at Great Lakes. When transferred he went to Bainbridge, Maryland, for further training. When he completed his course in October 1943, he had the rank of specialist 3rd class and was a physical instructor in the Naval Training School at Bainbridge.

In the spring of 1944 he returned to Great Lakes for a short time and then spent the summer of 1944 stationed at Norfolk Naval Training Station. He pitched for the base team during the summer of 1944. After the 1944 season he was sent, along with several other players, to San Francisco and then on to Honolulu. He arrived in Hawaii during the winter of 1944–45. He spent five months in Honolulu before being sent out to the islands with a baseball team to play exhibition games for the regular soldiers. He played on the islands of Kwajalein, Eniwetok, Peleliu, Tinian, Saipan, Guam, Roi-Namur, and Ulithi. In Saipan they played in front of 15,000 troops before the troops left that night for the invasion of Okinawa.

Rigney had some bad luck. On July 4, 1945, he strained his arm while pitching an exhibition game. He thought he would be okay after rest. He was discharged from the Navy on October 23, 1945. Rigney rejoined the White Sox for the 1946 season. However, the arm that he thought would be okay, wasn't. He had been a pitcher who averaged over thirty starts a year before the war; now he was a pitcher with a sore arm. He attempted to come back but was not successful. After pitching in fifteen games in 1946 and eleven in 1947, he retired from active playing. Rigney, who had married Dorothy Comiskey, daughter of the White Sox owner, in 1941 moved into the front office of the White Sox where he eventually became a vice president. The war had taken its toll on another successful pitcher.

AGE	YRS	ML	W	L	PCT	ERA	G	GS	CG	IP	H	BB	SO	SHO	SV
27-30	42-45	8	63	64	0.496	3.59	197	132	66	1186	1101	450	605	10	5
(4 YRS MINUS		3	48	45	0.516	3.59	135	96	49	844	796	322	429	8	4
7 GAMES)		11	111	109	0.505	3.59	332	228	115	2030	1897	772	1034	18	9

RUSSO, MARIUS U.   BR TL 6' 1"   190 lbs.
Born July 19, 1914, Brooklyn, N.Y.
Played for New York (A) (1939–43, 1946)

Marius Russo spent two-plus years at Newark in the International League before he was called up to the Yankees. He made his debut on June 6, 1939. In 1940 he became part of the regular rotation of Yankee starters and continued in that role until a sore arm put him on the shelf in 1942. He was the Yankee opening day pitcher in 1941. His activity increased in 1943, but he was not able to return to the status he enjoyed in 1940 and 1941. Russo pitched complete game victories in both the 1941 and 1943 World Series. In 1941, he bested the Dodgers with Freddy Fitzsimmons pitching by the score of 2 to 1. Russo hit a line drive off Fitzsimmons' knee which knocked him out of the game. The score was 0 to 0 at the time. He beat the Cardinals in game four of the 1943 Series when he allowed one unearned run as the Yankees won.

Russo was drafted by the Army in February 1944. After basic training, he was stationed at Fort Monmouth, New Jersey. He spent the summer of 1944 at that location and played baseball for Camp Edison there and for the base team. In the fall of 1944 he was transferred to Camp Crowder, Missouri, and also played baseball for their team. Later in 1944, he was sent on to Hawaii. He was the athletic director for the Signal Corps troops in Honolulu. While stationed in Hawaii, he wrote a sports column for a Hawaiian paper featuring sports in the service. In the spring of 1945 he had an operation on his elbow to remove bone chips. It was anticipated that this would not interfere with his ability to pitch. He had the rank of corporal. Russo was discharged from the Army on January 15, 1946. He rejoined the Yankees for the 1946 season. However, he was only able to pitch in eight games that season, winning none and losing two. The year 1946 closed out his major league career. Russo had experienced arm problems before he entered the service. His effectiveness had gone down after returning from the sore arm. However, spending two years in service and returning at age thirty-one helped end his career.

AGE	YRS	ML	W	L	PCT	ERA	G	GS	CG	IP	H	BB	SO	SHO	SV
29-30	44-45	6	45	34	0.57	3.13	120	84	48	681	618	253	311	6	5
		2	12	12	0.5	3.13	46	29	10	225	200	100	100	2	1
		8	57	46	0.543	3.13	166	113	58	906	818	353	411	8	6

SANFORD, JOHN F. (FRED)   BB TR 6' 1"   200 lbs.
Born August 9, 1919, Garfield, Ut.
Played for St. Louis (A) (1943, 1946–48, 1951), New York (A) (1949–51), and Washington (1951)

Fred Sanford got into three games in 1943 with the St. Louis Browns, pitching nine innings of relief. He spent most of the year with Toledo in the American Association. He was drafted in October or November 1943. He was stationed with the Infantry Training Battalion at Camp Roberts, California, in December 1943. He became part of the 41st Division based out of Fort Lewis, Washington. As part of the field artillery, he saw combat in the Philippines and the Netherlands East Indies. He earned two Bronze Stars while in service. He didn't, however, suffer any wounds or injuries during his tenure in the Army.

While in the Far East, Sanford was able to play on the Division baseball team on the island of Biak, located in the "neck" of New Guinea. He won fifteen games, lost only one (1 to 0) during that season, and pitched his team to the championship of the Southwest Pacific. He had the rank of lieutenant. During October and November 1945, he became part of the Asiatic Pacific Occupation Army and was stationed at Kure, Japan. While in Japan, he became part of a basketball team that got to play in a number of Japanese cities. They played in Hiroshima, Kure, Osaka, Kobe, and Nagoya, Japan. His team went on to win the Pacific championship after he was shipped home. Sanford was still listed on the Browns' defense list in December 1945. He did, however, return to baseball in time for the 1946 season. He got into three games with the Browns in 1946. This time it was three starts in which he won two and lost one, pitching two complete games.

Most of 1946 was spent in Toledo. He became part of the Browns' starting rotation in 1947 and continued in that position in 1948. The Browns teams were very bad, and Sanford led the league in losses in 1948 with twenty-one. The Yankees were impressed by his pitching. They traded four players and $100,000 to get Sanford and catcher Roy Partee. They may have been impressed because Sanford pitched a shutout against them in his first major league start on September 15, 1946. He had a winning record with the Yankees, but he was never considered to be a first-line pitcher for them. He closed out his major league career in 1951 by playing for the Yankees, Senators, and Browns (again) all in the same year.

AGE	YRS	ML	W	L	PCT	ERA	G	GS	CG	IP	H	BB	SO	SHO	SV
24-25	44-45	7	37	55	0.402	4.45	164	98	26	744	768	391	285	3	6
		2	4	4	0.5	4.45	14	8	2	64	66	34	24	0	0
		9	41	59	0.41	4.45	178	106	28	808	834	425	309	3	6

SCARBOROUGH, RAE W. (RAY)   BR TR 6'0" 185 lbs.
Born July 23, 1917, Mt. Gilead, N.C. — Died July 1, 1982, Mount Olive, N.C.
Played for Washington (1942–43, 1946–50), Chicago (A) (1950), Boston (A) (1951–52), New York (A) (1952–53), and Detroit (1953)

Ray Scarborough was signed by the Senators after he graduated from Wake Forest University. After two-plus years in the minors, he joined the Senators and made his debut on June 26, 1942. He remained with the Senators until he joined the Navy on August 5, 1943. He pitched mostly in relief during those two seasons, winning six and losing five. He attended Naval Pre-Flight School at Chapel Hill, North Carolina, that August. By the fall of 1944, he was stationed in California and pitched on an all-star team in the Army/Navy League.

During the spring and summer of 1945, he was stationed at St. Mary's, California, and played on the Pre-Flight baseball team. He was discharged on February 26, 1946. Scarborough had been considered a good prospect before the war, so when he returned, he joined the major league team. After pitching in both relief and starting for two years, he became one of the Senators main starting pitchers. He had his best year in 1948 when he won fifteen games and lost eight with an earned run average of 2.82 for a team that finished in seventh place. Twice in 1950 he was part of trades where large numbers of players changed teams. In the first deal on May 31, 1950, he was part of a six-player deal with the Chicago White Sox, and later that same year on December 10, 1950, he was sent to the Boston Red Sox as part of a deal where five players changed their team allegiance.

In 1952 he was sold to the New York Yankees on August 22. He pitched in nine games for the Yankees that season and won five and lost one as the Yankees won the American League pennant. He closed his career with the Yankees and Detroit Tigers in 1953. Scarborough played nine years after returning from World War II. He pitched between thirty-one games and thirty-eight games in each of those nine years.

AGE	YRS	ML	W	L	PCT	ERA	G	GS	CG	IP	H	BB	SO	SHO	SV
25-27	43-45	10	80	85	0.485	0.413	318	168	59	1429	1487	611	564	9	14
(3 YRS MINUS		2	14	25	0.358	3.72	71	40	15	339	364	153	120	3	2
24 GAMES)		12	94	110	0.461	4.05	389	208	74	1768	1851	764	684	12	16

SMITH, EDGAR (EDDIE)
BB TL 5' 10" 174 lbs.

Born December 14, 1913, Mansfield, N.J. — Died January 2, 1994, Willingboro, N.J.

Played for Philadelphia (A) (1936–39), Chicago (A) (1939–1943, 1946–47), and Boston (A) (1947)

Eddie Smith debuted with the Philadelphia A's on September 20, 1936, after winning twenty games for Williamsport in the NYP League. He was a starting pitcher his first full year, went to the bullpen for the second year, and then went back to the starting rotation to stay in 1939. Smith pitched for teams that were not the best in the league. As a result he only had one winning season in his ten-year career. In 1940 he won fourteen and lost nine as the White Sox finished fifth in the American League. Smith was the opening day pitcher in 1940 for the White Sox as they played the Indians. Smith only allowed one run but he still lost. Bob Feller pitched a no-hitter for the Indians that day. He also had some very difficult years. In 1937 he went 4–17, in 1938 his record was 3-10, and in 1942 he led the league in losses with twenty as he won only seven. During 1942, six of his losses were by scores of 2-0, 2-1, or 1-0. In 1941 he allowed the first hit that Joe DiMaggio got on the way to his fifty-six game hitting streak. It happened on May 15, 1941.

Smith was inducted into the Army on November 24, 1943. He served in the Mediterranean Theater during the winter and spring of 1944 and 1945. He was with the Fifth Army in Leghorn, Italy, during the summer of 1945. He did get to play some baseball while stationed there. Smith was discharged on November 16, 1945. White Sox manager Jimmy Dykes thought the odds were against him returning to play at the major league level. Smith was thirty-two years old when he reported to spring training for the 1946 season. However, he had a good year in 1946. He won eight and lost eleven, but his earned run average was a good 2.85. This would be his last good year. In 1947 he was not effective, and he closed his career that year with the Boston Red Sox.

AGE	YRS	ML	W	L	PCT	ERA	G	GS	CG	IP	H	BB	SO	SHO	SV
30-31	44-45	10	73	113	0.392	3.82	282	197	91	1596	1554	739	694	8	12
		2	16	24	0.4	3.73	58	37	21	346	331	152	150	2	1
		12	89	137	0.394	3.8	340	234	112	1942	1885	891	844	10	13

SUNDRA, STEPHEN R. (STEVE) BB TR 6' 2" 190 lbs.

Born March 27, 1910, Luxor, Pa. — Died March 23, 1952, Cleveland, Oh.

Played for New York (A) (1936, 1938–40), Washington (1941–42), and St. Louis (A) (1942–44, 1946)

Steve Sundra was the other player when the Indians traded Monte Pearson for Johnny Allen on December 11, 1935. He got a trial with the Yankees in 1936 and joined them to stay in 1938. He was both a starter and reliever during his time with the Yankees. He won his last four games in 1938 and his first eleven (three of the wins were in relief) in 1939 before losing his final start. He won the most games in 1943 for the St. Louis Browns. That year he won fifteen and lost eleven.

Sundra got into two games in 1944 before he entered the Army on May 9, 1944. He was thirty-three years old and working as a steamfitter in Atlantic City, New Jersey. They thought that he might receive a deferment for his war-related job. However, in February 1944, he was classified 1-A and notified to be ready for induction. He reported to Jefferson Barracks, Missouri, when he was inducted into the Army. He was transferred to Camp Sibert, Alabama, to take his basic training. Sundra was able to play baseball while stationed at Camp Sibert during that summer. In the fall of 1944, he was sent on to Camp Patrick Henry, Virginia. He stayed there that winter and the summer of 1945. He was part of the athletic department at Camp Patrick Henry. He was still listed on the Browns' defense list in December 1945.

He rejoined the Browns in time for the 1946 season at age thirty-six. However, his stay did not last long. He was dropped from the team two months into the 1946 season. He had pitched in two games for a total of four innings. His earned run average of the two games was 11.25, and his win/loss record was 0-0. Sundra filed charges against the Browns for violation of the G.I. Bill. The law allowed veterans to return to their old jobs if they were still able to perform them. The Browns contested the claim. They brought three experts to the St. Louis Federal Court House, their manager; Zack Taylor, *St. Louis Post-Dispatch* sports editor; and J. G. Taylor Spink, the publisher of *The Sporting News*, to say that Sundra could no longer do the job. Sundra lost his claim for back wages. The judge said, "Baseball not only is a business but also a sport and a source of entertainment. The position of each player is constantly subject to personal competition and the public demands the best in skill and ability. The will of the public is supreme" (Goldstein 1980, 273). This was the position taken by a team that played a one-armed outfielder primarily to draw fans to the park. The career of Steve Sundra ended in the federal court in St. Louis.

AGE	YRS	ML	W	L	PCT	ERA	G	GS	CG	IP	H	BB	SO	SHO	SV
34-35	44-45	9	56	41	0.577	4.17	168	99	47	859	944	321	214	4	2
(2 YRS MINUS		1	13	9	0.591	4.17	36	19	10	191	208	72	51	1	0
3 GAMES)		10	69	50	0.58	4.17	204	118	57	1050	1152	393	265	5	2

THOMPSON, EUGENE E. (JUNIOR)　　　　　　　　BR TR 6' 1"　185 lbs.
Born June 7, 1917, Latham, Il.
Played for Cincinnati (1939-42) and New York (N) (1946-47)

Junior Thompson joined the Reds in 1939 after a good year in 1938 with Columbia of the
South Atlantic League. During the 1939 and 1940 seasons, he helped the Reds win the National
League pennant and also the World Series in 1940. Pitching mostly in relief in 1939, he won
thirteen and lost five. Eight of the wins were relief wins, which led the league in that category.
In 1940, he shifted to the starting rotation. That year he won sixteen and lost nine. However,
he was hammered in both of his World Series starts, losing both games, one in each year. His
effectiveness went down after the 1940 season. He was dropped from the regular starting
rotation and pitched both as a starter and in relief during the 1941 and 1942 seasons as he
suffered some shoulder and elbow problems. He was on the voluntarily retired list in 1943.

Thompson was drafted into the Navy before the 1944 season. He was stationed at Great
Lakes Naval Training Center in February 1944. He did play briefly for the Great Lakes team.
By June 1944, he had been transferred to New London, Connecticut, Submarine Base. He was
able to play for New London during the summer of 1945. He was discharged in November
1945. Thompson did not leave the States during his stay in the Navy. However, he did suffer
an injury that would shorten his career. He said, "During some of our training exercises I
developed a knee problem. I was discharged because of the knee problem after serving 27
months" (Thompson letter 1997).

He rejoined the Reds for the 1946 season. The knee continued to be a problem. He said, "In
1946 I went to spring training with Cincinnati and then had a knee problem…" He continued,
"I was coming along pretty good in spring training but just before it ended my knee locked
up on me so Bill left me down there with a cast on. I was with the Reds a month into the
season when the team released me and the Giants picked me up" (Van Blair 1994, 198). He
served as a relief pitcher for the Giants during the 1946 and 1947 seasons. After he left the
majors, he continued his baseball career for a while at San Diego of the Pacific Coast League.

AGE	YRS	ML	W	L	PCT	ERA	G	GS	CG	IP	H	BB	SO	SHO	SV
26-28	43-45	6	47	35	0.573	3.26	185	68	27	687	602	328	315	6	7
		3	14	19	0.424	3.5	95	26	5	273	239	150	112	0	5
		9	61	54	0.53	3.33	280	94	32	960	841	478	427	6	12

WADE, JACOB F. (JAKE)　　　　　　　　BL TL 6' 2"　175 lbs.
Born April 1, 1912, Morehead City, N.C.
Played for Detroit (1936-38), Boston (A) (1939), St. Louis (A) (1939), Chicago (A) (1942-44),
New York (A) (1946), and Washington (1946)

Jake Wade joined the Tigers during the 1936 season after spending five-plus years in the
minors. During the balance of the 1936 season and for the 1937 season, he was part of the
Tigers' starting rotation. He had control problems during those years as he had during his
entire career. This, along with allowing an average of more than one hit per inning, caused him

to struggle as a major league pitcher. His earned run average for the two years he served as a starting pitcher was over 5.00. In 1938 he went to the bullpen for the Tigers.

After trades to Boston and St. Louis in 1939, he spent two years in the minors before returning to the majors in 1942 with the White Sox. He spent the next three years with the White Sox during the early war years. He pitched as a starter and reliever during that time. He was traded to the Yankees on December 11, 1944, and spent his time in service on their defense list. Wade entered the Navy in February 1945. He took his basic training at Bainbridge, Maryland, and was able to play some baseball that spring. In early summer he was transferred to Dahlgren Naval Proving Grounds, where he also was able to pitch for the base team. He was discharged in January 1946.

He joined the Yankees for the 1946 season. He pitched some of his best baseball while with the Yankees in 1946. In thirteen games he pitched a total of thirty-five innings. In those innings he allowed only thirty-three hits and fourteen walks. The Yankees sent him on to Washington during the season. His record there was not quite as good. However, during the 1946 season he struck out more batters than he allowed walks. This was the only year he was able to do this. Wade closed his major league career with the 1946 season.

AGE	YRS	ML	W	L	PCT	ERA	G	GS	CG	IP	H	BB	SO	SHO	SV
33	45	8	27	40	0.403	5	171	71	20	668	690	440	291	3	3
		1	4	6	0.4	4.9	20	8	2	77	80	52	35	0	0
		9	31	46	0.403	4.99	191	79	22	745	770	492	326	3	3

WAGNER, CHARLES T. (CHARLIE)   BR TR 5' 11"   170 lbs.
Born December 3, 1912, Reading, Pa.
Played for Boston (A) (1938–42, 1946)

Charlie Wagner had trials with the Red Sox in 1938, 1939, and 1940 before he stuck with the team in 1941 at age twenty-eight. During 1940 and 1941, he was part of the regular starting rotation. He won twelve games in 1941 and fourteen in 1942. He enlisted in the Navy on November 16, 1942, in Boston. He was stationed at Norfolk Naval Training Station in 1943. He was able to pitch for the their team and had seventeen wins and five losses for a team that went 75–25 that year. He pitched for the Navy in a game against the Washington Senators on May 24, 1943, to raise money for war bonds. The Navy won the game.

Wagner was transferred to Australia during 1944 and stayed there into early 1945. He was able to play baseball while in Australia. He was listed in the program of an Army/Navy all-star game on November 5, 1944, that was played at Brisbane, Australia. He was listed as an SP3C–Seabees. Wagner moved to Luzon in the Philippines during 1945. He did recreation and welfare work there. While he was stationed in the Philippines he contracted a severe case of dysentery and lost thirty pounds. He was discharged on November 10, 1945. He rejoined the Red Sox for spring training in 1946. However, he was still feeling the effects of the dysentery. He didn't have any strength and couldn't put anything on his pitches.

While the other players were rounding into shape, Wagner was trying to get over his illness. Wagner said, "I spent most of my time on the can" (Turner 1996, 86). He stayed on the team in 1946 because they were allowed to keep thirty players on the roster and because he was popular with the other players and the owner. He pitched in only eight games that year, winning one and losing none. Wagner commented on coming back to the majors after spending time in the service. He said, "My best years were spent in the service. Now, if I'd been twenty-two coming back, it might have been different. But I was thirty-three, and it was a little hard to crack it again. To lose those three years when you felt yourself coming was hard" (Turner 1996, 86). Wagner closed his major league career with the 1946 season.

AGE	YRS	ML	W	L	PCT	ERA	G	GS	CG	IP	H	BB	SO	SHO	SV
30-32	43-45	6	32	23	0.582	3.91	100	67	30	528	532	245	157	5	0
		3	39	29	0.573	3.18	87	76	43	588	538	270	155	7	0
		9	71	52	5.77	3.53	187	143	73	1116	1070	515	312	12	0

WHITE, ERNEST D. (ERNIE)   BR TL 5' 11"   175 lbs.
Born September 5, 1916, Pacolet Mills, S.C. — Died May 22, 1974, Augusta, Ga.
Played for St. Louis (N) (1940-43) and Boston (N) (1946-48)

Ernie White joined the Cardinals during the 1940 season after having three very good years in the minors. The final year in the minors, 1940, was at Columbus in the American Association when he led the league in earned run average and winning percentage. White's rookie year, 1941, was his best in the majors. He led the Cardinals with seventeen wins and an earned run average of 2.40. He suffered a sore arm in both of the next two seasons. He was limited to 128 innings in 1942 and only 78 innings in 1943. He started game three of the 1942 World Series against the Yankees, pitching a 2-0 complete game victory. This was the first time the Yankees had been shut out in a World Series game since 1926. The 1926 Series was also against the Cardinals.

White was inducted into the Army on January 20, 1944. He took his basic training at Fort Bragg, North Carolina. During his stay at Fort Bragg he was put in charge of the baseball team. In May 1944, he was sent on to Camp Butner, North Carolina, and then in June 1944 to Camp Pickett, Virginia. At Camp Pickett he played on the 78th Infantry Team before being sent to the European Theater. White was on the frontline as the Germans made their last major push in December 1944. He was pinned down in icy water for most of a day during the Battle of the Bulge. White was discharged from the Army in January 1946.

When he reported to spring training in 1946, he had arm problems that could be traced back to being pinned down in the icy water. He could never recover the skill he had before he left for the war. He thought he might have some tooth problems, so he had six teeth pulled. There was no change in his pitching. When he didn't improve, the Cardinals sold him to the Boston

Braves on May 14, 1946. He saw limited action with the Braves over the next three years, closing his major league career in 1948. Ernie White was another major leaguer who gave his career in service to his country. Following the 1948 season, he became a manager in the minor leagues for several years.

AGE	YRS	ML	W	L	PCT	ERA	G	GS	CG	IP	H	BB	SO	SHO	SV
27-28	44-45	7	30	21	0.588	2.78	108	57	24	489	425	188	244	5	6
		2	11	6	0.647	2.73	36	16	8	162	135	63	83	1	2
		9	41	27	0.603	2.77	144	73	32	651	560	251	327	6	8

CHAPTER 6

The position players whose careers were five years or fewer are covered in this chapter. In some cases, even though their careers were short, they contributed to the success of their team. In other cases, the career these players enjoyed came about because of the war. They were wartime substitutes who played before they in turn were taken into the service of their country. In some instances, they suffered the most of all. First, they suffered because their baseball careers were interrupted before they got the chance to prove themselves and with that got no chance to resume their career when they returned from service. Second, they were more often put in harm's way than "star" players because their names were not a household word. Because of their lack of "status," not as much is known about their careers or their service record. However, it was this group that responded to an inquiry about their careers and their service record. In many cases, the information presented here about their service to their country is from personal correspondence with the players.

Because the careers of these players were so short, there is no prediction of what might have happened to their numbers had they not gone into service in the military.

ANDERSON, ALFRED W. (ALF)   BR TR 5' 11"   165 lbs.
Born January 28, 1914, Gainesville, Ga. — Died June 23, 1985, Albany, Ga.
Played for Pittsburgh (1941–42, 1946)

Alf Anderson was a backup shortstop for the Pirates for two years before he entered the Navy. He was carried on the voluntarily retired list in the winter of 1943 before being added to the national defense list in the spring of 1944. He was stationed at and played for the Jacksonville Naval Air Station during the summers of 1944 and 1945. He was still on the Pirates' defense list in December 1945. He did return to the Pirates in 1946 for two games. Those two games concluded his major league career.

AGE	YRS	ML	G	BA	SA	AB	H	2B	3B	HR	HR%	R	RBI	BB	SO	SB
29-31	43-45	3	126	0.238	0.29	390	93	11	3	1	0.3	56	17	33	49	6

ANKENMAN, FREDERICK N. (PAT)   BR TR 5' 4"   125 lbs.
Born December 23, 1912, Houston, Tx. — Died January 13, 1989, Houston, Tx.
Played for St. Louis (N) (1936) and Brooklyn (1943–44)

Pat Ankenman had two years in which he only appeared in one game (1936 and 1943). He was listed as having spent some time in military service in 1943. He was classified as 1-A in April 1944, but no record was found of additional military service in 1944 or later. At 5' 4" and 125 lbs, Ankenman was one of the smaller players in baseball. He also had the distinction of being bought and sold by his father. The father owned the Houston team in the Texas League. His father purchased his contract from Greensboro in the Piedmont League and later sold that contract to the St. Louis Cardinals.

AGE	YRS	ML	G	BA	SA	AB	H	2B	3B	HR	HR%	R	RBI	BB	SO	SB
30	43	3	15	0.241	0.276	29	7	1	0	0	0	2	3	0	5	0

ARAGON, ANGEL V. (JACK)   BR TR 5' 10"   176 lbs.
Born November 20, 1915, Havana, Cuba — Died April 4, 1988, Clearwater, Fl.
Played for New York (N) (1941)

Jack Aragon was the son of Angel Aragon (Yankees 1914-1917). His career lasted only one game. In that game he did not get to bat, and he did not play in the field. He entered the Coast Guard in 1942 and served until 1944. At least during the middle part of that time (March and April 1943), he was stationed at Ellis Island in New York.

AGE	YRS	ML	G	BA	SA	AB	H	2B	3B	HR	HR%	R	RBI	BB	SO	SB
26-28	42-44	1	1	0	0	0	0	0	0	0	0	0	0	0	0	0

ARCHIE, GEORGE A.   BR TR 6' 0"   170 lbs.
Born April 27, 1914, Nashville, Tn. — Died September 20, 2001, Nashville, Tn.
Played for Detroit (1938), Washington (1941), and St. Louis (A) (1941, 1946)

George Archie volunteered for the Army before the start of the 1942 season. He had been the regular third baseman with the Senators in 1941, being in their opening day lineup that year, before being traded to the Browns late in the season. He entered the Army right after Pearl Harbor. In the beginning he was stationed at Jefferson Barracks, Missouri. By November 1943, he had been transferred to Fort Riley, Kansas, and by November 1944 was sent on to Camp Shelby, Mississippi, to join the 65th Cavalry Reconnaissance troop. Archie was sent overseas with that group, which included a number of other major league players. Harry Walker, Al Brazle, Rex Barney, and Ken Heintzelmann were part of the 65th. They landed at LeHavre and proceeded about 500 miles inland. As a reconnaissance troop, they were sometimes behind enemy lines laying out the plans for the Army that was to follow. Archie was involved in combat during that time in France, Germany, and Austria. However, he suffered no injuries.

Later, Archie was also part of a team that played at Traun and Linz, because the officer in charge wanted entertainment for the other troops. Archie was still listed on the Browns' defense list in December 1945. He did return to the Browns in 1946. However, he played in only four games following his four years in the service. He left for service as a starting third baseman and returned to a career that lasted only four more games. George Archie paid a high price for his service.

AGE	YRS	ML	G	BA	SA	AB	H	2B	3B	HR	HR%	R	RBI	BB	SO	SB
28-31	42-45	3	121	0.273	0.371	421	115	24	4	3	0.7	49	53	37	47	10

BARTLEY, BOYD O.   BR TR 5' 8"   165 lbs.
Born February 11, 1920, Chicago, Il.
Played for Brooklyn (1943)

Boyd Bartley was one the several shortstops the Dodgers tried out in 1943 as a replacement for PeeWee Reese after Reese was drafted. Bartley also entered the military in 1943. He was listed on the Dodgers' national defense list that summer and was still listed in December 1945. He did not return to the majors after the war.

AGE	YRS	ML	G	BA	SA	AB	H	2B	3B	HR	HR%	R	RBI	BB	SO	SB
23-25	43-45	1	9	0.048	0.048	21	1	0	0	0	0	0	1	1	3	0

BENSON, VERNON A. (VERN)   BL TR 5' 10"   160 lbs.
Born September 19, 1924, Granite Quarry, N.C.
Played for Philadelphia (A) (1943, 1946) and St. Louis (N) (1951-53)

Vern Benson signed with the Athletics in 1943 and had two pinch hitting appearances before being drafted into the Army in late 1943. He served for two years and saw combat in Europe but did not suffer any injuries in that combat. He was still listed on the A's national defense list in December 1945. He got a token appearance with the A's in 1946 after spending most of the year in the minors. After six more years in the minors, he got trials with the Cardinals. His baseball career is better noted by the time he spent as a minor league manager and as a major league coach. He managed for eight years at levels up to Triple A in the minors and coached at the major league level for eighteen years.

AGE	YRS	ML	G	BA	SA	AB	H	2B	3B	HR	HR%	R	RBI	BB	SO	SB
18-20	43-45	5	55	0.202	0.356	104	21	5	1	3	2.9	17	12	13	22	0

BLAIR, LOUIS N. (BUDDY)   BL TR 6' 0"   186 lbs.
Born September 10, 1910, Columbia, Mi. — Died June 7, 1996, Monroe, La.
Played for Philadelphia (A) (1942)

Buddy Blair was the 1942 replacement at third base after Al Brancato entered the military following the 1941 season. Blair had a respectable year, batting .279 with five home runs. However, his range in the field was very suspect. Phil Marchildon, A's pitcher, talked about the A's infield, saying, "That team was a bad one. They couldn't make a double play if you hit a line drive. Dick Siebert, he had a brace on his knee, and the other guy on third base, Buddy Blair, he had a brace on his knee. They couldn't move very far, either one of them. There was a fellow playing shortstop by the name of Davis; he wasn't too much of a player either" (Mead 1985, 50).

Blair was then taken into the military. In January 1943 he was listed on the national defense list. He achieved the rank of staff sergeant and spent most of his time in service at Selman Field, Louisiana. While there, he built a field and organized and played for the team. He also managed the team from 1943 to 1945. He was still listed on the national defense list in December 1945. He was not able to return to major leagues after his release from service.

AGE	YRS	ML	G	BA	SA	AB	H	2B	3B	HR	HR%	R	RBI	BB	SO	SB
32-34	43-45	1	137	0.279	0.397	484	135	26	8	5	1	48	66	30	30	1

BRANCATO, ALBERT (AL)　　　　　　　　　BR TR 5'9"　188 lbs.
Born May 29, 1919, Philadelphia, Pa.
Played for Philadelphia (A) (1939-41, 1945)

Al Brancato won the regular shortstop job with the A's in 1940 in spite of batting only .191. He continued as the regular shortstop the following year. His hitting improved some, .234, but his fielding suffered. In 1941 he committed sixty-one errors at shortstop. He became the last major league shortstop to commit sixty errors in one season.

Brancato enlisted in the Navy on January 13, 1942. He had run a sporting goods store, in addition to playing for the A's, prior to the war, so his rank as a second class storekeeper fit very well with what he had been doing. There were some rumors that he had made a deal with the Navy to enlist and get duty as a storekeeper in the States. The Navy denied this, and Brancato requested and got sea duty. He was stationed at League Island aboard a receiving ship at the start of his service, and later he was stationed in Boston.

Brancato served on the USS *Boston #69*, commissioned as a heavy cruiser. It was on this ship that he sailed to the Pacific in late 1943 or early 1944. He was stationed at the submarine base at Pearl Harbor and played on their baseball team. He also played in the Army/Navy World Series that took place in October 1944. Following that series, the Navy team was sent on a tour of the South Pacific islands. Brancato went with that team as far as Palalu and later was stationed on Tinian Island.

He returned to the States in May 1945 and was discharged on August 28, 1945. With the early release, he was able to play with the A's for a month at the close of the 1945 season. Before the 1946 season, he was sold to the Toronto team of the International League. He was never able to return to the major league level. He lost out on the pension fund because he was not kept on a major league team for one year following his release from service.

AGE	YRS	ML	G	BA	SA	AB	H	2B	3B	HR	HR%	R	RBI	BB	SO	SB
23-26	42-46	4	282	0.214	0.29	930	199	37	11	4	0.4	117	80	96	92	5

BURICH, WILLIAM M. (BILL)　　　　　　　BR TR 6'0"　180 lbs.
Born May 29, 1918, Camumet, Mi.
Played for Philadelphia (N) (1942, 1946)

"I did volunteer immediately after the 1942 season when with the Phillies," (Burich letter 1998.) He had gotten in twenty-five games that year, batting .287. Phillies manager Hans Lobert had told him he was ready for big league play. But when the need was there, Burich put baseball behind and joined the Army. He added, "[I] joined the 91st Division (1942) when in the States. I had injured my right quadriceps and had surgery, laid up for three weeks, went back to the division and shipped to Africa and went through three campaigns with Mark Clark's Fifth Army all in Italy" (Burich letter 1998).

Burich was able to play for the Fifth Army team while stationed in Europe. When the war was over, his leg was still bothering him. He was sent to General Hospital in Clinton, Iowa, for the 1946 season. He served as a utility infielder for the Indians in both 1946 and 1947 before being sold to the Giants to close out his major league career in 1948.

AGE	YRS	ML	G	BA	SA	AB	H	2B	3B	HR	HR%	R	RBI	BB	SO	SB
22-25	42-45	4	128	0.223	0.276	359	80	10	3	1	0.3	35	27	28	54	2

CRESPI, FRANK A.J. (CREEPY)   BR TR 5' 8"   175 lbs.

Born February 16, 1918, St. Louis, Mo. — Died March 1, 1990, Florissant, Mo.
Played for St. Louis (N) (1938–42)

Creepy Crespi won the regular second base job in 1941 after trials in 1938, 1939, and 1940. In 1941 he was considered to be one of the better second basemen in the league. However, in 1942 he lost the full-time role and shared the position with Jimmy Brown. After being reclassified from 3-A to 1-A and passing the physical early in 1943, Crespi was inducted into the Army on February 20, 1943. He was stationed at Fort Riley, Kansas. During the summer of 1943 Crespi was playing a baseball game for the Fort Riley team. In that game, he broke his left leg. Because of the accident, he was confined to the Army hospital. Bored with the lack of activity, a number of the patients got involved in a wheelchair race. Crespi was one who was involved. His wheelchair crashed into the wall during the race, and he broke the same leg in another place. The two fractures caused him a lot of trouble.

In April 1944 Crespi was still in the hospital at Fort Riley. He didn't have the cast removed until February 1944 and still needed a brace in order to walk. The second break was a compound fracture of the knee. In December 1944, he was a patient at Winter General Hospital in Topeka, Kansas. By November 1945 he had been transferred to Camp Atterbury, Indiana, and it was announced that he would soon undergo his fourteenth operation on his leg that was originally broken three years earlier. The leg would be in a cast for nine weeks. Crespi remained in the Army into 1946. He was not able to return to play major league baseball. He never fully recovered from the effects of the leg that was first broken in an Army game and later broken again in an act of horseplay.

AGE	YRS	ML	G	BA	SA	AB	H	2B	3B	HR	HR%	R	RBI	BB	SO	SB
25-28	43-46	5	264	0.263	0.321	911	240	32	4	4	0.4	125	88	90	102	8

CROSS, JOFFRE J. (JEFF)   BR TR 5' 11"   160 lbs.

Born August 28, 1918, Tulsa, Ok. — Died July 23, 1997, Huntsville, Tx.
Played for St. Louis (N) (1942, 1946–48) and Chicago (1948)

Jeff Cross got into one game with the Cardinals in 1942 after being called up at the end of the season. He went into the Navy after the 1942 season. He spent some time at Norfolk Naval Training Station and played on the base team during the summer of 1944. He was still listed on the national defense list in December 1945. He did return to the Cardinals in time for the 1946 season. He filled the role of a utility infielder for the next two years. Sold to the Cubs on May 2, 1948, he closed out his major league career that year.

AGE	YRS	ML	G	BA	SA	AB	H	2B	3B	HR	HR%	R	RBI	BB	SO	SB
24-26	43-45	4	119	0.162	0.19	142	23	4	0	0	0	22	10	20	18	4

CROUCHER, FRANK D.   BR TR 5' 11" 165 lbs.

Born July 23, 1914, San Antonio, Tx.– Died May 21, 1980, Houston, Tx.
Played for Detroit (1939-41) and Washington (1942)

Frank Croucher suffered from some injuries that hurt his career. He missed most of the 1938 season with a broken leg, which delayed his arrival in the majors. After he was traded to the Senators in 1942, he was out for most of that year with a sore arm, this after he had won the starting shortstop job with the Tigers in 1941. Following the 1942 season, he entered the military and spent the next three years serving his country. During that time, he was able to play some baseball. He was a member of the San Antonio Aviation Cadet Center team during the summer of 1944. Croucher was not able to return to the majors following his military service.

AGE	YRS	ML	G	BA	SA	AB	H	2B	3B	HR	HR%	R	RBI	BB	SO	SB
28-30	43-45	4	296	0.251	0.324	935	235	37	5	7	0.7	94	86	56	128	4

CULP, BENJAMIN B. (BENNY)   BR TR 5' 9" 175 lbs.

Born January 19, 1914, Philadelphia, Pa. — Died October 23, 2000, Philadelphia, Pa.
Played for Philadelphia (N) (1942-44)

Benny Culp got into a total of fifteen games during his three-year career with the Phillies. He had been classified 1-A in the spring of 1944 and took and passed the physical on May 25, 1944, but he was not called for duty until January 1945. He was thirty-one years old when inducted into the Navy. He took his boot training at Bainbridge, Maryland, completed that training on April 9, 1945, and enrolled in courses to qualify him as a physical instructor. He played on the Bainbridge team during that summer. He was still on the Phillies' defense list in December 1945. He was not able to return to the majors following his military service.

AGE	YRS	ML	G	BA	SA	AB	H	2B	3B	HR	HR%	R	RBI	BB	SO	SB
30-31	44-45	3	15	0.192	0.231	26	5	1	0	0	0	5	2	3	3	0

DAPPER, CLIFFORD R. (CLIFF)   BR TR 6' 2" 190 lbs.

Born January 2, 1920, Los Angeles, Ca.
Played for Brooklyn (1942)

Cliff Dapper ended with a career batting average of .471 and a slugging percentage of .706. Most baseball players would like to have those numbers. Unfortunately for Dapper, his career only lasted eight games. He played those games for the Dodgers in 1942. The next three years he would spend in the Navy. He volunteered for his military service. In a letter, he said that he didn't suffer any injuries and did not see combat (Dapper letter 1997). He was discharged by the Navy in December 1945. He was not able to return to play for the Dodgers after the war.

AGE	YRS	ML	G	BA	SA	AB	H	2B	3B	HR	HR%	R	RBI	BB	SO	SB
23-25	43-45	1	8	0.471	0.706	17	8	1	0	1	5.9	2	9	2	2	0

DAVIS, LAWRENCE C. (CRASH) BR TR 6' 0" 173 lbs.

Born July 14, 1919, Canon, Ga. — Died August 31, 2001, Greensboro, N.C.
Played for Philadelphia (A) (1940–42)

Crash Davis was backup for both shortstop and second base during the 1941 and 1942 seasons with the Philadelphia A's. It was said he "was shuttled between second and short; he could play neither" (Mead 1985, 50). Following the 1942 season, Davis entered the Navy. He did his basic training at Norfolk Naval Training Station. He was still listed on the A's national defense list on December 1945. Following the war, Davis did not return to play in the majors.

AGE	YRS	ML	G	BA	SA	AB	H	2B	3B	HR	HR%	R	RBI	BB	SO	SB
23-25	43-45	3	148	0.23	0.279	444	102	12	2	2	0.5	43	43	35	56	2

DAVIS, JOHN H. BR TR 5' 11" 172 lbs.

Born July 15, 1915, Laurel Run, Pa. — Died April 26, 2002, Laurel, Ms.
Played for New York (N) (1941)

John Davis got a trial at the end of the 1941 season. He got in twenty-one games at third base and batted only .214. In January 1942, he enlisted in the Army Air Corps and was assigned to a base in Savannah, Georgia. By December 1943, he had risen to the rank of sergeant and was stationed in India. He had been discharged and was listed on the Giants active roster in December 1945. In a letter, he indicated that he saw no combat and suffered no injuries. He also added, "In 1935 I signed my brother Bob's contract for $65.00 per month in Cardinal organization. [I] played three years before Social Security caught up with me in Houston, Texas, in 1937" (Davis letter 1997). Even though Davis was listed on the Giants' active roster, he did not play in major league games after the war.

AGE	YRS	ML	G	BA	SA	AB	H	2B	3B	HR	HR%	R	RBI	BB	SO	SB
26-29	42-45	1	21	0.214	0.257	70	15	3	0	0	0	8	5	8	12	0

DETWEILER, ROBERT S. (DUCKY) BR TR 5' 11" 178 lbs.

Born February 15, 1919, Trumbauersville, Pa.
Played for Boston (N) (1942, 1946)

Ducky Detweiler was able to get into twelve games during the 1942 season after he was called up in September 1942. He batted .318 during those games. After that season, on January 12, 1943, he was drafted into the Army. He was assigned to New Cumberland, Pennsylvania. By June 1944, he was with the 20th Armored Division at Camp Campbell, Kentucky, and then sent in July 1944, to Camp Sibert, Alabama. While stationed at Camp Sibert, he was able to play some baseball.

The summer of 1945 found Detweiler playing for Welch Convalescent Hospital in Florida. He was the playing coach for that team. He had risen to the rank of lieutenant. In a letter, he said he received no injuries and saw no combat while in service. He also added some comments about playing. He said, "The greatest thing about playing in my time was (1) getting to play professional baseball, (2) getting to the big leagues." He continued, "Naturally getting to the big leagues and getting a base hit my first time up to bat [was my biggest thrill]" (Detweiler letter 1997). Following the war, he got to play in only one game; he pinch-hit in the 1946 season.

AGE	YRS	ML	G	BA	SA	AB	H	2B	3B	HR	HR%	R	RBI	BB	SO	SB
24-26	43-45	2	13	0.311	0.4	45	14	2	1	0	0	3	5	2	7	0

DOYLE, HOWARD J. (DANNY)   BB TR 6' 1"   195 lbs.
Born January 24, 1917, McLoud, Ok.
Played for Boston (A) (1943)

Danny Doyle's career consisted of thirteen games in September of 1943. Following the 1943 season, he entered the military. He spent some time at Fort Sill, Oklahoma, during the summer of 1944. He was still on the Red Sox's defense list in December 1945. He did not play at the major league level following the war. However, he did make a significant contribution to the success of the Red Sox. He signed on as a scout for the Red Sox in 1949 and had success in signing good players for the Sox. His signees include Roger Clemens, Jim Lonborg, and Ellis Burks.

AGE	YRS	ML	G	BA	SA	AB	H	2B	3B	HR	HR%	R	RBI	BB	SO	SB
27-28	44-45	1	13	0.209	0.233	43	9	1	0	0	0	2	6	7	9	0

DUDRA, JOHN J.   BR TR 5' 11"   175 lbs.
Born May 27, 1916, Assumption, Il. — Died October 24, 1965, Pana, Il.
Played for Boston (N) (1941)

John Dudra made his debut on September 7, 1941, with the Braves. He played in fourteen games that season, batting .360 while playing all infield positions. Three months after his debut, the Japanese bombed Pearl Harbor. Dudra entered the war and missed four years in service to his country. Following the war, he was not able to resume his position with the Braves.

AGE	YRS	ML	G	BA	SA	AB	H	2B	3B	HR	HR%	R	RBI	BB	SO	SB
26-29	42-45	1	14	0.36	0.56	25	9	3	1	0	0	3	3	3	4	0

EPPS, HAROLD F. (HAL)   BL TL 6' 0"   175 lbs.
Born March 26, 1914, Athens, Ga.
Played for St. Louis (N) (1938, 1940), St. Louis (A) (1943–44), and Philadelphia (A) (1944)

Hal Epps didn't get much playing time until he signed with the Philadelphia A's in 1944 as a wartime replacement. He had trials with the Cardinals and Browns in previous years without much success. The Browns sold Epps to the A's on the last trading day, June 16. He became known for his speed and his ability to lay down a bunt.

Although he had received notice on May 16 that he would be inducted on May 26, Epps did not enter the service until after the end of the 1944 season. He was drafted by the Army and took his training at San Antonio, Texas. He was with the 25th Infantry Division, 1945. He saw combat at Combataarca, Philippines Islands, and was in Japan in 1946. Epps suffered no injuries during the war. He did get to play some baseball while stationed in the Pacific. He was still listed on the A's defense List in December 1945. Epps did not play any major league ball following the war.

AGE	YRS	ML	G	BA	SA	AB	H	2B	3B	HR	HR%	R	RBI	BB	SO	SB
31	45	4	125	0.253	0.34	391	99	13	9	1	0.3	58	21	37	43	5

FALLON, GEORGE D.   BR TR 5'9" 155 lbs.
Born July 8, 1914, Jersey City, N.J. — Died October 25, 1994, Lake Worth, Fl.
Played for Brooklyn (1937) and St. Louis (N) (1943-45)

George Fallon was a journeyman minor league infielder until he was called up to the Cardinals to back up the regulars during the player shortage of World War II. While his average was low during the 1944 season (.199), he contributed several key hits and backed up Marty Marion when he was injured. Fallon was summoned for a physical, which took place on May 16, 1944, at Jefferson Barricks, Missouri. He was rejected after that examination. The story his teammates told was that a psychiatrist had rejected him because he told the doctor that he was batting 1.000. The psychiatrist said that anybody who thought they were batting 1.000 was too balmy for the armed forces. The only truth to the story is that he was batting 1.000 at the time (1 for 1). After the examination, he was classified as 4-F for the rest of 1944.

Fallon was called for another examination at Jefferson Barricks, Missouri, on June 12, 1945. He was accepted after that examination, and was inducted into the Navy on July 25, 1945. Fallon was sent to the Sampson Naval Training Center in August 1945. While there, he played for the Sampson baseball team. He stayed there until he was discharged by the Navy in November 1945. He was available to the Cardinals for the 1946 season but did not play any major league games after returning from the Navy.

AGE	YRS	ML	G	BA	SA	AB	H	2B	3B	HR	HR%	R	RBI	BB	SO	SB
30	45	4	133	0.216	0.27	282	61	10	1	1	0.4	26	21	25	26	2

FELDERMAN, MARVIN W. (MARV)   BR TR 6'1" 187 lbs.
Born December 20, 1915, Bellevue, Ia. — Died August 6, 2000, Riverside, Ca.
Played for Chicago (N) (1942)

Marv Felderman got into three games in 1942 before entering the Navy in December 1942. He took his boot training at the Great Lakes base. He served as an athletic petty officer and was listed as a catcher on the Great Lakes team in 1943. In the fall of 1943, he was transferred to Bainbridge, Maryland, for further training. Early in 1944, he was sent from Bainbridge to Pearl Harbor, where he assisted with physical conditioning. He also played on a Navy team in Honolulu in the summer of 1944 and with the Kaneohe team in the 14th Naval District League in Hawaii in 1945. December 1945 found him discharged and signing a Cubs contract. However, he did not play baseball at the major league level after returning from the war.

AGE	YRS	ML	G	BA	SA	AB	H	2B	3B	HR	HR%	R	RBI	BB	SO	SB
27-29	43-45	1	3	0.167	0.167	6	1	0	0	0	0	0	0	1	4	0

FERNANDES, EDWARD P. (ED)   BB TR 5' 9" 185 lbs.
Born March 11, 1918, Oakland, Ca. — Died November 27, 1968, Haywood, Ca.
Played for Pittsburgh (1940) and Chicago (A) (1946)

Ed Fernandes got a brief trial with the Pirates in 1940 (28 games) and did not reappear on the big league scene until after the war. However, his only year of war service was 1945. He was drafted into the Navy on December 11, 1944, undergoing his boot training at San Diego. He played for the Fleet City club at Shoemaker Field, California, during the summer of 1945. He was still listed on the White Sox defense list in December 1945. He did, however, get his release in time to get another brief trial (14 games), this time with the White Sox during 1946.

AGE	YRS	ML	G	BA	SA	AB	H	2B	3B	HR	HR%	R	RBI	BB	SO	SB
27	45	2	42	0.185	0.231	65	12	3	0	0	0	5	6	15	13	0

FERNANDEZ, FROILAN (NANNY)   BR TR 5' 9" 170 lbs.
Born October 25, 1918, Wilmington, Ca. — Died September 16, 1996, Harbor City, Ca.
Played for Boston (N) (1942, 1946–47) and Pittsburgh (1950)

Nanny Fernandez won the starting third base job his rookie year (1942) with the Boston Braves. His hitting, while not great, was very adequate. He drove in fifty-five runs and stole fifteen bases. He joined the Army Air Corps on April 14, 1943. He was stationed with the Sixth Ferrying Group in Long Beach during 1943 and 1944. While he was there, he did play baseball for the base team. Early in 1945, he was transferred to Hawaii. He continued to be able to play ball and was selected to the Army Air Force all-star team in Hawaii.

Like many of the major league players, Fernandez was sent to the islands of the South Pacific. He played with the 313th Flyers in the Marianas and was again selected to an all-star team. He was stationed on Guam during this time. He arrived back in Los Angeles in November 1945 from the Pacific aboard the transport ship *Cecil* having achieved the rank of corporal. While still on the Braves' defense list in December 1945, he was discharged on January 10, 1946. He rejoined the Braves in time for the 1946 season and again reclaimed his job as starting third baseman. The 1946 season was not as good as 1942, and with the arrival of Bob Elliott, Fernandez was sent back to the minors in 1948. He was not as good a player as he had been before he lost three years in the service. He got another trial in 1950 to close out his major league career.

AGE	YRS	ML	G	BA	SA	AB	H	2B	3B	HR	HR%	R	RBI	BB	SO	SB
24-26	43-45	4	408	0.248	0.334	1356	336	59	5	16	1.2	139	145	109	142	20

FLAIR, ALBERT D. (AL)   BL TL 6' 4" 195 lbs.
Born July 24, 1916, New Orleans, La. — Died, July 25, 1988, New Orleans, La.
Played for Boston (A) (1941)

Al Flair debuted in the majors on September 6, 1941. He got into ten games, eight as a first baseman and two as a pinch hitter. He got six hits. By May 1942, he was listed as a player in the military. During the next four years, he would be in service to his country. He did have some opportunity to play baseball. He played on an Army barnstorming team that made a tour of the Southwest Pacific bases during the fall of 1944. He also played on a team in Australia during early 1945. Later that summer, Flair played on the 8th Army team in the Philippines. He was scheduled to return home on a transport out of Yokohama to arrive back to the States by December 1, 1945. He was still listed on the Red Sox defense list in December 1945. Flair was never able to play at the major league level after returning from service.

AGE	YRS	ML	G	BA	SA	AB	H	2B	3B	HR	HR%	R	RBI	BB	SO	SB
25-28	42-45	1	10	0.2	0.333	30	6	2	1	0	0	3	2	1	1	1

FOX, CHARLES F. (CHARLIE)   BR TR 5'11"   180 lbs.
Born October 7, 1921, New York, N.Y.—Died February 16, 2004, Stanford, Ca.
Played for New York (N) (1942)

Charlie Fox got into only three major league games in the fall of 1942 before going into service. He joined the Navy in the winter of 1942 and spent about three years working for them. Part of that service included making dangerous voyages to Murmansk in frigid northernmost Russia. He was released in time to be listed as a player on the Giants' active roster in December 1945.

Fox tried to make it as a player for the Giants following his return in 1946. He was not able to make the major league team and spent 1947 playing at the minor league level. It was the following year that he started managing at Class D level. He also continued playing as he managed until 1956. He then served as a scout and coach for the Giants before beginning another managing period, this time at the Triple A level. He became manager of the Giants in 1970 and managed them until 1974. Fox also managed with the Expos and Cubs for a short period of time. He was named as Major League Manager of the Year by *The Sporting News* in 1971 when he led the Giants to the pennant.

AGE	YRS	ML	G	BA	SA	AB	H	2B	3B	HR	HR%	R	RBI	BB	SO	SB
21-23	43-45	1	3	0.429	0.429	7	3	0	0	0	0	1	1	1	2	0

FRANKLIN, MURRAY A.   BR TR 6'0"   175 lbs.
Born April 1, 1914, Chicago, Il. — Died March 16, 1978, Harbor City, Ca.
Played for Detroit (1941–42)

Murray Franklin was a middle infielder with the Tigers in a reserve role during the 1942 season after a brief trial in 1941. He entered the Navy following the 1942 season and spent three years in service. He was at Norfolk Naval Air Station along with PeeWee Reese, Hugh Casey, and Al Evans. He achieved the rank of chief petty officer. By the summer of 1944, he had been transferred to the Pacific. Franklin was able to play baseball while stationed in the Pacific. His rank then was chief specialist (athletic). Franklin was discharged in December 1945 but was not able to return to the majors following his service in the Navy.

AGE	YRS	ML	G	BA	SA	AB	H	2B	3B	HR	HR%	R	RBI	BB	SO	SB
29-31	43-45	2	61	0.262	0.348	164	43	8	0	2	1.2	25	16	9	7	0

FREED, EDWIN C. (ED)
BR TR 5' 6"   165 lbs.

Born August 22, 1919, Centre Valley, Pa. — Died November 15, 2002, Rock Hill, S.C.
Played for Philadelphia (N) (1942)

Ed Freed got into thirteen games after making his major league debut on September 11, 1942.
In that first game he had four hits: two doubles, one triple, and one single. He was drafted
into the Army on January 14, 1943, at Allentown, Pennsylvania. In the summer of 1943, he
was stationed at Morriss Field, Charlotte, North Carolina, serving as a sergeant in the military
police. He said he suffered no injuries and saw no combat during his service. He was still on
the Phillies' defense list in December 1945. Following his service, he was not able to return to
the majors.

AGE	YRS	ML	G	BA	SA	AB	H	2B	3B	HR	HR%	R	RBI	BB	SO	SB
23-25	43-45	1	13	0.303	0.455	33	10	3	1	0	0	3	1	4	3	1

GALLAGHER, JOSEPH E. (JOE)
BR TR 6' 2"   210 lbs.

Born March 7, 1914, Buffalo, N.Y. — Died February 25, 1998, Houston, Tx.
Played for New York (A) (1939), St. Louis (A) (1939–40), and Brooklyn (1940)

Joe Gallagher was one of five major leaguers who were drafted in 1941 as the United States
prepared for war. He had made the majors in 1939 after a very good year at Kansas City in
the American Association. During the time that he spent in service, he didn't have a chance
to play any baseball. By the spring of 1944, he had achieved the rank of 1st sergeant and was
with the 474th Bombing Detachment stationed at Camp Hulen, Texas. A year later (1945),
he had been moved to Camp Howze, Texas, with the Infantry Replacement Center. He was
discharged by December 1945.

Gallagher was twenty-five when he made his first appearance in the majors. He was twenty-
seven when he entered the military. He was almost thirty-two when he was discharged from
service. With an absence of five years and at age thirty-two, he never was able to play at the
major league level following his release from service. When he was a player, he was known for
his muscles. Pete Reiser, his teammate in Brooklyn, remembered him. Reiser said, "He's a big,
good-natured guy, strong as hell" (Honig 1975, 305).

AGE	YRS	ML	G	BA	SA	AB	H	2B	3B	HR	HR%	R	RBI	BB	SO	SB
27-31	41-45	2	165	0.273	0.446	487	133	26	5	16	3.3	73	73	26	76	4

GALLE, STANLEY J. (STAN)
BR TR 5' 7"   165 lbs.

Born February 7, 1919, Milwaukee, Wi.
Played for Washington (1942)

Stan Galle got into thirteen games in the spring of 1942 before being enlisted in the Coast
Guard. Three of the games were at third base and ten as a pinch hitter. He would spend the
next four years in service. In a letter, Galle said that he saw no active combat nor suffered

any injuries during his stay in the Coast Guard. He did not play at the major league level after the war.

AGE	YRS	ML	G	BA	SA	AB	H	2B	3B	HR	HR%	R	RBI	BB	SO	SB
23-26	42-45	1	13	0.111	0.111	18	2	0	0	0	0	3	1	1	0	0

GARRISON, ROBERT F. (FORD)   BR TR 5' 10" 180 lbs.
Born August 29, 1915, Greenville, S.C. — Died June 6, 2001, Largo, Fl.
Played for Boston (A) (1943–44) and Philadelphia (A) (1944–46)

Ford Garrison was a wartime outfield replacement for the A's in 1944. He had a trial in 1943 with the Red Sox and was traded by them to the A's on May 8, 1944, for Hal Wagner. On April 26, 1945, he entered the Navy. He had gotten to play in six games that year before being inducted. He was twenty-nine years old when called. He was inducted at Philadelphia. Part of the time that summer he spent at Bainbridge, Maryland, where he was able to play baseball.

Garrison was still listed on the A's defense list in December 1945. However, he was able to rejoin the A's for the 1946 season. He played in nine games before being sent to Newark in the International League. His departure was quickened by an incident that occurred with a teammate. Garrison thought of himself as an expert knife-thrower. During a practice of his skill, Garrison stabbed pitcher Phil Marchildon in the hand. Garrison left for the minors right after the incident. He played in the minors until 1952 and did not return to the majors.

AGE	YRS	ML	G	BA	SA	AB	H	2B	3B	HR	HR%	R	RBI	BB	SO	SB
29	45	4	185	0.262	0.329	687	180	22	3	6	0.9	80	56	37	67	11

GEARY, EUGENE F.J. (HUCK)   BL TR 5' 10" 170 lbs.
Born January 22, 1917, Buffalo, N.Y. — Died January 27, 1981, Cuba, N.Y.
Played for Pittsburgh (1942–43)

Huck Geary was a weak-hitting shortstop with the Pirates. In addition to his trouble with pitchers, he also battled homesickness when he was a rookie. He left the team on occasion to visit his family in Buffalo. He was classified 1-A in the spring of 1944 even though he was married and had three children. He was accepted for active duty by the Army on May 24, 1944, at Buffalo, New York. Geary was ordered to report for induction April 16, 1945, when he was twenty-eight years old. While the June 1, 1944 edition of *The Sporting News* indicated that he had been accepted by the Army, he was inducted into the Navy in 1945. He was stationed at Sampson Naval Training Center during the summer of 1945 and was able to play baseball there. He was discharged by the Navy in December 1945. He did not play in the majors after the war.

AGE	YRS	ML	G	BA	SA	AB	H	2B	3B	HR	HR%	R	RBI	BB	SO	SB
27-28	44-45	2	55	0.16	0.197	188	30	4	0	1	0.5	20	15	20	9	3

He returned to the majors in 1946 with the Chicago Cubs. His time with them was limited to four games in which he went 0 for 10. He did not play in the majors after the 1946 season.

AGE	YRS	ML	G	BA	SA	AB	H	2B	3B	HR	HR%	R	RBI	BB	SO	SB
31-32	44-45	5	309	0.209	0.291	952	199	29	2	15	1.6	99	86	89	105	5

GOLDSTEIN, LESLIE E. (LONNIE)   BL TL 6' 2" 190 lbs.
Born May 13, 1918, Austin, Tx.
Played for Cincinnati (1943, 1946)

Lonnie Goldstein got a five-game trial with the Reds at the close of the 1943 season. He didn't play in the majors in 1944 and was drafted sometime during that year. In his letter, he indicated that he spent eighteen months in service but didn't see any combat (Goldstein letter 1997). He served in the Corps of Engineers while in service. He commented that the time he lost was at the "height of my career" (Goldstein letter 1997). He was still on the Reds' defense list in December 1945. He did rejoin the Reds in the 1946 season. He played in six games that year, five as a pinch hitter and one as a pinch runner. The year 1946 closed out his major league career.

AGE	YRS	ML	G	BA	SA	AB	H	2B	3B	HR	HR%	R	RBI	BB	SO	SB
27-28	45-46	2	11	0.1	0.1	10	1	0	0	0	0	2	0	3	2	0

GOLETZ, STANLEY (STAN)   BL TL 6' 3" 200 lbs.
Born May 21, 1918, Crescent, Oh. — Died July 7, 1997, Temple, Tx.
Played for Chicago (A) (1941)

Stan Goletz made it to the big leagues in September 1941. After the Japanese bombed Pearl Harbor in December 1941, Goletz tried to enlist on February 4, 1942, at Oklahoma City but failed to get grade as a volunteer and had to wait for a decision from the draft board. He was accepted that spring. January 1943 found him stationed at Williams Field Advanced Flying School, Chandler, Arizona. By the fall of 1943, he was stationed at Fort Sill, Oklahoma. He was transferred to the Pacific and spent some time in the Marianas where he was able to play some baseball for the 313th Flyers, 20th Air Force. In November 1945, he arrived in Los Angeles from the Pacific aboard the transport *Cecil* having achieved the rank of first lieutenant. He was still on the White Sox' defense list in December 1945 and did not rejoin the White Sox or another major league team after the war.

AGE	YRS	ML	G	BA	SA	AB	H	2B	3B	HR	HR%	R	RBI	BB	SO	SB
24-27	42-45	1	5	0.6	0.6	5	3	0	0	0	0	0	0	0	2	0

GREMP, LOUIS E. (BUDDY)   BR TR 6' 1" 175 lbs.
Born August 5, 1919, Denver, Co. — Died January 30, 1995, Manteca, Ca.
Played for Boston (N) (1940-42)

Buddy Gremp was able to play the role of a backup first baseman with the Braves in 1942 after two brief trials the previous years. He entered the military just after the season was over. He had

been expected to enter the Army on September 15 but did not. Instead, he enlisted in the Naval
Aviation program and reported on November 15, 1942. He entered the program with a number
of other major league players. They included Ted Williams, Johnny Sain, Joe Coleman, and Johnny
Pesky. They started their preliminary flight training at Amherst in November 1942, which
kept him busy fifteen hours a day. This training was completed in May 1943, and Gremp was
transferred to Chapel Hill, North Carolina, for preflight work. With the preflight training done in
August 1943, he was transferred to Kohomo, Indiana, for basic flight training.

During the spring of 1944, Gremp was stationed at Bunker Hill Naval Air Base where he was
able to play baseball. (Gremp had also gotten to play at Chapel Hill.) By November 1944, he
had been shipped to the South Pacific fighting zone. His son said that he did not see combat
while in the Pacific and indicated that Gremp wrote articles during the early part of the war
encouraging others to enlist. He was discharged by the Navy in November 1945. Gremp was
unable to return to the majors following his service.

AGE	YRS	ML	G	BA	SA	AB	H	2B	3B	HR	HR%	R	RBI	BB	SO	SB
22-25	42-45	3	113	0.223	0.302	291	65	14	0	3	1	19	31	18	24	1

HAMRICK, RAYMOND B. (RAY)   BR TR 5' 11"   160 lbs.
Born August 1, 1921, Nashville, Tn.
Played for Philadelphia (N) (1943–44)

Ray Hamrick debuted on August 14, 1943, as a twenty-one-year-old wartime replacement.
During the balance of 1943, he filled in at second base and shortstop. The following year he
was the regular shortstop until he was drafted during the season. In a letter, Hamrick said,
"I was drafted into the U.S. Navy, July 14th, 1944. The last games were a doubleheader in
Cincinnati" (Hamrick letter 1997). During the summer of 1944, he was stationed at Bainbridge,
Maryland Naval Training Station and played for the base team. Hamrick also added, "In the
spring of 1945 I was billeted to Barber's Point Naval Base north of Honolulu." He went on to
say, "There were many big league ballplayers stationed on the island and part of our duties
was to play ball and entertain the sailors and soldiers" (Hamrick letter 1997). Hamrick played
in the Navy Little World Series while he was stationed in Hawaii.

When the war ended in August 1945, Hamrick had not seen combat. He was still on the
Phillies' defense list in December 1945. After the war there was an overflow of players
wanting the 400 positions on the major league teams. Hamrick did not get one of those
positions. Casey Stengel was the manager at Oakland in the Pacific Coast League and brought
Hamrick to that team. Hamrick spent the balance of his career either with Oakland or San
Francisco. He added a postscript, "I have no regrets. I enjoyed every game I played and to
prove it I played hardball with the Oakland Old Timers until I was 65" (Hamrick letter 1997).

AGE	YRS	ML	G	BA	SA	AB	H	2B	3B	HR	HR%	R	RBI	BB	SO	SB
22-24	44-46	2	118	0.204	0.248	452	92	13	2	1	0.2	34	32	31	62	1

HARRIS, ROBERT N. (BOB)   BL TL 5' 11"   175 lbs.
Born July 9, 1916, Ames, Ia. — Died December 19, 1976, West Palm Beach, Fl.
Played for Detroit (1941–43, 1946)

Bob (Ned) Harris joined the Tigers at the start of the 1942 season and won a regular outfield
job. He kept that job until he entered the Navy on May 3, 1944. He took his boot training at
Great Lakes Naval Training Station and worked out with their baseball team. He spent the
summer stationed at the Iowa Pre-flight School and played on their baseball team, the Iowa
Seahawks. In the spring of 1945, he was sent to Shoemaker Field, California Naval Training
Distribution Center for further transfer. The transfer was to the commandant of the 14th Naval
District for duty. He was heading to the Pacific.

Harris spent the summer of 1945 stationed in the Pacific where he played on a Navy team and
took part in the Navy Little World Series in Hawaii in October 1945. He was still listed on the
Tigers' defense list in December 1945. He did return to the Tigers in 1946 and got into one
game as a pinch hitter. Even though he had been a regular for two seasons before the war, he
was able to get into only one major league game after the war.

AGE	YRS	ML	G	BA	SA	AB	H	2B	3B	HR	HR%	R	RBI	BB	SO	SB
27-28	44-45	4	262	0.259	0.393	814	211	33	14	16	2	107	81	102	77	12

HASENMAYER, DONALD I. (DON)   BR TR 5' 10"   180 lbs.
Born April 4, 1927, Roslyn, Pa.
Played for Philadelphia (N) (1945–46)

Don Hasenmayer got into five games as an eighteen-year-old rookie in 1945 before he entered
the service during that season. He was still listed on the Phillies' defense list in December
1945. He did rejoin the Phillies for six more games in 1946 after he was released from service.
The nineteen year old did not play any more major league games after 1946.

AGE	YRS	ML	G	BA	SA	AB	H	2B	3B	HR	HR%	R	RBI	BB	SO	SB
18	45	2	11	0.1	0.133	30	3	1	0	0	0	1	1	2	3	0

HEIM, VAL R.   BL TR 5' 11"   170 lbs.
Born November 4, 1920, Plymouth, Wi.
Played for Chicago (A) (1942)

Val Heim played in thirteen games at the end of the 1942 season. Heim said, "I was called by my
draft board to be drafted so I volunteered. [I was] in Navy from October 1942 to February 1946."
He went on, "I played two years of service baseball at Lambert Field in St. Louis. All or most of
the good players were in the service" (Heim letter 1997). After that two-year period, he was sent
to the Pacific and spent one year stationed on Saipan Island. He said, the "fighting was pretty
much over while I was there." Heim continued, "It was very hard to break into that group that
would play in 1946. I came close but in the end I didn't make the team" (Heim letter 1997).

In addition to trying to overcome the time away from the majors, Heim also had health problems in 1946. He was recalled to join the White Sox during the 1946 season but could not because of his health. During the following winter, he suffered rheumatic fever and spent three or four months in the hospital. His condition left him unable to play baseball at all during 1947. After coming back in the minors in 1948, he retired. He said, "I played at the top—the only place to play. To give up the game was hard but was the wise thing to do. I have a wonderful wife and we were able to raise two children" (Heim letter 1997). Health as well as the war kept Val Heim from having much of a major league career.

AGE	YRS	ML	G	BA	SA	AB	H	2B	3B	HR	HR%	R	RBI	BB	SO	SB
21-24	42-45	1	13	0.2	0.267	45	9	1	1	0	0	6	7	5	3	1

HELF, HENRY H. (HANK)   BR TR 6' 1"   196 lbs.
Born August 26, 1913, Austin, Tx. — Died October 27, 1984, Austin, Tx.
Played for Cleveland (1938, 1940) and St. Louis (A) (1946)

Hank Helf is probably more known for catching a ball dropped 708 feet from the top of the Terminal Tower in Cleveland than for his play on the field. On August 20, 1938, he caught a ball dropped from the tower by Ken Keltner. The catch broke the record that Gabby Street had made when he caught a ball dropped from the top of the Washington Monument. After trials in 1938 and 1940 with the Indians, Helf was drafted by the Browns from the Minneapolis Millers in the American Association in 1944. However, he was drafted into the military before he could play any games for the Browns.

Helf was in the Navy by February 1944. During 1945, he was stationed at the Naval Training Center, Gulfport, Mississippi. While stationed there, he played for and coached the baseball team. He was discharged by the Navy in December 1945. At age thirty-two, he rejoined the Browns for the 1946 season. He served as a backup catcher, catching in sixty-nine games. However, his batting suffered. He batted only .192 that year. The 1946 season was his last in the major leagues.

AGE	YRS	ML	G	BA	SA	AB	H	2B	3B	HR	HR%	R	RBI	BB	SO	SB
30-31	44-45	3	78	0.184	0.332	196	36	11	0	6	3.1	18	22	10	41	0

JARVIS, LEROY G. (ROY)   BR TR 5' 9"   160 lbs.
Born June 27, 1926, Shawnee, Ok. — Died January 13, 1990, Oklahoma City, Ok.
Played for Brooklyn (1944) and Pittsburgh (1946–47)

Roy Jarvis got into one game as a seventeen-year-old catcher in 1944 before going into the Navy that same year. During early 1945, he was stationed at a naval station in San Diego. He was still listed on the Pirates' defense list in December 1945. Jarvis spent part of the 1946 season still in the Navy but was released in time to play two games for the Pirates. He got another trial in 1947, but his hitting did not meet major league standards. Nineteen-forty-seven was his final major league season.

AGE	YRS	ML	G	BA	SA	AB	H	2B	3B	HR	HR%	R	RBI	BB	SO	SB
18-20	44-46	3	21	0.16	0.24	50	8	1	0	1	2	4	4	7	7	0

JONES, JAMES M. (JAKE)   BR TR 6' 3"   197 lbs.
Born November 23, 1920, Epps, La. — Died December 13, 2000, Delhi, La.
Played for Chicago (A) (1941–42, 1946–47) and Boston (A) (1947–48)

Jake Jones got trials with the White Sox in 1941 and 1942 after good years with Shreveport
in the Texas League. Jones volunteered after the 1942 season and went into Naval Aviation as
a pilot. He saw combat in the Pacific off the carrier *Yorktown*. His rank was lieutenant (j.g.).
In the spring of 1945, it was reported that he was on his way to becoming an ace in the Navy
Air Corps. He had seven confirmed kills of Japanese Zeros and was high man in his Hellcat
Fighter Squadron. Before the war was over, Jones did become an "Ace." Even with all that
combat, Jones confirmed that he did not suffer any war injuries.

Jones rejoined the White Sox for the 1946 season, but a broken wrist kept his games played
to twenty-four. During the 1947 season, he would finally earn the regular spot in the lineup.
Traded on June 14, 1947, to the Red Sox for Rudy York, Jones had a good year. Combined,
he hit nineteen home runs and drove in ninety-six runs. He lost the regular job to Billy
Goodman in 1948, his final year. He said, a "broken arm playing ball ended [my] ball career"
(Jones letter 1998).

AGE	YRS	ML	G	BA	SA	AB	H	2B	3B	HR	HR%	R	RBI	BB	SO	SB
21-24	42-45	5	224	0.229	0.368	790	181	31	5	23	2.9	80	117	69	130	8

KALIN, FRANK B.   BR TR 6' 0"   200 lbs.
Born October 3, 1917, Steubenville, Oh. — Died January 12, 1975, Weirton, W.V.
Played for Pittsburgh (1940) and Chicago (A) (1943)

Frank Kalin went 0 for a major league career. In seven at-bats during two seasons, he had no
hits. Five of the seven at-bats were as a pinch hitter. However, he did drive in a run and had
two walks. He went into the military during the 1943 season and missed both 1944 and 1945.
He did not play at the major league level after the war.

AGE	YRS	ML	G	BA	SA	AB	H	2B	3B	HR	HR%	R	RBI	BB	SO	SB
25-27	43-45	2	7	0	0	7	0	0	0	0	0	0	1	2	0	0

KELLEHER, FRANCIS E. (FRANKIE)   BR TR 6' 1"   195 lbs.
Born August 22, 1916, San Francisco, Ca. — Died April 13, 1979, Stockton, Ca.
Played for Cincinnati (1942–43)

Frankie Kelleher was brought up to the majors during July 1942. During that season, he hit
.182 in thirty-eight games. He also had a brief trial in 1943. Kelleher was inducted into the
Army in late 1944 or early 1945, undergoing his basic training at Camp Beale, California. After
completing that training, he was transferred to Fort Lewis, Washington, where he was able
to play baseball. He was stationed there during the spring and summer of 1945. He was still
listed on the Reds' defense list in December 1945. He did not return to the majors after the
war, but he played for the Hollywood Stars of the Pacific Coast League in the early 1950s.

AGE	YRS	ML	G	BA	SA	AB	H	2B	3B	HR	HR%	R	RBI	BB	SO	SB
27-28	44-45	2	47	0.167	0.283	120	20	3	1	3	2.5	14	12	18	20	0

KLEIN, LOUIS F. (LOU)   BR TR 5' 11" 167 lbs.
Born October 22, 1918, New Orleans, La. — Died June 20, 1976, Metairie, La.
Played for St. Louis (N) (1943, 1945–46, 1949), Cleveland (1951), and Philadelphia (A) (1951)

Lou Klein replaced Creepy Crispi at second base for the Cardinals in 1943. Crispi had been
called into service after the 1942 season. Klein, up from Columbus, Ohio, in the American
Association took over and played every inning of every game that year. He was successful,
batting .287 and scoring ninety-one runs as the Cardinals won their second of three pennants.
At one point during the 1943 season, he had a twenty-one game hitting streak. In turn, Klein
then was taken into the military after the 1943 season. He was inducted into the Coast Guard
on November 27, 1943. During the summer of 1944, he was stationed at St. Augustine, Florida.
By the spring of 1945, he had been transferred to Curtis Bay, Maryland. He was able to play
baseball while stationed at both St. Augustine and Curtis Bay.

Klein was released by the Coast Guard during 1945 in time for him to rejoin the Cardinals
and play in nineteen games. During that winter, he played ball in Cuba to prepare himself for
the following season. In the spring of 1946, he was in a three-way fight for the second base
job with Red Schoendienst and Emil Verban. Schoendienst won the job. Verban went to the
Phillies and Klein took the offer of a Mexican businessman who was recruiting major league
players for a league in Mexico. The baseball commissioner banned all the players who jumped
to the Mexican League from organized baseball.

Klein played 1947 and 1948 in Mexico. He had signed for the 1949 season with a league
in Canada, the Quebec Provincial League, when the banned players were reinstated. Klein
became the first of those players to return to the majors. However, with the time he had lost
to the military and in the Mexican League, he was unable to regain a regular role in the major
leagues. He played for the Cardinals in 1949 after being reinstated on June 15 and had another
chance with the Indians and A's in 1951. The service to his country hurt his major league
career and so did his decision to jump to the Mexican League.

AGE	YRS	ML	G	BA	SA	AB	H	2B	3B	HR	HR%	R	RBI	BB	SO	SB
25-26	44-45	5	305	0.259	0.381	1037	269	48	15	16	1.5	162	101	105	119	10

KONOPKA, BRUNO B. (BRUCE)   BL TL 6' 2" 190 lbs.
Born September 16, 1919, Hammond, In. — Died September 27, 1996, Denver, Co.
Played for Philadelphia (A) (1942–43, 1946)

Bruce Konopka got a brief five-game trial in 1942 and got to play in two games in 1943 before
being inducted into the Navy. He was ordered to report for duty on April 29, 1943. He spent
the balance of 1943 as well as 1944 and 1945 in the Navy. He was still on the A's defense list
in December 1945 but rejoined the A's for the 1946 season. Konopka got into thirty-eight
games that year, twenty games at first base, one in the outfield and seventeen pinch hitting
appearances. The 1946 season was his last year in the majors.

AGE	YRS	ML	G	BA	SA	AB	H	2B	3B	HR	HR%	R	RBI	BB	SO	SB
23-25	43-45	3	45	0.238	0.293	105	25	4	1	0	0	9	10	5	10	0

LAYNE, IVORIA H. (HILLY)   BL TR 6' 0" 170 lbs.
Born February 23, 1918, Whitwell, Tn.
Played for Washington (1941, 1944-45)

Hilly Layne made his debut on September 16, 1941. He was expected to be the starting
third baseman for the Senators in 1942 after Cecil Travis and Buddy Lewis had been drafted.
However, Layne was also drafted. He was inducted into the Air Corps at Fort Oglethrope on
February 7, 1942. In March 1942, he was transferred to the Army Hospital at Camp Shelby,
Mississippi because of leg problems. The leg problems came as the result of the typhus fever
that he had contracted during his first year of organized baseball (1938) at Americus, Georgia.
The problem emerged when Layne marched with a full pack. He was in the hospital for
fourteen weeks and was given an honorable medical discharge because of his condition. He
was released in November 1942 after nine months of service.

Layne did not rejoin the Senators until the 1944 season. That season, as well as 1945, he played
as a part-time third baseman and pinch hitter. Layne said, "The fever and complications after
cost me a promising major league career." He added, "From age 6 I had the goal of playing in
the major leagues and I wanted to play where Babe Ruth played in Yankee Stadium and hit a
home run. I did that and got to play against some of the better players" (Layne letter 1997). He
got to fulfill his dream even if it didn't last too long. While Layne's major league career lasted
only 107 games, he also played for a good while in the minors. He said he played in 1,993
games in total. He played in the Pacific Coast League in 1947, batted .367, and was named to
the all-star team.

AGE	YRS	ML	G	BA	SA	AB	H	2B	3B	HR	HR%	R	RBI	BB	SO	SB
24+25	42-43	3	107	0.264	0.335	284	75	9	4	1	0.4	37	28	20	22	3

LEIP, EDGAR E. (ED)   BR TR 5' 9" 160 lbs.
Born November 29, 1910, Trenton, N.J. — Died November 24, 1983, Zephyrhills, Fl.
Played for Washington (1939) and Pittsburgh (1940-42)

Ed Leip's career lasted four years, but he only played in thirty games and had a total of sixty-
two total at-bats during those four years. He entered the Army in late 1942. In the winter of
1943, he was known as the first Pittsburgh Pirate to go overseas. He was sent to Italy. It was
reported that he spent New Year's Eve on the side of a hill in the snow in Italy. He rose to the
rank of staff sergeant in the spring of 1945 during the Italian campaign. Leip won a battlefield
commission for valor during this time.

Leip was actively engaged in all of the Italian campaigns preceding the invasion of Germany.
In a published letter, he said, "Yesterday we crossed the Po River and I think our advance
has now reached a point which it will roll right into Germany" (*The Sporting News*, "In The
Service—Ed Leip Wins Battlefield Commission for Valor" 5-24-45, page 11). November 1945
found Leip on his way home from Naples, Italy, to be discharged. He was listed on the Pirates'
active roster in December 1945. However, he was not able to continue to play at the major
league level following his return from the war.

AGE	YRS	ML	G	BA	SA	AB	H	2B	3B	HR	HR%	R	RBI	BB	SO	SB
31-34	42-45	4	30	0.274	0.355	62	17	1	2	0	0	7	5	3	6	1

LETCHAS, CHARLIE   BR TR 5' 10"   150 lbs.

Born October 3, 1915, Thomasville, Ga. — Died March 14, 1995, Tampa, Fl.

Played for Philadelphia (N) (1939, 1944, 1946) and Washington (1941)

Charlie Letchas became a full-time utility player in 1944 after receiving brief trials in 1939 and 1941. As a wartime replacement, he backed up second, short, and third on the Phillies' infield and played in 116 games that year. He had been listed 4-F on the Phillies' list as late as January 1945, but he was taken into the military that year. He remained in the service until 1946. He was able to join the Phillies during the 1946 season and played six games that year but was not able to extend his major league career after the 1946 season.

AGE	YRS	ML	G	BA	SA	AB	H	2B	3B	HR	HR%	R	RBI	BB	SO	SB
29-30	45-46	4	136	0.234	0.262	461	108	10	0	1	0.2	32	37	35	31	0

LUBY, HUGH M.   BR TR 5' 10"   185 lbs.

Born June 13, 1913, Blackfoot, Id. — Died May 4, 1986, Eugene, Or.

Played for Philadelphia (A) (1936) and New York (N) (1944)

At age thirty-one, Hugh Luby became a wartime replacement for the New York Giants. He played second and third base in 1944 and batted .254 in 111 games. He had a brief trial in 1936 with the A's but did not return to the majors until the war had taken many of the current stars. His stay lasted only one year as Luby was drafted before the 1945 season.

Luby had been accepted for military service after taking his physical examination in New York on September 15, 1944. He was inducted into the Navy on April 4, 1945, at Alameda, California, and sent to San Diego for boot training. Following boot, he was stationed at St. Mary's, California, in the preflight program. That summer he was able to play baseball for the Armed Guard Club of Treasure Island, California. Later that fall, he played for the Bay Meadows team at San Mateo, California. He was still listed on the Giants' defense list in December 1945. He did not return to the majors following his release from the service.

AGE	YRS	ML	G	BA	SA	AB	H	2B	3B	HR	HR%	R	RBI	BB	SO	SB
32	45	2	120	0.247	0.305	361	89	11	2	2	0.6	33	38	52	22	4

LUKON, EDWARD P. (EDDIE)   BL TL 5' 10"   168 lbs.

Born August 5, 1920, Burgettstown, Pa. — Died November 7, 1996, Canonsburg, Pa.

Played for Cincinnati (1941, 1945–47)

Eddie Lukon got a brief taste of major league life in 1941 when he debuted on August 6. He got into twenty-three games that season. He then spent the next three years in the military. He registered for the draft on February 16, 1942, and was taken before the start of the 1942 season. He was released in 1945 in time for him to rejoin the Reds for two games that year. The following two years Lukon played the role of part-time outfielder and pinch hitter. In 1946 he played the outfield in 83 games, and in 1947 the number was reduced to 55 games.

While his batting average was not high, his power was respectable considering his number of at-bats. He had twelve home runs in 1946 and eleven in 1947.

AGE	YRS	ML	G	BA	SA	AB	H	2B	3B	HR	HR%	R	RBI	BB	SO	SB
22-24	43-45	4	213	0.236	0.408	606	143	17	9	23	3.8	64	70	60	72	4

MALLORY, JAMES B. (JIM)   BR TR 6' 1"   170 lbs.
Born September 1, 1918, Lawrenceville, Va. — Died August 6, 2001, Greenville, N.C.
Played for Washington (1940), St. Louis (N) (1945), and New York (N) (1945)

Jim Mallory played in four games in 1940 when he was a member of the Senators. He was taken into the Air Force and missed the 1942, 1943 and 1944 seasons. He served in a college training detachment, training Air Force Cadets. He didn't see any combat or suffer any injuries during his service time. He returned to the majors in 1945 and played thirteen games for the Cardinals before being sent to the Giants. Mallory played thirty-seven games for the Giants that year. He batted .277 during 1945. When the balance of the players returned for the 1946 season, Mallory was not able maintain his major league status. He said that illness forced his early retirement (Mallory letter 1998).

AGE	YRS	ML	G	BA	SA	AB	H	2B	3B	HR	HR%	R	RBI	BB	SO	SB
23-25	42-44	2	54	0.268	0.289	149	40	3	0	0	0	15	14	7	10	1

MARNIE, HARRY S. (HAL)   BR TR 6' 1"   178 lbs.
Born July 6, 1918, Philadelphia, Pa. — Died January 7, 2002, Philadelphia, Pa.
Played for Philadelphia (N) (1940–42)

Hal Marnie spent time with the Phillies before the war. In 1941 he got into sixty-one games as a middle infielder, backing up Danny Murtaugh and Bobby Bragan. His batting average slipped in 1942, and his playing time went down. He was taken into the military in 1943 and spent the next three seasons working for Uncle Sam. During his service time in 1943, he played in the all-star game in New York that raised $800,000,000 for war bonds. Following the war, he did not return to baseball at the major league level.

AGE	YRS	ML	G	BA	SA	AB	H	2B	3B	HR	HR%	R	RBI	BB	SO	SB
24-26	43-45	3	96	0.221	0.261	222	49	3	3	0	0	19	15	18	28	1

MARSHALL, MILO M. (MAX)   BL TR 6' 1"   180 lbs.
Born September 18, 1913, Shenandoah, Ia. — Died September 16, 1993, Salem, Or.
Played for Cincinnati (1942–44)

When Max Marshall joined the Reds in 1942, he had a solid minor league career to support the move to the major leagues. He secured a regular outfield position that year and retained it until he entered the Navy on August 5, 1944. He was twenty-eight years old when he made his debut. Marshall was almost thirty-one years old when he entered the Navy. He was called into service by the Randolph, Iowa, draft board. He spent his time during 1945 at Great Lakes and Bainbridge Naval facilities. He was able to play baseball for both of those bases while stationed at those locations. Marshall was the batting leader for the Great Lakes team in 1945. He was still on the Reds' defense list in December 1945. Marshall's major league time was spent during the World War II period. He had been a regular before the war, but following the war at age thirty-two, he was unable to make the team.

AGE	YRS	ML	G	BA	SA	AB	H	2B	3B	HR	HR%	R	RBI	BB	SO	SB
30-31	44-45	3	329	0.245	0.339	1267	311	41	16	15	1.2	140	105	89	100	15

MARTY, JOSEPH A. (JOE)   BR TR 6' 0" 182 lbs.
Born September 1, 1913, Sacramento, Ca. — Died October 4, 1984, Sacramento, Ca.
Played for Chicago (N) (1937–39) and Philadelphia (N) (1939–41)

Joe Marty was a part-time outfielder for the Chicago Cubs in 1937 and 1938. He was traded to the Phillies on May 29, 1939, and became a regular with the Phillies until he entered the military. He was the first Cub to hit a home run in a night game (Cincinnati, July 1, 1938). He also had an impact on the 1938 World Series. The Cubs scored only nine runs in the four-game sweep by the Yankees. Marty drove in five of those nine runs.

Marty enlisted in the Air Force on April 2, 1942, at age twenty-eight. He would spend the next four years in service to his country. He was stationed at Mathis Field in Sacramento, California, and was in charge of the athletic equipment room and played baseball for the base team. He was still at Mathis Field in 1943 and played for the service all-stars in a benefit game. Marty was injured in an automobile accident on Christmas Eve 1943. He suffered a knee injury that proved to be more serious than was first anticipated. He got blood poisoning and spent forty-four days in the post hospital. The injury required surgery.

Marty continued to be an athletic supply sergeant at Mathis Field until summer of 1944. At that time he was sent to Las Vegas to prepare for overseas duty. However, he continued to be Stateside. In the fall of 1944 he was at Fairfield-Suisun Air Base near San Francisco and then in early 1945 at Hamilton Field, California. He was able to play ball while stationed at Hamilton. The stay at Hamilton continued until the Army put together at baseball team that was to be sent to Hawaii to take on the Navy team that had just beaten the Army team in the Little World Series. The Army transferred a group of former major leaguers to Kerns, Utah, to train to play the Navy. Marty was one of those players. After training, they were sent to Hawaii by ship, but the Navy team was gone when they arrived. Those players then played in Hawaii for a while before being shipped out to the Pacific Islands to play exhibition games for the troops. Marty played on the 58th Wing 20th Air Force team in the Marianas. He spent the summer of 1945 in the South Pacific. He played in an all-star game in August in the Marianas and a second game on Iwo Jima.

Marty was sent home in November 1945, arriving in Los Angeles on the transport ship *Cecil* on November 2. He was still listed on the Phillies' defense list in December 1945. Marty was thirty-two years old at the close of the war. He was not able to play baseball for a major league team after the war.

AGE	YRS	ML	G	BA	SA	AB	H	2B	3B	HR	HR%	R	RBI	BB	SO	SB
28-31	42-45	5	538	0.261	0.4	1832	478	78	22	44	2.4	223	222	142	187	14

279

MAY, MERRILL G. (PINKY)   BR TR 5' 11" 165 lbs.
Born January 18, 1911, Lanconia, In. — Died September 4, 2000, Corydon, In.
Played for Philadelphia (N) (1939–43)

Pinky May got stuck in the Yankee farm system for several years. He spent four years at the
AAA level. In each of the years, he had a good record but not good enough to break into
the Yankee lineup. He was drafted by the Phillies after the 1938 season and became, at age
twenty-eight, their regular third baseman for the next five years. During that time he led the
National League in fielding three of the five years. He was chosen as a reserve for the 1940 All-
Star game. He said, "I think defense was my strong point." He added, "I was a line-drive hitter
with no power" (Van Blair 1994, 131).

After the 1943 season, May volunteered for service in the Navy. His number was close to
being called. He went into the Navy on October 22, 1943. He was only three months shy of
his thirty-third birthday. He spent the first part of his Navy career at Great Lakes. He stayed
there through 1944 and then in early 1945 was sent to San Francisco and from there was
transferred to Hawaii. He had played for the Great Lakes team during the summer of 1944
and batted .376. After five months in Hawaii, May, along with others, was sent to play baseball
on the Islands of the South Pacific to entertain the troops. They toured Johnston Island,
Kwajaleim, Eniwctok, Peleliu, Tinain, Saipan, Guam, Roi-Namur, and Ulithi and played one game
on Mog Mog Island. While stationed on Tinain, he watched the B-29s as they took off to bomb
the mainland of Japan.

Later in 1945 May was sent to Australia, where he directed an athletic program. He was still
listed on the Phillies' defense list in December 1945. He was able to join the Phillies for spring
training in 1946. After a trial he did not make the team. He was thirty-five years old. He went to
the U.S. Attorney's office to seek protection from the reemployment provision of the G.I. Bill. He
asked for the amount of money to make up the difference between what the Phillies had paid
him for spring training and what he would have made if he had played the 1946 season, $6950.
The Phillies agreed to pay two-thirds of the amount, and May settled. He did not play in the
majors after the war and because of that missed out on receiving a baseball pension.

AGE	YRS	ML	G	BA	SA	AB	H	2B	3B	HR	HR%	R	RBI	BB	SO	SB
33-34	44-45	5	665	0.275	0.337	2215	610	102	11	4	0.2	210	215	261	121	13

MAYNARD, JAMES W. (BUSTER)   BR TR 5' 11" 170 lbs.
Born March 25, 1913, Henderson, S.C. — Died September 7, 1977, Durham, N.C.
Played for New York (N) (1940, 1942–43, 1946)

Buster Maynard had a brief trial in September 1940 and returned in 1942 as a reserve
outfielder. He saw more playing time in 1943 as a wartime replacement. He struggled with the
bat even in wartime level of competition. He batted only .206 that year. Maynard was taken
into the Army before the 1944 season. By 1945 he had been transferred to Camp Lee, Virginia.
Even after a bout with pneumonia early in 1945, he was still able to play baseball during that

summer. He was still on the Giants' defense list in December 1945. He did return to Giants for the 1946 season but played in only seven games that year, going 0 for 4 during his stay.

AGE	YRS	ML	G	BA	SA	AB	H	2B	3B	HR	HR%	R	RBI	BB	SO	SB
31-32	44-45	4	224	0.221	0.328	616	136	14	5	14	2.3	68	66	46	53	6

MCCOY, BENJAMIN J. (BENNY)   BL TR 5' 9"   170 lbs.
Born November 9, 1915, Jenison, Mi.
Played for Detroit (1938–39) and Philadelphia (A) (1940–41)

Benny McCoy had trials with the Tigers in 1938 and 1939 before being declared a free agent by Commissioner Landis in January, 1940. McCoy was considered to be a very good prospect. Ten teams bid for his talent. Connie Mack with the A's paid him a bonus of $45,000 and signed him to a two-year contract for $10,000 a year. Both amounts were very good for that time. McCoy became the regular second baseman for the A's for the next two years. McCoy had been traded to the A's in exchange for Wally Moses earlier, but the deal was canceled when the Tigers were ordered, by the commissioner, to release McCoy because they had violated certain rules about the progression of prospects.

Shortly after Pearl Harbor, McCoy enlisted in the Navy. He was inducted as a coxswain on February 5, 1942. He spent his early time in the Navy at Great Lakes and was a member of the Great Lakes baseball team in 1942. While there he played in a benefit game against some American League All-Stars. They raised $193,000 for war relief. In February 1943, he was transferred to Norfolk Naval Training Station for advanced training. During the summer of 1943, McCoy played for the Norfolk team. They played a benefit game against the Senators and raised $2,125,375 for war bonds.

By the fall of 1944 he was stationed in Australia where he would stay until the summer of 1945. He was able to play baseball while stationed in Australia, playing in an Army-Navy all-star game on November 5, 1944, in Brisbane, Australia. He was listed as representing the CSP(A) Receiving Barracks Unit. During the summer of 1945 he went on to the Philippines. He was stationed on a tiny island in a harbor on the western coast of Luzon. He helped convert the island into a well-equipped recreation center.

McCoy was still listed on the A's defense list in December 1945. In a letter, McCoy said he suffered no injuries and did not see combat. He did not return to major league baseball following the war. Talking about his career, he said, "I feel I played in the greatest years of baseball—'39-'41—with and against some of the greatest players of all times" (McCoy letter 1997).

AGE	YRS	ML	G	BA	SA	AB	H	2B	3B	HR	HR%	R	RBI	BB	SO	SB
26-29	42-45	4	337	0.269	0.381	1214	327	52	18	16	1.3	182	156	190	122	8

MCELYEA, FRANK   BR TR 6'6"   221 lbs.
Born August 4, 1918, White County, Il. — Died April 19, 1987, Evansville, In.
Played for Boston (N) (1942)

Frank McElyea made his debut on September 10, 1942, and got into seven games during that
season. He went into the military before the start of the 1943 season and spent the next three
seasons in service to his country. In 1943 he had risen to rank of corporal. Also in 1943, he
spent some time helping during a flood in southern and central Illinois. He was still on the
Braves' defense list in December 1945. He did not return to baseball at the major league level
after the war.

AGE	YRS	ML	G	BA	SA	AB	H	2B	3B	HR	HR%	R	RBI	BB	SO	SB
24-26	43-45	1	7	0	0	4	0	0	0	0	0	2	0	0	0	0

MCHALE, JOHN J.   BL TR 6'0"   200 lbs.
Born September 21, 1921, Detroit, Mi.
Played for Detroit (1943-45, 1947-48)

John McHale got four pinch hitting appearances in 1943 and 1944 before volunteering for the
Navy. He served but did not see any combat. He suffered a perforated duodenal stomach ulcer
that required surgery while in the Navy. It was caused by his diet and unusual hours of travel,
etc. McHale was released in time to rejoin the Tigers in time for the 1945 World Series. He had
three pinch hitting appearances in the fall classic but did not get a hit. McHale played again
for the Tigers in 1947 and 1948. Of his 114 career at-bats, thirty-four came as a pinch hitter.

At age twenty-six, McHale moved from the playing side of baseball to the administrative side.
He started in the front office of the Tigers in 1948 and became general manager on April
30, 1957. He also served as general manager and later president of the Milwaukee Braves
(1959 to 1967) In addition, McHale became the president of the Montreal Expos when they
were formed in 1969. At one point in his career, he was considered for the commissioner of
baseball job but withdrew his name because of previous commitments.

AGE	YRS	ML	G	BA	SA	AB	H	2B	3B	HR	HR%	R	RBI	BB	SO	SB
21-22	43-44	5	64	0.193	0.281	114	22	1	0	3	2.6	10	12	9	29	1

MCQUILLEN, GLENN R.   BR TR 6'0"   198 lbs.
Born April 19, 1915, Strasburg, Va. — Died June 8, 1989, Gardenville, Md.
Played for St. Louis (A) (1938, 1941-42, 1946-47)

Glenn McQuillen played in 100 games in 1942 as an outfielder and pinch hitter and batted
.283. He had trials in 1938 and 1941 but at age twenty-seven he finally got his chance.
The war changed that. He entered the Navy before the start of the 1943 season. He was
stationed at Great Lakes during 1943 and was a member of their baseball team that year. He
was transferred to Bainbridge and became part of one of the most bizarre trades of all time.
Norfolk Naval Station needed an outfielder for their baseball team. McQuillen was traded by

Bainbridge to Norfolk for a life raft. It was discovered later that the life raft was defective, but McQuillen batted .367. He played for Norfolk during the summer of 1944.

At the beginning of 1945, McQuillen was sent to Hawaii and later became part of the group of baseball players that toured the islands of the South Pacific playing exhibitions in the war zone for resting troops. He was discharged by the Navy in December 1945. He rejoined the Browns in 1946 and played in fifty-nine games that year, batting .241. After a one game pinch hitting appearance in 1947, McQuillen closed out his major league career.

AGE	YRS	ML	G	BA	SA	AB	H	2B	3B	HR	HR%	R	RBI	BB	SO	SB
28-30	43-45	5	210	0.274	0.379	643	176	24	16	4	0.6	82	75	34	49	1

METZIG, WILLIAM A. (BILL)   BR TR 6' 1"   180 lbs.
Born December 4, 1918, Fort Dodge, Ia.
Played for Chicago (A) (1944)

Bill Metzig got into five games at the close of the 1944 season with the Chicago White Sox. But by December 1944, he had entered the service. He missed the 1945 season in service to his country. He was still listed on the White Sox's defense list in December 1945 but did not return to the majors following the war.

AGE	YRS	ML	G	BA	SA	AB	H	2B	3B	HR	HR%	R	RBI	BB	SO	SB
26	45	1	5	0.125	0.125	16	2	0	0	0	0	1	1	1	4	0

MOORE, D.C. (DEE)   BR TR 6' 0"   200 lbs.
Born April 6, 1914, Hedley, Tx. — Died July 2, 1997, Williston, N.D.
Played for Cincinnati (1936–37), Brooklyn (1943), and Philadelphia (N) (1943, 1946)

After brief trials in 1936 and 1937, Dee Moore became a wartime replacement for the Dodgers and the Phillies in 1943. He caught and played third base, outfield, and first base during that season. Moore then joined the Marines before the 1944 season. After training, he was stationed on a Marine base in San Diego and was able to play baseball while stationed there.

In the spring of 1945, Moore was sent to the Pacific, first to Hawaii and then to some of the islands of the South Pacific and back to Hawaii in the fall of 1945. In Hawaii, he played in the Navy Little World Series in October 1945. He had played on the FMF team in the 14th Naval District League in Hawaii. Moore had been able to play some baseball during the summer of 1945 as he was stationed on the islands. He had played for the Fleet Marine Force during that time. He was still listed on the Phillies' defense list in December 1945. Moore rejoined the Phillies for the 1946 season. However, after a one for thirteen batting performance, he closed his major league career.

AGE	YRS	ML	G	BA	SA	AB	H	2B	3B	HR	HR%	R	RBI	BB	SO	SB
30-31	44-45	4	98	0.232	0.303	228	53	9	2	1	0.4	29	22	34	24	1

MUELLER, EMMETT J.   BB TR 5' 6"   167 lbs.
Born July 20, 1912, St. Louis, Mo. — Died October 3, 1986, Orlando, Fl.
Played for Philadelphia (N) (1938–41)

Emmett Mueller got his start in the Cardinal organization, signing his first minor league
contract at age sixteen. After several years in the minors, he got to the majors with the
Phillies in 1938. In that year, he became their regular second baseman. In the following years,
he would be their number one utility player. During his career, he played the outfield and all
infield positions. His playing time was limited in 1941 by a broken finger. He hit a home run
off Van Lingo Mungo of the Dodgers in his first major league at bat on April 19, 1938.

Mueller volunteered for the Army on February 28, 1942, at Jefferson Barracks, Missouri. He
spent the first part of his Army time at Jefferson Barracks and was able to play some baseball
during the summer of 1942 with their team. On July 7, 1942, he got to play on a service all-
star team that played an American League All-Star team that raised money for war relief. They
raised $193,000. He stayed there until some time in 1943 when he was transferred to O'Reilly
Hospital, Springfield, Missouri, to serve as an educational advisor in the retraining unit.

By 1945 Mueller was transferred to Europe and was wounded in action in Germany. After the
time in Europe, he was returned to Jefferson Barracks. He again got to play baseball for that
team. He was discharged by the Army in December 1945. At age thirty-three and being gone
four years from the major leagues, Mueller was not able to return to baseball at the major
league level.

AGE	YRS	ML	G	BA	SA	AB	H	2B	3B	HR	HR%	R	RBI	BB	SO	SB
29-32	42-45	4	441	0.253	0.353	1281	324	55	11	17	1.3	144	127	156	124	10

MUELLER, WILLIAM L. (BILL)   BR TR 6' 1"   180 lbs.
Born November 9, 1920, Bay City, Mi. — Died October 24, 2001, Glenview, Il.
Played for Chicago (A) (1942, 1945)

Bill Mueller got a brief trial in 1942 after he made his debut on August 29 as an outfielder.
Following the 1942 season, he volunteered for the Navy. Mueller was injured in training at
Pensacola, Florida. In 1944 he was stationed at Lambert Field, St. Louis, and was able to play
for their team. He received his discharge in the summer of 1945 from Norfolk. He rejoined
the White Sox for thirteen games at the close of the 1945 season. However, the injury that
he had suffered required surgery. In the fall of 1945, he had his knee operated on at Mercy
Hospital, Chicago. He had hoped to be ready for spring training in 1946, but the injury kept
him from returning to the majors. After the close of his baseball career, Mueller spent thirty
years as a jeweler.

AGE	YRS	ML	G	BA	SA	AB	H	2B	3B	HR	HR%	R	RBI	BB	SO	SB
22-24	43-45	2	39	0.149	0.16	94	14	1	0	0	0	8	5	14	10	3

MULLEN FORD P. (MOON)   BL TR 5' 9" 165 lbs.
Born February 9, 1917, Olympia, Wa.
Played for Philadelphia (N) (1944)

Moon Mullen was a wartime replacement for the Phillies in 1944. He took over for Danny
Murtaugh and was the Phillies regular second baseman during 1944 and batted .267. After the
1944 season, he also entered the military. He had been classified 1-A early in 1944 but was not
taken until after the season ended. Mullen missed the 1945 and the 1946 season. At age thirty
and being a year later than the other returnees, Mullen was not able to return to the majors.

AGE	YRS	ML	G	BA	SA	AB	H	2B	3B	HR	HR%	R	RBI	BB	SO	SB
28-29	45-46	1	118	0.267	0.304	464	124	9	4	0	0	51	31	28	32	4

MURPHY, EDWARD J. (ED)   BR TR 5' 11" 190 lbs.
Born August 23, 1918, Joliet, Il. — Died December 10, 1991, Joliet, Il.
Played for Philadelphia (N) (1942)

Ed Murphy got into thirteen games at the end of the 1942 season for the Phillies as a first
baseman. He spent the next three years in the military. He was still listed on the Phillies' defense
list in December 1945. He did not return to the majors following his release from the service.

AGE	YRS	ML	G	BA	SA	AB	H	2B	3B	HR	HR%	R	RBI	BB	SO	SB
24-26	43-45	1	13	0.25	0.321	28	7	2	0	0	0	2	4	2	4	0

NAYLOR, EARL E.   BR TR 6' 0" 190 lbs.
Born May 19, 1919, Kansas City, Mo. — Died January 16, 1990, Winter Haven, Fl.
Played for Philadelphia (N) (1942-43) and Brooklyn (1946)

Earl Naylor was an outfielder and pitcher for the Phillies during the 1942 and 1943 seasons.
He was traded to the Cardinals on June 1, 1943, along with Danny Litwhiler, but he never
appeared in a game for the Cardinals. He went into the Navy after the 1943 season and spent
the next two years in the Navy. During the summer of 1945, he was stationed at Bainbridge
and pitched for their team. He was still listed on the Cardinals' defense list in December 1945.
He spent his military service time on the Cardinals' defense list, but he never played for them.
Following his release from the Navy, he did get two pinch hitting appearances for the Dodgers
in the three games he played for them in 1946. This closed out his major league career.

AGE	YRS	ML	G	BA	SA	AB	H	2B	3B	HR	HR%	R	RBI	BB	SO	SB
25-26	44-45	3	112	0.186	0.245	290	54	6	1	3	1	22	28	23	35	2

NOVIKOFF, LOUIS A. (LOU)   BR TR 5' 10" 185 lbs.
Born October 12, 1915, Glendale, Az. — Died September 30, 1970, South Gate, Ca.
Played for Chicago (N) (1941-44) and Philadelphia (N) (1946)

Lou Novikoff's nickname was "The Mad Russian." He earned it by his eccentric behavior. He
had been a batting champion in four different minor leagues, including batting .363, hitting

forty-one home runs, and driving in 171 runs with Los Angeles of the Pacific Coast League in 1940. His batting average for his minor league service was .365. He was named *The Sporting News* Minor League Player of the Year in 1939.

Novikoff could never translate the minor league success into major league stardom. His best year with the Cubs was 1942 when he batted .300 and was named to the all-rookie team. He hit only fifteen home runs in his entire major league career. He was also a bad outfielder. In addition, he was afraid of the ivy growing on the outfield walls of Wrigley Field in Chicago. He did not want to touch the ivy. An example of his eccentric behavior was stealing third base in a game when the bases were loaded. When asked why, he replied, "I got such a good jump on the pitcher" (Shatzkin 1990, 813). He was also known for his appetite and his wolfhound, which accompanied him wherever he went.

Novikoff was ordered to be inducted by the California draft board in Sacramento in the summer of 1945. He was inducted at Fort MacArthur, California, on July 17, 1945. He waited there for assignment before being sent to Sheppard Field, Texas. He stayed there until he was discharged by the Army in December 1945. In November 1945, Novikoff was drafted by the Phillies from the Los Angeles Angels. The Cubs had released him. He made fourteen pinch hitting appearances with the Phillies in the seventeen games he played in 1946. Novikoff had played softball before playing baseball. Following his baseball career he returned to playing softball and played until he was in his fifties. He was inducted into the Softball Hall of Fame at Long Beach, California.

AGE	YRS	ML	G	BA	SA	AB	H	2B	3B	HR	HR%	R	RBI	BB	SO	SB
29	45	5	356	0.282	0.384	1081	305	45	10	15	1.4	107	138	64	71	4

O'NEILL, HARRY M.

BR TR 6' 3"   205 lbs.

Born May 8, 1917, Philadelphia, Pa. — Died March 6, 1945, Iwo Jima, Marianasis
Played for Philadelphia (A) (1939)

Harry O'Neill was one of the two soldiers who were killed in World War II who had major league experience. His only appearance was in 1939 when he caught in one game for the Philadelphia A's. He did not get to bat in that game. He had been promoted to a first lieutenant in the Marines. He died in the assault on Iwo Jima. His obituary said, "Lieut. Harry O'Neill of the Marines, signed out of Gettysburg College by the Philadelphia Athletics in 1939 as a catcher and who was with Allentown and Harrisburg of the Inter-State League in 1940, was killed in action on Iwo Jima, March 6. His wife in Philadelphia has been notified. He was 27 years old" (*The Sporting News*, "Obituaries" 4-12-45, page 15). O'Neill paid the ultimate price in service to his country.

AGE	YRS	ML	G	BA	SA	AB	H	2B	3B	HR	HR%	R	RBI	BB	SO	SB
26-28	43-45	1	1	0	0	0	0	0	0	0	0	0	0	0	0	0

PARTEE, ROY R.

BR TR 5' 10"   180 lbs.

Born September 7, 1917, Los Angeles, Ca. — Died December 26, 2000, Eureka, Ca.
Played for Boston (A) (1943–44, 1946–47) and St. Louis (A) (1948)

Roy Partee was considered the number one catcher for the Red Sox in 1943 and 1944 even though he split the time behind the plate with others. He was a good fielding catcher and had the ability to handle pitchers and call a good game. During the early summer of 1944, he was rejected for service after he had his physical examination. However, he was reclassified from 4-F to 1-A on August 5, 1944. With that change, he entered the Army in October 1944. In the spring of 1945, he was stationed at Camp Howze, Texas, with the Infantry Advanced Replacement Training Center. Partee was sent to the South Pacific and was part of the invasion force that retook the Philippines from the Japanese.

Partee was still on the Red Sox defense list in December 1945 and was not discharged until April 1946. He rejoined the Red Sox for most of the 1946 season. However, he had lost his role as the number one catcher to Hal Wagner in 1946 and Birdie Tebbetts in 1947. He did appear in the 1946 World Series for the Red Sox and was the catcher when Enos Slaughter made his mad dash for home. He closed his career in 1948 with the St. Louis Browns after being traded to them as part of the deal that brought Vern Stephens and Jack Kramer to the Red Sox.

AGE	YRS	ML	G	BA	SA	AB	H	2B	3B	HR	HR%	R	RBI	BB	SO	SB
27	45	5	367	0.25	0.303	1090	273	41	5	2	0.2	89	114	132	120	2

PATRICK, ROBERT L (BOB)   BR TR 6' 2" 190 lbs.
Born October 27, 1917, Fort Smith, Ar. — Died October 6, 1999, Fort Smith, Ar.
Played for Detroit (1941–42)

Bob Patrick got brief trials with the Tigers in both 1941 and 1942. He played in a total of nine games during the two years, six games as an outfielder and three games as a pinch hitter. He was taken into the military before the 1943 season. He served three years in the service and was still on the Tigers' defense list in December 1945. He did not rejoin the Tigers following the war.

AGE	YRS	ML	G	BA	SA	AB	H	2B	3B	HR	HR%	R	RBI	BB	SO	SB
25-27	43-45	2	9	0.267	0.533	15	4	1	0	1	6.7	3	3	1	1	0

PATTON, GENE T.   BL TR 5' 10" 165 lbs.
Born July 8, 1926, Coatesville, Pa.
Played for Boston (N) (1944)

Gene Patton was a high school phenom who was signed by the Boston Braves at age seventeen, given a bonus, and sent straight to the Braves. He made his debut on June 17, 1944, in a pinch-running appearance. He would not appear in another game. During his high school career, he once went twenty-two for twenty-three and was robbed on a questionable call for the only out. He was scouted by all sixteen teams. Patton was the youngest of fifteen children (9 boys and 6 girls). Seven of his brothers were in service, so he didn't have to go into the military, but he did go. He went into the Army in 1944 at age eighteen.

Patton was a member of the 7th Infantry. He trained at Camp Wheeler, Georgia, in the swamps to get ready for the Pacific Theater. Patton was there for fourteen weeks, and as his unit was ready to ship out, he came down with rheumatic fever in the blood stream. He had an enlarged heart and numbness in his legs. He spent some time in an Army hospital. The doctors had trouble getting the disease under control and experimented with penicillin. The treatment worked, but it left him with an allergy to the drug.

When Patton was released by the Army, he went to Florida to train a month and a half before the rest of the team. He ran on the beach and swam in the ocean to try to get himself back in shape. He had a good spring but injured his shoulder when the team was coming north. Billy Southworth, the Braves manager, went out and got a proven third baseman to fill the void. Patton, when he recovered, never got a chance to play. He was sold to Milwaukee in the American Association, the sickness kept coming back, and his career was over. Patton said about his military service, "…7 of my brothers were in the service, one missing in action at the time and I just had to go because I'd never been able to live with myself if anything happened to any of my brothers." He added, "So I went and it cost me a wonderful baseball career. But I'd do it again because of the way things were at that time" (Patton letter 1997).

AGE	YRS	ML	G	BA	SA	AB	H	2B	3B	HR	HR%	R	RBI	BB	SO	SB
18	45	1	1	0	0	0	0	0	0	0	0	0	0	0	0	0

PETERMAN, WILLIAM D. (BILL)   BR TR 6' 2" 185 lbs.
Born April 20, 1921, Philadelphia, Pa. — Died March 13, 1999, Philadelphia, Pa.
Played for Philadelphia (N) (1942)

In some ways, Bill Peterman had a baseball career most only dream about. He had a career batting average of 1.000. The downside of his career is that he got to bat only one time. In his debut on April 26, 1942, he singled in his only plate appearance. He went into the Army before the 1943 season and spent three years working for Uncle Sam. In 1943 he played in an all-star game in New York that raised $800,000,000 for war bonds. He was still listed on the Phillies' defense list in December 1945 but did not play at the major league level following the war.

AGE	YRS	ML	G	BA	SA	AB	H	2B	3B	HR	HR%	R	RBI	BB	SO	SB
22-24	43-45	1	1	1	1	1	1	0	0	0	0	0	0	0	0	0

PHILLIPS, DAMON R.   BR TR 6' 0" 176 lbs.
Born June 8, 1919, Corsicana, Tx.
Played for Cincinnati (1942) and Boston (N) (1944, 1946)

After a trial with the Reds in 1942, Damon Phillips became a wartime replacement at third base and shortstop for the Boston Braves. During that time, on August 29, 1944, he tied a record for third basemen by making eleven assists in a nine-inning game. He was drafted by the Army before the 1945 season. He took his training in Texas and then was sent to the Philippine Islands. Phillips was in a combat zone but did not see actual combat. He heard the artillery fire and saw the planes dropping bombs on the Japanese holed up in the hills. He stayed in the Philippine Islands a short time and then was transferred to a very large training base to get ready for the invasion of Japan.

After the war was over, Phillips was with the second convey that entered Japan. He stayed in Japan until his service time was up and then came home. He commented on his military service, "Two years from baseball may or may not have had a bearing on my career. But it really doesn't matter. Thousands died in that war and thousands of others sustained injuries that would affect their lives for as long as they would live; I did not. For that I am grateful. I wish no one had [died or been injured]" (Phillips letter 1998). Phillips was still on the Braves' defense list in December 1945. He rejoined the Braves in 1946 and appeared in two games as a pinch hitter. Those two appearances closed out his major league career.

AGE	YRS	ML	G	BA	SA	AB	H	2B	3B	HR	HR%	R	RBI	BB	SO	SB
26	45	3	170	0.25	0.315	575	144	32	1	1	0.2	39	59	35	39	1

PLATT, MIZELL G. (WHITEY)   BR TR 6' 1" 190 lbs.
Born August 21, 1920, West Palm Beach, Fl. — Died July 27, 1970, West Palm Beach, Fl
Played for Chicago (N) (1942–43), Chicago (A) (1946), and St. Louis (A) (1948–49)

Whitey Platt spent most of 1942 and 1943 in the minors, but he did get a brief trial in both years with the Chicago Cubs. He entered the Navy before the start of the 1944 season. He spent 1944 stationed at Great Lakes and played baseball for their team that summer. He played outfield and batted .428. By early 1945, he had been transferred to Fort Pierce, Florida, as part of the Naval Amphibious Training. Later that spring, Platt was sent to the Pacific.

In the fall of 1945, in Hawaii, Platt played baseball in the Navy Little World Series and was named to the 14th Naval District all-star team representing the AIEA Barracks team. He was still on the Cubs' defense list in December 1945 but was released in time for the 1946 season. However, instead of rejoining the Cubs, he was released by them and signed with the White Sox for 1946. After a good year in the minors at Toledo in 1947, he returned to the majors with the St. Louis Browns in 1948, his only season as a regular. In 1949 his role changed to a reserve outfielder and pinch hitter. He led the league in the number of pinch hitting appearances in 1949 as he closed out his major league career.

AGE	YRS	ML	G	BA	SA	AB	H	2B	3B	HR	HR%	R	RBI	BB	SO	SB
23-24	44-45	5	333	0.255	0.369	1002	256	41	17	13	1.3	117	147	81	122	2

POLAND, HUGH R.   BL TR 5' 11" 185 lbs.
Born January 19, 1913, Tompkinsville, Ky. — Died March 30, 1984, Guthrie, Ky.
Played for New York (N) (1943), Boston (N) (1943–44, 1946), Philadelphia (N) (1947), and Cincinnati (1947–48)

Hugh Poland had only one year during his career in which he spent the entire season with a major league team. That was his rookie year in 1943. During that year he was traded by the Giants to the Braves, along with Connie Ryan, for Ernie Lombardi. It was not a very good trade for the Braves. Lombardi, even though he was close to the end of a hall of fame career, batted over .300 while Ryan and Poland batted .212 and .183 respectively.

After spending part of the year with the Braves in 1944, Poland was drafted as part of the military crackdown on 4-Fs who were professional athletes. He had tried to join the Navy but had been rejected because of an ankle injury he sustained playing basketball in high school. In early 1945, he was ordered to be reexamined. He was rejected again, but because he was a professional athlete, he was taken into the Army in spite of an injury that kept him from standing for long periods. The examiner said, "Mr. Poland, I'm going to tell you something. If you can play baseball on that leg of yours, you can go into the armed services" (Goldstein 1980, 206). He was taken even though he was married with two children. Poland said, however, "But I'm glad I went in and served some time. I was treated very good while I was in service. I'll say that. They didn't hold anything against me. I was treated very, very nicely" (Goldstein 1980, 206).

Poland did make an important contribution to the war effort. He was the regular catcher for the Fort Knox baseball team for the entire time he spent in the service. He was released by the Army by November 1945. He rejoined the Braves for part of the 1946 season and played in four games before being sent to the minors. He also got some major league time with the Phillies and Reds before closing his career. After his playing days, he became a scout for the Giants.

AGE	YRS	ML	G	BA	SA	AB	H	2B	3B	HR	HR%	R	RBI	BB	SO	SB
32	45	5	83	0.185	0.242	211	39	10	1	0	0	7	19	6	16	0

POOLE, RAYMOND H. (RAY)   BL TR 6' 0"   180 lbs.
Born January 16, 1920, Salisbury, N.C.
Played for Philadelphia (A) (1941, 1947)

Ray Poole made his major league debut on September 9, 1941. He got into two games during that season as a pinch hitter. In early 1942, Poole became part of the armed forces. He would serve for four years. He was still on the A's defense list in December 1945. He did not appear with the A's in 1946 but did rejoin for part of the 1947 season. During that season, he played in thirteen games, all as a pinch hitter. Poole's career is unique in that it was made up of only pinch hitting appearances. He pinch-hit two times in 1941 and thirteen times in 1947. He never played in the field during his major league career.

AGE	YRS	ML	G	BA	SA	AB	H	2B	3B	HR	HR%	R	RBI	BB	SO	SB
22-25	42-45	2	15	0.2	0.2	15	3	0	0	0	0	1	1	1	5	0

RICHMOND, DONALD L. (DON)   BL TR 6' 1"   175 lbs.
Born October 27, 1919, Gillett, Pa. — Died May 24, 1981, Elmira, N.Y.
Played for Philadelphia (A) (1941, 1946–47) and St. Louis (N) (1951)

Don Richmond was brought up to the A's at the close of the 1941 season. He appeared in nine games that year. Before the start of the 1942 season, he was added to the list of American Leaguers in service. He spent four years in the military. He was still listed on the A's defense list in December 1945. He made brief appearances with the A's in 1946 and 1947. After remaining in the minors for all of 1948 through 1950, he returned to majors with the

Cardinals in 1951. He was in the Cardinals' opening-day lineup in 1951 but played in only twelve games that season before closing his major league career.

AGE	YRS	ML	G	BA	SA	AB	H	2B	3B	HR	HR%	R	RBI	BB	SO	SB
22-25	42-45	4	56	0.211	0.316	152	32	6	2	2	1.3	11	22	6	17	1

RIEBE, HARVEY D. (HANK)   BR TR 5'9" 175 lbs.
Born October 10, 1921, Cleveland, Oh. — Died April 16, 2001, Cleveland, Oh.
Played for Detroit (1942, 1947–49)

Hank Riebe joined the Tigers at the end of the 1942 season and batted .314 in eleven games. When he made his debut on August 26, 1942, he went four for four, including two doubles. He had earlier tried to enlist in the military but was rejected because of bad teeth. He was taken in November of 1942 and reported to Camp Perry, Ohio. He took his basic training at Fort McClellan, Alabama, and was part of the Infantry Replacement Training Center. He was promoted to corporal while at Fort McClellan. He became an infantryman with the 66th Black Panther Division.

Riebe was sent to Europe to help support the war effort. Stationed in England, he was sent on a troop ship across the English Channel to help reinforce the troops under siege at the Battle of the Bulge. On Christmas Eve 1944, while crossing the Channel, his ship was torpedoed. Seven hundred and sixty-four of Riebe's fellow soldiers died in that sinking. Riebe survived nearly an hour in the icy water before he was rescued. He rejoined the 66th in Cherbourg and they were assigned to clear out pockets of Germans around St. Nazaire and Lorient. In the spring of 1945 he was hit in the right shoulder by shrapnel from a German 88. He was able to walk to the aid station but surgery was required because of the wound. When he was discharged from the service in early 1946, he had received two Purple Hearts.

Riebe spent 1946 in the minors at Buffalo and Dallas and most of 1947 at Memphis except for eight games at Detroit. In 1948, while playing only twenty-five games, he spent the year with the Tigers. He closed his major league career in 1949. He had gotten caught up in the numbers game because the Tigers had a number of good catchers during this time and Riebe didn't get to play very much. Hal Newhouser said, "So Harvey never really had a chance to show his ability" (*Autograph Times*, February, 1996). Johnny Lipon said, "Harvey Riebe was a good competitor, a fine handler of pitchers and definitely a winning-type player" (Autograph Times, February, 1996). Riebe commented on his service, "One of the articles mentions my career being cut short because of the service time, but I never really looked at it that way. I'm here today and I'm forever grateful for that." He added, "I played with and against some of the greatest players in the game and I'm very thankful for being part of that era" (Riebe letter 1997). Riebe missed qualifying for a baseball pension by thirty-five days.

AGE	YRS	ML	G	BA	SA	AB	H	2B	3B	HR	HR%	R	RBI	BB	SO	SB
21-23	43-45	4	61	0.212	0.241	137	29	4	0	0	0	2	11	3	18	1

RIKARD, CULLY
BL TR 6' 0"   183 lbs.

Born May 9, 1914, Oxford, Ms. — Died February 25, 2000, Memphis, Tn.
Played for Pittsburgh (1941–42, 1947)

Cully Rikard had a trial with the Pirates in late 1941 and also in 1942. His playing time in 1942 was cut short by a broken wrist. He was drafted into the Air Force in early 1943. He first was at the Army Modification Center in Memphis and then was sent to Camp Shelby, Mississippi, in the spring of 1943. By November 1943, he was with the 58th Training Group, Squadron 133, Kessler Field, Mississippi. He spent 1945 with Fourth Ferrying Group in Memphis where he was able to play baseball.

Rikard was still on the Pirates' defense list in December 1945. He did not play for the Pirates in 1946 but did reappear in 1947. At age thirty-three, he had a good year. He was the number-one backup outfielder and pinch hitter. He batted .287 with ninety-three hits in 324 at-bats. The 1947 season was his last in the majors. He missed being eligible for a pension by one year.

AGE	YRS	ML	G	BA	SA	AB	H	2B	3B	HR	HR%	R	RBI	BB	SO	SB
29-31	43-45	3	153	0.27	0.374	396	107	19	5	4	1	64	37	58	48	1

RIZZO, JOHN C. (JOHNNY)
BR TR 6' 0"   190 lbs.

Born July 30, 1912, Houston, Tx. — Died December 4, 1977, Houston, Tx.
Played for Pittsburgh (1938–40), Cincinnati (1940), Philadelphia (N) (1940–41), and Brooklyn (1942)

Johnny Rizzo was a member of the Columbus, Ohio, team in the American Association, a Cardinal farm team, in 1937. He had a very good year in 1937. He was recalled by the Cardinals and sold to the Pirates in late 1937. Rizzo had a very good year as a rookie with the Pirates in 1938. He batted .301, hit twenty-three home runs, and drove in 111 runs. The next year he fell victim to the sophomore jinx. He had half the RBIs and a fourth of the home runs, and his average fell to .261. After a slow start in 1940, the Pirates traded him to the Reds, who in turn traded him to the Phillies. He ended up having a good year for the Phillies. Two years of part-time duty followed with the Phillies and then with the Dodgers.

Rizzo enlisted in the Navy in March 1943. By June 1943, he had advanced in rating to Specialist (a) 3rd Class at Norman, Oklahoma. He continued to be stationed at Norman during 1943, 1944, and into 1945. In the summer of 1944 he made the all-star team in the Western Victory League of the Southwest representing the base at Norman. In early 1945, he was promoted to chief specialist while stationed at Norman. He was able to play baseball while stationed in Oklahoma. In the spring of 1945 Rizzo was to be shipped from Norman. He was still on the Dodgers' defense list in December 1945. At age thirty-three Rizzo did not return to baseball at the major league level following the war.

AGE	YRS	ML	G	BA	SA	AB	H	2B	3B	HR	HR%	R	RBI	BB	SO	SB
30-32	43-45	5	557	0.27	0.435	1842	497	90	16	61	3.3	268	289	200	197	7

ROBERGE, JOSEPH A.A. (SKIPPY)   BR TR 5' 11" 185 lbs.
Born May 19, 1917, Lowell, Ma. — Died June 7, 1993, Lowell, Ma.
Played for Boston (N) (1941–42, 1946)

Skippy Roberage was a utility infielder who spent the last half of the 1941 season with the Braves. He continued this utility role in 1942. However, his batting average never reached an acceptable level during that time. He batted .216 in 1941 and .215 in 1942. He entered the military before the start of the 1943 season. He was accepted at the Recruit Reception Center at Fort Devens, Massachusetts. By 1945 he was fighting in Germany where he was wounded in action. Roberge remained in Germany into the early winter of 1945. He was still on the Braves' defense list in December 1945 and he rejoined the Braves for the 1946 season. His role remained the same, that of a utility player. He had his best year hitting in 1946, but it was only .231. This was his final year in the majors.

AGE	YRS	ML	G	BA	SA	AB	H	2B	3B	HR	HR%	R	RBI	BB	SO	SB
26-28	43-45	3	177	0.22	0.283	508	112	19	2	3	0.6	35	47	25	49	2

ROCHELLI, LOUIS J. (LOU)   BR TR 6' 1" 175 lbs.
Born January 11, 1919, Staunton, Il. — Died October 23, 1992, Victoria, Tx.
Played for Brooklyn (1944)

Lou Rochelli got into five games as a second baseman in 1944 between the time he was discharged by the Navy and when he went back again. He was in the Iowa Pre-Flight Training Program in July 1944, then was discharged, then made his debut with the Dodgers on August 25, 1944, and then was back in the Navy by January 1945. In January 1945, he was stationed at Great Lakes Naval Training Center as an apprentice seaman. By the summer of 1945, he was back at Iowa where he was able to play baseball. Rochelli did not get another shot in the majors following the war.

AGE	YRS	ML	G	BA	SA	AB	H	2B	3B	HR	HR%	R	RBI	BB	SO	SB
25-27	44-46	1	5	0.176	0.294	17	3	0	1	0	0	0	2	2	6	0

RODGERS, WILLIAM S. (BILL)   BL TL 6' 0" 162 lbs.
Born December 5, 1922, Harrisburg, Pa.
Played for Pittsburgh (1944–45)

Bill Rodgers played in two games at the end of the 1944 season and in one game at the start of the 1945 season. He was listed 4-F early in 1945 but was accepted for service in the spring of 1945. He was drafted by the Army. He said about his service, "[I] was ready to be sent overseas, but at the ship they canceled the orders" (Rodgers letter 1997). He saw no combat and suffered no injuries. He was still listed on the Pirates' defense list in December 1945.

AGE	YRS	ML	G	BA	SA	AB	H	2B	3B	HR	HR%	R	RBI	BB	SO	SB
22	45	2	3	0.4	0.4	5	2	0	0	0	0	1	0	0	1	0

RUSZKOWSKI, HENRY A. (HANK)　　　　　BR TR 6' 0"　190 lbs.
Born November 10, 1925, Cleveland, Oh. — Died May 31, 2000, Cleveland, Oh.
Played for Cleveland (1944–45, 1947)

Hank Ruszkowski was an eighteen-year-old catcher when he made his first appearance in a major league game in 1944. He got into three games that year. In 1945 he was a nineteen-year-old catcher when he was inducted into the Army. He got to play in fourteen games before joining the Army at Fort Dix, New Jersey, on June 9, 1945. He was still on the Indians' defense list in December 1945. He made his last appearance in the major leagues in 1947 when he caught in sixteen games and pinch-hit in seven games.

AGE	YRS	ML	G	BA	SA	AB	H	2B	3B	HR	HR%	R	RBI	BB	SO	SB
19-20	45-46	3	40	0.238	0.369	84	20	2	0	3	3.6	8	10	6	16	0

SANFORD, JOHN H. (JACK)　　　　　BR TR 6' 3"　195 lbs.
Born June 23, 1917, Chatham, Va.
Played for Washington (1940–41, 1946)

Jack Sanford was a first baseman who got his first shot at the majors at the end of the 1940 season when he appeared in thirty-four games. He got into only three games the following year. He was drafted in October 1941. Sanford took his basic training in the Quartermaster Corps at Camp Lee, Virginia, where he was able to play some baseball. Following basic, he attended Officer Candidate School (O.C.S.) at Miami Beach where he was commissioned a second lieutenant in the Air Force in December 1942. In December 1943, he was listed with the 439th Fighter Group, Dale Mabry Field, Tallahassee, Florida, and in June 1944 with the 338th Fighter Group, North Florida. Sanford said, "I never saw active combat though I'll never understand why. I served in Special Services as a physical fitness officer at several bases" (Sanford letter 1997).

Sanford was promoted to first lieutenant, and he didn't suffer any injuries while in service. He did say, "But it hurt being able to play no baseball the last three years of my hitch. I literally started over at age of 28" (Sanford letter 1997). He was discharged in February 1946. Sanford did rejoin the Senators in 1946 but played in only ten games. The 1946 season was his last in the majors.

AGE	YRS	ML	G	BA	SA	AB	H	2B	3B	HR	HR%	R	RBI	BB	SO	SB
25-28	42-45	3	47	0.209	0.288	153	32	4	4	0	0	13	11	9	24	0

SCHALK, LEROY J. (ROY)　　　　　BR TR 5' 10"　168 lbs.
Born November 9, 1908, Chicago, Il. — Died March 11, 1990, Gainesville, Tx.
Played for New York (A) (1932) and Chicago (A) (1944–45)

Roy Schalk got a trial with the Yankees in 1932. He appeared in three games at the close of that season. That would be his only major league appearances for twelve years. In between he would serve his country. He served in the military for at least the 1943 season but was released from service. In 1944 he became a wartime replacement. He was the White Sox regular second baseman for both 1944 and 1945. In 1945 he led the White Sox in RBIs with sixty-five. However, he was released before the start of the 1946 season at age 37. He felt the effect of the returning players. His hitting was not strong, but he was among the league leaders in several fielding categories. Roy Schalk was one of the players who had a major league career because of the war.

AGE	YRS	ML	G	BA	SA	AB	H	2B	3B	HR	HR%	R	RBI	BB	SO	SB
34	43	3	282	0.233	0.281	1112	259	38	5	2	0.2	100	109	79	95	8

SCHMULBACH, HENRY A. (HANK)   BL TR 5' 11" 165 lbs.
Born January 17, 1925, East St. Louis, Il. — Died May 3, 2001, Belleville, Il.
Played for St. Louis (A) (1943)

Hank Schmulbach got into a game on September 27, 1943. He was a pinch runner and scored a run. That was his only major league appearance. Before the start of the 1944 season, he was drafted by the Air Force. He stayed in the Air Force for three years, not getting out until late in 1946. He did not see combat or suffer any injuries while in service, nor did he return to the Browns. About the effect on his career, he said, "I did miss 3 years during a time of my life I needed to hone my skills as a player" (Schmubach letter 1998).

AGE	YRS	ML	G	BA	SA	AB	H	2B	3B	HR	HR%	R	RBI	BB	SO	SB
19-21	44-46	1	1	0	0	0	0	0	0	0	0	1	0	0	0	0

SEARS. KENNETH E. (KEN)   BL TR 6' 1" 200 lbs.
Born July 6, 1917, Streator, Il. — Died July 17, 1968, Bridgeport, Tx.
Played for New York (A) (1943) and St. Louis (A) (1946)

Ken Sears was one of four catchers for the Yankees in 1943. By the end of 1944, all four were in service. Sears was one of the ones who backed up Bill Dickey in 1943. He caught in fifty games and pinch-hit in another ten. He had a reasonable .278 batting average that year. He entered the Navy on November 16, 1943. He was stationed at Bainbridge, Maryland, and helped line up baseball games. However, by spring of 1944, he was stationed on a cruiser in the Pacific. He was a gunner on the cruiser, which took part in the battles of Saipan and Guam. In the fall of 1944 he had been transferred to Honolulu with the rank of Seaman 1-C.

While stationed in Hawaii, Sears got to play baseball. In October 1944 he played for Navy in the Pacific World Series against Army. He continued to be stationed in Hawaii during 1945, playing on a subbase team in the 14th Naval District League and took part in the Navy Little World Series. He was discharged on December 10, 1945. Sears did not rejoin the Yankees following the war. The St. Louis Browns gave him a trial during the 1946 season and he appeared in seven games for the Browns in 1946, his last year in the majors.

AGE	YRS	ML	G	BA	SA	AB	H	2B	3B	HR	HR%	R	RBI	BB	SO	SB
26-27	44-45	2	67	0.282	0.347	202	57	7	0	2	1	23	23	14	18	1

SEPKOWSKI, THEODORE W. (TED)   BL TR 5' 11"   190 lbs.

Born November 9, 1923, Baltimore, Md. — Died March 8, 2002, Severna Park, Md.

Played for Cleveland (1942, 1946–47) and New York (A) (1947)

Ted Sepkowski got a brief shot in September 1942. After a year in the minors in 1943, Sepkowski was drafted by the Coast Guard and spent 1944 and 1945 in service. He spent time on a gun boat as well as having some time to play baseball. He commented on their Coast Guard team, saying, "On our ball club we had such players as Hank Sauer, Sid Gordon and Mickey Witek. We had a terrific team" (Sepkowski letter 1997). Following release from the Coast Guard, Sepkowski rejoined the Indians. He appeared in two games in 1946 and twelve games for the Indians and Yankees in 1947. In eight of the games in 1947, he appeared as a pinch hitter.

AGE	YRS	ML	G	BA	SA	AB	H	2B	3B	HR	HR%	R	RBI	BB	SO	SB
20-21	44-45	3	19	0.231	0.308	26	6	2	0	0	0	3	1	1	4	0

SESSI, WALTER A.   BL TL 6' 3"   225 lbs.

Born July 23, 1918, Finleyville, Pa. — Died April 18, 1998, Mobile, Al.

Played for St. Louis (N) (1941, 1946)

Walter Sessi joined the Cardinals in 1941 at the same time as Stan Musial. Both Sessi and Musial were from Pennsylvania. Finleyville and Donora, their hometowns, were not far apart. Sessi had been called up to the Cardinals from Houston club in the Texas League and Musial from the Rochester team in the International League. However, from that point their careers went in different directions; Musial went to the Hall of Fame, and Sessi appeared in a total of twenty games in his career.

The next year Sessi went into the service and spent four years in the military before being released. He did play some for the Cardinals in 1946 and made a contribution to the pennant. Sessi only had two hits in his career, but one of them was a home run in 1946. Stan Musial said, "He hit an important game-winning pinch homer in the 1946 National League pennant race" (Broeg 1964, 30). All of his fourteen plate appearances were in pinch hitting roles in 1946.

AGE	YRS	ML	G	BA	SA	AB	H	2B	3B	HR	HR%	R	RBI	BB	SO	SB
23-26	42-45	2	20	0.074	0.185	27	2	0	0	1	3.7	4	2	2	6	0

SHOKES, EDWARD C. (EDDIE)   BL TL 6' 0"   170 lbs.

Born January 27, 1920, Charleston, S.C. — Died September 14, 2002, Winchester, Va.

Played for Cincinnati (1941, 1946)

Eddie Shokes got one pinch hitting appearance in 1941. He attended Duke University and was signed by the Reds off the Duke campus. He joined the Reds for a couple of weeks before spending the balance of the season at Indianapolis, Indiana. He spent 1942 in the minors with the Syracuse Chiefs of the International League.

Shokes volunteered for the Navy in November of 1942 and spent some of his training time at Norfolk. He later was transferred to Hawaii where he got to play baseball. He was still on the Reds' defense list in December 1945. He said, "[I] saw no action nor received any injuries to affect my career" (Shokes letter 1998). He rejoined the Reds for the 1946 season, but his hitting was not good. He batted .120 in thirty-one games. He spent the following four years at Syracuse and retired after the 1950 season.

AGE	YRS	ML	G	BA	SA	AB	H	2B	3B	HR	HR%	R	RBI	BB	SO	SB
23-25	43-45	2	32	0.119	0.131	84	10	1	0	0	0	3	5	18	22	1

SHORT, DAVID O. (DAVE)   BL TR 5' 11" 162 lbs.
Born May 11, 1917, Magnolia, Ar. — Died November 22, 1983, Shreveport, La.
Played for Chicago (A) (1940–41)

Dave Short started his major league career in 1940 with three pinch hitting appearances and concluded it with two games in the outfield and one pinch hitting appearance in 1941. He entered the Army early in 1942 and stayed for four years. He was in the Army Aviation Corps and was qualified for a commission because of his college work at Louisiana Tech. He was not able to rejoin the White Sox at age twenty-nine when he was released from the Army.

AGE	YRS	ML	G	BA	SA	AB	H	2B	3B	HR	HR%	R	RBI	BB	SO	SB
24-28	41-45	2	7	0.091	0.091	11	1	0	0	0	0	1	0	3	3	0

SMITH, VINCENT A. (VINNIE)   BR TR 6' 1" 176 lbs.
Born December 7, 1915, Richmond, Va. — Died December 14, 1979, Virginia Beach, Va.
Played for Pittsburgh (1941, 1946)

Vinnie Smith joined the Pirates in 1941 and played in nine games. He then enlisted in the Navy on January 24, 1942. He spent his early time in the Navy at Norfolk. He played on Norfolk's baseball team in 1942 and on July 7, 1942, played for a service all-start team that played against an American League All-Star team to raise money for war relief. They raised $193,000. He stayed at Norfolk until early 1944 when he was transferred to Shoemaker Naval Receiving Barracks in California.

By the fall of 1944, Smith was sent to Hawaii. He got there in time to take part in the Army/ Navy Pacific World Series in October 1944. Following the "Series," the Navy team went to the Islands of the South Pacific to entertain the troops. Smith then spent time on Johnston Island, Kwajilein, Eniwetok, Peleliu, Tinian, Saipan, Guam, Roi-Namur, and Ulithi. In the fall of 1945, he played in an all-star game between the Fifth and Third Fleets. He was still listed on the Pirates' defense list in December 1945.

Smith rejoined the Pirates for the 1946 season; however, he spent most of that season on the disabled list with a knee injury. He also missed all of the 1947 season on the disabled list. After two years of managing at the minor league level, Smith turned to umpiring. After a stint as an umpire in the minor leagues he returned to the majors as an umpire in 1957 and stayed until

got to play some baseball. He played on the 313th Flyers Team and played in an all-star game on August 26, 1945. He was still listed on the Yankees' defense list in December 1945. He did return in time for the 1946 season. However, because of the injured hand and being gone for four years, Sturm was sent to the Yankee minor league team in Kansas City. At Kansas City, he suffered a broken wrist and was out for the entire season. With that injury, his playing career was over. The Yankees sent Sturm out as a scout, and he later became a manager in their farm system. In 1949 he was the manager at Joplin, Missouri, when Mickey Mantle got his start. Sturm had made the Yankees team in his rookie year in 1941. The combination of the four years absence and the hand injury he suffered at Jefferson Barracks ended any chance he had to continue that baseball career.

AGE	YRS	ML	G	BA	SA	AB	H	2B	3B	HR	HR%	R	RBI	BB	SO	SB
26-29	42-45	1	124	0.239	0.3	524	125	17	3	3	0.6	58	36	37	50	3

TATUM, V. T. (TOMMY)   BR TR 6' 0" 185 lbs.
Born July 16, 1919, Decatur, Tx. — Died November 7, 1989, Oklahoma City, Ok.
Played for Brooklyn (1941, 1947) and Cincinnati (1947)

Tommy Tatum got a brief trial with the National League champion Brooklyn Dodgers in 1941. Before the start of the 1942 season, he entered the military and spent the next four years in service. Following the war, he did return to the major leagues in 1947. In that year, after four games with the Dodgers, he was traded to the Reds and played in sixty-nine games for them. The 1947 season closed out his career. Author Frederick Turner said, "Tommy Tatum, a fleet Dodger outfield prospect before the war, suffered a serious arm injury in the service and was never the same player" (Turner 1996, 84).

AGE	YRS	ML	G	BA	SA	AB	H	2B	3B	HR	HR%	R	RBI	BB	SO	SB
22-25	42-45	2	81	0.258	0.325	194	50	6	2	1	0.5	20	17	17	20	7

TURNER, THOMAS R. (TOM)   BR TR 6' 0" 215 lbs.
Born September 8, 1916, Custer, Ok. — Died May 14, 1986, Kennewick, Wa.
Played for Chicago (A) (1940–44) and St. Louis (A) (1944)

Tom Turner spent four-and-one-half years as a backup catcher for the Chicago White Sox. He spent the second half of the 1944 season with the St. Louis Browns after the Browns purchased him on July 31, 1944, to shore up their injured catching corps. Turner played well for them until he also was injured by a foul tip at Fenway Park, Boston, on August 13. He batted .320 for the Browns during the time he played for them. He got into the 1944 World Series as a pinch hitter for Tex Shirley in the ninth inning of game four. He popped out to short center.

Turner had been classified as 4-F. However, in 1945 he entered the military. He was stationed for a time at Camp Roberts, California. He was still on Browns' defense list in December 1945. Turner did not return to the majors following the war. He was known for being one of the better "bench jockeys" in baseball.

AGE	YRS	ML	G	BA	SA	AB	H	2B	3B	HR	R%	R	RBI	BB	SO	SB
28	45	5	233	0.237	0.32	696	165	29	4	7	1	63	63	51	84	4

WALKER, HARVEY W. (HUB)   BL TR 5' 10"   175 lbs.

Born August 17, 1906, Gulfport, Ms. — Died November 26, 1982, San Jose, Ca.

Played for Detroit (1931, 1935, 1945) and Cincinnati (1936–37)

Hub Walker made his debut with the Tigers on April 15, 1931, at age twenty-four. In 1935, with the Tigers and in 1936 and 1937 with the Reds, Walker was a backup outfielder. He then entered the Navy shortly after the Japanese bombing of Pearl Harbor. By December 1942, he had completed his training and was a petty officer 1st class gunnery mate stationed at Great Lakes. By the summer of 1943, he risen to the rank of chief petty officer.

In the spring of 1944, Walker was stationed at the Shoemaker Naval Receiving Barracks in California. He was able to play baseball while stationed in California. He was transferred to the Pacific, where he suffered a knee injury in the line of duty that put him in the hospital. He was sent back to the States to a Naval hospital in San Diego. The knee required an operation and did not respond well to treatment. Walker was discharged by the Navy because of the knee injury in the summer of 1945. It was not certain if he would be able to play baseball again.

In the summer of 1945, the Tigers were locked in a pennant drive with the Senators, Browns, and Yankees. So Walker, after an absence of seven years, which included almost four years of military service, returned to the Tigers at age thirty-nine. He served as a pinch hitter and played a few games in the outfield. He should not have been eligible for the World Series, but the baseball commissioner made an exception for him. He appeared in two games in the 1945 World Series and got a double and scored a run in two at-bats.

AGE	YRS	ML	G	BA	SA	AB	H	2B	3B	HR	R%	R	RBI	BB	SO	SB
36-38	42-45	5	297	0.263	0.353	779	205	43	6	5	0.6	17	60	104	89	26

WALLAESA, JOHN (JACK)   BB TR 6' 3"   191 lbs.

Born August 31, 1919, Easton, Pa. — Died December 27, 1986, Easton, Pa.

Played for Philadelphia (A) (1940, 1942, 1946) and Chicago (A) (1947–48)

Jack Wallaesa had a brief trial in 1940 with the A's and then returned to them in 1942 as a backup shortstop. He entered the Army in June 1942 and saw plenty of combat. He went to Italy during the war and was stationed at Anzio. He was a stevedore and helped unload the ships. He spent forty-three days during the time unloading ammunition. He said of the experience, "I don't think any pitcher will ever scare me again after that experience." He added, "Dozens of times I got down on my knees and prayed as I saw ships blown up around me and my buddies tossed into the water" (Goldstein 1980, 253).

Wallaesa was discharged by the Army on November 27, 1945, at Indiantown Gap, Pennsylvania. He split time during the 1946 season between the A's and Toronto in the International League. The A's sold him to the White Sox on December 23, 1946. He closed out his career with the White Sox in 1947 and 1948. Wallaesa always struggled with the bat at the major league level. In his five years in the big leagues, he batted over .200 only one time. Because of that, he spent his time as a backup infielder.

AGE	YRS	ML	G	BA	SA	AB	H	2B	3B	HR	R%	R	RBI	BB	SO	SB
23-25	42-45	5	219	0.205	0.325	584	120	17	4	15	2.6	6	61	39	138	3

WELAJ, JOHN L. (JOHNNY)   BR TR 6' 0"   164 lbs.

Born May 27, 1914, Moss Creek, Pa. — Died September 13, 2003, Arlington, Tx.

Played for Washington (1939–41) and Philadelphia (A) (1943)

Johnny Welaj was a backup outfielder during his four-year major league career. He was known for being a very good base runner. However, his hitting was not as good. During his career, his best batting average was .274 during his rookie year. In spite of that, he made several pinch hitting appearances during his career.

Welaj was taken into service during the 1943 season and spent two years in the Army. In the spring of 1945, he was stationed in the Philippines as a corporal in the infantry. He was able to play some baseball during that summer and fall for the Fifth Replacement Depot Team. By December 1945, he had risen to the rank of sergeant and was in the training section of the 5th Replacement Depot near Manila. He did not return to the majors following his release from the Army.

AGE	YRS	ML	G	BA	SA	AB	H	2B	3B	HR	HR%	R	RBI	BB	SO	SB
29-31	43-45	4	293	0.25	0.323	793	198	40	3	4	0.5	115	74	53	73	36

WELLS, LEO D.   BR TR 5' 10"   180 lbs.

Born July 18, 1917, Kansas City, Ks.

Played for Chicago (A) (1942, 1946)

Leo Wells got in one partial year as a left side infielder and pinch hitter with the White Sox in 1942 before entering the military. He then spent the next three years in the Coast Guard. In January 1944, he was stationed at Alameda, California. He was scheduled to be transferred to New London, Connecticut, to go to officer school. He was still listed on the White Sox defense list in December 1945. He did rejoin the White Sox for the 1946 season. However, his hitting continued to be a problem. He batted only .189 in forty-five games that year. The 1946 season was his final in the major leagues.

AGE	YRS	ML	G	BA	SA	AB	H	2B	3B	HR	HR%	R	RBI	BB	SO	SB
25-27	43-45	2	80	0.19	0.265	189	36	6	1	2	1.1	19	15	16	39	4

WOOD, JOSEPH P. (JOE)   BR TR 5' 9"   160 lbs.

Born October 3, 1919, Houston, Tx. — Died March 25, 1985, Houston, Tx.

Played for Detroit (1943)

Joe Wood arrived on the major league scene on May 2, 1943, and proceeded to bat .323 as a backup infielder for the Tigers. He played in sixty games at second, third, and pinch hitting. He entered the Navy before the start of the 1944 season. During the spring of 1945, he was stationed at San Diego and was able to play some baseball. He was still on the Tigers' defense list in December 1945. He did not return to the major leagues following the war.

AGE	YRS	ML	G	BA	SA	AB	H	2B	3B	HR	HR%	R	RBI	BB	SO	SB
24-25	44-45	1	60	0.323	0.415	164	53	4	4	1	0.6	22	17	6	13	2

YANKOWSKI, GEORGE E.   BR TR 6' 0"   180 lbs.
Born November 19, 1922, Cambridge, Ma.
Played for Philadelphia (A) (1942) and Chicago (A) (1949)

George Yankowski's playing time was limited to six games in 1942 and twelve games in 1949.
Brought up in the late summer of 1942, he enlisted in the Army in October 1942. He served as
an aviation cadet and in the infantry. He was with the Third Army, 87th Infantry Division. They
went into combat in the Saar Region of Germany at the beginning of December 1944. During
the Battle of the Bulge, they moved north to help turn the Germans. They stayed in combat
until the end of the war. Yankowski earned a Bronze Star for his effort with the 87th. He was
not wounded but did suffer a back injury and hepatitis. He was hospitalized from October
1945 to January 1946.

When he was released by the Army, Yankowski reported to the A's training camp. He said, "My
spring training experience was physically very painful because of a back injury" (Yankowski
letter 1997). He was released by the A's. However, in 1948 the White Sox signed him to a
contract, and he returned to the majors one more time in 1949. He was not eligible for a
baseball pension; his service time was not counted because he was not under contract on a
specific date. Yankowski said, "Who is to say whether the three years in the Army affected my
baseball career. One thing is for sure: it didn't help my development as a baseball player to be
away from the game for three years during my early 20s" (Yankowski letter 1997).

AGE	YRS	ML	G	BA	SA	AB	H	2B	3B	HR	HR%	R	RBI	BB	SO	SB
20-23	43-46	2	18	0.161	0.226	31	5	2	0	0	0	0	4	0	4	0

YORK, ANTHONY B. (TONY)   BR TR 5' 10"   165 lbs.
Born November 27, 1912, Irene, Tx. — Died April 18, 1970, Hillsboro, Tx.
Played for Chicago (N) (1944)

Tony York played for the Chicago Cubs during his rookie season in 1944. He was a wartime
backup infielder. However, he spent his military service time listed on the Braves' defense
list. He was thirty-one years old when he broke into the majors. In the spring of 1945, he was
stationed at Fort Lewis, Washington. He was able to play some baseball during that time. He
was still listed on the Braves' defense list in December 1945. He did not return to the majors
following the war.

AGE	YRS	ML	G	BA	SA	AB	H	2B	3B	HR	R%	R	RBI	BB	SO	SB
32	45	1	28	0.235	0.247	85	20	1	0	0	0	4	7	4	11	0

ZIENTARA, BENEDICT J. (BENNY)   BR TR 5' 9"   165 lbs.
Born February 14, 1920, Chicago, Il. — Died April 16, 1985, Lake Elsinore, Ca.
Played for Cincinnati (1941, 1946-48)

Benny Zientara joined the Reds on September 11, 1941, after a good season at Indianapolis of
the American Association. He entered the Army before the 1942 season. He spent 1943 and

1944 stationed at Fort Benning, Georgia, where he played on and managed the baseball team. In 1945 he was sent to Europe. While stationed there he got to play baseball for the 71st Division both in Austria and Germany. He helped with a baseball school for German youths in the fall of 1945.

Zientara was still listed on the Reds' defense list in December 1945. He did return to the Reds for the 1946 season. He batted .289 as a backup second and third baseman that year. In 1947 he won the regular second base job. His hitting remained acceptable at .258. However, in 1948 his batting dropped to .187 and he lost the starting assignment. The 1948 season was his last in the majors.

AGE	YRS	ML	G	BA	SA	AB	H	2B	3B	HR	HR%	R	RBI	BB	SO	SB
22-25	42-45	4	278	0.254	0.304	906	230	29	5	2	0.2	106	49	50	48	5

CHAPTER 7

The pitchers who played for five years or fewer are covered in this chapter. In some cases, these pitchers filled in when the regular pitchers went to war and then, after a while, were themselves sent to spend their time in military service. Some of the pitchers listed here were on their way to good careers when they received the call from Uncle Sam. Several of them suffered career-ending arm injuries while in service. The pitching arm is very fragile. When pitchers had improper training or were not being allowed to warm up properly, they hurt their arms so they could not pitch again or, if they could, were ineffective after returning from service. Then, either because of age, inactivity, or injury, they were not able to pick up where they left off. The zip was gone off their fastball. Many were kids just out of high school, and they had their one shot and were done. Some got their chance because of the war and others had their chance taken away.

Because the careers of these players were so short, a prediction of what might have happened to their numbers if they had not gone to service was not calculated.

ALBOSTA, EDWARD J. (ED)   BR TR 6' 1"   175 lbs.
Born October 27, 1918, Saginaw, Mi. — Died January 3, 2003, Saginaw, Mi.
Played for Brooklyn (1941) and Pittsburgh (1946)

Ed Albosta started two games for the Dodgers when he came up to the major leagues in September 1941. After another season in the minors and a transfer to the Pirates organization, he was drafted into the Army in December 1942. He spent the early part of 1943 at Camp Claiborne, Louisiana. By the summer of 1944, he was stationed at Camp Livingston, Louisiana. He stayed there for the rest of 1944 and the first part of 1945 and achieved the rank of sergeant during that time.

Albosta was out of the Army by November 1945 and back on the Pirates' active roster in December 1945. He was able to make the Pirates team in 1946. He got six starts in his seventeen appearances that year. He started his career with a record of no wins and two losses with the Dodgers in 1941, and he concluded his career with six more losses, still without a win, when he pitched for the Pirates in 1946.

AGE	YRS	ML	W	L	PCT	ERA	G	GS	CG	IP	H	BB	SO	SHO	SV
24-26	43-45	2	0	8	0.000	6.15	19	8	0	53	52	43	24	0	0

ALDERSON, DALE L.   BR TR 5' 10"   190 lbs.
Born March 8, 1918, Belden, Ne. — Died February 12, 1982, Garden Grove, Ca.
Played for Chicago (N) (1943-44)

Dale Alderson had trials with the Cubs in both 1943 and 1944. Neither one proved to be successful. He got three starts in the sixteen games in which he appeared in the two years. He gave up fifty-two hits in 35 $^2/_3$ innings. Following the 1944 season, Alderson was taken into the military. He spent that season in service to his country. He had been released by

December 1945 and was on the Cubs' active roster. Even though he was on the December 1945 roster, he did not make the club for the 1946 season. In fact, he did not play in the majors following his return from the war.

AGE	YRS	ML	W	L	PCT	ERA	G	GS	CG	IP	H	BB	SO	SHO	SV
26-27	44-45	2	0	1	0.000	6.56	16	3	0	36	52	12	11	0	0

ANDERSON, ARNOLD R. (RED)   BR TR 6' 3"   210 lbs.
Born June 19, 1912, Lawton, Ia. — Died August 7, 1972, Sioux City, Ia
Played for Washington (1937, 1940–41)

Red Anderson got a trial with the Senators in 1937 after a great year at Sioux Falls in the Nebraska State League and another in 1940 after a year at Springfield, Massachusetts, in the Eastern League. In 1941 he spent the year with the Senators and was mostly used as a relief pitcher. He was with the Senators on opening day 1941 and caught President Roosevelt's season-opening pitch. He was classified 1-A early in 1942, but he appealed the classification because of his dependents. He was not successful and was taken into the Navy before the 1942 season. There is conflicting information regarding the amount of time he spent in the military. One reference only gives him credit for the 1942 season and another has him playing on a Navy team in Honolulu in 1944. In either case, he was not able to rejoin the Senators at the major league level following his release from the service.

AGE	YRS	ML	W	L	PCT	ERA	G	GS	CG	IP	H	BB	SO	SHO	SV
30	42	3	5	8	0.385	4.35	36	9	3	137	150	69	40	0	0

BESSE, HERMAN A.   BL TL 6' 2"   190 lbs.
Born August 16, 1911, St. Louis, Mo. — Died August 13, 1972, Los Angeles, Ca.
Played for Philadelphia (A) (1940–43, 1946)

Herman Besse played in the majors for five different years. His success was limited. He won five games and lost fifteen during his career. In 1942 he pitched in thirty games, by far the season with the most appearances. However, during the 133 innings, he gave up 163 hits and 91 earned runs. He appeared in only five games in 1943 even though the A's finished in last place. He went into the military before the 1944 season. In 1944 he was stationed at Page Field and was able to play some baseball there. In 1945 he had been transferred to Sherman Field, Texas, where he pitched for and managed the baseball team. He was still on the A's defense list in December 1945. He did return to the A's for a short while in 1946. He appeared in seven games that season, his last in the major leagues.

AGE	YRS	ML	W	L	PCT	ERA	G	GS	CG	IP	H	BB	SO	SHO	SV
32-33	44-45	5	5	15	0.250	6.97	65	25	5	243	298	128	118	0	2

BEVIL, LOUIS E. (LOU)   BB TR 5' 11" 190 lbs.
Born November 27, 1922, Nelson, Il. — Died February 1, 1973, Dixon, Il.
Played for Washington (1942)

Lou Bevil got into four games in 1942 after his debut on September 2. He had one start and
lost the game. At age nineteen, he had control problems. He walked eleven batters in the 9 $^2/_3$
innings he pitched in addition to giving up nine hits. He went into the military after the 1942
season. In the spring of 1943 he was stationed at Camp Beals, California. He did not return to
the majors following his release from the service.

AGE	YRS	ML	W	L	PCT	ERA	G	GS	CG	IP	H	BB	SO	SHO	SV
20-22	43-45	1	0	1	0.000	6.52	4	1	0	10	9	11	2	0	0

BISCAN, FRANK S.   BL TL 5' 11" 190 lbs.
Born March 13, 1920, Mt. Olive, Il. — Died May 22, 1959, St. Louis, Mo.
Played for St. Louis (A) (1942, 1946, 1948)

Frank Biscan pitched in eleven games in 1942 before joining the Navy in June. He had
good success. His earned run average for that year was 2.33. He allowed only thirteen hits
and seven earned runs in twenty-seven innings he pitched. Early in his military service, he
was stationed at Great Lakes, and then in the fall of 1943, he was transferred to Bainbridge,
Maryland, for further training at the physical instruction school. He was a member of their
baseball team while stationed at Great Lakes in 1943.

By the summer of 1944, Biscan had been transferred to the Pacific. He was stationed on
Guadalcanal during the summer of 1944 because he was interviewed by a sports announcer
during that period. He was still stationed on an island in the Pacific during the winter of 1944.
He was discharged by the Navy in December 1945.

Biscan returned to the Browns in 1946 but did not have the kind of success that he had
enjoyed in 1942. His earned run average ballooned to 5.16 in the sixteen games in which he
pitched. Then after a year's absence from the majors, he came back in 1948. He pitched in
most of his games during that year—forty-seven games, mostly in relief. However, again he had
trouble getting people out. In 98 $^2/_3$ innings, he gave up 129 hits and 71 walks. This was his
final season in the majors. It's hard to say that the war caused his lack of success. However, it
is easy to see the difference between his performance before his service in the Navy and his
performance following his return.

AGE	YRS	ML	W	L	PCT	ERA	G	GS	CG	IP	H	BB	SO	SHO	SV
22-25	42-45	3	7	9	0.438	5.28	74	4	1	148	170	104	64	0	4

BITHORN, HIRAM G. (HI)   BR TR 6' 1" 200 lbs.
Born March 18, 1916, Santurce, Puerto Rico — Died January 1, 1952, El Mante, Mexico
Played for Chicago (N) (1942–43, 1946) and Chicago (A) (1947)

Hi Bithorn was the Cubs' ace pitcher when he was inducted into the service. He had come to
the Cubs in 1942 after a good year at Hollywood of the Pacific Coast League in 1941. In 1942
he was both a starter and reliever. He pitched in thirty-eight games and 171 innings. In 1943
he became the leader of the staff. He started thirty games (plus nine in relief), completed
nineteen, pitched 249 innings, and led the National League in shutouts with seven. During
that year he had an earned run average of 2.60.

Bithorn was inducted into the Navy on November 26, 1943. He was one of the first major
league players to be born in Puerto Rico and was inducted into the Navy at San Juan, Puerto
Rico. He spent his time in service stationed at the Naval Air Station in San Juan. He was
released on September 1, 1945. He was back with the Cubs in time for the 1945 World Series
but did not play in the Series. The Cubs were counting on him for the 1946 season, but his
weight had gone up to 225 pounds, and he seemed to have lost his edge. He served mostly as
a relief pitcher. However, he did so with mixed success.

In 1947 the Cubs sold Bithorn to the Pirates, who released him in spring training. He
signed on with the White Sox and pitched in two games before a sore arm closed out his
major league career. He attempted a comeback in the Mexican League. On New Year's Day
1952, Bithorn was shot to death by a Mexican policeman at El Mante, Mexico. There were
discrepancies in the policeman's story on why Bithorn was there, what he was doing, and
how the shooting took place. But the outcome was the same: Bithorn was dead. Bithorn
had gone into the Navy in 1943 as the ace of the Cubs staff, leading the National League in
shutouts, and he came out as an overweight reliever who got a sore arm that ended his career.
It is clear that his service in the Navy cost him what might have been a good baseball career.

AGE	YRS	ML	W	L	PCT	ERA	G	GS	CG	IP	H	BB	SO	SHO	SV
28-29	44-45	4	34	31	0.523	3.16	105	53	30	510	516	171	185	8	5

BOWLES, CHARLES J. (CHARLIE)   BR TR 6' 3" 180 lbs.
Born March 15, 1917, Norwood, Ma.—Died December 23, 2004, Hickory, N.C.
Played for Philadelphia (A) (1943, 1945)

Charlie Bowles got two starts in the fall of 1943 after joining the A's on September 25, 1943.
He won one and lost one that fall, pitching two complete games. He was drafted into the
Army Air Corps that year. He worked with B-29s but didn't see any combat or suffer any
war-related injuries. He was, however, released from the Army because of a trick knee. This
occurred in the summer of 1945, and he rejoined the A's during that season. He got four starts
in eight games but did not have as much success as he did in 1943. He was not able to sustain
his position with the A's for the 1946 season.

AGE	YRS	ML	W	L	PCT	ERA	G	GS	CG	IP	H	BB	SO	SHO	SV
26-28	43-45	2	1	4	0.200	4.38	10	6	3	51	52	27	17	0	0

BRANCH, NORMAN D. (NORM)   BR TR 6' 3" 200 lbs.
Born March 22, 1915, Spokane, Wa. — Died November 21, 1971, Novasota, Tx.
Played for New York (A) (1941–42)

Norm Branch joined the Yankees in 1941 and became one of the main relievers with the team. He pitched in twenty-seven games, with five wins and two saves and a 2.87 earned run average. He was with the Yankees in 1942 when he was taken into the Coast Guard. In the fall of 1943, he was stationed at Groton, Connecticut. In 1945 he had moved on to New London, Connecticut. While he was stationed at New London, he was able to play some baseball on the base team. He was not able to rejoin the Yankees after his release from the service.

AGE	YRS	ML	W	L	PCT	ERA	G	GS	CG	IP	H	BB	SO	SHO	SV
27-30	42-45	2	5	2	0.714	3.73	37	0	0	63	55	42	41	0	4

BRANDT, WILLIAM G. (BILL)   BR TR 5' 8" 170 lbs.
Born March 21, 1915, Aurora, In. — Died May 16, 1968, Fort Wayne, In.
Played for Pittsburgh (1941–43)

Bill Brandt had trials with the Pirates in 1941 and 1942 before staying with the team in 1943. He was used mainly in relief. He pitched in twenty-nine games that year, and he won four games with an earned run average of 3.14. He went into the Navy after the 1943 season. He took his training at the Great Lakes Naval Station. He was able to play baseball for the Great Lakes team during 1944. By January 1945, he had been transferred to a base located on the site of the Tanforan Race Track in California. He was still on the Pirates' defense list in December 1945. He was not able to return to the major leagues following his service in the Navy.

AGE	YRS	ML	W	L	PCT	ERA	G	GS	CG	IP	H	BB	SO	SHO	SV
29-30	44-45	3	5	3	0.625	3.57	34	7	1	81	85	27	21	0	0

BROWN, NORMAN (NORM)   BB TR 6' 3" 180 lbs.
Born February 1, 1919, Evergreen, N.C. — Died May 31, 1995, Bennettsville, S.C.
Played for Philadelphia (A) (1943, 1946)

Norm Brown pitched in one game, which he started, when he made his debut with the A's on October 3, 1943. He went seven innings, allowed five hits, no walks, and no earned runs, although he did not get the decision. He then spent the next two years in the service for his country. He was still listed on the A's defense list in December 1945. He did rejoin the A's for part of the 1946 season. He pitched four games in relief that season. This time he allowed five earned runs and six walks in addition to eight hits in seven innings. This was the last season Brown would pitch on the major league level.

AGE	YRS	ML	W	L	PCT	ERA	G	GS	CG	IP	H	BB	SO	SHO	SV
25-26	44-45	2	0	1	0.000	3.14	5	1	0	14	13	6	4	0	0

BRUNER, WALTER R. (ROY)   BR TR 6' 0"   165 lbs.

Born February 10, 1917, Cecilia, Ky. — Died November 30, 1986, St. Matthews, Ky.

Played for Philadelphia (N) (1939–41)

Roy Bruner had a four-game trial in 1939 and a two-game chance in 1940 before staying with the Phillies in 1941. However, his opportunity was short as he entered the Army Air Force during the 1941 season. He got into thirteen games as a relief pitcher that year before he entered the service. By the summer of 1944, he was serving as a bombardier in the Army Air Force in the European war theater. He had achieved the rank of lieutenant. He returned to the States from Europe in the late summer of 1945 but was not able to rejoin the Phillies after he was released from service.

AGE	YRS	ML	W	L	PCT	ERA	G	GS	CG	IP	H	BB	SO	SHO	SV
24-28	41-45	3	0	7	0.000	5.74	19	5	2	63	80	44	28	0	0

BUTLAND, WILBURN R. (BILL)   BR TR 6' 5"   185 lbs.

Born March 22, 1918, Terre Haute, In. — Died September 19, 1997, Terre Haute, In.

Played for Boston (A) (1940, 1942, 1946–47)

Bill Butland pitched in three games in 1940. However, in 1942 he made the Red Sox team and stayed with them the entire year. He was used both as a starter and reliever. He pitched 111 innings as he started ten games and relieved in thirteen. He won seven and lost one as the Red Sox finished second to the Yankees, nine games out.

Butland entered the Army on December 11, 1942, at Evansville, Indiana. In January 1943, he completed his first training and was stationed at Camp Gordon, Georgia, in the field artillery. During 1943 he was transferred to Fort Sill, Oklahoma. By 1945 he was stationed in the Pacific. Butland was released by the Army in January 1946. He rejoined the American League champion Red Sox for the 1946 season. However, he lasted only sixteen innings while giving up twenty-three hits and thirteen walks. His earned run average was 11.02 that year. He got into one more game in 1947 before he closed out his major league career. Following the war, he was not able to duplicate the success he had before going into the Army.

AGE	YRS	ML	W	L	PCT	ERA	G	GS	CG	IP	H	BB	SO	SHO	SV
25-27	43-45	4	9	3	0.750	3.88	32	15	7	151	138	56	62	2	1

CALIGIURI, FREDERICK J. (FRED)   BR TR 6' 0"   190 lbs.

Born October 22, 1918, West Hickory, Pa.

Played for Philadelphia (A) (1941–42)

Fred Caligiuri joined the A's on September 3, 1941. He pitched in five games that year, including four complete games. He won two and lost two with an earned run average of 2.93. On September 28, 1941, he started the second game of a doubleheader against the Red Sox. That was the game that Ted Williams was trying to keep his average for the year over .400. Caligiuri allowed the Red Sox only six hits that day. However, two of the six were by Ted

Williams as he ended the season with an average of .406. Caligiuri struggled during the 1942 season. He played in thirteen games in 1942 and his earned run average ballooned to 6.38 as he lost three and won none. He went into the military after the 1942 season and spent the next four years in service. He also missed the 1946 season. He was not able to return to play at the major league level following his service in the military.

AGE	YRS	ML	W	L	PCT	ERA	G	GS	CG	IP	H	BB	SO	SHO	SV
24-27	43-46	2	2	5	0.286	4.52	18	7	4	80	90	32	27	0	1

CARPENTER, ROBERT L. (BOB)   BR TR 6' 3" 195 lbs.
Born December 12, 1917, Chicago, Il.
Played for New York (N) (1940-42, 1946-47) and Chicago (N) (1947)

Bob Carpenter earned a trial with the Giants at the end of the 1940 season. He took that trial and turned it into a regular spot in the starting rotation for the next two years. He won eleven games in each of those two years. Following the 1942 season, Carpenter entered the military. He was drafted in January 1943. He had been classified 1-B the previous year because of defective eyesight, but the Army took him anyway. Carpenter said, "I served in the US Medical Corp over three years" (Carpenter letter 1998).

In the summer of 1944, Carpenter had achieved the rank of sergeant and was stationed at Camp Grant, Illinois. *The Sporting News* reported in May 17, 1945, that he was pitching for the Norfolk Naval Air Station Flyers. He remained in the military through 1945. He was discharged in February 1946 and left immediately for spring training after his release. However, his return did not last long. He injured his throwing arm shortly after returning to the Giants, and his career was basically over. He stayed on the major league scene for two more years but only won one game in the two years. Carpenter commented that he did not receive any injuries during the war, but he also said, "However, over three years in not being in active baseball cannot but affect one's physical status" (Carpenter letter 1998). It did affect his career. The late release from the Army and the hurried effort to rejoin his team could both have been the cause of the arm injury that ended his career. Carpenter proved there is life after baseball. He became involved in the grain business and spent many years as a member of the Board of Trade in Chicago.

AGE	YRS	ML	W	L	PCT	ERA	G	GS	CG	IP	H	BB	SO	SHO	SV
25-27	43-45	5	25	20	0.556	3.60	80	54	23	400	411	132	134	4	2

CENTER, MARVIN E. (PETE)   BR TR 6' 4" 190 lbs.
Born April 22, 1912, Hazel Green, Ky.
Played for Cleveland (1942-43, 1945-46)

Pete Center came to the Indians in the fall of 1942. He spent the next year, 1943, with the Indians as a relief pitcher. He was drafted by the Army Air Corp before the start of the 1944 season. In April 1944, he was stationed at Daniel Field, Georgia. While Center said that he did not see combat and did not suffer any injuries, he was released by the Army on a medical discharge. The discharge came before the start of the 1945 season. He rejoined the Indians for the 1945 season. He continued to pitch mainly in relief, although he did start eight games during that season. He closed his major league career out in 1946 pitching twenty-one more games in relief.

AGE	YRS	ML	W	L	PCT	ERA	G	GS	CG	IP	H	BB	SO	SHO	SV
31-32	43-44	4	7	7	0.500	4.10	77	9	2	160	154	70	50	0	3

CIOLA, LOUIS A. (LOU)   BR TR 5' 9"   165 lbs.
Born September 6, 1922, Norfolk, Va. — Died October 18, 1981, Austin, Mn.
Played for Philadelphia (A) (1943)

Lou Ciola came up with the A's in July of 1943. He got three starts in the twelve games he pitched during that time. Of those three starts he pitched two complete games, winning one and losing two. He entered the Navy before the start of the 1944 season. He spent the spring and early summer of 1944 at Bainbridge, Maryland. He was able to play some baseball while stationed at Bainbridge. In July 1944, he was transferred to Norfolk Air Station. He played for their team during the rest of the summer of 1944. Early in 1945 he was sent to Hawaii and was also able to play ball there. He was still listed on the A's defense list in December 1945. He also missed the 1946 season because he was still serving in the Navy. Ciola was not able to return to baseball at the major league level following his release from service.

AGE	YRS	ML	W	L	PCT	ERA	G	GS	CG	IP	H	BB	SO	SHO	SV
21-23	44-46	1	1	3	0.250	5.56	12	3	2	44	48	22	7	0	0

CLEMENSEN, WILLIAM M. (BILL)   BR TR 6' 1"   193 lbs.
Born June 20, 1919, New Brunswick, N.J. — Died February 18, 1994, Alta, Ca.
Played for Pittsburgh (1939, 1941, 1946)

Bill Clemenson appeared in twelve games in 1939 and two games in 1941. He had been classified as 1-B because of an automobile accident that injured his left arm. However, he was taken into the Army before the start of the 1942 season. By December 1942, he had been promoted to the rank of sergeant. During the summer of 1944, he was stationed at Davis-Monthan Field, Tucson, Arizona. He continued to be located there during 1945. He was able to pitch for them during those two years. He was still listed on the Pirates' defense list in December 1945. He did rejoin the Pirates in 1946 for one game, which closed out his major league career. In his last game, he went two innings, struck out two batters, and allowed no hits or runs.

AGE	YRS	ML	W	L	PCT	ERA	G	GS	CG	IP	H	BB	SO	SHO	SV
23-26	42-45	3	1	1	0.500	5.57	15	2	1	42	39	27	19	0	0

CLYDE, THOMAS K. (TOM)   BR TR 6' 3"   195 lbs.
Born August 17, 1923, Wachapreague, Va.
Played for Philadelphia (A) (1943)

Tom Clyde was nineteen years old when he made his first appearance with the Philadelphia A's on May 31, 1943. He appeared in four games that year for a total of six innings. He gave up seven hits and eight runs, six of them earned during his six innings. He went into the military before the start of the 1944 season and stayed in service through the 1946 season. He was not able to return to pitching with a major league team following his return from the military.

AGE	YRS	ML	W	L	PCT	ERA	G	GS	CG	IP	H	BB	SO	SHO	SV
20-22	44-46	1	0	0	0.000	9.00	4	0	0	6	7	4	0	0	0

CONGER, RICHARD (DICK)   BR TR 6' 0"   185 lbs.
Born April 3, 1921, Los Angeles, Ca. — Died February 16, 1970, Los Angeles, Ca.
Played for Detroit (1940), Pittsburgh (1941–42) and Philadelphia (N) (1943)

Dick Conger pitched in two games in 1940, two games in 1941, and two games in 1942. As the pitching shortage took effect because of the war, he became a spot starter for the Phillies in 1943. He was not very successful, winning two games and losing seven with an earned run average of 6.09. Following the 1943 season, he went into military service. He stayed in the military during the 1944 and 1945 seasons. He did not return the major league scene following his release from the service.

AGE	YRS	ML	W	L	PCT	ERA	G	GS	CG	IP	H	BB	SO	SHO	SV
23-24	44-45	4	3	7	0.300	5.14	19	12	2	70	86	35	24	0	0

CURTIS, VERNON E. (VERN)   BR TR 6' 0"   170 lbs.
Born May 24, 1920, Cairo, Il. — Died June 24, 1992, Cairo, Il.
Played for Washington (1943-44, 1946)

Vern Curtis got into two games at the close of the 1943 season as he was called up during September 1943. He pitched in three games in 1944 before he went into service. He spent the balance of 1944 and all of 1945 in the military. He was still listed on the Senators' defense list in December 1945. He did rejoin the Senators when he returned in 1946. However, he had difficulty getting batters out. He allowed nineteen hits, ten walks, and thirteen earned runs in the sixteen innings he pitched in 1946, his final year in the majors.

AGE	YRS	ML	W	L	PCT	ERA	G	GS	CG	IP	H	BB	SO	SHO	SV
24-25	44-45	3	0	1	0.000	5.70	16	1	0	30	30	19	10	0	0

DICKMAN, GEORGE E. (EMERSON)   BR TR 6' 2" 175 lbs.
Born November 12, 1914, Buffalo, N.Y. — Died April 27, 1981, New York, N.Y.
Played for Boston (A) (1936, 1938–41)

Emerson Dickman had established himself in the Red Sox bullpen during 1938 to 1940.
However, he struggled during the 1941 season and was sent down to Louisville during that
year until he entered the military. He had pitched in nine games for the Red Sox that year
before he left the team. He was taken into the Navy and by August 1942 was classified as
storekeeper 3rd class. By February 1944, he had been assigned to the U. S. Merchant Marine
Academy, Kings Point, New York, to serve in the Department of Athletics and Morale as a
physical education instructor.

During the summer of 1944, Dickman helped conduct the cadet-midshipman regimental
league. He also coached the Academy team, which was made up of battle-toughened veterans,
although they were only seventeen to twenty-three years old. That fall he received the rank of
lieutenant. In 1945 he continued to be stationed at Kings Point and coached the baseball team
again that summer. By the close of the year 1945, Dickman was thirty-one years old. He did
not return to major league baseball following his release from the service. He later coached
baseball at Princeton University.

AGE	YRS	ML	W	L	PCT	ERA	G	GS	CG	IP	H	BB	SO	SHO	SV
26-27	41-42	5	22	15	0.595	5.33	125	24	6	350	403	153	126	1	8

DIETZ, LLOYD A. (DUTCH)   BR TR 5' 11" 180 lbs.
Born February 12, 1912, Cincinnati, Oh. — Died October 29, 1972, Beaumont, Tx.
Played for Pittsburgh (1940–43) and Philadelphia (N) (1943)

Dutch Dietz was one of players Commissioner Landis "freed" from the Detroit Tiger
organization in 1940. The Tigers had covered up the movement of players, a violation of
baseball rules. Dietz then signed with the Cincinnati Reds organization which optioned him
to Syracuse. Later that year, the Reds sold him to the Pirates. He got into four games with the
Pirates that year and then returned to the majors in 1941. Pitching primarily in relief, he led
the Pirates in winning percentage and ERA in 1941. He was one of the busiest pitchers for the
Pirates during the 1941 and 1942 seasons.

Dietz was traded to the Phillies on June 15, 1943, and finished the year with them. The
Dodgers traded for Dietz between the 1943 and 1944 season. However, he was taken into
the military before he could play for them. During the summer of 1944, he was stationed at
Brooke General Hospital in San Antonio, Texas, and pitched for their team. During the spring
of 1945, he was sent to Fort Lewis, Washington. He pitched for their team during 1945. He was
still listed on the Dodgers' defense list in December 1945. He was thirty-four years old before
the start of the 1946 season. He did not make the Dodger team that year and he did not play
major league ball following the war.

AGE	YRS	ML	W	L	PCT	ERA	G	GS	CG	IP	H	BB	SO	SHO	SV
32-33	44-45	4	14	16	0.467	3.87	106	21	7	295	303	113	79	1	6

DONOVAN, WILLARD E. (BILL)   BR TL 6' 2" 198 lbs.
Born July 6, 1916, Maywood, Il. — Died September 25, 1997, Maywood, Il.
Played for Boston (N) (1942-43)

Bill Donovan was drafted by the Cubs and then sold to the Braves organization. He was a roommate of Warren Spahn while they played in the III League. He made the Braves team in 1942 as a reliever and spot starter. Donovan won three games and lost six as he appeared in thirty-one games. He appeared in seven games in 1943 before he was drafted by the Navy.

Donovan's wife reported that he did not see combat or suffer any injuries while in service. She said, "When he was drafted into the service, he chose to be in the Shore Patrol in the Navy instead of playing baseball so he could remain near his family as we had a new baby" (Donovan letter 1998). He remained in the Navy through the 1945 season. He was not able to return to baseball at its highest level following his release.

AGE	YRS	ML	W	L	PCT	ERA	G	GS	CG	IP	H	BB	SO	SHO	SV
26-28	43-45	2	4	6	0.400	3.20	38	10	2	104	114	41	24	1	0

DORSETT, CALVIN L. (CAL)   BR TR 6' 0" 180 lbs.
Born June 10, 1913, Long Oak, Tx. — Died October 22, 1970, Elk City, Ok.
Played for Cleveland (1940-41, 1947)

Cal Dorsett's major league baseball career was not successful. He had trials in 1940 and 1941, pitching in one game in 1940 and five games in 1941. He had an earned run average of 9.00 and 10.32 for the two years. He went into the military before the start of the 1942 season. There he made a major contribution. He was involved in the taking of Saipan, Marianas Islands, from the Japanese during the summer of 1944. He landed the morning after the original invasion and helped haul supplies from the beaches to the frontlines. He went through twelve hours of continuous heavy enemy shelling. He also had a grandstand seat during the second Japanese counterattack. He said, "We had a field day knocking out their tanks and trucks" (*The Sporting News*, "In The Service" 7-13-44, page 13). He achieved the rank of corporal.

Before Saipan, Dorsett had pitched a Marine baseball team to a Divisional Championship. Dorsett was twenty-seven when he made his debut with the Indians. He was about twenty-eight when he entered the Marines, and he was thirty-two by the close of the war. However, he did make an appearance in the majors following his release. In 1947 he appeared in two games for the Indians. These appearances closed out his major league career.

AGE	YRS	ML	W	L	PCT	ERA	G	GS	CG	IP	H	BB	SO	SHO	SV
29-32	42-45	3	0	1	0.000	11.85	8	2	0	14	25	13	6	0	0

DREISEWERD, CLEMENT J. (CLEM)
BL TL 6' 1" 195 lbs.

Born January 24, 1916, Old Monroe, Mo. — Died September 11, 2001, Ocean Springs, Ms.
Played for Boston (A) (1944–46), St. Louis (A) (1948) and New York (N) (1948)

Clem Dreisewerd was purchased by the Red Sox from the Pacific Coast League to replace Tex Hughson when he was drafted during the 1944 season. He made his debut on August 29, 1944, and started seven games during the rest of the season. He won two and lost four, pitching three complete games. He got into two games at the start of the 1945 season before he was drafted by the Navy.

During the summer of 1945, Dreisewerd was stationed at Sampson Naval Training facility in New York. He was able to pitch for the Sampson team during that summer. He was still listed on the Red Sox defense list in December 1945 before returning to the Red Sox for the 1946 season to help them win the pennant that year. He also pitched a third of an inning in the 1946 World Series against the Cardinals. After a year's absence, he returned to majors in 1948, playing for the Browns and the Giants. Dreisewerd had a unique characteristic. He was superstitious. He demanded that only his wife, Edna, could serve as the catcher to warm him up in the bullpen.

AGE	YRS	ML	W	L	PCT	ERA	G	GS	CG	IP	H	BB	SO	SHO	SV
29	45	4	6	8	0.429	4.54	46	10	3	141	160	39	39	0	2

EAST, GORDON H. (HUGH)
BR TR 6' 2" 185 lbs.

Born July 7, 1919, Birmingham, Al. — Died November 2, 1981, Charleston, S.C.
Played for New York (N) (1941–43)

Hugh East got trials with the Giants in both 1941 and 1942. He had been a relief pitcher with Jersey City in 1942 before being brought back to the Giants. He got into thirteen games in 1943 before he was taken into the Navy. He struggled in all three of the years he was with the Giants. In 1943 he gave up fifty-one hits and twenty-five walks in only forty innings. During the summer of 1944, he spent time managing the Camp Endicott Seabees team. He was transferred to Bainbridge in time to pitch for their team in the spring of 1945. He was still on the Giants' defense list in December 1945. East did not return to major league baseball following the war.

AGE	YRS	ML	W	L	PCT	ERA	G	GS	CG	IP	H	BB	SO	SHO	SV
23-25	43-45	3	2	6	0.250	5.40	19	8	1	63	85	41	27	0	0

EYRICH, GEORGE L.
BR TR 5' 11" 175 lbs.

Born March 3, 1925, Reading, Pa.
Played for Philadelphia (N) (1943)

George Eyrich was eighteen years old when he got into nine games for the Phillies in 1943. Right out of Reading High School, he had signed with the Phillies on May 30, 1943, and went straight to the major leagues. In his first game, on June 13, he relieved against the Giants in the

Polo Grounds. He pitched against Carl Hubbell, threw two innings, and did not allow a run. His record during those nine games was acceptable. His earned run average for the eighteen innings he pitched was 3.38. During the time in the majors, he beat Mickey Cochrane's Great Lakes team 10-3. Eyrich said, "Beating them kept me in the big leagues till September when I went into the Navy" (Eyrich letter 1998).

Following the short stretch in the majors, Eyrich was drafted by the Navy in September. During his training, he was stationed at Treasure Island, California. He got to pitch for the Naval Armed Guard team while stationed there. Eyrich served as a seaman first class aboard the SS *Elwood Haymes,* a liberty ship. He was involved in combat for eighty-eight days during the invasion of the Philippines. During the battle of Leyte Gulf, the ship had to fight off several Kamikaze attacks. They were able to shoot down several Japanese planes during that battle. However, he did not suffer any injuries during his service in the Navy. Eyrich continued his military service into the 1946 season. Following his release from the Navy, he was farmed out to Utica. He spent the next ten years in the minor leagues but was never able to return to the majors.

AGE	YRS	ML	W	L	PCT	ERA	G	GS	CG	IP	H	BB	SO	SHO	SV
18-21	43-46	1	0	0	0.000	3.38	9	0	0	19	23	9	5	0	0

FAGAN, EVERETT J.
BR TR 6' 0"   195 lbs.
Born January 13, 1918, Pottersville, N.J. — Died February 16, 1983, Morristown, N.J.
Played for Philadelphia (A) (1943, 1946)

Everett Fagan joined the A's in the spring of 1943 and pitched in eighteen games before he entered the military. He won two and lost six, pitching mostly in relief that season. His earned run average was 6.27. He served the balance of 1943, all of 1944 and 1945, as well as part of 1946 season before he was released. He rejoined the A's for the rest of the 1946 season. He pitched in twenty games that year, all in relief. Fagan was not able to maintain the position on the major league team following the 1946 season.

AGE	YRS	ML	W	L	PCT	ERA	G	GS	CG	IP	H	BB	SO	SHO	SV
25-28	43-46	2	2	7	0.222	5.47	38	2	0	82	88	38	21	0	3

GORNICKI, HENRY F. (HANK)
BR TR 6' 0"   145 lbs.
Born January 14, 1911, Niagara Falls, N.Y. — Died February 16, 1996, Riviera Beach, Fl.
Played for St. Louis (N) (1941), Chicago (N) (1941), and Pittsburgh (1942-43, 1946)

Hank Gornicki threw a complete game shutout for the Cardinals in his first major league start. However, he was not able to break into the Cardinals' regular lineup. He spent most of 1941 in Rochester of the International League. Some of his teammates on that Rochester ball club were Stan Musial, Erv Dusak, and Whitey Kurowski. The Cardinals sold him to the Cubs on September 10, 1941. Commissioner Landis voided the deal on September 22, and Gornicki then was sold to the Pirates on December 1, 1941. He managed to pitch in one game while he was with the Cubs. Gornicki stuck with the Pirates next season. He was a spot starter and relief pitcher.

In 1942 he pitched in 112 innings and led the Pirates with an earned run average of 2.57. The next year he pitched in forty-two games, winning nine and losing thirteen.

Gornicki was inducted into the Army on March 10, 1944. He reported to Camp Wolters, Texas. He suffered a setback with a bout of pneumonia while stationed there. He was still on the Pirates' defense list in December 1945. Gornicki had been a thirty-year-old rookie in 1941. When the war was over, he was a thirty-five year old who had just spent two years away from baseball. He did rejoin the Pirates. However, he was not able to sustain his position. He pitched in only seven games during the 1946 season before he closed out his major league career.

AGE	YRS	ML	W	L	PCT	ERA	G	GS	CG	IP	H	BB	SO	SHO	SV
33-34	44-45	4	15	19	0.441	3.38	79	33	12	285	275	107	123	4	6

GRODZICKI, JOHN (JOHNNY)   BR TR 6' 2" 200 lbs.
Born February 26, 1917, Nanticoke, Pa. — Died May 2, 1998, Daytona Beach, Fl.
Played for St. Louis (N) (1941, 1946–47)

Johnny Grodzicki was the Cardinals' hottest pitching prospect in 1941. He had completed the year at Columbus in the American Association where he won nineteen games and led the league in winning percentage and earned run average. He got a short trial with the Cardinals that year, winning two games with an earned run average of 1.35. Burt Shotton, his manager, called him the best pitching prospect he had ever seen. Joe Garagiola said, "Grodzicki was a legend. You heard about him everywhere" (Turner 1996, 120).

All that changed when Grodzicki was inducted into the Army. He was taken on March 3, 1942, and was the only Cardinal taken in 1942. He was received in the Army at New Cumberland, Pennsylvania Reception Center. He was sent to Fort Knox to do his basic training and was part of the Armored Force Replacement Training Center. On July 7, 1942, he played in an all-star game against American League All-Stars that raised $193,000 for war relief. He went to paratrooper school in Georgia where his older brother was an instructor. He got no special treatment. At his first jump his brother said, "If you don't jump, I'm gonna kick you out" (Turner 1996, 120).

After completing training, Grodzicki was assigned to the European Theater. As the war was winding down, five weeks before V-E day, he was dropped on the other side of the Rhine River near Wesel, Germany. On March 30, 1945, as he and three of his fellow soldiers climbed over a wall, a German shell landed near them. The other three soldiers were killed and Grodzicki was wounded. He received a severe shrapnel wound in the right leg and thigh and had extensive muscle and nerve damage. It was discovered that the sciatic nerve had been severed. He had an operation in Germany and then was evacuated back to England. Several months of physical therapy and recovery followed his return to England. They saved his leg, but he did not have strength nor did he have complete control over his right foot.

Grodzicki was released from the Army on January 20, 1946. He went to the Cardinal spring training camp, wanting to play baseball. He was fitted with a steel brace, but he didn't have good balance, and he couldn't field the position. Even though the Cardinal trainer worked extensively with him on his leg, it did not respond. He went North with the team, but it was only as a batting practice pitcher. He spent most of 1946 on the disabled list. In 1947, when the Cardinals got very short of pitchers, they activated him to the big league roster. However, he was not effective during that time.

Grodzicki continued to play in the minors until 1951. Bob Broeg, a St. Louis sportswriter, had said prior to Grodzicki's induction that he had been universally regarded as the organization's best pitching prospect. Now five years later, he was not able to pitch effectively because of the injury. The war had ended what had been a very promising career. Author Frederick Turner reported that, "At night Grodzicki tossed and turned, haunted by thought of a career that might well be over and made physically uncomfortable by the leg which dripped with sweat all night long" (Turner 1996, 121).

AGE	YRS	ML	W	L	PCT	ERA	G	GS	CG	IP	H	BB	SO	SHO	SV
25-28	42-45	3	2	2	0.500	4.43	24	1	0	41	31	34	20	0	0

HANSKI, DONALD T. (DON)   BL TL 5' 11"   180 lbs.
Born February 27, 1916, LaPorte, In. — Died September 2, 1957, Worth, Il.
Played for Chicago (A) (1943-44)

Don Hanski's pitching career consisted of three games. He got into one game in 1943 and two games in 1944. In addition to his pitching, he played in five games at first base and three as a pinch hitter. As a batter he had a career average of .227 with two RBIs. He was summoned for a preinduction physical on May 6, 1944, at Argo, Illinois. His military service included the 1945 season. He was still on the White Sox defense list in December 1945 but did not return to major league baseball following his military service.

AGE	YRS	ML	W	L	PCT	ERA	G	GS	CG	IP	H	BB	SO	SHO	SV
29	45	2	0	0	0.000	9.00	3	0	0	4	6	3	0	0	0

HARMAN, WILLIAM B. (BILL)   BR TR 6' 4"   200 lbs.
Born January 2, 1919, Bridgewater, Va.
Played for Philadelphia (N) (1941)

Bill Harmon pitched in five games for a total of thirteen innings in 1941. He then was taken into the military for the 1942 season. Records indicate that 1942 was his only year of military service. However, he did not return to the Phillies after his release from the service.

AGE	YRS	ML	W	L	PCT	ERA	G	GS	CG	IP	H	BB	SO	SHO	SV
23	42	1	0	0	0.000	4.85	5	0	0	13	15	8	3	0	0

HARRIS, ROBERT A. (BOB)   BR TR 6' 0" 185 lbs.
Born May 1, 1917, Gillette, Wy. — Died August 8, 1989, North Platte, Ne.
Played for Detroit (1938–39), St. Louis (A) (1939–42), and Philadelphia (A) (1942)

Bob Harris got his chance at the end of the 1938 season with the Tigers after he had spent the year in Toledo of the American Association. He then was traded to the St. Louis Browns on May 13, 1939. After the trade, he pitched on a regular basis, first as a spot starter/reliever and then as one of the Browns' regular starters. After a one and five start in the 1942 season, the Browns traded Harris to the A's. He finished the season with the A's before entering the service after the season.

Harris enlisted in the Navy on November 10, 1942. He said, "I'd like to stay in baseball but I wouldn't feel as if I was doing my part in the war effort" (*The Sporting News*, "In The Service" 11-5-42, page 7). He started in the Navy at Great Lakes. He stayed there during the summer of 1943 and pitched on the Great Lakes team. In the spring of 1944, he was transferred to Bainbridge, Maryland, for more intensive training. By summer 1944, he had been shipped on to Honolulu to assist with physical conditioning.

Harris played for a Navy team during the summer of 1944 in Hawaii and pitched for the sub-base team in 1945. He was still on the A's defense list in December 1945. When he returned to the A's in 1946, they released him from the team. He appealed to the U.S. Attorney's office in Philadelphia that his job should be protected under the G.I. Bill. He demanded $3,300 in salary (the difference between what he would have made with the A's and what he would receive pitching in the minors). He did receive an undisclosed amount in settlement of his claim after a meeting with Connie Mack, the A's attorney, and the judge. Needless to say, Harris did not return to the majors following the settlement of his claim with the A's.

AGE	YRS	ML	W	L	PCT	ERA	G	GS	CG	IP	H	BB	SO	SHO	SV
26-28	43-45	5	30	52	0.366	4.96	127	89	26	646	770	294	205	4	2

HAUGHEY, CHRISTOPHER F. (CHRIS)   BR TR 6' 1" 180 lbs.
Born October 3, 1925, Astoria, N.Y.
Played for Brooklyn (1943)

Birthday presents come in many different forms. For Chris Haughey, it was being able to pitch in his first and only major league game. He came in relief in a game on October 3, 1943, his eighteenth birthday. Not only did he get to pitch, he finished the game, pitching seven innings. He took the loss, allowing only five hits but ten walks in the seven innings. He had been a high school phenom who was sought after by six different major league teams including the Yankees. The Dodgers were his favorite team, and he signed with them. Gil Hodges also made his debut with the Dodgers in that game.

Haughey was drafted into the Army on January 25, 1944, in New York. He spent two years at Fort Riley, Kansas, where he served as an instructor in the Communication School, basic training, weapons, and equestrian. He did not see combat or suffer any injuries while in service. While stationed at Fort Riley, Haughey played on the baseball team along with Pete Reiser, Joe Garagiola, John Lanning, Alpha Brazle, Murry Dickson, Rex Barney, Lonnie Fry, and Harry Walker. However, Haughey said he had a commanding officer who was an "out of work elevator operator" who did not like baseball (Haughey letter 1998). This officer tried to keep him from getting the opportunity to play. He was still listed on the Dodgers' defense list in December 1945. Following his release, Haughey was not able to rejoin the Dodgers or play baseball at the major league level.

AGE	YRS	ML	W	L	PCT	ERA	G	GS	CG	IP	H	BB	SO	SHO	SV
18-19	44-45	1	0	1	0.000	3.86	1	0	0	7	5	10	0	0	0

HEAD, EDWARD M. (ED)   BR TR 6' 1" 175 lbs.
Born January 25, 1918, Selma, La. — Died January 31, 1980, Bastrop, La.
Played for Brooklyn (1940, 1942–44, 1946)

Ed Head was brought up to the Dodgers in July 1940 after having a very good year at Elmira of the Eastern League. He didn't make the Dodgers in 1941. He spent that year in Montreal in the International League. Starting in 1942, he became a spot starter and reliever for the Dodgers for the next two years. During the 1943 season, he played in an all-star game that raised $800,000,000 for war bonds. He began the 1944 season very well. In nine games (eight starts), he won four games and lost three. However, his earned run average was a good 2.70 for the sixty-three innings.

Head entered the Army on July 15, 1944. He spent the summer of 1944 and the early part of 1945 stationed at Fort Hood, Texas. He was discharged from the Army on November 1, 1945. He rejoined the Dodgers for the 1946 season and was effective. On April 23, 1946, in a game against Mort Cooper and the Boston Braves, Ed Head pitched a no-hitter. He allowed three walks, struck out two batters, and the Dodgers made one error. Shortly after his no-hitter, he suffered a career-ending arm injury. He pitched in a total of thirteen games in 1946.

AGE	YRS	ML	W	L	PCT	ERA	G	GS	CG	IP	H	BB	SO	SHO	SV
26-27	44-45	5	27	23	0.540	3.48	118	53	22	465	434	174	208	5	11

HICKEY, JAMES R. (JIM)   BR TR 6' 1" 204 lbs.
Born October 22, 1920, North Abington, Ma. — Died September 20, 1997, Manchester, Ct.
Played for Boston (N) (1942, 1944)

Jim Hickey got into one game in 1942. He then returned to the Braves in time to play eight games in the 1944 season. However, he did enter the Navy sometime during that 1944 season. By the spring of 1945, he was stationed at Sampson, New York, Naval Training Center. He was able to pitch for the baseball team while stationed at Sampson. He did not return to the majors after his release from the Navy.

AGE	YRS	ML	W	L	PCT	ERA	G	GS	CG	IP	H	BB	SO	SHO	SV
23	44	2	0	1	0.000	6.75	9	1	0	11	19	7	3	0	0

HOERST, FRANK J.

BL TL 6' 3"   192 lbs.

Born August 11, 1917, Philadelphia, Pa. — Died February 18, 2000, Maple Shade, N.J.
Played for Philadelphia (N) (1940–42, 1946–47)

During the five years that Frank Hoerst pitched in the majors, the Phillies finished last three years, next to last one year, and fifth the other year. The teams were bad, and he didn't help too much. During the two years (1941 and 1942) when he did most of his pitching, he compiled a record of seven wins and twenty-six losses. He had an earned run average of 5.20 in both of those years. Even with the bad records of himself and his team, he said, "I loved what I was doing, so I don't see how you can fail when you do that" (Kaufman and Kaufman 1995, 10).

Hoerst volunteered for the Navy on August 12, 1942. That fall he was an ensign in the Naval Procurement Office in Boston. He later saw a lot of action as a gunnery officer on a freighter. His ship was active in transporting troops and supplies across the Atlantic to Russian ports that included Murmansk, Russia. This was called the "Boulevard of Bombs" because of the supplies transported to Russia. He also saw action in the Pacific, again transporting troops to prepare for the invasion of Japan. He achieved the rank of lieutenant in the Navy. He commented about injuries he might have suffered in the service, saying, "Just the inactive physical exercise causing arm trouble that shortened my career while in spring training at Clearwater" (Hoerst letter 1997).

Hoerst was still on the Phillies' defense list in December 1945. He did rejoin the Phillies in time for the 1946 season. However, he continued to suffer from a lack of success. After playing in four games in 1947, he left the major leagues for the last time. He continued to play baseball in the minor leagues until 1949 when he retired. He was also known as a good basketball referee. He said, "I refereed for about 20 years—high school, college, NBA" (Kaufman and Kaufman 1995, 88).

AGE	YRS	ML	W	L	PCT	ERA	G	GS	CG	IP	H	BB	SO	SHO	SV
25-27	43-45	5	10	33	0.233	5.17	98	41	8	348	381	175	105	0	1

HUGHES, THOMAS O. (TOMMY)

BR TR 6' 1"   190 lbs.

Born October 7, 1919, Wilkes-Barre, Pa. — Died November 28, 1990, Wilkes-Barre, Pa.
Played for Philadelphia (N) (1941–42, 1946–47) and Cincinnati (1948)

Tommy Hughes was one of the better pitchers that pitched for a very bad Phillies team during 1941 and 1942. In 1942 he won twelve of the forty-two games won by the entire team. His earned run average that year was 3.06, and he completed nineteen of the thirty-one starts. He was considered one of the better pitchers in the National League in 1942.

Hughes was inducted into the Army on December 19, 1942, at Wilkes-Barre, Pennsylvania, and he was to report to New Cumberland, Pennsylvania, on December 26. He stayed at New Cumberland during 1943 and was part of Company H, 1301st Service Unit. During that summer, he played in an all-star game that raised $800,000,000 for war bonds. By the summer of 1944, he had been transferred to Camp Sibert, Alabama. While stationed at Camp Sibert, he was able to play some baseball. That fall he moved on to Camp Patrick Henry, Virginia. He was there during the summer of 1945 and was able to pitch for their team.

Hughes was still on the Phillies' defense list in December 1945, and he was released from the Army on January 29, 1946. Hughes returned to the Phillies in 1946. However, he was not able to reach the same level of success that he had achieved before he entered the Army. In 1946 he won six and lost nine in 111 innings (he had pitched in 253 innings in 1942), and in 1947 he won four while losing eleven in 127 innings. On December 11, 1947, he was traded to the Reds where he closed out his career in 1948. He was only twenty-eight years old when he closed his career. He was still young enough, but he was not having the same success he had before he went into the Army, so his career was over.

AGE	YRS	ML	W	L	PCT	ERA	G	GS	CG	IP	H	BB	SO	SHO	SV
23-25	43-45	5	31	56	0.356	3.92	144	87	31	688	698	308	221	5	3

IOTT, CLARENCE E. (HOOKS)   BB TL 6' 2"   200 lbs.
Born December 3, 1919, Mountain Grove, Mo. — Died August 17, 1980, St. Petersburg, Fl.
Played for St. Louis (A) (1941, 1947) and New York (N) (1947)

Hooks Iott got into two games at the close of the 1941 season. After another year in the minors, he was taken into the military at Miami, Florida, before the 1943 season. By the summer of 1944, he had risen to the rank of sergeant and was stationed at the Kearns Overseas Replacement Center, Salt Lake City, Utah. He was able to play for their baseball team while stationed at Kearns. That fall he made the all-tourney team while playing for the AAF Overseas Replacement Depot team. He continued to be stationed at Kearns during 1945 and was able to play baseball again in the summer of 1945.

Iott was discharged by the Army in December 1945. He was not able to make the Browns team in 1946 but did in 1947. However, after four games, the Browns sent him to the Giants where he pitched in twenty games in 1947. While pitching mostly in relief, he did start nine games, completing two. His record was not good, winning three games and losing nine, with an earned run average of 7.00. He closed his career with the Giants in 1947.

AGE	YRS	ML	W	L	PCT	ERA	G	GS	CG	IP	H	BB	SO	SHO	SV
23-25	43-45	2	3	9	0.250	7.05	26	9	2	82	84	67	53	1	0

JOHNSON, ADAM R. (A. RANKIN)   BR TR 6' 3"   177 lbs.
Born March 1, 1917, Hayden, Az.
Played for Philadelphia (A) (1941)

The Adam Rankin Johnson, Jr., who played for the A's in 1941 was the son of Adam Rankin Johnson, Sr., who pitched in the majors from 1914-18. Johnson Jr. made his debut in April 1941, but he only played in seven games. All of the seven games were pitched in relief. He volunteered for the Navy twelve days after the Japanese bombed Pearl Harbor. He served for four years, two years aboard a ship and two years on shore duty. While serving on a transport and cargo ship, he was involved in the capture and defense of Guadalcanal. He was also involved at Midway Island.

Following the two years at sea, Johnson was transferred to a submarine base at Pearl Harbor. He spent the next two years stationed at the submarine base. He was able to play some baseball while he was stationed in Hawaii. He did not receive any injuries while serving in the Navy. He was released at Sampson, New York, in September 1945. Johnson returned to the A's after being released but did not make the team in 1946. After his retirement as an active player, he moved his baseball career to the front office. He served as a general manager as well as secretary and later president of the Eastern League.

AGE	YRS	ML	W	L	PCT	ERA	G	GS	CG	IP	H	BB	SO	SHO	SV
25-28	42-45	1	1	0	1.000	3.60	7	0	0	10	14	3	0	0	0

JOHNSON, ARTHUR H. (ART)   BL TL 6' 2" 185 lbs.
Born July 16, 1916, Winchester, Ma.
Played for Boston (N) (1940-42)

Art Johnson got a brief trial at the end of the 1940 season with the Boston Braves and then returned the following season to lead the Braves in strikeouts. His father had signed a contract for him while he was still in his third year of high school. After three seasons in the minors, he earned his chance with the Braves. He was a spot starter and reliever who pitched in 183 innings in 1941. He started the 1942 season with the Braves but entered the Navy during the season.

Johnson volunteered for his service in the Navy and served aboard the aircraft carrier, USS *Langley*. They were part of the advance attack force for the Marines at Saipan, Tinian, and Iwo Jima. He did not suffer any injuries, but he said, "I did not pick up a baseball for 3 years" (Johnson, Art letter 1997). To a baseball career, inactivity can be almost as much of a problem as a specific injury. For Johnson the inactivity caused a problem.

Johnson was released in time for spring training in 1946. It was during a spring training game that he felt a searing pain. The arm injury ended his baseball career. The Braves released him in July 1946. He found out forty years later that he had torn the deltoid muscle and, with today's medical care, could have repaired it. However, the injury occurred in 1946, and it stopped him from pitching.

AGE	YRS	ML	W	L	PCT	ERA	G	GS	CG	IP	H	BB	SO	SHO	SV
25-28	42-45	3	7	16	0.304	3.68	49	19	6	196	203	79	71	0	1

JONES, DALE E.   BR TR 6' 1" 172 lbs.
Born December 17, 1918, Marquette, Ne. — Died November 8, 1980, Orlando, Fl.
Played for Philadelphia (N) (1941)

Dale Jones made his debut on September 7, 1941. He got one start that fall, which he lost. He also pitched one game in relief. He entered the Navy on January 20, 1942. During the summer of 1944, he was stationed at Norfolk Naval Air Station and was able to pitch for the baseball team. He was still on the Phillies' defense list in December 1945. He did not play at the major league level following his release from the Navy.

AGE	YRS	ML	W	L	PCT	ERA	G	GS	CG	IP	H	BB	SO	SHO	SV
23-26	42-45	1	0	1	0.000	7.56	2	1	0	8	13	6	2	0	0

KEHN, CHESTER L. (CHET)   BR TR 5' 11"   168 lbs.
Born October 30, 1921, San Diego, Ca. — Died April 5, 1984, San Diego, Ca.
Played for Brooklyn (1942)

Chet Kehn started the season with the Dodgers in 1942. He appeared in three games, including one start. He didn't win or lose any games, but he did get a hit in each of his two at-bats. With two singles, he scored a run and drove one in. He took his Army physical on February 17, 1943. During his Army career, he spent some time in the Pacific. He arrived back in Los Angeles on November 2, 1945, from the Pacific aboard the transport ship *Cecil*. He achieved the rank of private first class. He was still on the Dodgers' defense list in December 1945, but his baseball career ended without another appearance in the major leagues.

AGE	YRS	ML	W	L	PCT	ERA	G	GS	CG	IP	H	BB	SO	SHO	SV
21-23	43-45	1	0	0	0.000	7.04	3	1	0	8	8	4	3	0	0

KENNEDY, WILLIAM G. (BILL)   BL TL 6' 1"   175 lbs.
Born December 22, 1918, Alexandria, Va. — Died August 20, 1995, Alexandria, Va.
Played for Washington (1942, 1946–47)

Bill Kennedy had a brief eight-game trial in 1942 before he entered the military. He then spent the next three years in the Army, spending time in the European Theater. After the actual fighting ended, he got to pitch for the 13th Airborne Division in France. He was still on the Senators' defense list in December 1945. He did, however, rejoin the Senators following his release from the Army. In 1946 Kennedy pitched in twenty-one games, mostly in relief. His total innings pitched that season was only thirty-nine. He closed out his major league career in 1947 by pitching in two additional games.

AGE	YRS	ML	W	L	PCT	ERA	G	GS	CG	IP	H	BB	SO	SHO	SV
24-26	43-45	3	1	3	0.250	6.79	31	4	1	64	71	44	23	0	5

KRAUS, JOHN W. (TEX)   BR TL 6' 4"   190 lbs.
Born April 26, 1918, San Antonio, Tx. — Died January 2, 1976, San Antonio, Tx.
Played for Philadelphia (N) (1943, 1945) and New York (N) (1946)

Tex Kraus joined the Phillies in the spring of 1943 and became one of their regular starting pitchers. In his rookie season, he pitched in thirty-four games and completed 199 2/3 innings. He had a record of nine wins and fifteen losses with an earned run average of 3.16 for a team that finished next to last in the National League.

Kraus went into the military before the start of the 1944 season. After training, he was sent to Brooke General Hospital in San Antonio, Texas. He was able to pitch for their team during the summer of 1944. By the spring of 1945, he had been shipped to Camp Brale in California. During the early part of the season, he was also able to pitch for the Camp Brale team. He rejoined the Phillies during the 1945 season in time to pitch in nineteen games. He got thirteen starts, but his record was not as good as it had been in 1943. After the 1945 season, the Phillies sent him to the Giants where he closed his major league career in 1946.

AGE	YRS	ML	W	L	PCT	ERA	G	GS	CG	IP	H	BB	SO	SHO	SV
26	44	3	15	25	0.375	4.00	70	39	10	306	318	133	83	1	2

KUCZYNSKI, BERNARD C. (BERT)   BR TR 6' 0" 195 lbs.
Born January 8, 1920, Philadelphia, Pa. — Died January 19, 1997, Allentown, Pa.
Played for Philadelphia (A) (1943)

Bert Kuczynski pitched in six games in 1943, starting with his debut on June 2. He got one start, which he lost, and had an overall earned run average of 4.01. He entered the Navy during the 1943 season. He was stationed at Bainbridge, Maryland, for a period of time during 1944. He was still on the A's defense list in December 1945. He did not rejoin the A's following his release from the Navy. Kuczynski was unique in that he played baseball for the A's in the same year he played professional football for the Detroit Lions. The year was 1943.

AGE	YRS	ML	W	L	PCT	ERA	G	GS	CG	IP	H	BB	SO	SHO	SV
23-26	43-46	1	0	1	0.000	4.01	6	1	0	25	36	9	8	0	0

LAMANNA, FRANK   BR TR 6' 2" 195 lbs.
Born August 22, 1919, Watertown, Pa. — Died September 1, 1980, Syracuse, N.Y.
Played for Boston (N) (1940–42)

After a trial in 1940, Frank LaManna became one of the Braves' main relief pitchers during the 1941 season. He recorded five wins and four losses during 1941. LaManna was a good hitter. In addition to pitching in thirty-five games in 1941, he also played four games in the outfield and pinch-hit in eight others. He had a .281 batting average that year. He only appeared in five games in 1942 before being sent down to the minors.

LaManna was inducted into the Army on February 19, 1943. He did his basic training at the Army Air Force Technical Basic Training Center in Atlantic City, New Jersey. During the summer of 1944, he was stationed at the Kearns Overseas Replacement Center in Salt Lake City, Utah, and was able to play baseball during that time. He made an all-tournament team that summer. In the spring of 1945, he was transferred to the Pacific. By December 1945, he was stationed in the Philippines where he got to play some baseball. He was still on the Braves' defense list in December 1945, but he did not return to major league baseball following his release from the Army.

AGE	YRS	ML	W	L	PCT	ERA	G	GS	CG	IP	H	BB	SO	SHO	SV
23-25	43-45	3	6	5	0.545	5.24	45	5	1	93	95	67	28	0	1

LAMBERT, EUGENE M. (GENE)   BR TR 5' 11" 175 lbs.
Born April 26, 1921, Crenshaw, Mi. — Died February 10, 2000, Germantown, Tn.
Played for Philadelphia (N) (1941–42)

Gene Lambert came up to the Phillies in the fall of 1941. He pitched in two games that fall, starting one of those games. He lost the game he started even though his earned run average for the two games was a good 2.00. The next spring he had a very good spring training. He was one of the best pitchers the Phillies had during the spring. However, because of his draft uncertainty, the Phillies sent him back to the minors. With the choice of Dallas or Memphis, he chose Memphis to be close to his family. He then was drafted into the Army in September 1942.

After basic training, Lambert was assigned to Fort Oglethrope, Georgia. He stayed there for a year. His duty at Fort Oglethrope was to teach soldiers who couldn't read or write. It was the intent to give them at least a third grade education. The Army wanted the soldiers to be able to communicate with their families. He was then transferred to Fort Jackson, South Carolina. He remained there for two-and-a-half years. He was with the 15th Armored Group Headquarters with the rank of first sergeant. Lambert didn't see any combat or suffer any injuries during his Army service. He was discharged in February 1946.

After being released from the Army, Lambert was again sent to Memphis. He said, "At that time I realized that my peak years were the years I spent in the service" (Lambert letter 1998). He had given himself five years to make the majors when he signed with the Phillies in 1939. His fifth year was 1946. He retired in 1947 and went to work for the Memphis Light, Gas, and Water Divisions. He remained there until he retired in 1984.

AGE	YRS	ML	W	L	PCT	ERA	G	GS	CG	IP	H	BB	SO	SHO	SV
22-24	43-45	2	0	1	0.000	2.70	3	1	0	10	14	2	4	0	0

LANFRANCONI, WALTER O. (WALT)   BR TR 5' 7" 155 lbs.
Born November 9, 1916, Barre, Vt. — Died August 18, 1986, Barre, Vt.
Played for Chicago (N) (1941) and Boston (N) (1947)

Walt Lanfranconi appeared in two games at the close of the 1941 season with the Chicago Cubs. Before the start of the next season, he had entered the Army Air Force. In the summer of 1944, he was stationed at Waco, Texas, Army Air Field and pitched for their baseball team. He made the all-tourney team that fall while pitching for Waco. That winter, with a rank of corporal, he was transferred somewhere in Europe. This service in the Army continued through the 1945 season. He did not make the Cubs roster in 1946, but he returned to the majors in 1947 as a member of the Boston Braves. Used mainly in relief, Lanfranconi won four games and lost four games while having an earned run average of 2.95. The 1947 season was his last in the majors.

AGE	YRS	ML	W	L	PCT	ERA	G	GS	CG	IP	H	BB	SO	SHO	SV
25-28	42-45	2	4	5	0.444	2.96	38	5	1	70	72	29	19	0	1

LAPIHUSKA, ANDREW (ANDY)

BL TR 5' 10" 175 lbs.

Born November 1, 1922, Delmont, N.J. — Died February 17, 1996, Millville, N.J.

Played for Philadelphia (N) (1942–43)

Andy Lapihuska was nineteen years old when he joined the Phillies on September 12, 1942. He pitched in three games that fall and one game in 1943. He was taken by the Army during the late summer of 1943. During the summer of 1944, he was stationed at Camp Howze, Texas, as part of the 410th Infantry. He was able to play some baseball while stationed at Camp Howze but was shipped to Europe in late 1944 or early 1945. During that summer, he was stationed in Austria and got to play baseball. He played for the 103rd Division in Austria. He was still on the Phillies' defense list in December 1945 but did not return to major league baseball following his release from the Army.

AGE	YRS	ML	W	L	PCT	ERA	G	GS	CG	IP	H	BB	SO	SHO	SV
21-22	44-45	2	0	2	0.000	7.04	4	2	0	23	22	16	8	0	0

LEFEBVRE, WILFRID H. (BILL)

BL TL 5' 11" 180 lbs.

Born November 11, 1915, Natick, R.I.

Played for Boston (A) (1938–39) and Washington (1943–44)

Bill Lefebvre joined the Red Sox on June 9, 1938, immediately after graduating from Holy Cross. He pitched in relief the following day for four innings. In his first at bat, he hit a home run off Monty Stratton of the White Sox. He was the first American League hurler to hit a home run in his first at bat. After the one appearance, the Red Sox sent him to Minneapolis where he played along with Ted Williams. He started 1939 in Louisville, along with PeeWee Reese, but returned to the Red Sox at the close of the 1939 season. PeeWee Reese was a member of the Red Sox organization in 1939.

Lefebvre went to San Francisco in 1940 as part of the deal that brought Dom DiMaggio to Boston. After stops in Little Rock, Arkansas; Scranton, Pennsylvania; and Louisville, Kentucky, he returned to Minneapolis and in 1943 was sold to Washington in the middle of the year. His only full year in the majors was 1944 with the Washington Senators. Lefebvre was a good hitter. During the 1944 season, he was used twenty-nine times as a pinch hitter. He led the American League in pinch hits that season with ten. He also played two games at first base.

Lefebvre entered the Army on March 23, 1945. He played baseball in the service. Smokey Burgess was his catcher. Lefebvre said, "Pitched a lot in service and my arm was never the same after" (Lefebvre letter 1997). He was released from the Army before the start of the 1946 season. The Senators sold him back to Minneapolis a week before the season started. He got off to a great start, but with a change in managers, he had problems. The new manager used him in both starting and relief, resulting in a torn rotator cuff. He retired from baseball after the 1946 season. Lefebvre taught junior high physical education, coached college baseball, and scouted for different major league teams until he retired.

AGE	YRS	ML	W	L	PCT	ERA	G	GS	CG	IP	H	BB	SO	SHO	SV
29	45	4	5	5	0.500	5.03	36	10	3	132	162	51	36	0	3

LOWRY, SAMUEL J. (SAM)   BR TR 5' 11" 160 lbs.

Born March 25, 1920, Philadelphia, Pa. — Died December 1, 1992, Philadelphia, Pa.
Played for Philadelphia (A) (1942-43)

Sam Lowry made his debut on September 19, 1942. He pitched three innings of relief in the
one game he played in that year. He returned the following year and pitched in five games
for a total of eighteen innings. He went into service before the start of the 1944 season and
stayed in service through the 1946 season. He did not return to the majors following his
release from his military service.

AGE	YRS	ML	W	L	PCT	ERA	G	GS	CG	IP	H	BB	SO	SHO	SV
24-26	44-46	2	0	0	0.000	5.14	6	0	0	21	21	10	3	0	0

LYNN, JAPHET M. (RED)   BR TR 6' 0" 162 lbs.

Born December 27, 1913, Kenney, Tx. — Died October 27, 1977, Bellville, Tx.
Played for Detroit (1939), New York (N) (1939-40), and Chicago (N) (1944)

Red Lynn pitched in thirty games in 1939 and thirty-three games in 1940 for a total of 100
innings. All of these games were in relief. His earned run average (3.87) and his win/loss
record (5-4) were not bad for those two years. However, he returned to the minors in 1941
and stayed there until the middle of the 1944 season. He had won twenty-one games for the
Los Angeles Angels in 1943 and was purchased by the Cubs on July 5, 1944, to take Jimmie
Foxx's place on the roster when Foxx retired from the Cubs. He won five and lost four during
the last half of the 1944 season as a spot starter and reliever. He pitched eighty-four innings
during that stretch. Lynn went into the military before the start of the 1945 season. He was
on the Cubs' voluntarily retired list in December 1945, and he did not return to the Cubs
following his release from service.

AGE	YRS	ML	W	L	PCT	ERA	G	GS	CG	IP	H	BB	SO	SHO	SV
31	45	3	10	8	0.556	3.95	85	7	4	185	175	85	85	1	5

LYONS, ALBERT H. (AL)   BR TR 6' 2" 195 lbs.

Born July 18, 1918, St. Joseph, Mo. — Died December 20, 1965, Inglewood, Ca.
Played for New York (A) (1944, 1946-47), Pittsburgh (1947), and Boston (N) (1948)

Al Lyons pitched in eleven games in 1944 before he entered the Navy. He had been classified
2-B earlier that spring. He was accepted for active duty on May 18, 1944, and was actually
summoned to active duty on August 9. He started his service at Sampson, New York, Naval
Training Center. He pitched for the baseball team at Sampson for the rest of the summer. On
April 13, 1945, he passed through the processing mill at Bainbridge and was scheduled for
early sea duty. By that fall, he was stationed in Hawaii, where he got to play in the Navy Little
World Series for the Base 8 hospital team in the 14th Naval District League. He was named to
14th Naval District second team all-stars as manager.

Lyons was still on the Yankees' defense list in December 1945. He did return to the Yankees in time for the 1946 season. However, he got into only two games in 1946 and six games in 1947 before the Yankees sent him to Pittsburgh. He finished the 1947 season in Pittsburgh and then on to the Braves in 1948. He closed his major league career following the 1948 season.

AGE	YRS	ML	W	L	PCT	ERA	G	GS	CG	IP	H	BB	SO	SHO	SV
25-26	44-45	4	3	3	0.500	6.30	39	1	0	100	125	59	46	0	0

MALLOY, ROBERT P. (BOB)   BR TR 5' 11"   185 lbs.
Born May 28, 1918, Cannonsburg, Pa.
Played for Cincinnati (1943-44, 1946-47) and St. Louis (A) (1949)

Bob Malloy signed with the Reds in 1941 and was called up to the parent club in 1943. He got into six games that year and nine the next. He was accepted for active duty on April 13, 1944, and was actually inducted in late October 1944 at Camp Dix, New Jersey. He was trained as a forward observer at Fort Bragg but ended up in the infantry. He was with the 3rd Division in Germany. He said, "Our outfit ended up in Salzburg. One horrible sight I did see was going into the concentration camp at Dacau. We were greeted with car loads of naked bodies waiting to be incinerated. We had smelled the horrible smell for miles and then to see why" (Malloy letter 1997). After the surrender his unit moved north for occupation to a little town of Badwildingun. Malloy was involved in a wreck there when Cal McLish tried to drive a jeep and failed. It turned over five times, and the only thing that saved them from serious injury was the wire cutter attached to the jeep.

Malloy was still on the Reds' defense list in December 1945. He missed part of the 1946 season but did return to the Reds in time to pitch in twenty-seven games. He had a record of two wins and five losses, pitching mostly in relief. He only got into one game with the Reds in 1947, and after a year in the minors, he reappeared with the St. Louis Browns in the 1949 season, his last in the majors.

AGE	YRS	ML	W	L	PCT	ERA	G	GS	CG	IP	H	BB	SO	SHO	SV
26-28	44-46	5	4	7	0.364	3.26	48	3	1	116	116	52	35	0	2

MALTZBERGER, GORDON R.   BR TR 6' 0"   170 lbs.
Born September 4, 1912, Utopia, Tx. — Died December 11, 1974, Rialto, Ca.
Played for Chicago (A) (1943-44, 1946-47)

Gordon Maltzberger was a successful starting pitcher in the Texas League for two years before the White Sox purchased him for $6000. He had been pitching in the minors since 1932. However, when he arrived, manager Jimmie Dykes converted him to a relief pitcher. He would pitch 135 games during his four-year career and never start a game in the majors. He was known for his curve ball. Dykes said, "I've never seen a pitcher with the control of a curve better than Maltzberger's" (Gilbert 1992, 133). Maltzberger was a successful relief pitcher for the two years he played before the war. He led the American League in saves for both the 1943 and 1944 seasons. He also led the American League in relief wins in 1944.

Maltzberger entered the Army in February 1945. He was thirty-two years old. In the spring of 1945 he was stationed at Camp Roberts, California. He was still on the White Sox defense list in December 1945 before being discharged from the Army on July 18, 1946. He rejoined the White Sox that year. He pitched in nineteen games and won two games while losing none. He had an earned run average of 1.59.

Maltzberger lasted one more year with the White Sox before closing out his major league career. He played seven more years in the minors before retiring. Most of that time was spent with the Hollywood team of the Pacific Coast League. Maltzberger's major league career happened because of the war and the resulting shortage of players, which gave him the chance to play in the major leagues. With that chance, he had a good, but short career. Chicago sportswriter Milt Woodard wrote, "Maltzberger represents, probably better than any other player in the majors today, that fraternity of bona fide major leaguers who might have been overlooked except for the war" (Gilbert 1992, 133).

AGE	YRS	ML	W	L	PCT	ERA	G	GS	CG	IP	H	BB	SO	SHO	SV
32-33	45-46	4	20	13	0.606	2.70	135	0	0	293	258	74	136	0	33

MARTIN, RAYMOND J. (RAY)

BR TR 6' 2"   177 lbs.

Born March 13, 1925, Norwood, Ma.
Played for Boston (N) (1943, 1947–48)

Ray Martin was eighteen years old when he broke in with the Boston Braves in August 1943. He pitched in two games before he was taken into military service that same year. He remained in service through the 1946 season. He returned to the Braves for a trial in both 1947 and 1948. In 1947 he appeared in one game, which he started. He pitched a complete game and won, allowing only one run. He closed out his major league career in 1948 by pitching in two more games in relief. He pitched a total of 14 2/3 innings in three years. Nine of those innings were in one game in 1947.

AGE	YRS	ML	W	L	PCT	ERA	G	GS	CG	IP	H	BB	SO	SHO	SV
18-21	43-46	3	1	0	1.000	2.45	5	1	1	15	10	6	3	0	0

MCCULLOUGH, PINSON L. (PHIL)

BR TR 6' 4"   204 lbs.

Born July 22, 1917, Stockbridge, Ga. — Died January 16, 2003, Decatur, Ga.
Played for Washington (1942)

Phil McCullough's major league career consisted of one game. In that game, he pitched three innings, faced seventeen batters, and allowed five hits and four runs (two earned runs). He finished that game for the Washington Senators. He volunteered later in 1942 for the Navy and was a Chief Specialist at Norfolk early in 1943. He spent some time in the South Pacific but did not suffer any wounds or injuries. He was not involved in direct combat but was close to the trouble and experienced some air raids.

While stationed in the Solomon Islands, McCullough got to play some "fun" games with a Seabees outfit. During this time, he had contact with other major league ballplayers, including Bobby Doerr. He was still listed on the Senators' defense list in December 1945. He said about his experience, "When I returned and mustered out I tried to return to B.B. [baseball] but three years in Pacific really took it out of me. I couldn't get into any kind of condition. Good Bye B.B." (McCullough letter 1997).

AGE	YRS	ML	W	L	PCT	ERA	G	GS	CG	IP	H	BB	SO	SHO	SV
25-28	43-45	1	0	0	0.000	6.00	1	0	0	3	5	2	2	0	0

MCKEE, ROGERS H.
BL TL 6' 1" 160 lbs.
Born September 16, 1926, Shelby, N.C.
Played for Philadelphia (N) (1943-44)

Rogers Hornsby McKee went from high school and American Legion baseball straight to the National League. He was sixteen years old when he made his debut with the Phillies. He had just turned seventeen in 1943 when he started and completed a game for the Phillies. It was a five-hit victory. He pitched in four games in 1943. In 1944, he pitched in one game before going to the minors.

McKee was drafted into the Navy in December 1944 at age eighteen. He didn't see any combat but did spent time in Hawaii and was in the occupation forces that went into Japan after the war ended. McKee remained in the Navy through 1946. He did not return to the Phillies' regular season roster when he was released from the Navy.

AGE	YRS	ML	W	L	PCT	ERA	G	GS	CG	IP	H	BB	SO	SHO	SV
18-19	45-46	2	1	0	1.000	5.87	5	1	1	15	14	11	1	0	0

MEERS, RUSSELL H. (RUSS)
BL TL 5' 10" 170 lbs.
Born November 28, 1918, Tilton, Il. — Died November 16, 1994, Lancaster, Pa.
Played for Chicago (N) (1941, 1946-47)

When Russ Meers came to the Cubs in 1941 and pitched in one game at the end of the season. He got to start a game on September 28, 1941. He pitched eight innings, allowing only five hits and two runs (one earned), but he still lost the game. The following year he was pitching for the Navy. He started his Naval career at Great Lakes in 1942 where he was listed as a pitcher for the Great Lakes baseball team. By the summer of 1943, he had been transferred to Norfolk Naval Training Center. He stayed at Norfolk through the spring of 1945. He played for the Norfolk team while stationed at that location.

By the summer of 1945, Meers was stationed in Hawaii. He pitched for the Kaneohe team there. He was released by the Navy in the late fall of 1945. He rejoined the Cubs in 1946, but he played in only seven games. In 1947, his last year in the majors, he became one of the regular relief pitchers for the team. He pitched in thirty-five games that year.

AGE	YRS	ML	W	L	PCT	ERA	G	GS	CG	IP	H	BB	SO	SHO	SV
23-26	42-45	3	3	3	0.500	3.98	43	4	0	84	76	48	35	0	0

MERTZ, JAMES V. (JIM)   BR TR 5' 10" 170 lbs.
Born August 10, 1916, Lima, Oh. — Died February 4, 2003, Waycross, Ga.
Played for Washington (1943)

Jim Mertz joined the Senators as a wartime replacement and helped the Senators to a second-place finish in the American League in 1943. He was used as a spot starter and relief pitcher. The next year he was drafted into the Army. He was stationed for a while in 1945 at Camp Blanding, Florida. He didn't see any combat, but he did hurt his pitching arm while in service. He said, "I hurt my right arm while in the Army, which ended my playing days" (Mertz letter 1997). His career was over. He was not released from the Army until after the 1946 season. He had pitched for the Atlanta Crackers in 1942 and, during an exhibition game, served up a pitch to Ted Williams that Williams hit so hard they thought it landed in downtown Atlanta.

AGE	YRS	ML	W	L	PCT	ERA	G	GS	CG	IP	H	BB	SO	SHO	SV
27-29	44-46	1	5	7	0.417	4.63	33	10	2	117	109	58	53	0	3

MILLER, ROLAND A. (RONNIE)   BB TR 5' 11" 167 lbs.
Born August 28, 1918, Mason City, Ia. — Died January 6, 1998, Ferguson, Mo.
Played for Washington (1941)

Ronnie Miller finished the game on September 10, 1941. He pitched two innings and allowed one run. This would be the only game that Miller would pitch in the major leagues. He entered the service in 1942, missing the 1942, 1943, 1944, and 1945 seasons in service to his country. He was still on the Senators' defense list in December 1945, but he did not rejoin the Senators at the close of the war.

AGE	YRS	ML	W	L	PCT	ERA	G	GS	CG	IP	H	BB	SO	SHO	SV
23-26	42-45	1	0	0	0.000	4.50	1	0	0	2	2	1	0	0	0

MODAK, MICHAEL (MIKE)   BR TR 5' 10" 195 lbs.
Born May 18, 1922, Campbell, Oh. — Died December 12, 1995, Lakeland, Fl.
Played for Cincinnati (1945)

Mike Modak came up to the Reds on July 4th, 1945, and pitched in twenty games before the end of the season. He was used mostly in relief that season. He was on the Reds' active roster in December 1945, but he was taken into the military before the start of the 1946 season. He was not able to return to baseball at the major league level following his release from service.

AGE	YRS	ML	W	L	PCT	ERA	G	GS	CG	IP	H	BB	SO	SHO	SV
24	46	1	1	2	0.333	5.74	20	3	1	42	52	23	7	1	1

MUELLER, LESLIE C. (LES)   BR TR 6' 3" 190 lbs.
Born March 4, 1919, Belleville, Il.
Played for Detroit (1941, 1945)

Les Mueller got a four-game trial in 1941 and then returned in 1945 after three years in service. He had been classified 1-B because of a bad knee, but he volunteered in early 1942 and was taken into the Army. In the summer of 1944, he was stationed at Jefferson Barracks near St. Louis, Missouri. Then on October 14, 1944, he was given a medical discharge at Jefferson Barracks. He had been stationed there for two years and had achieved the rank of sergeant while in the Army.

Mueller rejoined the Tigers in time for the 1945 season. He became one of the regular starters as the Tigers made their drive for the American League pennant. On July 21, 1945, he pitched nineteen and two-thirds innings in a game that was called after twenty-four innings tied one to one. His record was six wins and eight losses. However, his earned run average was 3.68. Mueller got into one game in the World Series against the Cubs that autumn.

AGE	YRS	ML	W	L	PCT	ERA	G	GS	CG	IP	H	BB	SO	SHO	SV
23-25	42-44	2	6	8	0.429	3.78	30	18	6	148	126	68	50	2	1

MULLIGAN, RICHARD C. (DICK)   BL TL 6' 0" 167 lbs.
Born March 18, 1918, Swoyersville, Pa. — Died December 15, 1992, Victoria, Tx.
Played for Washington (1941), Philadelphia (N) (1946), and Boston (N) (1946-47)

Dick Mulligan pitched in one game in 1941 for the Washington Senators. He started and threw a complete game but lost. Before the next season, he was traded to the Phillies and entered the Army. The trade came before the induction, so he spent his Army time on the Phillies' defense list. He entered the Army Air Corps on January 20, 1942, enlisting at Jefferson Barracks, Missouri. The Senators had sent him a contract and he sent it back, saying "[I] have decided to pitch for Uncle Sam" (*The Sporting News*, "From the Army Front" 1-29-1942, page 8). He spent four years in the Army.

Mulligan was listed on the Phillies' active roster in December 1945 but was not released in time to play any games for them in 1945. He rejoined the Phillies in 1946 and pitched in nineteen games before being sent to the Braves. Four games with the Braves in 1946 and one in 1947 closed out his major league career.

AGE	YRS	ML	W	L	PCT	ERA	G	GS	CG	IP	H	BB	SO	SHO	SV
24-27	42-45	3	3	3	0.500	4.44	25	6	2	81	82	39	23	0	1

NAHEM, SAMUEL R. (SAM)   BR TR 6' 1" 190 lbs.
Born October 19, 1915, New York, N.Y.—Died April 19, 2004, Berkley, Ca.
Played for Brooklyn (1938), St. Louis (N) (1941), and Philadelphia (N) (1942, 1948)

Sam Nahem started his career the way all pitchers want to start their careers. He pitched a complete game victory on October 2, 1938. He allowed six hits and three runs. He also got two singles in five at-bats, driving one run and scoring one run. Even with the good outing at the end of 1938, Nahem didn't reappear in the majors until 1941 and this time with the Cardinals. He had been traded to the Cardinals on June 12, 1940, as part of the deal that sent Joe Medwick to the Dodgers.

After a good year with the Cardinals in 1941, Nahem spent 1942 with the last place Phillies. He had been classified 1-B during the summer of 1942, but before the start of the 1943 season, he was in the Army. He volunteered for the infantry and ended up in the anti-aircraft artillery. In early 1944, he was with the Eastern Anti-Aircraft Command as a sportswriter for the *America's Alertman* that was published by the Command.

During the summer of 1944, Nahem was stationed at Fort Totten, New York. He was able to play some baseball there. The summer of 1945 found him in France. He ran two leagues for GI's at Rheims, France. He earned the rank of corporal. By fall 1945, he moved on to Germany. He played for OISE team and had risen to the rank of sergeant. Nahem said, "[I] led [a] ragtag team—I'm ragtag all the way—and won European Championship against major league team all-stars" (Nahem letter 1997).

Nahem didn't see any combat or suffer any injuries while in the Army. He was still listed on the Phillies' defense list in December 1945 but didn't make the Phillies team in either 1946 or 1947. However, he did return to the major league scene in 1948. He pitched in twenty-eight games that year, winning three and losing three. This was his last year in the majors.

AGE	YRS	ML	W	L	PCT	ERA	G	GS	CG	IP	H	BB	SO	SHO	SV
27-29	43-45	4	10	8	0.556	4.69	90	12	3	224	222	127	101	0	1

NEWLIN, MAURICE M. (MAURY)   BR TR 6'0" 176 lbs.
Born June 22, 1914, Bloomingdale, In. — Died August 14, 1978, Houston, Tx.
Played for St. Louis (A) (1940–41)

Maury Newlin got a start in 1940 and the won the game, the only game he pitched that year. He returned to the Browns in 1941 and appeared in fourteen games in relief. By January 1942, he was already in the Navy. He spent the next four years in service to his country. He was discharged by the Navy in October 1945 and was on the Browns' active roster in December 1945. However, he did not make the major league team in the spring of 1946 nor did he return at a later date. His major league career ended when he went into the Navy.

AGE	YRS	ML	W	L	PCT	ERA	G	GS	CG	IP	H	BB	SO	SHO	SV
28-31	42-45	2	1	2	0.333	6.42	15	1	0	34	47	14	13	0	1

NIEMES, JACOB L. (JACK)   BR TL 6'1" 180 lbs.
Born October 19, 1919, Cincinnati, Oh. — Died March 4, 1966, Hamilton, Oh.
Played for Cincinnati (1943)

Jack Niemes pitched in three games in 1943 and pitched a total of three innings. However, he was the pitcher who finished the game in all three of his appearances. He allowed five hits and three runs (two earned) in the three innings. Following the 1943 season, Niemes entered military service and spent 1944 and 1945 in the military. He was still on the Reds' defense list in December 1945, but Niemes did not play major league baseball after the war.

AGE	YRS	ML	W	L	PCT	ERA	G	GS	CG	IP	H	BB	SO	SHO	SV
24-25	44-45	1	0	0	0.000	6.00	3	0	0	3	5	2	1	0	0

OLSEN, VERN J. BR TL 6' 0" 175 lbs.
Born March 16, 1918, Hillsboro, Or. — Died July 13, 1989, Maywood, Il.
Played for Chicago (N) (1939–42, 1946)

After three very good minor league seasons, Vern Olsen got a trial with the Chicago Cubs at the end of 1939. He made the most of his opportunity and became one of Chicago's regular starting pitchers for the next three years. His rookie year was his best when he won thirteen games and lost nine. He had an earned run average of 2.97 that year.

Olsen enlisted in the Navy on November 21, 1942. He started his service at Great Lakes. Olsen pitched for the baseball team at Great Lakes during the summer of 1943. In January 1944, he was shipped to Bainbridge, Maryland, for more intensive training. The stay at Bainbridge was short. In late spring, he was transferred to Pearl Harbor to assist in physical conditioning. During his stay in Honolulu, Olsen played baseball for a Navy team. Navy food was agreeing with Olsen because it was noted that, "[he] has added weight to his 'skinny' frame since he had been in the Navy" (*The Sporting News*, "In The Service" 9-14-1944, page 13).

Olsen pitched for the Navy's Aila Hospital team during late 1944 and early 1945. He also spent some time in other locations in the Pacific. Olsen was discharged on October 26, 1945. It was anticipated that he would be able to help the Cubs in 1946. However, that was not the case. In 1946 he got into only five games, all in relief, before he closed out his major league career. When he went into service, he had been in the starting rotation; when he returned at age twenty-eight, he pitched in five games, 9 $^2/_3$ innings, and he was done. The war had taken its toll.

AGE	YRS	ML	W	L	PCT	ERA	G	GS	CG	IP	H	BB	SO	SHO	SV
25-27	43-45	5	30	26	0.536	3.40	112	60	23	516	547	192	201	7	2

PEEK, STEPHEN G. (STEVE) BB TR 6' 2" 195 lbs.
Born July 30, 1914, Springfield, Ma. — Died September 20, 1991, Syracuse, N.Y.
Played for New York (A) (1941)

At age twenty-six, Steve Peek made his debut with the New York Yankees on April 16, 1941. He appeared in seventeen games that year, starting eight for the World Champions. He enlisted in the Army on January 29, 1942, and reported to Fort Niagara, New York, on February 2 as an Army private. His Army career would take him to Europe. After the war ended in Europe on May 8, 1945, Peek was able to play some baseball. He pitched for the 11th Armored Division in games in Austria during the summer of 1945. He was still on the Yankees' defense list in

December 1945. By spring training 1946, Peek was thirty-one years old. He was not able to rejoin the Yankees following his release from the Army.

AGE	YRS	ML	W	L	PCT	ERA	G	GS	CG	IP	H	BB	SO	SHO	SV
27-30	42-45	1	4	2	0.667	5.06	17	8	2	80	85	39	18	0	0

PERME, LEONARD J. (LEN)   BL TL 6'0"   170 lbs.
Born November 25, 1917, Cleveland, Oh.
Played for Chicago (A) (1942, 1946)

Len Perme's career consisted of four games before the war and four games after he returned. He got into the four games in 1942 at the end of the season. Then in late 1942 he entered the Navy. He spent "3 years and 10 days in the Navy" (Perme letter 1998). He started out at the Navy Pier in Chicago. He spent several months there as he learned how to be an aviation mechanic. His next stop was Kansas, then on to Minneapolis, and, finally, to Camp Kearney in San Diego, California. At Camp Kearney, he was an instructor, teaching others how to work on airplanes. He also played a lot of baseball while stationed in California. He was still on the White Sox defense list in December 1945, and rejoined the White Sox in 1946. He said, "I hurt my arm and didn't have the stuff I had before the war." He added, "However, I enjoyed playing so I kept on as long as I could" (Perme letter 1998). After the four games with Chicago, Perme also played at Milwaukee.

AGE	YRS	ML	W	L	PCT	ERA	G	GS	CG	IP	H	BB	SO	SHO	SV
25-27	43-45	2	0	1	0.000	3.12	8	1	1	17	11	11	6	0	0

POSEDEL, WILLIAM J. (BILL)   BR TR 5'11"   175 lbs.
Born August 2, 1906, San Francisco, Ca. — Died November 28, 1989, Livermore, Ca.
Played for Brooklyn (1938) and Boston (N) (1939–41, 1946)

Bill Posedel started his career in the Navy. He enlisted as a teenager in 1925 and served until 1929. While in the Navy, he pitched for a team from the USS *Saratoga*. With Posedel pitching, the team won the Pacific Fleet Championship. After that success, he was offered a professional contract. It was not an instant trip to the majors. He pitched for nine years in the minors before he got his opportunity with Brooklyn in 1938. He was thirty-one years old when he made his debut. After a year with the Dodgers, he was sold to the Boston Braves. It was in Boston that Posedel had his two best years. In 1939 and 1940, he became one of the better pitchers for that team, but he slowed down in 1941. He pitched in fewer games with less success and changed from a starter to a relief pitcher. He did have some arm trouble during the 1941 season.

After the Japanese attack on Pearl Harbor, Posedel reenlisted in the Navy. After taking his physical in San Francisco on January 6, he signed up on January 19, 1942. He went back to sea. He was the chief of a gun crew on a ship in the Pacific. He spent three years in the Pacific fighting zone. In the spring of 1945, he was transferred to Treasure Island, San Francisco. He earned the rank of chief petty officer and was the chief master of arms of the Armed Guard at Treasure Island. With that job he had about 250 men under his command. He did not have much time to play baseball.

Posedel was discharged in October 1945. At age thirty-nine, he rejoined the Braves for the 1946 season. He won two games and lost none during 1946. While his major league playing career closed in 1946, his association with baseball did not end. He scouted and coached for a number of teams until 1972. His last coaching job was with the Oakland A's in 1972.

AGE	YRS	ML	W	L	PCT	ERA	G	GS	CG	IP	H	BB	SO	SHO	SV
35-38	42-45	5	41	43	0.488	4.56	138	87	45	679	757	248	227	6	6

RICH, WOODROW E. (WOODY)   BL TR 6' 2" 185 lbs.
Born March 9, 1916, Morganton, N.C. — Died April 18, 1983, Morganton, N.C.
Played for Boston (A) (1939–41) and Boston (N) (1944)

Woody Rich first appeared in the majors in 1939. In that year, he pitched in twenty-one games as a spot starter and reliever. He had some success, winning four games and losing three. He also suffered from a sore arm during that year. The following two years he would only appear in five games, three in 1940 and two in 1941. He didn't return to the majors until 1944 when the Braves purchased him from Indianapolis to serve as a wartime replacement. He then entered the military before the 1945 season. Rich was not able to return to major league baseball following his release from his military service.

AGE	YRS	ML	W	L	PCT	ERA	G	GS	CG	IP	H	BB	SO	SHO	SV
29	45	4	6	4	0.600	5.06	33	16	5	117	127	50	42	0	1

SAVAGE, JOHN R. (BOB)   BR TR 6' 2"   180 lbs.
Born December 1, 1921, Manchester, N.H.
Played for Philadelphia (A) (1942, 1946–48) and St. Louis (A) (1949)

Bob Savage graduated from Staunton (Va.) Military Academy in 1941 and joined the A's in 1942. After his debut in June, he pitched in eight games that year. He volunteered for the Army on March 10, 1943. After training, Savage had two years of active combat with Company D, 15th Infantry, 3rd Army Division. He was set to join the 3rd Division as a replacement in November 1943 with the rank of lieutenant. He was wounded on the way to join his new outfit. The wound was a shrapnel wound in his back near his right shoulder. This happened on the Mt. Casino front in Italy near the town of Casserta during his first night of combat. Savage would then spend five months in hospitals in Italy and Northern Africa. He wrote Connie Mack, the Philadelphia Athletics' owner and manager, from the hospital, saying, "I hope they will be able to dig it out, because more than anything else I want to pitch for you again" (*The Sporting News*, "In The Service" 3-2-1944, page 14). Mack responded, "I hope Bob will be able to pitch for me again, too. He's a fine lad and the team can use him" (*The Sporting News*, "In The Service" 3-2-44, page 14).

Savage rejoined his outfit in time to take part in the fighting at the Anzio beachhead. He went with his outfit on to Rome after they broke out. After the city was secured, they were pulled out of Italy to prepare for the invasion of France. On December 1, 1944, Savage was wounded a second time as they were trying to cross the Rhine River. He suffered a third wound just before the war ended in Germany. Savage commented that he believed he was the first professional athlete to be wounded in World War II and the professional athlete with the most Purple Hearts.

Following the surrender of Germany, Savage was able to pitch in some baseball games. He played for the 3rd Division in games in Austria. He was released by the Army in the fall of 1945. He said, "I do not believe the wounds caused me any problems as far as baseball was concerned, other than time lost" (Savage letter 1997). Like the attitude of so many of the men who served, Savage downplayed the effect on him and pointed to the service of others. He said, "Friends like Ted Williams were the ones more effected by the war, because they were the ones that were going to set records" (Savage letter 1997).

Savage got his wish to pitch again for the A's. He rejoined the team in time for the 1946 season. However, success was difficult to come by when pitching for the Philadelphia A's. As a starter/reliever, he won three and lost fifteen in 1946 and won eight and lost ten in 1947. In 1948 he was shifted to a reliever only and won five while losing only one. He closed out his career with the St. Louis Browns in 1949 after being sold by the A's on December 16, 1948.

AGE	YRS	ML	W	L	PCT	ERA	G	GS	CG	IP	H	BB	SO	SHO	SV
21-23	43-45	5	16	27	0.372	4.32	129	31	10	423	433	215	171	2	9

SAYLES, WILLIAM N. (BILL)   BR TR 6' 2"   175 lbs.
Born July 27, 1917, Portland, Or. — Died November 20, 1996, Lincoln City, Or.
Played for Boston (A) (1939), New York (N) (1943), and Brooklyn (1943)

Bill Sayles first appeared in the majors on July 17, 1939. He played in five games for the Red Sox that season and didn't reappear in the majors until 1943. He served as a wartime replacement in 1943, first for the Giants (nineteen games) and then for the Dodgers (six games). He went into the military before the start of the 1944 season. In the spring of 1945, he was stationed at Fort Lewis, Washington. He was scheduled to play for the post team that summer. Sayles was still on the Dodgers' defense list in December 1945. He was not able to return to the majors following his release from service.

AGE	YRS	ML	W	L	PCT	ERA	G	GS	CG	IP	H	BB	SO	SHO	SV
26-27	44-45	2	1	3	0.250	5.61	28	3	1	79	87	46	52	0	0

SCHMIDT, FREDERICK A. (FREDDY)   BR TR 6' 1"   185 lbs.
Born February 9, 1916, Hartford, Ct.
Played for St. Louis (N) (1944, 1946–47), Philadelphia (N) (1947), and Chicago (N) (1947)

Freddy Schmidt came to the Cardinals in 1944 with a blazing fastball and a nice change of pace. He had seen success in the minors, winning nineteen games at Allentown in 1942. In 1944 he was a spot starter and reliever for the Cardinals as they won the World

Championship. He pitched in thirty-seven games (nine starts) and 114 innings, winning seven games and losing three. He pitched in three and one-third innings in a losing cause in game three of the World Series that year. He allowed only one hit and no runs during his pitching performance.

In the spring of 1944, Schmidt had been classified 2-B. He was ordered to take a preinduction physical on July 5, 1944, at Asheville, North Carolina. He requested that the examination be transferred to St. Louis. On July 11, 1944, he took his physical at Jefferson Barracks and was accepted for active service. He was able to continue to pitch for the Cardinals that season because he was not actually inducted into the Army until December 8, 1944, in New Cumberland, Pennsylvania.

In the summer of 1945, Schmidt was sent to Camp Hood, Texas. He was able to pitch some baseball with the 95th Regimentation team while stationed there. By fall 1945, he had been sent to the Pacific. He again was able to play baseball while stationed in the islands. He was the leading pitcher in a league in the Marianas during the fall of 1945.

Schmidt was still on the Cardinals' defense list in December 1945 and rejoined the Cardinals for the 1946 season. However, he was not as effective as before the war. Baseball researcher Ed Walton said, "he went into military service and did not regain his form upon his return" (Shatzkin 1990, 970). He won one game in 1946 and was traded to the Phillies on May 3, 1947, as part of the deal that sent Harry Walker to the Phillies for Ron Northey. After twenty-nine games for the Phillies, he closed out his career that year with the Cubs. Again, the war had taken its toll. He did not return the same pitcher he was when he entered the Army.

AGE	YRS	ML	W	L	PCT	ERA	G	GS	CG	IP	H	BB	SO	SHO	SV
29	45	3	13	11	0.542	3.75	85	15	3	225	206	122	98	2	5

STANCEU, CHARLES (CHARLEY)   BR TR 6' 2" 190 lbs.
Born January 9, 1916, Canton, Oh. — Died April 3, 1969, Canton. Oh.
Played for New York (A) (1941, 1946) and Philadelphia (N) (1946)

Charley Stanceu made the Yankee team in the spring of 1941. He was used in relief, winning three games and losing three games. By February 1942, he was a member of the Army. He was stationed at Camp Wolters, Texas, as a private. He commented that he would soon be throwing hand grenades instead of baseballs. In the fall of 1942, he attended officer candidate school. He expected to qualify and be given a commission as a second lieutenant. He continued his service through the 1945 season and was still listed on the Yankees' defense list in December 1945. At age thirty, he rejoined the Yankees for the 1946 season. He pitched in only three games before being sent to the Phillies. He played in fourteen games for the Phillies in 1946 as he closed out his major league career.

AGE	YRS	ML	W	L	PCT	ERA	G	GS	CG	IP	H	BB	SO	SHO	SV
26-29	42-45	2	5	7	0.417	4.93	39	13	1	122	135	79	47	0	0

SWIGART, OADIS V. (OAD)

BL TR 6' 0" 175 lbs.

Born February 13, 1915, Archie, Mo. — Died August 8, 1997, St. Joseph, Mo.
Played for Pittsburgh (1939-40)

Oad Swigart got two brief trials in the majors. He pitched in three games at the close of the 1939 season, and he got into seven games during the 1940 season. He was one of the first four major league baseball players who was taken into the military in 1941. He spent the first part of his military career at Fort Leavenworth, Kansas, as the reception center athletic director. He helped organize, coach, and pitch for the base team. Ralph Houk, future New York catcher and manager, was the catcher for this team. Swigart continued his service in the Army through 1945. He was still listed on the Pirates' defense list in December 1945. Following his release from the Army, he was unable to rejoin the Pirates.

AGE	YRS	ML	W	L	PCT	ERA	G	GS	CG	IP	H	BB	SO	SHO	SV
26-30	41-45	2	1	3	0.250	4.44	10	5	1	47	54	16	17	1	0

THUMAN, LOUIS C. F. (LOU)

BR TR 6' 2" 185 lbs.

Born December 13, 1916, Baltimore, Md. — Died December 19, 2000, Baltimore, Md.
Played for Washington (1939-40)

Lou Thuman pitched in three games in the fall of 1939 and two games in 1940. He pitched a total of nine innings with limited success. His career earned run average was 12.00. He went into the Army in 1941. He was one of the first four major leaguers to be called into the military. The others were Oad Swigert, Joe Gallagher, and Hugh Mulcahy. Thuman said, "I was in spring training with the Washington Senators when I was called for the Army" (Thuman letter 1997).

After boot camp, Thuman was promoted to corporal as a member of Company B, 175th Infantry, 29th Division at Fort Meade, Maryland. After training was completed, Thuman's company was sent to England, and he had been promoted to sergeant. They were involved in the invasion of France and then on into Germany. He said, "I lasted about four days. I was wounded in my upper clavicle" (Thuman letter 1997). He spent about six months in England and in the United States in hospitals recovering from the wound. He added, "As a right-handed pitcher, this ended my baseball career" (Thuman letter 1997). Thuman was still on the Senators' defense list in December 1945. He did not return to major league baseball following his release from the Army.

AGE	YRS	ML	W	L	PCT	ERA	G	GS	CG	IP	H	BB	SO	SHO	SV
24-28	41-45	2	0	1	0.000	12.00	5	0	0	9	15	9	1	0	0

TOST, LOUIS E. (LOU)

BL TL 6' 0" 175 lbs.

Born June 1, 1911, Cumberland, Wa. — Died February 22, 1967, Santa Clara, Ca.
Played for Boston (N) (1942-43) and Pittsburgh (1947)

Lou Tost made the Braves' regular starting rotation when he joined the team in 1942 at age thirty-one. He had a good year at Hollywood in 1941 and had earned the promotion to the major league level. He was still with the Braves when he entered the Navy on May 26, 1943. During the summer of 1944, he was stationed at Norfolk Naval Air Station and was able to pitch for the base team.

That fall Tost was ordered overseas. He was sent to the Pacific and arrived in Hawaii early in 1945. Tost pitched for a subbase team in the 14th Naval District league. He pitched in a Navy all-star game and in the Little World Series in October 1945 and was also named to the 14th Naval District all-star team. He was still listed on the Braves' defense list in December 1945. Tost was thirty-five years old when the war ended. He did appear in one game following his return from the Navy, however. In 1947 he pitched one inning for the Pittsburgh Pirates as he closed his baseball career.

AGE	YRS	ML	W	L	PCT	ERA	G	GS	CG	IP	H	BB	SO	SHO	SV
33-34	44-45	3	10	11	0.476	3.65	39	23	5	155	159	56	46	1	0

TRINKLE, KENNETH W. (KEN)   BR TR 6' 1" 175 lbs.
Born December 15, 1919, Paoli, In. — Died May 10, 1976, Paoli, In.
Played for New York (N) (1943, 1946–48) and Philadelphia (N) (1949)

Ken Trinkle started the year with Giants in 1943; however, he spent most of that year at Jersey City. He went into the Army before the start of the 1944 season and was assigned to Fort Meade, Maryland. He became a member of the 9th Armored Division. He was in Luxembourg at the time of the German breakout. Trinkle was in a lot of combat during this period, shooting and getting shot at by the Germans. The 9th Armored was involved in the battle at vital sectors of the front at Bastogne, St. Vith, and Echternach. The outfit was called the "Phantom Division" by the Germans because it seemed to be everywhere. Trinkle received a Bronze Star medal for service on a reconnaissance patrol during the capture of the Ludendorff Bridge at Remagen, Germany.

After the fighting was over, Trinkle pitched for the 76th Division and the 9th Armored Division while still stationed in Germany. He earned the rank of corporal. He was discharged by the Army in late November or early December of 1945 and rejoined the Giants as a spot starter and reliever in time for the 1946 season. He pitched in 151 innings in forty-eight games. Starting in 1947, he was converted to strictly a reliever. That year he appeared in sixty-two games, all in relief. He led the National League in appearances in both 1946 and 1947.

Trinkle continued in the relief role through the balance of his career. Despite having some control problems, Trinkle had reasonable success. His career ERA of 3.74 is acceptable. He closed his career in 1949 with the Phillies after being sold by the Giants on December 14, 1948. Trinkle was a baseball player who made a difference in the war effort.

AGE	YRS	ML	W	L	PCT	ERA	G	GS	CG	IP	H	BB	SO	SHO	SV
24-25	44-45	5	21	29	0.420	3.74	216	19	3	435	442	208	130	0	21

VAUGHAN, CECIL P. (PORTER)   BR TL 6' 1" 178 lbs.
Born May 11, 1919, Stevensville, Va.
Played for Philadelphia (A) (1940–41, 1946)

Porter Vaughan came up to the A's in the middle of the 1940 season and pitched in eighteen games (fifteen starts). He won two games and lost nine. After a brief stint with the A's in 1941, he entered the Army before the start of the 1942 season. He was inducted into the Army on January 15, 1942, at Richmond, Virginia. He was stationed at Camp Lee during the spring of 1942, where he was able to play some baseball while stationed at Camp Lee.

In April 1942, Vaughan was injured when he was hit in the leg, and the leg became infected. The treatment for this injury required hospitalization at Camp Lee. Vaughan received a commission while in the Army. By the fall of 1944, he was stationed at Buckley Field, Colorado. He received a promotion from first lieutenant to captain while stationed at Buckley Field. He was the officer in charge of troop training. Buckley Field was an important Army Air Force installation training commandos. He was able to pitch for the Buckley Field team during the time he spent in Colorado.

Vaughan was still on the A's defense list in December 1945. He did rejoin the A's in 1946. However, he only got to pitch one inning in one game that year. The 1946 season ended his major league career.

AGE	YRS	ML	W	L	PCT	ERA	G	GS	CG	IP	H	BB	SO	SHO	SV
23-26	42-45	3	2	11	0.154	5.83	24	18	6	122	137	74	52	0	2

WALLACE, JAMES H. (LEFTY)   BL TL 5' 11" 160 lbs.
Born August 12, 1921, Evansville, In. — Died July 28, 1982, Evansville, In.
Played for Boston (N) (1942, 1945–46)

Lefty Wallace joined the Braves for the 1942 season after a year at Bridgeport in the Inter-State League in 1941. He was only twenty years old when he made his debut. He spent the season with the Braves until he enlisted in the Army on August 19, 1942. He pitched in nineteen games, mostly in relief, winning one and losing three. He served in the Army during the balance of 1942, 1943, and most of 1944. He received a medical discharge in late November 1944 because of a knee injury. He spent most of the 1945 season at Indianapolis. He was 17–4. Wallace rejoined the Braves in time to pitch in five games in 1945 and stayed with them for the 1946 season. He was used as a part-time starter and reliever. He pitched in twenty-seven games, winning three games and losing three games. The year 1946 closed out his major league career.

AGE	YRS	ML	W	L	PCT	ERA	G	GS	CG	IP	H	BB	SO	SHO	SV
21-22	43-44	3	5	6	0.455	4.11	51	14	4	145	133	64	51	0	0

WEILAND, EDWIN N. (ED)   BL TR 5' 11" 180 lbs.
Born November 26, 1914, Evanston, Il. — Died July 12, 1972, Chicago, Il.
Played for Chicago (A) (1940, 1942)

Ed Weiland had trials in both 1940 and 1942, pitching in five games each year. He pitched a total of twenty-four innings with an earned run average of 8.25. He was taken into the Navy before the start of the 1943 season. In the early summer of 1944, Weiland was stationed at Great Lakes and in late summer he was at the Iowa Pre-Flight Center. He pitched for both groups—the Great Lakes team in the spring and the Iowa Pre-Flight Seahawks in the late summer and fall.

In the spring of 1945, Weiland was transferred to Shoemaker Field, California, Naval Training Distribution Center for further transfer to the commandant of the 14th Naval District. This meant transfer to Hawaii and the Pacific. In the fall of 1945, Weiland got to play in the Navy Little World Series in Hawaii. He was not able to rejoin the White Sox and play on the major league level following his release from the Navy.

AGE	YRS	ML	W	L	PCT	ERA	G	GS	CG	IP	H	BB	SO	SHO	SV
28-30	43-45	2	0	0	0.000	8.25	10	0	0	24	33	10	7	0	0

WENSLOFF, CHARLES W. (BUTCH)   BR TR 5' 11" 185 lbs.
Born December 3, 1915, Sausalito, Ca. — Died February 18, 2001, San Rafael, Ca.
Played for New York (A) (1943, 1947) and Cleveland (1948)

Butch Wensloff was promoted to the Yankee team in 1943 after three good years at Kansas City in the American Association. He responded by moving into the starting rotation and winning thirteen games as the Yankees won the World Championship. His earned run average for 1943 was 2.54.

Wensloff was twenty-eight years old and classified 2-B in 1944. However, he did his part for the war effort. He voluntarily retired from the Yankees before the start of the 1944 season and went to work in a war plant. He worked in the plant for two years. He did play some baseball in the 1945 season for the San Diego team in the Pacific Coast League. Wensloff was drafted on July 14, 1945. He did not see any combat while he was in service and was discharged on July 1, 1946. He did not play professional baseball during the 1946 season after he was released.

Wensloff rejoined the Yankees for the 1947 season; however, his arm was dead. He pitched only fifty-one innings that year, winning three and losing one. He closed out his major league career the next year, pitching one game for Cleveland. He left baseball in 1944 to help his country. At that time, he was a regular starter for the Yankees. When he got back to baseball, he was only a shadow of what he had been before the war.

AGE	YRS	ML	W	L	PCT	ERA	G	GS	CG	IP	H	BB	SO	SHO	SV
28-30	44-46	3	16	13	0.552	2.60	41	32	19	277	222	95	125	1	1

WILKIE, ALDON J. (LEFTY)   BL TL 5' 11"   175 lbs.
Born October 30, 1914, Zealandia, Sask., Canada — Died August 5, 1992, Tualatin, Or.
Played for Pittsburgh (1941–42, 1946)

Lefty Wilkie joined the Pirates in 1941 after a good season at Seattle in the Pacific Coast
League in 1940. He was used primarily in relief, although he did start six games in his rookie
year. He pitched in a total of twenty-six games and seventy-nine innings in 1941. He returned
in 1942 and performed the same role. However, in 1942 he won six games while losing seven.
He pitched 107 innings in thirty-five games.

Wilkie went into the military between the 1942 and 1943 seasons. He served for three years.
He was still on the Pirates' defense list in December 1945 and returned to the Pirates in 1946.
However, his performance was not at the same level it had been before the war. His earned
run average went up to 10.57 in 1946 in the seven games in which he was the pitcher. His
earned run average had been 4.35 for the two years he had played before going into the
service. His final year in the major leagues was 1946.

AGE	YRS	ML	W	L	PCT	ERA	G	GS	CG	IP	H	BB	SO	SHO	SV
28-30	43-45	3	8	11	0.421	4.59	68	12	5	194	215	80	37	1	3

WILLIAMS, ROBERT F. (ACE)   BR TL 6' 2"   174 lbs.
Born March 18, 1917, Montclair, N.J. — Died September 16, 1999, Fort Myers, Fl.
Played for Boston (N) (1940, 1946)

Ace Williams' career consisted of two brief trials, one in 1940 before the war and another in
1946 after the war. In the first year, he pitched in five games for a total of nine innings. He
allowed twenty-one hits, twelve walks, and sixteen earned runs in those nine innings.

Williams entered the Navy after the 1942 season. By the spring of 1944, he had achieved the
rank of lieutenant (j.g.). He was assigned to the Colgate University's Navy Preflight School Staff.
He was still listed on the Braves' defense list in December 1945 and rejoined the Braves in
1946, getting his second major league trial. This time in one game he faced two batters. One
of the batters got a hit and the other walked. Williams did not get any outs. This last one-game
outing concluded his career in 1946.

AGE	YRS	ML	W	L	PCT	ERA	G	GS	CG	IP	H	BB	SO	SHO	SV
26-28	43-45	2	0	0	0.000	16.00	6	0	0	9	22	13	5	0	0

WILSON, MAX (MAXIE)   BL TL 5' 7"   150 lbs.
Born June 3, 1916, Haw River, N.C. — Died January 2, 1977, Greensboro, N.C.
Played for Philadelphia (N) (1940) and Washington (1946)

Maxie Wilson's major league time prior to the war was spent with the Philadelphia Phillies.
He was brought up to the major league team in September 1940. He got into three games
without a decision, although his earned run average for the seven innings he pitched was
12.86.

Wilson went into the Navy in 1942. He was stationed at Norfolk Naval Training Station and pitched very well for their baseball team in spring of 1942. Two of his fellow pitchers were Bob Feller and Fred Hutchinson. By the spring of 1944, he had been transferred to Bainbridge, Maryland Naval Training Center. He stayed there during the summer of 1944. He was also able to play baseball for that team during his tenure at Bainbridge.

Wilson received orders on September 1, 1944, to go overseas to the Pacific where he continued to get to play baseball. He played in the Navy Little World Series in October 1945 and was named to the 14th Naval District second team all-stars in the fall of 1945 while stationed in Hawaii. He was released from the Navy in time to be on the Senators' active roster in December 1945. The Senators had drafted him in the major league draft in the fall of 1945 while he was still in the Navy. He joined the Senators in 1946. However, he pitched in only nine games for a total of twelve innings. He continued to struggle in his attempt to get batters out. His final major league season was 1946.

AGE	YRS	ML	W	L	PCT	ERA	G	GS	CG	IP	H	BB	SO	SHO	SV
27-29	42-45	2	0	1	0.000	9.15	12	0	0	20	32	11	11	0	0

WITTIG, JOHN C. (JOHNNIE)   BR TR 6'0" 180 lbs.
Born June 16, 1914, Baltimore, Md. — Died February 24, 1999, Nassawadox, Va.
Played for New York (N) (1938–1939, 1941, 1943) and Boston (N) (1949)

Johnnie Wittig's career was up and down. He made the Giants team at the end of the 1938 season after a reasonable year at Baltimore of the International League. He got into thirteen games with six starts. In 1939 he started the year with the Giants and then was sent to Jersey City, also of the International League, after playing in only five games. He spent all of the 1940 season at Jersey City. In 1941 Wittig spent the entire season with the New York Giants, but in 1942 it was back to the minors. He spent 1942 back in Jersey City, and in 1943 he found himself back with the Giants. It was in 1943 he was used the most. He pitched in forty games with twenty-two starts. Pitching for the last place Giants, his record for the year was five wins and fifteen losses.

Because baseball did not pay much in those days, Wittig had a regular job he went to as soon as the season was over. He worked in a factory that built the frame and braces for the invasion barges needed by the country for the war effort. He got his draft notice and went to the office for induction. Everybody in the room was called except Wittig. He said, "As I sat there a man came out and asked me what I wanted. I showed him my papers" (Wittig letter 1998). Wittig's name had been taken off the list. His company had asked for and received a deferment for him because of the work he was doing. He voluntarily retired from baseball and continued to work at his defense plant job. He said, "I spent two full years at my job until it was over. I was not in the service but willing to go. My company was the ones who asked for my deferment" (Wittig letter 1998).

Wittig missed the 1944 and 1945 seasons working in the factory. He did get one more appearance in the majors before he retired from major league baseball. Wittig pitched two innings in one game for the Boston Braves in 1949. This closed out his major league career.

AGE	YRS	ML	W	L	PCT	ERA	G	GS	CG	IP	H	BB	SO	SHO	SV
30-31	44-45	5	10	25	0.286	4.89	84	39	7	307	343	163	121	1	4

CHAPTER 8

There have been several wars associated with baseball. Each of them has had some impact on the national pastime. During the Civil War, there were stories about Northern soldiers who were prisoners of war taking the game of baseball home with them when they were released from confinement. However, the game had probably already spread over the country before the start of the Civil War. A national magazine, as early as 1859, discussed whether baseball or football was the national pastime. During this period, doctors realized that exercise was important and had soldiers take part in all kinds of athletic games. Baseball was one of those games. There are many records about various individuals staging games and taking part in those games during this period.

Professional baseball came into existence in the late 1800s. Teams were organized, and leagues were formed. With that organization came rules and regulations that would govern the people who took part in the activity. The first major challenge to baseball that resulted from a war came during the years of 1918 and 1919. These were the years the United States took part in World War I. The nation was facing its first major war outside its borders, and the leaders were trying to cope with the problems presented by that war.

The conflict had started in 1914 when Archduke Francis Ferdinand of Austria-Hungary was assassinated. Over the course of the next four years, additional nations were drawn into the conflict. On April 6, 1917, the United States declared war on Germany. Over the next several months, the United States was at work building up its army. Baseball escaped much attention during the early months, but as the war went on, there was a push to have all nonessential individuals included in the war effort. This meant closing down those kind of activities. The order came on May 23, 1918, that men engaged in "nonessential activities" had until July 1, 1918, to either "work or fight." Baseball, along with other sports, was considered to be nonessential. Therefore, ballplayers either had to join the military or find work that was considered essential. General Enoch Crowder, the provost marshall of the armed forces, issued the order. Baseball players tried to get the deadline extended until the end of the season but were not successful. However, they did get the date moved to September 1, 1918, and also won the right to hold the World Series after that date. As a result, the baseball season in 1918 only lasted for 127 games on average (the teams played between 123 and 131 games). The effect on all players that year was that they played in about twenty percent fewer games than a normal season. In addition, several players were drafted into the military and lost either part or all of the season.

The war concluded on November 11, 1918, when Germany signed the Armistice Agreement. However, baseball continued to play a reduced schedule in 1919. The 1919 season averaged 140 games in length. The number of games played ranged from 138 to 142. While there were not many players in the military during 1919, the reduced schedule decreased the number of games played by about nine percent. This again reduced the chances of the players to amass additional numbers for the career statistics. In 1920 baseball returned to the regular number of games.

During the 1917 season, there were a few players with major league experience who were taken into the military. They included Hank Gowdy, Lou Guisto, Duster Mails, and Jim Scott. Hank Gowdy gained fame for his service in the military. He was the first major league player to enlist in World War I when he signed up on June 2, 1917. He served in the Rainbow Division at Chateau-Thierry, St. Mihiel, and Argonne. These were some of the bloodiest battles of the war. Gowdy was decorated because of his bravery under fire. He was still a patriot when it came time to serve in World War II. He was coaching for the Cincinnati Reds during this time. He said, "I have been the recipient of many honors in my lengthy baseball career and also have been in receipt of honors outside the realm of baseball." He continued, "But the highest honor of my entire life came through being privileged to wear the United States Army uniform and serve my country in the last war in which it was engaged" (Mead 1985, 86). He continued to show that love for country when, in 1943 at age 53, he enlisted in the Army again to serve in World War II.

Eddie Grant was the first person with major league experience to be killed during World War I. He had played for the Cleveland Indians, Philadelphia Phillies, Cincinnati Reds, and New York Giants during his career. He had closed out his ten-year career playing with the Giants in 1915. He was killed in Argonne, France, on October 5, 1918.

Some of the notable players of this era were Ty Cobb, Babe Ruth, Tris Speaker, Eddie Collins Sr., Rogers Hornsby, Harry Heilmann, Rabbit Maranville, Sam Rice, Max Carey, Jimmie Dykes, Hank Gowdy, Joe Jackson, Casey Stengel, Walter Johnson, Grover Cleveland Alexander, Dutch Leonard, Herb Pennock, and Eppa Rixey. Many others also spent some time in the majors and then spent some time in military service. There were probably in excess of 200 former and current major league players who spent some time in the military during these four seasons. Cobb, Ruth, Speaker, Hornsby, Carey, and Johnson did not spend any time in the military, so their records are only reduced by the shortened seasons of 1918 and 1919. Because of these shorter seasons, some of these players, who are in the top twenty-five all-time in several categories, may have suffered reduced chances to add to their career numbers. Based on their career numbers, they might have achieved the following additional production if they had had the chance to play the usual number of games for those two years: in hits, Cobb an additional 52, Speaker 45, Hornsby 39; in runs scored, Cobb an additional 26, Ruth 23, Speaker 23; in RBIs, Ruth an additional 28, Cobb 20, Hornsby 19; in stolen bases, Cobb an additional 10, Carey 15; in games played, Cobb an additional 35, Speaker 39; in total at-bats, Cobb 136, Speaker 144; in home runs, Ruth 5; in triples, Cobb 4, Speaker 3, Hornsby 3; in doubles, Speaker 10, Cobb 8, Hornsby 5; in walks, Ruth 25, Speaker 20. For pitchers, Walter Johnson was the one who is ranked in the top twenty-five of most career numbers who did not serve. The shortened seasons may have cost his career 10 games, 7 starts, 7 complete games, 85 innings pitched, 2 shutouts, 41 strikeouts, 6 wins, and 3 losses.

The effect on those players who served in the military in addition to having the seasons shortened is more dramatic. Collins, Heilmann, Maranville, Rice, Alexander, and Rixey all served in the military. Most missed all or part of the 1918 season because of their military service. They are also listed among the top twenty-five in a number of career statistics. The shortened seasons, along with their military service, cost them the opportunity to add to their career statistics. Based on their success during the balance of their careers, the following is an estimate of how they might have added to their numbers had they not missed the games while serving in the military: in hits, Collins 82, Rice 195; in runs scored, Collins 55; in stolen bases, Collins 15; in games played, Collins 69; in at-bats, Maranville 557, Collins 266; in triples, Collins 10, Rice 11, Maranville 11; in doubles, Heilmann 21; in walks, Collins 17; (pitchers) in games started, Alexander 40, Rixey 43; in complete games, Alexander 31; in innings pitched, Alexander 349; in shutouts, Alexander 10; in wins, Alexander 27; in losses, Rixey 20.

The effect on all of major league baseball was felt during this time. The players who suffered the pain of war suffered the most. They put their lives as well as the opportunity to play baseball on the line. The list of names that are included in Appendix B are those who were active in the major leagues at the time of the conflict. There probably are additional names that should be included, however.

After a long period of peace, the clouds of war once again covered Europe. Again, Germany was the aggressor. They, along with their ally Italy, overran Europe during the late 1930s and early 1940s. While the United States helped some of their European Allies, it wasn't until Japan bombed Pearl Harbor on December 7, 1941, that the United States declared itself at war. In the time between Germany's invasion of Europe and the Japanese bombing of Pearl Harbor, the United States had been getting ready in case it was forced into the war. The country expanded defense plants and began training soldiers.

As part of the preparation, the first peace time draft into the military was started. On Wednesday, October 16, 1940, American men between ages twenty-one and thirty-five registered for the draft. Some 16 million men registered during this time. Among those who registered were a number of baseball players, both from the major and minor leagues. As the war progressed, the number of baseball players who entered the military grew. The players who had major league experience before serving in the military are the ones featured in this book.

However, there were thousands of others who were playing in the minors and had their careers interrupted by their service to their country. Some of the these players returned to their baseball careers after the war and were successful in reaching the majors. Some died in service for their country. By December 1944, forty-one minor league players had died in the fighting. They were exposed to more combat because they were not as well known as their major league counterparts. Among those killed was Billy Southworth, Jr. He was a bomber pilot and son of Cardinal manager Billy Southworth, Sr. He was killed in the States when he took off from New York in a B-29. The plane developed engine trouble and Southworth tried to make an emergency landing. The plane overshot the runway and ended up in a bay with water that was twenty-five feet deep. Southworth's body was not found for six months when it finally washed up on a shore.

In addition to those killed, a number of other minor league players were never able to fulfill their dreams of a major league career because of injuries they received or because of the two to four years the war took away from their chance to improve their baseball skills, skills that were necessary to achieve major league status. Their story remains untold for the most part. They were like so many Americans who answered the call to service, served their country, and then returned to be part of the fiber that weaves the United States of America together. They were truly heroes, but their individual stories are, for the most part, only known to family and friends.

Each year the baseball record books — *The Sporting News' Baseball Register,* and *Baseball Magazine's Who's Who in Baseball* — record the career statistics for players who are scheduled to play in the majors that year. After examining these two record books for the years from 1942 to 1960, the names on the list presented in Appendix C are the players who are identified as serving in the military before they were able to play at the major league level. The players are listed by name, the last team and league where they played before military service, the first year they played at the major league level, and their first major league team.

A number of these players became stars in the major leagues after their service to their country. They played on pennant winning and world champion teams. They won batting titles. They played in All-Star games. Some of the others had only one day in the sun. In any case, all of their careers were delayed by giving their time in service to their country. Some played with pain because of the injuries they suffered during the war. For example, Lou Brissie was wounded in Italy and had to undergo twenty-three operations to help in his recovery. Even with those operations, he still had to wear a steel brace and a shin guard on his left leg while pitching. He overcame his injuries to pitch for seven years in the majors. His two best years were 1948 and 1949 when he won fourteen and sixteen games respectively for the Philadelphia Athletics. He pitched three innings in the All-Star game in 1949.

Another player on this list who was severely wounded was Gene Bearden. He was in the Navy serving in the Pacific. The ship he was on was attacked by the Japanese off Guadalcanal on August 9, 1942. Bearden was injured and ended up with aluminum plates in his skull and knee. In spite of these limitations, he joined the Cleveland Indians for one game in 1947 and then in 1948 won twenty games as the Indians won the American League pennant. He pitched the playoff game with the Red Sox when the season ended in a tie. He also started one game in the World Series and relieved in the sixth and final game. He won his start and saved the final game.

Another group of individuals also took part in baseball activities and served during World War II. They were players from the Negro Baseball Leagues.

During the history of America, people of color have made major contributions to a wide range of activities in American society. This includes the activity of baseball. Black baseball players also contributed to the war effort of the United States. They did this at a time when they were treated like second-class citizens. Many of the players in the Negro Leagues served their country during World War II. While they had not yet been permitted to play in the major leagues, their careers were affected by the war. Their career numbers in the major leagues were not reduced by the war because black players did not get a chance to accumulate statistics in the major leagues until 1947 when Jackie Robinson broke the color barrier. However, it would be an injustice not to at least list the members of the Negro Leagues who served their country during World War II. The players presented on the list in Appendix D, along with their teams, are those provided by the National Baseball Hall of Fame and Museum, Inc.

A few of these many players got a chance to play in the major leagues. Of those who did get the chance, many got a late start because of the discrimination against black players.

Jackie Robinson was the first black man to play major league baseball in the modern era. His work and effort paid off for him and all of the other black players who have followed him. He was called up to the Brooklyn Dodgers when he was 28 years old in 1947. He played for ten years, until 1956. His entire career was played for the Dodgers. During his career, he had a lifetime batting average of .311. He also had 1,518 hits, 137 home runs, 734 RBIs, and 197 stolen bases. He led the league in stolen bases in 1947 and 1949. He also led the league in batting average in 1949 with an average of .342. The Dodgers during this period had a lot of success. A good part of that success was because of the play of Jackie Robinson. They won the National League pennant in 1947, 1949, 1952, 1953, 1955, and 1956. The 1955 Dodgers were the first Dodger team to win the World Series.

Monte Irvin played eight years in the majors after making it to the "bigs" at age 30. During that time, he banged out 731 hits with 99 home runs and 443 RBIs. He had a lifetime batting average of .293. Monte played on two pennant winners. The best known was the 1951 Giants. He played left field in the final playoff game with the Dodgers. He had one hit in that game, a double in the seventh, and he scored the run that tied the game at that time. Monte also played on the 1954 Giants, which won the National League pennant and swept the Cleveland Indians in four games. His career lasted from 1949 to 1956. All of those years were played with the Giants except for 1956, which was with the Chicago Cubs.

Larry Doby got his start with the Cleveland Indians at age 22. His career lasted for thirteen years. His best years were 1952 and 1954. In 1952 he led the American League with 32 home runs, and in 1954 he duplicated that number to lead the league in home runs again as well as leading in RBIs with 104. He played on the Cleveland teams that won the American League pennant in 1948 and 1954. However, in both years, his team lost the World Series. His career totals with Cleveland, the Chicago White Sox, and Detroit were 1,515 hits, 253 home runs, 969 RBIs, and a lifetime batting average of .283. His career lasted from 1947 till 1959.

Hank Thompson was also a member of the 1951 and 1954 Giants. He played in the majors for nine years with the St. Louis Browns (1947) and the New York Giants (1949–1956). He had a lifetime batting average of .267. His best years were 1950, 1953, and 1954. In 1950 he batted .289 with 20 home runs, in 1953 he hit .302 with 24 home runs, and in 1954 it was .263 with 26 home runs. Hank solved the Cleveland Indians' pitching in the 1954 World Series. In the fall classic he batted .364. Hank was 22 years old when he first made the major league scene.

Others had less time with major league teams. Dan Bankhead pitched for the Brooklyn Dodgers from 1947 untill 1951. During that three-year career, he won nine games while losing five. He was 27 years old when he got his chance. Joe Black also pitched for the Brooklyn Dodgers when he came up in 1952. He stayed there until 1955 before finishing his career with the Cincinnati Reds (1955–1956) and the Washington Senators (1957). During his time in the majors, he won 30 games and lost 12. His best year was his rookie year in 1952 when he won 15 while losing 4. Black had an earned run average of 2.15 during that season and won the National League rookie of the year award. Willard Brown made the St. Louis Browns team in 1947, and Bob Thurman played for the Cincinnati Reds from 1955 till 1959. Thurman was 38 years old before he got his chance to play major league baseball.

The United States never got to relax following World War II. Immediately following the surrender of Germany and Japan, Russia, along with other communist countries, began to intensify the "Cold War." This "Cold War" became hot when the North Koreans invaded their neighbors to the south. This division of the country occurred in 1948 after Russian troops occupied the north and American troops occupied the south. Korea had been under Japanese control since 1910 before they were defeated in 1945. The Korean War began on June 25, 1950, when the North Koreans crossed the border into South Korea. South Korea was to be protected by the United Nations, and sixteen countries sent troops to help South Korea. The United States was among those countries. On June 27, 1950, President Harry S. Truman ordered the United States military into the war. Over the next four years, the fighting went back and forth across the peninsula called Korea. In the end, the line that separated those two countries was about where it was when the war started. However, there were two million troops killed or wounded during that time as well as one million civilians who were killed. The countries agreed to a truce, and the fighting stopped on July 27, 1953.

When the United States entered the war, it began calling up its young men to fight. Baseball again felt the effects of war. Many current major league players as well as those who would some day become major leaguers were called into service. The players listed in Appendix E include both those who played in the major leagues before serving in Korea and those who made it to the majors after doing their duty. They are listed by name, years in the military, their first year in the majors, and their first major league team. The list also includes those who served in the later 1950s. The sources of the list are *The Sporting News Baseball Register* and *Baseball Magazine's Who's Who in Baseball.*

Included on the list of players who served in Korea are two who took part in World War II. They played major league baseball, fought World War II, returned to play baseball, fought in the Korean War, and then returned to baseball again. They are Ted Williams and Bob Kennedy. Both individuals are listed in chapter two. Their records have been adjusted for their service in both wars.

A number of players who served in Korea had very good careers. Many led their teams to pennants, etc. Two of those pitchers who achieved this were Whitey Ford and Curt Simmons. Ford made the Yankee team in 1950 and had a record of nine wins and one loss. He also helped the Yankees defeat the Philadelphia Phillies in the 1950 World Series. He would have been one of the Yankees premier pitchers for the 1951 and 1952 seasons. However, he entered the military before the start of the 1951 season. Considering his start in 1950, his success in 1953, and the rest of his career, Ford would probably have won an additional thirty games during the time he spent in the military.

Curt Simmons also helped his team win the 1950 pennant. The Philadelphia Phillies won their first National League pennant since 1915. Simmons was one of the main pitchers on that team. He was taken into the conflict when his National Guard unit was activated. This caused him to miss the last month of the season after he had won seventeen games. This also caused him to miss the World Series when the Phillies held on to win the pennant. His presence would have helped the Phillies as the Yankees won the Series in four straight. Simmons missed the following year (1951) and returned to the Phillies in 1952. His service probably cost him a twenty-win season in 1950 and as many as seventeen wins the following season.

There are many others whose numbers would have been greater if they had not missed part of their career to serve in the Korean War. The one player who might have set a number of career marks was Willie Mays. He was drafted after getting to play in thirty-four games in the 1952 season. He missed the balance of that season as well as the 1953 season. If the numbers he might have achieved during that time were added to his actual career statistics, he would be ranked very high, if not first, in a number of categories. Currently Mays ranks in the top ten in seven major batting categories. They are hits (10th), runs scored (6th), RBIs (8th), games played (7th), at-bats (10th), home runs (3rd), and extra base hits (4th). If he had not served during 1951 and 1952, he probably would be ranked in the top five in each of the areas. He might be ranked number one in runs scored if he had had that time. A more interesting category is home runs. Hank Aaron broke Babe Ruth's record of 714 home runs in 1974. However, if Mays had not lost most of two seasons, he probably would have broken the record in 1971. He would have been the home run champion for three years before Aaron would have broken his estimated 729 home runs during the 1974 season. This is another major "what if" caused by service to his country.

Vietnam was another war in which the United States took part. While the first "advisors" arrived there in the late 1950s, it wasn't until 1964 that the United States had a major presence in the war. The United States engagement lasted until 1973 when the last troops left Vietnam. During that time, many soldiers took part in the battle against communism. Baseball players did not play as large a role in this war as others. In most cases, only one or two players were taken from any one team. The players that went into the military usually only missed part of a season or at the most one season. Only in a couple of cases (Rich Beck and Bobby Mercer, both of the Yankees) did a player miss two seasons. Other notables who spent some time in service included Larry Dieker, Ted Simmons, Mike Hegan, Ken Holtzman, Dave DeBusschere, Jimy Williams, Darold Knowles, Mickey Rivers, and Al Hrabosky. In all, fewer than fifty players who had prior major league experience went into the military during the 1960s. While any time gone affects the player and his statisitcs, the time lost for major leaguers did not have a major impact on their career numbers.

APPENDIX A
A COMPARISON OF ACTUAL TOP 25 IN SELECTED CATEGORIES TO TOP 25 ADJUSTED FOR ESTIMATED MISSED PERFORMANCE
(Through the 2003 season)

GAMES PLAYED

#	Player	Actual Record	#	Player	Actual Record	Estimated Additional Production for the Lost Years	Adjusted Total Record
1	Pete Rose	3562	1	Pete Rose	3562		3562
2	Carl Yastrzemski	3308	2	Carl Yastrzemski	3308		3308
3	Hank Aaron	3298	3	Hank Aaron	3298		3298
4	Rickey Henderson	3081	4	Stan Musial	3026	153	3179
5	Ty Cobb	3035	5	Rickey Henderson	3081		3081
6	Stan Musial	3026	6	Ty Cobb	3035		3035
7	Eddie Murray	3026	7	Eddie Murray	3026		3026
8	Cal Ripken, Jr.	3001	8	Cal Ripken, Jr.	3001		3001
9	Willie Mays	2992	9	Willie Mays	2992		2992
10	Dave Winfield	2973	10	Ted Williams	2292	682	2974
11	Rusty Staub	2951	11	Dave Winfield	2973		2973
12	Brooks Robinson	2896	12	Rusty Staub	2951		2951
13	Robin Yount	2856	13	Brooks Robinson	2896		2896
14	Al Kaline	2834	14	Robin Yount	2856		2856
15	Harold Baines	2830	15	Al Kaline	2834		2834
16	Eddie Collins	2826	16	Harold Baines	2830		2830
17	Reggie Jackson	2820	17	Eddie Collins	2826		2826
18	Frank Robinson	2808	18	Reggie Jackson	2820		2820
19	Honus Wagner	2794	19	Frank Robinson	2808		2808
20	Tris Speaker	2789	20	Enos Slaughter	2380	427	2807
21	Tony Perez	2777	21	Honus Wagner	2794		2794
22	Mel Ott	2730	22	Tris Speaker	2789		2789
23	George Brett	2707	23	Tony Perez	2777		2777
24	Greg Nettles	2700	24	Mel Ott	2730		2730
25	Darrell Evans	2687	25	George Brett	2707		2707

AT-BATS

#	Player	Actual Record	#	Player	Actual Record	Estimated Additional Production for the Lost Years	Adjusted Total Record
1	Pete Rose	14053	1	Pete Rose	14053		14053
2	Hank Aaron	12364	2	Hank Aaron	12364		12364
3	Carl Yastrzemski	11988	3	Carl Yastrzemski	11988		11988
4	Cal Ripken, Jr.	11551	4	Stan Musial	10972	603	11575
5	Ty Cobb	11434	5	Cal Ripken, Jr.	11551		11551
6	Eddie Murray	11336	6	Ty Cobb	11434		11434
7	Robin Yount	11008	7	Eddie Murray	11336		11336
8	Dave Winfield	11003	8	Robin Yount	11008		11008
9	Stan Musial	10972	9	Dave Winfield	11003		11003
10	Rickey Henderson	10961	10	Rickey Henderson	10961		10961
11	Willie Mays	10881	11	Willie Mays	10881		10881
12	Paul Molitor	10835	12	Paul Molitor	10835		10835
13	Brooks Robinson	10654	13	Brooks Robinson	10654		10654
14	Honus Wagner	10439	14	Honus Wagner	10439		10439

		Actual Record			Actual Record	Estimated Additional Production for the Lost Years	Adjusted Total Record
15	George Brett	10349	15	George Brett	10349		10349
16	Lou Brock	10332	16	Lou Brock	10332		10332
17	Luis Aparicio	10230	17	Charlie Gehringer	8860	1400	10260
18	Tris Speaker	10195	18	Luis Aparicio	10260		10260
19	Al Kaline	10116	19	Tris Speaker	10195		10195
20	Rabbit Maranville	10078	20	Al Kaline	10116		10116
21	Frank Robinson	10006	21	Ted Williams	7706	2405	10111
22	Eddie Collins	9949	22	Rabbit Maranville	10078		10078
23	Andre Dawson	9927	23	Frank Robinson	10006		10006
24	Harold Baines	9908	24	Eddie Collins	9949		9949
25	Reggie Jackson	9864	25	Andre Dawson	9927		9927

HITS

		Actual Record			Actual Record	Estimated Additional Production for the Lost Years	Adjusted Total Record
1	Pete Rose	4256	1	Pete Rose	4256		4256
2	Ty Cobb	4189	2	Ty Cobb	4189		4189
3	Hank Aaron	3771	3	Stan Musial	3630	215	3845
4	Stan Musial	3630	4	Hank Aaron	3771		3771
5	Tris Speaker	3514	5	Tris Speaker	3514		3514
6	Honus Wagner	3420	6	Ted Williams	2654	849	3503
7	Carl Yastrzemski	3419	7	Honus Wagner	3420		3420
8	Paul Molitor	3319	8	Carl Yastrzemski	3419		3419
9	Eddie Collins	3315	9	Paul Molitor	3319		3319
10	Willie Mays	3283	10	Eddie Collins	3315		3315
11	Eddie Murray	3255	11	Willie Mays	3283		3283
12	Nap Lajoie	3242	12	Eddie Murray	3255		3255
13	Cal Ripken, Jr.	3184	13	Nap Lajoie	3242		3242
14	George Brett	3154	14	Charlie Gehringer	2839	396	3235
15	Paul Waner	3152	15	Paul Waner	3152	55	3207
16	Robin Yount	3142	16	Cal Ripken, Jr.	3184		3184
17	Tony Gwynn	3141	17	George Brett	3154		3154
18	Dave Winfield	3110	18	Robin Yount	3142		3142
19	Cap Anson	3056	19	Tony Gwynn	3141		3141
20	Rickey Henderson	3055	20	Dave Winfield	3110		3110
21	Rod Carew	3053	21	Luke Appling	2749	316	3065
22	Lou Brock	3023	22	Cap Anson	3056		3056
23	Wade Boggs	3010	23	Rickey Henderson	3055		3055
24	Al Kaline	3007	24	Rod Carew	3053		3053
25	Roberto Clemente	3000	25	Lou Brock	3023		3023

DOUBLES

		Actual Record			Actual Record	Estimated Additional Production for the Lost Years	Adjusted Total Record
1	Tris Speaker	792	1	Tris Speaker	792		792
2	Pete Rose	746	2	Stan Musial	725	50	775
3	Stan Musial	725	3	Pete Rose	746		746
4	Ty Cobb	724	4	Ty Cobb	724		724
5	George Brett	665	5	Ted Williams	525	180	705
6	Nap Lajoie	657	6	George Brett	665		665
7	Carl Yastrzemski	646	7	Nap Lajoie	657		657

		Actual Record			Actual Record	Estimated Additional Production for the Lost Years	Adjusted Total Record
8	Honus Wagner	643	8	Charlie Gehringer	574	77	651
9	Hank Aaron	624	9	Carl Yastrzemski	646		646
10	Paul Molitor	605	10	Honus Wagner	643		643
11	Paul Waner	603	11	Hank Aaron	624		624
12	Cal Ripken, Jr.	603	12	Paul Waner	603	10	613
13	Robin Yount	583	13	Paul Molitor	605		605
14	Wade Boggs	578	14	Cal Ripken, Jr.	603		603
15	Charlie Gehringer	574	15	Robin Yount	583		583
16	Eddie Murray	560	16	Wade Boggs	578		578
17	Tony Gwynn	543	17	Eddie Murray	560		560
18	Rafael Palmiero	543	18	Billy Herman	486	71	557
19	Harry Heilmann	542	19	Mickey Vernon	490	66	556
20	Rogers Hornsby	541	20	Tony Gwynn	543		543
21	Joe Medwick	540	21	Rafael Palmiero	543		543
22	Dave Winfield	540	22	Harry Heilmann	542		542
23	Al Simmons	539	23	Rogers Hornsby	541		541
24	Barry Bonds	536	24	Joe Medwick	540		540
25	Lou Gehrig	534	25	Dave Winfield	540		540

TRIPLES

		Actual Record			Actual Record	Estimated Additional Production for the Lost Years	Adjusted Total Record
1	Sam Crawford	309	1	Sam Crawford	309		309
2	Ty Cobb	295	2	Ty Cobb	295		295
3	Honus Wagner	252	3	Honus Wagner	252		252
4	Jake Beckley	244	4	Jake Beckley	244		244
5	Roger Connor	233	5	Roger Connor	233		233
6	Tris Speaker	222	6	Tris Speaker	222		222
7	Fred Clarke	220	7	Fred Clarke	220		220
8	Dan Brouthers	205	8	Dan Brouthers	205		205
9	Joe Kelley	194	9	Stan Musial	177	18	195
10	Paul Waner	190	10	Joe Kelley	194		194
11	Bid McPhee	189	11	Paul Waner	190	1	191
12	Eddie Collins	187	12	Bid McPhee	189		189
13	Ed Delahanty	186	13	Eddie Collins	187		187
14	Sam Rice	184	14	Ed Delahanty	186		186
15	Jesse Burkett	182	15	Sam Rice	184		184
16	Edd Roush	182	16	Enos Slaughter	148	36	184
17	Ed Konetchy	182	17	Jesse Burkett	182		182
18	Buck Ewing	178	18	Edd Roush	182		182
19	Rabbit Maranville	177	19	Ed Konetchy	182		182
20	Stan Musial	177	20	Buck Ewing	178		178
21	Harry Stovey	174	21	Rabbit Maranville	177		177
22	Goose Goslin	173	22	Harry Stovey	174		174
23	Tommy Leach	172	23	Goose Goslin	173		173
24	Zach Wheat	172	24	Tommy Leach	172		172
25	Rogers Hornsby	169	25	Zach Wheat	172		172

HOME RUNS

#		Actual Record	#		Actual Record	Estimated Additional Production for the Lost Years	Adjusted Total Record
1	Hank Aaron	755	1	Hank Aaron	755		755
2	Babe Ruth	714	2	Babe Ruth	714		714
3	Willie Mays	660	3	Ted Williams	521	172	693
4	Barry Bonds	658	4	Willie Mays	660		660
5	Frank Robinson	586	5	Barry Bonds	658		658
6	Mark McGuire	583	6	Frank Robinson	586		586
7	Harmon Killebrew	573	7	Mark McGuire	583		583
8	Reggie Jackson	563	8	Harmon Killebrew	573		573
9	Mike Schmidt	548	9	Reggie Jackson	563		563
10	Sammy Sosa	539	10	Mike Schmidt	548		548
11	Mickey Mantle	536	11	Sammy Sosa	539		539
12	Jimmie Foxx	534	12	Mickey Mantle	536		536
13	Rafael Palmeiro	528	13	Jimmie Foxx	534		534
14	Willie McCovey	521	14	Rafael Palmeiro	528		528
15	Ted Williams	521	15	Hank Greenberg	331	194	525
16	Ernie Banks	512	16	Willie McCovey	521		521
17	Eddie Mathews	512	17	Ernie Banks	512		512
18	Mel Ott	511	18	Eddie Mathews	512		512
19	Eddie Murray	504	19	Mel Ott	511		511
20	Lou Gehrig	493	20	Eddie Murray	504		504
21	Fred McGriff	491	21	Lou Gehrig	493		493
22	Ken Griffey, Jr.	481	22	Fred McGriff	491		491
23	Stan Musial	475	23	Stan Musial	475	14	489
24	Willie Stargell	475	24	Ken Griffey, Jr.	481		481
25	Dave Winfield	465	25	Willie Stargell	475		475

RUNS SCORED

#		Actual Record	#		Actual Record	Estimated Additional Production for the Lost Years	Adjusted Total Record
1	Rickey Henderson	2295	1	Ted Williams	1798	597	2395
2	Ty Cobb	2246	2	Rickey Henderson	2295		2295
3	Hank Aaron	2174	3	Ty Cobb	2246		2246
4	Babe Ruth	2174	4	Hank Aaron	2174		2174
5	Pete Rose	2165	5	Babe Ruth	2174		2174
6	Willie Mays	2062	6	Pete Rose	2165		2165
7	Stan Musial	1949	7	Stan Musial	1949	115	2064
8	Barry Bonds	1941	8	Willie Mays	2062		2062
9	Lou Gehrig	1888	9	Charlie Gehringer	1774	219	1993
10	Tris Speaker	1882	10	Barry Bonds	1941		1941
11	Mel Ott	1859	11	Lou Gehrig	1888		1888
12	Frank Robinson	1829	12	Tris Speaker	1882		1882
13	Eddie Collins	1821	13	Mel Ott	1859		1859
14	Carl Yastrzemski	1816	14	Frank Robinson	1829		1829
15	Ted Williams	1798	15	Eddie Collins	1821		1821
16	Paul Molitor	1782	16	Carl Yastrzemski	1816		1816
17	Charlie Gehringer	1774	17	Paul Molitor	1782		1782
18	Jimmie Foxx	1751	18	Jimmie Foxx	1751		1751
19	Honus Wagner	1739	19	Honus Wagner	1739		1739

		Actual Record			Actual Record	Estimated Additional Production for the Lost Years	Adjusted Total Record
20	Cap Anson	1722	20	Cap Anson	1722		1722
21	Jesse Burkett	1720	21	Jesse Burkett	1720		1720
22	Willie Keeler	1719	22	Willie Keeler	1719		1719
23	Billie Hamilton	1697	23	Joe DiMaggio	1390	325	1715
24	Bid McPhee	1684	24	Billie Hamilton	1697		1697
25	Mickey Mantle	1677	25	Bid McPhee	1684		1684

RUNS BATTED IN

		Actual Record			Actual Record	Estimated Additional Production for the Lost Years	Adjusted Total Record
1	Hank Aaron	2297	1	Ted Williams	1839	581	2420
2	Babe Ruth	2213	2	Hank Aaron	2297		2297
3	Lou Gehrig	1995	3	Babe Ruth	2213		2213
4	Stan Musial	1951	4	Stan Musial	1951	93	2044
5	Ty Cobb	1938	5	Lou Gehrig	1995		1995
6	Jimmie Foxx	1922	6	Ty Cobb	1938		1938
7	Eddie Murray	1917	7	Jimmie Foxx	1922		1922
8	Willie Mays	1903	8	Eddie Murray	1917		1917
9	Cap Anson	1880	9	Joe DiMaggio	1537	380	1917
10	Mel Ott	1860	10	Willie Mays	1903		1903
11	Carl Yastrzemski	1844	11	Cap Anson	1880		1880
12	Ted Williams	1839	12	Hank Greenberg	1276	592	1868
13	Dave Winfield	1833	13	Mel Ott	1860		1860
14	Al Simmons	1827	14	Carl Yastrzemski	1844		1844
15	Frank Robinson	1812	15	Dave Winfield	1833		1833
16	Barry Bonds	1742	16	Al Simmons	1827		1827
17	Honus Wagner	1733	17	Frank Robinson	1812		1812
18	Reggie Jackson	1702	18	Barry Bonds	1742		1742
19	Cal Ripken, Jr.	1695	19	Honus Wagner	1733		1733
20	Rafael Palmeiro	1687	20	Reggie Jackson	1702		1702
21	Tony Perez	1652	21	Cal Ripken, Jr.	1695		1695
22	Ernie Banks	1636	22	Rafael Palmeiro	1687		1687
23	Harold Baines	1628	23	Johnny Mize	1337	340	1677
24	Goose Goslin	1609	24	Tony Perez	1652		1652
25	Nap Lajoie	1599	25	Ernie Banks	1636		1636

BASES ON BALLS

		Actual Record			Actual Record	Estimated Additional Production for the Lost Years	Adjusted Total Record
1	Rickey Henderson	2190	1	Ted Williams	2019	621	2640
2	Barry Bonds	2070	2	Rickey Henderson	2190		2190
3	Babe Ruth	2062	3	Barry Bonds	2070		2070
4	Ted Williams	2019	4	Babe Ruth	2062		2062
5	Joe Morgan	1865	5	Joe Morgan	1865		1865
6	Carl Yastrzemski	1845	6	Carl Yastrzemski	1845		1845
7	Mickey Mantle	1733	7	Mickey Mantle	1733		1733
8	Mel Ott	1708	8	Mel Ott	1708	78	1786
9	Eddie Yost	1614	9	Stan Musial	1599	78	1677
10	Darrell Evans	1605	10	Eddie Yost	1614	38	1652
11	Stan Musial	1599	11	Darrell Evans	1605		1605
12	Pete Rose	1566	12	Pete Rose	1566		1566

		Actual Record				Actual Record	Estimated Additional Production for the Lost Years	Adjusted Total Record
13	Harmon Killebrew	1559		13	Harmon Killebrew	1559		1559
14	Lou Gehrig	1508		14	Lou Gehrig	1508		1508
15	Mike Schmidt	1507		15	Mike Schmidt	1507		1507
16	Eddie Collins	1499		16	Eddie Collins	1499		1499
17	Willie Mays	1464		17	Pee Wee Reese	1210	268	1478
18	Jimmie Foxx	1452		18	Willie Mays	1464		1464
19	Eddie Mathews	1444		19	Jimmie Foxx	1452		1452
20	Frank Robinson	1420		20	Luke Appling	1302	143	1445
21	Wade Boggs	1412		21	Eddie Mathews	1444		1444
22	Hank Aaron	1402		22	Frank Robinson	1420		1420
23	Dwight Evans	1391		23	Wade Boggs	1412		1412
24	Frank Thomas	1386		24	Hank Aaron	1402		1402
25	Tris Speaker	1381		25	Dwight Evans	1391		1391

STOLEN BASES

		Actual Record				Actual Record		Adjusted Total Record
1	Rickey Henderson	1406		1	Rickey Henderson	1406		1406
2	Lou Brock	938		2	Lou Brock	938		938
3	Billy Hamilton	914		3	Billy Hamilton	914		914
4	Ty Cobb	892		4	Ty Cobb	892		892
5	Tim Raines	808		5	Tim Raines	808		808
6	Vince Coleman	752		6	Vince Coleman	752		752
7	Eddie Collins	745		7	Eddie Collins	745		745
8	Arlie Latham	742		8	Arlie Latham	742		742
9	Max Carey	738		9	Max Carey	738		738
10	Honus Wagner	723		10	Honus Wagner	723		723
11	Joe Morgan	689		11	Joe Morgan	689		689
12	Willie Wilson	668		12	Willie Wilson	668		668
13	Tom Brown	657		13	Tom Brown	657		657
14	Bert Campenaris	649		14	Bert Campenaris	649		649
15	Otis Nixon	620		15	Otis Nixon	620		620
16	George Davis	619		16	George Davis	619		619
17	Dummy Hoy	596		17	Dummy Hoy	596		596
18	Maury Wills	586		18	Maury Wills	586		586
19	George Van Haltren	583		19	George Van Haltren	583		583
20	Ozzie Smith	580		20	Ozzie Smith	580		580
21	Hugh Duffy	574		21	Hugh Duffy	574		574
22	Bud McPhee	568		22	Bud McPhee	568		568
23	Brett Butler	558		23	Brett Butler	558		558
24	Davey Lopes	557		24	Davey Lopes	557		557
25	Cesar Cedeno	550		25	Cesar Cedeno	550		550

PITCHING APPEARANCES

		Actual Record				Actual Record		Adjusted Total Record
1	Jesse Orosco	1252		1	Jesse Orosco	1252		1252
2	Dennis Eckersley	1071		2	Dennis Eckersley	1071		1071
3	Hoyt Wilhelm	1070		3	Hoyt Wilhelm	1070	0	1070
4	Dan Plesac	1064		4	Dan Plesac	1064		1064
5	Kent Tekulve	1050		5	Kent Tekulve	1050		1050

		Actual Record			Actual Record	Estimated Additional Production for the Lost Years	Adjusted Total Record
6	John Franco	1036	6	John Franco	1036		1036
7	Lee Smith	1022	7	Lee Smith	1022		1022
8	Goose Gossage	1002	8	Goose Gossage	1002		1002
9	Lindy McDaniel	987	9	Lindy McDaniel	987		987
10	Mike Jackson	960	10	Mike Jackson	960		960
11	Rollie Fingers	944	11	Rollie Fingers	944		944
12	Gene Garber	931	12	Gene Garber	931		931
13	Cy Young	906	13	Cy Young	906		906
14	Sparky Lyle	899	14	Sparky Lyle	899		899
15	Jim Kaat	898	15	Jim Kaat	898		898
16	Mike Stanton	885	16	Mike Stanton	885		885
17	Paul Assenmacher	884	17	Paul Assenmacher	884		884
18	Jeff Reardon	880	18	Jeff Reardon	880		880
19	Don McMahon	874	19	Don McMahon	874		874
20	Phil Niekro	864	20	Warren Spahn	750	115	865
21	Charlie Hough	858	21	Phil Niekro	864		864
22	Roy Face	848	22	Charlie Hough	858		858
23	Doug Jones	846	23	Roy Face	848		848
24	Tug McGraw	824	24	Doug Jones	846		846
25	Nolan Ryan	807	25	Tug McGraw	824		824

INNINGS PITCHED

		Actual Record			Actual Record	Estimated Additional Production for the Lost Years	Adjusted Total Record
1	Cy Young	7356	1	Cy Young	7356		7356
2	Pud Galvin	5941	2	Warren Spahn	5244	836	6080
3	Walter Johnson	5914	3	Pud Galvin	5941		5941
4	Phil Niekro	5404	4	Walter Johnson	5914		5914
5	Nolan Ryan	5386	5	Phil Niekro	5404		5404
6	Gaylord Perry	5350	6	Nolan Ryan	5386		5386
7	Don Sutton	5282	7	Gaylord Perry	5350		5350
8	Warren Spahn	5244	8	Don Sutton	5282		5282
9	Steve Carlton	5217	9	Steve Carlton	5217		5217
10	Grover Alexander	5190	10	Grover Alexander	5190		5190
11	Kid Nichols	5066	11	Bob Feller	3827	1232	5059
12	Tim Keefe	5050	12	Kid Nichols	5066		5066
13	Bert Blyleven	4970	13	Tim Keefe	5050		5050
14	Mickey Welch	4802	14	Bert Blyleven	4970		4970
15	Christy Mathewson	4789	15	Early Wynn	4564	379	4943
16	Tom Seaver	4783	16	Mickey Welch	4802		4802
17	Tommy John	4710	17	Christy Mathewson	4789		4789
18	Robin Roberts	4689	18	Tom Seaver	4783		4783
19	Early Wynn	4564	19	Tommy John	4710		4710
20	John Clarkson	4536	20	Robin Roberts	4689		4689
21	Tony Mullane	4531	21	Red Ruffing	4344	269	4613
22	Jim Kaat	4530	22	John Clarkson	4536		4536
23	Hoss Radbourn	4527	23	Tony Mullane	4531		4531
24	Fergie Jenkins	4501	24	Jim Kaat	4530		4530
25	Eddie Plank	4496	25	Hoss Radbourn	4527		4527

		Actual Record			Actual Record	Estimated Additional Production for the Lost Years	Adjusted Total Record
WINS							
1	Cy Young	511	1	Cy Young	511		511
2	Walter Johnson	417	2	Warren Spahn	363	56	419
3	Grover Alexander	373	3	Walter Johnson	417		417
4	Christy Mathewson	373	4	Grover Alexander	373		373
5	Warren Spahn	363	5	Christy Mathewson	373		373
6	Kid Nichols	361	6	Kid Nichols	361		361
7	Pud Galvin	361	7	Pud Galvin	361		361
8	Tim Keefe	342	8	Bob Feller	266	92	358
9	Steve Carlton	329	9	Tim Keefe	342		342
10	John Clarkson	328	10	Steve Carlton	329		329
11	Eddie Plank	326	11	Early Wynn	300	29	329
12	Nolan Ryan	324	12	John Clarkson	328		328
13	Don Sutton	324	13	Eddie Plank	326		326
14	Phil Niekro	318	14	Nolan Ryan	324		324
15	Gaylord Perry	314	15	Don Sutton	324		324
16	Tom Seaver	311	16	Phil Niekro	318		318
17	Roger Clemens	310	17	Gaylord Perry	314		314
18	Hoss Radbourn	309	18	Tom Seaver	311		311
19	Mickey Welch	307	19	Roger Clemens	310		310
20	Lefty Grove	300	20	Hoss Radbourn	309		309
21	Early Wynn	300	21	Mickey Welch	307		307
22	Greg Maddox	289	22	Lefty Grove	300		300
23	Tommy John	288	23	Red Ruffing	273	20	293
24	Bert Blyleven	287	24	Greg Maddox	289		289
25	Robin Roberts	286	25	Tommy John	288		288
STRIKEOUTS BY PITCHERS							
1	Nolan Ryan	5714	1	Nolan Ryan	5714		5714
2	Steve Carlton	4136	2	Steve Carlton	4136		4136
3	Roger Clemens	4099	3	Roger Clemens	4099		4099
4	Randy Johnson	3871	4	Randy Johnson	3871		3871
5	Bert Blyleven	3701	5	Bert Blyleven	3701		3701
6	Tom Seaver	3640	6	Tom Seaver	3640		3640
7	Don Sutton	3574	7	Don Sutton	3574		3574
8	Gaylord Perry	3534	8	Bob Feller	2581	990	3571
9	Walter Johnson	3509	9	Gaylord Perry	3534		3534
10	Phil Niekro	3342	10	Walter Johnson	3509		3509
11	Ferguson Jenkins	3192	11	Phil Niekro	3342		3342
12	Bob Gibson	3117	12	Ferguson Jenkins	3192		3192
13	Jim Bunning	2855	13	Bob Gibson	3117		3117
14	Mickey Lolich	2832	14	Warren Spahn	2583	372	2955
15	Cy Young	2803	15	Jim Bunning	2855		2855
16	Frank Tanana	2773	16	Mickey Lolich	2832		2832
17	Greg Maddox	2765	17	Cy Young	2803		2803
18	David Cone	2668	18	Frank Tanana	2773		2773
19	Chuck Finley	2610	19	Greg Maddox	2765		2765

#	Name	Actual Record	#	Name	Actual Record	Estimated Additional Production for the Lost Years	Adjusted Total Record
20	Warren Spahn	2583	20	David Cone	2668		2668
21	Bob Feller	2581	21	Chuck Finley	2610		2610
22	Tim Keefe	2564	22	Tim Keefe	2564		2564
23	Jerry Koosman	2556	23	Jerry Koosman	2556		2556
24	Curt Schilling	2542	24	Curt Schilling	2542		2542
25	Christy Mathewson	2507	25	Christy Mathewson	2507		2507

SHUTOUTS

#	Name	Actual Record	#	Name	Actual Record	Estimated Additional Production for the Lost Years	Adjusted Total Record
1	Walter Johnson	110	1	Walter Johnson	110		110
2	Grover Alexander	90	2	Grover Alexander	90		90
3	Christy Mathewson	79	3	Christy Mathewson	79		79
4	Cy Young	76	4	Warren Spahn	63	16	79
5	Eddie Plank	69	5	Cy Young	76		76
6	Warren Spahn	63	6	Eddie Plank	69		69
7	Nolan Ryan	61	7	Bob Feller	46	22	68
8	Tom Seaver	61	8	Nolan Ryan	61		61
9	Bert Blyleven	60	9	Tom Seaver	61		61
10	Don Sutton	58	10	Bert Blyleven	60		60
11	Pud Galvin	57	11	Don Sutton	58		58
12	Ed Walsh	57	12	Pud Galvin	57		57
13	Bob Gibson	56	13	Ed Walsh	57		57
14	Three-Finger Brown	55	14	Bob Gibson	56		56
15	Steve Carlton	55	15	Three-Finger Brown	55		55
16	Jim Palmer	53	16	Steve Carlton	55		55
17	Gaylord Perry	53	17	Jim Palmer	53		53
18	Juan Marichal	52	18	Gaylord Perry	53		53
19	Rube Waddell	50	19	Early Wynn	49	4	53
20	Vic Willis	50	20	Juan Marichal	52		52
21	Don Drysdale	49	21	Red Ruffing	48	4	52
22	Fergie Jenkins	49	22	Rube Waddell	50		50
23	Luis Tiant	49	23	Vic Willis	50		50
24	Early Wynn	49	24	Don Drysdale	49		49
25	Kid Nichols	48	25	Fergie Jenkins	49		49

SAVES

#	Name	Actual Record	#	Name	Actual Record	Estimated Additional Production for the Lost Years	Adjusted Total Record
1	Lee Smith	478	1	Lee Smith	478		478
2	John Franco	424	2	John Franco	424		424
3	Dennis Eckersley	390	3	Dennis Eckersley	390		390
4	Jeff Reardon	367	4	Jeff Reardon	367		367
5	Trevor Hoffman	352	5	Trevor Hoffman	352		352
6	Randy Myers	347	6	Randy Myers	347		347
7	Rollie Fingers	341	7	Rollie Fingers	341		341
8	John Wetteland	330	8	John Wetteland	330		330
9	Roberto Hernandez	320	9	Roberto Hernandez	320		320
10	Rick Aguilera	318	10	Rick Aguilera	318		318
11	Robb Nen	314	11	Robb Nen	314		314
12	Tom Henke	311	12	Tom Henke	311		311

							Actual Record	Estimated Additional Production for the Lost Years	Adjusted Total Record
13	Rich Goosage	310		13	Rich Goosage	310			310
14	Jeff Montgomery	304		14	Jeff Montgomery	304			304
15	Doug Jones	303		15	Doug Jones	303			303
16	Bruce Sutter	300		16	Bruce Sutter	300			300
17	Rod Beck	286		17	Rod Beck	286			286
18	Troy Percival	283		18	Troy Percival	283			283
19	Mariano Rivera	283		19	Mariano Rivera	283			283
20	Todd Worrell	256		20	Todd Worrell	256			256
21	Dave Righetti	252		21	Dave Righetti	252			252
22	Jose Mesa	249		22	Jose Mesa	249			249
23	Dan Quisenberry	244		23	Dan Quisenberry	244			244
24	Sparky Lyle	238		24	Sparky Lyle	238			238
25	Hoyt Wilhelm	227		25	Hoyt Wilhelm	227		0	227

APPENDIX B
BASEBALL PLAYERS WHO SERVED IN WORLD WAR I

Name	Team	Position	Age	Years in Service
Ainsmith, Eddie	Washington	Catcher	26	1918
Aldridge, Vic	Chicago (N)	Pitcher	24	1918
Alexander, Pete	Chicago (N)	Pitcher	31	1918
Allen, Nick	Cincinnati	Catcher	29	1918
Anderson, Fred	New York (N)	Pitcher	32	1918
Anderson, Walter	Philadelphia (A)	Pitcher	20	1918
Bailey, Fred	Boston (N)	Outfield	22	1918
Bailey, Gene	Philadelphia (A)	Outfield	24	1918
Baird, Al	New York (N)	Infield	23	1918
Baird, Doug	St. Louis (N)	Infield	26	1918
Barnes, Jesse	New York (N)	Pitcher	25	1918
Barry, Jack	Boston (A)	Infield	31	1918
Bates, Ray	Philadelphia (A)	Infield	25	1918
Benton, Rube	New York (N)	Pitcher	31	1918
Billings, Josh	Cleveland	Catcher	26	1918
Blackwell, Fred	Pittsburgh	Catcher	22	1918
Boeckel, Tony	Pittsburgh	Infield	25	1918
Brady, Neal	New York (A)	Pitcher	21	1918
Bressler, Rube	Cincinnati	Pitcher	23	1918
Brottem, Tony	St. Louis (N)	Catcher	26	1918
Cadore, Leon	Brooklyn	Pitcher	27	1918
Camp, Howie	New York (A)	Outfield	25	1918
Canavan, Hugh	Boston (N)	Pitcher	21	1918
Carlson, Hal	Pittsburgh	Pitcher	26	1918
Caton, Buster	Pittsburgh	Infield	21	1918
Cobb, Joe	Detroit	Unknown	23	1918
Collins, Eddie	Chicago (A)	Infield	31	1918
Conway, Rip	Boston (N)	Infield	22	1918
Cooney, Jimmy	Boston (A)	Infield	23	1918
Cooper, Claude	Philadelphia (N)	Outfield	25	1918
Couch, Johnny	Detroit	Pitcher	27	1918
Covington, Sam	Boston (N)	Infield	25	1918
Craft, Molly	Washington	Pitcher	22	1918
Cruise, Walton	St. Louis (N)	Outfield	28	1918
Davis, Dixie	Philadelphia (N)	Pitcher	27	1918
DeBerry, Hank	Cleveland	Catcher	23	1918
Debus, Adam	Pittsburgh	Infield	25	1918, 1919
Dilhoefer, Pickles	Philadelphia (N)	Catcher	23	1918
Driscoll, Paddy	Chicago (N)	Infield	23	1918
Duncan, Pat	Cincinnati	Outfield	24	1918, 1919
Dyer, Ben	Detroit	Infield	26	1918
Dykes, Jimmy	Philadelphia (A)	Infield	21	1918
Ehmke, Howard	Detroit	Pitcher	24	1918
Elliott, Rowdy	Chicago (N)	Catcher	27	1918
Ellison, Bert	Detroit	Outfield	22	1918
Erickson, Eric	Detroit	Pitcher	26	1918

Name	Team	Position	Age	Years in Service
Evans, Bill	Pittsburgh	Pitcher	25	1918
Evans, Joe	Cleveland	Infield	23	1918
Faber, Red	Chicago (A)	Pitcher	29	1918
Felsch, Happy	Chicago (A)	Outfield	26	1918
Ferguson, Alex	New York (A)	Pitcher	21	1918
Fillingim, Dana	Boston (N)	Pitcher	24	1918
Fisher, Ray	New York (A)	Pitcher	30	1918
Fitzpatrick, Ed	Boston (N)	Infield	28	1918
Flagstead, Ira	Detroit	Outfield	24	1918
Gainer, Del	Boston (A)	Infield	31	1918
Geary, Bob	Philadelphia (A)	Pitcher	27	1918
Gerber, Wally	St. Louis (A)	Infield	26	1918
Goodwin, Marv	St. Louis (N)	Pitcher	27	1918
Gowdy, Hank	Boston (N)	Catcher	28	1917, 1918, 1919
Guisto, Lou	Cleveland	Infield	24	1918
Haley, Pat	Philadelphia (A)	Catcher	27	1918, 1919
Hamilton, Earl	Pittsburgh	Pitcher	26	1918
Hardgrove, Pat	Chicago (A)	Unknown	22	1918
Harris, Joe	Cleveland	Infield	27	1918
Heilmann, Harry	Detroit	Outfield	23	1918
Heitmann, Harry	Brooklyn	Pitcher	21	1918
Hickman, Jim	Brooklyn	Outfield	24	1918
Hitt, Bruce	St. Louis (N)	Pitcher	20	1918
Hobitzell, Dick	Boston (A)	Infield	29	1918, 1919, 1920
Holke, Walter	New York (N)	Infield	25	1918
Horstmann, Oscar	St. Louis (N)	Pitcher	27	1918
Jackson, Charlie	Pittsburgh	Outfield	25	1918
Jackson, Joe	Chicago (A)	Outfield	28	1918
Jacobson, Baby Doll	St. Louis (A)	Outfield	27	1918
James, Bill	Boston (N)	Pitcher	26	1918
James, Bill	Detroit	Pitcher	31	1918
Janvrin, Hal	Boston (A)	Infield	25	1918
Jenkins, Joe	Chicago (A)	Catcher	27	1918
Johnson, Jing	Philadelphia (A)	Pitcher	23	1918
Jourdan, Ted	Chicago (A)	Infield	22	1918
Kauff, Benny	New York (N)	Outfield	28	1918
Keefe, Dave	Philadelphia (A)	Pitcher	21	1918
Kelly, Joe	Boston (N)	Outfield	31	1918
Kelly, George	New York (N)	Infield	22	1918
Kiduff, Pete	Chicago (N)	Infield	25	1918
King, Lee	Pittsburgh	Outfield	25	1918
Klepfer, Ed	Cleveland	Pitcher	30	1918
Kopf, Larry	Cincinnati	Infield	27	1918
Kopp, Manny	Philadelphia (A)	Outfield	26	1918
Koob, Ernie	St. Louis (A)	Pitcher	25	1918
Krueger, Ernie	Brooklyn	Catcher	27	1918
Lamar, Bill	New York (A)	Outfield	21	1918
Lambeth, Otis	Cleveland	Pitcher	28	1918
Lawry, Otis	Philadelphia (A)	Infield	24	1918, 1919

Name	Team	Position	Age	Years in Service
Leonard, Dutch	Boston (A)	Pitcher	26	1918
Leonard, Joe	Washington	Infield	23	1918
Lewis, Duffy	Boston (A)	Outfield	30	1918
Mails, Duster	Brooklyn	Pitcher	22	1917, 1918
Malone, Lew	Brooklyn	Infield	21	1918
Mamaux, Al	Brooklyn	Pitcher	24	1918
Maranville, Rabbit	Boston (N)	Infield	26	1918
Marriott, Bill	Chicago (N)	Outfield	25	1918
May, Jackie	St. Louis (N)	Pitcher	22	1918
Mayer, Wally	Boston (A)	Catcher	23	1918
McGaffigan, Patsy	Philadelphia (N)	Infield	29	1918
McGraw, Bob	New York (A)	Pitcher	23	1918, 1919
McGuire, Tom	Chicago (A)	Pitcher	26	1918
McInnis, Stuffy	Boston (A)	Infield	27	1918
McNally, Mike	Boston (A)	Infield	24	1918
Menosky, Mike	Washington	Outfield	23	1918
Mijus, Johnny	Brooklyn	Pitcher	23	1918
Milan, Horace	Washington	Outfield	24	1918
Miller, Dots	St. Louis (N)	Infield	31	1918
Miller, Ray	Pittsburgh	Infield	30	1918
Mitchell, Clarence	Brooklyn	Pitcher	27	1918
Mitchell, Willie	Detroit	Pitcher	28	1918
Monroe, Ed	New York (A)	Pitcher	25	1918
Morton, Guy	Cleveland	Pitcher	25	1918
Musser, Paul	Boston (A)	Pitcher	29	1918, 1919
Myers, Elmer	Philadelphia (A)	Pitcher	24	1918
Naylor, Rollie	Philadelphia (A)	Pitcher	26	1918
Nicholson, Fred	Detroit	Outfield	23	1918
North, Lou	St. Louis (N)	Pitcher	27	1918
Noyes, Win	Philadelphia (A)	Pitcher	29	1918
Pennock, Herb	Boston (A)	Pitcher	24	1918
Pfeffer, Jeff	Brooklyn	Pitcher	30	1918
Picinich, Val	Washington	Catcher	21	1918
Pipp, Wally	New York (A)	Infield	25	1918
Ponder, Elmer	Pittsburgh	Pitcher	25	1918, 1919
Powell, Ray	Boston (N)	Outfield	29	1918
Rath, Morrie	Cincinnati	Infield	31	1918
Rehg, Wally	Boston (N)	Outfield	29	1918
Rice, Sam	Washington	Outfield	28	1918
Rico, Art	Boston (N)	Catcher	21	1918
Risberg, Swede	Chicago (A)	Infield	23	1918
Rixey, Eppa	Philadelphia (N)	Pitcher	27	1918, 1919
Robertson, Dave	New York (N)	Outfield	28	1918
Ruel, Muddy	New York (A)	Catcher	22	1918
Ruether, Dutch	Cincinnati	Pitcher	24	1918
Rumier, Bill	St. Louis (A)	Outfield	27	1918
Russell, Jack	Brooklyn	Pitcher	23	1918
Schick, Morrie	Chicago (N)	Outfield	26	1918
Schmandt, Ray	Brooklyn	Infield	22	1918

Name	Team	Position	Age	Years in Service
Schreiber, Hank	Boston (N)	Infield	26	1918
Scott, Jim	Chicago (A)	Pitcher	30	1917, 1918
Seibold, Socks	Philadelphia (A)	Pitcher	22	1918
Severeid, Hank	St. Louis (A)	Catcher	27	1918
Shaw, Ben	Pittsburgh	Infield	25	1918
Shawkey, Bob	New York (A)	Pitcher	27	1918
Sheridan, Red	Brooklyn	Infield	21	1918
Shocker, Urban	St. Louis (A)	Pitcher	27	1918
Shore, Ernie	New York (A)	Pitcher	27	1918
Shorten, Chick	Boston (A)	Outfield	26	1918
Sicking, Eddie	New York (N)	Infield	21	1918
Sloan, Tod	St. Louis (A)	Outfield	27	1918
Smallwood, Walt	New York (A)	Pitcher	25	1918, 1919
Smith, Elmer	Cleveland	Outfield	25	1918
Smith, Jackie	St. Louis (N)	Outfield	23	1918
Smith, Sherry	Brooklyn	Pitcher	27	1918
Snyder, Frank	St. Louis (N)	Catcher	25	1918
Stengel, Casey	Pittsburgh	Outfield	27	1918
Terry, Zeb	Boston (N)	Infield	27	1918
Tesreau, Jeff	New York (N)	Pitcher	29	1918
Thomas, Fred	Boston (A)	Infield	25	1918
Tincup, Ben	Philadelphia (N)	Pitcher	27	1918
Torkelson, Red	Cleveland	Pitcher	24	1918
Tragresser, Walt	Boston (N)	Catcher	31	1918
Vick, Sammy	New York (A)	Outfield	22	1918
Walsh, Jimmy	Boston (A)	Outfield	22	1918
Ward, Aaron	New York (A)	Infield	21	1918
Ward, Chuck	Brooklyn	Infield	23	1918
Warner, Hooks	Pittsburgh	Infield	24	1918
Weaver, Harry	Chicago (N)	Pitcher	26	1918
Webb, Billy	Pittsburgh	Infield	22	1918
Williams, Ken	St. Louis (A)	Outfield	28	1918
Williams, Lefty	Chicago (A)	Pitcher	25	1918
Witt, Whitey	Philadelphia (A)	Infield	22	1918
Woodward, Frank	Philadelphia (N)	Pitcher	24	1918
Yingling, Earl	Washington	Pitcher	29	1918
Zachary, Tom	Philadelphia (A)	Pitcher	22	1918, 1919

APPENDIX C
BASEBALL PLAYERS WHO SERVED IN MILITARY BEFORE GOING TO MAJOR LEAGUES

Name	Years in Military	Team Prior to Military Service	League Prior to Military	First Year in Majors	First Major League Team
Abrams, Calvin R.	1943-1945	Olean	Pony	1949	Brooklyn
Addis, Robert G.	1944-1945	Wellsville	Pony	1950	Boston (N)
Anderson, Andrew H.	1943-1945	Springfield	Three I	1948	St. Louis (A)
Arft, Henry I.	1943-1945	Springfield	Three I	1948	St. Louis (A)
Ashburn, Richie	1946	Utica	Eastern	1948	Philadelphia (N)
Asthroth, Joseph	1944	None	None	1945	Philadelphia (A)
Babe, Loren R.	1946	Norfolk	Piedmont	1952	New York (A)
Basgall, Romanus	1943-1945	Valdosta	Georgia-Florida	1948	Pittsburgh
Batts, Matthew D.	1943-1945	Canton	Middle Atlantic	1947	Boston (A)
Bauer, Henry A.	1942-1945	Oshkosh	Wisconsin State	1948	New York (A)
Baumholtz, Frank C.	1943-1945	Odgen	Pioneer	1947	Cincinnati
Bearden, H. Eugene	1943-1944	Savannah-Augusta	South Atlantic	1947	Cleveland
Behrman, Henry B.	1943-1945	Durham	Piedmont	1946	Brooklyn
Berry, Cornelius J.	1943-1945	Winston-Salem	Piedmont	1948	Detroit
Bickford, Vernon E.	1943-1945	Welch	Mt. State	1948	Boston (N)
Bishop, Charles T.	1944-1945	Jamestown	Pony	1952	Philadelphia (A)
Blake, Edward J.	1945	Mobile	Southern Association	1951	Cincinnati
Blatnik, John L.	1943-1945	Charleston	Middle Atlantic	1948	Philadelphia (N)
Bockman, Joseph E.	1942-1945	Norfolk	Piedmont	1946	New York (A)
Bollwig, Donald R.	1943-1945	Washington	Pennsylvania St. Assn.	1950	St. Louis (N)
Boone, Raymond O.	1943-1945	Wausau	Northern	1948	Cleveland
Boyer, Cloyd V.	1945-1946	Johnson City	Appalachian	1949	St. Louis (N)
Bradley, Fred L.	1943-1945	Tacoma	Western International	1948	Chicago (A)
Brinkoff, Leon C.	1945-1947	Newark	Ohio State	1952	Chicago (N)
Brissie, Leland V.	1942	None	None	1948	Philadelphia (A)
Burgess, Forrest H.	1945-1946	Portsmouth	Piedmont	1949	Chicago (N)
Burris, Paul R.	1943-1945	Durham	Piedmont	1948	Boston (N)
Burtschy, Edward F.	1943-1945	Columbia	South Atlantic	1950	Philadelphia (A)
Cain, Robert M.	1944-1945	Bristol	Appalachian	1949	Chicago (A)
Castiglione, Peter P	1943-1945	Harrisburg	Interstate	1947	Pittsburgh
Chakales, Robert E.	1946	Wilmington	Interstate	1951	Cleveland
Chambers, Clifford R.	1943-1945	Los Angeles	Pacific Coast	1948	Chicago (N)
Chesnes, Robert V.	1943-1945	Salt Lake City	Pioneer	1948	Pittsburgh
Clark, Alfred A.	1943-1945	Newark	International	1947	New York (A)
Clark, Michael J.	1943-1945	Mobile	Southeastern	1952	St. Louis (N)
Cole, Richard R.	1945	Allentown	Interstate	1951	St. Louis (N)
Coleman, Gerald F.	1943-1945	Wellsville	Pony	1949	New York (A)
Coleman, Raymond L.	1942-1945	Springfield	Three I	1947	St. Louis (A)
Collins, Joseph E.	1944-1945	Springfield	Eastern	1948	New York (A)
Combs, Merrill R.	1942-1945	Greensboro	Piedmont	1947	Boston (A)
Conatser, Clinton A.	1942-1945	Charleston	Middle Atlantic	1948	Boston (N)
Connor, Kevin	1943-1945	Norfolk	Piedmont	1949	Brooklyn
Corbitt, Claude E.	1942-1945	Montreal	International	1945	Brooklyn
Crimian, John M.	1945	Wilmington	Interstate	1951	St. Louis (N)

371

Name	Years in Military	Team Prior to Military Service	League Prior to Military	First Year in Majors	First Major League Team
Davis, Thomas O.	1945-1946	Hollywood	Pacific Coast	1949	Philadelphia (A)
Deal, Ellis F. (Cot)	1943-1945	Hutchison	Western Association	1947	Boston (A)
Delsing, James H.	1944-1945	Lockport	Pony	1948	Chicago (A)
Dente, Sam J.	1944-1945	Scranton	Eastern	1947	Boston (A)
Diering, Charles E.	1943-1945	Albany	Georgia-Florida	1947	St. Louis (N)
Dillinger, Robert B.	1943-1945	Toledo	American Association	1946	St. Louis (A)
Dixon, John C.	1943-1945	Charlotte	Piedmont	1953	Washington
Dobernic, Andrew J.	1943-1945	Los Angeles	Pacific Coast	1948	Chicago (N)
Dorish, Harry	1943-1945	Scranton	Eastern	1947	Boston (A)
Dyck, James R.	1943-1945	Fond du Lac	Wisconsin State	1951	St. Louis (A)
Edwards, Bruce	1943-1945	Durham	Piedmont	1946	Brooklyn
Ennis, Delmar	1944-1945	Trenton	Interstate	1946	Philadelphia (N)
Erautt, Edward L.	1944-1945	Hollywood	Pacific Coast	1947	Cincinnati
Fain, Ferris R.	1943-1945	San Francisco	Pacific Coast	1947	Philadelphia (A)
Ferriss, David M.	1943-1944	Greensboro	Piedmont	1945	Boston (A)
Flowers, Bennett Jr.	1947	Roanoke	Piedmont	1951	Boston (A)
Fox, J. Nelson	1946	Lancaster	Interstate	1947	Philadelphia (A)
Frazier, Joseph F.	1943-1945	Cedar Rapids	Three I	1947	Cleveland
Furillo, Carl A.	1943-1945	Montreal	International	1946	Brooklyn
Fusselman, Lester L.	1943-1945	Columbus	South Atlantic	1952	St. Louis (N)
Garagiola, Joseph H.	1944-1946	Columbus	American Association	1946	St. Louis (N)
Garcia, E. Mike	1943-1945	Appleton	Wisconsin State	1948	Cleveland
Gardner, William F.	1946-1947	Jersey City	International	1954	New York (N)
Ginsberg, Myron N.	1945-1946	Jamestown	Pony	1948	Detroit
Gionfriddo, Albert F.	1943	Oil City	Pennsylvania State Assn.	1944	Pittsburgh
Glaviano, Thomas	1943-1945	Springfield	Middle Atlantic	1946	St. Louis (N)
Goodman, William D.	1945	Atlanta	Southern Association	1947	Boston (A)
Graham, John B.	1944-1945	Montreal	International	1946	Brooklyn
Grasso, N. Michael	1942-1945	Trenton	Interstate	1946	New York (N)
Gray, Ted G.	1943-1945	Winston-Salem	Piedmont	1946	Detroit
Greengrass, James R.	1946-1947	Binghamton	Eastern	1952	Cincinnati
Grissom, Marvin E.	1942-1945	San Bernardine	California	1946	New York (N)
Hall, Robert L.	1943-1945	Winston-Salem	Piedmont	1949	Boston (N)
Hamner, Ralph C.	1943-1945	Shreveport	Texas	1946	Chicago (A)
Harris, Charles Jr.	1945	Roanoke	Piedmont	1948	Philadelphia (A)
Harrist, Earl	1942-1945	Syracuse	International	1945	Cincinnati
Hartsfield, Roy T.	1944-1945	Atlanta	Southern Association	1950	Boston (N)
Hartung, Clinton C.	1943-1946	Eau Claire	Northern	1947	New York (N)
Hatfield, Fred J.	1943-1945	Danville-Schoolfield	Bi-State	1950	Boston (A)
Hatton, Grady E.	1943-1945	None	None	1946	Cincinnati
Hatton, Joseph H	1943-1945	Montreal	International	1946	Brooklyn
Hearn, James T.	1943-1945	Columbus	South Atlantic	1947	St. Louis (N)
Hetki, John E.	1943-1944	Birmingham	Southern Association	1945	Cincinnati
Hicks, Clarence W.	1945-1946	Newport News	Piedmont	1956	Detroit
Hoderlein, Melvin A.	1943-1945	Columbia	South Atlantic	1951	Boston (A)
Hofman, Robert G.	1945	Springfield	Ohio State	1949	New York (N)
Hogue, Robert C.	1943-1945	Winston-Salem	Piedmont	1948	Boston (N)

Name	Years in Military	Team Prior to Military Service	League Prior to Military	First Year in Majors	First Major League Team
Hooper, Robert N.	1943-1945	Oklahoma City	Texas	1950	Philadelphia (A)
Houk, Ralph G.	1942-1945	Augusta	South Atlantic	1947	New York (A)
Howell, Homer E.	1944-1945	Montreal	International	1947	Pittsburgh
Jansen, Lawrence	1943-1945	San Francisco	Pacific Coast	1947	New York (N)
Johnson, Donald R.	1945-1946	Newark	International	1947	New York (A)
Johnson, Ernest T.	1943-1945	Hartford	Eastern	1950	Boston (N)
Johnson, Kenneth W.	1943-1945	Asheville	Piedmont	1947	St. Louis (N)
Jones, Sheldon L.	1943-1945	Ft. Smith	Western Association	1946	New York (N)
Jones, Vernal L.	1944-1945	Sacramento	Pacific Coast	1946	St. Louis (N)
Jorgensen, John D.	1942-1945	Santa Barbara	California	1947	Brooklyn
Jurisich, Alvin J	1943	Rochester	International	1944	St. Louis (N)
Kazak, Edward T.	1943-1945	Houston	Texas	1948	St. Louis (N)
Kellner, Alexander R.	1943-1945	Muskogee	Western Association	1948	Philadelphia (A)
Kennedy, Montia C.	1943-1945	Richmond	Piedmont	1946	New York (N)
Kennedy, William A.	1943-1945	Rocky Mount	Bi-State	1948	Cleveland
Kinder, Ellis R.	1945	Memphis	Southern Association	1946	St. Louis (A)
Klippstein, John C.	1946	Allentown	Interstate	1950	Chicago (N)
Kozar, Albert K.	1943-1945	Scranton	Eastern	1948	Washington
Kress, Charles S.	1943-1945	Columbia	South Atlantic	1947	Cincinnati
Kucab, John A.	1942-1945	Columbia	South Atlantic	1950	Philadelphia (A)
Kuzava, Robert L.	1943-1945	Charleston	Middle Atlantic	1946	Cleveland
La Palme, Paul E.	1943-1945	Erie	Middle Atlantic	1951	Pittsburgh
La Sorda, Thomas C.	1946-1947	Conord	North Carolina State	1954	Brooklyn
Labine, Clement W.	1945-1946	Newport News	Piedmont	1950	Brooklyn
Lade, Doyle M.	1943-1945	Shreveport	Texas	1948	Chicago (N)
Lafata, Joseph J.	1943-1944	Minneapolis	American Association	1947	New York (N)
Lang, Donald C.	1943-1945	Kansas City	American Association	1948	St. Louis (N)
Lohrke, Jack W.	1943-1945	San Diego	Pacific Coast	1947	New York (N)
Lombardi, Victor A.	1943-1944	Durham	Piedmont	1945	Brooklyn
Lown, Omar (Turk)	1943-1945	Valdosta	Georgia-Florida	1951	Chicago (N)
Maddern, Clarence J.	1943-1945	Los Angeles	Pacific Coast	1946	Chicago (N)
Maguire, Jack	1944-1945	Jersey City	International	1950	New York (N)
Main, Forrest H.	1943-1945	Norfolk	Piedmont	1948	Pittsburgh
Malone, Edward R.	1945	Rochester	International	1949	Chicago (A)
Mancuso, Frank O.	1943	San Antonio	Texas	1944	St. Louis (A)
Mapes, Clifford F.	1944-1945	Wilkes-Barre	Eastern	1948	New York (A)
Marsh, Fred F.	1943-1945	Zanesville	Middle Atlantic	1949	Cleveland
Martin, Fred T.	1942-1945	Houston	Texas	1946	St. Louis (N)
Martin, Morris W.	1943-1945	St. Paul	American Association	1949	Brooklyn
McCahan, William G.	1943-1945	Wilmington	Interstate	1946	Philadelphia (A)
McCall, Robert	1944-1945	Nashville	Southern Association	1948	Chicago (N)
McLeland, Wayne G.	1943-1945	LaCrosse	Wisconsin State	1951	Detroit
Medlinger, Irving J.	1946	Durham	Piedmont	1951	St. Louis (A)
Merson, John W.	1941-1946	Newport	Appalachian	1951	Pittsburgh
Meyer, Russell C.	1943	Superior	Northern	1946	Chicago (N)
Miggins, Lawrence E.	1945	Jersey City	International	1948	St. Louis (N)
Milne, William J.	1944-1945	Batavia	Pony	1948	New York (N)

Name	Years in Military	Team Prior to Military Service	League Prior to Military	First Year in Majors	First Major League Team
Minner, Paul E.	1943-1945	Elizabethton	Appalachian	1946	Brooklyn
Morgan, Bobby M.	1945-1946	Olean	Pony	1950	Brooklyn
Moss, John Lester	1944-1945	Elmira	Eastern	1946	St. Louis (A)
Moulder Glen H.	1943-1945	Durham	Piedmont	1946	Brooklyn
Murray, Joseph A.	1943-1945	Butler	Pennsylvania St. Assn.	1950	Philadelphia (A)
Murray, Raymond L.	1942-1945	Tarboro	Coastal Plain	1948	Cleveland
Nelson, Glenn R.	1943-1945	Johnson City	Appalachian	1949	St. Louis (N)
Niarhos, Costantine	1943-1945	Binghamton	Eastern	1946	New York (A)
Okrie, Leonard J.	1943-1945	Lockport	Pony	1948	Washington
Ostrowski, Joseph P.	1943-1945	Greensboro	Piedmont	1948	St. Louis (A)
Palm, Richard P.	1944-1945	Allentown	Interstate	1948	Boston (A)
Papai, Alford T.	1942-1944	Springfield	Western Association	1948	St. Louis (N)
Parnell, Melvin L.	1943-1945	Canton	Middle Atlantic	1947	Boston (A)
Pellagrini, Edward	1942-1945	Louisville	American Association	1946	Boston (A)
Perkowski, Harry W.	1943-1945	Bluefield	Mountain State	1947	Cincinnati
Phillips, Jack D.	1944-1945	Newark	International	1947	New York (A)
Pramesa, John S. Jr.	1944-1945	Bristol	Appalachian	1949	Cincinnati
Rackley, Marvin	1943-1945	Dayton	Middle Atlantic	1947	Brooklyn
Ramazzotti, Robert L.	1942-1945	Durham	Piedmont	1946	Brooklyn
Ramsdell, James W.	1943-1945	Muskogee	Western Association	1947	Brooklyn
Rapp, Earl W.	1943-1945	Buffalo	International	1949	Detroit
Raschi, Victor J.	1943-1945	Kansas City	American Association	1947	New York (A)
Reeder, William E.	1943-1945	Merdian	Southeastern	1949	St. Louis (N)
Reich, Herman C.	1942-1945	Portland	Pacific Coast	1949	Washington
Restelli, Dino P.	1944-1945	San Francisco	Pacific Coast	1949	Pittsburgh
Rhawn, Robert J.	1941-1945	Asheville	Piedmont	1947	New York (N)
Rice, Harold H.	1943-1945	Asheville	Piedmont	1948	St. Louis (N)
Richter, Allen G.	1946	Roanoke	Piedmont	1951	Boston (A)
Rigney, William J.	1943-1945	Oakland	Pacific Coast	1946	New York (N)
Rosen, Albert L.	1943-1945	Thomasville	North Carolina State	1947	Cleveland
Rossi, Joseph A.	1945	Sacramento	Pacific Coast	1952	Cincinnati
Saffell, Thomas J	1943-1945	Kingsport	Appalachian	1949	Pittsburgh
Sarni, William F.	1946	Los Angeles	Pacific Coast	1951	St. Louis (N)
Schenz, Henry L.	1943-1945	Portsmouth	Piedmont	1946	Chicago (N)
Schoendienst, Albert R.	1944	Rochester	International	1945	St. Louis (N)
Shea, Frank J.	1943-1945	Kansas City	American Association	1947	New York (A)
Shelly, Hollis	1943-1945	Greensboro	Piedmont	1951	Chicago (A)
Silvera, Charles R.	1943-1945	Wellsville	Pony	1948	New York (A)
Sima, Albert	1944-1945	Jersey City	International	1950	Washington
Sisler, Richard A.	1943-1945	Asheville	Piedmont	1946	St. Louis (N)
Smalley, Roy F. Jr.	1945	Los Angeles	Pacific Coast	1948	Chicago (N)
Souchock, Steve	1943-1945	Binghamton	Eastern	1946	New York (A)
Staley, Gerald L.	1943-1945	Boise	Pioneer	1947	St. Louis (N)
Stallcup, T. Virgil	1943-1945	Canton	Middle Atlantic	1947	Cincinnati
Starr, Richard E.	1943-1945	Butler	Pennsylvania St. Assn.	1947	New York (A)
Stephens, Bryan M.	1943-1945	Ceder Rapids	Three I	1947	Cleveland
Strickland, George B.	1944-1945	New Orleans	Southern Association	1950	Pittsburgh

Name	Years in Military	Team Prior to Military Service	League Prior to Military	First Year in Majors	First Major League Team
Stuart, Marlin H.	1943-1945	Springfield	Three I	1949	Detroit
St. Claire, Edward J. Jr.	1943-1944	Albany	Eastern	1951	Boston (N)
Suchecki, James J.	1945-1946	Scranton	Eastern	1950	Boston (A)
Surkont, Matthew C.	1943-1945	Rochester	International	1949	Chicago (A)
Taylor, Benjamin	1946	Olean	Pony	1951	St. Louis (A)
Taylor, James H.	1941-1945	St. Paul	American Association	1946	Brooklyn
Thomas, Leo R.	1943-1945	Olean	Pony	1950	St. Louis (A)
Thompson, David F.	1943	Thomasville	Eastern	1948	Washington
Thompson, John S.	1942-1945	Greensboro	Piedmont	1948	Philadelphia (N)
Thomson, Robert B.	1943-1945	Rocky Mount	Bi-State	1946	New York (N)
Tipton, Joseph J.	1943-1945	Charleston	Middle Atlantic	1948	Cleveland
Torgeson, Clifford Earl	1943-1945	Seattle	Pacific Coast	1947	Boston (N)
Upton, Thomas H. Jr.	1945-1946	Norfolk	Piedmont	1950	St. Louis (A)
Usher, Robert R.	1944-1945	Birmingham	Southern Association	1946	Cincinnati
Vico, George S.	1943-1945	Winston-Salem	Piedmont	1948	Detroit
Wade, Benjamin S.	1943-1945	Syracuse	International	1948	Chicago (N)
Walsh, James R.	1944-1945	York	Interstate	1946	Pittsburgh
Weigel, Ralph R.	1943-1945	Charleston	Middle Atlantic	1946	Cleveland
Werle, William G.	1945	San Francisco	Pacific Coast	1949	Pittsburgh
Wertz, Victor W.	1943-1945	Buffalo	International	1947	Detroit
Westlake, Waldon T.	1943-1945	Oakland	Pacific Coast	1947	Pittsburgh
Westrum, Wesley N.	1943-1945	Little Rock	Southern Association	1947	New York (N)
White, Donald W.	1942-1945	San Francisco	Pacific Coast	1948	Philadelphia (A)
Whitman, Dick C.	1943-1945	Durham	Piedmont	1946	Brooklyn
Wight, William R.	1943-1945	Norfolk	Piedmont	1946	New York (A)
Wilber, Delbert Q.	1942-1945	Columbus	South Atlantic	1946	St. Louis (N)
Wilson, George W.	1943-1945	Statesville	North Carolina State	1952	Chicago (A)
Wilson, James A.	1945	Louisville	American Association	1946	Boston (A)
Wojey, Peter P.	1942-1946	Miami	Florida East Coast	1954	Brooklyn
Wood, Kenneth L.	1944-1945	Wilmington	Interstate	1948	St. Louis (A)
Wright, Thomas E.	1943-1945	Danville-Schoolfield	Bi-State	1948	Boston (A)
Yuhas, J. Edward	1943-1946	Fond du Lac	Wisconsin State	1952	St. Louis (N)
Zernial, Gus E.	1943-1945	Waycross	Georgia-Florida	1949	Chicago (A)

APPENDIX D
NEGRO BASEBALL LEAGUE PLAYERS

Player Name	Team Name	Player Name	Team Name
Awkard, Russell	Newark Eagles	Johnson, Ralph	Philadelphia Stars
Bankhead, Dan	Birmingham Black Barons	Kimbrough, Larry	Philadelphia Stars
Barbee, Bud	Baltimore Elite Giants	Lewis, Rufus	Newark Eagles
Barber, Sam	Cleveland Buckeyes	Manning, Max	Newark Eagles
Barnes, Bill	Baltimore Elite Giants	McCord, Butch	Baltimore Elite Giants
Black, Joe	Baltimore Elite Giants	Mitchell, Bud	Philadelphia Stars
Blair, Garnett	Homestead Grays	Moore, Red	Baltimore Elite Giants
Bolden, Jim	Cleveland Buckeyes	O'Neil, Buck	Kansas City Monarchs
Bostock, Sr., Lymon	Birmingham Black Barons	Parker, Tom	New York Cubans
Bracken, Herb	Cleveland Buckeyes	Parks, Charlie	Newark Eagles
Brown, Barney	Philadelphia Stars	Patterson, Andrew	Philadelphia Stars
Brown, James	Newark Eagles	Perkins, Bill	Philadelphia Stars
Brown, Willard	Kansas City Monarchs	Pigg, Len	Indianapolis Clowns
Bryant, Lefty	Kansas City Monarchs	Pollard, Nat	Birmingham Black Barons
Buchanan, Chester	Philadelphia Stars	Richardson, Earl	Newark Eagles
Carlisle, Matthew	Homestead Grays	Robinson, Henry F.	Baltimore Elite Giants
Clarkson, James	Philadelphia Stars	Robinson, Jackie	Kansas City Monarchs
Cohen, Jim	Indianapolis Clowns	Romby, Robert	Baltimore Elite Giants
Cooper, Bill	Philadelphia Stars	Ruffin, Leon	Newark Eagles
Crutchfield, Jimmie	Chicago American Giants	Russell, Frank	Baltimore Elite Giants
Davis, Spencer	New York Black Yankees	Scott, Joe	Birmingham Black Barons
Day, Leon	Newark Eagles	Seay, Dickie	New York Black Yankees
Doby, Larry	Newark Eagles	Sharpe, Robert	Memphis Red Sox
Duckett, Mahlon	Philadelphia Stars	Smith, Gene	New York Black Yankees
Dunn, Jake	Philadelphia Stars	Smith, John Ford	Kansas City Monarchs
Easterling, Howard	Homestead Grays	Smith, Raymond	Philadelphia Stars
Elam, Jim	Newark Eagles	Strong, Ted	Kansas City Monarchs
Fields, Red	Homestead Grays	Summers, Lonnie	Chicago American Giants
Fillmore, Joe	Philadelphia Stars	Taylor, Schoolboy	New York Cubans
Gaines, Jonas	Baltimore Elite Giants	Taylor, Olan "Jelly"	Memphis Red Sox
Gibson, Jerry	Homestead Grays	Thompson, Hank	Kansas City Monarchs
Greene, Joe	Kansas City Monarchs	Thurman, Bob	Homestead Grays
Griffith, Bob	New York Black Yankees	Washington, Johnny	Baltimore Elite Giants
Hardy, Paul	Birmingham Black Barons	Watts, Andy	Cleveland Buckeyes
Harvey, David "Bill"	Baltimore Elite Giants	Welmaker, Roy	Homestead Grays
Hayes, Johnny	New York Black Yankees	Whatley, David	Homestead Grays
Henderson, Curtis	New York Black Yankees	Williams, Frank	Homestead Grays
Henry, Preacher	Indianapolis Clowns	Williams, Jesse	Kansas City Monarchs
Horne, Billy	Cleveland Buckeyes	Williams, Wilmore	Newark Eagles
Hughes, Sammy T.	Baltimore Elite Giants	Wilmore, Al	Philadelphia Stars
Irvin, Monte	Newark Eagles	Wilson, Fred	Indianapolis Clowns
Israel, Pint	Homestead Grays	Wright, Johnny	Homestead Grays
Jefferson, Willie	Cleveland Buckeyes	Zapp, James	Baltimore Elite Giants
Johnson, Connie	Kansas City Monarchs		
Johnson, Josh	New York Black Yankees		

APPENDIX E
BASEBALL PLAYERS WHO SERVED IN THE KOREAN WAR

Name	Years in Military Service	First Year in Major League	First Major League Team
Aber, Albert J.	1951–1952	1950	Cleveland
Abernathy, Ted W.	1953–1954	1955	Washington
Acker, Thomas J.	1952–1956	1956	Cincinnati
Adams, Herbert L.	1951–1952	1948	Chicago (A)
Altman, George L.	1957	1959	Chicago (N)
Anderson, Harry W.	1955	1957	Philadelphia (N)
Antonelli, John A.	1951–1952	1948	Boston (N)
Aspromonte, Kenneth J.	1954–1955	1957	Boston (A)
Bailey, L. Edgar	1951–1952	1953	Cincinnati
Barclay, Curtis C.	1953	1957	New York (N)
Bartirome, Anthony J.	1953	1952	Pittsburgh
Bauman, Frank M.	1954–1955	1955	Boston (A)
Baxes, Michael	1952–1953	1956	Kansas City
Bell, William S.	1953–1954	1952	Pittsburgh
Bella, John Jr.	1952–1953	1957	New York (A)
Berberet, Louis J.	1951–1952	1954	New York (A)
Birrer, Werner J.	1953–1954	1955	Detroit
Black, William C. (Bud)	1953–1954	1952	Detroit
Blanchard, John E.	1953–1954	1955	New York (A)
Blyzka, Michael J.	1951–1952	1953	St. Louis (A)
Bolling, Frank E.	1955	1954	Detroit
Borland, Thomas B.	1956–1957	1960	Boston (A)
Bouchee, Edward F.	1953–1954	1956	Philadelphia (N)
Boyer, Kenton	1952–1953	1955	St. Louis (N)
Brandt, John G.	1957	1956	St Louis (N)
Breeding, Marvin E.	1957–1958	1960	Baltimore
Bressoud, Edward F.	1953–1954	1956	New York (N)
Brewer, Thomas A.	1952–1953	1954	Boston (A)
Brodowski, Richard S.	1953–1954	1952	Boston (A)
Brosnan, James P.	1951–1952	1954	Chicago (N)
Brown, Robert W.	1953	1946	New York (A)
Bruce, Robert J	1957	1959	Detroit
Brunette, Wallace H.	1951–1952	1956	Kansas City
Buddin, Donald T.	1957	1956	Boston (A)
Buhl, Robert F.	1951–1952	1953	Milwaukee
Burk, Mack E.	1957	1956	Philadelphia (N)
Burnside, Peter W.	1953	1955	New York (N)
Calderone, Samuel F.	1951–1952	1950	New York (N)
Casale, Jerry J.	1957–1958	1958	Boston (A)
Cash, Norman D.	1957	1958	Chicago (A)
Castleman, Foster E.	1952	1954	New York (N)
Ceccarelli, Arthur E.	1951–1952	1955	Kansas City
Cheney, Thomas E.	1958	1957	St. Louis (N)
Chiti, Harry Jr.	1953–1954	1950	Chicago (N)
Chrisley, B. O'Neil	1952	1957	Washington

Name	Years in Military Service	First Year in Major League	First Major League Team
Churn, Clarence N. Jr.	1952	1957	Pittsburgh
Cicotte, Alva W.	1949-1951	1957	New York (A)
Clark, Philip J. III	1951-1952	1958	St. Louis (N)
Cohen, Hyman	1952-1953	1955	Chicago (N)
Coleman, Gerald F.	1952-1953	1949	New York (A)
Covington, J. Wesley	1954	1956	Milwaukee
Craig, Roger L.	1952-1953	1955	Brooklyn
Crandell, Delmar W.	1951-1952	1949	Boston (N)
Cunningham, Joseph R.	1952-1953	1954	St. Louis (N)
Dahlke, Jerome A.	1952-1953	1956	Chicago (A)
Daley, Peter H.	1951-1952	1955	Boston (A)
Daniels, Bennie Jr.	1953-1954	1957	Pittsburgh
Davie, Gerald L.	1953-1954	1959	Detroit
Ditmar, Arthur	1951-1952	1954	Philadelphia (A)
Dobbek, Daniel J.	1957-1958	1959	Washington
Dotterer, J. Henry	1953-1954	1957	Cincinnati
Drake, Solomon L.	1952-1953	1956	Chicago (N)
Duliba, Robert J.	1956-1958	1959	St. Louis (N)
Durham, Joseph V.	1955-1956	1954	Baltimore
Eaddy, Donald J.	1956-1958	1959	Chicago (N)
Esposito, Samuel	1954	1955	Chicago (A)
Ferrarese, Donald H.	1951-1952	1955	Baltimore
Finigan, James L	1951-1952	1954	Philadelphia (A)
Fischer, Willaim C.	1952-1953	1956	Chicago (A)
Ford, Edward C. (Whitey)	1951-1952	1950	New York (A)
Francona, John P. (Tito)	1954-1955	1956	Baltimore
Freeman, Mark P. Jr.	1955	1959	Kansas City
Friend, Owen L.	1951-1952	1949	St. Louis (A)
Gabler, John R.	1952-1953	1959	New York (A)
Garber, Robert M	1951-1952	1956	Pittsburgh
Giel, Paul	1956	1954	New York (N)
Giggie, Robert T.	1957	1959	Milwaukee
Graff, Milton E.	1952-1953	1957	Kansas City
Gray, Richard B.	1953-1954	1958	Los Angeles
Grba, Eli	1957-1958	1959	New York (A)
Green, Fred A.	1957	1959	Pittsburgh
Grim, Robert A.	1952-1953	1954	New York (A)
Groat, Richard M	1953-1954	1952	Pittsburgh
Grob, Conrad G.	1953-1954	1956	Washington
Gross, Donald J.	1953	1955	Cincinnati
Haddix, Harvey Jr.	1951-1952	1952	St. Louis (N)
Hall, William L.	1949	1954	Pittsburgh
Hardy, Carroll W.	1956-1957	1958	Cleveland
Harrington, William W.	1953-1954	1955	Kansas City
Hazle, Robert S.	1952	1955	Cincinnati
Herbert, Raymond E.	1951-1952	1950	Detroit
Herriage, William T.	1953	1956	Kansas City
Herzog, Dorrell N. (Whitey)	1953-1954	1956	Washington

Name	Years in Military Service	First Year in Major League	First Major League Team
Hicks, William J.	1956-1957	1959	Chicago (A)
House, H. Frank	1952-1953	1951	Detroit
Houtteman, Arthur J.	1951	1945	Detroit
Howard, Elston G.	1951-1952	1955	New York (A)
Hunt, Kenneth L.	1955-1956	1959	New York (A)
Hyde, Richard E.	1951-1952	1955	Washington
Johnson, Benjamin F.	1952-1953	1959	Chicago (N)
Johnson, Kenneth T.	1953-1954	1958	Kansas City
Jones, Gordon B.	1951-1953	1954	St. Louis (N)
Kasko, Edward M.	1952-1953	1957	St. Louis (N)
Kennedy, Robert D.	1952	1939	Chicago (A)
Kiely, Leo P.	1952-1953	1951	Boston (A)
King, Nelson J.	1951-1952	1954	Pittsburgh
Kipp, Fred L.	1954	1957	Brooklyn
Kirkland, Willie C.	1957	1958	San Francisco
Kirrene, Joseph J.	1951-1952	1950	Chicago (A)
Kline, Ronald L.	1953-1954	1952	Pittsburgh
Kokos, Richard J.	1951-1952	1948	St. Louis (A)
Konikowski, Alexander J.	1952-1953	1948	New York (N)
Korcheck, Stephen J.	1956-1957	1954	Washington
Koski, William J	1952-1954	1951	Pittsburgh
Kravitz, Daniel	1953-1953	1956	Pittsburgh
Kucks, John C.	1953-1954	1955	New York (A)
Landis, James H.	1954-1955	1957	Chicago (A)
Larson, Donald J.	1951-1952	1953	St. Louis (A)
Lary, Alford A.	1953-1954	1954	Chicago (N)
Lary, Frank S.	1951-1952	1954	Detroit
Lau, Charles	1953-1954	1956	Detroit
Law, Vernon S.	1952-1953	1950	Pittsburgh
Lehman, Kenneth K.	1951	1952	Brooklyn
Lemon, James R.	1951-1952	1950	Cleveland
Lennon, Robert A.	1951	1954	New York (N)
Lillis, Robert P.	1954-1955	1958	Los Angeles
Locke, Lawrence D.	1957-1958	1959	Cleveland
Locklin, Stuart C.	1952-1954	1955	Cleveland
Loes, William	1951	1950	Brooklyn
Lonnett, Joseph P.	1951-1952	1956	Philadelphia (N)
Lumpe, Jerry D.	1953-1954	1956	New York (A)
Luttrell, Kyle K.	1952-1953	1956	Washington
Lynch, Gerald T.	1951-1952	1954	Pittsburgh
Maas, Duane F.	1951-1952	1955	Detroit
Mabe, Robert L	1952	1958	St. Louis (N)
MacDonald, William P.	1951-1952	1950	Pittsburgh
Madison, David P.	1951	1950	New York (A)
Malkmus, Robert E.	1952-1953	1957	Milwaukee
Malzone, Frank J.	1952-1953	1955	Boston (A)
Mangan, James D.	1953-1954	1952	Pittsburgh
Margoneri, Joseph E.	1952-1953	1956	New York (N)

Name	Years in Military Service	First Year in Major League	First Major League Team
Martin, Billy M.	1954–1955	1950	New York (A)
Martyn, Robert G.	1953	1957	Kansas City
Mays, Willie H.	1952–1953	1951	New York (N)
McCardell, Roger M.	1953–1954	1959	San Francisco
McDevitt, Daniel E.	1953–1954	1957	Brooklyn
McMahan, Donald J.	1952	1957	Milwaukee
Melton, David O.	1951–1952	1956	Kansas City
Merriman, Lloyd A.	1952–1953	1949	Cincinnati
Merritt, Lloyd W.	1955	1957	St. Louis (N)
Micelotta, Robert P.	1951–1952	1954	Philadelphia (N)
Milliken, Robert F.	1951–1952	1953	Brooklyn
Minarcin, Rudy A.	1952–1953	1955	Cincinnati
Mizell, Wilmer D.	1954–1955	1952	St. Louis (N)
Monroe, Zack C.	1953–1954	1958	New York (A)
Moran, William N.	1955–1956	1958	Cleveland
Morgan, Joseph M.	1954–1955	1959	Kansas City
Morgan, Thomas S.	1953	1951	New York (A)
Morgan, Vernon T.	1952–1953	1954	Chicago (N)
Muffett, Billy A.	1952–1953	1957	St. Louis (N)
Murphy, Richard L	1955–1957	1954	Cincinnati
Naragon, Harold R.	1952–1953	1951	Cleveland
Naton, Peter A.	1953–1954	1953	Pittsburgh
Necciai, Ronald A.	1953	1952	Pittsburgh
Neeman, Calvin A.	1951–1952	1957	Chicago (N)
Newcombe, Donald	1952–1953	1949	Brooklyn
Nichols, Chester R.	1952–1953	1951	Boston (N)
O'Brien, Edward J.	1954	1953	Pittsburgh
O'Brien, John T.	1954	1953	Pitttsburgh
O'Connell, Daniel	1951–1952	1950	Pittsburgh
O'Dell, William O.	1955	1954	Baltimore
Oldham, John H.	1956	1957	Cincinnati
Olson, Karl A.	1952	1951	Boston (A)
Oravetz, Ernest E.	1953–1954	1955	Washington
Owens, James P.	1957–1958	1955	Philadelphia (N)
Pagliaroni, James V.	1956–1957	1955	Boston (A)
Paine, Phillips S.	1952–1953	1951	Boston (N)
Palica, Ervin M.	1952	1945	Brooklyn
Palys, Stanley F.	1951	1953	Philadelphia (N)
Pavietich, Donald S.	1957–1958	1957	Cincinnati
Peterson, William H.	1952–1953	1955	Pittsburgh
Phillips, John M.	1953–1954	1955	Detroit
Phillips, William T.	1954–1955	1956	Milwaukee
Pignatano, Joseph B.	1951–1952	1957	Brooklyn
Pilarcik, Alfred J.	1953–1954	1956	Kansas City
Pisoni, James P.	1951–1952	1956	Kansas City
Pitula, Stanley Jr.	1952–1953	1957	Cleveland
Plews, Herbert E.	1951–1952	1956	Washington
Podres, John J.	1956	1953	Brooklyn

Name	Years in Military Service	First Year in Major League	First Major League Team
Poholsky, Thomas G.	1952–1953	1950	St. Louis (N)
Porter, Daniel E.	1952–1953	1951	Washington
Porter, J. W.	1953–1954	1952	St. Louis (A)
Portocarrero, Arnold M.	1952–1953	1954	Philadelphia (A)
Powell, Robert L.	1956	1955	Chicago (A)
Powers, John C.	1952–1953	1955	Pittsburgh
Purkey, Robert T.	1951–1952	1954	Pittsburgh
Rabe, Charles H.	1953–1954	1957	Cincinnati
Roach, Melvin E.	1955–1956	1957	Milwaukee
Roig, Anton A.	1951–1952	1953	Washington
Romonosky, John Jr.	1951–1952	1953	St. Louis (N)
Roseboro, John	1954	1957	Brooklyn
Roselli, Robert E.	1954	1955	Milwaukee
Ross, F. Robert	1952–1953	1950	Washington
Rudolph, Frederick D.	1953	1957	Chicago (A)
Sadowski, Edward R.	1954–1955	1960	Boston (A)
Sanford, John S.	1955	1956	Philadelphia (N)
Saucier, Frank F.	1952–1954	1951	St. Louis (A)
Sawatski, Carl R.	1951–1952	1948	Chicago (N)
Schaive, John E.	1956–1957	1958	Washington
Schmidt, Robert B.	1953–1954	1958	San Francisco
Schoonmaker, Jerald L.	1956	1955	Washington
Schult, Arthur W.	1951–1952	1953	New York (A)
Semproch, Roman A.	1952–1953	1958	Philadelphia (N)
Shannon, Walter C. Jr.	1953–1954	1959	St. Louis (N)
Sherry, Norman B.	1952–1953	1959	Los Angeles
Siebern, Norman L.	1954–1955	1956	New York (A)
Simmons, Curtis T.	1951	1947	Philadelphia (N)
Sisler, David M	1954–1955	1956	Boston (A)
Skinner, Robert R.	1952–1953	1954	Pittsburgh
Skizas, Louis P.	1952–1953	1956	New York (A)
Smith, Harold R.	1951	1956	St. Louis (N)
Smith, Paul L.	1955–1956	1953	Pittsburgh
Smith, Robert G.	1952–1953	1955	Boston (A)
Snyder, Gene W.	1953–1954	1959	Los Angeles
Spangler, Albert D.	1956–1957	1959	Milwaukee
Speake, Bob C.	1952–1953	1955	Chicago (N)
Spencer, Daryl D.	1954–1955	1952	New York (N)
Stephenson, Robert L.	1952–1953	1955	St. Louis (N)
Striker, Wilbur S.	1956–1957	1959	Cleveland
Stuart, Richard L.	1953–1954	1958	Pittsburgh
Sturdivant, Thomas V.	1951–1952	1955	New York (A)
Sullivan, Franklin L.	1951–1952	1953	Boston (A)
Sullivan, Haywood C.	1953–1954	1955	Boston (A)
Susce, George D.	1953	1955	Boston (A)
Tappe, Theodore N.	1953	1951	Cincinnati
Taussig, Donald F.	1953–1954	1958	San Francisco
Taylor, Samuel D.	1952–1955	1958	Chicago (N)

Name	Years in Military Service	First Year in Major League	First Major League Team
Taylor, William M.	1951–1952	1954	New York (N)
Templeton, Charles	1953	1955	Brooklyn
Throneberry, M. Faye	1953–1954	1952	Boston (A)
Tomanek, Richard C.	1951	1953	Cleveland
Torre, Frank J.	1952	1956	Milwaukee
Triandos, Gus	1951–1952	1953	New York (A)
Trowbridge, Robert M.	1951–1953	1956	Milwaukee
Turley, Robert L.	1952	1951	St. Louis (A)
Umbricht, James	1954–1955	1959	Pittsburgh
Urban, Jack E.	1952–1953	1957	Kansas City
Valentine, Harold	1951–1952	1954	Cincinnati
Valentinetti, Vito J.	1952	1954	Chicago (A)
Wagner, Leon L.	1957	1958	San Francisco
Walters, Kenneth R.	1954–1955	1960	Philadelphia (N)
Ward, Preston M.	1951–1952	1948	Brooklyn
Weik, Richard H.	1951–1952	1948	Washington
Wheat, Leroy W.	1951–1952	1954	Philadelphia (A)
Whisenant, T. Peter	1951	1952	Boston (N)
White, William D.	1957–1958	1956	New York (N)
Wiesler, Robert G.	1952	1951	New York (A)
Willey, Carlton F.	1953–1954	1958	Milwaukee
Williams, Donald F.	1954–1955	1958	Pittsburgh
Williams, Theodore S.	1952–1953	1939	Boston (A)
Wilson, Robert E.	1957–1958	1959	Boston (A)
Wilson, William D.	1951–1952	1950	Chicago (A)
Witt, George A.	1951	1957	Pittsburgh
Woodeschick, Harold J.	1953–1954	1956	Detroit
Zauchin, Norbert H.	1952–1953	1951	Boston (A)

REFERENCES

Blake, Mike. 1994. *Baseball Chronicles, An Oral History of Baseball Through the Decades.* Cincinnati: Betterway Books.

Blattner, Robert G. (Buddy). 1997. Letter to author. November 29.

Block, Seymour (Cy). 1997. Letter to author. December 7.

Bloodworth, James H. (Jimmy). 1997. Letter to author. December 15.

Broeg, Bob. 1964. *Stan Musial: The Man's Own Story As Told to Bob Broeg.* Garden City, N.Y.: Doubleday and Company, Inc.

Bruun, Erik, and Robin Getzen, eds. 1996. *The Book of American Values and Virtues: Our Tradition of Freedom, Liberty, and Tolerance.* New York: Black Dog and Leventhal.

Bucek, Jeanine, ed. 1996. *The Baseball Encyclopedia, Tenth Edition, Revised, Updated, and Expanded, The Complete and Definitive Record of Major League Baseball.* New York: Macmillan.

Burich, William M. (Bill). 1998. Letter to author. February 2.

Byrne, Thomas J. (Tommy). 1997. Letter to author. December 16.

Campbell, Clarence (Soup). 1997. Letter to author. November 29.

Carpenter, Robert L. (Bob). 1998. Letter to author. January 26.

Castiglia, James V. (Jim). 1997. Letter to author. December 1.

Cataneo, David. 1991. *Peanuts & Crackerjack, A Treasury of Baseball Legends and Lore.* San Diego: Harcourt Brace and Co.

Chapman, Samuel B. (Sam) 1997. Letter to author. December 17.

Coleman, Bruce Reaves. 1998. *True Stars of the Major Leagues.* Madison, Miss.: Circuit Clout Press, Inc.

Collins, Edward T. Jr. (Eddie). 1997. Letter to author. December 1.

Danning, Harry. 1997. Letter to author. November 30.

Dapper, Clifford R. (Cliff). 1997. Letter to author. December 1.

Davis, John H. 1997. Letter to author. December 5.

Detweiler, Robert S. (Ducky). 1997. Letter to author. December 1.

Dickson, Paul. 1991. *Baseball's Greatest Quotations.* New York: Harper Collins.

DiMaggio, Dominic P. (Dom). 1997. Letter to author. December 9.

Donovan, Willard E. (Bill). 1998. Letter to author from wife. January 20.

Eisenbath, Mike. 1999. *The Cardinals Encyclopedia.* Philadelphia: Temple University Press.

Eyrich, George L. 1998. Letter to author. January 17.

Feller, Robert W.A. (Bob) 1997. Letter to author. December 9.

Feller, Bob, with Bill Gilbert. 1990. *Now Pitching, Bob Feller.* New York: Carol Publishing Group.

Gentile, Samuel C. (Sam). 1998. Letter to author. February 3.

Gilbert, Bill. 1992. *They Also Served, Baseball and the Home Front, 1941-1945.* New York: Crown Publishers, Inc.

Gilbert, Thomas. 1997. *Baseball at War: World War II and the Fall of the Color Line.* New York: Franklin Watts.

Goldstein, Leslie E. (Lonnie). 1997. Letter to author. December 2.

Goldstein, Richard. 1980. *Spartan Seasons, How Baseball Survived the Second World War.* New York: MacMillan Publishing Co., Inc.

Gumpert, Randall P. (Randy). 1997. Letter to author. December 1.

Hamrick, Raymond B. (Ray). 1998. Letter to author. March 22.

Hanks, Stephen, Perry Barber, Allen Barra, Thomas W. Gilbert, Joe Glickman, Owen Kean, and Berry Stainback. 1989. *150 Years of Baseball*. Lincolnwood, Ill.: Publications International, Ltd.

Haughey, Christopher F. (Chris). 1998. Letter to author. January 5.

Heim, Val R. 1997. Letter to author. December 1.

Hitchcock, William C. (Billy). 1997. Letter to author. December 2.

Hodgin, Elmer R. (Ralph). 1997. Letter to author. December 2.

Hoerst, Frank J. 1997. Letter to author. December 1.

Honig, Donald. 1975. *Baseball When the Grass Was Real, Baseball from the Twenties to the Forties, Told by the Men Who Played It*. Lincoln: University of Nebraska Press.

——————. 1976. *Baseball Between the Lines, Baseball in the Forties and Fifties, As Told by the Men Who Played It*. Lincoln: University of Nebraska Press.

Hirshberg, Al. 1970. *The Greatest American Leaguers*. New York: G. P. Putnam's Sons.

Hudlin, George W. (Willis). 1997. Letter to author. November 29.

Hudson, Sidney C. (Sid). 1997. Letter to author. December 1.

Johnson, Arthur H. (Art). 1997. Letter to author. December 15.

Johnson, Dick, ed., and Glenn Stout. 1991. *Ted Williams: A Portrait in Words and Pictures*. New York: Walker and Company.

Johnson, William R. (Billy). 1998. Letter to author. February 28.

Jones, James M. (Jake). 1998. Letter to author. February 10.

Kaam, Herbert. 1944. "Keller, Former Pill Pounder for Yankees, Now Medicine Man for Merchant Marines." *The Sporting News*. St. Louis: August 24.

Karst, Gene, and Martin J. Jones, Jr. 1973. *Who's Who in Professional Baseball*. New Rochelle: N.Y.: Arlington House.

Kaufman, Alan S., and James C. Kaufman. 1995. *The Worst Baseball Pitchers of All Time*. New York: Carol Publishing Group.

Kennedy, Robert D. (Bob) 1997. Letter to author. December 1.

Kiner, Ralph M. 1997. Letter to author. December 1.

Koy, Ernest A. (Ernie). 1997. Letter to author. November 28.

Kvasnak, Alexander (Al). 1997. Letter to author. December 1.

Lahsche, Jerry. 1994. *Stan "The Man" Musial: Born To Be a Ballplayer*. Dallas: Taylor Publishing Company.

Laird, A. W. 1990. *Ranking Baseball's Elite: An Analysis Derived from Player Statistics, 1893–1987*. Jefferson, N.C.: McFarland and Co., Inc.

Lambert, Eugene M. (Gene). 1998. Letter to author. January 30.

Lanier, Hubert M. (Max). 1997. Letter to author. November 29.

Layne, Ivoria H. (Hilly). 1997. Letter to author. December 16.

Lefebvre, Wilfrid H. (Bill). 1997. Letter to author. November 29.

Liebman, Glenn. 1994. *Baseball Shorts, 1000 of the Game's Funniest One-Liners*. Chicago: Contemporary Books.

Lodigiani, Dario A. 1998. Letter to author. January 12.

MacLean, Norman, ed. 1990. *All-Time Greatest Who's Who in Baseball, 1872–1990*. New York: Who's Who in Baseball Magazine.

Mallory, James B. (Jim). 1998. Letter to author. January 28.

Malloy, Robert P. (Bob). 1997. Letter to author. December 7.

Mauch, Gene W. 1998. Letter to author. March 2.

McCoy, Benjamin J. (Benny). 1997. Letter to author. December 19.

McCullough, Pinson L. (Phil). 1997. Letter to author. December 11.

Mead, William B. 1985. *Baseball Goes To War.* Washington, D.C.: Farragut Publishing Co.

Mertz, James V. (Jim). 1997. Letter to author. December 6.

Milnar, Albert J. (Al). 1997. Letter to author. December 1.

Mullin, Patrick J. (Pat). 1998. Letter to author. February 2.

Nahem, Samuel R. (Sam). 1997. Letter to author. December 3.

Nemec, David, Stephen Hanks, Dick Johnson, Thomas W. Gilbert, Andy Cohen, Joe Glickman, Danny Green, and David Raskin. 1992. *20th Century Baseball Chronicle: A Year-by-Year History of Major League Baseball.* Lincolnwood, Ill.: Publications International, Ltd.

Nemec, David, and Pete Palmer. 1993. *1001 Fascinating Baseball Facts: Facts, Records, Anecdotes, Quotes, Lore, and More!* Stamford, Conn: Longmeadow Press.

Okrent, Daniel, and Steve Wulf. 1989. *Baseball Anecdotes.* New York: Harper Collins Publishers.

Patton, Gene T. 1997. Letter to author. December 1.

Peary, Danny, ed. 1994. *We Played the Game: 65 Players Remember Baseball's Greatest Era, 1947-1964.* New York: Hyperion.

————. 1990. *Baseball's Finest: The Greats, the Flakes, the Weird, and the Wonderful.* North Dighton, Mass.: JG Press.

Perme, Leonard J. (Len). 1998. Letter to author. February 6.

Peters, Russell D. (Rusty). 1997. Letter to author. December 2.

Phillips, Damon R. 1998. Letter to author. January 8.

Pietrusza, David, Matthew Silverman, and Michael Gershman, eds. 2000. *Baseball, The Biographical Encyclopedia.* Kingston, N.Y.: Total/Sports Illustrated.

Raffensberger, Kenneth D. (Ken). 1997. Letter to author. December 1.

Reichler, Joseph. 1981. *Baseball's Great Moments.* New York: Bonanza Books.

Riebe, Harvey D. (Hank). 1997. Letter to author. December 1.

Ritter, Lawrence. 1984. *The Glory of Their Times: The Story of the Early Days of Baseball Told by the Men Who Played it.* The Enlarged Edition. New York: Quill William Morrow.

Ritter, Lawrence, and Donald Honig. 1984. *The Image of Their Greatness: An Illustrated History of Baseball from 1900 to the Present.* Updated Edition. New York: Crown Publishers Inc.

Rodgers, William S. (Bill). 1997. Letter to author. December 7.

Romeo, Blues. 1944. "In the Service—Phil Rizzuto, Navy's Lend-Lease Star, Flashed Yankee Form in GI Series." *The Sporting News.* St. Louis. November 23.

Rumill, Ed. 1946. "Battleaction." *Baseball Magazine.* January.

Salsinger, H.G., Harry E. Heilmann, and Don H. Black, eds. 1945. *Major League Baseball, Facts, Figures and Official Rules.* Racine, Wisconsin: Whitman Publishing Company.

————. 1946. *Major League Baseball, Facts, Figures and Official Rules.* Racine, Wisconsin: Whitman Publishing Company.

Sanford, John H. (Jack). 1997. Letter to author. December 4.

Sargent, Jim. 2000. "Where Are They Now? Former Outfielder, Gene Woodling Recalls Career in Majors." *Baseball Digest.* Evanston, Ill. February.

Sauer, Henry J. (Hank). 1998. Letter to author. January 12.

Savage, John R. (Bob). 1997. Letter to author. December 8.

Scheib, Carl A. 1998. Letter to author. January 6.

Schmitz, John A. (Johnny) 1997. Letter to author. December 17.

Schmulbach, Henry A. (Hank). 1998. Letter to author. February 26.

Sepkowski, Theodore W. (Ted). 1997. Letter to author. December 15.

Shatzkin, Mike, ed. 1990. *The Ballplayers: Baseball's Ultimate Biographical Reference*. New York: Arbor House William Morrow.

Shokes, Edward C. (Eddie). 1998. Letter to author. January 26.

Sisti, Sebastian D. (Sibby). 1997. Letter to author. December 1.

Slaughter, Enos B. 1997. Letter to author. December 23.

Smith, Ron. 1993. *The Sporting News, Chronicle of Baseball*. New York: BDD Illustrated Books.

Solomon, Burt. 1997. *The Baseball Timeline: The Day-by-Day History of Baseball from Valley Forge to the Present Day*. New York: Avon Book.

Sturgeon, Robert H. (Bobby). 1997. Letter to author. December 11.

Sturm, John P.J. (Johnny). 1998. Letter to author. January 14.

Thompson, Eugene E. (Junior). 1997. Letter to author. December 12.

Thuman, Louis C.F. (Lou). 1997. Letter to author. December 10.

Turner, Frederick. 1996. *When the Boys Came Back, Baseball and 1946*. New York: Henry Holt and Co.

Van Blair, Rick. 1994. *Dugout to Foxhole: Interviews with Baseball Players Whose Careers Were Affected by World War II*. Jefferson, N.C.: McFarland and Co., Inc.

Van Lindt, Carson. 1994. *One Championship Season: The Story of the 1944 St. Louis Browns*. New York: Marabou Publishing.

Ward, Geoffrey C., and Ken Burns. 1994. *Baseball: An Illustrated History*. New York: Alfred A. Knopf, Inc.

White, Harold G. (Hal). 1998. Letter to author. February 28.

Williams, Ted, with John Underwood. 1988. *My Turn at Bat, The Story of My Life*. New York: Simon and Schuster.

Wittig, John C. (Johnnie). 1998. Letter to author. February 5.

Yankowski, George E. 1997. Letter to author. December 16.

Yost, Edward F. (Eddie). 1998. Letter to author. January 15.

Statistical References

Abramovich, Joe, ed. 1964. *Baseball Register, 1964 Edition*. St. Louis: C.C. Spink and Son.

Bloodgood, Clifford, ed. 1941. *Who's Who in Baseball* 26th ed. New York: Baseball Magazine Co.

—————. 1942. *Who's Who in Baseball* 27th ed. New York: Baseball Magazine Co.

—————. 1943. *Who's Who in Baseball* 28th ed. New York: Baseball Magazine Co.

—————. 1944. *Who's Who in Baseball* 29th ed. New York: Baseball Magazine Co.

—————. 1945. *Who's Who in Baseball* 30th ed. New York: Baseball Magazine Co.

—————. 1946. *Who's Who in Baseball* 31st ed. New York: Baseball Magazine Co.

—————. 1947. *Who's Who in Baseball* 32nd ed. New York: Baseball Magazine Co.

—————. 1948. *Who's Who in Baseball* 33rd ed. New York: Baseball Magazine Co.

—————. 1949. *Who's Who in Baseball* 34th ed. New York: Baseball Magazine Co.

—————. 1950. *Who's Who in Baseball* 35th ed. New York: Baseball Magazine Co.

—————. 1951. *Who's Who in Baseball* 36th ed. New York: Baseball Magazine Co.

Duxbury, John, ed. 1966. *Baseball Register, 1966 Edition*. St. Louis: The Sporting News.

Feder, Sid, ed. 1953. *Who's Who in Baseball*. 38th ed. New York: Baseball Magazine Co.

James, Bill, John Dewan, Neil Munro, and Don Ziminda, eds. 1998. *Bill James Presents STATS Inc. All-Time Major League Handbook.* Skokie, Ill: STATS, Inc.

————. 1998. *Bill James Presents STATS Inc. All-Time Baseball Sourcebook.* Skokie, Ill: STATS, Inc.

Lilly, Joseph, ed. 1952. *Who's Who in Baseball.* 37th ed. New York: Baseball Magazine Co.

Neft, David S., Richard M. Cohen, and Michael L. Neft. 2000. *The Sports Encyclopedia: Baseball 2000.* New York: St. Martin's Griffin.

Pickard, Charles, and Clifford Kachline, eds. 1965. *Baseball Register.* St. Louis: The Sporting News.

Reichler, Joseph. Revised by Ken Samelson. 1993. *The Great All-Time Baseball Record Book.* New York: MacMillan Publishing Company

Roth, Allan, ed. 1954. *Who's Who in Baseball.* 39th ed. New York: Baseball Magazine Co.

————. 1955. *Who's Who in Baseball* 40th ed. New York: Who's Who in Baseball Magazine Co., Inc.

————. 1956. *Who's Who in Baseball* 41st ed. New York: Who's Who in Baseball Magazine Co., Inc.

————. 1957. *Who's Who in Baseball* 42nd ed. New York: Who's Who in Baseball Magazine Co., Inc.

———— 1958. *Who's Who in Baseball* 43rd ed. New York: Who's Who in Baseball Magazine Co., Inc.

————. 1959. *Who's Who in Baseball* 44th ed. New York: Who's Who in Baseball Magazine Co., Inc.

————. 1960. *Who's Who in Baseball* 45th ed. New York: Who's Who in Baseball Magazine Co., Inc.

————. 1961. *Who's Who in Baseball* 46th ed. New York: Who's Who in Baseball Magazine Co., Inc.

————. 1962. *Who's Who in Baseball* 47th ed. New York: Who's Who in Baseball Magazine Co., Inc.

————. 1963. *Who's Who in Baseball* 48th ed. New York: Who's Who in Baseball Magazine Co., Inc.

————. 1964. *Who's Who in Baseball* 49th ed. New York: Who's Who in Baseball Magazine Co., Inc.

————. 1965. *Who's Who in Baseball* 50th ed. New York: Who's Who in Baseball Magazine Co., Inc.

Spink, C.C. Johnson, ed.. 1963. *Offical Baseball Register.* St. Louis: C.C. Spink and Son.

Spink, J.G. Taylor, ed. 1943. *Baseball Guide and Record Book.* St. Louis: Charles C. Spink and Son.

————. 1944. *Baseball Guide and Record Book.* St. Louis: Charles C. Spink and Son.

————. 1945. *Baseball Guide and Record Book.* St. Louis: Charles C. Spink and Son.

————. 1946. *Baseball Guide and Record Book.* St. Louis: Charles C. Spink and Son.

————. 1942. *Official Baseball Record Book, 1942.* St. Louis: Charles C. Spink and Son.

————. 1940. *Official Baseball Register.* St. Louis: C.C. Spink and Son.

————. 1941. *Official Baseball Register.* St. Louis: C.C. Spink and Son.

————. 1942. *Official Baseball Register.* St. Louis: C.C. Spink and Son.

————. 1943. *Official Baseball Register.* St. Louis: C.C. Spink and Son.

————. 1944. *Official Baseball Register.* St. Louis: C.C. Spink and Son.

————. 1945. *Official Baseball Register.* St. Louis: C.C. Spink and Son.

————. 1946. *Official Baseball Register.* St. Louis: C.C. Spink and Son.
————. 1947. *Official Baseball Register.* St. Louis: C.C. Spink and Son.
————. 1948. *Official Baseball Register.* St. Louis: C.C. Spink and Son.
————. 1949. *Official Baseball Register.* St. Louis: C.C. Spink and Son.
————. 1950. *Official Baseball Register.* St. Louis: C.C. Spink and Son.
————. 1951. *Official Baseball Register.* St. Louis: C.C. Spink and Son.
————. 1952. *Official Baseball Register.* St. Louis: C.C. Spink and Son.
————. 1953. *Official Baseball Register.* St. Louis: C.C. Spink and Son.
————. 1954. *Official Baseball Register.* St. Louis: C.C. Spink and Son.
————. 1955. *Official Baseball Register.* St. Louis: C.C. Spink and Son.
————. 1956. *Official Baseball Register.* St. Louis: C.C. Spink and Son.
————. 1957. *Official Baseball Register.* St. Louis: C.C. Spink and Son.
————. 1958. *Official Baseball Register.* St. Louis: C.C. Spink and Son.
————. 1959. *Official Baseball Register.* St. Louis: C.C. Spink and Son.
————. 1960. *Official Baseball Register.* St. Louis: C.C. Spink and Son.
————. 1961. *Official Baseball Register.* St. Louis: C.C. Spink and Son.
————. 1962. *Official Baseball Register.* St. Louis: C.C. Spink and Son.
Thorn, John, Pete Palmer, Michael Gershman, and David Pietrusza, eds. 1999. *Total Baseball*.
    6th ed. New York: Total Sports.

General References
Not Specifically Quoted in the Text

Archie, George A. 1997. Letter to author. December 12.
Baker, William P. (Bill). 1997. Letter to author. December 2.
Benson, Vernon A. (Vern). 1998. Letter to author. February 25.
Borst, Bill. 1995. *The Best of Seasons: The 1944 St. Louis Cardinals and St. Louis Browns*.
    Jefferson, N.C.: McFarland and Company, Inc.
Bowles, Charles J. (Charlie). 1997. Letter to author. November 28.
Bragan, Robert R. (Bobby). 1998. Letter to author. January 29.
Brancato, Albert (Al). 1997. Letter to author. November 29.
Candini, Mario C. (Milo). 1998. Letter to author. February 7.
Carnett, Edwin E. (Eddie). 1997. Interview with author. November 25.
Center, Marviln E. (Pete). 1998. Letter to author. February 3.
Clemens, Chester S. (Chet). 1997. Letter to author. November 29.
Dawidoff, Nicholas. 1995. *The Catcher Was a Spy: The Mysterious Life of Moe Berg*. New York:
    Vintage Books.
Doerr, Robert P. (Bobby). 1997. Letter to author. December 1.
Eisenstat, Harry. 1997. Letter to author. December 5.
Epps, Harold F. (Hal). 1997. Letter to author. December 15.
Fleming, Leslie F. (Bill). 1997. Letter to author. December 3.
Franks, Herman L. 1997. Letter to author. December 1.
Freed, Edwin C. (Ed). 1997. Letter to author. November 29.
Frey, Linus R. (Lonny). 1998. Letter to author. January 31.
Galehouse, Dennis W. (Denny). 1997. Letter to author. December 1.
Galle, Stanley J. (Stan). 1997. Letter to author. December 6.

Gremp, Louis E. (Buddy). 1998. Telephone call to author from son. February 3.
Heintzelman, Kenneth A. (Ken). 1998. Letter to author. February 6.
Johnson, Adam R. (A. Rankin). 1997. Letter to author. December 8.
Johnson, Lloyd, and Brenda Ward. 1994. *Who's Who in Baseball History.* New York: Barnes and Noble.
Lewis, John K. (Buddy). 1997. Letter to author. November 29.
Litwhiler, Daniel W. (Danny). 1997. Letter to author. December 1.
Lockman, Carroll W. (Whitey). 1997. Letter to author. November 28.
Lupien, Ulysses J. (Tony). 1998. Letter to author. February 14.
Lyons, Jeffrey, and Douglas B. Lyons. 1998. *Out of Left Field: Over 1,134 Newly Discovered Amazing Baseball Records, Connections, Coincidences, and More!* New York: Times Books/Random House.
————. 2001. *Curveball and Screwballs: Over 1,286 Incredible Baseball Facts, Flukes, and More!* New York: Random House Games and Puzzles.
Marshall, Willard W. 1998. Letter to author. January 27.
Martinez, David H. 1996. *The Book of Baseball Literacy.* New York: Plume/Penguin Group.
Masterson, Walter E. (Walt). 1997. Letter to author. December 1.
May, Merrill G. (Pinky). 1997. Letter to author. December 9.
McHale, John J. 1997. Letter to author. December 6.
McKee, Rogers H. 1997. Letter to author. December 4.
McLish, Calvin C.J.C.T. (Cal). 1998. Letter to author. February 2.
Moore, Jack B. 1987. *Joe DiMaggio, Baseball's Yankee Clipper.* New York: Praeger Publishers.
Mueller, Leslie C. (Les). 1997. Letter to author. December 3.
Mueller, William L. (Bill). 1997. Letter to author. December 2.
Myers, Doug, and Brian Dodd. *Louisville Slugger Presents Batting Around, A Comprehensive Collection of Hitting Achievements, Anecdotes, and Analyses.* Lincolnwood, Ill.: Contemporary Books.
Neft, David S., and Richard M. Cohen. 1990. *The World Series: Complete Play-by-Play of Every Game 1903–1989.* New York: St. Martin's Press.
Nemec, David, Matthew D. Greenberger, Dan Schlossberg, Dick Johnson, and Mike Tully. 1994. *Players of Cooperstown: Baseball's Hall of Fame.* Lincolnwood, Ill. Publications International Ltd.
Okrent, Daniel, and Harris Lewine, eds. 2000. *The Ultimate Baseball Book, The Classic Illustrated History of the World's Greatest Game.* Boston: Houghton Mifflin Co.
Owen, Arnold M. (Mickey). 1998. Letter to author. March 2.
Pesky, John M. (Johnny). 1997. Letter to author. November 30.
Reichler, Joseph. Ken Samelson revised edition. 1993. *The Great All-Time Baseball Record Book.* New York: Macmillan Publishing Company.
Rikard, Cully. 1997. Letter to author. December 3.
Ritter, Lawrence, and Donald Honig. 1999. *The Story of Baseball.* 3rd ed. New York: William Morrow and Co.
Robinson, William E. (Eddie). 1998. Letter to author. February 25.
Russo, Marius U. 1998. Letter to author. January 12.
Sain, John F. (Johnny). 1997. Letter to author. December 15.
Salsinger, H.G., Harry E. Heilmann, and Don H. Black, eds. 1943. *Major League Baseball, Facts, Figures and Official Rules.* Racine, Wisconsin: Whitman Publishing Company.

———. 1944. *Major League Baseball, Facts, Figures and Official Rules.* Racine, Wisconsin: Whitman Publishing Company.

Sanford, John F. (Fred). 1998. Letter to author. January 10.

Stevens, Charles A. (Chuck). 1997. Letter to author. December 9.

Stewart, Edward P. (Bud). 1997. Letter to author. December 10.

Suder, Peter (Pete). 1997. Letter to author. December 12.

Sullivan, John Paul. 1997. Letter to author. December 1.

Trucks, Virgil O. 1997. Letter to author. December 12.

Vernon, James B. (Mickey). 1998. Letter to author. February 6.

Vincent, David, Lyle Spatz, and David W. Smith. 2001. *The Midsummer Classic: The Complete History of Baseball's All-Star Game.* Lincoln: University of Nebraska Press.

Walker, Harry W. 1998. Letter to author. January 29.

Weinstein, Stephen. 1993. *The Random House Pro Baseball Dictionary.* New York: Random House.

Wensloff, Charles W. (Butch). 1998. Letter to author. January 14.

Woodling, Eugene R. (Gene). 1998. Letter to author. January 14.

Newspapers and Periodicals
Used for References and Quotations

Autograph Times. February 1996.

Baseball Digest. February, 2000. Evanston, Ill. Century Publishing Company.

Baseball Magazine. January, 1946. New York: The Baseball Magazine Company.

Boston Globe. April 27, 1978. Boston:

Cleveland Plain-Dealer. December 21, 1941. Cleveland:

New York Herald Tribune. April 7, 1943. New York:

New York Times. December 11, 1941. New York:

Sarasota Herald-Tribune. December 8, 1997. Sarasota, Florida.

Sports Collector Digest. July 17, 1992.

Sports Illustrated. July 16, 2001.

The Philadelphia Inquirer. August 8, 1976. Philadelphia:

The Sporting News. 1942 (all issues). St. Louis: The Sporting News.

The Sporting News. 1943 (all issues). St. Louis: The Sporting News.

The Sporting News. 1944 (all issues). St. Louis: The Sporting News.

The Sporting News. 1945 (all issues). St. Louis: The Sporting News.